THE AGE OF CHOICE

THE AGE OF CHOICE

A HISTORY OF FREEDOM IN MODERN LIFE

SOPHIA ROSENFELD

PRINCETON UNIVERSITY PRESS

PRINCETON & OXFORD

Published by Princeton University Press
41 William Street, Princeton, New Jersey 08540
99 Banbury Road, Oxford OX2 6JX

press.princeton.edu

All Rights Reserved

Library of Congress Cataloging-in-Publication Data

Names: Rosenfeld, Sophia A., author.
Title: The age of choice : a history of freedom in modern life / Sophia Rosenfeld.
Description: Princeton : Princeton University Press, 2025. | Includes bibliographical references and index.
Identifiers: LCCN 2024015381 (print) | LCCN 2024015382 (ebook) | ISBN 9780691164717 (hardback) | ISBN 9780691261621 (ebook)
Subjects: LCSH: Liberty—History. | Choice (Psychology)
Classification: LCC HM1266 .R67 2025 (print) | LCC HM1266 (ebook) | DDC 153.8/3—dc23/eng/20240701
LC record available at https://lccn.loc.gov/2024015381
LC ebook record available at https://lccn.loc.gov/2024015382

British Library Cataloging-in-Publication Data is available

Editorial: Rob Tempio, Chloe Coy
Production Editorial: Elizabeth Byrd
Production: Erin Suydam
Publicity: James Schneider (US), Carmen Jimenez (UK)

Jacket Credit: Elliott Erwitt / Magnum Photos

This book has been composed in Arno with Oscine

Printed in the United States of America

10 9 8 7 6 5 4 3 2 1

For Matthew, always

One of the indispensable foods of the human soul is liberty. Liberty, taking the word in its concrete sense, consists in the ability to choose.

—SIMONE WEIL, *THE NEED FOR ROOTS* (WRITTEN 1943, PUBLISHED POSTHUMOUSLY IN 1949)

Wer die Wahl hat, hat die Qual (He who has choice has torment).

—GERMAN PROVERB

And he thought, The women have more courage than we do. Then he thought, Maybe they don't have any choice.

—JAMES BALDWIN, *ANOTHER COUNTRY* (1962)

CONTENTS

Color plates follow page 214

THE AGE OF CHOICE

INTRODUCTION

WRITING THIS BOOK has involved a steady stream of choices, large and small, from what to write about in the first place to whether the initial word of this sentence should be "writing" or "drafting" or even "crafting." If you plan to read any further, you too will have to make a number of choices: To read straight through in the order I've imposed? To read only the chapters that interest you? To look in the index and pick where to land? The table of contents and index, even the chapter headings, are there largely to help you decide.

You are unlikely to be rattled by having to choose among these several, discrete alternatives, however. A great deal of contemporary life is given over to studying menus of various kinds and then making deliberate, preference-driven selections from among the options presented—which is generally what choice today entails. We shop for goods we desire in supermarkets, at flea markets, in chain stores, and, increasingly, online. We pick what we want to watch, read, hear, follow, even (sometimes) believe to be true. We vote our favorites: for bond issues, for presidents, for winners on television game shows. We select—or hope to select—friends, lovers, and spouses, places to live or travel, subjects to study, jobs, hobbies, even insurance and health plans to hedge our bets when something we cannot choose occurs.

A few years ago, when I boarded a flight to Japan on Air Canada (whose slogan at the time was "Choice is good"), my own choices of the day started on a screen with hundreds of entertainment possibilities available at the touch of a finger. There was even a weepy Nicholas Sparks movie on offer called, appropriately, *The Choice*. The necessity of making such determinations only concluded when, after disembarking, I had successfully eaten dinner by grabbing at what I took to be the most attractive sushi options in a Tokyo restaurant as they came endlessly around a snaking conveyor belt, a menu come to life. The business of selecting and the logic of the menu of options have become both a way of life and, it is widely assumed, a means to build a life—or what we now call a "lifestyle."[1]

For choices, from this vantage point, not only help each of us get what we want. We *are* the sum of our choices. (Even opting out, like Herman Melville's Bartleby the Scrivener, has come to represent one among many possible choices about how we want to live and who we want to be.) Although we rarely make up the rules of the game or craft the banquet of possibilities, we like to think that when we are expressing our personal preferences, we are engaged in the business of self-realization as distinctive and independent people. Both having choices and making choices are largely what count these days as being, indeed feeling, free.[2]

This conception of the self, and even more of freedom, spans the political spectrum in the contemporary United States. It forms the basis of what the sociologist Pierre Bourdieu once called a *doxa*, the set of largely taken-for-granted assumptions that undergird all explicit fights in a given era.[3] Consider "reproductive choice" on the left and "school choice" or even choice in health-care providers on the right. One reason for this recurrent rhetoric is that few Americans today see themselves as opposed to the maximization of either alternatives from which to make selections or occasions to do so. We generally only disagree about what those alternatives are supposed to be.

This *doxa* is not, though, limited to North America, even if that's perhaps where it exists right now in its most exaggerated form. The language of democracy and human rights, running parallel with capitalism and advertising campaigns like Air Canada's, has spread globally, if highly unevenly, the idea that human autonomy, dignity, and even happiness and fulfillment depend on the ability to make one's own, personally satisfying choices, with a minimum of impediments, from among a range of options. Today that faith even anchors official charters and constitutions in many parts of the world. A commitment to individual choice has become fundamental to the kind of formal statements of equality of opportunity, if not outcome, that nowadays suggest a free society (which is also why even autocratic regimes usually pay lip service to this ideal, instituting sham forms of voting, for example, no matter how little they count in practice).

The "free choice of employment" (art. 23), the "right to choose the kind of education that shall be given to their children" (art. 26), and the "right to take part in the government of his country, directly or through freely chosen representatives" (art. 21): all already appear in the original Universal Declaration of Human Rights of 1948 as basic principles states should uphold.[4] Religious rights were reworded by the United Nations in a similar way in the 1960s as a right to choose a religion.[5] So were marriage rights, where talk of the "free and full consent of the intending spouses" gave way by the late 1970s to "the same right [for men and women] to choose a spouse and to enter into marriage only with their free and full consent."[6]

Since then, the range of those choice-based rights has continued to expand, at least in theory. The Indonesian constitution states that "every person shall be free to choose and to practice the religion of his/her choice" (though the choice is among six official religions, in effect a limited menu of state-sanctioned possibilities). The constitutions of Ethiopia, Ukraine, and Finland guarantee choice in place of residence. In Fiji, India, and Zimbabwe, citizens have the right to consult a legal practitioner of their own choosing. Ecuador protects citizens' right to join trade unions and other organizations of "their choice." In Nepal there is even a provision in the 2015 constitution laying out one's "right to choose" when it comes to "endemic seeds and agricultural species."[7]

The categories of peoples purportedly holding these rights have grown as well, from the disabled to the gender nonconforming to (with limits) youths. Partly this is rooted in the assumption that, as the Canadian philosopher Michael Ignatieff puts it in a rousing twenty-first-century defense of human rights, individuals are only free when they have agency, which he defines as the "right to choose the life they see fit to lead."[8] But this momentum also stems from the widely shared notion that being able to choose is not just worthy of our attention on instrumental grounds. What has "intrinsic value," explains the American philosopher Gerald Dworkin, is "being recognized as the kind of creature who is capable of making choices. That capacity grounds our idea of what it is to be a person and a moral agent equally worthy of respect by all."[9]

Indeed, it follows that if more and better choices on the part of more people is considered the desired effect of good policy in what we now call liberal democracies, good policy depends on the aggregated but democratically determined choices of individual citizens. According to the great late twentieth-century liberal political theorist John Rawls, people cannot and should not be expected to agree on preferences, aspirations, or even the conditions for a good life. However, they *can* agree on the need for the state to establish stable institutions by which to adjudicate equitably among different and conflicting goals. And they can agree on the process.[10] Democratic theory turns today on the idea of the individual citizen as a rational maker of personally sound choices who has consented, largely out of self-interest, to follow a set of collectively proscribed choice-making rules and to live by the results. Ideally, these results will guarantee the further expansion of personal choice, albeit with certain necessary if often controversial limits, going forward.

The modern economy is supposed to work on a very similar premise. Choices, rooted in individual wishes and desires, are created by and then work to drive effective markets. In response, effective markets generate more options for more people to pick among.[11]

We should not be surprised, then, that the notion of the human as an autonomous choice-maker acting on his or her closely held and distinctive penchants, values, and tastes is currently at the core of standard explanatory mechanisms as well. This conception of the self animates rational choice theory in the social sciences, with its reliance on the model of the utility-maximizing subject. It also holds weight when we are engaging in more prosaic talk at kitchen tables or in courtrooms about individual actors "taking personal responsibility" for choices freely made. That includes the ones that turn out badly.[12] In fact, stories about the deliberate choices we have made and their consequences are major parts of how we narrate our own existences today, albeit with varied cultural inflections among those of different backgrounds. Truly alternative versions of the self generally make us a bit nervous. As the commentators in a recent American updating of the traditional Passover Haggadah point out, people who identify as Jews have a much easier time these days thinking of themselves as choosers than as chosen.[13]

Arguably, though, it is feminism where the full power of the concept of choice is most evident today, and it is women's lives and identities that have been most buffeted and ultimately transformed globally in this concept's wake. It was in the last quarter of the nineteenth century that Isabel Archer, the central character of Henry James's great novel *The Portrait of a Lady*, announced that she wanted to know even the things one shouldn't do, not to do them, but "so as to choose."[14] Since then, what counts as a good (virtuous) choice versus a bad (unvirtuous) one has become less and less clearly defined. The range of possible paths has also greatly expanded. But from Isabel Archer's time onward, more or less, the mainstream women's rights movement has adopted and made good use of the idea that emancipation requires extending to women the same choice-making opportunities, conditions, and options as those previously accorded to men, plus a few others that are sex-specific. Fundamental still to most strains of feminism is the conviction that women become empowered precisely at that moment when (a) they each get to choose for themselves what they most desire (following Ignatieff's logic), and (b) they are recognized by themselves and others as capable, autonomous choosers (following Dworkin's).

This was certainly the reasoning behind the decision of American feminist organizations like NOW to advocate for legal abortion services in the 1970s with the slogan "the right to choose." Such language was intended, as we will see, to tie a controversial medical procedure to what had become a relatively uncontroversial economic, political, and moral outlook.[15] We now know it didn't work out quite as hoped. Still, the basic premise continues to hold sway: choice *is* freedom as we conceive of it in much of the world. This is, bluntly, the Age of Choice.

So, how did this happen? How did we—meaning primarily residents of the West but increasingly the people of all places around the globe that bill themselves as capitalist democracies—come to turn choice-making into a proxy for freedom in so many different realms of modern life and transform the social roles of both women and men in the process?

Not everyone would agree that this is a question for a historian to tackle at all. To a certain degree, of course, to choose is natural to people of both sexes. We humans have probably always had preferences for some things over others, from particular foods to particular persons. Scientists, along with philosophers, have also helped us see people, across space and time, as hardwired for certain kinds of autonomous decision-making tasks.[16] Sociobiologists and evolutionary psychologists, in particular, have insisted in recent years that how and what we choose are shaped by the long-term process of evolution—meaning the needs of our species—as much as anything else.[17] Women, for instance, much as they think they are expressing personal predilections when it comes to mates, are biologically programmed over time to choose men with certain characteristics that will ensure their own replication. These choices then further shape the evolutionary process.[18]

Such claims are, perhaps, reinforced by the apparent dominance, even hegemony, of choice—as a term, as a value, and as a social practice—today. To be asked to make a choice, even an essentially meaningless one between, say, two or three or twenty different shampoos in the pharmacy or one hundred different profiles on Tinder, has come to seem such a natural, unexceptional part of life in much of our globalized world that it is rarely considered as culturally or historically specific behavior. On the contrary, it can often feel, especially among the earth's more prosperous inhabitants, as if what we confront is just a ceaseless expansion of opportunities and options, both material and abstract, to do what we were meant to be doing all along.

But to the historian—and particularly one with a long-standing interest in the history of the *doxic*—it is evident that the specific forms choosing has taken and, even more, the significance that we have accorded it as a hallmark of freedom from consumer capitalism to human rights and feminism *are* historical developments. This claim holds even if we accept that the ability to choose is part of what makes us human. It holds even if we accept that many of our choices are a lot more biologically determined than they appear to us. Our investment in choice-making as a lived experience, and the special weight we attribute to this experience despite its clear limitations and exclusions, constitutes a crucial element of the story of Western modernity. So is seeing the world as structured by these choices and humans as fundamentally freely choosing selves. "Take your choice!," as Major John Cartwright urged his British contemporaries in 1776, is, in fact, a deeply culturally and temporally distinctive battle cry.[19]

For we also know that not only did people, male or female, have and make quantitatively fewer choices in the distant past, but understandings of what freedom means or feels like have also changed substantially over the last few hundred years. Until relatively recently, to be free in the Western world actually had almost nothing to do with having the capacity to make unconstrained decisions at every turn about how to forge a life path or worldview out of the possibilities available. What made a nobleman in early modern Europe free was quite the opposite: the knowledge that, as a result of his status, he was not dependent on or dominated by anyone else (an ideal that never fully went away either).[20] That, and the security of having a predetermined set of beliefs, life partner, landholdings, income, belongings, and social role before, in many cases, even reaching adulthood.[21] In a world where continuity and stability were exceptionally prized and so much was handed down, maximizing choice-making opportunities was not just of limited appeal. It was also unlikely to matter much, especially for those at the top of a relatively fixed social hierarchy.

For women this was even more obviously true, even if liberty was long personified as a heroic female holding a flag or staff or book. Plus, where alternative paths did exist for either sex, they were, as we will see, typically framed in the register of "Hercules' Choice," a popular, early modern allegory (and subject of much great literature, music, and art) in which decision making boiled down to two, unequal options. One could do the right and proper thing associated with the good of others. Or one could choose badly by acting on one's fleeting and selfish instincts and, as a result, head down the path of licentiousness and vice.[22]

The rest of what happened generally came down to luck, fate, God's larger plan, or something else quite outside human control. Even the point of the biblical story of Eve was, for most Christians, that it was important for humans not to misuse their divinely given capacity for free choice unless they sought to bring suffering upon themselves.[23] Freedom, in a spiritual and moral sense, traditionally meant living in inner peace with a set of already widely agreed-upon rules and obligations. This is quite different from how we usually think about choice *or* liberty in the twenty-first century. In other parts of the world, notably South and East Asia, conceptualizations of freedom traditionally took even more radically alternative premodern forms and, to a certain degree, still do. Consider, for example, Gandhi's "non-willing" freedom, which was all about relinquishing rather than affirming one's will or surrendering without subordination.[24]

The Age of Choice is thus an account of how a very particular transformation establishing, first, liberal and, then, what is sometimes now called "neoliberal" freedom came about, from its initial stirrings in early modern commercial and religious contexts across the North Atlantic world (albeit always with some connection to specific extra-European developments) to its mid- to late twentieth-century quasi-global turn (though without denying that it has been remade with distinctive variations in every context and fiercely rejected in plenty too).[25] This is the previously untold story of an idea and way of life that have been fundamental to defining the modern world—told now as their future looks increasingly unsure.

Four key propositions about how best to narrate this complex tale govern this inquiry from the get-go. The first concerns the time frame—and historical time more generally. The current hegemony of freedom-as-choice was, I want to suggest, the result of a long-term, staccato, and in no way inevitable or even unidirectional historical process. Commitment to this conception of the world did not suddenly spring full-blown into life in the Western Hemisphere in the 1970s and 1980s, as some historians of neoliberalism or second-wave feminism would have it.[26] But neither did it spontaneously emerge back in the age of democratic revolutions as a natural extension of transatlantic enlightened rights talk, as is sometimes imagined by other scholars.[27] Early statements of the *droits de l'homme*, such as the Declaration of the Rights of Man and of the Citizen of 1789, make no mention of the protection of individuals' "choice" or "choices." Classic early texts concerned with "the woman question" say nothing of the sort either. And when Thomas Paine did urge Americans in 1776 to make a "choice" about a new political order, he was referring to a collective determination and never indicated that this plan would require the adoption of a procedure to measure, then aggregate the specific preferences of every individual, or even adult male individual, person by person.

On the contrary, I submit, our contemporary attachment to freedom-as-choice (and choice-as-freedom) has deep if loose roots stretching all the way back both to the first age of empire, as new elements of consumer culture started to take root around much of the globe, *and* to the intellectual fracturing of Europe in the aftermath of the Reformation and Wars of Religion. That's especially the case when it comes to material goods and to beliefs. We can in both arenas trace the origins in broad strokes of a move away from choices on the model of Hercules and toward those predicated on the satisfaction of one's own preferences in a world rich with increased, as well as less morally freighted, options.

However, this distinctive way of seeing the world only very gradually and fitfully came to fruition, with different timing and different sources and effects in every domain. Individuated political choice, in particular, was a very late piece in the puzzle—for men and, especially, for women. The end of the nineteenth century and the first half of the twentieth, when the secret ballot combined with universal male and then female suffrage became the global norm, might actually be thought of as encompassing a second major age of democratic revolutions quite distinct from the first. For only after this moment did different spheres of life and different parts of the world become entwined and, to a certain degree, synchronized around notions of individual choice in ways that began to feel natural even if they weren't—and also to generate resentments that continue to this day.[28] That story continues into the twentieth century with the foundation of whole sciences dependent on the naturalization

of the act of personally motivated choice and, finally, through the growing fusion of liberal democracy with capitalist values, the reinvention of
choice as itself the critical moral value for our times.

The larger point, though, is that conventional periodization around
established turning points like regime changes and major wars is mostly
irrelevant here. So is any kind of strict chronology. When it comes to
big stories, historians are sometimes better off, I believe, telling them in
discontinuous ways, cutting even jarringly across time as well as space,
as will repeatedly happen here. Past and present illuminate each other in
what follows because we see new things when we pay attention to contrast
and continuity at the same time.

Which leads to my second proposition: that to understand how any
of this came about, we need to turn our gaze, at least initially, less to
philosophy or political theory than to mundane social practices. By this
I mean the ordinary, often formulaic behavior that men and women
have long engaged in around the business of selection from among defined alternatives, whether of goods for sale, ideas and beliefs, romantic
partners, candidates for office, occupations, or most anything else. For
I am also convinced that new attitudes about choice-making, not to
mention freedom, developed largely in the *doing*, or what the French
call *usage*, especially in people's "free" time.[29]

Outside of working hours and at the nexus between public and private life, men and women from varied backgrounds increasingly took
up varied physical as well as mental rituals of choice-making (think
shopping or voting or picking a dancing partner, for example). They did
so in a variety of specialized spaces using a range of small-scale technologies (think restaurant bills of fare, election ballots, dance cards,
catalogs and advertising circulars, library registers, commonplace
books, surveys and quizzes, and a whole new world of largely paper
inventions related to organizing, determining, and registering their
choices).[30] As such, they allowed the experience of picking from sets of
options to be understood in a very specific way: as the externalization
of self-defined interior preferences and thus an act of independent self-
making. This happened even as other people and forces almost always
defined who got to pick which options from which menus and with

what implications. Over time, the constant repetition and routinization of such activities, indeed their intellectual *and* corporeal performance by ordinary people in the role of "choosers," did much to make this association second nature or *doxic* in the sense of no longer consciously feeling chosen.[31] Eventually this was true even for the poor and the illiterate, despite the reliance on paper and print.

One of Hannah Arendt's great insights for historians was, to my mind, that political norms always depend on historically specific but socially widespread mental habits.[32] A liberal order, for example, needs distinctive ways of thinking, judging, seeking truth, and more, both for its creation and for its reinforcement. From the work of Bourdieu, we have also come to appreciate that such norms, or what he calls "political mythologies," are first and foremost embodied.[33] They require, for solidification, physical enactment according to directives and patterns set out in advance but soon learned by heart. That is why the metaphor of choreography is important to this book as a whole and not only in the discussion of social dance to follow.[34]

I do not mean, however, that we should ignore the claims of great thinkers of the past or discard the history of concepts and their expression when it comes to the story of freedom-as-choice or choice-as-freedom. What you are reading is still primarily an intellectual history, even if built out of the history of ordinary activities, and you can rest assured that you will still meet familiar figures here and there—Cotton Mather, Voltaire, John Stuart Mill, Betty Friedan—talking about big abstractions. My contention is simply that doing, thinking, and talking about, or what might also be called conduct and culture, are always linked and multidirectional. Existing ways of describing and basic cultural presuppositions shape how new practices are understood by those performing or watching them; but social practices, especially if frequently repeated over time, also reshape language and, ultimately, meaning. This is how *doxic* ideas gain their power.

Just as significantly, this book is also a study of obstacles to and constraints on free choice, from official rules, to customs and social conventions, to lack of funds or even locks on doors. My third proposition is that these multiple factors, along with those imposing them, limited at every turn who within any population got to choose; what choices were on offer; and how those choices were to be made, registered, put to work, and, ultimately, valued. New forms of choice-making were, in short, always built on new forms of exclusion and prohibition. Simultaneously, though, these same impediments—formal and informal, externally imposed and also eventually internalized—made choice-making navigable. In addition, they rendered it sufficiently organized and circumscribed for it to be relatively safe for mass participation. What needs recognition is that, paradoxically, freedom of choice has always required, and still requires, rules, regulations, even restrictions of multiple kinds in order to prevent it from threatening individual well-being or the stability of the social order as a whole. That's also why all the choices discussed in this book, no matter how open-seeming, are necessarily what I term "bounded choices," limited by parameters both visible and not.[35] One might even say that the proliferation of impersonal laws of all kinds in the modern world should be seen as a function of and complement to the proliferation and celebration of individuated, personalized choice.[36]

But for the historian, this claim requires a shift in thinking. At the very least, it means moving away from any binary distinctions, as famously introduced at the height of the Cold War by the philosopher Isaiah Berlin, between "freedom from," or the elimination of external barriers to picking to do what one wants, and "freedom to," or the creation of the conditions that make it possible for one to achieve self-fulfillment.[37] In fact, one cannot exist without the other. That means any story about choice necessarily becomes a double one. Even as we chart the growth of deregulation and the apparent rise of laissez-faire attitudes and policies, we must also pay attention to enhanced state reach—evident, for example, in new forms of street lighting or new laws governing the institution of marriage—and the flourishing of unofficial regulative ideals in civil society, such as standards of taste, reason, truth, virtue, and decorum. As this book tries to make clear, the nineteenth century was the great age of rules, offering up protocols for everything from how to flirt before dancing with a chosen member of the opposite sex to how to register political opinions (though there was always some room for playing with the possibilities). All of these kinds of constraints—not to mention the often unrecognized "choice architects" behind them, from shopkeepers to dancing masters to party leaders and election officials to, now, the makers of algorithms—are central to the story of how choice has been distributed, experienced, protected, promoted, occasionally thwarted, and understood.[38] They, too, along with all of those doing the actual choosing, are an overlooked part of the long story of today.

Fourth and finally, as might already be apparent, I am convinced that women deserve special attention on all sides of this story's unfolding. That's partly because of their distinctive roles in it and partly because of the way their example brings the big issues here into sharp focus. Long denied many opportunities for individuated choice and disparaged for doing badly those they were afforded (to the detriment of this innovative kind of choice-making too), women might seem marginal to the main action. Yet women actively made use of this particular power going back to the eighteenth century, and a small subset eventually hitched their destiny to this specific ambition, twinning it with liberation more broadly in an effort both to challenge and to capitalize on mainstream liberalism. Ultimately, they both succeeded and failed, entrenching this core idea still further. Uncovering women's fraught role in the long history of choice-making illuminates something important about the peculiar kind of feminism we have inherited from our foremothers and forefathers. But even more, to understand how and why such unprecedented stature has been accorded to preference-driven, increasingly value-neutral choice-making in so many different realms of life today, it pays to keep an eye on women—and especially women with some social power—and their evolving struggles over the last few centuries around autonomy and freedom.[39]

Of course, the long story of freedom-as-choice and choice-as-freedom is *also* necessarily interlaced in much of the West with that of chattel slavery and abolition, real and metaphoric, as will be evident throughout this book as well. Freedom and slavery have historically depended on each other for force.[40] And even as coerced labor and reproduction have formally ended and been replaced with equality under the law in most democracies, including our own, freedom has remained thoroughly racialized. New social hierarchies established around the outcomes of choices made, rather than explicitly around conditions of birth, have not dispelled that reality. Perhaps they have even made it more invidious by making it less visible. This feature of the modern choice landscape renders it all the more important to highlight those who have been, and in some cases remain, often shut out of its terrain: children, the seriously poor, the institutionalized, many rural people, and, in much of the West, people of color of both sexes. To a considerable degree, individualized choice eventually came to define all of their horizons anyway, whether as aspiration or as rubric for pathologizing their fates.

But what needs emphasizing is that over the last few hundred years, adult women of a certain level of privilege and prosperity—and by extension largely urban, white women in Western Europe and its former colonial domains for much of this time—both repeatedly found themselves excluded from choice-making rituals *and* became the paradigmatic modern choosers. As such, they will feature especially heavily among the cast of characters in this book. My last proposition is that focusing on women as both tropes and historical actors, from the fictional Isabel Archer to the many real women who filled out reader surveys in twentieth-century women's magazines, brings the tensions and contradictions around the equation of choice with freedom—and thus liberal democracy itself—into high relief.

And those trade-offs matter. For there is also a growing body of contemporary (and decidedly nonhistorical) scholarship indicating that the model of self-as-chooser and freedom-as-choice that we are so collectively enamored of today and that is so central to our reigning political-economic paradigms is a flawed one.

How so? Let's start with the chooser. Several decades of research by psychologists, behavioral economists, and now neuroscientists have helped us see that even fully adult men and women are not as good at making choices as we have long tended to think they are. Or at least they are not as good as rational choice theorists, who imagine every choice

as the externalization and optimization of a standing interior preference, would have us believe (though, arguably, this is something that
Freudians, Marxists, and, before them, fiction writers and key religious
thinkers have long known).[41] It turns out we humans suffer from faulty
intuitions, context dependence, risk aversion, short-term thinking, and
simply not knowing our own minds. When choosing among different
options, we are too driven by our emotions and transient desires, too
likely to overvalue our own judgment (snap or not), and too easily
swayed by the wrong factors. We overestimate what we know. We fail to
accurately predict what we will want in the future.

We are also inconsistent about our preferences and value the objects
we possess over the ones we lack in ways that do not make objective
sense. More information doesn't always help either. That is because
we also tend to ignore facts that do not jibe with the outcome we desire,
focus on the wrong information, or see patterns where they do not exist.
Add to that the discovery that we are also easily manipulated by those
designing the menus as well as by peer pressure and the desire for external approval. Even our desires, in other words, are rarely entirely of
our own invention—and to think otherwise is just to engage in another
kind of self-deception.

Choice can also, at its worst, turn into compulsion or addiction,
meaning choice-making without any actual control. The upshot of all
of this, say psychologists, is that, whether shopping or picking a mate,
people frequently end up selecting what is not in their own best interest.
Or what they pick is not consonant with what they thought were their
preferences. Poor choices then come with serious economic and also
psychic costs.

This phenomenon, says yet another group of social scientists, has
only been magnified in recent years, as technology has expanded beyond anyone's wildest dreams both our need to make choices and our
options, not to mention the time, energy, and know-how required to
navigate them all.[42] It is not only a matter of exhaustion, it turns out
(though I suspect I am not alone in finding that even selecting an electric teakettle or a vacuum cleaner has become an arduous task insofar
as one aims to find the "right" or "best" one). We have taken on so much

imagined responsibility for crafting our own happiness and success that many of us find ourselves feeling guilty over the last choice, anxious about the next one, and potentially overburdened, even paralyzed by such mundane questions as what to eat for lunch.

This may be especially true for those of us without sufficient means to employ others—consultants, advisors, experts, guides, managers of all kinds, both human and algorithmic—who promise to map out the choices we confront and make "suggestions" or even "selections" for us. (And the wealthy *do* get a lot of help, including help in making bad choices go away in an era when, thanks to the internet, their traces otherwise live on indefinitely.)[43] Consider here Immanuel Kant's prescient proposition on the eve of the French Revolution that the discovery of choice might well have given the initial human beings their first taste of freedom, but it came at a high cost. This same realization also introduced stress and fear into their lives for the duration. For the possibility of choice opened up what Kant called an "infinite range of objects," with little guidance on how to select among them, one choice foreclosing another with no way of knowing in advance what the different effects would be.[44]

Nearly two centuries later, in her 1963 novel *The Bell Jar*, Sylvia Plath transposed this same ambivalence onto her female heroine's imaginary confrontation, in an age of ever-increasing options for women of her class, with a fig tree: "I [Esther] saw my life branching out before me. . . . From the tip of every branch, like a fat purple fig, a wonderful future beckoned and winked," including one fig representing a husband and a happy home and children, another becoming a famous poet, yet another adventures in Europe, Africa, and South America, and many others, including some futures she can't yet even make out. The point is that a world of delicious possibility lies before her—at least in theory. Yet the Garden of Eden has its own traps for this modern Eve. Esther continues, "I saw myself sitting in the crotch of this fig tree, starving to death, just because I couldn't make up my mind which of the figs I would choose. I wanted each and every one of them, but choosing one meant losing all the rest, and, as I sat there, unable to decide, the figs began to wrinkle and go black, and, one by one, they plopped to the ground at my feet."[45]

Similar experiences of required choices with few obvious directives have today prompted a flourishing market for self-help guides, on the one hand, and for so-called libertarian paternalist policy manifestos, on the other, all purporting to employ the latest experimental cognitive science for assistance in the business of selection. Neither genre is designed to challenge choice's proliferation. Nor is either intended to undermine the understanding that to choose by and for oneself is broadly constitutive of freedom.[46] But their collective promise is that we *can* be helped, whether with a book in hand or with a "nudge" from the state, to choose a little better (however defined), and with a little less mental anguish, henceforth.[47]

Meanwhile, in ways that diverge from the behavioralists and often from each other, a diverse group of political philosophers has drawn our gaze to the larger, negative social and political consequences of all this attention to maximizing choice and thinking of it as a synonym for liberty. Their arguments often begin from the premise that there is much that this preoccupation either distracts us from or elides. At a minimum, goes one strain of critique, we have become so preoccupied with needing to choose so much and so often, from teakettles and vacuums onward, that we no longer have much residual appetite for collective decision making or, indeed, for investment in community affairs. That is, beyond Facebook "likes." The only exception, perhaps, is when the agenda is to promote the creation of more opportunities for individual choice or choices themselves. This is a theme that recurs in postcolonial literature too, like Vivek Shanbhag's haunting novel *Ghachar Ghochar* (2013), where the new experience of consumer society and individualized choice leaves a once-poor extended family of spice traders in Bangalore in moral disarray, no longer able to act as one to advance their common well-being.[48]

Just as seriously, claim other contemporary critics, a discursive focus on choice and personal responsibility has come to function not as a fig but as a fig leaf: a way of covering over or even reinforcing structural inequalities inherent in our democratic, capitalist order.[49] We blame the poor, in particular, for their bad choices as individuals, or even for the choice of poverty itself, rather than recognize the ways in which opportunities to choose and the choices themselves, starting with the menu of options, are constantly and everywhere inequitably defined by race, gender, location, education level, social expectations, age, and especially wealth. Most of those factors themselves fall outside the realm of choice. In fact, all people are not equally free to choose, regardless of what human rights decrees say.[50] All choices also aren't equal. They aren't even all real. More often than not, the language of choice is, as one legal scholar puts it, a "rhetoric of the powerful" that helps those already on top and harms the powerless.[51]

This is also a major theme of Margaret Wilkerson Sexton's 2017 American novel, *A Kind of Freedom*, which focuses on several generations of an African American family and the array of suboptimal choices its members confront even as formal equality, the legal possibility of determining one's own life course, grows.[52] The protagonists only get to be full-fledged individuals at the cost of being repeatedly punished, formally and informally, for what they pick. Something similarly punitive happens disproportionately to women across racial, class, and ethnic differences, albeit with different effects depending on these variables. In practice, women are still often tasked with full responsibility for risk management, not least when it comes to their reproductive "choices." Or they are left with impossible choices, like family *or* income-producing job. This hardly counts as liberation.

One result has been public efforts to regulate further the lives of the disadvantaged and sometimes quite literally tell them what to do. Food subsidy programs for the poor, for example, generally specify what recipients can and cannot purchase to eat. But even laws framed around respect for choice can, in practice, end up functioning to curtail the rights of the vulnerable rather than expand them, rendering greater freedom an illusion. Consider, for example, the "freedom of choice" laws enacted in some southern American states in the 1950s and 1960s in the wake of the *Brown v. Board of Education* Supreme Court decision that let parents determine what schools their children would attend, but also intimidated nonwhite parents into "picking" nonwhite options, thereby violating the promise of equal opportunity associated with school desegregation.[53] Or consider the 1993

Méhaignerie Law or Second Pasqua Law that modified the French citizenship code (until it too was overturned a few years later), replacing birthright citizenship for individuals born in France to immigrant parents with a system in which such individuals would need henceforth to demonstrate their allegiance to the state through "an expression of choice" in order to become citizens.[54] Or, still more recently, we might think about how laws preserving "choice" in health insurance plans in the United States leave much of the public exposed to the coercion of the marketplace, with the result that health care costs more rather than less.[55]

Little wonder, then, that some commentators argue that to create real freedom for *all* people, we need a change of course. To realize many of our most important collective aims—say, clean air to breathe—we may need more policies that encourage shared responsibility and resist marketization as individual choices. On occasion, we may also need to place formal limits on the choices of the most privileged sectors of society (what if, for example, one couldn't "choose" a private or magnet school for one's own children?) with the goal of increasing the number and quality of options available to others. Otherwise the sum of our choices may well be a world no one would actually choose.

In just this vein of critique, some contemporary feminists have struck back at mainstream women's rights discourse too, calling it, following Linda Hirshman's clever pejorative tag, "choice feminism."[56] The name is intended to shine a negative light on two particular qualities of this discourse. One is advocates' tendency to see empowerment as a matter of women having the widest range of lifestyle and career options possible for self-invention. The other is proponents' suggestion that any choice counts as a feminist one if a woman who understands herself as a feminist has freely made it, thereby discouraging any criticism of those choices whether they involve kitchens or boardrooms, burqas or G-strings.

According to philosopher Nancy Fraser, among others, such attitudes assume the existence of a world of value-neutral freedom, where neither money, nor internalized social attitudes, nor relations with others from families to bosses function as constraints on choice. That world is, though, purely imaginary, especially for women. Still worse, such "respect for all choices" attitudes in the here and now make feminism complacent in or even a buttress for the status quo rather than a challenge to it—to the benefit of media, advertising, and retail outfits, not women themselves.[57]

Instead, say these critics, feminists today need to make clear that some things are too morally weighty or dangerous to be described as a legitimate "choice." This is why, for example, we cannot legally buy children, or sell our own organs, or even opt for a decidedly unsafe job. What's more, today's feminists need to acknowledge that some choices, whether made by women or men, are trivial from a political standpoint (lipstick shades, for example?) or, more seriously, detrimental, exacerbating sexist stereotypes, inequalities of power and money, or the destruction of the earth we all share.[58] The "choice" to engage in sex work is one obvious site of contention. But so is something as small as what kind of vehicle one drives to work; one person's freedom to choose can come at the expense of another's or the well-being of the planet and its inhabitants as a whole. As the Black feminist legal scholar Dorothy Roberts pointed out some time ago, focusing repeatedly on choice as liberty "does nothing to dismantle social arrangements that make it impossible for some people to make a choice in the first place"—which is precisely what she believes feminism should be about.[59] The Canadian journalist Meghan Murphy puts it in historical terms: "Choice is no longer a rallying cry for change."[60] It has, from this perspective, lost its emancipatory bite for all of us.

Can the historian do more than simply show it was once otherwise or flesh out the details in the story? Can she use the evidence of the past to address normative issues alongside properly historical ones and thus have something to contribute to today's lively debates about choice?[61] Demonstrating that possibility constitutes my other key ambition in writing this book.

The Age of Choice is structured primarily as a work of history. Each chapter hones in on a specific social practice or ritual in the place(s) where and at the moment(s) when it also became a new arena for individuated, preference-based, and increasingly value-neutral choice-making in daily life, apart from the demands of labor. But each chapter also explores the promises and perils that these developments entailed, as well as their relation to changing notions of freedom that remain central to liberal democratic theory and capitalist culture today.

The first two chapters take up choices in what are "defined objects" from the perspective of contemporary choice theory. Chapter 1 focuses on *consumer* or *aesthetic choice*. Chapter 2 takes up *intellectual choice*. Two middle chapters then consider the selection of other people, as well as the development of ever-more restricted or "bounded" (in my terms) versions of choice. Chapter 3 looks at "interdependent choice" through an exploration of *affective choice*. Chapter 4 addresses the emergence of *political choice*, including the establishment of formal rules for "group choice." Chapter 5, finally, tells the story of the invention of *sciences of choice* centered on study of the abstract human as a choice-maker realizing his or her personal preferences and tastes in these various domains. It also relays how researchers and their subjects together helped turn choice-making into the moral telos of modern life. The epilogue then comes full circle, using the war over abortion rights since the early 1970s to reconsider the liberal conception of choice and what this might mean for future framings of freedom.

Throughout I pay attention to what has been left out of the hegemony of choice too. Think for a moment of recent discussions of gay rights that downplay the role of agency or motivated choice in the determination of one's sexual orientation—much as one might have done, in an earlier moment, in conversations about national character. The political implications of such bio-essentialism, with its starting point of born-this-way-ism rather than optionality, are enormous, sometimes fueling new forms of discrimination and sometimes leading to new areas of liberation, as in the marriage equality struggle.[62] Debates about gender identity today similarly draw on rationales related to both choice and birth, fueling yet more political fights (though this book will follow my historical actors in generally taking women to be a biological category along with a political and social one).[63] And consider, too, the distinction between people advocating choice who want to be able to opt out of something that the government requires (i.e., vaccination in the age of Covid-19), claiming they are being denied their autonomy or coerced by the state, and people advocating choice who want to be able to do something that the government threatens to disallow as a possibility because of potential harms (as in the abortion debate, but also the debate around gun ownership). The subject of this book, in the end, is human actors' evolving choices about choices: what should be subject to choice, how should choosing happen, who should be able to do it, what should it mean.

Finally, a word is needed on the sources for all of this. Occasionally, I insert myself and my own experience into the story. Often, I turn to obsolete material objects, from preprinted paper dance cards to wooden ballot boxes, to see what they can tell us about choice in the past. I do something similar with works of visual art; precisely because choice is such a difficult idea to capture in images, efforts at its representation can make for especially revealing sources. I also draw on a wide range of different written texts (which is what historians generally do), including how-to manuals, laws, polemics, travelogues, and various forms of reportage. But a comment is needed about one particular kind of textual source that I have taken the liberty of employing frequently and not just in this introduction: novels.

The specific type of fictional story that we call a novel—itself a new commercial product of the late seventeenth and eighteenth centuries—took up the subject of choice almost immediately. Not only did early (often female) novelists offer their (often female) readers detailed images of new (often female) forms of choice-making in action, placing their (often female) protagonists in the front rooms of shops, at writing tables and library counters, and in ballrooms and polling stations. These same writers also made the psychological experience of choice, that seeming hinge between interior preference and outward action, a central theme of the genre. Think of all the plots of novels ever since that turn on their heroes and heroines wrestling with what to do in the face of conflicts between, on the one hand, their innermost desires and, on the other, laws, customs, expectations, obligations, and even the effects of past choices, all of which function to enable and constrain current options and opportunities. Think, too, of the discourse of rewards and punishments afterward. In crafting fiction this way, authors from Frances Burney to Sylvia Plath to Margaret Wilkerson Sexton have steadily helped invent, through their characters, the association between choice-making and the construction of an autonomous, free self.[64] For this reason, we might even call the realist novel the choice-genre *par excellence*; characters' particular situations become case studies in the psychology, sociology, and even ethics of choice. Isabel Archer did not—and does not—stand alone. She and her peers have much to tell us still.

As for you, the reader of *this* book: you can, of course, decide to follow along, disagree, modify what I say with a new interpretation, or even close the book in disgust! (More on how those possibilities came into being can be found in chapter 2.) I do not, in any case, ask you to accept any single, seamless, inexorable storyline about the rise of choice idolatry or even to read in any one particular way. But if this book contains a polemic about anything, it is about seeing clearly what we are doing and considering the implications when we go about our mundane business as pickers from menus of options, rather than just following the guidelines that we've internalized in a haze. For if I am shirking my responsibilities in not being more directive in my authorial or "choice architect" role, as the libertarian paternalists might put it, I am potentially overstepping them in attempting to use history to tell us something about not only the past but also where we might go in the future.

My hope is that by laying bare an obscure history, I might have something to contribute to a conversation begun by cognitive scientists, economists, feminist political theorists, and others, including novelists, that needs to make itself heard in larger circles. My belief is that study of choice's past effectiveness as well as its serious limitations as a means to emancipation can help us think freshly about when choice-making does and does not serve larger social goals; how opportunities for choice can expand but also become more just for more people; and even what other modes for envisioning our future, beyond choice, are worth cultivating starting now, in light of current challenges to liberal democracy. For it seems that today's critics of American-style choice feminism are ultimately right: our reigning concept of freedom has lost its way, and it will be up to the next generation to right it, remake it, or replace it with something else.

CHAPTER 1

SHOPPING FOR GOODS—OR CHOICE IN THINGS

Mr. Cock's Auctions

One part of the story of choice begins in the marketplace. Or more precisely, it begins with a European historical artifact: an activity that we still routinely call shopping.

"Shopping," or sometimes "going a shopping," only entered the English language as a term of art in the last few decades of the eighteenth century.[1] It shows up in period novels about fashionable ladies and their newly fashionable pursuits like visiting, gossiping, and dressing for dinner. But the business that this neologism was meant to describe—the specific act of not just buying but first looking over, considering, selecting, and only then making purchases from a range of displayed goods—actually got its start some decades earlier. That is in good part thanks to ambitious, if now obscure, entrepreneurs like Mr. Cock, London auctioneer.

Christopher Cock did not invent the marketplace or the shop. He did not invent the provisioning of one's home or body with premade goods. He did not even invent the auction. All have ancient origins, though auctions did not get a lot of modern play until they were revived for selling secondhand goods in Amsterdam, Stockholm, and other cities in continental Europe in the seventeenth century—and, in another important aspect of our story, became a standard means of distributing human cargo in the form of enslaved Africans and their descendants in Europe's American outposts.[2]

What the London-based Mr. Cock did come up with between the 1720s and 1740s was a clever set of new sales techniques, or maybe more accurately gimmicks, that put *his* auctions on the map. With a few tricks, he turned miscellaneous luxury (and sometimes not-so-luxury) items into a set of discrete options—or something like what we'd now call a "choice set." Then he made potential purchasers and even onlookers— male and female, fancy and not—into individual competitors. Finally, he engaged them all in a form of carefully choreographed choice-making behavior, at once mental and physical, that would soon enough be known, innovatively, as shopping.[3]

Cock's initial insight was that the auction had the potential to be more than a practical way to dispose of inventory. It could be an experience, a participatory and even haptic event suitable for a socially ambitious urban clientele of the sort that early eighteenth-century London already boasted. From his start in the 1710s to just before his death at mid-century, Cock was, it seems, a seller of anything inanimate that he could get his hands on. Sometimes those wares were used books or whole libraries, long the primary kind of goods distributed through the auction mechanism within Europe. Other times they were decorative objects, fine furnishings, paintings, and/or prints, ideally from far-off places like Italy or India that could be name-checked for their cachet. Many of his auctions revolved around household miscellany, including beds and tables, cooking utensils, clothing, carpets, and fabrics of many kinds, not to mention the real estate that contained them too. Old, used, or secondhand stuff was, after all, central to economic life everywhere in a world without cheap, mass-manufactured goods.[4] But regardless of this heterogeneity of wares, Cock had his methods, one might even say formula, for drawing crowds to him and getting them to do what he wanted, which was eventually to make off with a lot of stuff.

To begin with, the auctioneer delimited the space. Cock's dealings transpired variously in the estates of the deceased at the edges of London (especially when the goods were the entire content of those people's lives and property), in rented city locations like Mrs. Savage's India Warehouse in the Strand, and, in his later years, in his own professional quarters attached to his home near Golden Square and then the Great

Piazza, Covent Gardens. In each of these settings, his opening move was laying out all the objects he hoped to sell—or making them "expos'd to view."[5] Then, initially by way of newspaper advertisements, he invited Londoners of both sexes, during set dates and hours for the few days before the actual sale, to come take a look at all the exposed goods, which is to say, survey all the alternatives, either in anticipation of bidding and buying or just for entertainment. Occasionally he offered viewing times "when ladies only will be admitted."[6] But one of the features of these auctions was that even when the items for sale had a fancy provenance, doors chez Cock opened widely to what his contemporary James Ralph called, with a certain amount of exaggeration, "all Ranks, from the Duke and Duchess to the Pick-pocket and Street-walker," to come linger and peruse the options.[7] They just had to agree to follow Cock's procedures. For only once Cock had successfully stoked desires at many social levels did he conduct single- or many-day sales, still in the same spaces, with possession going to the highest bidder in ascending order, lot by lot, and himself at the helm, directing the whole spectacle. Indeed, Cock became so famous as a kind of impresario of sales in the second quarter of the eighteenth century that he was parodied by both the painter William Hogarth and the writer Henry Fielding, a real distinction in this moment (fig. 1.1).[8]

But that's not all that makes Cock important to our larger story. Several decades before the founding of Sotheby's and Christie's, the high-end British auction houses that survive to this day, Cock also made substantial use of a specific paper technology for realizing his commercial aims: printed catalogs. On the model of booksellers' ones from the previous century,[9] they were given out for free or, at most, one shilling at select locations, including the auctioneer's home and, sometimes, the printer's or local coffeehouses and pubs. (These sales catalogs are also how we can know so much about these auctions now, from the items on offer to Cock's sales techniques.)

Consider first the cover page for a catalog associated with a Cock production. Its function, like the "puffery" or ads that Cock also placed in the papers, was to lure potential customers and, in the process, to whet their appetites for purchasing as well as the overall event. In big

Fig. 1.1. William Hogarth, *The Battle of the Pictures* (1744–45), etching and engraving. This is a bidder's ticket for a Cock auction in which Christopher Cock himself is depicted as a weathervane on the auction house. But it is also a satire, as the compass points on the weathervane have been replaced by P, V, F, S, for "puffs," a Cock specialty, and the image suggests that Hogarth's paintings will lose in the upcoming battle against battalions of traditional paintings.

type, covers gave a hint of the category of goods to be auctioned (books, china, paintings, what-have-you). They almost always linked those goods to an eminent institution or person, like "the Most Noble Charles, Earl of Haifaix, deceas'd" (1727), or "the ingenius Mr. John Price, surgeon" (1746), or the book collector "Mrs. Katherine Bridgeman" (1743), who could be counted on to have had good taste or expertise and whose name still added prestige and thus value to the items on sale, much like the goods that people still wildly overpay for at estate auctions of deceased celebrities like Yves St. Laurent or Jackie O. or Joan Didion. What's more, these covers usually laid out the ground rules, including when, where, and how much one had to spend up front to take anything home. With the auctioneer's name in the place usually accorded to the author controlling the action inside, such covers looked a lot like the novels with which they came to compete for fashionable attention in the first half of the eighteenth century (fig. 1.2).[10]

As for the stuff: the interior pages that followed were given over to inventories, sometimes descriptive and sometimes not, of an array of tantalizing goods, antique and modern, disaggregated into discrete "lots." When it came to paintings, for example, entries could be brief and specific: "Hercules Chuseth Virtue by Mr. Zeeman," a most eighteenth-century title. They could be brief and rather general: "a piece of dead fowls." Or they could be inventive descriptions with narrative power of their own: "Sophonisba, Anguisciola (the famous Italian Paintress) playing upon a Harpsichord with another Figure done by herself; this is the only picture in England, of that Excellent Paintress."[11] The same held for furniture or even fabric for sale. It was, in good part, Cock's catalogs—an early form of mechanically reproduced consumer technology meant to be read and used by his patrons every step of the way (and many of those that still exist today contain handwritten annotations, including of prices noted in the moment)—that defined these events and made them into early markers in the history of shopping.

For finally, using as a framing device this same catalog but likely also his live auction banter, Mr. Cock gave his customers a way to make sense of just what they were engaged in doing. He embedded the whole ritual, from start to finish, in the idea and language of "choice." Or to put it a bit differently: he inaugurated one of the great modern marketing terms, destined to be repeated for the next three centuries from soda ads to bank promotions to health-care plans. We are, after all, still constantly urged to make the "right" choice, the "smart" choice, the "best" choice, or just be damn glad we have such good choices before us—including the product in question. Drive down any highway in billboard territory in the United States or glance at the signage around your town, and you will see what a cliché this idea has become.

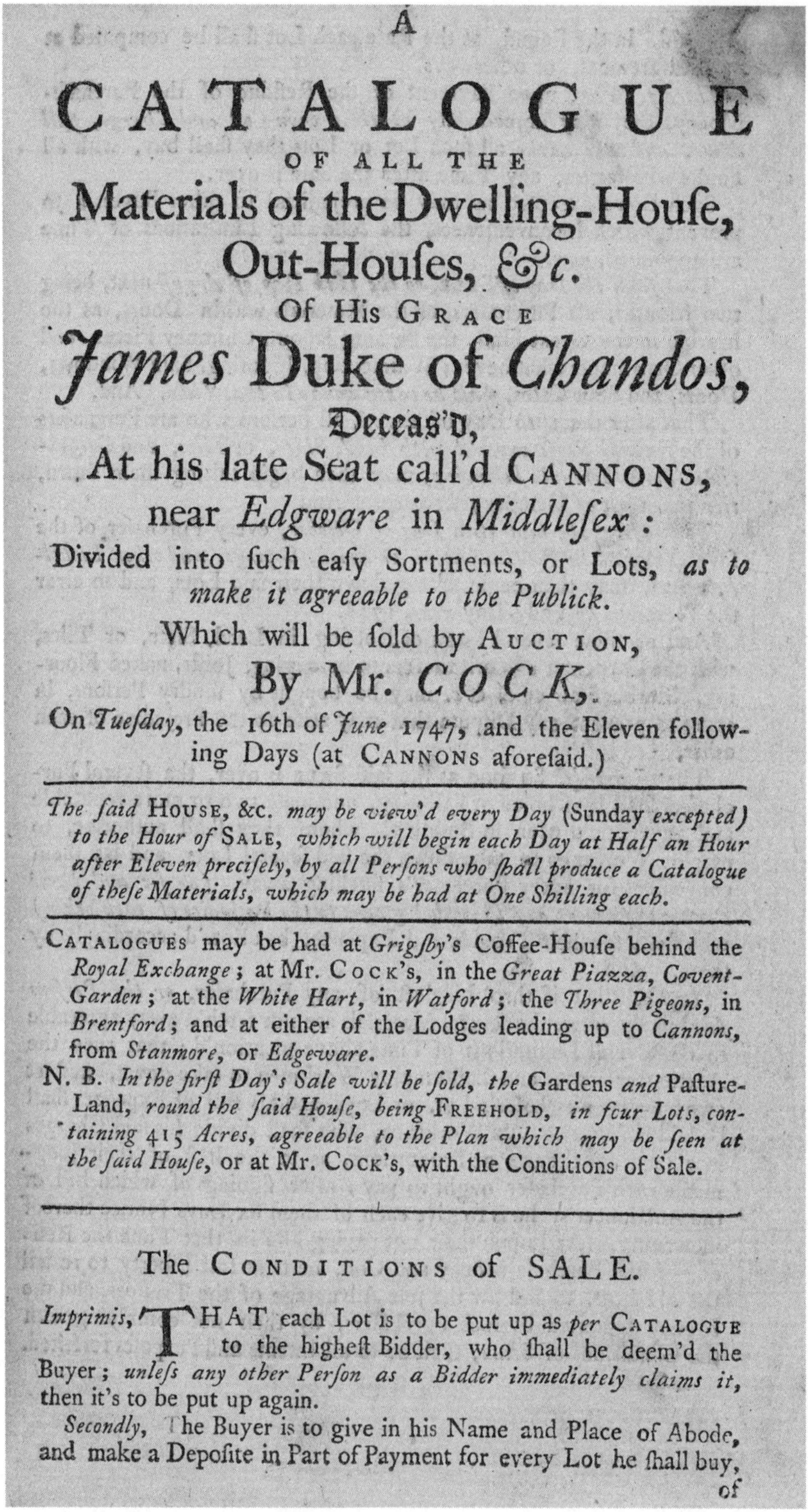

A

CATALOGUE

OF ALL THE

Materials of the Dwelling-House, Out-Houfes, &c.

OF HIS GRACE

James Duke of Chandos,

Deceas'd,

At his late Seat call'd CANNONS,
near *Edgware* in *Middlesex* :

Divided into fuch eafy Sortments, or Lots, *as to make it agreeable to the Publick.*

Which will be fold by AUCTION,

By Mr. COCK,

On *Tuesday*, the 16th of *June* 1747, and the Eleven following Days (at CANNONS aforefaid.)

The faid HOUSE, &c. *may be view'd every Day (Sunday excepted)
to the Hour of* SALE, *which will begin each Day at Half an Hour
after Eleven precifely, by all Perfons who fhall produce a Catalogue
of thefe Materials, which may be had at One Shilling each.*

CATALOGUES may be had at *Grigfby*'s Coffee-Houfe behind the
Royal Exchange; at Mr. COCK's, in the *Great Piazza, Covent-
Garden*; at the *White Hart*, in *Watford*; the *Three Pigeons*, in
Brentford; and at either of the Lodges leading up to *Cannons*,
from *Stanmore*, or *Edgware*.

N. B. *In the firft Day's Sale will be fold,* the Gardens *and* Pafture-
Land, *round the faid Houfe, being* FREEHOLD, *in four Lots, containing* 415 *Acres, agreeable to the Plan which may be feen at
the faid Houfe, or at Mr.* COCK's, *with the Conditions of Sale.*

The CONDITIONS of SALE.

Imprimis, THAT each Lot is to be put up as *per* CATALOGUE
to the higheft Bidder, who fhall be deem'd the
Buyer; *unlefs any other Perfon as a Bidder immediately claims it,*
then it's to be put up again.

Secondly, The Buyer is to give in his Name and Place of Abode,
and make a Depofite in Part of Payment for every Lot he fhall buy,

of

Fig. 1.2. Cover for the catalog of a 1747 auction of "all the materials of the
dwelling-house, out-houses, etc. of His Grace James Duke of Chandos,"
organized by the great auction empresario Christopher Cock.

But meanings and usages also multiply and diminish over time. In eighteenth-century British English, choice was employed in two ways. As an adjective, it meant preselected for quality, elegance, and significance—that, or worthy of being selected in the future because of those special qualities, something not always so obvious in an era before brands. Think of having in one's possession "a choice book." Alternately, as a noun, choice meant (as it still does) a range of options from which one could make a deliberate selection based on one's preferences or, in more formal terms, a field for the action of consciously selecting some things and rejecting others. One could, therefore, also have "a choice *of* books." Significantly, both the adjective and the noun had their specific function in this auction business. The Cock auction experience turned these two meanings into distinct, if related, stages of the same process on the path toward acquisition and, finally, possession.

Cock insisted repeatedly upon the importance of choice in the first and now slightly archaic sense. Whatever inventory was on view (and regardless of how accurate or fictional his claims actually were), Cock promised that it was made up exclusively of the most superior or ultimately "choice" items, in the sense of chosen by someone with knowledge, standing, taste, or skill. Beginning in the 1720s, he routinely announced that what he would have on offer to his undefined public was not only "a choice Parcel of Books" or a "choice library" or even a collection marked by "the Choiceness and Scarceness of the Editions"; these are all designations that can already be found in book sales catalogs from the previous century as well as at the head of publishers' compendiums like *Choice Sermons, preached upon selected occasions* (1640) or *Choice Songs and Ayres* (1673) or, in French, *Recueil choisi des plus beaux traits d'histoire, pris des anciens et des modernes* (1693).[12] Our high-end London auctioneer additionally proclaimed that he would be displaying, variously, "choice pictures," "choice and noble Pieces of Antiquities," "a choice collection of medals in gold and silver," "sundry choice and valuable Jewels," "a very Choice and Curious parcel of . . . China," and, more generally, "choice effects."[13] Even the fictional Mr. Cock, satirically rechristened by Fielding as Mr. Hen, arrives in his "pulpit," offers up a rhetorical question ("I hope you like the Catalogue, Ladies?"), and goes on immediately to offer, in the grandest of terms, a "choice Cabinet" (aka *un cabinet choisi*) for sale.[14] Today we might, pretentiously, say "curated" or "well chosen," meaning selected for good reasons. Yet the real Mr. Cock had lots of synonyms in his arsenal too. Other things up for sale he described variously as "exquisite" or "rich" or "valuable," but also "curious," "rare," "scarce," "matchless," or "uncommon" to emphasize both their singularity and their monetary value. What gave his objects these powers was, in good part, their provenance: the fact that they had *already* been chosen based on the acumen and superior critical determinations of particular previous, prestigious owners (now deceased or, sometimes, merely bankrupt or retired to the country) and then vouched for by Cock himself.

It must be noted that in the same moment and in almost the same vocabulary, a similar parade of options animated the fateful slave auctions of the New World. Eighteenth-century South Carolinian importers and auctioneers of enslaved persons, for example, frequently offered buyers "a choice cargo." Sometimes they inadvertently stressed this cargo's humanity as made up of actual "handy boys and girls," and sometimes they emphasized only its status as a "parcel" of valuable goods. But either way, merchants enmeshed in the world of slave trading routinely drew attention to the distinguishing feature—that, for example, this cargo had arrived fresh from a quick trip across the ocean or, alternately, was native born—which, they hoped, would make buyers of other humans see this particular set as "choice" (fig. 1.3).[15]

But that still wasn't the end. Cock's spectators, whether Londoners or tourists, serious purchasers or merely "the curious," were—much like buyers in a slave market or estate auction in colonial Charleston—then offered a second opportunity, should they show up for the actual events or even just chance upon a catalog for perusal. That was to use their *own* powers of discernment to decide among this assortment of exotic, obscure, or rarely seen offerings—or to choose among all these choice items themselves. And in neither case could the "cargo" choose back. When Cock announced the sale in 1744 of "Part of the Valuable Spanish Silks and Other Effects of the St. Joachim Prize, taken by His Majesty's Ship the Monmouth, Capt. Charles Wyndham," he informed potential

CHARLESTOWN, *April* 27, 1769.

TO BE SOLD,

On WEDNESDAY *the* Tenth *Day of* MAY *next*,

A CHOICE CARGO OF

Two Hundred & Fifty

NEGROES:

A RRIVED in the Ship
COUNTESS of SUSSEX, THOMAS DAVIES, Mafter, directly from GAMBIA, by

JOHN CHAPMAN, & Co.

** *THIS is the Veffel that had the Small-Pox on Board at the Time of her Arrival the* 31ft *of March laft : Every neceffary Precaution hath fince been taken to cleanfe both Ship and Cargo thoroughly, fo that thofe who may be inclined to purchafe need not be under the leaft Apprehenfion of Danger from Infection.*

The NEGROES *are allowed to be the likelieft Parcel that have been imported this Seafon.*

Fig. 1.3. A broadside advertising the sale of a "choice cargo of two hundred & fifty Negroes" from Gambia, to be held in Charleston, South Carolina, in May 1769, part of a joint effort by enslavers and auction houses in the Americas to turn other humans into commodities who could be sorted and sold just like other "choice" imported goods.

attendees that they would find themselves presented with a "Great Choice of the richest Gold and Silver Brocades," as well as a "great Variety of Gold and Silver Lace for Petticoats and Robings, of the most beautiful Patterns" and a number of other elegant-sounding fabrics (e.g., "taffety," "colour'd Genoa velvet"), including those described quite honestly as "mildew'd," from which to pick.[16] The same held true on other occasions for a "great Choice of the old fine Japan China" and a "great Choice of the finest Editions of the Classicks."[17]

It was obviously a sales pitch that worked—and trickled down. From book and fine art auctions in Paris, to dockside sales generated by British ships pulling into Boston harbor, to Forster's Linen Warehouse in central London or the shops of minor Liverpool drapers and chinamen, customers were repeatedly told by the mid-eighteenth century that they would confront situations in which plentiful "choices" or "a great Choice" or "the greatest of choice" would be available, but also required of them.[18] By the 1770s, this double meaning of choice as *choisi* or *de choix* was evident in French sales promotion materials too. An ultimately rather ordinary leisure activity, one turning on the idea of individuals of both sexes being authorized to select particular objects from among a set of possibilities correlated to pocketbook, but also knowledge, social aspirations, and personal inclination as opposed to either survival or moral desideratum, was coming into existence. Out of an explicit protocol, some very basic technology in the form of sales catalogs matched to a display of varied goods, and, finally, an act of naming, Cock had concocted a new arena for a new activity: consumer choice.

Cotton for Sale

A full account of the invention of "shopping" as a new experience in choice-making goes back, though, to significantly larger forces than Mr. Cock, who is really just a single, if now unjustly neglected, player in this tale. So does any account of this experience's growing popularity and eventual ubiquity in much of the world. Shops as spaces, and shopkeepers as a growing corps of professionals in the business of selling goods in cities and towns all over western Europe and its colonial outposts, matter to this story as much as auction rooms and auctioneers. The advent and expansion of consumer choice also has a demand side—in the form of "shoppers" and their desires—that, in the end, has been an equally important force. This particular commercial activity quickly gained a gendered dimension too; by the close of the eighteenth century, the ritual of shopping had become strongly associated with women and women with shopping, with lasting implications for both. Furthermore, though books may have been the key product in early marketing efforts, and paintings and objets d'art may have been most subject to discussions of taste, it was a humbler and more everyday good—one with extra-European roots and surprisingly wide social penetration—that was at the center of the remaking and then expansion of a new kind of marketplace experience across much of Europe and the Americas.

That commodity was calicoes or *indiennes*: printed cottons initially from the Indian subcontinent. Starting in the latter half of the seventeenth century, following centuries of prior circulation around the Indian Ocean and as far afield as the Horn of Africa and Japan, this product of long-haul trade routes began arriving in substantial quantities in the main cities of northwestern Europe. Eventually it found its way deep into the European hinterland and well down the social scale from the urban upper bourgeoisie to whom it was originally targeted. It also found varied buyers across the North and South Atlantic. The fabric's appeal was partly due to its price point, especially when compared with silk. Mainly its allure stemmed from the fact that it allowed ordinary people to clothe their homes and themselves in an array of bright colors and elaborate, quasi-exotic patterns, many of them originally customized by Indian manufacturers specifically for European and other international buyers. That, and the fact that the colors of these new textiles also, quite amazingly, held fast in the wash.[19]

The so-called calico craze—the growing market in the late seventeenth through eighteenth centuries in cottons adorned with intensely hued stripes, checks, and flowers and birds that was aggressively promoted by multiple state-sponsored East Indian trading companies— soon spawned protectionist opposition almost everywhere it had made itself felt. Between the 1680s and the 1720s, state-mandated bans on the importation, sale, purchase, even wearing of Indian cotton were imposed in much of Europe, including France and England, though significantly not in their North American and Caribbean possessions. Moral arguments against the widespread adoption of these gaudy cottons abounded, extensions of an old debate about the pernicious effect of luxury items. So did economic arguments about the way consumption of foreign goods threatened local livelihoods in practical terms. Yet even these bans did not really stem demand, and in the latter part of the eighteenth century, the bans themselves were mainly abandoned. (Prohibitions on imported paintings, so important to the early auction economy, were already almost gone by this period, leaving auctions in England, as opposed to the continent, largely unregulated in the Cock era.)[20] In the interim, smuggling and subterfuge continued unabated. More importantly, especially after 1750, domestic European and Latin American manufacturers of textiles, often working in materials other than cotton or in cotton-linen blends, produced cloth with new patterns, not to mention new kinds of decorative accessories, at an accelerated rate, thus replacing Indian goods with similar products (aka "knock-offs") for customers on both sides of the northern and southern Atlantic.[21]

To be clear: cotton or imitations of cotton did not suddenly exceed in popularity or displace all other kinds of cloth. That development belongs to a considerably more modern moment that we generally associate with industrialization and full-blown imperialism.[22] However, as the eighteenth century wore on, printed cotton fabric became not just a coveted commodity in Europe and its colonies, former and current, but the centerpiece of an explosion of novel stuff for sale, used and new.

What characterized this particular type of stuff—and what ultimately makes it central to the history of choice—was that it satisfied no essential need. It was, despite its ubiquity, meant to be purchased on an exceptional basis rather than repeatedly. It was also designed to be cherished as much for its appeal to the eye, that is, its aesthetic or decorative properties, as for anything else. One version could be substituted for another (red v. blue, checked v. striped, flowers v. curlicues) with no important practical or ethical consequences for the chooser. Beyond price, the lure of any particular design was, seemingly, almost entirely a question of what appealed on an individual sensory level to the purchaser.

In this way, colored and patterned calicoes can be said to have joined ranks with decorated porcelain dishes, patterned carpets, lacquered cabinets, and elaborate clocks, some imported ready to sell, some "finished" in Europe, and some out-and-out domestic imitations. Cheaper indulgences with similar properties, like colored ribbons, stockings, and tea, formed part of this crowded field as well. Such tantalizing items helped extend the reach of so-called luxury goods to ever more western European and colonial families' lives, starting with the well-off in Amsterdam and London in the seventeenth century and spreading steadily outward and downward in a range of qualities, styles, and prices.[23] Ultimately, in the course of the eighteenth century, all of this inessential stuff for sale—and especially calico and its imported and domestic imitators—engendered what historian Michael Kwass calls "a buying spree of historic proportions."[24]

Many historians before me have, in fact, described the geopolitical origins and then the socioeconomic repercussions of all this increased purchasing activity in the era of the Enlightenment. They have pointed, for example, to the rising percentage of income even poor people in western Europe spent on clothing as the eighteenth century progressed,[25] and they have explored the relationship between all this buying and such major historical trends as the (relative) decline of fixed social hierarchies and the growth of the bourgeoisie, capitalism, colonialism, and dependency on various forms of enslaved and exploited labor, as well as global integration. But historians have only rarely assimilated this story about cotton, except in the bluntest of terms, to the larger one of the changing cultural and ethical status of choice in the modern world. What many historians call, with considerable exaggeration, "the consumer revolution" or even "retail revolution" of the eighteenth century had a complex impact on Europeans' everyday habits and behavior.[26] It did the same (paradoxically, given the amorality implied by choices of this type) for their value system.

Most obviously, the stigma long associated with the purchase of inessential or luxury goods began, in the eighteenth-century Atlantic world, to meet more resistance, including arguments in some quarters for acquisitiveness as a stimulant of national prosperity and cultural progress rather than sin and corruption.[27] This has been well-documented ever since, though we will shortly hear counterarguments too. Just as significantly (though maybe less obviously, since the effects were longer term), cotton and related consumer goods were at the heart of what initially turned the making of deliberate, personally motivated, and largely value-neutral choices in manufactured goods—a process not unlike that encouraged and celebrated by Mr. Cock and disciples originally for selling rarities and oddities—into both a newly ordinary *and* a newly sought-after experience. At least it did so for the growing population with financial and geographical access. The calico craze marks one important origin point for the democratization of discriminating and picking from various kinds of menus of options as an obtainable, if ultimately cramped, form of freedom.

Agents of Choice

Let's look first at the case for the supply side of this transformation. The new fabrics, as they arrived in Europe starting in the seventeenth century and were remade domestically in the eighteenth, formed the linchpin—initially in the biggest cities of England,[28] France,[29] and the Low Countries,[30] and gradually in smaller ones in much of Europe too[31]—of a new system of marketing and distribution that would make increasingly familiar that particular form of selection that we now call consumer choice. As we've seen, this system was, in the early years of the eighteenth century, coterminous with practices associated with auctions and auction houses. But when it came to printed cottons and their cousins, it was tied very much to the introduction and then proliferation of fixed location shops. Envision small, enclosed venues, typically clustered in galleries or specially dedicated urban streets and designed purely for the business of selling, rain or shine.[32] Such shops matter considerably to our story even as many other settings for retail activity, from markets to fairgrounds to peddlers' carts, continued apace. That's also because, in these particular spaces, mercers, linen drapers, and other dealers in textiles did not simply advance the art of closing the deal. Very much in the Cock spirit, they developed the practice of, first, displaying the options and, then, creating, fostering, and finally organizing and managing shoppers' desires so that each of these individuals might make the "right" (i.e., optimal) choice, however defined, by themselves.[33]

Before the late seventeenth century, whether in a shop or market stall, you, the ordinary purchaser, typically began any ordinary commercial transaction with an idea of what you needed. You asked for specific goods from the other side of a counter. A salesman or saleswoman scurried back to locate what you were looking for. The announced price being found satisfactory and coinage or, more likely, credit accepted, the goods were handed over and the exchange was then completed. Only luxury purchases conducted in private for a tiny elite were different. This was a world characterized for most people by provisioning more than shopping.

Then, around the turn of the new century, in "better" stores in England and France, this encounter started to change. The options available were increasingly arranged to dramatic, sensory effect in order to attract into the space both serious customers and random passersby, but also to make clear to them what they would be able to choose among. Fabric was hung from hooks inside shops or on the sides of entranceways in enticing folds that stretched down to the floor in a simulation of women's copious skirts. It was also increasingly presented in bolts on shelves or in open presses, where it could be reflected in mirrors and illuminated by the candles, lamps, and sconces that soon became standard decoration in high-end city shops, not to mention an effective means to convey the exclusiveness of their goods and clientele. Eventually fine fabrics, like many other kinds of goods, were featured on bars behind the panes of glazed glass store windows, an innovation of the later eighteenth century that resulted in something like a visual menu of perfectly framed lots from which the shopper, wandering in from the street without appointment, could pick what he or she most wanted.[34] As Daniel Defoe already put it in 1726 in his *Complete English*

Tradesman, "It is true, that a fine shew [*sic*] of goods will bring customers . . . but that a fine shew of shelves and glass windows should bring customers, that was never made a rule in trade 'till now."[35]

Shop windows continued to improve in size and luminosity and thus potential for display well into the nineteenth century.[36] The spa town of Bath (as Jane Austen readers well know) became famous for its elegant bowed ones, which allowed considerable daylight into shops while also accommodating the showing of even more goods for sale. Similarly, Parisian builders began constructing sky-lit arcades, starting with the Galerie de Bois in 1786, to make what we'd now call browsing, or lingering to look at all possibilities, even easier. Presenting multiple goods to the purchaser's selective eye mattered more and more to urban commerce.

At the same time, in larger stores in both Paris and London, fixed prices on goods sometimes appeared by the late eighteenth century (especially at haberdashers and drapers), ensuring yet more opportunity for consumers to make informed comparisons, whether between different products for sale in one setting or between similar products in different shops. The shopkeeper Verrier described this kind of set pricing as "an excellent means to win the public's confidence . . . because it puts artisans and *connoisseurs* [knowledgeable people] in a state to be able to judge if an object is overvalued."[37] English retail drapery "warehouses," as they became known, experimented with cash sales to similar effect, making the ultimate financial transaction less rooted in personal exchange or reputation than when dependent entirely on credit.[38] In such newfangled places, workshops were often situated just next door, close by but out of sight, so that, once purchased, finished goods could be taken away immediately but without in any way enmeshing the consumer in the system of production. Even the specific act of ringing up the sale was sometimes moved to a space separate from where all the stuff was displayed.[39]

With these innovations, choosing increasingly became—for initiates—but one step, one transitional moment even, in the process that led from manufacturing to consumption and, often, from private life to public life and then back again. Picking from a set of concrete, visible consumer options was remade as a distinctive and discrete activity with a set of rules but also pleasures and benefits unto itself.[40] By the start of the nineteenth century, such models of retailing were being copied all across Europe. As the city government of The Hague bragged at mid-century, "Everywhere magnificent shops arise and in most of them one finds a rich choice of various articles of necessity and luxury."[41]

Even in the considerably less populous North American colonies—which were, after all, initially established in a good number of cases as commercial enterprises—the same pattern held. In the early 1700s, according to Sarah Kemble Knight's colonial travel diary, shops were beginning to dot the landscape, but rural customers especially had to "take what they [the merchants] bring [out to the counter] without Liberty to choose for themselves."[42] By the end of the century, shops had, at least in the case of Virginia, become the most common nondomestic, single-function buildings from urban centers all the way to the backcountry frontier. Merchants, in competition with each other, also increasingly developed specialized inventories, including both local artisanal production and goods imported from Britain and France, with finished cloth assuming pride of place.[43] Furthermore, North American shopkeepers focused more and more on display. Setting goods out in windows and on shelves behind the ubiquitous counter and adding heat and light to their interiors were two ways fixed-location shops in North America also gave consumers' eyes and hands access to all the options available to them for keeps, should they agree to pay the requisite price (fig. 1.4).[44] By 1800, some Philadelphia shops were very consciously emulating London ones, right down to the luscious fabrics in the window.[45]

What is more, for those who could not witness it all up close, the shop and its ethos of plenty could, in a sense, now come to them. Sample books and cards displaying minute examples of the available options in fabric and other commodities were sent by post to smaller retailers and shoppers alike (though such books were banned in the mid-1760s in France, where they had led, it was thought, to the plagiarizing of patterns) and by ship as far as Japan and South America (fig. 1.5).[46] So too regional newspapers, especially in France and North America, regularly ran paid announcements with long lists of exotic-sounding goods for sale rife for imagining in all their bounty.

Fig. 1.4. Ralph Earl, *Elijah Boardman* (1789), oil on canvas, a portrait of the elegant dry-goods merchant in his Connecticut shop, which was advertised in the local press as offering "a very extensive assortment of European, East, and West-India Goods." The viewer can see, just behind Boardman, a storeroom stacked with bolts of various kinds and designs of imported cloth.

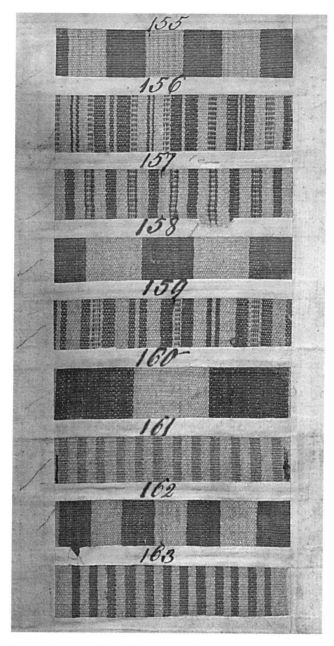

Fig. 1.5. A page of a pattern book for imported textiles, originating in the Manchester, England, firm of Benjamin and John Bower and sold also by Henry Remsen Jr., New York, 1767. The forty-one pages of small swatches, with up to twenty different examples per page, served as an innovative marketing tool, allowing customers to preview fabric trends up close before choosing what they preferred.

Perhaps we can think of these products as precursors to other, more familiar paraphernalia for categorizing and facilitating consumers' choices (and extracting their money). This was also the moment when enormous, single-page printed menus, then called "bills of fare" or *cartes*, started to appear in those new Parisian dining establishments known as restaurants. With their extensive inventories of invisible but mouth-watering-sounding dishes and drinks, all available in individual portions, these novel choosing aids encouraged the restaurant customer—unlike the patron of a traditional inn or communal *table d'hôte*—to pick whatever fit his or her tastes and pocketbook, as English guidebooks marveled. And that was regardless of what others were consuming or at what moment. The food selected (which sometimes came with the "recommendation" of an equally invisible chef) could even be delivered to one's home or served in a private room (fig. 1.6).[47] Or jump a century to American mail-order catalogs like those of Sears, Roebuck or Montgomery Ward, thick tomes that arrived in mailboxes via the postal service and that promised, upon completion of a paper form, to transform home and body and mind wherever one lived. Options ranged from pianos to parasols even for those unwilling, unwelcome, or unable to set foot in a brick-and-mortar department store.[48] Or consider our current dependence on elaborate commercial websites offering not just goods but also services, credit, entertainment, courses of study, and more, replete with electronic "baskets" meant to hold one's choices. All have certain common formal properties, starting with lists of options and instructions on selection, even as their technological foundations, offerings, and mode of use, from penciled-in checks to clicks, have varied considerably. They are advertisements and finding-and-selecting aids all in one.

But in the early years, most of all there were trade cards, collectable then as now (as Samuel Pepys already made clear in his diaries of the 1660s and 1670s),[49] like most other forms of visual ephemera associated with choice. Early eighteenth-century ones frequently featured images of desirable goods, including fabrics, spilling out of the frame. Later in the century they also depicted specific, product-rich shop windows. Still others displayed the charms of a particular shop's interior, often

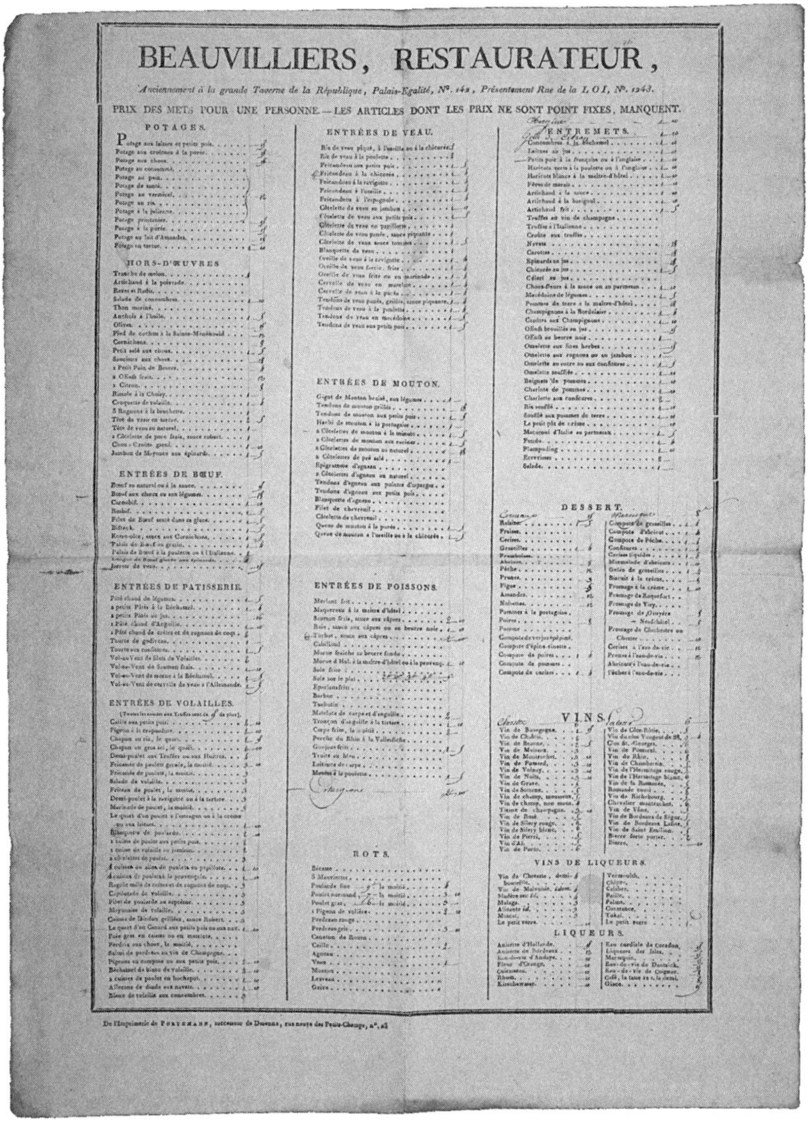

Fig. 1.6. The menu for Antoine Beauvilliers's restaurant, Paris, c. 1800–1805, listing vast numbers of options for food and drink organized into categories— an early example of what would become a standard form for the presentation of choices, culinary or other.

enlivened with views of members of both sexes being shown all the attractive stuff. The purpose, clearly, was not just luring but also steering the future customer in the business of choosing, first, where to shop and, second, what he or she might actually consider purchasing from within this panoply of options (figs. 1.7 and 1.8).[50]

For in effect, up-to-date eighteenth-century retailers became stage managers and promoters of their goods in ways that proprietors of traditional market stalls had never been. What mercers and other cutting-edge urban merchants tended to emphasize was the quality and gentility of their stock, or its "choiceness" in the Cock tradition, which could also mean either its association with the socially eminent or its rarity. Sometimes (as in the case of French mercers, who were unrestrained by all the regulations that governed most other French trades prior to the 1770s), it was also innovation or so-called fashion. This was a novel and difficult concept to realize in that it required constant renewal of the options available amid all that abundance. But it also kept those who could afford to do so repeatedly buying to satisfy new preferences.[51] Today's "fast fashion" suggests only an acceleration of the pace, not a real departure, judging from journals like the *Mercure galante*, founded in 1672, which already put considerable emphasis on what was truly new, especially in fabric design itself.

Mainly, what shopkeepers emphasized was range and variety, the many possibilities of *toutes sortes* available at every price point, for the benefit of the customer and his or her sensibility. As one eighteenth-century merchant in the Connecticut Valley bragged rather typically, his shop contained "the most universal assortment of goods, that can be found at any one store in the Commonwealth."[52] Defoe qualified slightly for the sake of shopkeepers themselves: merchants needed to offer "great choice [of wares] to please the curious," but not so much that it included that which was out of date or undesirable.[53] That, of course, is just what contemporary marketing psychology guru Sheena Iyengar has counseled marketers today. *Too* many options, whether in flavors of jam or kinds of insurance plans, and the customer becomes overwhelmed and fails to part with any cash.[54] But that did not always stop merchants, especially in the second half of the eighteenth

Fig. 1.7. Trade card for Lillington's Hosiery, Glove and London Hat Warehouse, Birmingham, England, c. 1800–1820, showing the store exterior, with a wide variety of items for sale, each highlighted as an option in a discrete windowpane.

Fig. 1.8. Trade card for James Wheeley's Paper Hanging Warehouse, London, c. 1760, showing the store interior with customers of both sexes being presented various possibilities in wallpapers, with an emphasis on multiplicity as well as elegance.

century. Not content to leave shoppers to choose among an enormous variety of types of cloth, including silks, velvets, damasks, woolens, Hollands, cambrics, muslins, and crepes, mid- to late-century advertisers and purveyors of textiles came up with a seemingly endless assortment of different names for cottons alone, differentiating them into distinct products based on small gradations of appearance (printed, bordered, flowered, etc.), quality, place of manufacture, and kind alike.[55]

The same strategy was taken up in the 1790s by French *restaurateurs*. Routinely they listed hundreds of items in multiple categories, from soups to desserts to liqueurs, in sizes and forms that were, despite a stated price, difficult to distinguish one from the next based on what an English writer called their "pompous, big-sounding name[s]" alone.[56] The point was clearly, as with paint colors today called heather, stone, and steel, not just to stimulate fantasies about alternative ways to live and be. It was also to convey the sense that the range and number of options for how to do so went beyond one's wildest imagination.

For, needless to say, no one was expected to buy it all. The eighteenth-century shopkeeper's job was, ultimately, to assemble a stock of desirable goods from which consumers, whether in search of beauty, novelty, social advantage, or pleasure, not to mention what they took to be a good price, could determine and land exactly what they most desired. (That's also why some shoppers and retailers alike railed against the advent of fixed prices—it took out the personal dimension, including the help with choice when there so were many variables to consider in determining what made one object more desirable than another.) The upscale shopkeeper was reimagined, largely by himself, as an intermediary and active facilitator, someone who could properly and appropriately, with some "gentle hints," then "direct his [the customer's] choice," as one British luxury cabinet maker put it after the turn of the century.[57] The novelist and essayist Louis-Sébastien Mercier, writing just before the French Revolution, said similarly of the true *maître* purveyor of luxury goods, "He animates, he supervises all the articles he sells, he imagines what will be pleasing."[58]

Today we might even describe him or, sometimes, her as a "choice architect" (using an expression made popular by the legal scholar Cass Sunstein) or a "choice agent."[59] For then, as now, the shopkeeper was understood to be someone with the responsibility for creating and arranging the menu of options in just such a way as to maneuver purchasers along a particular socially and economically suitable course. But he or she was also imagined to be capable of fulfilling this mandate in such an undisruptive and, indeed, invisible manner (with just a "nudge"?) that those same customers believed they had made the selections entirely by themselves to suit their own, self-generated desires. That is also why, finally, some merchants in cities with advanced shopping cultures took it upon themselves to invent and promote rules, both explicit and tacit, that would help make the whole ritual into a kind of performance unto itself.

One new possibility, which a minority of shopkeepers-turned-agents-of-choice adopted, was to offer to fill an information void (since the purchasing of luxury goods was still a novel activity for all but the true elite), writing primers for those shoppers who could no longer count on custom alone, matched with cost, for guidance in their selections. As early as the second half of the seventeenth century, yet another kind of ephemeral commercial print—how-to (and how-not-to) manuals for purchasers, such as the anonymous *The Merchant's Ware-house laid open; or the Plain Dealing Linnen-Draper: Shewing how to Buy all sorts of Linnen and Indian Goods* (1696)—started to appear for sale in small numbers. We cannot miss the important role as honest broker in such transactions that the tradesman-author accorded to himself. Some even made explicit reference to their vital function as human aids (eventually "experts") in the business of choosing in the new world of plenty, as in *The Tea Purchaser's Guide; or, The Lady and Gentleman's Tea Table and Useful Companion, in the Knowledge and Choice of Teas* penned by "A Friend to the Public" almost a century later.[60] We might see a small irony in notions of independent choice developing early around mind-altering substances such as tea, coffee, and tobacco. But such pamphlets can also be seen as the precursors to the great consumer education magazines of the second half of the twentieth century, with their to-the-point names like

Que Choisir? (France, 1951–), *Which?* (Britain, 1957–), and *CHOICE* (Australia, 1960–), though they presented themselves as objective checks on the standard puffery of merchants. What early shopper's guides detailed is how to pick well given one's needs and station, yes, but also how not to be deceived by faulty goods or faulty price tags, how not to be seduced by luxury, how, in short, to avoid picking badly according to the conventions of the moment.

Mainly, though, shopkeepers, aided all century in northwest Europe by a burgeoning commercial press including both general interest newspapers and illustrated specialty fashion magazines, cultivated some powerful social norms. These norms, in turn, helped to regulate but also to stimulate the very specific and modern practice of going to shops with the aim of buying new goods to match new desires for oneself or others. This was an important task, as the early nineteenth-century *Guide dans la choix des étrennes* (Guide in the choice of gifts) put it, "in an era in which everyone is eager to explain the sentiments in his heart through his purchase of presents."[61] By offering customers informal guidelines—about who should shop and where and how and also what to pick and when—the frequenting of streets or arcades rife with stores containing inessential options available for selection and purchase became less likely to result in moral or social disaster for the shopper (as traditional critics of luxury would have predicted).[62] But even more, doing it right became yet another way to demonstrate respectability, even, at times, exclusivity, while also participating in an organized social activity that, in principle, was open to all.

One such norm was what the English called "politeness." Think of it as a largely unwritten code of proper behavior or manners designed to be internalized as a form of self-discipline by genteel (or even aspirationally genteel) men and women, albeit differentially according to sex. Throughout the eighteenth century, English tastemakers like the editors of *The Spectator* but also merchants themselves extended its dictates to cover a variety of new, interactive leisure activities, including acquiring things in auction houses and boutiques. On the one hand, questions about who spoke to whom with what degree of familiarity made shopping into a kind of nerve-wracking performance that needed to be done correctly, by shopper and shopkeeper alike, in order for the larger goals of propriety and social harmony in a highly stratified world to be upheld. The standards associated with politeness—and the corresponding threat of vulgarity or excessive display, its chief antagonists at the two outer ends of the social scale—could be seen as having placed deliberate, if informal, brakes on anything reeking of excessive individualism and, indeed, individualized choice (though it was often violated in practice, as we will see). But on the other hand, for the middling or socially ambitious commercial classes, learning to make marketplace choices in the right establishments and with all the right, communally sanctioned words, actions, and bodily comportment and style became, in and of itself, advantageous. It aided in the goal of moving through that stratified world and gaining the esteem of one's peers or even social betters—to the advantage of the act of shopping itself.[63]

The same was true of the eighteenth-century social norm known as "taste," which provided a complex set of largely aesthetic criteria for what to admire and then buy *following* the presentation of a wide array of possibilities and polite exchange about them. Here, too, taste could be said to have functioned as a form of regulation or constraint, in lieu of formal law. As money or appearance decreasingly indicated true social standing and as the appeal of fashion undermined established conventions regarding goods and social referents, taste—which depended on one's knowledge and breeding as much as wealth—stepped into the void. It became, starting in the seventeenth century in France, an important benchmark by which one's aesthetic and then consumer choices could be made and, ultimately, measured by others. Moreover, it could be learned as well as inherited. And insofar as it was seen as objective and universally valid, an agreed-upon communal standard like "reason" or "truth" or "common sense" to which one *ought* to conform in the realm of decision making, it too worked to temper nascent individualism and encourage a kind of class-bound conformity—as it arguably still does. Think of how, even when it comes to buying a pair of new shoes, existing standards of good taste and one's own predilections can seem, somehow, to seamlessly merge.

Nevertheless, the significance accorded to taste, from magazine spreads to the new discipline of aesthetics, also encouraged the choosing of things for the house and body for a new purpose: as a way to display one's cultivation in the sense of savvy about how to discriminate effectively among the options. "Good" taste made one's choices, even when there were a lot of them, respectable. That assumption applied to women as well as men and to the middling orders as much as the upper ones, though once the overt display of lots of unnecessary goods had seemed suitable only for the powerful. (There was, however, always room for parody, as in Charles Branston's 1733 ditty "The Man of Taste": "My taste in Sculpture from my choice is seen, I buy no Statues that are not obscene.")[64] By the nineteenth century, that rule would extend to mass-produced goods, from buttons to carpets. Now, in the age of brands, it could be said to extend to the choice of Moët & Chandon over Amstel Light as well. Thus, even if taste, like politeness or price tags, worked to restrain an excess of choice at a moment when it seemed already that too much was for sale in too many places, it did so in the service of promoting choice-making (along with acquisition and accumulation) as a practice, and, increasingly, a value unto itself.[65] Thanks to ambitious professionals, namely, shopkeepers and the creators of their media and technology, the infrastructure for a culture of consumer choice was born at the nexus of new forms of agency and new forms of constraint, including keeping everyone in their own lane.[66]

The Choosers

But let's not forget the buyers. Needless to say, not all choice-related activity came about in eighteenth-century western Europe or, after 1776, the early American republic as a result of ordinary people capitulating to merchants and business owners' directives, explicit or not. We miss a lot if we concentrate only on Mr. Cock, or better-known salesmen of the eighteenth century like the pottery magnate Josiah Wedgwood, or even Mrs. Savage and her India warehouse and all those now anonymous drapers and mercers in eighteenth-century cities, big and small, who set local standards in England and beyond. The frequenters of auctions and shops—those we now label *customers*—themselves also helped set the culture of choice into motion. They also often derailed the process from the ambitions of auctioneers and, later, mercers, drapers, and the like. Faced with an array of carefully selected options displayed for their consideration, including vast quantities of beautifully patterned cottons, shoppers on both sides of the Atlantic invented their own set of retail habits and expectations.

And, importantly, women played an outsized role in this part of the story. That was not so much because they were the only people doing the choosing. Rather, women did so because they—especially in the innovative role of polite, tasteful consumers surveying, selecting, then finally buying what they wanted—both reinforced long-standing gender norms and threatened to blow them open. Consumer choice, along with aesthetic choice, was feminized and thus wrapped up in the politics of sexual difference from the start.

In practice, the culture of consumption invented in the eighteenth century thoroughly involved men and women alike, just as it did multiple social strata (apart from the truly poor, who were increasingly conspicuously excluded and marked by that fact). That doesn't mean, of course, that male and female members of households always went for the same things any more than members of different classes did. Broadly speaking, for example, English men of the gentry and middling classes lavished attention on tools, books, watches, large furniture, wine, silver, paintings, and carriages (which might be called the cars of yesteryear). Women across class, by contrast, were attuned to things for the home and body, a predilection made acceptable by its close linkage to women's traditional role as stewards of family and hearth. Some things clearly haven't changed, though today men might also take charge of home electronics. According to the account books of the well-off Cottons of Cambridgeshire analyzed by historian Amanda Vickery, for example, in the sample year 1761, the wife bought china, glass, candles, heating material, and every sort of textile, and her husband bought primarily luxury goods as well as anything that came from the tailor.[67] All of this is consonant with a preexisting tradition of women making many of the regular purchasing decisions for their households, whether in fashionable shops or from private middlemen for the better-off or among peddlers and hawkers of secondhand goods for the less affluent. It was also consistent with the antique idea of women as superior patrons of the arts.

But what must be emphasized is that, in the eighteenth century, inessential, fashionable consumer goods, from shawls to wigs, were developed for both sexes. Moreover, going into shops and placing orders or making purchases became, especially in chic locations, what could be called a mixed-sex activity, as were many newer leisure-time pleasures. In London at least (much to the amazement of women travelers from some other parts of Europe),[68] in the upper, middling, and even to some extent lower classes, women went "a shopping" with other women, women went with male family members or escorts, and men went alone or in packs, too, sometimes making purchases for wives or daughters. In Paris and in northern cities like The Hague, women could often be found on both sides of the counter, selling as well as buying, in luxury spaces and in more humble ones alike, as could men.[69] Even enslaved peoples of both sexes frequented stores on behalf of their "masters" in rural North America.[70]

This transatlantic drive to consume, according to historians of commerce and commodities, was in good part also a result of larger processes that depended upon and affected whole families in the seventeenth and eighteenth centuries. Here we are not just talking about the decline in prices for what would have been real luxury goods in earlier centuries, a trajectory fueled in part by both low-paid and, in the case of cotton by the end of this period, unfree labor outside of Europe.[71] New consumer habits were—according to the famous thesis of the economic historian Jan de Vries—also spurred by greater full household effort within Europe going to market labor. European families as units became more industrious if not yet industrial in this era, he proposes, precisely so as to be able to buy more and in new ways, a process that soon became self-reinforcing: the more people of both sexes participated in the expansion of market-based commerce, the more market-based commerce expanded.[72]

At the same time, states did not simply get out of the way of families eager and able to purchase more stuff either (as commentators

committed to a "negative liberty" or deregulatory account have sometimes imagined). Governments of varied kinds, even well before the age
of revolutions, actively stoked and then facilitated this process to the
benefit of whole households made up of members of varied ages and
sexes. Yes, shops themselves were, in the eighteenth century, generally
less highly regulated spaces than were traditional marketplaces. Sumptuary laws dictating who could wear what, not to mention when and
where, were also long in retreat in eighteenth-century western Europe,
albeit not in the American South, where requirements surrounding
"negro cloth" were enforced with an eye to obscuring individual identity
among Black people as well as reinforcing broader caste difference.[73]
Both trends do lend some credence to later arguments that modern
freedom was a result of eliminating state-dictated, legal obstacles to personal choice, including various forms of monopoly, whether in clothing
or anything else. But we need also to recognize that the English and
Dutch states and, to a lesser degree, the French one were, by the late
eighteenth century, actively helping construct and then maintain an
economy of consumer choice for men and women alike.

They did so through imperial ventures along the lines of East and
West India trading companies designed to expand the range of choices;
through protectionist policies meant to shore up home industries like
textile manufacturing; through the creation and upholding of laws intended to make commerce more secure; and even through the sponsorship of all kinds of infrastructure improvements helpful to producers
and consumers alike.[74] Wide, raised pavements constructed in London
after the 1766 Paving and Lighting Act, for example, transformed the
cleanliness and safety of that city's public shopping streets in ways that
facilitated men and women strolling and looking in all those private
shop windows, day or night. So did better street lighting, the building
of post offices and roads, effective waste removal, and the creation of
new forms of ground transportation.[75] Such innovations were also
widely copied in smaller and provincial cities all across Europe and
its imperial domains in the latter half of the eighteenth century, sometimes sponsored by royal authorities and sometimes by city governments.[76] And all of this happened to the advantage of new classes of

consumers of both sexes who, in practice, accepted the invitation to remake themselves as choosers in a world of goods for selection and then sale.

Still—and here is where things get complicated for a history of choice—the particular act that came to be known as "shopping" was, in the course of the eighteenth century, increasingly coded as feminine. It was also marked as elite, a "fashionable female amusement" in the words of William Alexander, M.D., in his grandly titled *The History of Women, from the earliest antiquity, to the present time.*[77] The stereotypical "shopper" (to use a subsequent coinage) became a well-off woman of the leisure class or, at times, an excessively feminized man with income (i.e., a fop), even as most women had no formal independent economic power and male heads of households often wrote the checks. What is more, the joys and pitfalls of this very particular activity of making personal choices in public spaces about what to wrap around one's body or consume inside the private home became increasingly associated with womanly qualities and attributes. That was true even in the early days of the auction, when satires of the institution already singled out female clients ("I hope you like the Catalogue, Ladies?") for ridicule. It was even more true by the century's close, when the activity of browsing in stores acquired its modern name.

Partly this association reflects the novelty of both the extramural activity called "shopping" and urban women's enthusiastic participation in it, from looking at all the goods to displaying its aftereffects. To a significant degree, though, this association suggests a society trying to come to grips with what these new spaces and occasions for choice in the commercial realm will ultimately mean for all involved—and using women as stand-ins for that exercise. For the Scottish doctor William Alexander, who was not unique, women offered a metric for measuring the "progress" of civilization as a whole. Consequently, in writing today the history of shopping it becomes very hard to disentangle the woman as a social actor, going about her everyday business, from the woman as trope, soon to be the very emblem of the desirous and desiring modern, leisure-time chooser (and in implied contradistinction to the public-minded male producer increasingly associated with the workplace). This is a duality with substantial implications for the future course of feminism or the imagination of women's emancipation. It has been equally consequential, as we shall see, for the history of choice as our modern *doxa*.

We know something about this rush to feminize consumer choice partly from a century of travel accounts and tourist diaries recounting noteworthy encounters in London and other metropolises with reams of fabulous goods to choose among and transport home. Such details became a stock feature of such accounts, especially when written by those coming from places with decidedly less for sale. Robert Southey's fake Spanish tourist Don Manuel Alvarez Espriella, writing in mock amazement about London in 1807, practically drools with enthusiasm describing all the kinds of stores—drapers, stationers, confectioners, pastry cooks, seal cutters, silversmiths, booksellers, print sellers, hosiers, fruiterers, china sellers, and more—he encounters, as well as all the opulent stuff they hold, from giant sturgeons, to exotic birds, to scissors and walking sticks, all "so beautifully arranged." He also remains very alert to the peculiar gender dynamics involved in the exchanges that these object displays produced: "That so many young men should be employed in London to recommend laces and muslins to the ladies, to assist them in the choice of a gown . . . excited my surprise."[78] About twenty years earlier, the very real German tourist, the writer Sophie von La Roche, peering in wonder inside the glass cases in London pastry shops and through the windows of London print shops and mercers, where fabrics were hung to replicate "the ordinary folds of a woman's dress," modeled the same. Gushing over both the range of possibilities and the elaborate displays that promised new pleasures for the eyes of her mainly female readers, she established herself as an early evangelist for the culture of choice.[79]

The Anglophilic Sophie von La Roche was, however, herself imitating the sentimental style of the English novel in her reportage (she was also thrilled to meet on her travels the famous younger novelist Frances Burney, who privately reported feeling considerably less warmly toward her German counterpart).[80] And it is novels themselves, a relatively new consumer product with a large female fan base by the mid-eighteenth century, that really cemented the linkage of women with a specific activity that female novelists themselves promoted as "shopping." Fictional stories, and especially novels of manners of the last quarter of the eighteenth century, gave readers (then, as now) detailed pictures as to how shopping happened in practice. Simultaneously, they spelled out shopping's incipient moral and psychological significance for those enmeshed in its newfangled ways. Indeed, it was novels that first put the experience of women as choosers in the world of plenty but also price tags under the microscope for anyone to witness and assess.

The Lady Shopper Revealed

The "fashionable language" of shopping made its actual fictional debut in Frances Burney's hit novel *Evelina* of 1778 and less appreciated *Cecilia* of 1782.[81] Soon talk of it was everywhere in the English-language print world, as a host of imitators got in on the game. In just the last fifteen years of the eighteenth century, "going shopping" or "going a shopping" made appearances in *Adeline, Terentia, Belinda, Rosella, Ellinor, Louisa, Fanny, Madeline, Constance, Georgina, Ethelinde,* and *Julia,* too, not to mention *The Beggar Girl, The Posthumous Daughter, The Hapless Orphan, The Platonic Guardian,* and *A Tale of the Times.* All were commercial fictions designated "a novel" on their respective title pages. All were also clearly intended by their exclusively female authors for female purchasers-turned-readers alone.[82] What emerges from reviewing them together is a kind of paradox.

Shopping, done right, holds a certain amount of promise for its most passionate female fans: as entertainment, as a means of potential social mobility (since it could help make oneself into a more desirable object), even as a source of temporary liberation from the rules of other social spaces. "A charming amusement" that got women out of the house in the morning, it was also a way to see and be seen.[83] Occasionally it could even turn into a profession, as women shopped for others, bringing back the latest in city fashions to less urban settings for redistribution.[84]

But all those opportunities for choice-making, with their close associations with wants and ambitions, also made this highly treacherous terrain, a potential minefield for the women who engaged in it and, in fact, a potential problem for society as a whole—despite what merchants and other advocates said. Frances Burney and her authoress-followers made such risks clear well before Jane Austen's genteel shoppers in Bath stepped onto the scene, walking its commercial streets, putting down money for desired items, and changing literature as a result. This too is an important part of the legacy of eighteenth-century commercial culture for our larger story.

Typically, at the heart of these late Enlightenment, post-Richardsonian novels there lived a central character, herself female, who found herself torn. On the one side lay her personal desires, whether for suitors or goods, and the particular interior forces behind them, including often a whiff of lust. On the other side were virtue and propriety, meaning attention both to obligations and to expectations. The latter often took the form of the desires and ambitions of more powerful figures, male and female, around her but also appeared simply as internalized norms. Plots then turned on the heroine's attempts to chart a life course, which is to say in the world of the early novel, navigate the field of existing options as circumscribed by these moral and social boundaries along with economic realities and make her own choices in that context. For importantly, in these fictions there was no sacred master plot, like that of a "chosen people," ruling the day. Causality, outcomes: both were generally left in human hands rather than the hands of fate or God. Women could make choices with real-world effects because they were, in fact, despite all social and legal limits, free moral agents with open-ended futures.

Novelists thus increasingly narrated for their readers not simply what their main character or characters decided to do, given the possibilities. Nor did they stop with the material consequences that followed, including what would now be called the "opportunity costs" associated with paths not taken. Our eighteenth-century authors also tried, through innovative literary devices like epistolarity and occasional free indirect discourse, to provide readers with access to the interior realm of their characters' thought processes. That is, writers worked to reveal the (fictional) combination of emotions and reasoning behind their (fictional) characters' impending choices, as well as the (fictional) psychological effects of choices made—all with a moralizing cast. In the late eighteenth-century novel, choice-making, otherwise so hard to witness in others since so much of it took place in the private realm of one's inner consciousness, was laid out to be dissected and judged. How characters dealt with this responsibility in different settings became a kind of test. Certainly, this was the case when it came to scenes of active shopping.[85]

"Shopping expeditions" show up intermittently in women's novels as a distinctly modern pursuit of the well-heeled woman, like novel reading itself. Scenes set in and around fashionable commercial venues like shops were, in the 1780s and 1790s and into the nineteenth century, an easy way for an author to convey up-to-datedness, spatially and in terms of behavior, and, indeed, for a book itself to participate in the world of commercial fashion. But simultaneously, shops (like libraries and ballrooms, which we will get to in subsequent chapters) served as microcosms of the larger world and its pressures. These were small but meaningful stages where the character of the heroine was determined or reflected in response—though not all authors conveyed the psychological torment of either the voluntary or coerced chooser as effectively as Frances Burney did. For the stakes in such literary scenes were often high: nothing less than that character's efforts to forge a self, which is to say, to be someone who, to a certain degree, controls her own destiny through the weighing of options and the making of decisions large and small, perhaps sometimes even exceeding the expected fate associated with both her class and gender position.

Importantly, though, this increasing sense of autonomy comes *not* because shopping allows the heroine to craft her own style and thus "identity," making herself the eighteenth-century equivalent of a hippie, a punk, a goth, or a member of some other cultural subgroup. And neither is it because she is empowered through consumption to adopt the "lifestyle" she wishes, subversive or not. We are not talking here about Plath's young woman under the fig tree. Those are all much later developments in this story, despite what some literary critics and historians— eager to link political with economic independence from way back and to locate the commercial origins of modern identity politics and "self-fashioning"—have to say, partly in an effort to justify how we live now.[86]

Instead, what's striking in English novelistic discussions of "shopping" at their debut moment is how much focus there is specifically on the heroine's desire to engage in the seemingly modest gesture of choosing among the possibilities that she is offered, a process right at the boundary between interior meditation and outward action, private experience and public life. The real appeal for women of visiting the mercers, mantua makers, milliners, trimming makers, perfumers, and jewelers, according to Mrs. Gomersall's *The Citizen, A Novel* (1790), is actually the opportunity to "be judges of the articles to be viewed," quite apart from what one actually purchases and brings home.[87] In such claims lie some of the first explicit connections between individual consumer choice and independence for late adolescent and adult women.

The stock literary figure in this regard—and maybe the best place to see this dynamic in action in its original form—is the *coquette*. Typically, she's a young, attractive, and still unmarried woman whom we come to know, whether she is central or peripheral to the narrative, by her actions and psychology alike. What defines the *coquette* is that she finds satisfaction but also unexpected power in exercising choice where and when she can, whether that be in examining trinkets or surveying potential husbands. And when she shops, it is, in fact, rare that she is looking for anything specific. Her authority in the situation comes from the act (or potential act) of making acquisitions in line with her desires but also, at times, from refusing to do so, meaning choosing not to choose at all despite all the pressure. Ladies gone "a-shopping," Southey explained, tongue-in-cheek, no matter how cajoled by (male) linen drapers and mercers eager to direct their choices, "spend their money or not, according to the temptations which are held out to gratify and amuse."[88] For the true *coquette*, driven by the conjoined pursuit of pleasure and a small dose of independence, aims while she can (since marriage will usually signal the end and a return to a male-dominated world) neither to limit her options nor to give up her ability to act on them. As the literary critic Theresa Braunschneider notes, having alternatives, weighing and comparing them, and finally deciding on her own how to proceed is what makes the literary *coquette* a modern and recognizable type; her very identification with this series of activities, especially within a burgeoning commercial culture, is also what makes such characters "a testing ground for a society of choosers."[89]

But therein also lies the problem. What ultimately happens to the eighteenth-century *coquette* or "shopping lady" in her fictional life, where she typically refuses standard constraints on her ability to choose? Usually, nothing good. That's because "going a shopping," whether for ribbons or gowns or toys, was also full of social, moral, and psychological traps no matter what choice agents did to mitigate them. (Sayings that attest to the almighty power of the consumer's pocketbook, like the nineteenth-century British one made famous by Mark Twain, "You pays yer money and you takes yer choice," seem written for men.) And for all the carefully detailed stuff that pops up in late eighteenth-century novels, a strong current of distaste and even critique makes itself felt as well, much of it only a later variant of arguments that had long identified women with luxury by way of lust and sex. Right along with the *coquette*'s rise as a type, all the anxieties of the age were also projected onto female consumers and, to a lesser degree, effeminate male ones.

Women shoppers were deemed responsible, through their consumer choice-making habits, for a variety of forms of social and moral decay. What's more, many of those same women were represented in late eighteenth-century English novels, including those by women, as battered by the experience. Some found themselves incapable of coping with so many choices even as they were psychologically and physically vulnerable to its seductions. Others became disruptive, wrestling dangerous public power through the exercise of their (economic) clout as consumers in ways that were socially and morally destructive to themselves. Either way, their behavior permanently tainted consumer choice as contrary to public life. To a certain extent it still does, even as Amazon delivery trucks pull up to curbs and into driveways every day over and over again.

One big reason shopping caused so much hand-wringing in late eighteenth-century British and European print culture is the same reason some later feminist writers extoll it: it seemed to upset the existing social hierarchy, allowing status to be decoupled from appearance. There were, after all, many variants of the old "what if servants find a way to purchase fine or fashionable clothes and it's no longer possible to judge a book entirely by its cover" lament, all rooted in the traditional assumption that any suggestion of choosing beyond one's station would result in sexual and social disorder.[90] This was not an idle anxiety either. New retail conditions in cities, along with an increase in transitory encounters, anonymity, and blurring of social lines that expanding urban life increasingly produced, including inside shops, seemed to make this kind of confusion around status and virtue a very real possibility. As one French guidebook of 1715 explained to visitors in reference to a Parisian shop selling premade clothes, "There are clothes for all sexes, all sizes, and all sorts of ranks [conditions], and one has only to choose [choisir]."[91] By the early 1770s, London Magazine or Gentleman's Monthly was reporting that "the lower orders of the people (if there are any; for distinctions are now confounded) are equally immerged in the fashionable vices," buying, for example, bright-colored cottons with no attention to rank.[92] With their fashion choices, women especially threatened to upend the very social order of which they were traditionally supposed to be the guardians. Choices in the sartorial realm, backed up by money and circumstance, potentially destabilized old status lines (or benefited from their prior destabilization) at the same time as they helped erect new ones.[93]

But the bigger, more abstract threat was identified with the spread of the new values associated with consumer choice—and thus with women's distinctive ways of responding to their desires, along with the money behind them—into the larger, extracommercial world. That could mean either the intimacies of family life or the workings of the public sphere, including political life. Furthermore, where once the desire and possession of luxury goods were linked to lax morality and the potential for sin, now the problem seemed to stem from women's particular psychology as it manifested itself in the business of shopping.[94] New forms of choice behavior, rooted in women's assumed innate (and largely negative) moral, emotional, and epistemic predispositions, potentially compromised male civic virtue as well, turning men into quasi-women and contributing to what John Trusler, author of *The Way to Be Rich and Respectable: Addressed to Men of Small Fortune*, called the "effeminacies of the age."[95]

One of those key qualities was fickleness, the fact that women had a tendency—according even to their champions—to be indecisive, vacillating, and incapable of knowing their own minds in any reliable way, and, therefore, to act capriciously. The anonymous author of the previously mentioned *The Merchant's Ware-house* of 1696 assumed that more information—about quality, price, and use value—would necessarily lead to objectively better decisions on the part of drapers, seamstresses, and consumers alike. Later advocates of the rules of politeness and taste felt the same. This is indeed just what most classical economists wedded to a rational choice model still take for granted, as we will soon see. However, the rise of patterned calicoes, along with advertising playing on their visual allure, moved much purchasing in the eighteenth century in what contemporaries believed to be the other direction. That was toward decisions made on the basis of unstable, irrational, and insufficiently public-minded criteria (a "fancy" or "whim," in the language of the time) that even the purchasers themselves ill understood. Here the novel took on the job of highlighting the existence of a human quality otherwise not very visible in Enlightenment culture: *akrasia*, or the act of failing to follow the path of virtue and reason in one's choices despite one's good intentions.[96] But we might also see echoes of what will become the behavioralist critique much closer to our own moment, when those ostensibly womanly qualities—faulty (read: superficial, vain, overly emotional, or self-indulgent) motives and faulty (read: irrational) logic—have become *everybody's* property when it comes to the now essential experience of consumer choice.

Eighteenth-century businesses quickly learned to cater to and, indeed, to build upon this gendered psychology. To be successful, European pattern drawers and printers, according to a 1747 English guidebook, needed to have (much as Indian designers had already discovered) "a fruitful Fancy, to invent new Whims to please the changeable Foible of the Ladies . . . [and] a wild kind of Imagination, to adorn their work with a regular sort of Confusion, fit to attract the Eye but not to please the Judgment."[97] Shopkeepers found themselves ostensibly competing with each other for the same reason (which is why Mercier insisted shopkeeping was a dangerous profession from an economic point of view). By the start of the century, it was already a commonplace to claim, as Bernard Mandeville did in *The Fable of the Bees*, that "in the choice of things we are more often directed by the Caprice of Fashions, and the Custom of the Age, than we are by solid Reason, or our own Understanding," but also "the reasons some of the Fair Sex have for their choice [of shop] are often very Whimsical and kept as a great Secret."[98] In other words, it was acknowledged that most shoppers were *coquettes*—and in a negative sense. This, in fact, is what many eighteenth-century novels underlined: even those written *by* women authors *for* women readers typically depicted their heroine-consumers at critical moments as imprudent or indecisive or rash. Flitting from object to object or place to place, they were easily seduced by novelty, flattery, and the promise of immediate gratification. So much for either standing duties or long-term rewards.

But that's not all. Perhaps most worryingly to the moralists, there was also women's propensity, again exacerbated by the new world of shopping, for overindulgence or gluttony, understood as the failure to tame temptation (whether sexual or commercial) and, in a sense, attempt to take it all. The hedonistic heroine of the epistolary novel *Fanny* (1785) by Margaret Holford whittles away some hours in shops and at an auction and then declares, if only she had "money to squander," there were "many toys" that she would have been "tempted to purchase."[99] Others, like the star of Burney's *Camilla; or, A Picture of Youth* (1796), go all the way and do try to purchase everything they see; when a milliner, despite being cautioned to be reasonable in her choices, picks for Camilla items "too pretty to disapprove," our heroine finds herself parting with considerably more money than she ever intended (or can afford).[100] There is often a hint in these novels that, unsupervised, women could be acquisitive to the point where they were unable to control their own desires and exhibit any restraint at all. Then the risk becomes what we'd now call shopaholism: a compulsion to buy that mitigates against free or reasonable choice, not to mention self-discipline, entirely.[101]

Or, conversely, like the eponymous heroine of Helen Williams's *Julia* (1790), who is quickly made bored and weary by flitting from milliner to milliner, they could decide to forgo the whole thing.[102] By the era of Jane Austen, it was also clear that one could cycle through all those stages at once in the course of a single shopping trip; witness *Sense and Sensibility*'s Mrs. Palmer, "whose eye was caught by every thing pretty, expensive, or new; who was wild to buy all, could determine on none, and dawdled away her time in rapture and indecision."[103] In popular discourse, the eighteenth- and early nineteenth-century female shopper seems to oscillate among choosing inconsistently by not knowing her own mind; choosing badly by "over-valu[ing] her own Judgment as well as the Commodity she would purchase" (in Mandeville's terms);[104] choosing too much through lack of restraint; and, quite often, failure to choose at all (though we know from probate inventories that an awful lot of stuff did end up in people's homes). This was hardly a foundation for individual choices to produce any kind of collective good.

And in the world of late eighteenth-century English fiction, shopping plagued shoppers too—much as today's commentators on the "tyranny of choice" and its nefarious effects on middle-class peace of mind note anew. The earliest novels with shopping scenes repeatedly demonstrate that excessive choice, whether in numbers of objects or in number of opportunities, takes a serious psychic toll, especially, though not exclusively, on the women who confront it. Because having to make consumer choices stokes unwanted feelings, it also occasions fights within the self with unpleasant secondary emotional effects. Foremost among them are shame (at wanting too much or buying too much or any other socially frowned-upon impulse); embarrassment (at not knowing what to do or doing it wrong); and disorientation (in the face of too many dazzling options to consider or too many pressures from different quarters, a state that was liable to leave one overwhelmed and incapable of making any choices at all). Today's equivalent might be the familiar trope of the recently arrived foreigner, looking with befuddled dismay at all the practically identical cereal boxes or toothpaste tubes lined up in a U.S. grocery store aisle, where the number of different products continues to explode. Choice is stressful, not least for those who want to consider themselves—not to mention be considered by others—both morally upstanding and culturally competent.

Recall Immanuel Kant insisting, in his high-Enlightenment *Conjectures on the Beginning of Human History* of 1786, that the initial discovery of choice both opened up the freedom for people to craft their own futures and introduced unending anxiety into human history.[105] That same year, Sophie von La Roche wrote breathlessly but nervously of window-shopping in London: "Behind great glass windows absolutely everything one can think of is neatly, attractively displayed and in such abundance of choice as almost to make one greedy."[106] In the same spirit, the fictional Miss Larolles in Burney's *Cecilia; or, Memoirs of an Heiress* describes wrestling with her desires at an auction as leaving her "ready to cry" and "in an agony the whole morning" when she cannot bid on it all.[107]

Yet Burney's slightly earlier satirical novel of manners *Evelina; or, The History of a Young Lady's Entrance into the World* inverts this anxiety: when the title character is taken out "to go *a shopping*" in fashionable London, milliners and mercers, "bowing and smirking to be noticed," show her so much stuff—"silks, caps, gauzes, and so forth"—that she is "almost ashamed" not to be able to buy everything in sight.[108] Choice is repeatedly something of an ordeal for the unsophisticated and virtuous Evelina even in those few, exceptional moments in her story, usually concerning some form of entertainment, in which she is explicitly offered the chance of a "vote." That's partly because, as a seventeen-year-old country girl, she has had no real experience in this regard; she describes herself repeatedly as "ignorant what choice was in my power." But it is also because choice, and especially choice in the commercial world, triggers intense emotions, including recurring feelings of embarrassment. She's also well aware of the scorn of others insensitive to her plight (when Evelina tries to put off making a choice until after everyone else has spoken, her male tormenter says sarcastically, "Why, pray . . . who have we left out? would you have the cats and dogs vote?").[109] Choosing is something Evelina must learn to perform to make her way in the new world of elite urban sociability. But it does not come naturally to her. She has had access to neither the opportunities, nor the menu of options, nor the necessary mindset and performance codes before now.

Outside the pages of the novel, others describe feeling not powerful but overcome in the face of shopping's seductions. Another literary German traveler to London, the *salonnière* and future novelist Johanna Schopenhauer, seeing "the beautiful draperies . . . behind large plate glass windows," claims the display "bewitches the visitor."[110] French commentators seemingly agreed; fashionable *marchands de modes*, notes the prolific writer Nicolas-Toussaint Des Essarts in his *Dictionnaire universel de police* (1786–90), feed on women's "frivolity" and "coquetry," leaving them unable to "resist the attraction they feel when seeing [other] women of all ages and all conditions entering these enchanted places."[111] This was a full century before Émile Zola's famous description in *Au bonheur des dames* (1883) of the tempting manipulations of the department store, that late nineteenth-century feminine Shangri-La. Choosing in a commercial context is, from the eighteenth century onward, a pleasure but also a burden. It's an occasion for self-recrimination in addition to being a ritual that must be properly performed. One has, after all, also to live with the consequences on one's own. Even today, that's a reason why people—myself included—often prefer the hit-or-miss quality of the thrift shop or the "curated" boutique to the vast online emporium or even that nineteenth- or twentieth-century leftover, the majestic department store. It also explains why so many people only shop now where there is the promise of the redo in the form of the (highly wasteful) "returns department."[112] There *is* such a thing as too much choice for the nonexpert going it alone.

The Shopping Duet

Yet the eighteenth-century habitué of shops was never really solo. As early as the first decades of the eighteenth century, Mandeville and Defoe both pointed out that the shopper's battle was not entirely internal either. The actual business of buying and selling involved a complex power struggle between generally polite but determined adversaries—choice architect and chooser—both afraid of manipulation by the other. That the two sides were frequently of the opposite sex and likely of different classes did not make matters any easier.

One repeat motif of novels and travel accounts of the second half of the century was the male merchant (and earlier, auctioneer) taking advantage of the dazzled female consumer and robbing her, via the presentation of seductive goods, of more money than she had. In many a novel, the virtuous heroine is made so uncomfortable by the pressure of shopkeepers that she likens it to a form of assault (and of course sexual seduction, where a woman becomes the object to be chosen, is always lurking as a possibility). Just as the stereotype of the auctioneer was as the orchestrator of a temple of deception with gullible ladies as victims, so did the male shopkeeper in the eighteenth-century Atlantic world get pegged as a tempter, a flatterer, a hyperbolic faker of gentility, in hot pursuit of women's money or bodies or both, cheating whenever he saw an advantage. Yes, in his professional capacity, the shopkeeper may have been rewritten in some quarters as an important economic actor on behalf of the nation. But more often and especially in the fashionable trades, the men and occasional women on the far side of the counter were identified with sleaze (fig. 1.9).

Still, even more common in eighteenth-century literary discourse was the motif of the frequenting of shops in town as a ritualized social activity that involved groups of women of some standing throwing their weight around and finding pleasure by actually *resisting* the final step in the game of consumer choice, which is to say, endlessly looking, conversing, and browsing without buying. For if women were frequently pawns of shopkeepers, women shoppers were even more ready, according to literary tradition, to thwart the ambitions of middlemen eager to close the deal. "Shopping, as it is called," according to our Scottish expert on the history of women, is an activity distinct from mere purchasing whereby "two, three, or sometimes more ladies, accompanied by their gallants, set out to make a tour through the most fashionable shops, and to look at all the most fashionable goods, without any intention of laying out one single sixpence. After a whole forenoon spent in plaguing mercers and milliners, they return home, either

Fig. 1.9. Charles Williams, *The Haberdasher Dandy* (c. 1818), etching with hand-colored additions, in which an unctuous and overdressed salesman selling fabric, lace, and ribbons is waiting on two fashionable ladies and cutting cloth to their specifications, though they are sure he is cheating them on the measurements all the while.

thoughtless of their folly, or which, perhaps, is worse, exalting at the thoughts of the trouble and disturbance they have given."[113]

This was a stereotype with a long life. The caricature of the woman shopper who simply refuses to make a selection and lay out the money required already populates the first half of the century, from Defoe's *Complete English Tradesman* to the pages of *The Female Tatler* and *The Spectator*. It was the latter that introduced the term "silk worms" for women who "ramble" a few times a week from shop to shop and get shop assistants to unravel long lengths of cloth only to buy nothing in the end, though they might later publicize new wares much like today's "influencers."[114] Late in the century, the stereotype was still alive. Johanna Schopenhauer was explicit about this English custom too: "going a shopping" involved trying the "patience of shopkeepers" by "having a thousand things shown to us which we do not wish to buy" in ways that ultimately hindered rather than advanced the business of selling.[115] And it wasn't just London either. Louis-Sébastien Mercier, in his great *Tableau de Paris*, noted that when one is visiting shops in Paris, "often times one leaves the store after a long discussion without having bought anything," though he blamed this effect on the customer having been made "dizzy from the merchant's babble."[116]

Once again it is women's novels, themselves both commercial products and often anticommercial tracts, where this motif was most developed. The greatest exponent of the practice is Mrs. Mittin, who—to the horror of local shopkeepers—takes the titular Camilla out for a day in Southampton in Burney's great novel of that name to take "a near view of the various commodities exposed to sale" in shop after shop, regarding "all that was smartest" and "routing over every body's best goods" and "yet not laying out a penny."[117] That, we learn, is precisely her game. A few years later, in a novel of the last year of the eighteenth century called *A Tale of the Times* by Jane West, one Lady Arabella is described as enjoying most fully her present situation in which "some mornings she went a shopping to cheap warehouses; at others she was waited upon by different tradesmen at home: she ordered and counter-ordered; bought and returned; thought this monstrous pretty, and that monstrous frightful; gave as much trouble as her rank would possibly enable her to impose, and then complained of the impertinence and imposition of the trades-people."[118] And when Burney finally turns the tables and gives her readers a heroine, Juliet, working on the other side of the counter in a milliner's shop in *The Wanderer; or, Female Difficulties* (1814), we learn that she "found herself in a whirl of hurry, bustle, loquacity, and interruptions. Customers pressed upon customers; goods were taken down merely to be put up again; cheapened but to be rejected; admired but to be looked at, and left; and only bought when, to all appearance, they were undervalued and despised." Burney continues satirically, "the good of a nation, the interest of society, the welfare of a family, could with difficulty have appeared of higher importance than the choice of a ribbon, or the set of a cap."[119]

But making the most of the opportunity to ponder this choice, or really any choice, was clearly the point, as Burney makes clear. With this particular, if limited, power accorded to them, women buyers had—commentators worried—found a way to be proudly and assertively disruptive even if they were otherwise economically disempowered. For all the talk of the hyperfeminine consumer imposing her womanly values on commercial exchange, the other great fear rooted in the circumstance was that same female person perversely usurping male power as a decision maker, and thereby thwarting the rules of commerce, even when the things to be chosen were of no great import.

In other words, what comes through in all these accounts, fictional and not, is that choosing in the mercantile world of inanimate goods should be understood as a relational game requiring a certain measure of cunning on both sides of the counter. Yet women bore the brunt of the blame as essentially ill-suited to the task. Either their innate weaknesses made them bad at this kind of bounded choice-making or, in performing bounded choice, they lost what made them distinctively female, a process that threatened to upset relations between the sexes permanently. These arguments in many ways anticipate those that would be deployed more than a hundred years later in opposition to women's suffrage or formal engagement in political choice-making. Moreover, the linkage went the other way too. Precisely the kind of morally neutral selection process associated with the fashion of shopping to match one's (increasingly) personal aesthetic preferences became itself tainted by its feminine associations, much as voting by ballot was decried as unmanly for much of the nineteenth century.

Here, then, is the rub. In practice, consumer choice takes off first in the eighteenth-century North Atlantic world, with London as its epicenter. It becomes a self-consciously modern pastime, produced by the invention and production of new consumer options, by the establishment of new kinds of entrepreneurs from shopkeepers to novelists to oversee the process, and by the actions of voluntary choosers as well as by laws and norms governing choice's operation on both ends of the deal. It also becomes an increasingly ordinary pastime from the age of revolutions onward, performed by a wide swath of the North Atlantic world population under varied political conditions and then by various people in the southern Atlantic world too. By the early nineteenth

Fig. 1.10. Joseph Brown (English), untitled watercolor (c. 1840), based on a drawing by the Colombian artist and Catholic polemicist José Manuel Groot, showing a modern store on the main street in Bogotá, Colombia, in which mule drivers are purchasing cloth after choosing among the many options displayed on the walls.

century, European immigrants in major Latin American city centers, taking over old, colonial shops called *cajones*, had created similar experiences for affluent customers, again with local and imported textiles at their core (fig. 1.10).[120] Department store windows and print advertising campaigns would, by the last quarter of the century, entrench the culture of European-style shopping even further in places like Buenos Aires and Mexico City where, for most people, London and Paris were only abstractions.[121]

And yet, the appearance of something like an expanded menu of options along with the cultivation of consumer choice-making did not, by itself, initially provide a model for other arenas of behavior, public or private, political or not. Shopping was never, despite some twentieth-century historians' wishes, coterminous with those late eighteenth- and early nineteenth-century political revolutions that came wrapped in the language of rights. It did not create, except in fleeting glimpses, anything like the liberal subject, imagined as a model of free- dom and rationality when engaged in the business of informed and independent choice. Mainly, the act of selecting consumer goods re- mained highly gendered in meaning and, no matter the nature of the choices, inextricable from the censorious eye of an alternate and older moral framework than the one cultivated inside the burgeoning world of shops.

Which brings us back to the topic of one of Mr. Cock's many paint- ings for sale in the 1720s and 1730s, not to mention a century's worth of didactic essays, operas, paintings, prints, and poems by figures from Shaftesbury to Bach: the Choice of Hercules.[122] One of the appeals of this traditional theme was the way it brought into view and indeed pro- moted a different, more traditional form of choice-making. If choice in an emerging commercial culture meant men and women alike selecting among numerous options, none of them with a clear moral valence or use value, and thus engaging in an activity suggestive of a certain kind of cultural decadence, the subject as offered up by the many eighteenth- century representations of the Hercules story, visual or textual, was the inverse. Here women were allegorized as options to choose between, not choosers themselves. And here the man at the center of the story, Hercules, was given a choice that was morally clear-cut even in the face of temptation. He could do the right and, consequently, the more dif- ficult and manly thing and follow the path of civic responsibility labeled Virtue. Or he could choose wrongly and follow the open road toward Vice—now sometimes called Pleasure or Happiness. As the century wore on, the latter was a pathway increasingly associated with the world of baubles, fashion, and the opportunity, as the poet and anecdote- compiler Joseph Spence put it in his mid-century version of the classic story, to "satiate yourself with Things."[123]

Needless to say, in the didactic art of the eighteenth century, the for- mer option always wins in the end. The Hercules myth gave painters, poets, composers, rhetoricians, and even novelists the opportunity to take on the role of anticommercial moralist for themselves. They did so by finding concrete ways to depict a mythic moment of high-stakes decision making—generally precisely when Hercules is torn, physically and mentally, but nevertheless on the cusp of making the right choice between his two options—in an effort to shape similar moments of decision making in the present and future. As Spence announced: "There can be no virtue without choice."[124] This was a basic principle of self-rule and indeed freedom. But the opposite was widely propounded by thinkers in the civic humanist tradition too, namely, that there can be no meaningful choice (i.e., weighing the options and coming to a deliberate decision) without the guidance of virtue or discipline over one's own passions and desires. This was also the argument of British abolitionists in the 1790s who called for spurning "proffered temptation" and abstaining from purchasing sugar as a commodity dependent on slave labor. There was only one correct choice, and that choice entailed, in this instance, not choosing at all when it came to this particular consumer good.[125] For Hercules's choice was ultimately, and similarly, the conscious, moral choice to live righteously or not, a position that over time had become thoroughly intertwined with Christian teachings and assumptions about manliness as well (fig. 1.11).[126]

The only catch? Paintings, for eighteenth-century artists, were also opportunities to show off their decorative powers, including depictions of fashions arrayed to sensual effect on female bodies in the form of Vice or Pleasure and, like that by Zeeland being auctioned by Cock, for sale in the marketplace themselves. In fact, Cock's Hercules painting was just one choice among many ripe for bidding on, in keeping with personal inclinations, already in the first part of the century. The same went for commercial novels and most other artistic products of the time. They were almost all operating as parts of markets. Even abolitionism was simultaneously commodified at the close of the eighteenth century, including by that most clever of marketers and merchants, Josiah Wedgwood, in antislavery tableware.[127] As Mandeville had announced early in the century, in real life there is no single and decisive moment of choice, no clear-cut right path or obviously wrong one to pick between, no choice that impacts no one else, and no choice that thoroughly escapes the passions. Stoical self-mastery, on the one hand, and amoral commercial choice rooted in self-fulfillment or something

Fig. 1.11. Paolo de' Matteis, *The Choice of Hercules* (1712), an allegorical painting of a classical theme in which Hercules, at the center, has a choice between the rocky path of virtue, on one side, and hedonism and vice, on the other, both represented as women. Hercules, though his body is torqued, is clearly turning toward the former as the better choice.

more akin to the choice of the *coquette*, on the other, were going to be hard to reconcile (fig. 1.12).

The Future of Choice

The problem has never actually gone away. Ambivalence about shopping and, more specifically, the kind of choice it entails has lasted—and lasted some more. Ever since the eighteenth century, consumer choice has steadily displayed two faces, both of them highly gendered: as emancipatory *and* as selfish and indulgent. This dualism holds whether one is considering the DIY shop of the small business owner in the 1700s, the arcade or grand department store in the 1800s, or the suburban shopping center ("the mall" in the parlance in the part of the world

LA COQUETTE FIXÉE

Fig. 1.12. Jean Couché and Jacques Dambrun, *La Coquette fixée*, a 1785 engraving after a 1752–55 painting in the Rococo style by Jean-Honoré Fragonard. A flirtatious young woman (*coquette*), dressed as a shepherdess, has just made her selection between the two male suitors, dressed as shepherds, who flank her. Neither is clearly a better choice than the other, except in terms of her personal predilections. Note too the gender reversal of the Choice of Hercules theme.

where I grew up) in the 1900s and beyond, though now in its period of decline.

Certainly the appeal of consumer choice has grown steadily, in practice and in theory, since the eighteenth century. It has been aided by the exponential worldwide expansion and intensification of shopping's domain, from venues to products, as well as by what would become liberal thinkers, who have pegged it as desirable and, ultimately, freeing both as a personal experience and in relation to broader economic and political trends. Importation of exotic, extra-European luxury goods during the Middle Ages began the process for Europeans. But that flow has long gone the other way too, and the more recent globalization of trade under the banner of capitalism has also meant the export of consumer choice itself, especially in the latter half of the twentieth century, from Western Europe and the United States outward. Among the defenses: consumer choice creates prosperity; it equalizes; but above all, it is empowering, a form of aesthetic and personal self-fulfillment, even liberation, for the person who aspires to live and define him- or herself precisely how he or she wants, unimpeded by the traditional boundaries of family, class, gender, taste, race, religion, age, or local culture. Eventually, in looser form, it became a key component of a global ideology known as human rights, linking consumer culture with democracy promotion based on the analogy that freedom in a market economy should mean the chance to be a chooser of *this* rather than *that* in multiple domains. Consider the Japanese philosopher, critic, and playwright Yamazaki Masakazu, who pushed this notion in the early 1980s, just as Japanese shopping culture was exploding but in a very different ethical and cultural environment in which thrift and obligation continued to hold real weight too. The argument he advanced was that a form of "soft" or "gentle" individualism, derived from selecting among differentiated commodities based on "individually determined preferences," was actually a path to satisfaction in life.[128]

Such outlooks (and accompanying practices) were made possible in Japan and elsewhere around the globe in the nineteenth and twentieth centuries even as—or, more likely, because—all those ordinary people making small-bore choices in goods and services were subject both to considerable formal regulation by lawmakers and to extensive informal, often unacknowledged regulation by tastemakers, family members, peers, and others, not to mention voluntary constraints. Global consumer culture has also necessarily continued to produce new forms of exclusion, leaving certain objects (e.g., body parts, many stimulants) and certain people (e.g., the destitute, the stateless, the incarcerated) out of the world of commercial choice entirely or granting them deeply unequal chances or options but now on a global rather than local scale. Consider the old saw "beggars can't be choosers." Yet this has not prevented the rise of an almost worldwide political creed since the second half of the twentieth century emphasizing that, given a chance and full information, individuals know best how to maximize their own happiness, indeed, that they would benefit from an extension of the model of market freedom associated with shopping to multiple domains of their existence. By now, it can sometimes seem as if we have no choice but choice, with consumer choice as the primordial form. How else, for example, can we explain the rise of the twentieth-century practice of giving even small children personal "allowances" if not to acclimate them early to the experience of making their own marketplace selections, in keeping with their own predilections, even if only for a pack of gum?[129]

But that said, consumer choice, understood as primarily the product of interior, personal preferences, has never been viewed as an entirely unadulterated good. That includes within places that have subsequently billed themselves as liberal democracies. On the contrary, ever since our eighteenth-century commentators got wind of it, consumer choice has remained suspect as potentially unserious, hedonistic, and troubling to the psyche when acted upon. Jean-Jacques Rousseau sensed, and just a little while later than Shaftesbury did, that if current trends continued, both men and women would ultimately find themselves dominated by the objects that they chose; in pursuit of the esteem of others, they would end up separated from their true selves. Plus, as the Genevan philosopher argued in his *Discourse on the Origin of Inequality* (1755), they would inadvertently make social and economic competition the hallmark of civilization too, with deleterious effects on all our social institutions.

Karl Marx, writing as industrialization took off a century later, didn't disagree. By performing the very act of choosing goods with prices attached, consumers, he claimed, aided in the process of "commodity fetishism" whereby both the productive labor and the actual exploitative labor relations behind all those desired objects were obscured from view to the detriment of equality and liberty alike.[130] In the twentieth century, his Frankfurt School followers and many progressives, including some liberal thinkers, went even further. When citizens turned into consumers in a world permeated with advertising urging nonstop consumption, they imagined needs that they did not have. What's more, the time-consuming but empty and ultimately joyless project of repeatedly picking inconsequential things to purchase ended up replacing meaningful civic and community engagements—just as Shaftesbury and eighteenth-century moralists, eager to punish imagined *coquettes*, shopping ladies, and fops, worried that it would. Indeed, in such anticapitalist critiques (which sometimes overlapped with antisemitic ones by the late nineteenth century),[131] advertising and then shopping became key elements in the long story of how the people of today—and women especially—built their inauthentic, alienated, and ultimately both aesthetically and intellectually impoverished modern lives, reshaping all other values in the process.[132]

Many traditional conservatives have agreed as well. At the start of the 1970s, the writer Iris Murdoch suggested that we moderns, in our novels, our philosophy, and our politics alike, had gone so far in this new direction that even our understanding of morality had been "assimilated to a visit to a shop."[133] The self, she continued, had become nothing more than an "empty choosing will" in which, metaphorically, "I [as in individual self] enter the shop in a condition of totally responsible freedom, I objectively estimate the features of the goods, and I choose. The greater my objectivity and discrimination, the larger the number of products from which I can select"—and the greater that self's ostensible freedom, since all that matters ends up being the point of action or moment of willed choice.[134] Here was the worst fear of Hercules's champions coming to fruition.

Enter movements of resistance, that is, efforts of various sizes to undermine the power of choice in goods in the modern world, not least in the twentieth century, when consumption seemed to reign especially triumphant. The biggest and most obvious were all-encompassing political movements—forms of state socialism and communism, in particular—that tried, from the Russian Revolution onward, to change not just the mode of production but also the habits associated with consumption and the realm of finished goods. The tamped-down and heavily regulated consumer spheres of the Soviet Union and of post-revolutionary China constituted deliberate efforts to evade the materialistic, commodity culture of modern capitalist societies, including the fetishization of marketplace choice, and to remake women's roles in the process. Even when opportunities for acquiring commercial products increased in the USSR in the later 1930s, they mainly took the form of rewards made available by the state, as neither competition among purveyors nor free choice among consumers ever ruled the roost.[135]

But this wasn't just a question of the efforts of central planners. Visual artists of the twentieth century, working in commercial cities and towns, also found themselves obsessed with the model of glass storefronts filled with goods for sale, that iconic image of modern urbanity, aesthetic allure, and the psychology of consumer desire. Then they wondered if art were the place to consciously challenge its power.

Of course, that wasn't true of artists tout court. From German Expressionists to International Pop artists, a certain current of twentieth-century art self-consciously celebrated the ever-looser boundaries between art and commerce, frequently placing women at the center as both subjects and objects of desire. Think of August Macke trying to capture on canvas his own voyeurism directed toward female shoppers gazing at the merchandise alluringly displayed just out of reach in Swiss shop windows on the eve of World War I (fig. 1.13). Or think of certain American Pop artists (some of them veterans of "doing" store windows themselves) only semi-ironically conjuring up cornucopias of very contemporary goods, whether painted, sculpted, or real; organizing them into advertisement-like visual "choice sets"; and refusing to distance themselves from, as New York gallerist Stanley Kunitz put it in the early 1960s, "the supermarket that is our world." Some artists even went so

Fig. 1.13. August Macke, *Modes: Frau mit Sonnenschirm vor Hutladen* (Fashion: Woman with parasol in front of a milliner's shop) (1914), oil on canvas.

far in that same decade as to set up fake stores in which viewers could pick out premade objects in open acknowledgment of art's complicity in consumer culture, as in the famous *American Supermarket* show.[136]

But there were always also the oddballs, the dissenters, most notably Marcel Duchamp, who avoided the moralizing of, say, Frances Burney but volunteered to be the anti-Mr. Cock when it came to the orchestra-tion of choice. One might even say Duchamp's central project, one of the most aesthetically influential of the last hundred years, was an act of imagination: to try to invent both a form of art object that did not function as a commodity and a type of artist who, while maintaining his or her autonomy, operated neither as conventional choice architect nor as conventional chooser in a world increasingly made up of menus.

Already in 1913, Duchamp offered up a short, cryptic critique of the effects of the shop window, suggesting its pull on the spectator and the ultimately coercive and depressing way that it shaped desire and under-cut the viewer's imagined freedom and thus pleasure. "One's choice," said Duchamp, speaking of the exigency of shop windows, is "'round trip' [aller et retour]. From the demands of the shop windows, from the inevitable response to the shop windows, my choice is determined. . . . [And] the penalty consists in cutting the pane and in feeling regret as soon as possession is consummated."[137] But the impact of Duchamp lies less in the profundity of his resistance to the shop window's power than in the nature of his response. At almost the same moment, this wily artist—a transplant from Paris to New York—was coming up with counterstrategies, ways to break the hold of choice, and especially con-sumer choice, as a practice and ideology in which both art and artist, and indeed everything in the modern world by the early twentieth century, were fully embedded.

One of those strategies was to introduce chance: finding ways to eliminate human agency from artistic decision making as much as pos-sible and letting fate or luck or even pure arbitrariness, as in a coin toss, shape outcomes instead. It was an approach that artists of every type would try in the course of the twentieth century over and over.[138] Ready-mades, Duchamp's name for works fashioned from repurposed man-made objects, from a bottle rack to a defunct urinal turned on its head and renamed "Fountain," was another—and equally subject to imita-tion (fig. 1.14).

In one sense, such appropriations could be said to turn artists into consumers rather than producers: as one of his surrogates explained in 1917, "Whether Mr. Mutt [one of Duchamp's aliases] with his own hands

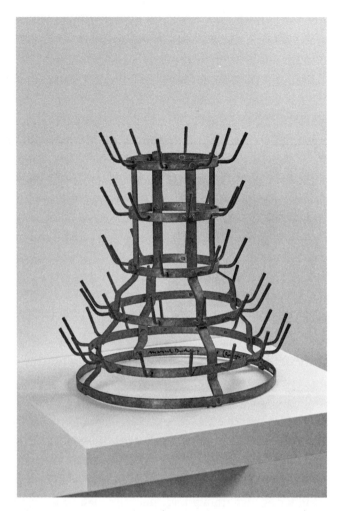

Fig. 1.14. Marcel Duchamp, *Bottlerack* (1961, replica of 1914 original), a "ready-made" the choice of which, the artist insisted, owed nothing to preference or taste or any personal inclination.

made the fountain or not has no importance. He CHOSE it. He took an ordinary article of life, placed it so that its useful significance disappeared under the new title and point of view—created a new thought for that object."[139] But the novelty of the readymade lay in good part in the fact that the choosing behind it happened not, ostensibly, according to the assumed rules of modern consumer choice or what had, by the

1910s, become everyday experience. On the contrary, the selection of
the object was a result—claimed Duchamp many years later, truthfully
or not—of pure "indifference." It was untainted by bourgeois notions
of good or bad taste, *or* aesthetic value, *or* utility, *or* pleasure, *or* exchange
value, *or*, most significantly, even a hint of any manufactured desire to
express one's own inner preferences and personality through the work
of art.[140] This refusal of self-expressive choice became particularly true
in subsequent decades, as he let others purchase for him even the raw
materials ripe for repurposing.

Furthermore, Duchamp's strategies for evading the conventions of
modern consumer behavior extended to the deliberate confusion of
gender norms, as he gave himself, as artist, both female and male per-
sonas at different moments. That way he also refused the role of either
male producer or female consumer, a precursor to more recent efforts
to thwart all binaries of this sort. Anything to break out of the close association of artistic practice with marketplace behavior and "the game
of taste," as one key contemporary critic has put it, even as shopping and
the shop window remained touchstones of a sort.[141] By seeking both to
demystify the once bourgeois and ultimately mass-market conceit of
choice-as-freedom *and* to create works of (quasi-) art that were utopian
because they could not easily function as store-window commodities
or auction lots ripe for picking, Duchamp could be said to have devoted
his career to dispelling the enduring magic of Mr. Cock and the like.
Here was what individualism and freedom apart from market-based
capitalism and bourgeois self-determination along traditional gender
lines could look like.

But that option wasn't available in the eighteenth-century Atlantic
world, as a new kind of consumer choice was just getting off the ground.
Furthermore, art can critique, but it necessarily remains marginal in its
power to transform practice itself; no one—including Duchamp—
found a way to break the logic of consumer choice, as established by
tastemakers like Mr. Cock, except at the margins (which is partly what
kept strategies like that of Duchamp always in the avant-garde). What
was clear by the end of the eighteenth century was only that (a) history
was moving toward ever greater engagement in the world of markets

and goods, and (b) the fate of women as consuming subjects, on the one hand, and the fate of commercial culture with its attachment to individual, preference-driven choice, on the other, were going to be bound up with one another. *Coquetterie* was essentially "innate" for almost all women, according to one mid-century French commentator.[142] Plus, as long as there were baubles to consider, the *coquette*, just as much as the choice architect, was here to stay.

Nevertheless, that's only one part of the big story of this book. It would take the emergence of other areas of choice-making—beyond the sphere of consumer goods—for anyone to recognize the political potential in the idea of a life governed by personal choice as a life of freedom and, ultimately, for that idea to become banal. That was especially true for the cause of women's emancipation. The self-governed conscience also had a key role to play.

CHAPTER 2

DECIDING WHAT
TO BELIEVE—OR CHOICE
IN IDEAS

EVERY BIG STORY has more than one beginning. Forget about restaurant menus and sales catalogs for the moment. Scissors and knives can also be useful as instruments of choice. So can glue, once choices are made. All found their way into the tool kits of readers, male and female, as printed material got cheaper and more abundant starting in the late eighteenth century and direction in how best to consume it got scarcer. By the beginning of the nineteenth century such implements had become essential paraphernalia for what might be described as a fad for intellectual *collage*.

The most obvious residue of this process is commonplace books. Close cousins of diaries and scrapbooks and, maybe, today's vision boards, these homemade organizational tools are a frequent presence still in repositories of family papers. Philadelphia's archives, like those of most Atlantic seaport cities, are full of striking examples. In the first few decades of the nineteenth century, Deborah Logan, a prominent well-educated Quaker woman with a large private library and famous book-collecting ancestors on her husband's side, copied out select bits of poems, prose, and magazine articles she'd read into seventeen different notebooks and, scissors in hand, stuck in printed illustrations. Just a few years earlier, the esteemed evangelically inclined physician Benjamin Rush similarly used blank books to combine newspaper clippings, reports on sermons, and exegesis of his readings and conversations, picking from the pieces of his own eclectic intellectual life in Philadelphia's professional circles.

This happened almost the same moment as Rush's friend Thomas Jefferson, secretly and several hundred miles to the south, began cutting up a single book—the Bible—and sorting and reassembling the chosen pieces—and by extension, Christianity—to his own liking. For Jefferson, even the New Testament could quietly be turned into a set of menu items from which a proper choice would result in a satisfying meal.[1] But the authors of many other such experiments remain obscure. Commonplacing was the result of an old technique of selection and recombination that was repurposed and turned into a private, leisure-time activity in just about the same years as "going a shopping" grew into its own. It now looks like another emblem of the growing power and reach of individuated, preference-based choice-making, in this instance directed toward ideas and beliefs—or what we might call "worldviews."

Still, just because we are talking again about objects and unidirectional choice (printed matter can't, after all, pick you back any better than a calico can), we should not be jumping to any pat conclusions about the long arm of commercial development overriding everything else. The story of the growing significance of choice is not one in which it is sufficient to think only about the emergence of capital and new kinds of markets, whether for books or anything else. Sellers and buyers, or shopkeepers and consumers, aren't the right terms here either. Different kinds of choice architects and theorists, as well as active choosers, populate this part of the tale. For the practice and, ultimately, veneration of choice-making have equally deep roots in another grand—and largely distinct, even if ultimately mutually reinforcing—process in the history of Europe and its global outposts. That is the Protestant Reformation, which, rather ironically, ended up producing as one of its accidental, long-term aftershocks a new form of religious diversity and then a new emphasis on deliberate, personal selection from among the new options available. Choice, in other words, was once just as much a Christian practice and concept as a commercial one. The long history of listening, reading, "cutting and pasting," and, ultimately, appropriating and adopting cannot be separated from a largely post-Reformation, Protestant conviction about interiority and the necessity of individual deliberation and judgment, following consideration of the existing possibilities, about what to take to be true.

The implications of this aspect of the long history of choice are enormous. Most obviously, a distinctively Protestant way of understanding and thus living the experience of faith lies, controversially in our postcolonial era, at the root of what today is considered "freedom of religion" in global human rights terms.[2] But it is also, in a largely secularized form, at the core of equally contested notions of freedom of information and expression, or the rights of listeners and speakers more generally, which were also adopted as core principles from the eighteenth century onward by liberal states, democratic and not.[3] Eventually, this essentially religious notion was to shape early feminist claims around choice, never entirely co-opted by its economic cousins. This is something that historians fixated on the "neoliberalism" of recent years as almost entirely an outgrowth of rapacious capitalism and market thinking are less likely to talk about. There are, though, good reasons to pay it heed, as we will see.

Choice after the Reformation

On the surface, the Protestant Reformation of the sixteenth century seems a poor place to look to understand the origins of anything like intellectual or spiritual choice-making. By most accounts, mainstream Reformation theology placed new limits on the idea of free will or choice, commonly called *liberum arbitrium*. Martin Luther conceded that humans might have choice when it came to most (relatively unimportant) areas of life, or *adiaphora*, but not when it had anything to do with salvation. The "elect" are predestined, meaning nothing they decide or do will make much of a difference in terms of their ultimate fate; the choice or selection lay entirely in God's hands. Calvin was even less inclined to see much scope or value in free will, given humans' inclination toward sin. For the great early thinkers of what came to be known as the Protestant tradition, freedom was defined quite differently. It had little to do with the exercise of anything we might call autonomy or going at it one's own way. It had everything to do with the recognition, through the grace of God, of the necessity of following the moral truths of the Gospel. True liberty meant the freedom to live in accordance with the Word and thus with a clear conscience.[4]

And yet, committed religious challenges to this narrow construction of the realm of choice began in theoretical terms almost immediately after Luther nailed his ninety-five theses to the castle church door in Wittenberg. They continued through the sixteenth and seventeenth centuries, from the teachings of Reformed theologians like Franciscus Junius, who insisted that though man had lost the total freedom he had had before the Fall, including the ability to do good, an essential kind of freedom of choice remained intact, to those of Arminians, who re-defined freedom of the will to require the possibility that one could have made a contrary choice. We might do well to imagine the Refor-mation inadvertently but effectively fracturing any doctrinal consensus in northern Europe and then producing two centuries of heated debate about just what free will meant, what it governed, and what remained of it after Eve's fateful "choice" that brought about the Fall.[5] And even more importantly for the history of choice that was to follow, by the end of the sixteenth century and right at the heart of what came to be mainstream Protestantism, there emerged, paradoxically, the corner-stone of the modern idea of freedom in the spiritual realm. This was the notion, often referred to as "liberty of conscience" but also some-times as "religious choice," that for faith to be legitimate, it had to be a matter of private judgment, a decision on the part of the individual, sovereign mind.

At one extreme, recall those radical Protestants who came to be known (pejoratively) as Anabaptists. What distinguished them, starting in the sixteenth century, was their insistence that church membership should be an active "choice" made deliberately by individual men and women. Thus they rejected the standard (Protestant *and* Catholic) prac-tice of baptism before a boy or girl was old enough to make a free and conscious decision to adopt the Christian faith and follow Christ, pre-ferring instead to delay baptism to adulthood. Their descendants—the

Mennonites, the Amish, the Hutterites, and, eventually, New World Baptists—still do.[6]

Not all went so far, certainly. Yet across many pockets of the Protestant world a more crucial conviction developed starting in the sixteenth century that coerced choice was not a choice at all when it came to faith. The argument went something like this. Belief cannot actually be willed, as it is a product of experience and understanding. The correct way to deal with mistaken belief is thus to persuade the intellect of the person who is mistaken—as Christ himself had done—not to compel him or her. For the conscience is ultimately subjective, meaning that each person, or group of persons, has to be free to follow its dictates, rightly or wrongly, in word and (some believed) in deed too. The future would entail churches filled with people of both sexes who had made conscientious and voluntary choices to believe and to live by what was being professed.[7]

This conception of religious freedom took off especially in England, with its multiple dissenting sects and its late religious wars. John Locke is now the most famous defender of the "liberty of choosing" when it came to belief, but he was hardly alone or even early in the game when he composed his *Letter Concerning Toleration* in the 1680s. Mainly he put all the pieces, many of which had been established earlier in the century during the English Civil War, together. Importantly, Locke did not appropriate choice to the register of natural "rights." Rather, following Christian reasoning, he took up the problem of dissenting belief as a chance to clarify the limits of civil authority over the individual. The main point, according to Locke, was that one should not and could not be forced by any kind of magistrate on questions of faith. The state has other, distinctive concerns that are properly its own. But even more, Locke insisted that religious compulsion necessarily creates an untenable situation for the individual; as he put it, "No man can so far abandon the care of his own salvation as blindly to leave it to the choice of any other, whether prince or subject, to prescribe to him what faith or worship he shall embrace." Furthermore, in the realm of belief, coercion on the part of magistrates is ineffective. The understanding must be appealed to, via reasoned argument, for faith to mean anything, since "all the life and power of true religion consists in the inward and full persuasion of the mind."[8] Force simply fosters hypocrisy, a disconnect between interior belief—which is what really matters—and outward expression.

Others looked for metaphors and similes to convey the same points. Similarly rejecting "blind choice" as unbecoming of reasonable creatures, Jonathan Clapham, author of a marvelously titled effort at persuasion called *A Guide to The True Religion; or, A Discourse Directing to make a wise Choice of that Religion Men venture their Salvation upon: Seasonable for these Times wherein there are such Diversities of Opinions and Wayes of Religion: To inform the Ignorant, to resolve the Wavering, to confirm the Weak* (1668), explained that religious choice is properly performed by the understanding much as "the palate judges of what it tastes and then the stomach or appetite craves it."[9] In both domains, one had to try more than one thing to figure out what truly appealed.

By this way of thinking, the only legitimate real-world policy could thus be some degree of "toleration"—or what might be called the decriminalization of choice and the acceptance of multiple, even competing, paths in the realm of belief. That was especially the case when it came to *adiaphora*, or the realm of "things indifferent" to God, including precisely how He was to be worshipped.[10] In the Dutch Republic, the exiled Huguenot Pierre Bayle not only reinforced the idea that coerced acts have no real religious value since they don't involve the soul. He also argued, quite radically and at almost the same time as Locke, that, practically speaking, if religious persecution stopped, "the Diversity of Persuasions, of Churches, and Worship, wou'd breed no more Disorder in Citys or Societys, than the Diversitys of Shops in a Fair, where every honest Dealer puts off his Wares, without prejudicing his Neighbor's Market,"[11] as if buyers and believers were ultimately engaged in analogous activities. This was not an entirely exceptional idea either. A decade earlier, the English ambassador to the Netherlands, William Temple, had insisted that something along these lines was already happening in Dutch lands, also drawing a comparison with mercantile activity. By making "every Man's choice . . . with whom he will pray or go to Church," just as "with whom he will eat or lodge, with whom go to Market, or to Court," the state had made it so that "Nor is any more notice taken . . . of what every one chuses in these cases, than in any other."[12]

The Dutch Republic was, of course, distinctive in terms of its early investment in religious choice.[13] (Even conservatives were liable to point out by the end of the eighteenth century that this was yet another exceptional characteristic of a society where every man is "free to choose his clothing, his food and drink, his profession, his friends and entertainments, his entire way of life.")[14] But well before Jefferson began cutting up Bibles in different languages, clerics in British North America had already picked up elements of these trans-European arguments, adding, too, that moral character and even self-fulfillment came from being accorded the opportunity for choice-making in the realm of belief. Early eighteenth-century New England Congregationalists Charles Chauncy and Ebenezer Gay defended the "free Choice" of "rational and free Agents" in matters of belief as at the heart of what it meant to be human ("men"), though they also conceded that "Explanation of the Manner of its [freedom of choice] operating, is difficult."[15] So did the leaders of the Great Awakening and their defenders starting in the late 1730s, like the New Light preacher Gilbert Tennent, who tried to reassure all Pennsylvanians that religion is a "reasonable service . . . founded on argument, a matter of choice," whose truth humans must "examine and judge" for themselves.[16] Such arguments had become truisms in much of the Anglo-Protestant world by the middle of the eighteenth century, a way of conceiving of self and faith that was theoretically extended to all adult women too, even as pulpits and theology remained dominated by men. These were also claims that women, starting with female Levellers at the time of the English Civil War, had a history of promulgating themselves.[17]

Before we get ahead of ourselves, however, a few caveats are in order. None of this talk was actually premised on the position that all choices were equally good. Instructive books with titles like *A Conference with a Lady about Choice of Religion* (1638), by a Catholic author, and *The Englishman Directed in the Choice of His Religion* (1740), by a Protestant one, offered readers, male and female alike, something much closer to Hercules's Choice. That was help in figuring out how to take the right path rather than the wrong one, not how to pick among morally neutral options.[18] (Bayle remains something of a striking exception here, though the author of *The Sincere Christian's Guide, in the Choice of Religion* [1734] also notes, "In our *Clothing, Eating, and Dwelling*, etc. there is no Regard to what our parents us'd, but we take Care to make Choice of that which is *Best* for us.")[19] Moreover, it was clear even to advanced thinkers on these questions like Locke that one can and should be compelled *not* to choose atheism or Godlessness or, for that matter, Catholicism, which Locke believed failed as a choice worthy of toleration, in part because it did not itself recognize either conscience or free choice in matters of faith. None of these thinkers made a case for what we now call relativism or choice based on purely personal appeal, with truth and established morality as beside the point. Neither did any of them claim the "right" to think however one wants.

It also followed well into the eighteenth century that spiritual heterogeneity, or having multiple options on the religious front, was not a net positive for society, though occasionally its advantages for trade were pointed out. Rather, diversity in the realm of belief was more something to be "tolerated," in the sense of put up with, for reasons that were sometimes epistemic (human uncertainty—can we ever be sure we are 100 percent right?) and more often practical (avoiding big fights and preventing the kinds of hatreds, persecution, and oppression that produce them). Sometimes that also meant treating choice as a purely private or interior matter, not something that required visible public expression at all. And very few people saw competition among religions, or even just the existence of explicit difference, as something to cherish in and of itself, not least those sincere about winning souls to Christ. The conviction held fast that in an ideal world, the one *true* religion would, at the end of the day, be the possession of everyone.

Then there's another hitch in the story. The choice of religion in the early modern period meant, as it still does to a certain degree, adopting a creed that would minimize future choices once it had been fully chosen. That was especially the case for women. To accept any one faith not only required giving up all other options, in life and death alike. It also demanded choosing an existence of piety marked by obedience and future behavioral constraints, including on sexual, consumer, and even intellectual choice—think "commandments"—which is why the choice of no faith seemed to most commentators a dangerous and intolerable recipe for anarchism and licentiousness. At the time of the American Revolution, liberty, as opposed to license, still generally meant the chance to live a life of righteousness, understood as freedom from sin.[20] Should we be surprised that, in 1776, John Adams suggested that the Great Seal of the new United States take as its model none other than the engraving of Hercules's Choice originally outlined by Shaftesbury?[21] We are very far here from the world of Karl Marx, who argued in "On the Jewish Question" (1844) that "the right to be religious—to be religious in whatever way one chooses and to practice one's chosen religion" had already become a hallmark of modern life but was not actually compatible with true emancipation since it only concerned the egotistic man, separated from his community.[22]

The significance of the early discourse of liberty of conscience for our inquiry is that, despite what we might now see as its limitations or at least differences from later liberal ideals, rhetorically it attached that old, amorphous concept of "choice" to the equally abstract idea of "freedom." Then it linked them both, if not with a set of personal preferences in any modern sense, then with the idea that all of us possess some kind of private, inner self.[23] This was a self that could, and indeed should, make its own subjective determinations—albeit always following familiar regulative norms like reason and taste, along with family obligation, ministerial authority, and godly direction—about what to take to heart from among the range of possibilities this self had already encountered.

We might thus also see this self as part and parcel of a new belief about the nature and origins of belief. In an age that became increasingly attached to the contractual notion of reasoned consent as the theoretical foundation for all sorts of political arrangements, a related early Protestant discourse about the significance of private, subjective judgments and the value of toleration of spiritual difference helped widen notions of individual autonomy quite apart from going shopping or a related consumer discourse. At least it did so for that circumscribed part of the adult population, male and female, accorded the theoretical authority to make deliberate, individualized choices in the realm of ideas and then their expression. In this newfangled form, the distinctive logic of "modern belief," as the historian Ethan Shagan characterizes it, gradually expanded its domain over much of our world.[24]

New States and Old

Theory, though, never has much sway on its own. Specific developments at the level of the state and an emergent civil society, as well as the behavior of various kinds of social actors, created the conditions in which such an abstract view of self and world made sense and, even more, proved useful. Or to put it slightly differently, the theory should be seen as much as a strategic response to changing circumstances on the ground as an instigator of them. Moreover, as with the rise of markets for exotic goods, that circumstance was multiplicity, which, in this case, meant the proliferation of various rival claims. Being presented, whether on the page or in places of worship or even in daily life, with multiple, competing possibilities in belief, not to mention a decline in clear guidance about or penalties for how the chosen alternatives were to be weighed so that they ultimately came to seem more like commensurate options, made personal intellectual and spiritual choice actionable and even a necessity, if not (yet) a value unto itself. Here, too, choosing was well on its way, from the late seventeenth century onward, to becoming a form of behavior, or a way of being and acting in the world, orchestrated by new kinds of choice agents and enacted by new kinds of people in the role of choosers. Only in this instance it was happening in the realm of ideas.

Let's consider initially the function of states in fostering the practice and experience of spiritual choice-making among ordinary people. Starting in the seventeenth century, when it came to religion, a variety of secular rulers in different corners of Europe took actions that both changed the rules governing the menu of options and widened the pool of choosers. This happened initially in Protestant Europe and its colonial outposts in the northern New World and then, in the next century, in parts of Catholic Europe too. Even if we shouldn't exaggerate the degree of tolerance, as in forbearance, that was established by the Toleration Act of 1689 in England, we need to acknowledge that, by making attendance at Church of England services voluntary and exempting Protestant dissenters from most penalties, the Act helped make multiple possibilities for worship, first, visible and, second, subject to choice in practice on a wide, family-by-family or even person-by-person basis. For just as in the Dutch Republic, in England and its outposts the decision about where and how to worship increasingly became something circumscribed by informal social pressures (family, community, tradition, and other prior duties and allegiances that exerted a power of their own) rather than by formal laws, even as states established the parameters and imperial projects like trading companies helped spread them.

In addition, well before the French Revolution shook up the world by codifying certain "rights," *reversals* of the doctrine *cuius regio, eius religio*, according to which the religious choice of the ruler had long been the default confessional identity of all his subjects, had begun to be enshrined in new legal codes in multiple large continental European states. France, Prussia, and the Habsburg Empire all enacted in the course of the eighteenth century limited toleration decrees with an enlightened ring, moving increasingly from framing them as grants of tolerance (in hopes of one day achieving religious uniformity staked on truth) to a broader notion of liberty of worship premised on civil rights (that is, opportunities for choice related to individual conscience) for individuals and minority religious groups that states had a responsibility to protect and even foster.[25] Such laws made heresy—once related to the need to constrain choice (*hairesis*) in order to enforce orthodoxy or uniformity of belief—essentially obsolete in the political realm.

Certainly, the rhetoric of monarchs and assemblies, not to mention Enlightenment polemicists, continued in the late eighteenth century to owe something to its religious roots when it came to the legalization of religious freedom. Voltaire, writing in the wake of Locke and Bayle almost a century later in the 1760s but far from either London or Amsterdam, insisted rather unoriginally in his *Philosophical Dictionary* upon what he now called the "unalterable rights of conscience." He also reaffirmed that one who is enslaved by a sovereign or master or coerced in any way cannot really be said to be religious because "religion . . . in its nature presumes choice and liberty."[26] This became a standard Enlightenment position. The difference from earlier polemics? The case for a policy of toleration turned, in various parts of Catholic and Protestant Europe, more strident. It also became more explicitly secular, infused with the desire of men like Voltaire, despite the Christian language, to strip clerical influence from the public realm. Indeed, it was reconfigured as the political corollary—along with, eventually, a new, related "right" to self-expression—of the necessity of each individual leaving behind his self-imposed intellectual dependency, in Kantian terms, on the path toward Enlightenment.[27] Over time, these positions helped both create the preconditions for and anchor new forms of representative government just as much as more familiar (North American) arguments about the separation of church and state as a way to avoid Caesarism or theocracy.

It is important to keep in mind, though, that political rulers, including quasi-absolutist ones like Austria's Joseph II, initially latched onto these arguments for toleration of varied beliefs (including offending religious ones) for strategic reasons as much as for intellectual or spiritual ones. Enshrining religious liberty in law offered kings and princes a way simultaneously to maintain internal peace in an era of growing confessionalization *and* to increase their own might at the expense of any one church and its authorities. New legislative assemblies characteristic of the age of revolutions similarly saw possibilities for state building, national consolidation, and even imperial expansion in such claims. And considerable Catholic resistance to all of these related doctrines endured well into the nineteenth century for equally political reasons, as the Papal Encyclical Mirari Vos of 1832 condemning both liberty of conscience and freedom of expression makes clear.[28]

The key point here is that legal guarantees of freedom of expression, belief, and worship—as in the French Revolutionary Constitution of Year III (1795), which declared in very forward-looking language: "No man can be hindered from exercising the worship he has chosen"—did

not come out of nowhere in the 1790s.[29] They were, like contemporaneous economic decrees, ways of shrinking certain sources and types of
moral policing in favor of increasing state power overall. In much
European and colonial law, though with important exceptions, a post-
Reformation Christian idea was repurposed so as to make the state itself
the guarantor of a wide field of choice. In those places, protection from
religion (i.e., separation of obligations as a citizen and as a believer) also
came to mean protection for religion (i.e., granting individuals the possibility to believe, worship, and express themselves of their own volition
in many different ways) and thus for spiritual pluralism as a result.

A changing media landscape in the eighteenth century, with similarly
transnational contours, did much the same. As formal places of worship
grew in number, variety, and visibility, especially in urban centers in
Europe and its outposts, so did other places, mainly nongovernmental,
designed for the diffusion of information, ideas, and opinions: schools,
learned societies, taverns, coffeehouses, tent revivals, clubs, lending
libraries, bookshops, masonic lodges, general stores, and peddler's
backs. The same pattern held from Stockholm to Turin, Boston to Cap
Français. Something similar happened to printed matter itself, an
eighteenth-century "growth industry" (to use today's terms). Certain
ideas newly promulgated in printed matter were consonant with existing religious languages or even linked to religious institutions; the
eighteenth-century explosion of outlets for ideas aided orthodoxy as
well as dissent. Others expanded the realm of belief in new directions—
heterodox or even atheistic—via underground networks or new official
policies of toleration and freedom in the sphere of print and expression.
Still others were resolutely secular. Supply grew faster than literacy itself, at least in England.[30] What matters is that all of these books and
pamphlets and newsletters and prints also became valuable goods in a
larger world of trans-European and transatlantic commerce both alongside and in concert with other kinds of markets. In this space, traditional
choice agents and orderers of the world of ideas, from academicians to
preachers and priests to printers themselves, were forced to compete
with one another for public attention and financial rewards and thus
also ended up growing the sphere of ideas.

Finally, we can't forget all the ordinary readers and churchgoers, famous and obscure, who remade the world of intellectual choice in practice too. Confronted with this new, expanded menu of possibilities, some chose to dig in their heels and stick with what they already knew. Alternately, others brought new sources to themselves and their family dwellings. Or, they followed new ideas to new destinations, traveling in previously unfamiliar directions to attend a new church or other intellectual hub. In the most extreme cases, that meant moving across continents or oceans as part of a diasporic religious or ideological community and setting out into the larger world of alternative options. Some overseas colonies like South Carolina even began marketing themselves to buyers in part by promising respect for "liberty of conscience."[31] In this context, everyone was potentially a heretic in the sense of an explicit chooser in the realm of belief.[32]

Men were in the forefront of this emerging world, especially as they constituted a larger portion of both the literate classes and the geographically mobile. Still, women also seized new opportunities for intellectual and spiritual consumption, combining them with more obviously domestic roles. The late eighteenth-century high-volume London bookseller James Lackington, like some other shopkeepers of this moment, saw himself very much as an entrepreneur in the world of choice. Yet in his own account of his remarkable success published as the century drew to a close, he insisted that his customers, across both gender and class divides, had no trouble making up their own minds when confronted with all the options he had on offer. "There are some thousands of ladies, who frequent my shop," he noted in his characteristic exaggerated fashion, "that know as well what books to choose, and are as well acquainted with works of taste and genius, as any gentleman in the kingdom," even as their tastes in reading material diverged.[33] Such women gradually turned the making of choices in ideas from an interior process associated with religious responsibility into an ordinary, lived activity, another form of participation in the new world of deliberate choice-making, apart from the world of labor but at the very nexus of the public and private realms.

Nowhere did all these forces come together in a more conspicuous fashion than in the colonial and then early national city of Philadelphia—my key (and hometown) example here, as it was for eighteenth- and early nineteenth-century commentators on religious freedom everywhere. When William Penn, an English Quaker dissenter, wrote about "liberty of conscience," as he called it, and published his words in London in 1670, he sounded many of the same themes that Locke, an unconventional Anglican, would just a few years later and others had before. That included belief understood as an intellectual phenomenon that is unresponsive to coercion or force and the limited powers of any civil magistrate when it comes to matters of faith and salvation. Choosing for himself some extraordinary analogies, Penn insisted that just as "Men have their Liberty and Choice in External Matters; they are not compelled to *Marry this Person, to Converse with that, to Buy here, to Eat there, nor to Sleep yonder*," they also require "the Right of Inquiry and Choice" in the realm of belief.[34]

But it was the legal framework for the cross-oceanic province that Penn established in 1682 based on an enormous land grant from King Charles II that really astonished. Penn was convinced that social and political harmony required not only a commitment to English contractualism, or consent of the governed in the political sphere, but also a guarantee of full freedom of conscience and choice in the religious sphere.[35] Or, to put it differently, state neutrality about who worshiped when and how was deemed by Penn the essential recipe for the experiment's success.

That meant the colony of Pennsylvania would be characterized by full disestablishment, a policy that went well beyond the English Toleration Act in that it accorded no body the status of official, state-sanctioned church. That also meant there would be no persecution of dissenters, including unbelievers, who—it was hoped—would come to God of their own volition.[36] All added to the idea, advanced by people just like Voltaire across both Catholic and Protestant Europe, of Pennsylvania and especially Philadelphia as that rarest of places, distinguished by diversity of population, the rejection of all dogma, and relative harmony and peacefulness as a result.

Mythology it largely was, too. It has to be emphasized again that, despite the desire of some contemporary economists to imagine a "marketplace" for religion steadily developing in North America since the eighteenth century, with preferences in consumer goods simply translated into preferences in the religious sphere, the analogy is misplaced here.[37] Pennsylvania was not an early liberal paradise. There is no evidence, contra the claims of some historically minded rational choice theorists, that simply because an official policy of toleration allowed for multiple legitimate options in terms of worship, early Philadelphia churches acted like enterprising private businesses in a common market, competing with each other in selling different brands. Nor is there evidence that the religious choices of early Philadelphians were based on maximization of benefits by people who saw themselves as consumers in the realm of belief or acted as utility-maximizing beings. "Liberty of conscience" remained primarily a mechanism for protecting what one historian calls "sincerely held beliefs and deeply valued practices."[38] The right to choose meant according to one's divinely guided conscience and reasoned judgments rather than simply what appeals or an arbitrary preference. Even today it is hard to say persuasively that we "shop" for God or beliefs or even congregations in the same way we "shop" for home appliances, fabric, or novels or that we have the same investment in the results. (That may be one reason why older expressions like "right of private judgment" and "liberty of conscience" have stuck around and remained more common than the language of choice when it comes to religion—they sound potentially less frivolous.)

What's more, the point of Penn's original "holy experiment" with religious liberty was ultimately to lead settlers in one direction: to Quakerism, which meant to him true Christianity. And in practice, the seemingly laissez-faire position of Penn not only produced much doctrinal, intergroup strife of the kind it was supposed to snuff out. It was also, from the beginning, rooted in myriad formal prohibitions and efforts at policing daily life. By the early eighteenth century, extensive state intervention, including both missionizing designed to bring the Truth to light *and* behavioral codes instituted to encourage properly moral conduct and limit options from the kitchen to the bedroom to the tavern, was considered essential to making freedom of conscience possible. Some scholars call Penn's colonial experiment, despite the absence of any official established church, a powerful theocracy.[39] It is also vital to emphasize that Penn's plan, from its start into the nineteenth century, involved the subjugation of Indigenous peoples already on the land that became Pennsylvania and the subordination of all peoples of African descent, enslaved or "free." At the very least, here too we should not see anything like modern liberalism, premised on freedom for everyone to follow and express their own views without impediment, or what Isaiah Berlin called "negative" freedom, alone.

Yet the menu of options *did* continually grow in Philadelphia—and in ways that surprised and worried the Quakers and eventually put them out of business as the dominant power in the city. Three-quarters of the way into the eighteenth century, congregations associated with at least sixteen different sects and denominations could be found in the colony of Pennsylvania.[40] Think Quakers, Huguenots, Mennonites, the Amish, Lutherans, Anglicans, Baptists, Moravians, African communities, Catholics, and Jews, among others. In Philadelphia alone, there were, by the time of the American Revolution, eighteen or so churches, including (thanks to schisms) multiple varieties of Presbyterian and Methodist ones, and a synagogue.[41] All were understood at least in theory to be voluntary devotional communities rooted in the conscious choices of individual believers, even as there was no presumed equality between them. Deists and nonbelievers gradually gained a foothold as well.

Moreover, even as family ties, neighborhood pressure, and ethnic, racial, and linguistic identifications continued to shape initial determinations, city records show Philadelphians of various races, ages, and genders attending multiple kinds of services and reading multiple kinds of religious tracts in the course of their lives. Sometimes that meant choosing to change affiliations or even denominations and creeds along the way. Sometimes that just meant they were eager to hear different interpretations of Scripture, or to experience the various options without making a single determination, or even to mix and match the parts, subverting the menu. No taboo seems to have existed on merely testing out the alternatives. Quaker ministers recall both backcountry and city Meetings visited by curious Presbyterians, Germans, and Baptists. Conversely, Anglican, Reformed, and Lutheran churches in Pennsylvania regularly hosted various kinds of nonconformists and dissenters.[42] Black ministers and churches were a draw for mixed-race crowds. As for women, the majority of North American parishioners in the eighteenth and nineteenth centuries: they went everywhere. Sunday morning in Philadelphia and its orbit offered multiple options, and doors opened widely to women, who filled the pews across denominations even as they enjoyed few official roles and even fewer chances to preach except among the Quakers and a small number of other truly dissenting groups.[43]

Trends were similar in various other North American port cities, including Charleston, Newport, and New York, and their environs. A Lutheran pastor in New York noted in 1749 that "everyone does what he considers right," and "one who is today a Lutheran, he or his child may tomorrow be a Reformed, a Moravian, or a Quaker." A Long Island woman named Mary Cooper, who left a diary of the years 1768–73, tells her reader (perhaps herself) that she went to services in four different town churches (Anglican, Quaker, Regular Baptist, and new Light Baptist) as well as listened to the sermons of itinerant preachers and even the occasional female, Black, or Indian preacher.[44] Tourists visiting Philadelphia from elsewhere, meanwhile, often made a point of trying to attend as many churches as possible while in town—and of leaving records of the fact afterward. Historian Jane Calvert gives us the example of William Black of Scotland, who showed up in Philadelphia for a visit in 1744 and sat in on the services of Moravians, Anglicans, Presbyterians, and New Lights; went to several Quaker meetings; and heard a sermon by Gilbert Tennent. Sometimes he listened to part of one and withdrew to another in the same afternoon. Then, in his journal, he weighed in with his opinions.[45]

It was, in fact, the First Great Awakening of the late 1730s and 1740s—well before the First Amendment to the U.S. Constitution set religious liberty and freedom of expression on a particular and permanent, transregional legal foundation—that introduced de facto into Pennsylvania and other colonies up and down the Atlantic coast the business that is now pejoratively known as "church shopping" or even "church hopping." Beginning in those years, itinerant evangelical preachers like Tennent and, most famously, George Whitefield, whom contemporaries sometimes denigrated as a mere "retailer of trifles" or a "peddler in divinity,"[46] traversed the sacred and secular spaces of British North America from New England to Virginia. In the course of their journeys, these men hawked an emotional brand of Christianity that some scholars now describe as an atavistic reaction against Enlightenment rationalism that both the transatlantic press and much of the colonial public ate up. But paradoxically, in the process, these preachers, soon known as "New Lights," effectively burst the monopolies of the established churches and their clergy. Under the guise of the spiritual equality of all souls before God, they doubled down on the old idea of religious liberty, including the "right of conscience" and "private judgment" and even the right to "choose" one's own church and principles (ideas all borrowed from Great Britain and continental Europe over the previous century and a half and already widely accepted as American creed).[47] They also, in practice, opened up to lay men and women veritable new choices in forms of worship and in sources of wisdom and truth, now increasingly untethered from geography, denomination, and deference to established authority.[48] Or as the historian Chris Beneke puts it, "To the theoretical right of choosing one's affiliation, the Great Awakening added the concrete possibility of having a choice."[49]

Spokesmen for the Great Awakening importantly extended those principles to mean choice of minister too, letting congregants determine just whom and what they wanted to hear, a close corollary of the question of whom they wanted to read. The Virginian Presbyterian minister Samuel Davies, writing to a fellow clergyman in 1750, insisted that just as individuals had the right to pick a medical doctor of their choice for their bodies, so they were "entitled to the same Liberty in chusing a Physician for their Souls," emphasizing that openness to multiple possibilities meant an openness to the Spirit of God himself.[50] Others went back to the taste metaphor: according to a writer in the 1732 *South Carolina Gazette* (a paper partly owned by Benjamin Franklin, who profited off the printing of revivalist sermons and images even as he personally took a very different religious tack), "Every Man, who is in earnest in his Religion, must chuse his own Priest, as well as his own Cook, accordingly to his Sentiments and his palate: and if he can find neither Priest nor Cook to his Mind, he must be content to say his own Prayers and dress his own Victuals."[51] And in the Middle Colonies, Tennent—for whom religion was nothing less than a "reasonable service . . . founded on argument, a matter of choice"[52]—explicitly extended the right to pursue spiritual fulfillment wherever they could find it to women too.

This early (and often very limited) freedom of the layman or laywoman, rich or poor, Black or white, to accept what one heard, to reject it, or even, when needed, to say what one's conscience dictated or to offer one's own interpretation was precisely what distinguished (true) American Christianity from popery and European intolerance. Or at least that was what supporters claimed. Well before the American Revolution, the colonial public, including women from a range of backgrounds, some of them acting independently of the rest of their family units and acutely aware they were going it alone "with no earthly prop" (in the words of one female convert), took this idea to heart.[53] They famously responded in ritualized and dramatically physical ways, fainting, weeping, convulsing, and more. Such acts cannot really be called chosen in the sense of directly willed. Converts, in particular, saw themselves as externally called to take this decisive step toward embracing a new faith and to do so in a communal setting. But in the end, conversion, apart from or within a specific church, increasingly constituted, in both act and rhetoric, an example of individual, lived choice.[54]

Resistance was swift in coming. Established clergy horrified by this "awakening," men like the Boston Congregationalist Chauncy, insisted that they had never meant *that* much choice, including do-it-yourself versions of Christianity. Ordinary people, Chauncy argued quite vehemently, most certainly still needed to hear from learned professionals about the right way to go; choice was supposed to be the product of reasoned reflection following a proper education—or what he calls persuasiveness and we might call indoctrination.[55] Others, like the Boston Congregationalist Jonathan Mayhew, stressed that if there is a right to choose in the realm of belief, that does not mean there is a right to choose or judge wrongly.[56] Itinerant preachers were seen by many established church leaders as serious threats to the social and intellectual order, turning everything upside down, relying on emotion and physical response over rational persuasion, and confusing who should be doing the teaching and who should be doing the listening.

Furthermore, the hostile response to the proliferation of spiritual and ministerial choices was again given a female face. Women, it was feared, with their weak minds and emotional natures, were particularly susceptible to making bad choices in response to new forms of religious freedom. That could mean falling for perceived charlatans like Whitefield (which could be pegged an irrational kind of choice). Or it could mean forgetting their place entirely and developing aspirations beyond their station (which might be called a case of being carried away by having the power of choice at all). As women especially seized the opportunities afforded by the revivalist movement, they did not simply find themselves attacked for trying out new options. Too much choice-making or simply poor choice-making in the religious sphere also reinforced the association of religious inconstancy with the negative qualities of women, much as happened with shopping at almost the same moment (fig. 2.1).

The story for children was similar. Though they were often encouraged by their parents to read and to attend meetings, children in the eighteenth century were increasingly deemed, on account of age, incapable of making good or rational choices rooted in understanding.[57] Which meant that adults' bad choices (from the vantage point of established choice architects like mainline preachers) could be linked to and analogized with childishness or underdevelopment as well as effeminacy, as if rational agency were a life stage that not everyone could reach. Indeed, capacity for sound choice-making in the realm of ideas and beliefs became something like a litmus test; failure provided just the evidence needed to deny the status of independent beings to whole categories of people, including most white women, Black people of both sexes, the mentally disabled, and the poor, as well as the young. Arguably, it often still does.

Fig. 2.1. John Wollaston, *George Whitefield* (c. 1742), portrait of the Great Awakening preacher with an enthralled woman listener, possibly Elizabeth James, née Burnell.

Overall, though, we can now surely conclude, men like Chauncy were fighting a losing battle in taking on the democratization of choice, even with all these restrictions on access. Predestination was largely finished. And rarely did the basic idea of private choice on the path to salvation itself come under attack in these debates so established was it as a solidly Protestant value by the mid-eighteenth century. (One exception to the rule might be the Congregationalist minister Isaac Stiles of New Haven, who despaired over those who act "as tho' they had their Religion to chuse," making him sound almost like a European Catholic conservative.)[58] Even the former-slave-turned-best-selling-author and abolitionist Olaudah Equiano, a convert to Protestant Christianity, wrote in 1789 about faith as a matter of personal choice, despite his eloquent disdain for choice as it could and did involve the sale of other humans.[59]

In addition, up and down the Eastern Seaboard, spiritual and intellectual diversity increasingly became a fact of life. Itinerant preaching expanded enormously after the Revolutionary War right along with denominational heterogeneity and schisms of various kinds; in the first fifty years of the republic, more and more Americans, white and Black, male and female, attended more and more different kinds of churches.[60] Partisan newspapers and other forms of contentious print proliferated too, further spreading competing ideas—unevenly— beyond their regional borders and to an ever-larger body of literate people of both sexes.[61] Consider Philadelphia once again for its outsized stature in this story. By the 1730s and 1740s, it had dueling printers, who, in good eighteenth-century fashion, busied themselves commissioning new texts, reproducing existing English ones, and importing still others. By 1805, according to city directories, it had fifty-one, as well as a host of retail booksellers who also sold writing paper, pens, notebooks, and other authorial and reader supplies.[62] All of these enterprises now promoted their wares, religious and secular alike, to readers as if they were autonomous consumers with a mandate to choose among a range of goods, properly differentiated according to age, gender, education, and income.

Lending libraries, with varied levels of exclusivity, took off in the city from the 1760s onward as well, offering either open stacks or catalogs for browsing the options (which increasingly diversified to include novels, plays, and romances too) and then, it seems, lending out just about as many books to women per month as to men.[63] As one London bookseller wrote to the Library Company in Philadelphia in 1794, using a culinary metaphor once again in response to a request for a new set of alternatives for new kinds of patrons, "Our aim is to assist you in setting before your Company some wholesome and well-dressed Dishes among which every one may consult his own taste, and indulge his appetite with Moderation and Profit." Heads of other American libraries, like that of Charleston in South Carolina, echoed this message after the turn of the century in slightly embarrassed terms, for example apprising

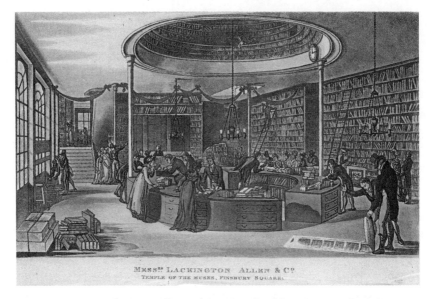

Fig. 2.2. *Messrs. Lackington, Allen and Co., Temple of the Muses, Finsbury Square* [London], (c. 1809), a print showing the great bookstore and circulating library that James Lackington and his wife built up over the last quarter of the eighteenth century, as well as its patrons of both sexes.

the prominent London booksellers Lackington, Allen and Company that "as our Society is numerous, and of course variant in the taste, that we trust you will adapt your selection to suit as well those who are fond of serious and erudite subjects as those who love to amuse themselves with light and trivial reading."[64] By the first decades of the nineteenth century, thanks to the menu-building of the men at the helm of all such institutions, commercial and not, there was simply more to pick from when it came to ideas, and for more kinds of people (fig. 2.2).

Just as importantly, the volunteerism behind all this picking and choosing took on new weight, especially in the religious domain. In the aftermath of the American Revolution, both the direct authority of the government over traditional churches and of traditional churches over laypeople took a substantial hit. Dependent now on voluntary support alone, places of worship would henceforth need to court the public—that is, put forth competing arguments in an effort at persuasion in a crowded field—in order to survive. But as a result, personal identity, or conception of one's place in the world, increasingly became a matter of chosen commitments (or at least commitments derived from social pressures like family expectations rather than from formal legal ones), especially as immigration brought more varied newcomers to North America. Even Jews in the early republic, though still subject to various forms of official discrimination, could pick how they wanted to be Jewish once there was no compulsory model imposed.[65]

In the first decades of the nineteenth century, that growing sense of an autonomous, willing self, responsible for its own destiny, led in two directions. In one, it jumpstarted an expanding realm of moral reform efforts. Most often that took the form of membership in (largely Christian) voluntary societies designed either to combat the bad choices of others, from excessive drinking to prostitution, or to restore the possibility of free moral choice to those without, including, via abolitionism, the enslaved.[66] The common idea was, as the historian Daniel Walker Howe puts it, "to substitute for external constraint the inner discipline of responsible morality" or self-regulation.[67] Women often took the lead, in a few cases organizing and forming associations around their own rights and futures too, as we will see, in yet another public moral crusade.

But, in the other direction, this same impulse toward self-management also eventually underlined a new emphasis on the benefits of diversity, or the existence of multiple, even rivalrous alternatives in the realm of belief[68] and novel forms of intellectual bricolage. Here the so-called Second Great Awakening in North America (and its English counterpart) played as vital a role as it did in generating moral reform movements.[69] For even as revivalist movements of the first three decades of the 1800s stressed once again the necessity of internal constraints on the self as a hotbed of depravity, not least for women, a growing number of preachers, many of them untrained and unaffiliated, were welcoming into the fold an ever-wider part of the population. These same clerics were also spelling out an expanded set of options and, finally, granting audiences, person by person, the opportunity to literally make a choice (albeit a predetermined one) about their *own* way of life and ultimate fate. From hymns to sermons, preachers like the impassioned Presbyterian Charles Grandison Finney provided ordinary men and women of all backgrounds and races with ever more concrete and individual-ized ways to take responsibility, demonstrate moral agency, even "vote" for their own salvation.[70] Many people—women especially—responded.[71] Americans still, to this day, both consider themselves followers of religious traditions *and*, of their own accord, change their affiliations and beliefs to an unusual degree.[72]

What is more, by the time the United States was constituted as a re-public, it had become possible to choose to eschew religion altogether (even though well into the nineteenth century, many states made of-ficeholding a matter still of professing adherence to Christianity).[73] To not believe in God became, social penalties aside, just one more option among others. Or as Robert Baird put it optimistically in 1844 in one of the first histories of religion in America, "The voluntary system rests on the grand basis of perfect religious freedom. I mean a freedom of conscience for all; for those who believe Christianity to be true, and for those who do not; for those who prefer one form of worship, and for those who prefer another."[74]

All of this is, in fact, now part of American lore, a set of ideas fre-quently still weaponized on both the right and the left in a battle over American values. It also distinguishes the United States from its hemi-spheric counterparts to the south. In the U.S. republic between the eigh-teenth and nineteenth centuries, the old idea of freedom of conscience was secularized (though it never lost its Protestant undergirding) and individualized (though belief, as one more set of independently chosen attributes, remains unusually tied to informal constraints compared to many other kinds of choices). It was also turned into the very founda-tion of an everyday culture, quite apart from the workplace, that com-bined voluntarism at the community level, self-discipline, and the idea of self-rule, all with the backing of the law.[75] As such, choice became not just a way of talking about life but, for those with access, a way to engage in many aspects of it. Those choice-based practices, some of them ex-ceptional and some of them habitual, generated new forms of belief in turn. One might even say that in the antebellum period choice became the foundation of a new national religion, even as many were left out (fig. 2.3).

Fig. 2.3. Samuel Jennings, *Liberty Displaying the Arts and Sciences, or The Genius of America Encouraging the Emancipation of the Blacks* (1792), an allegorical painting made for display in the Library Company of Philadelphia, based on instructions from Benjamin Franklin and the other library directors. The painting shows three emancipated slaves kneeling before Liberty, who is holding the book catalog of the Library Company in one hand. But note that the former slaves are not picking out books for themselves; they are, like the female liberty figure, employed as abstract symbols to stand for the benefits of freedom for knowledge.

Commonplacing as a Game of Ideas—or the Reader's Choice

The story of the transformation of religious choice in the early republic also takes us back, in a roundabout way, to the quotidian realm of commonplacing activities, including cutting and pasting, where this chapter began. Commonplacing, complete with its own small-scale technologies, rules, rituals, and versions of choice sets, took off as one important instantiation of a commitment to the experience of intellectual choice in the late eighteenth and, even more, early nineteenth centuries on both sides of the North Atlantic, including the new United States. Our Philadelphia commonplacers, starting with Rush and Logan, got some of their ideas from listening to sermons and talking with religious leaders. They also took in new thoughts or concepts from hearing other kinds of lectures and the dinnertime chatter of visiting dignitaries. Mainly, though, they got their ideas from reading—books, pamphlets, magazines, newspapers, lots of handwritten letters, poems, devotional tracts, eventually novels too, a menu both religious and not. Commonplacing reflected all of this, as men and women alike in the postrevolutionary era recopied, reworked, and reported not on *all* of the "content" they had exposure to in daily life—this was no longer possible, especially for the more connected among them—but rather that which they took to be personally significant in some way. Commonplace books became leisure-time repositories of those items, secular and sacred, that women and men purposefully chose to preserve as they sorted through their experiences in the realm of information, ideas, and beliefs.

Much like buying goods in a marketplace, recording snippets of eloquence or meaningful passages in a notebook was, by the close of the eighteenth century, a very old activity. Since antiquity, commentators had been lamenting the perceived superabundance of texts, many of them seemingly expressing ideas at odds with one another. Since antiquity, too, commonplacing had been considered a potential coping strategy for those confronted with this bounty. Renaissance Humanist educators, in an effort to revive the practices of the ancients, had insisted on the usefulness of getting students to appropriate exemplary aphorisms from their readings and occasional lectures or conversations and then copy them into notebooks under thematic headings like Matrimony or Faith or Jealousy or Chance or even Choice. Not only was the end result meant to be a kind of homemade reference work, a portable storage and retrieval system for the world of past ideas and their expression. From the very business of extraction and transcription, it was thought, lasting benefits to the compositor—meaning reader—would accrue. Students employing commonplace books made up of "choice" extracts of the words of others could hope to enhance their memories, learn of what eloquence consists, and develop their moral character (assuming the passages taught good lessons) all at once.[76]

It was a scholarly tradition that would last. John Locke maintained various commonplace books starting in his student days at Oxford, which he attended just after the middle of the seventeenth century. Many can still be found in the Bodleian Library there.[77] Cotton Mather would keep one in colonial Boston a half century later and urged the next generation of New England students to do the same.[78] Jefferson, in colonial Virginia, subsequently kept a literary commonplace book alongside a legal one and dipped into them both to read and reuse their contents for years.[79] Late in his career, Locke would also offer concrete instructions on how to simplify the practice of commonplacing that would prove exceptionally popular on both sides of the Atlantic for more than a century after they were posthumously published in English in 1706 (fig. 2.4). Perhaps that's because his "method" was so adaptable to new uses, including those that were decidedly less traditional than what Locke actually had in mind.[80]

Commercial publishers well into the nineteenth century churned out essentially blank books, often prefacing them with Locke's original instructions or updated versions promising ever greater utility and efficiency in the organization of one's selections.[81] Publishers shilled too for their own already assembled "treasuries" and "store-houses," telling schoolboys, merchants, gentlemen, and autodidacts of "both sexes" that they, like other kinds of merchants, had done the work of preselecting or identifying "choice" items for their target audience, usually on the solid grounds of community standards. That way all those new readers could access premade compendia of all the best moral essays, aphorisms, devotional texts, literary examples, and/or sayings around.[82] Consider such titles as *Elegant Extracts; or, Useful and Entertaining Pieces of Poetry, Selected for the Improvement of Youth, in Speaking, Reading, Thinking, Composing; and in the Conduct of Life* (1789), in which the reader was promised pieces that "are loudly recommended by the voice of fame, and indeed have already been selected in a variety of volumes of preceding collections" (though of course the reader isn't let off the hook entirely, as he or she will

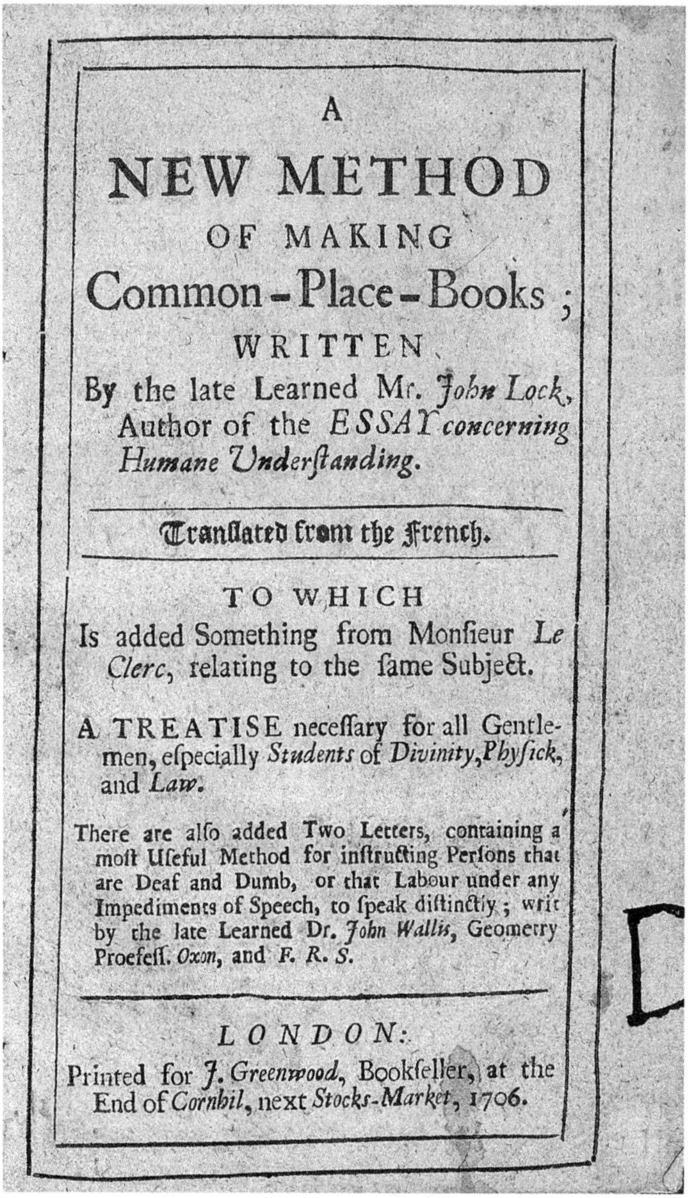

A

NEW METHOD

OF MAKING

Common - Place - Books ;

WRITTEN

By the late Learned Mr. *John Lock*,
Author of the *ESSAY concerning
Humane Understanding*.

Translated from the French.

TO WHICH

Is added Something from Monſieur *Le
Clerc*, relating to the ſame Subject.

A TREATISE neceſſary for all Gentle-
men, eſpecially *Students* of *Divinity*, *Phyſick*,
and *Law*.

There are alſo added Two Letters, containing a
moſt Uſeful Method for inſtructing Perſons that
are Deaf and Dumb, or that Labour under any
Impediments of Speech, to ſpeak diſtinctly ; writ
by the late Learned Dr. *John Wallis*, Geometry
Proefeſſ. *Oxon*, and *F. R. S.*

LONDON:

Printed for *J. Greenwood*, Bookſeller, at the
End of *Cornhil*, next *Stocks-Market*, 1706.

Fig. 2.4. John Locke, *A New Method of Making Common-Place-Books* (1706), a posthumous translation of his *Méthode nouvelle de dresser des recueils* of 1685.

still have to choose from among all the selections, as with collections of "Choice Sermons," "Choice Songs," "Choice Poems," and more).[83]

By the 1720s, keeping a commonplace book made up of what Locke's own publisher, Jean Le Clerc, called "only those Things which are Choice and Excellent" and not easily remembered on one's own had become such a common affectation that it readily lent itself to satire.[84] Employing his alter ego Simon Wagstaff, the great Anglo-Irish writer Jonathan Swift made good fun of the kind of man who has at his disposal, thanks to his commonplace book, what he insists are the "choisest expressions," all "at least one hundred Years" old and therefore "genuine, sterling, and authentick." For what distinguished this character was that he lacked actual knowledge or reasoned opinions about anything of significance.[85] If Montaigne had once told his readers that they should judge his work by seeing "in what I borrow whether I have known how to choose what would enhance my theme,"[86] the eighteenth-century English-language commonplacer was increasingly publicly ridiculed as the mere collector of the words and wisdom of others, devoid of any independent thoughts.

Social practices, however, evolve over time. Starting late in that same century, and just as all that personal investment in memorization was coming to seem rather antithetical to polite culture and maybe even the mark of a pedant, the commonplace book began to be remade to serve new goals. Indeed, a second use emerged: as a tool for the construction and expression of one's own personal take on the world. Commonplacing was rebranded by users as a strategy of personal decision making within the domain of the library, a matter of choosing what one took personally to be the choicest passages or parts from among the range of options one had already assembled, whether through purchase or loan. The right choice turned into the preferred one. This shift would hold whether we are talking about fictional characters or real people, literal reconstruction with scissors and glue or simply recopying. Eventually it became metaphoric, a mental habit and a way of living in the world rather than a specific activity. Furthermore, this transformation was largely accomplished by ordinary, albeit literate and relatively leisured people on both sides of the Atlantic—our early choosers—as they both followed the rules laid out by Locke and others and, then, strategically broke them.

First, the content that filled these blank books expanded and diversified in ways that would likely have horrified a Humanist schoolmaster. Eighteenth- and early nineteenth-century commonplace books are hard to read now because they can seem like information dumps. Poetry, literary excerpts, and aphorisms and maxims rub shoulders with recipes, financial accounting, lists of debts, plant specimens, and social appointments, that is, the stuff generally of calendars or diaries or scrapbooks. Some contain hand-drawn illustrations. Some mix in jokes, riddles, humorous anecdotes, or epigrams. Others showcase Scripture or drafts of sermons or other Christian teachings, while others stick to secular philosophical musings (ancient or modern), or science and medicine, or history, and still others do all of the above. Plenty also make space for the compiler's own writing, whether in verse or prose. Often it is clear that the compiler has opted to edit, paraphrase, rearrange, or otherwise adapt the passages chosen, sometimes adding personal commentary as well. Letters and (later as the price of paper dropped) newspaper and magazine clippings had a way of squeezing in by means of paste or copying too, right along with accounts of interesting exchanges, especially with guests from out of town bearing news.[87] The range of possibilities from which one could make selections grew ever greater.

As for the organization of all those "choice" bits: after Locke it gradually came apart. His alphabetical indexing system, minus any kind of preexisting conceptual grid, encouraged the process of disorganization insofar as it eschewed established categories or hierarchies in the conceptualization of knowledge. Many later commonplacers then abandoned even the pretext of alphabetization or the use of any kind of headings, creating what can seem now to be randomly put-together anthologies in which the compiler and his or her tastes, interests, and experiences (and practically speaking, remembering them) became the only constant thread. Even the written hand can seem to go in every which direction in this era when notebook paper was too valuable to leave much untouched.

For to work our way backward from the finished form, the purpose of such repositories seems to have become, by the early nineteenth century, less to find a way to conform to gentlemanly social and intellectual expectations than to construct a particular, even potentially idiosyncratic self. That is to say, a person who has a specific and distinctive intellectual identity rooted in the mind and the liberty to act as "the Mind shall chuse or direct," as Locke was to put it in his 1694 *An Essay Concerning Human Understanding*.[88] Here again many scholars of post-Humanist commonplacing have drawn connections between this literary activity and what they have frequently called self-fashioning or self-arrangement or self-management or even self-representation.[89] What these scholars sometimes forget (but that Locke reminds us) is that prior to any version of self-fashioning was always a process of selection, or choice-making within an existing field of limited options, that deserves to be highlighted as well. For this very kind of bounded intellectual choice-making was to become a distinct, embodied, and increasingly commonplace habit of modern life.

Of course, all of this print-based activity was initially primarily an elite phenomenon. The necessity of an education that resulted in literacy, the scarcity of leisure time for all but the well-off, the cost of supplies from books to blank paper: all functioned as barriers. Those barriers then functioned as new social fault lines. In every realm, choice, as we've seen, is always the prerogative of some, not all, especially as it became a source of power and status.

But in an era in which a reading habit was increasingly spreading among white Europeans and their descendants across class lines, middle-class and occasionally working-class people got in on the game on both sides of the Atlantic as well. Consider, for example, the "choice Farrago of new Poems" assembled or, rather, "collected from the papers of that wonder-working Genius S[tephen] Simpson," a Coventry weaver in the 1770s.[90] Or mull over the postrevolutionary democratic musings of the New England farmer William Manning, who fashioned his own ideas out of his self-selected and wide-ranging readings and an extensive archive of newspaper clippings.[91] The working-class autobiography could take a lot of different forms, but it was conventional to evoke a self that existed through building on the chosen sentiments of others.

Across the social ranks, this shift in practice affected women too. As commonplacing became tied less to scholarship than to pleasure reading and the quotidian; as the dominant language of the genre became the vernacular rather than Latin; and as the rules generally loosened regarding how best to do it, amateur bookmaking in the commonplace mode became more and more something that literate white women, rural and urban, did. Maybe that's unsurprising insofar as they constituted a growing percentage of both churchgoers and readers too.[92] The great international best-selling novelist Samuel Richardson gives us an early hint of the significance of women as cultural consumers in this regard. Not only did he ask his female and male friends alike to weigh in on alternative endings for some of his work and to try their own hand at producing sequels in the choose-your-own-adventure game mode, "so that everyone of my Correspondents, at his or her own Choice, assume one of the surviving Characters in the Story, and write in it; and that . . . I shall pick and choose, alter, connect, and accommodate, till I have completed from [the contributions] the requested Volume."[93] In his great bestseller *Pamela; or, Virtue Rewarded* (1740), he informed his (heavily female) audience of readers that his literature-mad heroine of the same name keeps "a Common-place Book, as I may call it; In which, by her Lady's Direction, from time to time, she had transcribed from the Bible, and other good Books, such Passages as made most Impression upon her, as she read."[94]

That feminine association carried over to both the production and consumption sides of this business. Books of all types, including blank books, were increasingly marketed to readers of the "fair sex" or "ladies."[95] And even when publishers of commercial commonplace books announced they were made for the male reader (or more precisely, the man of letters, the man of observation, the traveler, or the student), that message could be undercut—as in the case of *A New Commonplace Book* published in London in 1799—by the inclusion of examples taken straight from the pages of none other than the most controversial female writer of the era, Mary Wollstonecraft.[96] Moreover, filled-in books suggest women readers were even less likely than men in the late eighteenth and early nineteenth centuries to follow all the rules as to who should be using a commonplace book and to what ends and how.

For women, in practice if not yet theory, took the lead in shifting from commonplacing as a form of "collecting" or "harvesting" in a finite space (dominant metaphors in the Humanist tradition)[97] to commonplacing as a form of selecting and conscious choosing and reassemblage in a world rife with intellectual and literary options. Perhaps that was sometimes the result of a feminine effort to economize and save (expensive, especially in the eighteenth century) paper. Or maybe it was because women were more detached from formal schooling and its traditions; certainly, that educational difference made them more likely to be "extensive" rather than "intensive" readers, to evoke the famous dichotomy of the historian of reading Rolf Englesing, who himself based his claim exclusively on men.[98] But possibly it was also because, without yet attaching the cause of women rhetorically to the idea of enhancing choice, many were eager to seize upon small opportunities for self-definition. Choice-making in the world of reading offered women one path, right at the boundaries between the public and private spheres, to greater intellectual autonomy. Female commonplacers might even be said to have crafted their own subjectivities centuries before collage or sampling, the names we've given to the more modern practices of building a new composition out of pieces and possibilities chosen from what one has on hand.

The image of the reader specifically as a "chooser," free to make selections in an abundant and varied landscape rather than collect it all, actually had an old and serious pedigree that predated this shift in commonplacing culture. As early as the English Civil War of the mid-seventeenth century, John Milton, a dissenting Protestant and briefly the keeper of a commonplace book himself,[99] had famously and imaginatively envisioned readers in just this guise, tying the image back to the biblical Adam. In Milton's conception, it was wrongheaded to think of a person, unless exceedingly vulgar, confronting a text as a passive consumer in the world of ideas, simply swallowing every notion encountered (as book censors might have imagined). On the contrary, as Milton saw it, books themselves were living repositories of ideas, full of potency. And humans had been fashioned by God precisely to be the makers of *active* selections within and among them.

In Milton's great poem *Paradise Lost,* published in 1667, when God wishes to emphasize that humans have free will and are thus accountable for their own decisions, He refers to them as "authors to themselves in all / Both what they judge and what they choose."[100] In *Areopagitica* of 1644, Milton's earlier argument for the end of book licensing (and subsequently a foundational text of free speech literature), the same metaphor appears at intervals throughout. But this time it is in close association specifically with readers and their confrontation with books. As Milton explains in his characteristic Arminian fashion: "when God gave him [Adam] reason, he gave him freedom to choose, for reason is but choosing; he had bin else a meer artificiall Adam," meaning fully controlled by God.

Milton's point was that contemporary readers, as humans created in Adam's image and endowed with the ability to make rational judgments, should be free to wrestle unimpeded with the choice of what to consume on the road to the choice of what to believe—or the truth.[101] It was a striking reversal of the very old Christian conception of the chooser in the realm of belief as, by definition, a heretic or *homo hairesis*. Milton's view also did not go away. Echoes of his concern with the benefits of access to all the options reemerged in some of the earliest laws protecting freedom of expression, specifically those of Sweden and Denmark in 1766 and 1770, respectively. Both emphasized the right to read, hear, and judge all the possibilities—or the necessity of *Offent-lighetsprincipen* (the principle of public access)—more than the right to speak oneself.[102]

But still, from the vantage point of 1800, Milton's great argument for readers as choosers belonged to an earlier intellectual world, one still invested in a largely Christian vision of the operation of judgment in the world of belief and of freedom of conscience as the foundational form of liberty. Milton's tracts were not in any sense tributes to relativism or all choices in the end being equally valid. There were for him, clearly, good books in the world, and there were bad ones. There was also right faith, and there was wrong. *Paradise Lost,* after all, is entirely a story on the model of Hercules's choice. One needed to encounter evil on the page precisely so as to have the opportunity to make the correct choice, which is to say, "distinguish" what is vice and "prefer" that which is truly better. Ditto, in fact, for the Swedish government which similarly insisted more than a century later that many ideas, including Catholicism and atheism, were too dangerous for this game.

That's also why, for Milton, the analogy between books and cloth as similar kinds of goods ripe for picking *does not* actually hold. It might be fine for the state to continue to regulate the market and allow for monopolies when something as inert and inconsequential as broadcloth is at stake, says Milton. But the state must step to the side when it comes to books precisely so that they may be "promiscuously read" and then compared, judged, and ultimately, through consultation with others and "incessant labour to cull out, and sort asunder," deemed good and true or, alternately, dangerous and wrong.[103] Options in reading material—unlike in textiles—must be manifold and unrestricted because this is the only way moral truth becomes apparent (though Milton has not much empirical evidence for why clarity and not, say, confusion or error will just as likely result, especially as the amount of reading material continues to increase). Plus, that reader doing all the choosing was also assumed to be male, the replica of Adam. And Adam, though a chooser, was not the ancient prototype for the shopper.

What's new about the practice of commonplacing in its later stages is not simply that it depended upon commercial products for its execution. It is also that commonplacing largely echoed a postmercantilist logic in which consumers, theoretically, had a kind of carte blanche to weigh their information by their own criteria, including personal taste and temperament, as well as communal judgments of value. Moreover, women entered the fray in significant numbers. All of which means we need not read such homemade tomes now solely to learn what they tell us about which texts and topics once interested various people, male and female alike. Postrevolutionary commonplace books can also tell us how those same people encountered, sorted, and reassembled ideas, which is to say, approached the more abstract problem of intellectual selection in an era of growing abundance and variety along with declining strictures on just how much one could forge one's own path.[104]

Take Benjamin Rush. The esteemed Philadelphia doctor's "Commonplace Book," as he called it, functioned as a kind of intellectual diary for the more than two decades between 1789 and his death in 1813. Rush used it to record, in no particular order, his own thoughts on a miscellany of topics: love, solitude, evil, aristocracy, salvation, politics, the Latin and Greek languages, dreams. He also copied in extracts, passages, even phrases that appealed, the fragmentary ideas of others that he had selected more than collected from his voluminous and varied reading. Even clippings from contemporaneous newspapers, such as the death notice of Dr. Priestley and, under the headline "A Great Curiosity," a story of a Black man whose "natural color [had] rubbed off," found their way into the book. And to all of these, he added further lessons drawn from his experience and from conversation as a prominent Philadelphian, active in medical, scholarly, and political circles; many passages begin "Mrs. Ferguson informed me" or "Chas. Brown informed me" or describe a conversation with a visiting dignitary like the Venetian doctor Jean Baptiste Scandella (and sometimes Rush's own points of disagreement). Rush further worked in those encounters that occurred in a fragmented but vibrant religious sphere of which he took full advantage: interspersed comments include "Heard the Revd. Dr. Coke preach in the African Methodist Church," followed by a brief description of what the reverend had said of interest about Black Methodists and a meal with the Black minister Richard Allen, and "Heard the Revd. Mr. Murray preach in the Universal Church," with an account of how Murray had explained a passage in Corinthians 1. Rush seems to have had no qualms about bringing together in one space the sacred and secular, the high and the low, and the personally meaningful, the polemical, and general information.[105] These were indeed all part of his own makeup.

As Rush explained in another one of his self-reflexive writings, his "Travels through Life" begun in 1800, his religious identity had shifted of its own accord at various junctures over the years since his birth. But Rush was also comfortable with heterogeneity in life as well as on the page. Moreover, he was clearly uninterested in denominational purity, at one moment finding ways of "delight[ing] in public worship, and particularly, in hearing evangelical ministers of all denominations," and in another, attending both Episcopalian and Presbyterian churches and making his own personal (and often negative) judgments about what ensued.[106] In light of such practices, Rush's commonplace book became the place to try to reassemble, much like Jefferson and his bricolage Bible, the bits of religious as well as literary and scientific culture that the doctor had chosen for himself. It now appears a similarly creative act to that of Jefferson, a means of using the varied options out there to compile a distinctive sense of self—a project that continues to resonate with us now.

Yet Rush also had the moral disposition of the evangelism of his time. That meant that when it came to others, he was worried by too wide a realm for personal discretion and not least in the realm of ideas and beliefs. In one of his many writings on education, he announced himself alarmed by the fashionable opinion that "it is improper to fill the minds of youth with religious prejudices of any kind, and that they should be left to choose their own principles, after they have arrived at an age in which they are capable of judging for themselves." After all, he insisted, even the young mind is never a perfect blank slate, and much that is wrongheaded will certainly be absorbed long before the age of reason, in a sense refuting the Miltonian argument for unimpeded access on the grounds that it was inappropriate for the young.[107] In addition, as a physician with an interest in what we would now call mental health, he took note of all the varied kinds of faulty reasoning—he details twenty-six in his satirical "On the Different Species of Mania" (1786)—that regularly plagued the act of decision making, or what might be called sound choice, on the part of adults.[108] He also (unusually for his time) worried about addiction, which he called a "disease of the will" and equated metaphorically with slavery.[109] The picture of Rush that emerges from his "Commonplace Book" along with his other writings is of a man who relished his independence, meaning the opportunities to pick and choose his own intellectual life that his membership in Philadelphia's well-educated, white, Christian elite allowed him at the start of the nineteenth century. But that isn't the full story. He simultaneously reveals himself as someone obsessed with elucidating the weak points in the epistemology of choice and less than sanguine about what a generalized culture of autonomous choosers would mean, given that "good" choices, whether scientific or religious or moral, could not be taken for granted on the part of others.

What is perhaps more striking is that Deborah Norris Logan, a generation later, was similarly self-reflexive about intellectual choice-making, including her decision to record her own choices of text and image in the form of commonplace books. Still, gender difference pervades the comparison of Logan and Rush. Logan kept a series of notebooks starting in 1815 and continuing in various forms almost to the moment of her death in 1839. She also repeatedly reflected on the meaning and purpose of her amateur literary activities in terms of her own life. In the first volume, which she called "Diary and missellanious articles," she explained that she wrote down what seemed to her, whether fact or anecdote, to be "worthy of preservation." But she also quickly qualified their potentially subjective appeal insofar as the category included items that are "for my own satisfaction likewise that may be irrelevant to others."[110]

Logan's choices in terms of what to preserve were, in fact, largely derived from personal experience: what she had read in newspapers, magazines, and books (her own private library was extensive), what she received in the mail from correspondents, what she heard from visitors or while out at "a [Quaker] meeting" or "at Shops." Like Rush, Logan had a taste for extracts, both printed and not, along with diary keeping. Her notebooks contain her own poems alongside news, reports on weather and popular science (often with her own corrections), and both prose and verse by writers famous and not, much of it drawn from still other compilations, anthologies, or collections.[111] Her glue supply also did extra duty with visual materials to a considerably greater degree than did Rush's; even lithographs made their way into Logan's blank books, turning them into composites of commonplace books, journals, and scrapbooks (fig. 2.5).

In this she was actually not that distinctive. Many other literate, white American and British women readers of the early nineteenth century were to create equally heterogeneous books of multilingual "selections" (French women sometimes called them "extraits et mélanges," Italians of looking at things, in which I seem as if just entered into existence — and so I am with reference to immortallity.

Fourth Day

I was very unwell, indeed, nervous and lame, but Stepey and myself went down to Somerville to tea; where we found Poor Maria still a sufferer, and more especially now, her spirits too have failed at her long long confinement.

Fifth Day,

at home all day miserably lame and poorly, but yet a little better than yesterday — it was not at all an agreeable sort of day, damp, warm and windy with the thousand generations of leaves whirling about like the Ghosts in 'Leonora'. sometimes what is not agreeable at the time furnishes an interesting theme notwithstanding for the Diary — but such is not the case now — but instead of such a one I will paste in here a little lithographic view of the Tomb of St Helena, said to be 'drawn from Nature, on the spot.' when I first saw it I did not discover the Profile fi-gure, now I cannot look on it without seeing it. — But what a lesson to towering ambition is that humble tomb.

In St Helena the Tomb
of
Napoleon.

Fig. 2.5. A page from the last volume (1839) of Philadelphia Quaker Deborah Norris Logan's multivolume commonplace book/diary, written just before her death at age eighty-two, on which she has glued in an image of Napoleon's tomb in St. Helena that is a visual pun (note the profile of the emperor that emerges between the trees) beneath her complaints about her health.

"zibaldone"), though perhaps not generally over as many years and volumes. Elizabeth Phillips Payson kept a commonplace book from 1806 to 1825 in which she recorded 341 titles, along with "extracts from and remarks upon some of the books I have read," including novels, that made her an amateur book reviewer of considerable capacity.[112] Amy (Hornor) Coates at the turn of the century produced a list of scraps organized alphabetically by topic, e.g., Affliction, Acceptable Sacrifice, Advice to a Young Woman on the Subject of Marriage, Coquetry, Cheerfulness, Criticism, and Death—before stopping with Employment under the letter E and turning the book the other way for a collection largely of verse. The sources for Coates's musings? Everything from the Bible to Sir William Jones's *Institutes of Hindu Law*, the journal *The Mirror*, and her own son's schoolboy compositions.[113] Then there's Elizabeth Galloway, who, in the late 1810s and 1820s, inventoried at one end of a blank book her whole household, including what could be found in the kitchen, a mahogany chest, and the safe, before turning the book the other way to record hymns, songs, some things "suggested by reading some lines of Lord Byron," and an "Address to a cottage."[114] Some women's commonplace books were purely devotional or were committed to a particular theme, like death and loss.[115] For others, like Anna Jane Mitchell McAllister in the 1830s, widely circulated literary journals played a critical role in supplying material, as did an unnamed source on the language of flowers.[116] Pencil or pen and ink drawings, watercolors, and miniatures, many of them of places these women had visited, show up too, along with hand-colored engravings by others.[117] The heterogeneity seems to be the point.

What is noteworthy about Logan, then, is not so much the sources themselves as how she telegraphed her own self-consciousness about her engagement in all this reading and choosing. The first epitaph to open the series comes from Oliver Goldsmith but is modified in what appears to be her own hand: "A [wo]man shews [her] Judgment in these Selections and [s]he may be often 20 years of [her] life cultivating that Judgment."[118] And while at times she downplayed her investment in activities like commonplacing as antiquarian and "old-fashioned" pursuits, the work of a preservationist at heart, she seems to have been very aware that the cumulative effect of all of this effort at selection and compilation was to forge an enduring picture of herself. As she notes, "Will my Books and Diaries Survive me . . . if they do, I should like them to convey a faithful view both of myself and of my venerable Old Mansion."[119] It is also a hybrid public/private portrait. Most of the materials were themselves once part of public, published documents or rooted in relations with others. But they have been perused, selected, and copied in private reading sessions, in private spaces, for personal development or self-fulfillment. Yet at the same time, the resulting notebooks are clearly designed to be shared with others, maybe even read aloud, into posterity. (The actual Frances Burney's famed commonplace book was, not unusually, a whole family affair.) Extensive reading—in the sense of many people and many texts—becomes, through culling and choice, potentially intensive once again.

And if Logan was fixated on the doing, with its promises and pitfalls, she was also determined to record the obstacles that often kept her, frustratingly, from this particular cherished activity. She notes with pleasure the moments that allow her to read and write: "on one day of this month being alone and spending the Day agreeably to myself" or "I spent this day pretty comfortably according to my own ideas, for I have been alone and have read til my eyes became tired."[120] Being alone—being unaccounted for, even briefly—is clearly something of a treat. At other moments she is "meditating an Escape to the Library" when a kind neighbor shows up or another intrusion occurs.[121] Or she complains that she is missing the supplies that commonplacing requires, like pens or fresh books.[122] She is less the master of her own intellectual life than was Rush, and this she records too—even as her notebooks display a similar commitment to all that made commonplacing an appealing kind of choice-making activity in the early nineteenth century. With these journals, she and many other female commonplacers turned themselves into characters in the stories of their own lives.

Moralizing critics, needless to say, attacked all aspects of women's deep involvement in reading, writing, and literary culture, including commonplacing, much as they did shopping or church hopping. Logan sometimes sounds defensive, and unsure if she is taking too great liberties, for a reason. Into the nineteenth century, intellectual choice was more elevated as an idea than was consumer choice, especially in majority-Protestant urban spaces like Philadelphia. But that did not mean that it wasn't also seen as potentially disruptive. Once again, a similar negative focus on women's choice-related actions even at the margins of the public sphere suggests that anxiety about the socially and psychologically destabilizing effects of expanded choice—this time, choice in ideas—was ultimately displaced onto women every bit as much as women's actual behavior constituted an offense, especially since intellectual choice was not initially coded feminine in the same way as consumer choice. These anxieties were then further exacerbated when the reader was young or not of the elevated class position of either Rush or Logan.

Ideally, for both sexes, reading and commonplacing alike reinforced piety and virtue, deepened understanding and judgment, and made one a better conversationalist—that is, if they were performed right. That meant by the "right" people, in the "right" places, following the "right" steps and even comportment, and with the "right" foundational texts. That aim also explains why, as with consumer purchasing, written guides to printed matter of different kinds proliferated into the nineteenth century, including ones promising to help in the making of good choices rather than bad ones according to one's circumstances. Here was the beginning of a classic self-improvement strategy. By the mid-eighteenth century, one could consult professional book reviews giving thumbs up or down to publications hot off the press.[123] One could imitate the choices of one's social betters by perusing published catalogs of their collections. Or one could turn to self-help books replete with instructions on how to choose from scratch a private library suitable to one's own situation and goals, whether one was a young person wracked with doubt, a parent of girls, or a gentleman looking to build a prestigious country library and not from the kind of family already in possession of one.[124] Word of mouth was surely important too.

That's because the choice as to what to assign to one's private library holdings, or what to borrow, to hear, or to save for posterity, was so wrapped up both in one's own self-presentation and in others' perceptions of that self's moral and social worth that it could not be trusted to instinct or preference alone. We are a far cry here from Amazon's algorithms, which are all about imagining what will produce individual-ized "likes." In the eighteenth and well into the nineteenth century, books belonged to a pecking order, just like people, even if that order was often ignored. Arguably they still do for elites, whether we are talk-ing about fiction or not. In this context, it seemed especially vital, as any number of etiquette books were to insist, for proper women to read properly, meaning the correct sorts of things, fully worthy of their choice given their social context.

But the ideal image of the pious female reader consuming a diet suit-able for ethical self-improvement and thus the morality of her home also generated a set of stark opposites. Many of them took the form of warnings. All of them also got coded feminine, which meant they were linked to poor choice-making habits. The alternatives were several.

There was the frivolous lady reader hopping from fashion to fashion, obsessed with the trivial, which is to say, choosing by the most superfi-cial of criteria. That would be today's consumer of beach reading. (Here the overlap of the critique of the shopper or restaurant-goer was substantial—consider the claim in the British *Critical Review* that "fe-male readers, in particular have voracious appetites, and are not over delicate in their choice of food, every thing that is new will go down.")[125] There was also the undisciplined or indiscriminate reader who had no ability to prioritize among her responsibilities and thus ended up ne-glecting her more important wifely and maternal duties to stare at the printed page—the precursor to the mommy on the playground pushing the swing absent-mindedly or even absent, glued to her cell phone. There was the overly emotional or oversexed reader, who read only for pleasure and personal gratification, preferring especially those new-fangled novels with passion and desire at their core. One recurring worry is that such a reader was so exceptionally impressionable that she was incapable of maintaining any critical distance from the book's char-acters or plot; as such she could easily end up herself an easy mark for a seducer, incapacitated by her literary selections in terms of making good and proper choices when it came to her own future conduct. (Today we sometimes imagine that fate for the consumer of too many soap operas and romances or, in the case of men, too much porn.) How-ever, the woman reader could conversely, with too dry a reading diet,

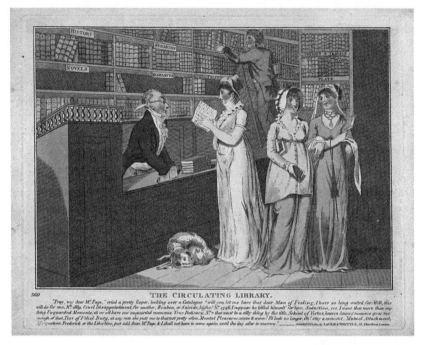

Fig. 2.6. *The Circulating Library* (1804), a hand-colored print after a watercolor by Isaac Cruikshank, in which a reading-addicted young woman, on an outing with her female companions, is depicted going through a circulating library's catalog, picking out all the salacious titles and rejecting all the ones about virtue, while also explaining her preferences to the man behind the counter. The subject of the satire is the choices of the undiscerning and profligate female novel reader.

become unnaturally unsexed or too much like a man in her sense of her own power and independence, the very stereotype of the bluestocking.[126] Here was an equal challenge to the gender division on which nineteenth-century liberalism depended.

Whichever way, moralizing commentators made it clear that the effects of reading were at once potentially mentally and physically transformative for women. This was a fact that novels themselves often dramatized with their intradiegetic, reading-obsessed heroines and their frequently tragic fates. Humorous images, like Isaac Cruikshank's *The Circulating Library*, did the same (fig. 2.6).[127] The young ones were predictably the most at risk.

Men, as well as parents of both sexes, were urged to reassert control. Proposing yet another use for that particular choice-enabling object, the pair of scissors, the Anglo-Irish writer Maria Edgeworth recommended in her best-selling turn-of-the-century educational guide not simply that parents carefully select all books for their children. She told those same parents to take shears to any passages of even seemingly harmless books that might be age-inappropriate or morally dangerous for their offspring, encouraging them to create something like a scrapbook in reverse.[128] For though generally reading itself happened at home, in private spaces, books both hailed from and established new relationships between their readers and the larger world. The more there was to read, the more dangerous it got. In the age of abundance, reading needed boundaries, limits on both the options and the readers themselves.

Ideology

Perhaps we should not be surprised, then, that a broader embrace of an ideology of unfettered personal choice, even when it came to ideas, had little obvious appeal in either the United States or Europe in the immediate aftermath of the age of revolutions. It had even less purchase in the so-called first wave of feminist writing that developed starting in the 1790s to capitalize on the revolutionary vogue for the idea of citizenship entailing individual "rights." That was despite the significance of social contract theory and the idea of collective choice as hallmarks of a new republican sensibility. As long as choice-talk evoked the frivolity of the individual consumer in the burgeoning capitalist marketplace or the religious freedom of the questioning believer remade as the oversexualized or undersexualized autonomous reader in the new world of deregulated and metastasizing print, it held relatively little promise as a concept to get behind in the service of any larger cause. Indeed, as these stereotypes suggest, too much choosing or too many possible choices remained potent sources of social anxiety at least in the transatlantic Anglophone world. So did the fact that bad choices and bad choosing subjects were bound to have negative social consequences for all involved.

The association of choice with women both provided an outlet for this anxiety and fueled it. A few female writers also publicly took note. The radical Englishwoman Mary Wollstonecraft, in her seminal feminist treatise *A Vindication of the Rights of Woman* (1792), promoted the progressive idea of women being given the leeway to "choose for themselves" when it came to reading material, suggesting that the end result of more opportunities for mental stimulation would be women with greater "liberty of mind."[129] In this, she echoed Jean-Jacques Rousseau's ideas about the natural education of the boy child Emile (though not his counterpart Sophie), about whom Rousseau said, "We will not attach him to any sect, but we will give him the means to choose for himself according to the right use of his own reason" even if, as Rousseau was to admit later, it might prove very hard for poor Emile ever to be sure what to take as true.[130] Wollstonecraft's partner, the equally radical philosopher William Godwin, said something similar in his own, slightly later essay "Of Choice in Reading": let children make up their own minds about what they read and believed, since exposure develops judgment and autonomy.[131] It was the lesson of Milton, here applied to the young—exactly what got Benjamin Rush so worried at almost the same moment.

But just as importantly, Wollstonecraft also sneered (in the lingo of the moment) at "the reading of novels," as at "shopping," "bargain-hunting," and all forms of "coquetry," as degrading upper-class female pursuits rooted purely in vanity and narcissism.[132] Furthermore, she promoted greater mental stimulation for women as one of her primary causes with the clever argument not that women would find greater fulfillment for themselves but that it would be a boon to society as a whole. For education would change women's nature. It would make them less prone to the superficial forms of self-determination accorded them under the unnatural conditions of "civilization" and more able to make good (which is to say, essentially reasonable, morally upstanding, and manlike) choices in the future—to the benefit of men too.

In the meantime, it still made sense to most women to create rhetorical distance between themselves and the world of personal, preference-based choice. As late as the 1850s, an author named Mrs. Jameson, who went as far as to publish her several-hundred-page-long *Commonplace Book of Thoughts, Memories, and Fancies, Original and Selected* rather than leave it in manuscript on her bedside table, saw a need to downplay any connection to choice as well as originality. As she noted in the preface, after worrying that her book could seem "supremely egotistical and subjective": "The passages from books are not, strictly speaking, *selected*; they are not given here on any principle of choice, but simply because that by some process of assimilation they became a part of the individual mind. They 'found me'—to borrow Coleridge's expression—'found me in some depth of my being'; I did not 'find *them*.'"[133] She almost sounds like a prototype for Marcel Duchamp, who said much the same about his readymades.

There is, though, another way of reading this evidence. All this alarm about, first, shopping and, then, new reading habits also suggests the possibility that when women like Mrs. Jameson were, de facto, engaged in making choices in these specific realms, they were, even within the constraints they encountered, experiencing a certain kind of power that was otherwise elusive—and they knew it, as did their male counterparts. Yes, those constraints were evidently and consistently material. Virginia Woolf was still explaining in the 1920s that the mental independence of women was hard to foster insofar as it first required an income and space, ideally with a key.[134] To this day, those are critical reasons why real opportunities for choice remain elusive for so many women. Yes, constraints also continued to inhere in the existing corpus of ideas, especially about what constitutes virtue. Only some things are ever thinkable in any place or time, and some are always more elevated or socially acceptable than others even as we claim the contrary. The rules for a woman, no matter her class, were strict in Wollstonecraft's moment, and the truly permissible options were few, as she was well aware. Nevertheless, we need also note that to navigate within these boundaries, to choose what George Orwell was to call "the furniture of one's mind," became, in practice, something of a key eighteenth- and nineteenth-century aspiration, one often associated with female heroines, from Richardson's Pamela onward, in that dangerous genre called the novel. Jane Austen pokes good fun at her fictional heroine Fanny Price in *Mansfield Park* (1814), who, when she gets up her nerve to subscribe to a lending library, is "amazed at her own doings in every way; to be a renter, a chuser [*sic*] of books!"[135] Austen seems to be suggesting to her own readers just how absurd or retrograde this kind of female timidity in the face of proliferating choice has become. In the imaginary space of the nineteenth-century European novel, the chooser resembles Eve as often as Adam.

What is more, in some quarters, post-Wollstonecraft and indeed the whole first age of revolutions, that same impulse began to be translated into an aspiration toward mitigating the constraints, whether that meant making more opportunities for real choice-making available to more women or expanding and revising the options themselves. By the second half of the nineteenth century, America's first self-proclaimed (and much lampooned) "women's rights" activists were not just making scrapbooks of their own, culling and selecting from newspapers to craft alternative histories of their movement and themselves.[136] In the case of Elizabeth Cady Stanton (whose dogged advocacy for white women's suffrage led her to promote a racial hierarchy in which Black people of either sex were deemed less deserving of choice), the emancipation of her perceived sisters required, at the century's close, cutting up the Bible once again. This time the purpose was identifying and lifting out those particular parts that helped her show Christianity as, in fact, the key source of women's ongoing oppression. As she explained in *The Woman's Bible*: "The time has come to read it as we do all other books, accepting the good and rejecting the evil it teaches."[137] We might call that critical judgment. The language of choice was not, at least initially, linked to women's rights movements. But the practice of choice—and the appeal of choice-making activities right at the boundary between the public and the private—was on its way to becoming the unspoken backbone of a postrevolutionary liberalism. Here was an ideology, if not yet a *doxa*, that would eventually turn the very *act* of choice-making in multiple arenas into a perceived agent of women's emancipation too.

What Women Need Is Choice:
Reconsidering Mill and Taylor

How did that happen? To explain, we have to run roughshod over chronology and geography and talk about John Stuart Mill and Harriet Taylor's capture and repurposing of choice as a concept and term on behalf of women. Living and writing in London in the middle decades of the nineteenth century, both famously made the case that the world around them was increasingly structured around personal ambition and competition—and rightly so. Yet women, this duo insisted both together and apart, were still saddled with a combination of both formal legal restrictions and informal social expectations that worked systematically to keep them out of the game. Not only did these factors thwart women's true natures, which were not fundamentally different from men's (and Mill and Taylor both denied that women had any "special" qualities that made them suited only for domesticity). These conditions also denied women, as individuals, the same kind of "unfettered choice" and "freedom of individual choice" in their myriad life "pursuits" that had now become routinely available to men.[138]

To end women's collective subjugation, Mill and Taylor thus insisted in a then-unusual argument, laws and conventions alike had to catch up with the times. It had to be possible for women, too, to engage in rational, positive, preference-based choice-making in all domains of importance to their fates: in their educations, in their occupations, in their marriages, even in the voting booth. And they had to be able to do so with moral approbation regardless of the option chosen, even (or especially) if it went against custom or the mentality of the crowd. What mattered was primarily that the choice was their own choice, not whether it was the right choice in society's terms.

Harriet Taylor took the lesson from news of the first women's rights conventions held in 1848 in Seneca Falls, New York, and then in 1850 in Worcester, Massachusetts, that, as she put it in the *Westminster Review*, "the proper sphere for all human beings [including women] is the largest and highest which they are able to attain to." Then she added, moving rhetorically well beyond the mid-century arguments of Elizabeth Cady

Stanton and her American confreres, "What this is, cannot be ascertained, without complete liberty of choice."[139] By the next national women's rights convention, held again in Worcester in 1851, the identical language had crossed the Atlantic back again, thanks to the white abolitionist and women's rights advocate Wendell Phillips, establishing choice as a key element of self-discovery and, indeed, liberation in a way that earlier rights movements of various kinds had not.[140]

Mill, working at least partially in concert, then extended this logic further. As with men, Mill concurred more than a decade later in his *The Subjection of Women* (written in 1861 and published in 1869), every preference-based choice that could transpire "short of injury to others," even if it went against the norm, should be there for the taking by women too. That meant without attendant public stigma or penalty (though both the menu that he imagined being open to women and what he imagined women would subsequently choose—marriage *or* career—were more limited than he seemed to realize).[141] Moreover, again as with men, the only acceptable external fetter on such choices should be wealth because, he insisted, everyone in the contemporary world was now ostensibly free to chase it (and it is also quite clear that he really only had middle- and upper-middle-class English women like his own partner, Harriet Taylor, in mind anyway, despite other comments suggesting caste and race should not decide one's aspirations any more than gender).[142] The benefits would accrue to women, he argued, in the opportunity to realize their personal aspirations. They would also accrue to society as a whole, since women's full entry into it would ultimately expand "the field of selection" for the competition to follow.[143]

Such innovative talk of women, preferences, and choice was, despite these limitations, to reshape the way the woman question was imagined not just in the English-speaking world but globally in the last decades of the nineteenth century and the start of the twentieth. *The Subjection of Women*, in particular, was published between 1869 and 1928 in multiple English editions and in at least twenty-six non-English editions in seventeen countries, making it the first feminist text with that kind of reach. Rather quickly, translations found their way into circulation as far afield as colonial India, Russia, and Chile, as did spin-off arguments by local champions of women's causes.[144] Partly this was a result of Mill's prior fame in the global arena of ideas in the heyday of British imperial power. Partly, though, this must have been a result of the seeming universality of the message, which could be lightly adapted to different contexts (as in the shift in title in the Chilean edition from subjection to slavery). In Mill's hands and those of his late nineteenth-century disciples invested in "women's rights," liberal and socialist alike, choice was rescued from its negative and distinctly feminine implications around the consumption of consumer goods (despite Mill's prior, thirty-five-year day job with the East India Company).[145] It was also secularized and individualized well beyond its Protestant roots. By the 1870s, preference and choice were on their way to becoming a standard and enduring part of the vocabulary associated with the "woman question," not least, as we will see, when it came to suffrage campaigns.

Today, when women's issues are often subsumed under talk of human rights on a global scale, many late nineteenth-century arguments evoking the significance of choice on behalf of women can seem almost banal. Think of the Black American abolitionist Frederick Douglass's emphasis on "the fact that woman has the power to say 'I choose *this* rather than *that*'" as "all-sufficient proof that there is no natural reason against the exercise of that power"[146] or the white French feminist Maria Deraismes's insistence on women as autonomous "individuals" requiring the opportunity to exercise their faculties.[147] These appear to be the prerogatives of already-existing masculine individuality, including the theoretical chance to shape (and take responsibility for) many aspects of one's own existence, simply extended to include women too.

But for all the same reasons, "feminism," as it came to be known by the 1890s,[148] became linked across much of the globe with some combination of consumer culture, Christianity, Westernization, imperialism, and the liberal utilitarianism and rights-based individualism out of which this argument was born. (And it is important to note that this is a linkage which Mill himself directly encouraged by associating the rest of the world with barbarity and backwardness and "Christian Europe" with being temporally far ahead—except when it came to the treatment of women, who still constituted a civilizational metric.)

Moreover, resistance to this approach to the "woman question" was soon rendered of a piece with a larger case against all individuated and choice-centered ways of considering human existence, including active struggles against capitalism, colonialism, and even globalization lasting to this day. From this vantage point, a liberal feminism focused on individual choice became but one, albeit prominent, facet of an imported or imposed ideology that threatened much of the non-European world with cultural (and often also economic and political) domination. It still often plays this role.

For it is also essential to recognize that precisely in the years that this innovative feminist argument was taking form, Mill—with Taylor's substantial input until her death in 1858[149]—was invested in an equally influential redefinition of freedom itself. That vision was also historically and culturally particular, despite the universalizing package. *On Liberty* (1859) built very specifically on a post-Reformation Christian and Western tradition of thinking about, but even more practicing, liberty of conscience and expression and then updated this tradition for a new economic and political climate. Freedom is no longer, in these pages, a result of surrendering to a life of righteousness and virtue that a community helps you to obtain. It is not even a result of consciously choosing the correct path by oneself, as it might have been for Kant. It inheres instead in the very act of selecting among options, unshackled from any conventional menu, independent of others' needs or judgments, and beholden only to an internalized sense of what constitutes the good and right and personally fitting, as long as no one else is harmed in the process. What Mill proposed at mid-century is that this act is itself what turns us—women and men alike—into not just abstract humans endowed with equal rights, as in the era of the French Revolution, but autonomous and distinctive individuals, fundamentally different one from another. As each of us engages in the making of, first, choices about belief but then, more generally, choices about how to live in accord with our own internal values, interests, talents, and desires, we learn to be, indeed become, fully realized, unique, and ultimately free persons within a larger community.[150]

The argument was spun out as follows. The process of selecting a good, in the sense of personally meaningful, set of beliefs requires a large field of diverse options, or a wide range of ideas and opinions, to consider. Hence the necessity for Mill (as for Milton long before him) of freedom of "thought and discussion" as the first freedom and the one from which all others stem. But it is largely in the business of intellectual consumption, starting in the private realm of the mind or conscience, that the individual self—Mill's primary concern—is actually formed. As Mill explained in *On Liberty*, "The human faculties of perception, judgment, discriminative feeling, mental activity, and even moral preference, are exercised only in making a choice" from the alternatives on offer. What Mill then concluded was not just that "he who does anything because it is the custom, makes no choice" and is engaged only in "ape-like" imitation; it was also that "the mental and moral, like the muscular powers, are improved only by being used." In other words, self-development, or the forging of a distinctive and upstanding character, stems directly from the active experience of gathering, observing, evaluating, comparing, sorting, selecting, and then finally putting into play one's particular and distinctive ideas, derived from one's own desires and preferences, combined with exposure to the ideas of others— or "choos[ing] his plan for himself."[151] In this way, unstructured, expansive choice lost the stigma of being associated with selfishness or whim. On the contrary, it was given social and moral value in and of itself: as the key component of what Mill called liberty.

This was certainly an idea that Mill saw running through his own existence. His *Autobiography* is rife with discussion of the tension between choice and parental coercion in his own education, starting with what books he read on the way to adulthood and his own father's efforts to "impress" upon him "the lesson of the Choice of Hercules" that remained a staple of the English literary canon.[152] This was also an idea that Taylor and Mill tried to live out together in their unconventional relationship. For though Mill long advanced a myth about the total mental synergy that they experienced as a couple, once they finally married, he emphasized their radical separateness in all other ways. He sought no rights over Taylor's person or property and granted her an extraordinary (and extralegal) degree of independence to go her own way, writing in 1851 that she was to retain "in all respects whatever the same absolute freedom of action, and freedom of disposal of herself . . .

as if no such marriage had taken place."[153] In a sense, he invented his own set of rules for choice.

Mainly, though, we need recognize that no matter how conceptually innovative in its application to both sexes in the form of texts like *The Subjection of Women*, Mill and Taylor's emphasis on choice-as-freedom resonated because of a certain kind of familiarity. The message already conformed to nineteenth-century Anglo-American, Victorian, Protestant (or even post-Protestant) cultural norms, where occasions for choosing among various possibilities were, for both sexes, on the rise. Mill's argument for more opportunities for women to make more choices in order to benefit both themselves and the world could not have been heard or maybe even have been articulated in the first place except in a culture in which the experience of personalized choice-making and its small rituals and technologies, successes and frustrations, were starting to feel ordinary—and intuitively, if not yet explicitly, already linked to individual freedom. Otherwise, the argument would have sounded not just unnatural but, likely, nonsensical.

He also wasn't alone. At precisely the same moment, the other great British thinker of the era, Charles Darwin, was to write, even as he was making a case *against* human intentionality in generating change over time, "I have called this principle, by which each slight variation, if useful, is preserved, by the term Natural Selection, in order to mark its relation to man's power of selection. We have seen that man by selection can certainly produce great results."[154] Darwin, too, was rewriting the story of choice.

The point, then, is not to make the case for Mill or Taylor or any other philosopher as *the* source of modern feminism or even one of its dominant strains. It is instead to show how Mill and Taylor (like Darwin) drew out the implications of an already existing culture of active choice-making and gave it new moral and practical significance and a new gender cast. They effectively elevated it for men and then handed it back in this enhanced form to (some) women too, legitimating their engagement in a variety of market-like spheres and spaces as a social good. And alongside a host of new choice agents, crafting menus and directing the business of choosing, Mill added the role of theorist of choice, defining its meaning and value, attacking the obstacles to its realization from slavery to public opinion, and creating a new—and enduring, if also ultimately limited—moral and political vision in its wake. That vision eventually became the core of modern liberalism.[155]

The Issue

But there remained a key dilemma: How could the risks of anarchy, sexual impropriety, atheism, social disorder, psychic hurt, and more be mitigated in this newly individualized and competitive world, where free will mattered more than ever and authorities' control over the ordering of the options seemed to be steadily declining? It is a problem that would worry a range of postrevolutionary thinkers, from Alexis de Tocqueville to Émile Durkheim, going forward.

The nineteenth century's main answer was, paradoxically, that for the idea of freedom of choice to be actualized and rendered mainstream, more, not fewer, constraints were needed. As the liberal theorist (and later, Mill translator) Charles Dupont-White noted bluntly just before the revolutions of 1848, "There is no liberty without regulation."[156] What was essential were institutions that would enable choice's effective functioning by creating and enforcing underlying rules, laws, and other kinds of limits, formal and customary alike, on who and what and when and where and how. Another major aspect of the nineteenth-century segment of this story is the development of an expanded choice infrastructure under the aegis of both informal community pressures *and* the state. Indeed, we might even say that the more women got in on the picking, the more all kinds of protocols and boundaries proliferated but also tightened around them. Again, it happened without almost any notice. And this too was consonant with the advance of liberalism. To grasp this part of our history, we must look to one more choice practice with a long pedigree, specifically the only choice that was already widely understood to be the special province of women: marriage.

CHAPTER 3

SELECTING A PARTNER—OR ROMANTIC CHOICE

Dance Cards

Twenty-first-century people collect a lot of odd things. Today dance cards, like most outmoded technologies related to choice-making, are one of those things. With a little effort, you can, as I did, search eBay .com under "dance card" or *carnet de bal* or *Balspende* and find a wide range of vintage options available to purchase.

You will likely land on a few expensive late eighteenth-century or early nineteenth-century jeweled and enameled versions, some made out of silver, others bone, still others ivory or tortoiseshell or mother-of-pearl, that work hard to announce their preciousness. Inside are usually silk linings into which well-heeled young women once inserted fresh papers before heading out to a ball. The small gold pencil that accompanied the papers is often now missing. Occasionally, though, the whole tiny package is preserved intact, making a dance card a luxury item still. Museums already contain some of the best, decorated by well-known miniaturists and fine jewelry makers.

Mid- to late nineteenth-century exemplars exist in greater quantities—and, you will discover, at lower prices, since many, though not all of them, were constructed of ordinary rather than sumptuous materials. Sometimes they resemble notebooks or diaries. Other times they double as expanding fans (fig. 3.1). A collectors' market also exists today for the entirely paper ones, created for a single occasion.

Preprinted, ephemeral *carnets de bal*, which grew in popularity in the course of the century, listed the evening's planned order of dances on one side, with spaces on the other in which to write in the names of the gentlemen who had requested the pleasure of each number, giving them a superficial resemblance to a paper ballot (fig. 3.2). Frequently those for sale now still have names in different hands—Mr. X for the gavotte, Mr. Y for the quadrille—and clips and ribbons for attaching the list to their female owner's wrist or skirt, along with the essential pencil.[1]

Contemporary enthusiasts surely like these objects for their formal, decorative qualities but also for their strangeness in today's world. Dance cards have become collectors' items, much like snuff boxes or other paper ephemera like trade cards, as relics of the mores and customs of another time. Even the dealers for these varied keepsakes are often the same, brokers in sales of the charming and obsolete.

Once, though, dance cards had a real function. They were designed (mostly by men) and used (mostly by women and older adolescent girls) across the Western world to facilitate and organize micro-level choice-making in a very specific context. That was the ballroom. Clues to their significance dot the nineteenth century and its better-known printed matter, including story collections and novels. This is especially the case for France. In Émile Zola's "Le Carnet de Danse" (1864), the object of the title is so potent that it literally speaks to the adolescent female at the center of the story after the fact of her first ball. Intended to be practical, a way of structuring an evening, the little booklet and its annotations now remind the young, so-called *coquette* of the many, small amorous dramas behind her: the various men who took the occasion to choose her for the next dance.[2]

When a man wanted time on the dance floor with a woman in any proper urban nineteenth-century setting from Paris to the main cities of Latin America, he could not make this happen without following a series of quite literal steps that would set the process in motion (and the inverse—women choosing men directly—was normally quite impossible even to imagine). At both public and private balls, the gentleman in question had first to survey the whole field of female possibilities seated around the perimeter of the room. Then, making his mental

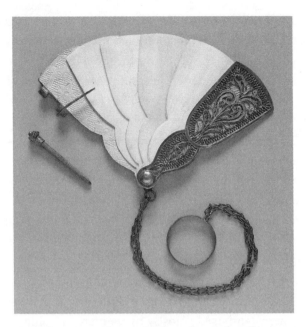

Fig. 3.1. An early nineteenth-century French or Italian fan, now in the MFA Boston, made of ivory, mother-of-pearl, and gilt metal and originally intended for use as a *carnet de bal*. The blades were suitable for inscribing the names of dance partners using the accompanying pencil.

Fig. 3.2. A paper dance card designed for a single special occasion: the Citizens' Ball in Honor of the Prince of Wales, Montreal, August 27, 1860.

selection, he had to get the permission of the floor manager or host or chaperone to act upon it, make his way to the particular seated lady with whom he wished to sally around the dance floor, bow slightly toward her at a respectable distance, and then finally request her partnership for a specific dance—now or later—among the evening's preselected and preordered offerings. That's where dance cards, like other kinds of menus, came into play.

A lady's dance card provided one possible out for the so-chosen: she could show, if it were indeed the case, that her dance card was already full (giving rise to a later but enduring English expression for "otherwise committed") or even possibly suggest that she'd gotten her card scrambled and wasn't sure if she were free at the precise moment requested. But otherwise, the expectation for the woman was a yes. The dance card was primarily meant to make that agreement a reality. Following a carefully and correctly worded ask on the part of the gentleman, the woman would present her card to him. He would then affix his name to the blank line or space on the card corresponding to the specific dance he'd inquired about, making use of either the diminutive pencil attached to the dance card that she was visibly wearing (which also made it clear that she was available for picking) or his own, stored in a little case, perhaps together with a tiny notebook, in one of his interior pockets. That way, he could secure each of his preferred partners for the full evening—one couldn't, after all, keep repeating any of the offerings any more than order repeatedly the same course in a restaurant—and she could remember to whom she had made promises for later. As both menu and record of choices, a *carnet de bal* scripted ahead of time what would be happening throughout the evening and, as a bonus, helped women recall it all afterward.

Thus, as insignificant as they might seem to us now, after all these years, dance cards (called "ball books" or "ball programmes" in English at the time) render concrete for the historian a central aspect of nineteenth-century transatlantic and continental European urban culture, elite and more modest alike. They demonstrate something vital about how choice was facilitated but also systematized and tamed in the affective or romantic sphere in an era before datebooks or dating. For dance cards, as a popular kind of choice paraphernalia, provided one small, unexceptional but effective means for coping with the growing problem of how best to select a partner or mate, whether for the next fifteen minutes or for life, in what we might now describe as an expanding and also increasingly fraught choice landscape.

On the one hand, dance cards, like the writings of that quintessential Victorian thinker John Stuart Mill, place us firmly in a world rife with new opportunities and occasions for picking among multiple options for both sexes. Nineteenth-century people of various classes in Europe and throughout the Americas not only encountered ever more special spaces and aids for doing so; as the century wore on, the principle of the menu of options also became increasingly entrenched as a central organizing schema that made many aspects of life loosely homologous. Even those without access to much by way of choice for themselves became more aware of its work, as elite habits became harder for those of other classes to ignore.[3]

It is no accident, after all, that this was the same era in which chattel slavery was beginning its slow demise across the Atlantic world, granting at least some minimal level of choice to enormous numbers of people—people who had been denied almost any before—in two forms: wage or "free" labor and the ability to form lasting, voluntary families. Even as colonialism expanded and created new kinds of barriers, many Europeans and white Americans patted themselves on the back for this achievement as signaling a new development in the annals of freedom. It is in this context that the ability to choose, especially when it came to the deployment of one's own body, came to seem like something akin to a superpower. Increasingly, it was treated as an essential way to shape one's own existence. What's more, it became a marker of an independent, adult self. Even in the ballroom, for those so empowered, sealing the deal on the next dance demonstrated to the world that one was in possession of one's own affections and physical being and could dispose of them as one wished, a new standard for liberty.

On the other hand, though, the prevalence of dance cards—much like those considerably more important nineteenth-century instruments of choice regulation, contracts—testifies to something else: a growing need for increased rules and order in the selection-making process, that is, for both formal and customary forms of restraint.[4] That was especially the case when it came to what a modern game theorist would call "interdependent choice," or choice that required multiple parties to anticipate each other's desires and actions and to persuade, as opposed to coerce, the other person or persons to pick them too. For the extension of the logic of personalized choice beyond objects and ideas to include other humans, who were understood to have agency and feelings themselves (unlike in an auction of enslaved persons), presented unusual risks to both self and society that required careful managing. Or at least they did until all contracts were signed and sealed and choice was put, once again, on hold until such moment as the contract came to an end. What dance cards demonstrate in a small way is also the practical transformation of freedom, especially in the affective and romantic sphere, into something like *bounded* choice—for men and, especially, for women.

Of course, this is not to suggest that in the course of the nineteenth century everyone everywhere simply got on board with this nascent postrevolutionary Western equation of freedom and choice, bounded or not. Challenges surfaced almost immediately from the political right and left alike; the new power accorded to choice had its detractors from the start. Some people chafed against the whole idea of a society structured around the pseudo-egalitarian concept of mutual selection. We know, for example, that an increasingly contractual view of social relations produced dilemmas of justification for those eager to perpetuate human bondage and, later, strict racial codes in the Americas, giving rise to the argument that not all people deserve or even have the capacity to benefit from freedom of choice. (Today that argument is often deployed against initiatives like universal basic income.) The same went for defenders of monarchical, aristocratic, and/or clerical privilege across Europe. Older ideas did not simply evaporate, and in some cases they gained new strength after the age of revolutions.

Others, following the line of Marx from the mid-nineteenth century onward, insisted that an emphasis on choice could be pernicious in its own right, a cover for structural inequality and new forms of subordination no matter how couched, a critique that has also only grown over time.[5] After all, in a postrevolutionary, postemancipation world that defined freedom this way, coercion was for most people still, in practice, frequently the norm, and the choices themselves often looked less like Hercules's and more like Hobson's—meaning, this or none.[6] Or they looked like a slate of only bad options. For the powerful, by contrast, having choices often meant dominating and even erasing the choices of those with less capital or clout.

And still others declared that choice, as a form of self-ownership, was largely an illusion since fate, temperament, chance, providence, and other quasi-natural processes out of our control will ultimately always win out. Think of Johann Wolfgang von Goethe's haunting 1809 novel *Die Wahlverwandschaften* (translated alternately as *Elective Affinities* or *Kindred by Choice*) in which the great German novelist tried to show, by way of a story of a married couple and an extra man and an extra woman who embark on a romantic "experiment," just how wrong we are when we think we are in control of our emotional destinies. The tragedy of Goethe's novel was that none of them could see how fate had already determined their choices. Mill himself was convinced that, in his own moment, public opinion and the pressure of social conformity were playing almost the same role.

Still, the primary response to the growing power of choice in everyday life in the nineteenth-century Western world was not to reject it but to figure out how to make it work. That meant trying to use it to reorder many kinds of human relationships. It also meant trying to quell its anarchic and destructive potential, whether through courts and legislative bodies, civil and religious customs, the threat of harm to reputation and standing, or even voluntary forms of constraint. This is something we've largely lost sight of in the age of seemingly endlessly proliferating and relatively value-neutral online options, including for dates. In retrospect, the *carnet de bal* also demonstrates an inverse concern about how best, in a world of emancipated "individuals" empowered to contract with one another in a series of different leisure-time marketplaces, to contain the dangerous forces unleashed by this seemingly extreme form of freedom. The real question was whether choice could operate on the dance floor, and by extension in romantic life more broadly, in such a way as to protect the established social order and, even more, the individual men and women who constituted it.

One set of worries certainly circled around class, race, and social status, as it always had. Mid-nineteenth-century Europeans and their brethren in North and South America were ensconced in a world in which hierarchy was very much an explicit and valued norm. It remained impossible, for example, even as political orders came and went, to imagine a man of a lower or inferior class in most circumstances asking a socially superior woman to pencil in his name for a dance. Nevertheless, it was also the case, just as critics of luxury shopping had worried in the eighteenth century, that it was increasingly hard to tell precisely who was who, especially in urban environments, as networks expanded and people of different social or civic status intersected, accidentally or as a matter of course. Social rank, with its noncongruent axes around money and family and professional status, had also, by the nineteenth century, typically become ambiguous in new ways, further complicating the business of figuring out the degrees of deference required in different settings, including the dance floor. Plus, in an age of increasing social and economic mobility, all evidence suggested that choices, if made well, could indeed change fortunes in multiple senses. Dance cards must have seemed a small way to try to control the potential chaos and establish some basic order.

Equally central to the nineteenth century, though, were questions about choice and gender. Some of these questions concerned the relative autonomy that *should* be accorded to men versus women in this new social landscape. Could a man's sphere for choosing be expanded without either granting women too much independence in the process or, conversely, rendering women entirely passive and dominated? Or to put it the other way, how much choice, and over what domains, became a woman—a being who generally had few other claims to independence, especially when it came to her own feelings, affections, and desires regarding others—before she endangered either herself and her virtue or society as a whole? The other set of questions concerned mitigating techniques. What kind of procedural norms or "best practices" would offer ways to reduce or bypass the particular dangers and stresses of the world of choice? Could manners be brought in line with morals when it came to the deployment of sentiments and bodies?

Dance cards should not, despite their association with the female sex and the fantasies about girls' fantasies spun by Zola, be seen as a tool of incipient feminist liberation. The *carnet de bal* is better understood as one element of an elaborate ritual designed to keep the tightest of controls on the sexual politics of the ballroom in terms of who got selected and how and by whom. Mainly, this minor piece of ephemera illustrates the limited opportunities and options available to women vis-à-vis men. Men appear to have worked all century to maintain their traditional and largely exclusive prerogative as fully formed and autonomous individuals in the business of decision making on the dance floor as well as in almost every other space.[7] Women largely acquiesced.

And yet, that might be a bit of an oversimplification too. In the great flirtation scene in Jane Austen's *Northanger Abbey* (written at the end of the 1790s but not published until 1817), Henry Tilney explains to Catherine Moreland, the single young woman with whom he is (very happily) dancing in an assembly room in Bath, that women can't choose—and that's one important way in which contracting for a dance resembles contracting for a lifelong partnership. As he bluntly puts it to her, "I consider a country-dance as an emblem of marriage" and, what's more, "You will allow, that in both, man has the advantage of choice, woman only the power of refusal."[8] It is hard not to hear here a positive echo of Mary Astell's famous critique of marriage inequality of a century earlier: "A Woman, indeed, can't properly be said to Choose; all that is allow'd her, is to Refuse or Accept what is offer'd."[9] We would call that consent—at best.[10] But our heroes in Bath are, of course, also engaging in a kind of two-way courtship ritual as they discuss this social norm. And while dancing and chatting, Austen makes clear, they are also proceeding to develop further their affection for each other. Their lightly mocking banter about what amounts to the inequity of male and female choice, in concert with the very rituals in which they are engaging, only strengthens their mutual regard, as Austen narrates it—and chance of a fulfilling and lasting engagement for both parties. One imagines the ritualized use of the dance card, essentially a choice-facilitating fashion accessory, quite often produced similar effects. Like other protocols, it could be manipulated to work in one's favor in all sorts of small ways, if one knew the right moves.

Affective choice, in other words, was a complicated business to navigate for men and women alike in the nineteenth century. Neither the rules nor their implications were identical to those established for consumer/aesthetic or religious/intellectual choice, the bifurcation of the previous two chapters. That was in part because of their different ethical weightings, in part because personal desires were, in such situations, more entangled with those of others. But from the end of the age of revolutions until well into the new century, the *practical* working through of questions about how and upon whom to bestow one's affections and with whom to share one's body set the stage for our contemporary obsession with choice and the uses made of one's own mental and physical self, with sexuality and sexual difference at the center.

Now one might well wonder: Can we possibly draw any meaningful lines from the business of courtship and flirtation in the first three quarters of the nineteenth century to twentieth- and twenty-first-century debates about reproductive rights, gay marriage, trans politics, and the dominance of so-called choice feminism? The argument of this chapter is that a full history of the "right to choose" requires reckoning with the nineteenth-century ballroom and its innovative techniques and technologies for regulating how men and women were going to engage in the world of choice, especially when it came to such powerful emotions as love and desire and their social and psychic consequences. Performed in specific leisure-time spaces, presided over by dancing masters and other sorts of hosts and hostesses in the roles of both professional and amateur choice architects, choosing a partner, or choice in others, increasingly in this era became a matter of elaborate, gender-specific choreography quite apart from the dance steps themselves. And those fundamental moves—most of them laid out and codified first in France—would ultimately help provide a scaffolding for modern liberalism and its feminist offshoots considerably farther afield.

Getting Married: "The" Choice

Our small story about dance cards has first, then, to be anchored in a bigger and longer one focused on the history of the institution of marriage and, more specifically, the history of that critical moment of transition from single to hitched. In the eighteenth- and nineteenth-century Anglophone world, the phrase "The Choice" meant one thing only: the decision about with whom to form a lifelong pact and new family unit.[11] Especially for women, this was understood to be *the* pivotal and decisive event of late adolescence or early adulthood—and also the only one over which they had much say. "The Choice" would ultimately define full adulthood for both parties even though, for women, it meant leaving one dependency (on a father) for another (on a husband, the chief provider and representative of a new family) once it formally began.

None of this was new to the era of dance cards. The long history of pre-Reformation Christianity, combined with most Western legal traditions, points toward the deep significance of mutual consent in the creation of marriages. It also points, at least in theory, toward fixed gender roles, meaning the subordinate role of wives and mothers once new family ties were created.[12] As John Winthrop, leader of the Massachusetts Bay Colony, succinctly explained the English Protestant tradition in the middle of the seventeenth century, "The woman's own choice [in marriage] makes such a man her husband; yet being so chosen, he is her lord, and she is subject to him, yet in a way of liberty, not bondage."[13] The clearest analogy for Winthrop was to be found in the husband's relation to Christ. This is a distinction that survived, though not without its challengers, well into the modern era among Protestants and Catholics alike, perhaps only strengthened in the aftermath of the Council of Trent.

Historians have, however, also long documented how understandings of the institution of marriage—and of the attendant idea of freedom—began to evolve, first in England and then across much of northwestern Europe and its colonies, in response to both new affective ideals and broader social changes in the era of the Enlightenment. Indeed, historians have even developed a term to describe the new ideal conception of weddedness that first made itself felt among the gentry and middling classes in England sometime in the eighteenth century: companionate marriage. What changed initially was less the framework within which marriage occurred (since the contract ideal, in conjunction with the idea of marriage as a sacrament or covenant, goes back to Roman law and canon law alike) than perceptions of marriage's aim or goals. Especially novel was the idea that something as subjective and as potentially fleeting as affection or even love—conceptualized as a strong emotional attachment to and preference for one specific person of the opposite sex among one's circle of acquaintances based on the appeal of that person's distinctive personal qualities—could be not simply an aspiration for a marriage. It could, and should, be the foundation on which a strong marriage got built.[14]

Now we should not, of course, imagine that this notion instantly produced, in either theory or practice, anything like the end of concern with traditional considerations in the selection of a life partner. We know that men, women, and their parents, extended kin, and even neighbors continued to weigh a variety of factors associated with the larger and enduring function of marriage as the bedrock of social, economic, and political order. Social status, wealth, profession, and connections all remained vital, even paramount. In France, this was especially true at the very top and at the bottom of the social scale, that is, among aristocrats, where marriages functioned as alliances among powerful families, and among peasants, where marriages remained an essential economic survival strategy. Still, much of this held for the incipient bourgeoisie too, as is clear from the extensive self-help literature starting in the eighteenth century on "choice of wife" and "choice of husband," as well as from actual correspondences in which relative equality in status and fortune among bride and groom continued to be taken very seriously as critical criteria for a good match.[15]

Endogamy, in other words, remained the norm everywhere and among everyone—as it largely does today when similar economic, professional, and educational attainments bind couples too. Consider that "Date Someone in Your Own League," meaning with the same pedigree in schooling, is the explicit motto of one early twenty-first-century American matchmaking company. Moreover, parents and their extended circles continued well into the twentieth century (and up to the present in some parts of the world) to be central to the process of enabling the union of two young people, whether by facilitating introductions or by arranging new unions in their entirety, an unremarkable fact given that family needs remained at the heart of what made for a "good" choice. Today algorithms do much the same for many.

But eighteenth-century western Europe did see the slow growth of attention to additional criteria—including subjective, sensible qualities like wit, charm, style, manners, and beauty—as well as new weighting to compatibility and even general attraction between oneself and a prospective mate, right along with incomes and ranks and family names. The invention of companionate or sentimental marriage was anchored by the burgeoning idea that the success of such life partnerships on both a personal and institutional level was only possible with a union of hearts as well as economic conditions. As such, parents and other relatives were only of limited value in the process; the individual men and women in question needed to play an active role in sussing each other out as distinctive persons, with distinctive traits and virtues, even if fathers still had the power of ultimate approval.[16] Or, to put it slightly differently, potential suitors needed to be able to compare the options before them on multiple fronts prior to making any major determinations.

It was the French Revolution, near the century's end, that transformed these ideas into laws. These laws, in turn, both changed behavior and, at least in France, cemented in formal terms the relationship among marriage choice, desire, and freedom. The so-called *mariage d'inclination*—as opposed to the *mariage de convenance* or *mariage de raison*—was slower to take hold in that nation than in England. But in France, too, as in much of western and central Europe, sentimental norms seemingly derived first from literary models gradually began to affect real people's decisions—or at least the way they talked about them with each other.[17] Purely mercenary nuptial arrangements increasingly came in for stinging rebukes from many quarters in the eighteenth century. Moreover, a late Enlightenment taste for the critique of dominant institutions, rooted in revised understandings of human nature, generated a countertradition that can be said to have lasted to this day. From Étienne-Gabriel Morelly to Denis Diderot, Enlightenment *philosophes* attacked long-standing Western truisms about marriage, in part by posing new questions about the centrality of choice in the social organization of human sexuality.

One strategy was to ask why anyone should *ever* make "The Choice" insofar as it, paradoxically, required that individual to give up all subsequent ones in the sexual or romantic sphere. Through the example of an imaginary Tahitian paradise, for example, Diderot indirectly asked what if it were actually unnatural to vow to channel all one's affections in one direction in a permanent way?[18] But the challenge also extended to asking why "The Choice," once made, should be irrevocable except by death. The hallmark of eighteenth-century (male) libertine thought—think of the Marquis de Sade—became the refusal to abide by prevailing moral norms and to make a definitive pick when it came to either sexual partners or sexual acts (so-called *plaisirs de choix*).[19] A minority of women writers meanwhile, not least in the feminine genre of the novel, turned such critiques toward new ends (and at a time when few male writers about domestic questions were interested in women's emancipation per se). They argued for more autonomy for women in determining the uses to which their bodies and property were put in marriage but also advocated for having the option to opt out—or choose not to get married at all. And they challenged enforced marriage, or the power of fathers in determining women's futures without their input or sometimes even consent prior to the big event.[20] The French Revolution could be said to have extended and then actualized all of these nascent arguments insofar as the family was subjected to the same sorts of radical rethinking after 1789 as all the other dominant institutions of the so-called Old Regime.

However, when, in 1791, the lawmakers of revolutionary France mandated a dramatic break in practice around the questions of both *who* got to make the choice when it came time to marry and *what* would be the nature of the choice they would be making, these representatives did so in an effort to strengthen the institution of marriage, not dissolve it.[21] The idea was that putting this venerable institution on more firm footing would help solidify the new social order. For central to revolutionary politics were two principles that would profoundly affect subsequent family life—in France and, ultimately, in many other states that moved toward liberal norms in the nineteenth century too. One was laicization, or wresting power away from the Catholic Church and locating it more fully in the state (and here, new speech and new religious freedom laws can be seen as parallel efforts). The other was the notion of an original social contract among all citizens, who had consciously and freely, if tacitly, chosen to form affective and formal bonds with one another for mutual protection and, indeed, to create a different kind of freedom as a result. That was freedom from domination by anyone but themselves and their self-made laws. Marriage, French revolutionaries believed, required reformulation on both axes—laicization or another variant of secularism, on the one hand, and voluntary contractualism, on the other. For the family, from the position of the French revolutionaries, was poised to become both the training ground for new forms of civic virtue and a metonym for the revolutionary social order.

And if love and affection were states of emotion that could be said to exist *prior* to the law, it was still the law, as crafted by the revolutionary state, that would legitimate them, define their acceptable boundaries, and render them more than a private agreement. Not long after the writing of the Declaration of the Rights of Man, members of the French National Assembly put their energies into reformulating the role of choice in the formal construction of the revolutionary family. First, in the Constitution of 1791, marriage defined as a sacrament gave way to marriage as purely the product of a civil contract, a legal agreement between consenting parties, with specific benefits and obligations to follow. Then, a little more than a year later and just as significantly, those consenting partners, once over the age of twenty-one, were redefined as self-sovereign or independent individuals who could freely choose their (opposite sex) life partner and then contract with one another without the permission of their families, meaning especially fathers. The aim was to institutionalize the conviction that potential brides and grooms would best know their own preferences and wills, as well as to tamp down on the potentially despotic quality of paternal or clerical authority. Further, should the original choice have been faulty or an error, divorce also became legal in France on that same day in 1792, just after the fall of Louis XVI, as the lowering of the age of majority. This final piece of legislation gave couples a way out of the unpleasantness that came from breach of contract on one or both parties' part or simply from "incompatibility." It also enabled the possibility—rooted in "individual liberty"—of each person in the couple making a new, more fruitful selection in the future.[22]

In principle, this chance to "contract again," or remarry, offered new leverage, especially to women, just as "free labor," or the chance to continually enter and exit labor contracts, did to workers.[23] Legalizing divorce meant granting women not just a collection of rights, passively held, but also the freedom to engage in active choice-making about future plans as independent agents, acting of their own volition and without coercion by or undue interference from priests, fathers, uncles, brothers, or husbands. But it is important to emphasize again that this form of emancipation was also predicated on the state acting in its capacity as rule-maker, laying out and determining all the steps in the process. Moreover, the state's justification for the policy change was not personal fulfillment for women; rather it was the production of new citizens and the promotion of general well-being and social stability. As the historian Suzanne Desan explains, the French revolutionaries envisioned heterosexual marriage as "the social contract in miniature, ideally tying each citizen to the state and integrating individual liberty and free choice [especially around one's affections] with a profound commitment to society as a whole."[24] The state would, in this vision, regulate and encourage choice-making in marriage, as in other domains, precisely because choice-making of this kind was in its interest.

None of this radical legal change in the world of marriage actually lasted in France in its Revolution-era incarnation. Almost immediately after the start of the new century, Napoleon raised the age of consent; severely curtailed the possibility of divorce, which was outlawed once again in 1816; and reasserted the power of husbands over wives, restricting the latter's ability, once married, to make contracts of any kind. He did so in the belief that the traditional family, rooted in male authority, was the foundation of the social order. But that was not the end of the story. A whole century of debate, agitation, and new legislation about family questions, much of it focused on the proper roles of women in public and private life alike, including the permissibility of divorce, was to follow. The argument also spread across the European continent and much of the New World, turning global by the start of the new one.

Some of this ferment was spurred by self-proclaimed champions of what came to be known after 1848 as "women's rights," that is, women and a few men who tried initially to agitate for more space for women to act as autonomous beings. As contracts among independent individuals increasingly became the standard emblem of freedom, the literal sign of economic or sexual relations constructed in contrast to slavery, agitators for "women's rights" had, since well before Taylor and Mill, encouraged an association between marriage, as entered into and as practiced following existing Western law, and bondage, the ultimate form of unfreedom. The (unmarried) novelist Mademoiselle de Scudéry had said as much way back in the seventeenth century, noting, "We are not given even the freedom to choose our masters, since we are often married against our inclination."[25] Then, early in the nineteenth, French, British, and American abolitionists and women's rights advocates joined forces (though never without conflict) both in organizational terms and in rhetorical ones. The explicit goal was to paint free white women and enslaved Black people of both sexes as similarly subjected to the choices of others (i.e., white men) and thus tragically prevented from allocating their bodily labor and, even more, their sexualized bodies at will.[26] Talk of slavery gave moral weight to women's reformist causes. But Black abolitionists, in particular, drew on newer notions of marriage to turn the old analogy on its head, arguing that slaveowners' refusal to countenance personal "preference," in the words of the formerly enslaved abolitionist Harriet Jacobs, and instead to perpetuate what other opponents derisively called "slave breeding" or sexual coercion, constituted one of slavery's greatest moral failings.[27] It is impossible to miss the way such arguments were also consonant with those of radical nineteenth-century white abolitionists like William Lloyd Garrison, who insisted that slavery is a sin because it also deprives humans of both sexes of the freedom they need to choose their own salvation in their own way.[28]

And then some French socialist women, influenced by the Saint-Simonians and Fourierists in the 1830s, 1840s, and 1850s, went one step further and rejected conventional marriage entirely. Calling it necessarily a form of legalized prostitution or sexual slavery, they advocated in its place either staying single and chaste *or* what the writer Claire Démar called "free love" and "the right of election" in the government of the family and in the public realm alike.[29] This, too, was a position that would long taint emancipation for women as serial license.

But the fight over marriage and family was also taken up by conservatives looking for the reverse: a way to protect traditional gender arrangements in the realm of choice, including male prerogatives as the choosers. One might even say the same battle has continued to this day—consider feminist arguments about whether sex work by women should be seen as a valid choice by autonomous individuals about how to deploy one's own body and earn a living or, conversely, as an unnatural and unconscionable form of subordination of self similar to enslavement, even if contractual. Debates around commercialized sex played out differently in the nineteenth century, but were no less intense, with prostitutes themselves standing (largely for male commentators and artists) for everything that was right or wrong about modern culture, including its seemingly voluntary transactionalism.[30]

What's salient for our purposes is that despite the fact that domestic law in France continued to evolve in the aftermath of Napoleon, two shifts proved permanent. One was a tendency to treat romantic love within marriage and, consequently, strong affection beforehand as vital to another new ideal: personal happiness. The other was a trend toward giving young men and women, as opposed to patriarchs, more independence to act on these affections and desires in contracting with each other. Indeed, as the nineteenth century progressed, the importance of an independent version of "The Choice" in creating the fulfilled (male) individual, and that individual's fully realized (female) soulmate, only grew and extended itself through more of the social order, especially in urban settings.

As a consequence, when it came to the formation of new families, freedom was gradually reconceptualized too. It became the source of any legitimate marriage contract. It also became the result of having made a good choice of spouse in the first place. As the anonymous author of one French revolutionary pamphlet of 1790 imagined this ideal: "Liberty elevates all the sentiments. . . . At last, all the caresses will be like the first one, confirming their choice [of each other]: 'I love you' in their language will continue to mean 'You are my favorite' [*je te préfère*]; and for them, marriage will be a treaty agreed upon anew every day."[31] This trifecta—an imagined synergy among love, happiness, and freedom (of choice) that was to be realized in marriage alone—would only expand in assumed validity in the decades to come.[32] Developments in religion, politics, the growth of free trade: all could be said to be consonant with this new ideal. This was true as much in the young, largely Protestant United States as it was in majority-Catholic France.[33]

All ideas, however, have peripheral effects, both intellectual and practical. So do new laws. One major result of the redefinition of marriage in the aftermath of the age of revolutions was a new pressure on young people of both sexes. They were now entrusted with the responsibility of guaranteeing their own future welfare. When it came to partners of any kind, it would henceforth be essential to pick well from the get-go.

The Attractions and Dangers of the Ball

It was the imperative of choosing successfully, and (ideally) definitively, that added so much weight in the nineteenth century to social dance and the world of the ballroom. Not surprisingly, long-term developments in both the criteria for forming alliances and conceptions of how consent should operate produced profound changes in the backstory process of getting to the altar—or what might be called the rituals of courtship. What the particular redefinition of marriage characteristic of the age of revolutions made essential was the creation of specific spaces, social practices, and occasions tailored to young people's romantic needs. The requirements included, first, producing effective "choice sets" out of other humans and, second, allowing for the blossoming and, ultimately, expression of appropriate preferences or "inclinations" among those who were expected to be both choices and choosers themselves. That, and a means for preventing serious misalliances.

Many French revolutionaries, from elected members of various representative assemblies to anonymous concerned citizens, recognized this practical problem immediately. In a world increasingly too big and impersonal for everyone to already know intimately all the suitable possibilities, suggestions about how to facilitate the new secular marriage order (and the babies sure to follow) filled tracts, journals, and letters to the state. Plans were hatched for places called marriage offices that would help men and women "who have not up to present been able, in their Cities, to meet a suitable object for their intentions [*l'objet qui lui convenient*] . . . to locate such a person, without difficulty, in another location, close or far."[34] Newspapers too were reenvisioned as depots for those seeking spouses. Ads for would-be brides were the bread-and-butter of the short-lived *Courrier de l'Hymen* (February–July 1791), which, just like many other contemporary commercial circulars, billed itself as especially directed toward women's happiness. Indeed, the content of the ads suggests that the whole format was particularly popular with mercers, clothing merchants, and other members of a prosperous shop-owning class catering already to women buyers.[35] Similar efforts continued through the nineteenth century, as French people took to advertising in regular newspapers too, both offering and seeking, at different times, possessions, a place to live, a job, a servant, or a spouse.[36] On the romantic end, one can't help but think of such initiatives as early, off-line equivalents of OkCupid, Tinder, or the other prominent online, algorithmically driven "dating sites" of today.[37] These revolutionary and postrevolutionary initiatives can also be seen, though, as no more than newfangled ways to update traditional customs, including veritable "marriage markets" like the Belgian *foires aux amoureux* and the informal wife-selling tradition in England, for a new political culture.[38] In any case, none of them actually took off as a critical mode of establishing lasting unions.

From the end of the Napoleonic era through most of the nineteenth century, the less overtly crass (and considerably more successful) nonfamilial solution to the business of creating marriage options was the expansion of assemblies, parties, and especially balls to which young and old alike might be socially sorted by means of invitation or ability to purchase a ticket. Participatory social dancing was a phenomenon with incredible reach in the nineteenth century; balls dominated the social life of Vienna, Florence, Bath, Stockholm, Leipzig, Buenos Aires, Philadelphia, and many points in between. Paris, though, remained the epicenter of this world. Although the French had taken much of the pomp out of marriage by insisting so fully on its contractual rather than sacred nature, French dances—as well as those frequently mocked experts in the business, French dancing masters—spread out across this world, shaping fashions and rules alike *à la française*, albeit always lightly adapted to local mores and tastes.[39] If marriage remained a metonym for the social order writ large, then the ball became a metonym for courtship and marriage (just as Austen's Henry Tilney insisted). To secure a desirable dancing partner was not only to take a practical, if still entirely reversible, step in the business of locating and securing a desirable spouse. It was also to participate in an elaborate second-level choreography that extended well beyond the actual dance steps and music. Its purpose was to help men and women alike, though necessarily differentially, to make their way effectively through the business of affective and sexual choice-making required by the modern world.

This might sound like a perverse or far-fetched reading of the world of ballroom dancing. We tend to look to explicitly political processes—the crafting of arguments in legal cases or the drafting of petitions to the state or new legislation, for example—to discern how, in the past, freedom, unfreedom, and choice did and did not coincide, especially for women. But the study of comportment in the ballroom, much like shopping or commonplacing, gets us to the implicit politics of everyday life, even if dancing was always only an occasional leisure-time activity. Exploring the norms around social dance helps us grasp how politics and the law shaped ordinary habits, including those associated with marriage. Even more, such inquiries let us see how following the basic rules around bodies and choice—including both taboos, on the one hand, and learned and subsequently internalized "best practices," on the other—worked to reinforce certain political notions, often with significant social consequences. Those consequences extended to ideas about freedom and its limits.

How, though, do we know what transpired on the nineteenth-century French dance floor, particularly when it came to choice in people with whom to pair up? For starters, the end products of a flourishing contemporaneous culture of printed instruction manuals tell us an awful lot about the newfound significance accorded to selecting dancing partners in the social imagination of the period. Hundreds of how-to guides, some anonymous and many explicitly authored by celebrated dancing masters like Henri Cellarius (to whom we will return), could be bought in nineteenth-century Paris or Lyon or really any city in the Western Hemisphere, in French or in an array of local languages. Socially ambitious Latin Americans could, for example, consult Domingo Ibarra's *Colección de bailes de sala, y método para aprenderlos sin Ausilio de Maestro, dedicada a la juventud mexicana,* published in Mexico City in 1860, or the section "De los bailes" of Manuel Antonio Carreño's popular *Manual de Urbanidad y Buenas Maneras, para uso de la juventud de ambos sexos,* published in Caracas in 1853. Most such manuals contained information on how to navigate or, maybe better, micromanage every stage of one's interactions with the opposite sex at a ball, from exiting a carriage on the night of the event, to garnering and accepting introductions once inside, to the dance steps themselves (figs. 3.3 and 3.4). Published in multiple editions and tailored to different parts of the social spectrum, some of these guides laid stake to comprehensiveness (as in Eugène Giraudet's massive 1885 *La Danse, la tenue, le maintien, l'hygiène et l'éducation, seul guide complet approuvé par l'Académie,* which promised 1,000 dances for every kind of ball or concert, 500 drawings and figures, and 2,000 choreographed steps from all countries of the world). Still others were so tiny they could be kept in a pocket right along with a *carnet de bal,* the miniature pictures or written descriptions consulted as the need might arise. All were ripe with promises and warnings alike. They can be read right alongside dance cards in the hopes of seeing both the ideal and the reality, respectively, of the performance.

And again, there are novels—in abundance. The other great source for understanding nineteenth-century social dance is fiction, where

Figs. 3.3 and 3.4. Paul Gavarni's illustrations of the proper way to invite a lady to dance and the proper waltzing position, designed for Henri Cellarius's *La Danse des salons* (1847).

plots continued to turn on the question of how to reconcile multiple, conflicting impulses and desires with recognizable obligations, especially for female characters. Sometimes that meant before marriage (giving us the so-called marriage plot), sometimes after (the adultery plot). But in all of the above, social dance and the protocol of the ballroom, right down to those overdetermined dance cards with their tiny pencils, loomed large.[40] The ball, whether public or private, whether set in western Europe or farther afield, became *the* setting for considering, negotiating, and finally enacting choices around affection and desire, a vital and, alternately, conventional and eventful stage in the path toward "The Choice" or its dissolution.

In certain instances, these ballroom encounters, as chronicled in fiction, made for spectacularly happy endings. That was especially true in early sentimental novels in which reconciliation of personal desires and romantic attraction, on the one hand, and familial or larger social demands, on the other, often presented itself as a real possibility. In such cases, we can see gender, class, and sexual desire mapping onto one another and choice-making working out to the ultimate benefit of all those so deserving. Often, though, and increasingly, the result was spectacular failure. What changed? Let's start with form. The major development in urban European and North and South American social dance in the nineteenth century was the rise of so-called closed couple dances. That meant, first, the waltz (fig. 3.4).

Early in the century, the quadrille or contredanse still held sway in most social settings. What distinguished such dances was their collective ethos, the fact that they were danced by sets of couples. That, and their attention to hierarchy; the groupings themselves were often organized with social distinctions in mind (albeit less so than in court dancing of the previous century), even as these dances were suitable for all ages and stations. Dancers were also expected to follow established patterns that required little real technical ability by the nineteenth century and little physical intimacy aside from hand holding. They were, in fact, to engage in lots of changes in partners or brief encounters within each dance.[41] (One version required so much swapping that it was known by the 1830s as the *saint-simonnienne* after the great utopian socialist, which tells you how closely dance was assumed both to facilitate and to mirror social and marital arrangements.)[42]

The "scandalous" waltz challenged all of that. It was the Congress of Vienna, hosted by the Austrian emperor Francis I following the end of the Napoleonic Wars in 1814–15, that made this dance fashionable with Europe's upper classes. The Congress is remembered, apart from its redrawing of the European map, for its enormous, glittering international balls, which required numerous dancing masters on hand for an unusual form of leisure-time diplomatic aid. In this context, a much older peasant dance (*die Walser*) was prettified and transformed—as is often the case in the history of social dancing—into a standardized form of entertainment appropriate even for aristocratic use.[43] The modern waltz was, however, slow to be taken up in high society inside France simply because it was so risqué. It took until the 1830s—that is, considerably longer than in London or Vienna, even though it came to be thought of elsewhere as a French dance—for the waltz to begin its rise to full respectability and become dominant across multiple milieus in France too. Celebrity dancing masters, looking to profit, continued to help ease the way, despite their own often obscure origins and ambiguous social positions. But the waltz itself never fully shed its associations with sex and, indeed, with the *coquette*, male or female. The great 1936 modernist Catalan novel *The Waltz* by Francesc Trabal still uses the trope of the waltz to structure a story about a man who simply can't make up his mind. Robert Schumann's piano masterwork of the 1830s, *Carnaval*, got there first.[44]

As dance steps go, the waltz can, in certain ways, be considered egalitarian or at least socially leveling. It was performed by many couples at once; it was organized without leaders or attention to hierarchy (or even much by way of onlookers, since it was so participatory); and it required even less technique than the quadrille, especially when compared with court dances in the past. At the same time, it repeatedly left each couple in its own world, spinning clockwise around itself, as well as around a giant counterclockwise circle, all the while touching intimately in something of an extended embrace, unmoored from everybody else. Soon after the waltz's ascension, the old quadrilles were relegated primarily to the role of fillers, opportunities for catching one's breath between the main attractions: waltzes and, by the 1840s, close variants with similarly mysterious central or eastern European roots, like the polka, the galop, and the mazurka. All of these newer genres were danced everywhere from private society balls requiring an invitation to popular Parisian dance halls and outdoor venues in parks, where one paid an entrance fee to engage in the collective entertainment. The waltz and its successors could be said to mark the final separation of the ballroom from the stage, the rendering of the former a world unto itself.[45]

It is actually not hard to understand the popularity of these closed-couple ballroom dances—or what became known in France as la dansomanie in the 1840s and 1850s—at either a visceral or a social scientific level. They represented a rare opportunity for men and women alike. Dancing a waltz or polka offered a thrill, sometimes called "the charms of liberty," in a culture with almost no other sanctioned physical contact, or even unchaperoned conversation with a focus on each other, between unmarried men and women.[46] Waltzing allowed one to engage, voluntarily, in a kind of intimate and daringly physical, even sexual behavior with a stranger or mere acquaintance that would have been totally taboo in all other settings. Even dance teachers indirectly admitted as much. Cellarius, who was celebrated across Europe for having brought a Bohemian peasant-dance, the polka, to Paris (or so he insisted) and then becoming that city's most famous instructor in the new couple dances of the mid-century, praised them with introducing "abandonment, naturalness and freedom of movement" and, in the case of the polka, a dance world "revolution."[47]

But simultaneously for many attendees, waltzes, along with other fashionable dances, became an aid in the serious business of finding a spouse—or making "The Choice"—in precisely the kinds of new contexts in which they took off. For the upper classes in the post-Napoleonic period, both public and private balls were spaces for the forging of social ties between the titled and the merely rich and ambitious, a playing field on which both could thrive after a few lessons. With the help of dancing masters, young people of means could cultivate a new kind of endogamy, dependent on the recognition of shared cultural norms, including gestures, carriage, and bodily comportment.[48]

For the urban working class, often far from their families of birth, big-city public balls, some of them organized around particular occupations or places of origin and some of them sporting a clientele that ranged from servants to students to gentlemen of standing slumming it for the evening, offered opportunities for matchmaking too. *Guinguettes, salles d'hiver, opéra-bals*: the range of types of Parisian commercial dance venues that were also places of encounter was vast by the 1840s. Some of these sites of commercial entertainment even took making matches, whether for the night or for life, as their primary purpose, despite the fact that partners were supposed to change frequently. Elysée Montmartre bluntly promised at the end of the nineteenth century that its ballroom was *the* place "where gentlemen and pretty women can joyously meet."[49]

Therein, of course, also lay their great perceived danger. For aside from the promise of a heady new kind of freedom (to experiment with physical contact across the boundaries of self and other, to form a temporary couple of one's own accord) and even happy endings (in the form of a choice proved just and good), there was every chance of everything going wrong.[50] That was especially the case when it came to selecting from among the many candidates, suitable and not, for even a trip around the dance floor or, in the case of women, consenting to an ask. For choosing properly with whom to have all this consensual, if discreet, bodily contact could potentially lead to love and a successful marriage, indeed fulfillment in the domestic sphere (or more temporary pleasures for a certain kind of man). But if navigated incorrectly, choice in partners could also result in thwarted ambition, humiliation, heartbreak, ruin, and, once again, social discord. That was particularly true for women. Poor choice of partner or poor performance of the whole could, in the world of the waltz, also end—as doctors, social critics, dance instructors, and novelists all explained in different ways—with terrible denouements from which one could not easily escape. What's more, with deliberate choice came personal responsibility for the consequences, whatever they might be.

Medical authorities warned that the euphoria of the new couple dances, and especially the turning waltz, easily gave way in women to dizziness, sickness, losing control, and thus easy seduction, especially if the wrong partner were enlisted.[51] Women were liable to become either too exhausted or too excited if presented with so much sensual experience combined with physical exertion, they and their male partners were both told. This was a danger even greater than luxury shopping or frivolous reading. Social critics, from conservative Catholic moralists like Joseph de Maistre to socialists like Charles Fourier, went further, comparing balls to "Oriental bazaars" (in the words of the former) where women were exposed "like a piece of merchandise offered to the highest bidder" (in the words of the latter), thus drawing on a familiar analogy in the world of choice, only with women turned into objects of consumption to be then discarded at will.[52] For social critics of the left in particular, it was a slippery slope from being "chosen" on the dance floor to abandonment, unwanted children, prostitution, and worse (even though some nineteenth-century men imagined prostitutes not as women without choices but as women who had, against the odds, held on to them).[53]

But bad ends were not just for poor *grisettes* or coquettish working-class women either. Disaster at the ball knew neither class nor gender limits. Dance instructors warned, too, of the torturous mortification that awaited ambitious men without proper ballroom skills, who would likely experience nothing but shame as they failed in their interactions with ladies, as well as the terrible experience for women of finding themselves "wallflowers," unchosen and alone.[54] Consider the plight of the man who blunders as he begins his quest and causes "the eyes of many to be directed upon him," one English dancing manual author admonished his readers: "Of course, scrutiny but adds to his confusion. . . . If, on being asked to dance, he should *venture* to approach a young lady in order to make her his partner—will she accept him?—and if she should, what a fate were hers! He must necessarily throw the whole set into confusion, tread upon the ladies' toes, come into rude collision with them and their partners, be voted a vulgar bore, and make everything more conspicuously ridiculous by his apology."[55] A constant theme for ballroom dancing's greatest promotors was that both love and social standing would elude those who failed in the performance of a ball, from the crucial "ask" onward through the evening and subsequent life.

Above all, though, it was (primarily male) novelists who dramatized how it could all go downhill, for men and women of all classes, with one bad choice in dancing partner or bad set. In the postrevolutionary French and, more generally, European novel, balls, as meeting places for future couples and places for the public observation of courtship, offered a chance for both male and female characters—as one imagines they did for real people too—to express what could not be otherwise said, whether through a glance, a fleeting moment of touch, a small gesture, a flirtatious turn of phrase. Yet basic miscommunication, deliberate or not, and failures of timing or insight, authors also remind their readers, remained a constant possibility in this artificial space that was at once so short on explicit statements of intention and so sensually charged. Sex, desire, marriage—creating them, evading them, thwarting them, failing to pursue them properly—hover constantly on the horizon of the ballroom in nineteenth-century fiction, sealing fates down the line. Moreover, in ballroom scenes, as alliances are forged and sundered, readers (in the very real role of spectators) not only learn of individuals' characters and interior motives. These same readers often discover, in granular detail, the whole nature of the social order at that moment, including the values and complexities around gender, rank, wealth, and standing that ran through the larger culture. Sometimes that meant authors could also illuminate the rightness of this culture in fostering successful unions. But often, as the century wore on, such scenes let writers make clear why most real love matches could only be doomed.

Consider Honoré de Balzac's wonderful novella "Le Bal de Sceaux" (1830), one of many parts of La Comédie humaine in which ball scenes turn out to be pivotal. In this instance, the story centers on Emilie, the beautiful, coquettish, and irredeemably snobby youngest daughter of a Restoration-era count, who is herself determined to marry only a high nobleman. Emilie is so enamored of her own power to attract and then to reject all suitors, and so unwilling to compromise (what we might call "picky") about her ultimate selection, that her father, in desperation, relieves himself of "the heaviest of paternal functions" and grants her the full authority to make her own nuptial choice. "You are at this moment under the necessity of making such a choice of husband as may secure you durable happiness," he declares early in the story, and "from this day forth you [alone] are the arbiter of your fate."[56]

Thus temporarily empowered to the greatest degree a woman might be in Restoration France by reason of rank and age and release from parental constraint, Emilie attends one day the ball at Sceaux, one of the most celebrated of the outdoor commercial summer attractions newly established on the edges of Paris. What made this space distinctive—we learn directly from Emilie, as well as from the historical record—was that within its confines members of the aristocracy, the commercial bourgeoisie, artists and students, and even more common people, rural and urban alike, mingled. Further, status differences were not always as self-evident to onlookers as they were during the Old Regime (though Emilie trusts she will attract all eyes as a result of her self-evident social standing and beauty alike). And in this festive but hermeneutically complex setting, Emilie surprises herself by spotting and then dancing with a man who appears to be everything of which she has dreamed: rich, handsome, intelligent, charming in his manners. The only problem for a young woman determined to uphold an increasingly dated attachment to hierarchy and to marry only a peer of the realm is that, though he comports himself, to her eye, like a nobleman, his true social standing remains ambiguous.

Emilie continues for much of this novella to be unsure just *who* this partner is, even as she dances with him again at her home, feeling "their fingertips thrill and tremble as they were married in the figures of the dance," and announces afterward to her father "you left me at liberty to make my choice; my choice is irrevocably made."[57] This uncertainty, encouraged by her suitor as a kind of test of her devotion, proves to be her downfall. When Emilie encounters her would-be husband quite by accident in a thoroughly mercantile role, selling muslins, calicoes, and printed cottons (in an echo of chapter 1 in this book), she jumps to the wrong conclusion and determines that he is, in fact, her social inferior, a mere consumer choice purveyor. In keeping with her rigid snobbery and the blinders it produces, she turns away from her own happiness and shuns the man whom she loves. Her punishment comes in the form of her own reluctant, unhappy marriage, when all other options have expired, to her extremely elderly uncle—and the too-late discovery, at yet another ball, this time thrown by the Neapolitan ambassador in Paris, that her former suitor was nobly making a sacrifice for his brother by engaging in the fabric trade that fateful day and was destined to be a peer after all. Reading the offerings in partners incorrectly in the socially complex spaces of various Restoration entertainments, combined with her own retrograde and flawed system of selection, leaves our haughty heroine ultimately without any choices at all—even as she is living in a new world of social fluidity and proliferating choice. In "Le Bal de Sceaux," Balzac gives his readers a political parable, worked out over a series of different kinds of balls. What we glimpse is a world in which liberty, dramatized as the temporary but previously unimaginable escalation of both opportunities for and range of choices, including for women, goes horribly awry for those who have not learned to play the new game with its new values and, yes, practices. *Coquettes* still do not win in the end.

Emilie does not waltz with her suitor, however. All the sexual thrill that Emilie experiences, in Balzac's telling, is through the collision of fingertips in the course of a contredanse at home. The social treacherousness of the nineteenth-century ballroom was further exacerbated by the newly intimate couple dances of a decade or so later—or so we learn from other nineteenth-century French novelists. Think of Madame Bovary, who does famously waltz. It is the overtly sexual nature of the description of her first try at waltzing, among a few other "voluptuous scenes" in Gustave Flaubert's 1856 novel of that name, that helped land the author before a French court, on trial for offending public morality and religion.[58]

Early on, in one of the novel's most consequential (and infamous) moments, the bourgeois Madame Bovary, attending her first real high-society ball in the late 1830s or early 1840s with her stolid, bourgeois husband, is asked to waltz by an elegant "Viscount" in a form-fitting waistcoat. She agrees, despite not knowing how. And almost as soon as they begin, Emma (as she is also known) is made dizzy and almost delirious from the turning motion of the dance as well as its physical intimacy. We grasp from Flaubert's remarkable and economical description of the sensations she experiences that Emma herself has barely any idea what is happening to her:

> They started slowly, then got faster. They turned, and everything turned round them—the lamps and chairs, the paneling, the parquet floor—like a disc on a pivot. As they swept past a door, Emma's skirt swirled out against her partner's trousers. Their legs intertwined. He looked down at her and she looked up at him; a numb feeling came over her, she stopped still. Then they were off again, and the Viscount whirled her away still faster, till they were out of sight at the end of the gallery. She was panting for breath, she nearly fell, for an instant she leaned her head on his chest. Still turning, but more gently, he brought her back to her seat. She sank back against the wall and covered her eyes with her hands.[59]

But then, just a sentence later, Flaubert snaps the reader and his main character back to reality—and to order. When Emma opens her eyes again in a passage much less frequently cited, "there was a lady sitting on a footstool in the center of the floor, with three gentlemen kneeling at her feet; she chose the Viscount, the violin struck up again." The other guests, we learn, go on selecting each other for new amusements, unmoved by the extraordinariness that Emma feels; the Viscount simply turns for another round of waltzing to the next available woman who has, in fact, chosen him for reasons that we will come to in a moment. All of this was quite ordinary ballroom behavior in aristocratic circles of France's July Monarchy, the reader is meant (along with Emma) to conclude. But waltzing in the wee hours of the night at the opulent Vaubyessard ball in the countryside of Normandy turns out to be a life-changing experience for the sensitive Madame Bovary, a quasi-sexual moment, outside of regular time or space, enjoyed with a very different man from her husband. The Viscount's selection and cultivation of Emma constitutes a ritual of "initiation" (as the prosecutor at Flaubert's trial termed it in 1857) that his heroine will be able to return to repeatedly as a source of reverie. It will also cause her to disrupt her quotidian life as she tries continually to rediscover its effects in new forms, from excessive consumption to serial adultery, all dangerous indulgences in female choice-making. Flaubert does not condemn his heroine in the fashion of Balzac; the moral message remains ambiguous, as the prosecutor also complained.[60] Still, this one-paragraph waltz, danced in the middle of a complex orchestration of choice-making that the provincial, middle-class Emma hardly grasps, leads inexorably to her ruin.

Playing by the Rules

The great nineteenth-century solution, the only imagined protection against seduction, temptation, embarrassment, or any of the personal or social risks associated with engaging in the business of ballroom choice, was a strict code of etiquette. Even though public balls in Paris, where fights sometimes broke out over the picking of partners, certainly depended upon the presence of the police,[61] balls at every social level were primarily regulated by an elaborate armature of informal laws. Such laws were rooted in and reinforced by community standards, as well as by dancing masters and social elites, and went well beyond anything imagined for shopping or most other leisure-time pursuits in terms of reinforcing bodily and emotional self-control. Ever-increasing vigilance was demanded in terms of not only mastery in the execution of the steps before setting out on the dance floor but also avoidance of any kind of indecorous or unseemly or antisocial behavior along the way (though novels like *Madame Bovary*, whose author was also charged with making "art without rules," further illustrate the limitations of such strictures in practice).[62] For when it came to interactions between men and women, with all their potential for transgression, it was widely understood that nothing should be left to chance. And very little should be left to one's own discretion either. From high-society events to servants' balls, the rules and regulations of the dance floor, designed as much to protect against hurt feelings as to preserve honor, reputation, and order, were encouraged and upheld by everyone assembled (fig. 3.5). But ultimately, such strictures were meant to be internalized, much like the forms of the dances themselves, by all participants individually. And that meant, above all, the conventions for sorting and selecting partners, including who, when, where, and, especially, how.

Lest one forgot or did not know in the first place, scores of dancing instruction manuals, which often featured back pages advertising yet more varieties of commercial etiquette guides, made these gender-specific and difference-reinforcing rules of ballroom conduct explicit. Cellarius was an exception; despite setting himself up as an expert, he left much unstated in his manual, apart from the details of the dances themselves, so as to be able to compliment his readers for being the kind of people for whom such social guidance was surely, at mid-century, unnecessary. What most others tell us (and, again, readers of Jane Austen already surely know, since her subjects are routinely hampered as well as abetted by them) are the protocols for how precisely to go about choosing with whom to dance—a business that Cellarius does concede is one of those "details, which once were so indifferent and now are so

Fig. 3.5. James Gillray, *A Broad Hint of Not Meaning to Dance* (1804), a hand-colored etching satirizing the strategies that women were required to develop to avoid unwanted dance partners, with the strong suggestion that the rules were not always effective for either party. Note the unchosen "wallflower" as well.

important, [that] have sufficed to re-animate the ball."[63] All participants *needed* to be aware, whether from lessons, observation, or simply practice and habituation:

- that the man must always ask the lady to dance and never the other way around, whether in public or private venues
- that she has the power of refusal on account of needing rest or if otherwise occupied (as generally demonstrated by her dance card) but must not then choose to dance with someone else until considerably later in the evening or not at all
- that no man can occupy any woman for more than two or three dances in an evening—even fiancées should have limits
- that the cavalier must escort the lady after each dance to her seat, her left hand in his right, without delay or small talk, just a bow as he takes his leave

- that women should keep track of who has chosen them and for what dance (again with the dance card), though it would be bad manners to have reserved too many dances ahead of time
- that if a woman should violate one of these rules, it is better for the man not to make a scene or otherwise take offense, especially as it is hard to control all sentiments and impulses
- that, nevertheless, staring or compliments or explicit displays of personal preference should have no place in any of this

In a book that was repeatedly reprinted, translated, and simply copied from its first edition in 1804 through mid-century, J. H. Gourdoux-Daux, a Parisian dancing master with a great interest in the rules of civility, came down hard on that last dictate. On the essentialness of avoiding any overt display of preferences at private balls, he announced: "It is not only impolite but rude [or worse: *malhonnête et indécent*, in the French original] to choose the lady with whom you are to dance, or to single out one and continue as her partner during the whole of the entertainment. . . . Besides, being all invited by one gentleman [the host], he would be offended if preference or partiality were shown to some and neglect to others."[64] Other commentators agreed on the importance of the "no preference" standard as essential for propriety even as one was called upon to discriminate among available options (which meant also not asking any woman seated near one who has declined to dance, since it might be taken to suggest that the former is a second-tier option, but also that women should in almost all cases say yes to avoid conveying any preferences in return). Restraint in the expression of personal tastes or inclinations helped one avoid compromising situations or hurt feelings. It was also a way to convey one's attachment, even in the ballroom, to social duty rather than selfishness. Giraudet felt so strongly about the importance of protocol that, late in the same century, he even tried to spell out the full verbal scripts appropriate to every kind of request.[65] The idea was that in such ritualized formulas, one could separate the messiness of personal desires and affections, or self-expression, from the business of securing one's choices.

Small variances and modifications were required, of course, depending on the persons in question, the precise type of event, and, even more, location. Such subtle adjustments were understood to reflect the distinctive social and political worlds, with their different norms around gender, class, age, and status, of which balls were always a microcosm. The rules got stricter as one went up the social chain, even as they brought rituals once associated with court culture to the middle and working classes. They were also always inseparable from dominant forms of political rule.

As the English author of a guide called *The Ballroom Preceptor* (1846) noted: "The etiquette of the ball-room differs essentially in France and England, and seems remarkably to illustrate the idea that the dance even assimilates itself to political institutions." In this telling: "In democratic France, a gentleman without an introduction may ask a lady to dance with him; but then he must restore her to her seat immediately after the set is concluded, and may not enter into individual conversation with her after the dance is over; such being deemed a wise precaution, rendered the more necessary, perhaps from the greater liberty allowed in forming the partnership." Across the Channel, by contrast, where the Lady Patronnesses of Almack's Assembly Room were famous in the era of Jane Austen for arranging matches for dancing as preludes to life matches for the top of the social hierarchy, the reverse was the case: "In aristocratic England, on the other hand, a regular introduction must take place between the parties before a gentleman can be entitled to offer himself as the partner of a lady. But this indispensable ceremony having been gone through, he is at full liberty, both before and after the dance, to take his seat by her side, or promenade with her through the room, without being considered guilty of presumption in so doing."[66] The same English rule on introductions generally held in the nineteenth-century United States as well, though some American guides insisted: "Ladies in American cities have much more license [to speak or move about with men on their own] than in European society, nor is this license often abused."[67]

But it is the very attention to such subtleties in affective and personal choice-making behavior that suggests how much was basically shared, especially by the upper classes of the 1800s, from St. Petersburg and Vienna to Chicago, Mexico City, and Buenos Aires, when it came to thinking about the management of that enduring tension between propriety with an emphasis on honor and reputation, on the one hand, and inevitable emotional attachment or sexual desire, on the other. Dance cards make this tangible, which is probably why they frequently entered nineteenth-century fiction right along with detailed descriptions of ball-room practices.

Among their functions was certainly, as we have seen, the regulation of choice in a hazardous arena. With their "air" of what Zola calls "necessity and disinterestedness," they helped create order and process out of desires.[68] They could even be employed by young women strategically to avoid an undesirable pairing without causing offense, as when "a girl is able to account for a mistake by saying that her programme had got into such a state of confusion that she thought she was engaged when she was not."[69] Dance cards were handmaidens to the etiquette of dispassionate, depersonalized, structured choice for men and women alike. True, they also worked, as both Zola's "Le Carnet de Danse" and Julien Duvivier's classic 1937 movie of almost the same name (*Un carnet de bal*) demonstrate, as aide-mémoires, objects useful for conjuring up affective states in the past. The original ones of the eighteenth century, with their precious stones and metalwork, were often stamped "souvenirs." Zola, after an evocative description of a dance card of the 1860s, from its soft, perfumed paper to its golden clasp and pencil holder, also calls them "tablets of love" in which each signature functions as a discrete but distinct "love letter."[70] Indeed, an encounter with this commonplace object after it has ceased to be useful for its original purpose provokes an almost sexual reverie in Zola's young protagonist—until the chambermaid enters her bedroom and the spell is broken. But part of their poignancy, one of the reasons that emotion always burst through their pages, is precisely because ball programs conjured sentiments on which women had little power to act, which is to say choose freely, either before or after the fact.

Rules for Breaking the Rules, or the *Cotillon*

There is, however, in Cellarius's *La Danse des salons*, as in many subsequent dance manuals right up until the eve of World War I, something else of interest to the historian of choice. Once Cellarius has finished going over all the basic dances of Parisian high society at mid-century, he turns his attention to the so-called *cotillon*, a distinctive ballroom fad of the 1840s built upon the popularity of the waltz, that is best described as a series of dance games frequently involving props.

Cotillons were designed to be played or performed in the latest hours of the night as a final, post-supper menu item at a private ball. Cellarius describes eighty-three possible variations or figures for this kind of dance game. Later in the century, some dancing masters listed well over two hundred. Eugène Giraudet, always eager to outdo everyone else, claimed to document 3,333 cotillon figures by the century's close.[71] To us they seem shockingly silly—chasing the opposite sex with a butterfly net while waltzing, forcing the opposite sex to try to eat a biscuit off the end of a fishing rod as a prelude to a galop, dancing around chairs much like the contemporary children's birthday party game. But their popularity was replicated almost immediately in the 1840s and 1850s in cities across continental Europe, Great Britain, the United States (where the cotillon was often referred to, oddly, as the German Cotillion or simply the German), and eventually Latin America, and they soon reached the middle and upper classes alike. What is rarely noted in discussions of Flaubert's great waltzing scene at the Vaubyessard ball is that Emma Bovary's trip around the floor with her Viscount takes place explicitly in the context of a very late-night cotillon. And what is important from our perspective is that the cotillon, whether danced by Emma Bovary's fictional fellow attendees or her real-life contemporaries, turns out to be all about making the business of picking partners work. In fact, choosing with whom to pair up functions in these strange and often rather sexual dance games not as the precursor to the real action or choreography. It becomes the focus of the dance games themselves.[72]

A good number of Cellarius's (and others') cotillon variations, not surprisingly, involve men doing the choosing from among the assembled women, much as all the major nineteenth-century ballroom dances do. Some variants even seem to have turned on humiliating the gentlemen's potential female partners insofar as they required the public rejection of certain of the human options before them as part of the fun. Cellarius describes, for example, one that is actually called "Les Dames

Trompées" (translated as The Deceived Ladies or The Ladies Mocked, depending on the English edition) in which the gentleman "approaches several ladies pretending to invite them to waltze [*sic*] or dance. The moment the lady rises to accept his offer, he turns away quickly to address himself to another, on whom he plays off the same game, til at last [he] really makes a choice."[73] It is hard not to see such activities as actualizations, albeit in a humorous vein, of the old metaphor of the ballroom as an auction or bazaar with women as the items on offer.

Yet significantly, a good number of the games chronicled by Cellarius involve a form of role reversal: women picking men—and explicitly leaving some men out in the cold—an activity that had little counterpart in the world outside the ballroom in an era before female suffrage, though maybe some scenes at the mercers or drapers could qualify. Let us not forget that when Madame Bovary opens her eyes after her first experience of the waltz, the reader sees her seeing (and coming to terms with the fact) that "there was a lady sitting on a footstool in the center of the floor, with three gentlemen kneeling at her feet," one of whom— the Viscount—*she* proceeds to "choose." Then consider two common cotillon figures that, even though in both cases a man (the *conducteur* or host) still initiates the activity and constructs the "choice set," fit this same, seemingly gender-reversing mold.

In "Le Coussin" (The Cushion), Cellarius tells us: "The first gentleman sets out, holding a cushion in his left hand. He makes the round of the room . . . and leaves the cushion to his partner, which she must present to several gentlemen, inviting them to kneel upon it. The lady should draw back quickly from the gentleman she means to mock and let it fall before the one she intends to choose."[74] One of Cellarius's contemporaries, a dancing master named Laborde, elaborates that, in this figure, the woman should keep drawing away the cushion from the assembled cavaliers until she lands on one who "agrees with her" (*lui convienne*).[75] Then there is a popular one called "L'Eventail" (The Fan), done with a waltz or polka step: "Three chairs are placed in the middle of the room upon the same line. The two at the ends should be turned contrarywise to that in the centre. . . . The first couple sets out waltzing. The gentleman seats his lady upon the centre chair, and seeks two other

L'Eventail

Fig. 3.6. "L'Eventail" (The Fan), an illustration of a cotillon variation in which a lady ultimately gives her fan to one man and then picks a different one to dance with, from Laborde, *Le Cotillon* (1853).

gentlemen whom he places in the two other chairs. The lady offers her fan to one of the gentlemen at her side, and waltzes with the other. The gentleman with the fan must follow the waltzing couple, fanning them and hopping about the circle" (fig. 3.6).[76]

Other, similar figures took root as the century wore on. The woman dancer might be tasked with putting a hat on the man she has chosen or picking him from a mirror. One of the simplest, described by a mid-century dancing master named Gustave Desrat, is called "The Conversation" and operates a little bit like a speed date: "The master of ceremonies [*cavalier conducteur*] introduces two dancers to a seated lady. Both must address her in a single sentence, and she will choose for waltzing the man who has been able to please her most."[77] Still others conveyed the spirit of their proposed figures with names like "Les Dames ont le Choix" (Ladies' Choice) or "L'Invitation" (The Invitation), "Les

Cavaliers Présentés" (The Proposed Gentlemen), "Le Cavalier Trompé" (The Cheated Gentleman), "La Trompeuse" (The Deceiving Lady), and "Le Refusé" (The Rejected Man).[78] A number too specifically play on the idea of the *coquette*, picking as she desires and leaving the rejected man to suffer.[79] And a few, like "Les Cavaliers Ensemble" (The Gentlemen Together), even conclude with what was surely intended to be the humiliating, albeit titillating, consequence of the two leftover men having to dance with each other.[80]

Cellarius, who managed to popularize and spread the fad for the cotillon in the wake of the polka, leaves us—much as Flaubert did—to draw our own conclusions about all this highly orchestrated but temporary role reversal, which seems to have functioned something like a modern-day charivari or an antique version of Bumble (a contemporary American dating site distinguished by the fact that women "make the first move"). Cellarius's is strictly a how-to manual aimed at hosts and guests, male and female alike. It is hard to know if he saw turning the indignities of not being chosen into a consensual game of this sort as a way of affirming or mocking the growing power of choice.

But others point to the political subtext of the cotillon, as is often the case in discussions of social dance. Some writers note, for example, that *conducteurs* were encouraged to invent their own variants following the news or political developments of the day.[81] More significantly, from the beginning there are hints of a sort of feminine inflection to the whole exercise of the cotillon, starting with its name redolent of women's petticoats and continuing to its unusual gender politics in the realm of partner choice.[82] The social dance expert Lily Grove, writing in England near the end of the century, noted, "Women like the cotillon . . . for it gives them the rare chance of showing their preferences and of enabling them to pay out now and again the men who, through conceit, neglect, or indolence, have displeased them." It is, she prophesied, an innovation likely to last in this "age of woman."[83] Some French writers, as well as painters, made similar points about the role reversal in choice-making aided by female costuming and masks in the public opera balls of mid-century (fig. 3.7). Alphonse Karr, author of *Encore les femmes* of 1858, noted that though "women in life must wait to be invited

Fig. 3.7. Edouard Manet, *Masked Ball at the Opera* (1873), an extraordinary painting of modern sexual commerce in which women are both the objects of interest and—masked and costumed, unlike the well-dressed men who surround them—active participants in this charged ritual.

to love, just as, in the salon, they wait to be invited to dance," masked in the special space of the opera ball, something else transpired: "They [women] chose before being chosen, chose outside the circle of their acquaintances, and spoke for once with unmanned tongues."[84]

And other variants of the cotillon, as described by Cellarius and his contemporaries, played with decision-making alternatives in different ways. Some figures used chance, including dice, to get rid of the obligation for men *and* women to pick at all, thereby depersonalizing the whole process of choice (a technique more often associated, as we've seen, with a twentieth-century artistic avant-garde eager to sever links to the realm of commercial culture and its fixation on consumer preferences). Additional figures employed combinations of choice and

Le Colin-Maillard assis.

Fig. 3.8. "Le Colin-Maillard Assis" (Blind-Man's Bluff), another common cotillon variation illustrated in Laborde's *Le Cotillon* in which choice is partially hampered by blindfolding, this time of the "cavalier."

chance, as in games like the "Mysterious Sheet," "The Secret Hands," or "Blind Man's Bluff" that involved selecting with limited visual access, or blind choice, and thus without full information about the options on offer (fig. 3.8). Still others involved competitions in which one tried literally to "catch" one's choice, whether with nets or lowered arms, while the objects of this attention, male or female, attempted to avoid being "caught"—or not. Finally, a good number depended upon a *conducteur* or master of ceremonies to do the selecting and to create new couples from the crowd, though one imagines that a word in his ear ahead of time might have produced predetermined results.

The important point is that all these games introduced *both* sexes to a kind of temporary freedom from the normal constraints, whether verbal or physical, on making and expressing sentimental and erotic choice. That was clearly their intended purpose, along with some brief relief from the need to choose at all (as in the case of those employing limited vision or serendipity). Cotillons, we might say, provided a lighthearted outlet from the increasingly dominant values of romantic life and a way to briefly violate certain gender- and class-based taboos, all under the guise of humor and fun for its initiates. We might even conclude that with these flirtatious and competitive dance games, the knowing banter of Austen's *Northanger Abbey* couple was finally rendered physical. The dancing master Charles Périn had perhaps the best description: the co- tillon is a "tournament" in which skill, force, agility, intelligence, malice, and even wit are called upon; surprise is the norm; and other people are literally the rewards.[85]

But here's the rub: far from authorizing a free-for-all or real relaxation in the regime of choice, cotillons, as the century wore on, actually made romantic choice-making a matter of ever more elaborate rules and pro- cedures. That is, cotillons subjected the business of selection to increasingly stylized, repetitive choreography, with limited room for im- provisation. Women surely embraced such essentially ridiculous oppor- tunities for both agency and chance in good part because the cotillon's elaborate, scripted protocols made it possible for them, as well as men, to do so largely risk-free, without threat to their virtue or reputation or chance of generating discord. Game-like regulations mitigated against the psychological or social toll of interpersonal choice (unless, like Emma Bovary, one didn't know the drill). Even more, they helped facili- tate multiple people doing the same complex thing—that is, choosing each other—at the same time and in the same defined space. We might even say they made the ballroom something like today's highway inter- change in which everyone knows, after learning the rules, how to move at once without causing chaos. Cotillons ultimately imposed a literal pattern on the collective performance of individualized affective choice.

What is more, cotillons also forged a concrete association between choice in the romantic or sexual domain and consumer choice. As the nineteenth century wore on, hosts of cotillons were increasingly told that guidance was needed not only in picking from a menu of dances and dancers but also in picking from a menu of masks, dice, fans, hair accessories, and other inessential, largely decorative objects, to be em- ployed as props in various games or rewarded as prizes at the end. That's because there was bound to be competition and comparison among hosts and hostesses as well. As one 1885 *Guide du Cotillon* published by a store in the cotillon-supply business noted on its first page, "The Choice of objects [for a cotillon] is often difficult. That's why we have put together a very pretty collection of Souvenirs, called 'Bibelots du Cottilon,' along with all the newest and most attractive figures."[86] Here the domains of material and affective choice became linked in ways that recall the horrified protagonist of "Le Bal de Sceaux" several decades earlier when she encountered her beloved in the guise of a fabric merchant, or the values of de Maistre or Fourier denouncing women for sale, or the *Courrier de l'Hymen* advertising for brides. Late twentieth-century economists like Gary Becker, who would one day claim behavior in marriage markets and markets for any commodity could be explained in much the same way, might not be surprised.[87]

It thus seems necessary to conclude that these popular nineteenth-century dance games, even as they provided a short respite from choice's normal reign under the guise of late-night fun and humor, worked much like those dance cards with which this chapter began. At the level of the body, they reinforced the power and significance of organized choice-making to multiple domains of modern life. Only those without any resources were directly left out. For everyone else: playing games of choice was becoming a matter of habit, an activity governed by elaborate instructions that were actually so well-known and consensual that they could, following yet more rules, temporarily be subverted without risk to the social order—and still feel like a form of freedom.

When, in 1851, a New York sheet music provider wanted to make fun of the new vogue for women's emancipation, the company issued its latest polka and mazurka with a cover image of two women eyeing each other in front of an urban shop window filled with objects for sale. One is dressed in an exaggerated version of the skirt-over-bloomers costume associated with faddish women's health movements at mid-century, the other in an even more scandalous bloomers get-up, also called "freedom dress," associated with women's nascent, post-1848 political activism. Both are out in public. What did the publisher then title this wordless score? "Women's Rights. Ladies Take Your Own Choice," suggesting

Fig. 3.9. "Women's Rights. Ladies Take Your Own Choice, Polka and Mazurka," the cover to sheet music, published in New York in 1851, as one of a number of compositions referring to the "freedom dress" movement that appeared in the wake of the first U.S. women's rights conventions.

(by way of ridicule) the mid-century applicability of both phrases, in concert, to popular dance modes, window-shopping, sartorial options, and political commitments alike (fig. 3.9). Modern life had become a game of choosing among tightly choreographed options for both how to present oneself and how to forge alliances with others.

After Mill

Now I realize that dance cards for waltzes, the trinkets or *bibelots* of the cotillon, and polkas scored for piano might seem like rather minor stuff to bother lifting out of the realm of the antique store—except for the timing. Note that they all took off in the middle of the nineteenth century, just when new social norms related to affective choice were being embodied and internalized as part of such leisure-time activities as courting. This was, moreover, the moment when an explicitly liberal conception of women's rights, building on a conception of freedom tied to the practice of choice-making, was starting on both sides of the Atlantic to come into existence as a lived politics. Mainly, the latter took the form of movements: collective, civil society efforts that would splinter and grow in various ways through the end of the century in response to changes in both women's ideas and women's experience. That, and the possibility, also generated by liberalizing regimes, of ordinary people of both sexes assembling and organizing to forge yet more cultural changes.

Of course, any kind of activism that could be called feminist (to use an anachronistic expression until at least the 1890s) was still very much a minority current through the century's end. This is also, importantly, not a story of steady ascension; the cause of women's liberty and equality has waxed and waned in various parts of the globe to this day. What's more, we need to recognize its distinctive inflections over time as well as space. Nineteenth-century framings, which remained as attached to the good of society as to that of individuals, are a far cry from today's "choice feminism," with its considerably wider arena of acceptable options and considerably diminished concern with either judgments of or responsibilities to others. Much of the emphasis in the early years also focused on gaining access—say, to property or to education—rather than gaining choice as the means to autonomy.

Yet, in the second half of the century, associations of women's "rights" with expanded opportunities for choice-making, not to mention enhanced choices, did more than pop up on the pages of treatises. They became, for the first time, the foundation for recognizable causes in a political sense. They were also enlisted to cover more domains of human action, some already in Mill and Taylor's sights and some newer. What these domains shared is that they were built upon the continuing salience of "The Choice" as a critical decision, given a set of acknowledged options, about the future uses of one's own (at times female, at times unspecified) body and affections in relation to those of others.

These varied efforts also very clearly extended the question of women's self-determination and, ultimately, self-definition beyond the question of getting into or out of a permanent heterosexual pair. As the American novelist and lecturer Charlotte Perkins Gilman announced at the close of the century, it was the differential range of choice-making opportunities available to (white) men and women *beyond* marriage that now defined their distinct horizons: "To the young man confronting life, the world lies wide. Such powers as he has he may use, he must use. If he chooses wrong at first, he may choose again, and yet again. . . . To the young woman confronting life there is the same world beyond, there are the same energies and human desires and ambition within. But all that she may wish to have, all that she may wish to do, must come through a single channel and a single choice . . . all, must come to her through a small gold ring."[88] And it was this difference that ultimately required rectifying.

What spheres did Gilman have in mind? Where else in the course of the human life cycle, beyond marriage, did the female half of the population require more access to choice itself? One area of growing political agitation in the latter part of the nineteenth century all across the industrial West concerned women's participation in *productive labor*, which is to say, the world of paid employment outside their own homes. A debate emerged in much of the Western Hemisphere about what jobs, with what provisions, should be made explicitly available to women, but also how much autonomy individual women should have in terms of which professions (and professional training) or even specific positions they could legitimately pursue. Did women's entitlement to an education contain a "right to a choice of vocation; that is, the right to a choice of the end to which those faculties should be trained,"[89] as the American transcendentalist women's rights advocate Caroline Healy Dall insisted in the 1850s? This was both an extension of a debate about marriage and a related question insofar as the answer was typically thought to depend (as it did for Mill) on whether the woman in question was unmarried, married, or once-married, even as many women in the industrial age had, in fact, no choice but to engage permanently in the world of remunerative work. Employment had started to become a symbol of a certain kind of independence and stature that went beyond the pocketbook.[90] For male characters in nineteenth-century novels, by contrast to female ones, it is choice of profession that is typically *the* choice.

At the same time, new arguments also took off about what kinds of sorting mechanisms could be developed, beyond informal connections, to help individuals (including women) choose one another with the least harm or financial risk to either party in this second contractual landscape. The era of the cotillon was, after all, also the era of the expansion of a formal labor marketplace that depended, ostensibly, upon matching employers' and employees' desires. It was also another important moment for the development of new tools and institutions—from job placement bureaus, to private and trade union–based employment agencies, to newspaper want-ads—as well as new forms of training and certification, to abet the selection process.[91]

Moreover, while a small number of women sought a new vision of unfettered power to contract without interference outside the family context, many others (and their male advocates) increasingly demanded more formal rules surrounding the workplace. Those ranged from a limit on the length of the workday to safety precautions while there. The argument for mandated shorter hours was, in good part, the imperative of guaranteeing both married and unmarried women's choice of work, if not choice of how to spend the hours on the job. It was also protecting some modicum of "free" time outside the job. Competition and the expansion of consent went too, after 1848, with labor reform efforts largely focused on regulating just how exploitative a labor contract could be, especially for poor women, women bearing children or likely to, and children themselves. This is a well-known story, often told by labor historians and historians of feminism alike, though it is rarely framed in terms of the history of choice or, especially, bounded choice.[92]

For closely related, and with less initial support or success, choice also became, as the century drew to a close, an important concept and term in a fight concerning maternity or *reproductive labor*. Originally, the argument revolved around what was known as "voluntary motherhood."[93] If women were to have an enhanced sphere of choice when it came to the moment of marriage, some women's rights advocates both in the United States and in Europe asked, why should they not have a similar prerogative when it came to whether to have children within that marriage or, at least, how many and when? But then came a more scandalous ask, especially from socialist women: for access to birth control, including before marriage, and even—by 1900—abortion, when all else failed. For as the pioneering French psychiatrist, socialist, and women's rights advocate Madeleine Pelletier put it just after the turn of the century, "It is up to the woman, and the woman alone, to decide if and when she wants to be a mother."[94] At stake was partly a pragmatic (and enduring) question about how to reconcile raising children with work *and* marriage. In Pelletier's framing, though, this was also a question about bodily and sexual freedom for the individual, which meant a profound challenge to expectations for family life and long-established gender roles within. When Nora, the female protagonist of Henrik Ibsen's notorious play *A Doll's House* (1879), walks out on her husband and family, what so shocked late nineteenth-century audiences was that this was not thought to be an option on any woman's existing menu—until then.

Such arguments would ricochet around the world for the next few decades, producing variants as well as counterarguments from Stockholm to Boston to the cities of colonial India, at the same time as new means of family planning were simultaneously being developed, employed, and formally restricted.[95] Children and families themselves lost some of their autonomy with the rise in much of the world of compulsory schooling and formal restrictions on child labor. But adult women's trajectory was different. Eventually, as we will see, choice in, first, employment and, then, marriage and family formation would become enshrined as human rights principles, and specific women's ones at that, even as they remain among the most contested issues around the globe today.

We can even point to a certain kind of continuity at the level of argu-mentation since the late nineteenth century, though accelerated in the twentieth and into the twenty-first. Most of the etiquette of the ball-room, along with small-scale technologies like the dance card, died away with World War I, only ever to be revived again in moments of deliberate nostalgia. So did the intense strictures around gender and status; the range of choices available to both sexes about, for example, whom they can love and how they can court has continued to expand in much of the world, albeit with certain newer limitations, such as those related to the age at which one can legitimately give consent. But remnants of this discourse about bodily autonomy and choice still ap-pear in many passionate defenses of abortion, a subject to which we will return at this book's end. Just as importantly, they also suffuse recent battles over gay marriage.

Being homosexual or bisexual is not, at present, typically framed as a lifestyle choice or preference, like something one can try on in a dress-ing room, any more than being heterosexual is; sexual identity is instead generally understood as being intrinsic to who one is in some deeper sense. But the fight for the legalization of gay marriage in the early twenty-first century in many places successfully combined this basically bio-essentialist claim with a recognizably liberal conception of marriage that was all about the significance of unfettered choice as a way both to achieve what one most desires and to have dignity as an individual.

In a decisive Massachusetts Supreme Court case of 2003 (*Goodridge v. Department of Public Health*), which marked a turning point on the path toward the legalization of gay marriage in the United States, for exam-ple, the majority of the court found the existing state law on civil mar-riage unconstitutional because it denied the plaintiff the "right to marry a person of one's choice." That meant the person most suitable in one's *own* estimation, not the person judged to be most suitable by others. As such, it reaffirmed individual, if interdependent, choice, rooted in the fulfillment of one's own interests and wishes, as the essential ele-ment in the institution of marriage. What was at stake, according to the majority opinion, was nothing less than "personal liberty."[96] Ultimately, by the time of the Supreme Court's decision in *Obergefell v. Hodges*

(2015), which legalized gay marriage across the United States, questions of sexual equality had become central to the winning argument as well. But the movement as a whole was framed around considerably older notions of freedom, which is to say, freedom of choice and freedom-as-choice, independent of birth family or community wishes or social norms and expectations and without social penalties or stigma, when it came to one's desires. In fact, responding to this essentially liberal conception of choice formed the heart of the arguments of the opposition too.[97]

There is, however, a crucial missing piece in this story as I've narrated it so far. Choice in the domain of sexuality has, from the beginning, been just as much a political question as either a legal or a customary one. Furthermore, from the tail end of the age of revolutions onward, arguments for expanded choice for women in areas related to the private, familial sphere were increasingly coupled—in a direct challenge to fundamental liberal norms—with demands for choice in the political sphere as well. Think elections, the hallmark of democracy, from which female citizens were almost entirely excluded in the postrevolutionary world. More and more in the second half of the nineteenth century and into the twentieth, women (like other excluded populations) around the world agitated for the right to take part in this particular kind of *collective* choice-making, again focused on other people (i.e., representatives of their political views). For the vote, pro-suffrage women believed, would ultimately allow them to determine the scope and scale of most other choices that they would be afforded. Plus, as choice-making became more important as a general social action, being denied this fundamental one became a more offensive form of subordination. And this time proponents not only made that case in public; they also demanded that the state itself make or, really, remake the rules.

This effort came to fruition surprisingly slowly. Individualized, preference-based, and largely value-neutral choice-making was itself exceptionally late to be put into practice in the domain we might have thought would be first—national political life—despite the wave of quasi-democratic revolutions that swept across continental Europe and the North and South Atlantic in the second half of the eighteenth

century and the first half of the nineteenth. That was true in the case of
men, as heads of households, even as the ranks of voters among them
grew steadily. It was even more true for women, for reasons we will see.

And yet, what's perhaps more remarkable is how thoroughly the
change became normalized, even naturalized, once it happened—and
how little trace of its controversial past it ultimately left behind. For
once laws establishing secret balloting alongside mass and, eventually,
universal male suffrage were enacted in one nation after another across
much of the world in the last three decades of the nineteenth century,
voting for candidates for office as yet another instantiation of personalized, individual choice-making quickly came to seem altogether ordinary
and even mundane. Arguably, such laws then also helped make it easier
to take seriously the long-standing minority cause of women's suffrage,
which, by the start of the twentieth century, had small but dedicated
adherents around the globe eager to build on a century of changes in
choice-based behavior in both politics and social life. That's despite lingering negative associations of women with the act of choosing in any
form. The public performance of private balloting by men *and* women
with which we are all intimately acquainted (at least for the moment)
should be seen as a critical element of the growing standardization of
rule-bound practices of choice, or bounded freedom, that liberalism
ultimately imposed between the last quarter of the nineteenth century
and the middle of the twentieth on much of the world.

CHAPTER 4

VOTING BY BALLOT—OR POLITICAL CHOICE

Pontefract

This chapter starts not with a single person, practice, or technical innovation but instead with a single event—or, really, nonevent. In mid-August 1872, reporters and election agents from all over Great Britain and beyond descended on the small West Yorkshire town of Pontefract to observe an "experiment" or "trial" in a new form of choice-making. The result was almost uniformly described as successful. It was also called remarkably dull. Newspaper accounts of the fateful day focus, significantly, on all that did not occur.

Few drunken people appeared in the streets. The town's many tavern owners racked up no more sales than on an ordinary day. The market center was quiet, as church bells fell silent along with local bands. Crowds bearing banners or wearing politically significant colors failed to make a show of themselves. There were few arrests for either disorderliness or, as some anticipated, public declarations of where one's loyalties lay. Speeches were kept to a minimum, and no one pelted anyone else with eggs. Even at the polls, confusion was limited, though the relatively high number of illiterate men in the Pontefract area had been a cause in some quarters for condescending concern. The same went (despite the town's contrary reputation) for "crowding," "delay," "rioting," "tumultuous conduct," or "political saturnalia" on anyone's part. The *Bristol Mercury* told readers "not the slightest breach of the peace was reported."[1] The *Daily News* of London noted "a total absence of excitement and apparently of interest."[2] The London *Times* relayed that the tradespeople of Pontefract and neighboring Knottingley had said: "'It hardly seemed like an election,' . . . and they were right."[3]

As for what actually *did* take place on the occasion of an off-year by-election that became England's first parliamentary election ever to be conducted by secret ballot: reporters could really only, at the risk of illustrating dullness firsthand, describe what the *Times* characterized as the vote's "practical workings" and the *Leeds Mercury* called "mechanical operations."[4] So readers learned that on the stated day, at "that unearthly and unwholesome hour" of 8 a.m. (as one Dublin-based reporter put it), a requisite five makeshift polling stations opened across the district.[5] To these schoolrooms-turned-suffrage headquarters—"remarkable," in one case, primarily for its "bare walls, empty benches and small windows," according to the *Daily News*—enfranchised men alone were admitted, just a few at a time, and under the watch of local police.[6] Posters had already appeared all over town in previous days stating the terms of the Ballot Act of 1872 that made this new method of suffrage now obligatory across Great Britain and detailing how and when and where voters should proceed in their performance of this critical civic responsibility. The two candidates had already handed in their nominations at the Pontefract Town Hall the afternoon before, a by-product of the Ballot Act abolishing traditionally raucous public nomination days right along with the standard practice of open voting. The next step in the procedure was the casting of the vote itself.

For the local elector, continued the Dublin correspondent reporting by "special wire" for *Freeman's Journal and Daily Commercial Advertiser*, was required to follow a novel series of physical acts, or what we might call a different kind of formal choreography, for registering his personal choice between the two nominees for Member of Parliament (MP) for Pontefract borough:

> The elector enters [the polling station] and produces a card, which he obtained from the town clerk yesterday in token of his right to

vote. He presents this to the presiding officer, who consults the number and name on the card and then refers to the electoral roll. Finding all correct he tears out a voting paper [paper ballot], which is connected by a perforated line with a counterfoil or block, exactly as in a cheque book. He writes the elector's number on the roll on the counterfoil or block and on the paper. He hands the paper to a clerk, who stamps it back and front with an official stamp, the presiding officer observing. The paper is then handed to the voter, who steps into one of the little boxes, like a pawnbroker's box (I have seen such a thing), and places a cross thus (X) at the right hand side of the name of the candidate for whom he votes. This done, he doubles the paper in two, keeping his X on the inside and showing the official stamp on the outside. He then presents this stamp outward to the presiding officer, who nods assent if all be right, and the voter then drops the paper into the ballot box and retires.

Just to be clear, the correspondent went on, "this ballot-box"—which was the other key innovation, along with the paper ballot and the enclosed voting booth—"is like any other box, about two and a-half feet square, with an opening about a quarter of an inch in depth and four or five inches in length," the implication being that for such an important technology in making manifest the people's preferences, it too could hardly be called remarkable.[7]

At the close of the polls at 4 p.m., the contents of the five sealed ballot boxes were then unfolded and counted by a similarly elaborate procedure. This, too, was largely hidden from public view, though it was overseen inside the Pontefract Town Hall by a phalanx of election officials, assistants, candidates' agents, and the candidates themselves. Four hours later, after a slight uptick in merriment in the streets around the town's eighteenth-century marketplace, the suspense was ended. The mayor, acting as returning officer (i.e., election overseer), announced at 8 p.m. from the balcony of the Town Hall the winning candidate's name. In this exceptional public moment, the meaning of the entire exercise— the quantifiably determined aggregation of all of the district's male electors' personal choices into a collective selection of a single parliamentary representative—was made clear to the people of Pontefract and their unusual number of out-of-town guests.

Reporters tried, in some cases, to add a bit of local color to this rather dry account of operations. A few journalists turned to history, noting that the town was an ancient one, home of a castle of significance at the time of the Civil War and now a picturesque ruin, a place where elections for MPs had been taking place since 1297. Others mentioned the surrounding landscape, marked by pasture, coal beds, and the cultivation of licorice. (A stamp from the leading local manufacturing plant for licorice cakes, Dunhill's, was used to seal the wax on at least one of the original Pontefract pine ballot boxes, as the totemic item displayed in the Pontefract Museum indicates today [fig. 4.1].) The state of the hotels at which election officials and journalists congregated, the prettiness of the local women, the economic conditions of the residents, the strange Yorkshire dialect: they all drew commentary as well. Our amateur ethnographer, "come all the way from Dublin to see how the Ballot worked," tried to heighten the sense of observing a strange people at an alien pursuit by noting, "I do believe that Telegu is a much nicer and more intelligible form of speech than the dialect which prevails in Yorkshire. I have been as totally dumbfounded by these people as I should have been were I beside Dr. Livingston in the heart of Central Africa."[8]

Still others tried to imagine the inner psychology of the 1,941 (presumed to be largely backward) enfranchised male inhabitants who were engaging in this ritual exercise in individual choice-making for the first time—or who chose to sit it out, presumably out of fear of falling afoul of the process in some way or because, as a writer for the *Times* speculated, "a good many uneducated persons hate handling a pen even to make their mark."[9] Our Dublin reporter assumed that at least at first, "in the mind of the yokel," the entire process must have seemed both unnatural and a bit burdensome: "The voting is so solemn—secrecy is always solemn—that men go to the booth with quite a serious air, and a deep sense of responsibility."[10] The local *Leeds Mercury* followed the *Times* in judging the humbler class of voters acutely nervous about what was being asked of them by way of performance, since the instructions required "going alone and unbefriended to a compartment" as well as having to make a mark "in the right place and opposite the right name."[11]

Fig. 4.1. An 1872 Pontefract ballot box, saved as a local treasure to mark the town's place in the history of secret voting in England.

Both newspapers claimed that those who managed to complete the final step in the process, dropping their ballot in a box, then generally bolted for the door in relief and only took a deep breath once they were back on the street. But other observers imagined that though secret voting might now be something of an acquired taste, electors would soon be studying politics to "see what is to be said for men and measures," as Lord Frederick Cavendish put it in a speech excerpted by the *Pall-Mall Gazette*, and "a positive taste for the exercise of the franchise" would develop.[12] Eventually, even ordinary men in their capacity as voters would appreciate their "power and independence," in the words of the correspondent for *Lloyd's Weekly Newspaper*.[13] They would, in sum, feel themselves growing confident as full-fledged, autonomous choosers in the realm of public affairs.

Such commentary on local customs and mentalities helped as much to bolster preexisting political positions (for the Ballot Act was very much a Liberal party effort in 1872) as to gussy up otherwise dry accounts of an operating procedure smoothly executed. Pro-secret-ballot newspapers emphasized how few ballots were spoiled by voter incompetence (25 out of 1,236 cast)[14] and how the uneventfulness of the election proved that even the most ignorant, rural men could, in the end, handle the business of independent choice-making. The antiballoting press stressed, by contrast, the simplicity of the voters' task (only two candidates to choose between meant marking one of only two squares), not to mention the relative paucity of enfranchised men or strong party passions in such an out-of-the-way, "sleepy" borough.[15] They then used this information to urge that no generalizations about efficacy be drawn from this one, albeit successful, experiment in the individuation and privatization of political choice—except for the unusual degree of absenteeism, or refusal to choose, that it had engendered.

On both sides, though, there seems to have been an implicit awareness that there could be no turning the clock back, despite the limited duration of the Ballot Act's terms, that what was to follow would be a matter of tinkering with procedure rather than a return to the old communal electoral status quo (which we will come to shortly). The *Times* was already predicting, based on "the single instance of Pontefract," the rise of a new kind of expert, the adept in "the art and science of [the] Ballot."[16] Furthermore, in Victorian terms, an increase in uneventfulness and proceduralism marked progress, and what had transpired in Pontefract was nothing less than a triumph in the precincts of the boring. *The Way We Live Now*, Anthony Trollope's great novel of Victorian politics serialized in 1874–75, contains an extended satire of an election by secret ballot right down to the reporter "looking for paragraphs as to the conduct of electors." Alas, the polling station at Covent Garden on the occasion of this fictional election is "wonderfully quiet." For "with the ballot,—so said the leader of the understrappers [junior officials],—there never was any excitement."[17] No wonder historians have not had much to say about this "event" either.

In the end, even the results of the 1872 Pontefract parliamentary by-election were anticlimactic. The introduction of the ballot produced a victory for the Liberal incumbent, Hugh Childers, though by a smaller margin than the previous time around. (It hurt Childers's Conservative opponent, the young Lord Pollington, that the latter had announced that he would surely win since he had had the good fortune to pick a four-leaf shamrock upon arriving in town—that, and the fact that not long before he, too, had been a Liberal.) Not only was this result an anticipated finale to their respective campaigns, proving the advent of the secret ballot would have few direct consequences for the makeup of Parliament; it did not engender much by way of public celebrating or remonstrating after the fact either. Normal quotidian life continued up through the polling and after. As the local *Leeds Mercury* reported, "Men went about their work during the day just as though no election were taking place."[18] The ballot had already begun the process of pushing the action of choosing in the political realm into the hidden recesses of the voter's mind, on the one hand, and the indoor, makeshift voting booth, on the other. Voting in public spaces but privately—in the dual senses of according to one's interior inclinations and away from the scrutiny of others, including one's peers and bemused journalists—had accomplished just what it was supposed to, according to its long-standing proponents. That was to make the act of selecting a preferred representative feel free because uncoerced (financially, physically, or psychologically). But it was also to produce a result that would collectively be taken as fair and closed to challenge or even excitement precisely because of this fact.

All of this likely sounds rather obvious to us now too, so used are we to doing it almost precisely this way. Voting is widely understood to be a means to express or instantiate individual choice in the service of group choice (in this case about individual people—representatives—who will themselves eventually be voting on matters of concern to the collectivity). And voting shielded from fellow citizens' eyes and ears, albeit publicly performed in a central location, is understood to be the only effective way to protect those self-generated choices, that is, to make sure they are freely given. (After all, coerced choices cannot be genuine ones, as Protestant theologians had insisted long before.) For almost three-quarters of a century now, use of the secret ballot—shorthand for both a state-mandated technology and a state-mandated procedure centered on removing the elector from external pressure at the magic moment of casting his or her vote so as to protect his or her self-generated choices reflective of his or her personal preferences—has been an established part of human rights doctrine. Indeed, it too is enshrined in the Universal Declaration of Human Rights as a basic requirement that a democratic state must protect.[19] This is despite wide geographical variance across nations in terms of eligibility to vote, the organization of polling stations, the forms of ballots and booths, the days and hours of voting, and the frequency of elections, not to mention differences in local electoral cultures, including whether one is obliged to choose as a democratic duty (as in Australia or Argentina) or to choose is itself a choice (as in the United States).[20]

But that is also what draws us back to that signal day in the Yorkshire town of Pontefract. For all its seeming banality, the trial run of the secret ballot in August 1872 should actually be viewed as a major (albeit largely unacknowledged even in its moment) historical landmark. It suggests the concretization of a conceptualization of popular sovereignty quite distinct from that which galvanized revolutionaries on both sides of the North Atlantic at the close of the previous century. At a minimum, this observation indicates a need for reperiodization of the stages in the invention of contemporary democracy.[21] More importantly for our purposes here, the unspectacular proceedings at Pontefract demand to be seen as the culmination of the ongoing reimagining of choice-making of which this book tells the story.

When put back into a history of voting procedures and, indeed, of choice-making across multiple arenas, the adoption of the secret ballot in the place of open, communal voting in late nineteenth-century Britain marks the importation and incorporation of certain kinds of choice-making behaviors already long familiar from other realms of western European and American social life (which may explain why it caused so little agitation in its moment) into what had been one of the last areas of theoretical resistance. That is the political life of the nation. Ultimately, the introduction of the secret ballot on a national and then global scale helped cement several assumptions that were new to political thinking even in the second half of the nineteenth century but that were central in the enshrinement of choice-making as the defining activity of the modern citizen, just as they were for the consumer, the reader-turned-commonplacer, and the spouse, if not wage laborer on the job. Only in this case, they were, initially, exclusively the prerogative of adult men.

What were these assumptions? The first is that when it comes to politics, "independent" people—the definition of which was and is permanently subject to debate and long excluded almost all women regardless of age—have judgments and preferences that can be discerned and measured, just as they can when we are talking about consumer goods or worldviews or romantic partners. What follows from this presupposition is a second, which takes the form of a problem: these judgments and preferences are not likely to be shared across the board, even if focused on the collective good, precisely *because* they are rooted largely in personal and privately held values, tastes, aspirations, and consciences. For all people are at once roughly alike in their capacities and singular in their preferences; there can be no single correct choice for all. Moreover, that's okay. So, third, what people can and should agree on is procedure or means, not ends. The state and its agents have a responsibility to equitably organize, manage, and adjudicate, via formal laws, regulations, and technical solutions, the performance of collective choice-making in politics (even if we are just talking about electing representatives or proxies to do the actual decision making), as well as the menu of options itself. But the state must remain neutral about the content of those choices both before and after they are made. Finally, and contrary to older traditions, the right procedure or means for conducting this business, with the right degree of oversight, constitutes not just a path to freedom. The act and experience of engaging in this semipublic procedure—literally, entering a secure compartment in a public space, privately marking a ballot with an X next to one's preferred option or options, and dropping that ballot in the specially designated box—constitutes freedom tout court. This is what modern freedom is supposed to feel like.

What we need to keep in mind, despite how it might seem today, is that there is nothing obvious or inexorable about the process by which these essentially liberal assumptions developed or turned into truisms in the course of the nineteenth century, just as there is nothing natural about the turn to the secret ballot as their carrier. Neither the new election ideology nor the new election process of the Victorian age was an immediate outgrowth of the old idea of popular sovereignty. Neither was the direct result of the arrival of market-based consumption, the pluralization of the world of ideas, or new forms of courtship and marriage either, though these various domains would structurally come to have more in common with one another over time. On the contrary, the business of politics was slower to be subject to individuated choice *or* extended to all adults regardless of class, race, religion, or gender than was the world of consumer goods or, for that matter, that of beliefs or romantic and sexual attraction. It was also stimulated by different impulses and regulated and constrained by a different set of institutions and authorities. The story of Pontefract and the subsequent late nineteenth-century mainstreaming of the secret ballot around much of the world is the story of the late transformation of politics, on its own terms, into yet another distinct arena for the sanctification of personal, preference-driven, and bounded choice-making as constitutive of freedom. It was also complicated from the start by preexisting gender norms that would ultimately be manipulated by both men and women to change the face of political life in the twentieth and twenty-first centuries.

The Deep History of the Secret Ballot

Victorians did not invent the ballot, the ballot box, the voting booth, or even the idea of declaring one's political predilections in semi-secret, away from the prying eyes and ears of one's neighbors. Experiments in balloting—Victorian advocates were happy to note—went back to antiquity, and enthusiasm for these antique efforts had, as early as the mid-seventeenth century, taken on new life in the hands of self-declared republicans. James Harrington, in his utopian tract *The Commonwealth of Oceana* (1656), had memorably extolled the complex secret voting methods of the great city-state of Venice and, before that, Rome. In a passage that was resuscitated as a rhetorical crutch everywhere from an obscure 1705 tract with the title *The Patriot's Proposal to the People of England Concerning the Ballot: The Best Way of Choosing their Representatives in Parliament* to the columns of reporters covering Pontefract in 1872, Harrington had already defended the ballot with the claim that it "increased the freedom of their [male voters'] Judgment." For, according to Harrington's reasoning, "the election or suffrage of the people is freest, where it is made or given in such a manner, that it can neither oblige (*qui beneficium accepit libertatem vendidit*) nor disoblige another; nor through fear of an enemy, or bashfulness toward a friend, impair a man's [*sic*] liberty."[22]

It was also widely noted in the nineteenth century that secret societies and private clubs, also all-male, had long-standing rituals for selecting members that operated quite similarly to a Venetian election. The term "blackballing" comes from the practice of using white and black balls to vote secretly for or against the admission of new members (a point of which Childers reminded his constituents while urging them to, in effect, "black-ball Lord Pollington").[23] Moreover, paper balloting, with greater and lesser degrees of secrecy and success, had been used intermittently and with regional variance in both the United States and France since the late eighteenth century as a means to choose representatives for popular assemblies.

Yet we have largely forgotten (unlike our Victorians) that in neither nation had the age of revolutions, with its celebrated declarations of individual rights and popular rule, made voting in this now obligatory fashion obvious or anything like a standard. Quite the opposite: surprisingly little discussion of mechanisms of selection for political representatives took place anywhere in the Atlantic world in the late eighteenth century. (The Marquis de Condorcet, who has lent his name to a kind of voting still in use, was the rare exception in taking up such questions.)

In France and North America too, multiple methods of voting, in multiple kinds of elections, survived well into the late nineteenth century, including voting viva voce or *à haute voix*, by raising of hands, by moving to one side of the room or exiting it entirely, by depositing beans or lots or even bullets in boxes, as well as by paper balloting—and sometimes in combinations thereof. So did all kinds of versions of publicity for one's stance, from poll books recording individual votes to be tallied at the end of the proceedings to voting by general, collective acclamation.[24]

Yes, suffrage, at the level of symbolism, was central to the new constitutional order, a marker of the significance accorded to the consent and then rule of the people. Consider how much voting mattered in the buildup to the meeting of the Estates-General in France in 1789; as Thomas Jefferson put it then, "All the world here is occupied in electioneering, in chusing [*sic*] or being chosen."[25] Consider, too, how little attention either French or American revolutionaries ever gave to the ancient (and actually rather practical) idea of a lottery, or chance rather than conscious choice, as a means to determine representatives of "the people." Political choice, as represented by events called elections, was, in fact, established early on as a vital element of both nations' modern founding myths.[26] But in most instances, traditional early modern *means* of selection, from beans to balls to written forms, were simply adapted with little discussion or fanfare to new circumstances, most likely to avoid any discussion of the possibility of dissension or conflicting choices. Choice generally assumed the same level of abstraction in late eighteenth-century discussions of elections as consent did in early contract theory.

Moreover, when the subject did come up for debate, particular suffrage methods and particular political inclinations did not always find themselves similarly allied. In France during the Revolution, for example, it was radicals who most favored fully public and preferably consensual voting—not surprisingly, as they were eager to use suffrage to express an indivisible and consensual general will. Conservatives and moderates were more likely to demand secrecy, as evidenced by the first (and extremely short-lived) constitutional requirement of a secret ballot in 1795, which was motivated by a fear of collusion on the part of ordinary working people or pressure from below.[27] Either way, no one in France imagined, except in conjunction with this brief experiment, offering the voter a slate of declared candidates from which to pick or menu of concrete options. Instructions to voters posted in electoral assembly halls starting in May 1790 required them to swear under oath to name "only those whom you have chosen [*choisis*] in your soul and conscience as the most worthy of public confidence, without it having been determined by gifts, promises, solicitations or threats," but also without giving any further guidance as to who those people might be.[28] The idea was that the enfranchised would use their power simply to identify the most virtuous or appropriate-seeming embodiment of the will and sentiments of the community as a whole. (After all, it was also assumed that anyone actually suitable by these criteria would refuse to put himself forward for public choosing, lest it look like he thought he deserved to rule over others.) The objective was unlimited choice, or leaving all options open, even if it led on occasion to such a profusion of different names being put forth that "the people" were left with no real choice at all.

Still, the opposite could also be the case, as it was for the agitators associated with the New York Sons of Liberty, who fought for the secret ballot in 1769–70 explicitly as a way to protect themselves against bosses and landlords, or pressure from on high to cast their vote in ways that benefited the powerful only. Sounding much like Harrington, these Radical Whigs demanded that viva voce voting be replaced by balloting, as was already the norm in Philadelphia and Boston, for the sake of "all honest Burghers and Tradesmen who may incline to Vote contrary to the Sentiments, of their Employers or Landlords."[29] The policy was not adopted. But over the next few decades, the drafters of many of the new U.S. state constitutions proposed "experiments" with secret balloting, seeing similarly good reasons to break with the English mode—though, in the nineteenth century, balloting also became a way, much like literacy tests, to disenfranchise Black and immigrant voters, and earlier, balloting was used to suppress Native ones.[30] In practice, methods of polling the electorate varied in the late eighteenth and nineteenth centuries from colony to colony and then from state to state and sometimes even town to town, with regular reversals of policy depending on the political winds.[31] This heterogeneity is a condition that has lasted in the United States, within the parameters of a now obligatory secrecy, to this day.

We are thus left to conclude that there was never any single ideological bias inherent in the secret ballot, only a technology that, in most places, ran counter to custom. It could enable dissent and become a tool of empowerment for oppressed or disgruntled parts of the electorate. It could also, literally, keep an electorate in line and marginalize what were perceived to be dangerous voters and their worrisome impact. But then again, there was no consensus in the age of revolutions, before the true age of party, that an election was an occasion for competition rooted in individual voters' personal and freestanding choices among clearly stated options. There was also no agreement that those options represented varied, mutually exclusive visions of the community's future course from which one had an obligation, right, or even capacity to make a selection by oneself. What's more, the idea that women would participate in the process was not initially much discussed, even as gender and choice remained tightly wrapped up in one another conceptually.

English Tradition

And ironically, nowhere was hostility to the secret ballot as an election technology quite so deeply ingrained as a matter of custom and quite so attached to standards of masculinity and class-based morality as in England, home of some of the first experiments in the institutionalization of menu-based choice in other domains. The Glorious Revolution of the late seventeenth century had enshrined the notion of popular sovereignty as a principle, in contradistinction to most of continental Europe. But it had not followed that this idea required translation into a new electoral system that helped secure regular, individualized determinations of political preferences. On the contrary: at the end of the seventeenth century and well into the eighteenth, voting in England remained strictly limited by gender, income, and status; it was a prerogative of the few and the privileged among men alone. Moreover, even the affirmation in the early eighteenth century of the requirement of regular elections for MPs (every seven years became the new maximum wait as of 1716) did not necessitate that there be clearly delineated and multiple selections from which electors were to choose or even standardized districts in which one could do so. By the early nineteenth century, enfranchised residents of some counties and boroughs had not experienced a contested parliamentary election for many generations.[32] If late eighteenth-into-nineteenth-century French elections featured too many candidates and hence too much choice, their English counterparts were characterized by a long tradition of rarely having anything to do with choice at all.

At the heart of the English conception of suffrage was the idea that the vote was a privilege and obligation held by "independent" men on behalf of nonelectors. Electors were entrusted with collective determination of the collective good, an idea that was thought to require neither competition among candidates nor a way to measure the population's preferences, sentiments, and judgments on a person-by-person basis. In all their superior wisdom, well-off, property-owning men—those who were independent in both the economic and intellectual sense—were to decide on representatives on behalf of and, in principle, in the interest of their social, economic, and (it duly followed) intellectual inferiors, much as adults theoretically vote on behalf of children's interests today.[33]

As for those *without* the franchise, a category that included all women, all young people, and most poor men: they could consider themselves perfectly free, in the long-established sense of experiencing no direct interference in their lives as English people, without belonging to the voter rolls. Furthermore, in practice, lacking the vote no more hindered one person's ability to participate in civic or public activity at the local level than having the vote gave another a chance for self-expression or sharing his (and it was always "his") personal political sentiments, including approval or disapproval of a candidate or situation and desired future path. By the eighteenth century, it was a long-standing principle in English life, going back centuries, that elections were primarily rituals of affirmation and legitimation—for voters and nonvoters (including women) alike.[34] Even as they were often accompanied by a good deal of violence and even as money played a large role in the proceedings, their goal was ultimately mass participation and agreement rather than competition, selectivity, and choice in anything like a consumer vein. As historian Mark Kishlansky notes, before the mid-seventeenth century, voters "gave voices" rather than votes, and potential MPs said they were "standing for a seat" rather than running for one, precisely so as to downplay the sense of a battle for loyalties.[35] As elections became more frequent in the following century, no longer held only at the whim of the monarch, some greater competition for places did emerge. But old forms of electioneering survived, along with notions of honor (for those who presented themselves as potential MPs or shaped public opinion), deference (on the part of the socially subordinate), and unanimity that those forms supported.

Indeed, according to the landmark work on traditional election culture by Frank O'Gorman, the ritual, celebratory aspects of English elections actually intensified and reached their peak between the last decades of the eighteenth century and the first third of the next one.[36] Elections of this era constituted a form of extended theater that, at certain junctures, took over space (in the form of town halls, marketplaces, squares, inns, and city walls) and time (in the form of multiple days), as well as whole populations in urban centers and towns all across the nation. Though the Borough of Pontefract, as the English correspondent for the *New York Times* was to point out, had a reputation before that important day in August 1872 as "not very steady in its politics, and not indisposed to sell its votes to the highest bidder,"[37] it had traditionally fully committed itself, just like many other counties and boroughs in England, to making parliamentary elections into major local events.

How then, when it became necessary, did a broad public make its preferences among candidates known in the pre-1872 English system of suffrage? Imagine all the elements of a parliamentary election that our Pontefract correspondents claimed, with some considerable exaggeration, to have missed, starting with boisterous crowds in the streets. Now put most of them back into place.

In the days preceding a poll in the era before the Pontefract by-election of 1872, agents of the candidates would already have distributed a wealth of material objects pertinent to the event to come, from ribbons to handbills. The extended festivities, known as an election, would formally begin with a ceremony reminiscent of a royal entry: each candidate would be pulled into town in his carriage surrounded by cheering spectators of both sexes sometimes numbering in the thousands. Then, over the next few days, the candidates, accompanied by the local elite, would begin canvasing or courting the general population, electors and nonelectors alike, in a ritual rich with hints of (temporary) social inversion. In the same spirit, the business of lining up supporters generally produced a variety of treating rituals, namely, food and drink for the many at the candidates' expense. Such treats ostensibly offered candidates a way to express gratitude to their essential backers.

But it is what happened next, toward the end of the formal nomination day (which was abolished with the Ballot Act of 1872, along with written nominations), that was most strange from the perspective of the new kinds of rituals that developed afterward. That day, once the electoral breakfasts, the hours of additional processions to the hustings, and all the speeches that went with the business of nomination were finally over, the returning officer would typically ask for a show of hands during which it was often hard to tell voters from nonvoters among the assembled. The less popular candidate could demand a poll or an actual numerical calculation of support at this point. But if his chances seemed negligible, he would likely concede, and no formal tallying of votes would ever take place. The crowd would turn its attention immediately to the chairing of the victorious candidate, an event that symbolized community solidarity as well as, loosely, the power of the people over their parliamentary representative.

Alternately, when a poll was called for, it would likely start almost immediately, especially in smaller places, and could last anywhere from hours to days (until it was finally limited by law to one day for borough polls in 1835 and one day for county polls in 1853). The polling process would also be accompanied by more speeches by the candidates, more "competitive parading," since voters sometimes arrived in tallies with banners and music,[38] the cheering and jeering of spectators, and yet more treating, all aimed at swaying the voter's mind, or determining his choice, up to the last second. For at some point, the elector, often in earshot of his family members, neighbors, and employers or customers, would finally be asked to step up to a specially designed small wooden structure furnished with chairs and a table, give proof to a poll clerk that he was entitled to vote (usually his name, address, and occupation), sometimes swear an oath or two, and then publicly state his choices. Those choices would then be recorded, along with the elector's name, in a poll book that would be published by a local printer, allowing anyone interested to check after the fact precisely who chose whom.

It is a mistake to imagine this business as a free-for-all despite the noise of bands, the cheering of crowds, and the copious amounts of food and drink that marked the day and the celebrating that followed. Heavy police presence made sure that all the talk of the Englishman's liberty on the part of candidates eager for votes was also accompanied by the semblance of social order, not to mention deference to traditional elites when it counted. Laws on the books, including the Bribery Act (1729) and, later, the Corrupt Practices Act (1854), did much the same thing, as did highly scripted parade routes and roles. This was regulated unruliness.

But it is also worth keeping in mind that through much of the nineteenth century—and in great contrast to the Pontefract by-election in 1872, when only the formally enfranchised were let indoors, and only in small batches, to make their preferences known—every part of the process in the traditional culture of elections was open to all, including women and the poor, who had multiple ways to make their influence felt.[39] Even the one exclusive activity in the business of elections, casting a vote when called for, took place with the voter in close proximity to people who would remind him of his social position and obligations, starting with his family and his employees or bosses. And though political and religious issues were, at times, acknowledged by the candidates, suggesting differences of opinion that duplicated similar divergences in the population at large, and though candidates were constantly stressing the "independence" of the English voter, the whole business of elections in pre-1872 England was not primarily about giving "the people," or even a majority thereof, an opportunity to select a national political course. Elections were statements about community. They were also occasions for the extended, cross-class entertainment of residents, opportunities for the display of various loyalties and emotions, and chances to cement or enhance the

Plate 1. Paolo de' Matteis, *The Choice of Hercules* (1712), an allegorical painting of a classical theme in which Hercules, at the center, has a choice between the rocky path of virtue, on one side, and hedonism and vice, on the other, both represented as women. Hercules, though his body is torqued, is clearly turning toward the former as the better choice. The painting was commissioned by Anthony Ashley-Cooper, 3rd Earl of Shaftesbury, and completed based on his instructions about the attitudes and expressions of the figures; but Matteis also drew, as did many eighteenth-century painters on this subject, on Annibale Carracci's famed *Choice of Hercules* (1596), designed for the Palazzo Farnese in Rome.

LA COQUETTE FIXÉE

Plate 2. Jean Couché and Jacques Dambrun, *La Coquette fixée*, a 1785 engraving after a 1752–55 painting in the Rococo style by Jean-Honoré Fragonard. A flirtatious young woman (*coquette*), dressed as a shepherdess, has just made her selection between the two male suitors, dressed as shepherds, who flank her. Neither is clearly a better choice than the other, except in terms of her personal predilections. Note, too, the gender reversal of the Choice of Hercules theme.

Plate 3. Edouard Manet, *Masked Ball at the Opera* (1873), an extraordinary painting of modern sexual commerce in which women are both the objects of interest and—masked and costumed, unlike the well-dressed men who surround them—active participants in this charged ritual. The painting, with its subject spilling beyond the canvas and leaving only parts of bodies visible at the edges, works against either narrative closure or moralizing about its very contemporary subject. In the right foreground is a fallen dance card with the painter's signature on it.

Plate 4. William Hogarth, *Canvassing for Votes* (1754–55), a satire of Hercules's Choice insofar as the non-elite voter is being given a choice between two corrupt options—Tory and Whig—and, extending the corruption, is taking both in the form of two different bribes. As for the other figures in the image, they are all thoroughly engaged in the activities that led up to an eighteenth-century English election, but they are also profiting as best they can.

Plate 5. Jacob Lawrence, *The Migration Series, panel no. 59: In the North they had the freedom to vote* (1940–41), tempera on hardboard, The Phillips Collection, Washington, D.C. Black men and women, seen only from the back, wait in line to vote. They do so before a white policeman with a nightstick who represents the authority of the state but is not interfering in their orderly progress toward the voting booth, where they will each be able to register a political choice— unlike in the U.S. South in this moment. This radically spare, modernist image represents a new vision of freedom extended to a new group of people.

Plate 6. John Peto, *Take Your Choice!* (1885). In trompe l'oeil paintings of this era, objects often appear to be either projected toward the viewer into real space (as they are here) or arranged in an implied space behind the picture frame, such as a cupboard or cabinet. With the injunction to the viewer to "Take your choice!" this image plays both on the viewer's desire to actually select from among the used books on display and on his or her enjoyment of the pictorial fiction.

Plate 7. Jan van Eyk, photograph of young woman choosing a record at a coin-operated vending machine called, in Dutch, a *Grammofoonplatenautomat*, 1960. The history of both vending machines and automats to dispense food goes back to the late nineteenth century, but this image stands for the burgeoning American-style consumer culture of postwar Europe and the increased emphasis on choice for young men and women.

Plate 8. Barbara Kruger, *Untitled (Your body is a battleground)* (1989), photographic silkscreen on vinyl. Since the 1970s, Kruger has made work in multiple mediums that straddle the boundaries among art, political protest, and advertising. Her iconic 1987 image of a black-and-white photographic hand holding a small sign reading "I shop therefore I am" in her signature typography and color scheme can be read either as a condemnation of consumerism or as a factual statement about how we have been encouraged to define ourselves as individuals today: through our commercial choices. In the image above, she suggests the limits to that autonomy when it comes to women. Made initially for the 1989 Women's March on Washington, this image has been repeatedly deployed in defense of abortion rights ever since. One of the nine big questions Kruger went on to pose in her 1990 work *Untitled (Questions)* is "Who Is Free to Choose?"

reputation of an exalted local family. We might additionally (as today) look upon them as fund-raising events, since they were quickly followed by a wide range of payments, not least to lawyers who ran the local operations, tavern owners who enabled the treating, printers who created the copious campaign literature surrounding elections, and shopkeepers who supplied all of the necessary election furniture and related paraphernalia. These are all reasons why open elections, with both voters and hangers-on at the core, were to make such great set pieces for Victorian novelists, from Charles Dickens to George Eliot to (repeatedly) Trollope.[40] In this, open elections had much in common with balls.

"Take Your Choice!"

It was against this suffrage system that Major John Cartwright, in the paper equivalent to a public scream, exhorted his fellow British citizens just at the outbreak of the American war of independence in 1776 to "Take Your Choice!" The counterargument that arose with Cartwright's little tract of this name and that this English radical assiduously continued to promulgate in almost the same terms for the next sixty years had very limited impact in its moment. Only a small group of radicals and Nonconformists—men like the famed pottery merchant Josiah Wedgwood who were also invested in the politics of antislavery, free trade, and freedom of conscience—paid it much heed.[41] Its social reach was initially shallow too. But with his taste for exclamation points and heated prose, Cartwright made a strong case for suffrage reform by linking the vaunted old idea of English "independence" to the securitization of political choice on the part of individual citizens. The plea was less for a new political order than for practices that would allow the current one to work as promised. As Cartwright admonished his readers in the last lines of his introduction to this pamphlet: "Trust not, I say, in princes nor in ministers; but trust in YOURSELVES, and in representatives chosen by YOURSELVES alone! TAKE YOUR CHOICE!"[42] In his hands, making or taking a choice became a rallying cry and a symbol of freedom from political dependence or, indeed, enslavement.

Despite all the street-level action common at election time, Cart-wright, a country gentleman, burned with hostility to what he perceived to be oligarchic politics. From his perspective, what was ordinarily taken to be (legitimate and moral) "influence" over others—including in the business of voting—needed to be reconfigured as (illegitimate and im-moral) "corruption." American colonists, he believed, had been reduced to dependency and servitude by being denied the right to choose their own rulers or levels of taxation.[43] War in the North Atlantic gave him the opportunity to extend this argument to the political system at home. The same could be said, Cartwright claimed at the same moment as the American Declaration of Independence, of the individual Englishman. For the major failing of the current electoral regime was that the English voter's traditional independence, understood as the ability to make a choice for himself without being subject to the will of anyone else, was constantly being thwarted.[44]

A kindred message about the absence of anything like free, indi-vidual determinations on the part of English voters can be found earlier in William Hogarth's famous election image, *Canvassing for Votes*, inspired by the highly divisive Oxfordshire contest in the gen-eral election of 1754 (fig. 4.2). One of a series of paintings by Hogarth focused on election behavior and subsequently adapted as prints for wider circulation, *Canvassing for Votes* (1754–55) depicts what appears to be blatant corruption in many of the standard rituals leading up to the casting of the vote. In an obvious parody of Hercules's struggle between Virtue and Vice, the elector at the center is most promi-nently being given a tantalizing "choice" prior to arriving at the poll-ing station.[45] He has been offered competing bribes: from the Tories on one side and the Whigs on the other. Quite seriously, he is taking both. This is a satire of a choice that is, in effect, nothing of the sort, again more Hobson's than Hercules's. (The voter's only *real* choice, it seems, would be to sit the whole thing out.) But Hogarth's actual feel-ings about this state of affairs are ambiguous, with the comic and moral sitting uneasily together, just as in his depictions of auctions. This is, after all, much like the next painting in the series, *The Polling* (1754–55), also a great picture of unrestrained ambitions and desires and of the liveliness of the English crowd. The all-too-human voters

Fig. 4.2. William Hogarth, *Canvassing for Votes* (1754–55), the second painting in the series *Humours of an Election.*

are operating under the literal banner of liberty in both senses of the word (fig. 4.3).

Cartwright, by contrast, thought he had landed upon an actual solution to this state of affairs: not just more voters, more frequent elections, and more balanced electoral districts but also a new method of voting. A key piece of his reform program was a suffrage system in which the secret ballot assumed center stage as a proxy for liberty, understood as the preservation of the capacity of independent men to make their own choices in the public realm without hindrance. Cartwright's starting point was the recognition of mental equality, the idea that almost all men—and he meant men—have the psychological and intellectual resources necessary to participate in public life, as the proper basis of political equality. As he saw it, "natural reason and justice . . . abound in every honest man's mind," as do the "fundamental maxims of our law which he carries in his heart, and understands by his common sense."[46] Moreover, he argued in *Take Your Choice!*, his major text on the subject,

Fig. 4.3. William Hogarth, *The Polling* (1754–55), the third painting in the series *Humours of an Election.*

"*personality* [i.e., a man's personal character] is the *sole* foundation of the right of being represented; and . . . *property* has in reality, nothing to do in the case."[47] But recognition of this basic equality, in the form of the institution of universal manhood suffrage without regard for property qualifications, was not for Cartwright an end unto itself. In no way did he translate this principle into a demand for economic equity or any kind of social leveling either. Instead, this commitment constituted a precondition for the attachment of the act of voting to the condition of liberty. Or as Cartwright put it, "All are by nature free; all are by nature equal; freedom implies choice; equality excludes degrees in freedom."[48] Why insist upon the secret ballot to ensure that choice? Because balloting "would prevent undue influence, personal offence, and self reproach. But it would not prevent that influence which ought to follow worth, wisdom and a right use of wealth."[49] The secret ballot would, in other words, preserve hierarchy in general while also protecting choicemakers from the kinds of negative social pressures, including intimidation and bribery, that could distort their specific elective dispositions and thus limit their personal liberty and autonomy.

In the United States, too, as new voting laws were enacted on a state-by-state basis at the conclusion of the eighteenth and into the nineteenth century, the sense of the ballot as the instantiation of individual, preference-based choice, rather than merely an instrumental piece of paper, could sometimes be heard as well. The Tennessee Acts of 1796, for example, clarified that a ballot is "a ticket or scroll of paper, purporting to express the voter's choice given by the voter to the officer or person holding an election, to be put into the ballot-box."[50] The ballot box, in all its physical banality, consequently became an abstract but mythical site for determining, via aggregation, the meaning of those individuated choices. The Germans called it *Die Wahlurne*, literally a choice-vessel or choice-urn. It spelled out a single collective decision even if a product of initially conflicting preferences and judgments. Cartwright was soon imagining similarly concrete solutions, including suitable furniture for the process that he had in mind; his 1817 pamphlet *A Bill of Rights and Liberties* includes a plan for a polling table for which he had an actual model built for his house (fig. 4.4).[51]

Subsequent prominent suffrage reformers could not resist this same impulse to focus on machinery, that is, the technology that would finally make true independent choice possible, as well as the physical actions necessary for its orderly registration. (Today, the quest goes on electronically, albeit increasingly in the United States with a literal paper trail.) In 1836, the radical historian and MP George Grote developed a machine with his equally political wife, Harriet Grote, that enabled voters, at the culmination of an extended electoral ballet, to punch holes in a ballot paper next to the names of their favored candidates and then to shoot the paper into an attached ballot box, all in privacy.[52] Chartists, too, published diagrams in the later 1830s not just of polling places and the steps required of voters but of newfangled voting machines, also to be called ballot boxes, that depended on voters, behind curtains for secrecy, dropping brass balls into holes marked with their preferred candidates' names. The balls would advance a clockwork counter one step before dropping into a tray on the front of the machine where they could be seen and registered by election judges alone (fig. 4.5).

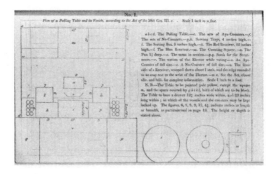

Fig. 4.4. Major Cartwright's design for a balloting table, reproduced in his *Bill of Rights and Liberties* (1817).

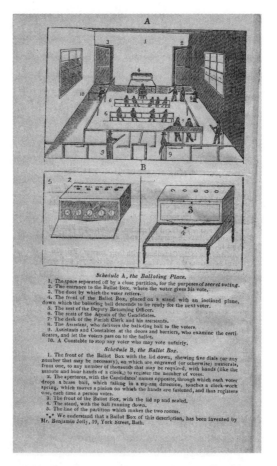

Fig. 4.5. Diagrams detailing a new way to organize a polling place and a new kind of ballot box, designed by Benjamin Jolly of Bath, published by the London Working Men's Association in *The People's Charter: Being the outline of an act to provide for the just representation of the people of Great Britain in the Commons House of Parliament* (1838).

In these essentially utopian drawings of choice-registering technologies, we can see the broad contours of an emerging ideology, however minoritarian at the start of the nineteenth century. What their authors did was link together (a) independence, or freedom from economic, social, or intellectual dependency; (b) individualized political determinations (even if conceptualized as referring exclusively to the public good); and (c) the secret ballot as a form of technology and, even more, linchpin of a set of formal rules for registering those independent and private determinations or choices. This combination would simultaneously come to define respectable English manhood.[53] As the Grotes explained to the press, with this method of voting, "He [the voter] will no longer be called upon to bawl out as the squire or his landlord directs, but will have to express a conscientious preference by an act which can give no evidence of the manner of its performance"—even as that voter's general electoral behavior and the series of sequential movements and actions that he would have to undertake would be highly scripted.[54]

Political philosophers today sometimes refer to voting as occurring according to either a judgment ideal or a preference ideal.[55] The judgment ideal depends upon imagining each voter weighing and aggregating diverse ideas in his (and only later, her) mind prior to voting as to what will best serve the collectivity. A preference ideal reflects primarily the private interests of a voter, who ranks the persons or policies that compete for his support based on his own personal criteria; only after everyone eligible has voted are all those individual expressions of self-interest aggregated. For Cartwright and his contemporaries, though, no such distinction yet applied. To make one's own choice and to express oneself without hindrance—that is, to make sure no one could link the individual with a specific choice and thereby potentially suppress or thwart that individual's chance for self-expression even as the focus remained the common rather than personal good—was to experience being part of a community in which one could maintain one's essential (male) dignity and thus call oneself independent and free.[56]

What, though, of voting as lived experience or in practice? For those among Cartwright's contemporaries not content to build secret ballot tables in their living rooms or write marginal screeds, the taste for "independence" could also mean taking matters into their own hands.

A subset of English anti-oligarchic voters of the late eighteenth and early nineteenth centuries attempted simultaneously to enact their freedom from dependency, or at least hostility to being told what to do, via the very business of casting their vote. "Plumping," or casting only one vote even though most boroughs returned two MPs and thus allowed electors to cast two votes at once, was one tried-and-true way of accomplishing this trick. Another venerable method was known as "splitting," essentially voting for one candidate from each party so as to be controlled by neither.[57] Getting a third party or "independent" candidate to run as a spoiler or disruptor could work too.[58] The effect and indeed goal was the same: messing up the electoral process, exact results be damned in either a numerical or ideological sense. The logic was again that choice and deference (whether to aristocratic, corporate, or clerical authority or even party) were antithetical. Independence, in the sense of being governed exclusively by one's own will and inclinations, was a friend only to the former. To be prevented from choosing as one wished, or to be forced through expected servility to act on behalf of a patron, marked the perversion or corruption of the whole system.

This was a moral question before all else, a matter of the ability to exercise a right, whether an election was seriously contested or not (though this isn't to say that venal motives weren't often a factor too, as some independent voters also insisted on suffrage as a voter's "property" to do with as he pleased). As one elector wrote indignantly in the Stamford Poll Book of 1809 against the influence of a particular local family, "Have the Inhabitants of Stamford a right to choose their own Representatives, or have they not?"[59] In the same spirit, the ground rules of the Wiltshire election of 1818 began with the pronouncement: "First, that independence of election consists in every freeholder exercising his right of voting in the choice of a representative in parliament, unawed by rank and power, and uninfluenced by hope of reward, or fear of injury."[60]

Such statements were also, to be sure, expressions of resentment, effects of a kind of local, atavistic reaction to what felt like "usurpation" of a customary role on the part of a subset of the male country gentry.[61] But the idea of "taking your choice" independently was to become a staple of nineteenth-century campaign literature even as the authors of this literature dedicated themselves to persuading voters on the benefits of one course of action and the dangers of the other—or what we might describe as trying to force how those choices were to be made.[62] Independence in a political sense was gradually being attached to the solo performance of the act of choosing itself.

A Choice Like Any Other?

Yet such self-proclaimed independence *movements* proved largely to be a dead end for British suffrage reformers. Cartwright's line of argument had little official success for almost another hundred years; the French Revolution did it no favors by tainting electoral reform, wherever it was proposed, with an air of French radicalism. Moreover, independent "plumpers" and "splitters"—who had a similarly narrow reach, especially beyond the English countryside—often favored public, performative voting as a national tradition, just without regard for class-based deference or party pressure. By the 1830s, independents no longer constituted much of a force in English politics in any case. And never did the demand for the secret ballot morph into a fundamental working-class cause. In fact, no truly mass movement around voting methods and procedures ever arose in England at all, even in the prelude to the Ballot Act of 1872.

Certainly, Cartwright's secret ballot always had its vocal champions who, at various moments in the first seventy years of the nineteenth century, made their enthusiasm widely known. The high point of general interest came in the late 1830s when the Chartists—following the logic of earlier philosophical radicals like Jeremy Bentham, James Mill, and John Stuart Mill (before he very publicly changed his mind)—designated the secret ballot one of their Six Points.[63] Again, the dominant argument was that the purpose of an election was primarily for the electorate to determine a new government. The individual voter of modest means needed secrecy to be able to vote his convictions, his true, uncompromised, "independent" sense of what would serve the public good, apart from unwanted pressure, or what James Mill had called in his influential 1830 essay "The Ballot" "the power of some opulent man."[64]

Furthermore, experiments in the actual institutionalization of the secret ballot, particularly in some American states and then (thanks to Chartist-inspired immigrants) much of Australia, continued well into the middle of the century to provide illustrations of the efficacy of the process.[65] Or at least it did for white men in racially divided societies. (In an excellent coincidence, it was none other than the winner of the 1872 Pontefract by-election, Hugh Childers, who, as a newly elected MP in 1860 and commissioner of Trade and Customs for the State of Victoria before that, made one of the first major pro-ballot speeches in Parliament, drawing attention to the smooth workings of the secret ballot even among a population "far more excitable than . . . you have in this country.")[66] After introducing ballot measures repeatedly, MP George Grote and his wife, Harriet, gave up. But in much the same language, though with less philosophical backing, Francis Henry Berkeley—with little chance of success—took over the cause within Parliament for the whole middle of the century, founding the moderate liberal Society for Promoting the Adoption of the Vote by Ballot in 1853 and introducing a ballot measure every year thereafter.[67]

And all the while, and probably more significantly for the history of political choice-making, new means of organizing and registering choices, from selecting items arranged in "departments" of so-called department stores to picking jobs to apply for from newspaper help-wanted ads, had become mainstream in many other arenas in British life. So had a wide variety of kinds of voting from clubs to churches. Furthermore, British election practice was itself evolving at the local level in the course of the nineteenth century in ways that made the introduction of voting in national elections via secret ballot, with aggregation of individual preferences to follow, feel like less of a fundamental break with political custom when it finally occurred.

This tendency was not only a matter of the decline around mid-century of some of the most traditional election rituals, including chairing and extended days of polling, victims of changing taste and changing laws, including the Great Reform Act of 1832, alike. It was also a matter of new habits of political choice-making acquired in the doing. Three successful reform efforts in the 1830s—the 1831 Vestries Act, the 1834 Poor Law Amendment Act, and then the 1835 Municipal Corporations Act—introduced forms of balloting into elections at the local level well before any change was instituted in the process for choosing MPs.[68] Granted, the Poor Law Amendment Act and the Municipal Corporations Act required signatures on ballot papers, rendering secrecy impossible. Granted, too, that the Municipal Corporations Act allowed for papers to be filled out at home, eliminating the public, performative aspect of the modern parliamentary election. What these measures succeeded in doing was attaching the practice of voting to contemplation in private, on the one hand, and to new notions of order and proceduralism, on the other—both of which required expression via the preferred modern (pre-electronic) choice technology of printed paper forms.[69]

At the same time, popular attention to political life as something which required choices on the part of ordinary people also grew in the nineteenth century. Partly this was a result of the expansion of basic education, including in civics, as a national priority. More, this was a result of the rise of the commercial newspaper business, including the penny press, which armed ordinary and increasingly literate people with up-to-the-minute political news and opinions. Mainly, though, responsibility can be traced to the growth of national political parties and their leaders, who did much the same thing, especially after 1867, in an effort to divide voters into competing camps and, ultimately, steer their political behavior one way or another.[70]

In practice, new voter laws, on the one hand, and the expansion of extramural systems like parties and newspapers for defining and then coordinating voters' choices, on the other, reinforced one another. The rise of the paper municipal ballot, for example, led to parties issuing optional preprinted ballots (as were already in use in many American states in the nineteenth century). That, in turn, seems to have encouraged greater party loyalty on the part of voters, meaning a tendency to repeatedly pick candidates with the same party affiliation when it came time to contemplate local or national political life. Similarly, the unsensational requirement in the 1832 Great Reform Act of annual voter registration as a formal procedure, separate from the casting of a vote, reinforced the status of the (now explicitly male) elector as an autonomous agent, with a special role to play in the political decision-making process, whether an election was occurring that year or not.[71] Registration also helped undo "independence" as a political stance if not as an abstract idea or expression.[72]

By the 1870s, in other words, the state and its schools, the press, and national political parties had all begun to expand the popular constituencies for formal choice-making, while also circumscribing and regulating the options from which voters could choose and then streamlining and individuating the process for making those choices. And electors were, in a sense, primed well before 1872 to imagine themselves fulfilling this role. Published guides dedicated to laying out the new rules governing the culture of suffrage helped do the same.[73] Once again, popular understanding seems to have shifted almost imperceivably through small alterations in practice and procedure, this time driven by formal laws as well as social convention.

But, that said, the idea of establishing the secret ballot as the norm for parliamentary elections in Great Britain was largely abandoned (*pace* Berkeley) as a major issue in the 1840s. Enthusiasm was slow to develop both inside and outside Parliament, with workingmen, in particular, remaining suspicious of ballot debates as a distraction from their chief agenda item: expanding the franchise to more of their own. More than a half century after the revolutions of 1776 and 1789, protection for the individual voter's independent judgment was still not a central concern, belying any notion of the steady advance of democracy around individual voting rights, whether for men or for women. Moreover, the case for the opposition remained strong, with its advocates advancing not only an argument about the dangers of abandoning English tradition but, just as alarmingly, the idea that the secret ballot would ultimately make choosing a representative to determine the future and texture of public life a choice just like any other.

It was John Stuart Mill who most famously, and influentially, laid out this case. Mill fully accepted the idea that voting constituted a vital method of choice-making. He had, as we've seen, insisted in the context

of *On Liberty* (1859) that a man must "choose his plan of life . . . for himself," rather than simply follow convention, if he were to be fully realized
as a person.[74] In addition, his *Considerations on Representative Government* (1861) contained a long discussion of the stages of elections and
whether electors should "choose the choosers" or make a "direct choice"
when it came to MPs.[75] But in chapter 10 of that same work, titled "Of
the Mode of Voting," Mill, perhaps surprisingly, developed a formidable
argument against the position of George and Harriet Grote and other
nineteenth-century advocates of the ballot, Mill's own younger self
included.

Mill was not actually convinced that *all* people, including the prop-
ertyless and uneducated ("the poorest and rudest class of labourers")
and colonial subjects, needed to be able to choose for themselves when
it came to political determinations, even as he was to very publicly support suffrage for property-owning British women later that decade.[76]
The more significant point was that, in Mill's estimation, even those
worthy of being electors required publicity rather than secrecy in exe-
cuting this function. At the heart of the argument was his claim that if
voting were indeed a trust and duty, oriented toward the public good,
as was still widely accepted, then the public should be privy to how that
trust was being used. Otherwise, if the elector could not be held accountable, voting would, in practice, come to be seen as *merely* a personal right, something that one could buy or sell or use any way one
liked. For the great worry unleashed by the idea of the ballot was that
the voter would be emboldened by secrecy to "use a public function for
his own interest, pleasure or caprice" and to bestow his vote "simply as
he feels inclined."[77] Selection measures rooted in nothing more than
expressing one's inner inclinations might be acceptable in a private club
where balloting was already a norm, according to the author of *On Liberty*. But that conclusion in no way carried over into public life.

In fact, claimed Mill writing at the start of the 1860s, times had
changed: "Thirty years ago it was still true that in the election of members of Parliament, the main evil to be guarded against was that which
the ballot would exclude—coercion by landlords, employers, and customers. At present, I conceive, a much greater source of evil is the

selfishness, or the selfish partialities, of the voter himself." Well before the Ballot Act of 1872 turned the secret ballot into the norm, Mill identified what he perceived to be a dangerous drift toward voters casting their vote "to please themselves" or, as he further explained, to make heard their "personal interest, or class interest, or some mean feeling in his [the voter's] own mind." Mill had no hesitation in imagining the existence of those private preferences: "Everybody has as many different interests as he has feelings, likings or dislikings, either of a selfish or of a better kind."[78] But in a communitarian or civic republican spirit, he insisted on the importance of guarding against the actualization of those preferences in public life, where common agreement about common interests, not the aggregation of private or partisan ones, was supposed to be the guiding spirit. Mill (who was to be pelted by the crowd in his own first foray into electoral politics, though it resulted in him serving as the MP of the city of Westminster from 1865 to 1868) imagined audible, visible, open voting as essential both to the production of virtuous citizens and to the exchange of influence and opinion that would produce the public good. Or to put it the inverse way, and in terms that he never did, a voter was not a consumer, and picking an MP should not become an act akin to selecting new upholstery or a carriage.

Indeed, to this argument against the turn toward secrecy, others added the charge that anything other than open, public, communal voting was essentially unmanly, which was to say, contrary to all things British. (This was Trollope's point in his *Autobiography* as well.)[79] For a man to vote alone, behind a curtain, would be a sad form of capitulation. It would indicate to his fellow citizens that he lacked regard for the collective good, or was afraid to stand for his convictions, or had something to hide. It would also, according that long-term foe of the secret ballot, the *Times* of London, inevitably compromise the very principle of freedom and (male, white) autonomy that was so dear to Cartwright's intellectual forefathers and descendants. Claimed the *Times* more than two decades before its editors grudgingly had to accept that the Pontefract by-election of 1872 had gone off largely without a hitch, "A man votes to record his opinion, to influence others, to testify to a principle, or express a personal regard—for all which purposes publicity is needed."[80] To vote any other way would abandon the most important moral principle: freedom, here conceptualized *not* as the ability to make choices free of social and economic pressure from others but instead as a form of public-minded participation in public life. As the *Times* declared in 1856, inverting Cartwright's old argument in a burst of patriotism: "the Ballot is impossible in England, because it is utterly inconsistent with the publicity and self-respect that are essential to freedom, and that, should the institution ever become possible here, it will be because we have lost those national characteristics which alone make freedom durable, or even desirable—the manly pride that scorns concealment, and the sturdy will that refuses to bend to coercion."[81] It was an argument that was to be made in similar terms, with a recognizable emphasis on masculinity as compromised by certain kinds of choice redolent of women, in late nineteenth-century France and Germany too.[82]

The Ground Shifts

Only in the wake of 1867 Reform Act, and then the general election of the following year, did the secret ballot become a real possibility in practice. Even then, it generated little by way of extraparliamentary, popular agitation. In fact, it was greeted with considerable reluctance even by many of its supporters, who deemed it a necessary evil. The immediate cause that returned the issue to the fore was the violence and evidence of corruption that, along with the election of more pro-ballot MPs, accompanied the 1868 elections. More critical and immediate, though, was the Reform Act's introduction of mass (if not even close to universal) manhood suffrage in England and Wales, as large portions of the male working class found themselves, for the first time, in possession of the vote.[83]

In some ways, *who* should have suffrage rights was the great question of the age, considerably more substantive than the question of *how* those given the right to vote should go about exercising it.[84] For the expansion of the franchise depended not only on rethinking what the political historian James Thompson calls "the social distribution of political wisdom" within the population[85] but also on explaining what made it necessary for individual English men's sentiments regarding suitable representatives to be registered on a one-by-one basis rather than collectively or by means of proxies and surrogates. The winning argument involved accepting that while "respectable" urban workingmen held an unequal share of the nation's wealth, they had roughly equal moral and intellectual capacities—including the ability to make reasonable, ethical choices about who and what pertained to their lives in common— compared with other, long-standing voters. Such men were, in short, independent in moral and intellectual terms if not always in economic ones. Equity thus required according to each of them equal influence over national government (though importantly, this argument did not extend to imperial subjects).[86] That, and a growing faith that a limited expansion of the domestic electorate, as managed by political parties, would not lead to revolutionary ends but rather forestall them.

But this next step in the gradual, almost century-long extension of the English voting rolls immediately brought a new set of concerns to the fore connected to the social position of these new voters—concerns for which the secret ballot came to seem as much a solution as a further provocation, just as in postrevolutionary France. One of those concerns was a way to control what promised to be a new class of potentially unruly men participating directly in what was already seen as an unruly mode and moment of choice-making. Hence the eventual pleasure of the pro-ballot advocates in reporting that the Pontefract elections went off without the slightest disturbance or even an excess of enthusiasm. The secret ballot, along with the end of public nominations, promised— claimed its now mainstream Liberal champions—to make the chaotic, noisy scene of a traditional English election in the Hogarthian or Dickensian vein a relic of the past. The other concern was the old one of voter intimidation, but this time rooted as much in fear of pressure from "beneath," as Prime Minister Gladstone himself put it, as from "above."[87] The potential influence of "mobs" and trade unions seemed as problematic in light of the expanded franchise as the financial pressure of landlords or the spiritual pressure exercised, ostensibly, by Irish priests. And here, too, secrecy seemed a potential antidote. By isolating the voter from all the social constraints in which he was normally both literally and symbolically enmeshed, the ballot and the voting booth became emblems of the production of what was now deemed a "pure" choice.

Naturally, some disagreement ensued about the epistemological foundations for the pure choices that the secret ballot would help elicit. The safest bet was to imagine the voter's selection by ballot as the result of individual intelligence and reason, combined with some accounting of public opinion, or what might also be called legitimate influence. The standard argument, as laid out by the former MP and diplomat William Dougal Christie in *The Ballot and Corruption and Expenditure at Elections* (1872), a reprinting of all Christie's writing on the subject since 1839, went like this: "It is intended by the state, that each man to whom the elective franchise is entrusted, should exercise his own judgment on the merits of the candidates between whom he has to choose, and vote for him whom, on the several grounds of honesty, intelligence, and the general tenor of political opinion, he himself holds most worthy of a seat in Parliament." But this would hardly be possible, Christie insisted, if voters could only make choices as a result of bribes and intimidation, which is to say, could, as a result of affiliation, clientage, and dependence, make no real choices at all. The beauty of the secret ballot was that it would enable voting "in opposition to the wishes of landlords, masters and customers," while still allowing for the reciprocity of opinion on which collective life depended.[88]

Others, though, in the wake of the expansion of the franchise in 1868, imagined instituting something closer to what the French would later envision in the context of the *isoloir* and the Germans in the *Isolierräume*: a space and procedure that produced reason alone, unaffected not only by specific, individual influences and interests but also by the swirl of collective opinion. Declared Liberal MP Edward Leatham in a speech before the House of Commons in 1869, "Put the voter into a closet, and he may see what the philosopher sees."[89] In what literary critic Elaine Hadley calls the imagined "cognitive privacy" of the voting booth, the voter would become detached from *all* social relations, affiliations, and constraints, past or future, familial or professional, and become simply a rational, impartial mind at work.[90] He would be answerable only to "his own conscience," a clear reference to earlier religious arguments around choice.[91] What's more, he would himself, for a limited time, be transformed in the process. We are not far here from how the *Lloyd's Weekly* reporter would, in the aftermath of the 1872 Pontefract election, imagine the first-time voter by secret ballot, suddenly aware of his (temporary) "power and independence" as a choice-maker.

For in the most radical of cases, voting in secret was redefined as a purely personal affair, a matter of inclination, much like selecting a bride or, indeed, a destination for a carriage ride or a carriage itself. In an argument that was to have little immediate impact but that was to be oddly prescient, the self-proclaimed "agitator" George Jacob Holyoake imagined voting by secret ballot as primarily a means of satisfying one's individual tastes, without regard for either public opinion *or* reason. *A New Defence of the Ballot, In Consequence of Mr. Mill's Objections to It* (1868) began from an older, Cartwright-like argument linking the secret ballot with manly independence and opposing it to slavery: "The Ballot is the weapon of the strong and of the strong only—a condition of individuality of action and a necessary complement of enfranchisement." But what Holyoake called "personal" rather than secret voting became, contra Cartwright or Mill, a proudly private act in which "my interests, my preferences" are "in my own keeping" and no one else's business. The key comparison here was with marriage: "A man votes, as he marries, not for his neighbor's satisfaction, but for his own."

Some years earlier, Berkeley had famously said something similar in comparing a man voting by ballot to driving a carriage he owned "where, when, and how he pleased."[92] This, for Holyoake, is what made voting by ballot ultimately an exercise in freedom: "It is no affair of my neighbor *how* I vote, or *for whom* I vote, or *why* I vote—since I exercise no power or freedom which he does not equally possess, and which I do not equally concede to him." In the end, even the turn to secrecy came down to a matter of safeguarding the possibility of unhindered choice: "If I *choose* to vote openly, that is my bravery, my pride, my ostentation, or my hardihood—if I am *forced* to vote openly that is the *badge of my inferiority*—it is the sign that I am not to be trusted."[93] The ballot made a man free because it allowed not only for self-determination but also for self-expression, the sense that one's distinctive, closely held tastes, values, and preferences were being actualized in one's public decisions or choices. In Holyoake on the ballot, the "preference ideal" by itself, with its whiff of consumer culture and feminine desire, albeit here rendered a new standard for masculinity, found an early expression.[94]

This was, of course, precisely what Mill feared the secret ballot would produce. And in the long run, Mill turned out to be largely right in his apprehensions. What rational choice and public choice theorists of voting now take for granted is that a vote is, by definition, an expression of a strongly held inner preference, rooted in a prior comparison of the available options, much as in consumer purchasing. Many twentieth- and twenty-first-century histories of elections and electoral behavior are, in fact, written as if this has always been the case precisely because it is now so widely held to be true.[95] However, this assumption—correct or not—has a history. The technology of the secret ballot did not create this effect as an obvious function of its design. But in the second half of the nineteenth century, the secret ballot seemed, in England and soon elsewhere too, to instantiate in practice a burgeoning idea of the individual, male voter as an independent chooser and of voting as a marker of interior preferences that the ballot's use could help reproduce as a new norm.

For what all of these partisans of the ballot did ultimately agree upon was that the way the state and its choice agents, from municipal officials to party leaders, could best put themselves in the business of ensuring something that felt like electoral freedom was by establishing and overseeing the logistics of the process, from the protection of individual choice-making at the neighborhood level to the tallying and homogenization of the results afterward. That would be the case even if this oversight, or choice-management process, might leave up to half the electorate, not to mention the formally disenfranchised, seeing its own preferences rejected at the end. Equity would result not only from the limited expansion of rights—allowing more people to participate in the process of choosing representatives—but also from the expansion and enforcement of the formal rules or procedures tied to majoritarianism themselves. In the end, balloting was an electoral system advocated for, molded, and instituted by the mid-century English political elite, primarily within Parliament. It was also heavily orchestrated by mainstream political parties, signaling the decline of the more informal influence of local patrons as architects of political choice. And it was designed to keep a growing electorate simultaneously liberated and in check. In an odd way, top-down regulation and freedom for the white, male individual were, in the promise of the ballot, rendered one.

The Ballot Act and After

For finally, in 1872, with the backing of the Liberal party, the Liberal press, and, rather reluctantly, Gladstone himself, the ballot became the law of the land across Britain—to bring us back to where we started. Alongside an outpouring of speeches and pamphlets making various philosophical cases for the ballot and against the position of J. S. Mill,[96] a Parliamentary Select Committee had gone to work in 1869, studying the question in practice the world over, from the United States to Greece to Australia, before eventually endorsing the idea. The committee's charge had been dual: to "inquire into the present modes of conducting Parliamentary and Municipal Elections," but also to consider "further guarantees for their tranquility, purity and freedom."[97] To this end, scores of witnesses of election practice, from mayors to ministers to grocers, bookkeepers, ironmongers, dentists, engine fitters, and agriculturalists from all across Britain, had been summoned to London to tell the committee both what they had observed at home and abroad and what they and their neighbors believed, primarily about the ballot question. Much of the conversation had turned on whether the witnesses felt that voters would be aided by the ballot in seeing elections as representations of their "convictions" and the "dictates of their conscience[s]" and thereby "just," as Mr. Daniel Collen, a corn factor (i.e., grain dealer) residing at Chippenham, put it, or if, on the contrary, they felt, in the words of a stuff merchant (i.e., cloth seller) in Bradford named Mr. Storey, "a man's whole life is a lie under the ballot."[98]

In fact, though, the Select Committee and the direction of the questioning itself had leaned heavily on the former side. And after several tries on the part of Liberal MPs, the Parliamentary and Municipal Elections Bill, soon known as the Ballot Act, passed in 1872, formally changing the mechanics of voting in all the ways that would be reported by Pontefract's election observers. That included the adoption of the Australian practice of listing all the options (i.e., candidates' names) on a printed menu, designed and distributed by the state, with squares to be marked with Xs for choices made, a format slowly adopted in the United States after 1888 as well (fig. 4.6).[99] That also included, as in Australia, requiring privacy in the performance of this task even as it was to occur within a public space.[100] A flurry of new how-to guides and new choice-making paraphernalia, from ballot boxes to instructional handbills, then set the policy in motion in time for the Pontefract experiment and, eventually, its generalization across Great Britain—though, importantly, again not its Empire—in 1874.[101] Pontefract's mayor and returning officer, Richard Moxon, complained to the London *Times* a few days after the Pontefract by-election about how little time there had been beforehand to get the process in order.[102] But he also conceded that the election there had been a surprising success in terms of how easily ordinary people took to their new roles. He furthermore predicted that what had been witnessed that August 1872 day would soon be the new norm.

Moxon was right. Subsequent years produced only small, procedural adaptations based on a steady stream of reports from overseas (the *Times* issued positive reports on the practice almost immediately from parts of the United States and Belgium) and from local examples, starting with Moxon's own. Despite dire predictions prior to Pontefract's election about inhabitants of "old-world" places being "slow to fall in with new-fangled ways," even the *Times* had to admit that the difficulty of the shift was proven "rather fancied than real" and that philosophical complications did not mean complications in practice.[103] Election officials reporting to parliamentary committees established after that date to ruminate on the meeting of Pontefract and other subsequent electoral experiments also happily insisted that voting by ballot had done away with much of the "noise" surrounding elections, which might be taken to mean alternative methods of expressing collective dissent, especially on the part of non-elites, or an actual excess of sound. Positive

Fig. 4.6. An example of an "Australian ballot," this one dating from 1886 and issued by the state of New York, that required the voter to put an X next to all the options that he chose. The party symbols at the top were intended to help those with limited literacy, though balloting in other instances served as a tool for disenfranchising those who could not interpret a menu of names alone.

claims of "quietness" and lack of "popular excitement" persisted.[104] The change in process, furthermore, had been accomplished without producing much by way of resistance from either the respectable or the "very poor" and without causing any radical change in the makeup of Parliament itself.

Many older election rituals did, needless to say, survive past the Ballot Act and the Pontefract by-election, as did what election observers and officials deemed "corruption." The very next experiment with the ballot, an election in Preston (Lancashire) where Conservatives carried the day, was rife with official accusations of bribery, including vote buying and treating with food and drink. The general election in 1880 was deemed so corrupt that more legislation was required in 1883—the so-called Corrupt and Illegal Practices Act—to deal with the bribery issue.[105] Can we be surprised? We continue to this day in the United States to debate, in highly partisan terms, just what constitutes potentially "undue influence," from ballot harvesting to "election selfies" to the funding of advertising that distorts the choices before the electorate or drowns out one side's case. Corruption is always partly in the eye of the beholder, when it isn't a partisan accusation itself. Even secrecy has remained relative when it comes to voting by ballot. In the first half of the nineteenth century, in the United States and in France, ticket distribution—or the handing out by party officials of already completed ballots, often distinguishable from the outside by color and size—meant limited privacy existed for voters' choices even when balloting was the norm.[106] To a lesser degree, semi-secrecy continued in Britain as well. Raucous popular politics, meanwhile, soon also found itself a new home in the form of local election meetings.

And yet, the mythology of the ballot as the embodiment of free, unconstrained political choice was never really contested again post-Pontefract, as if in a definitive answer to Cartwright's plaintive question of 1795: is the ballot "utterly inconsistent with the very character of freedom" or "a principle of security to liberty"?[107] After 1880, the Ballot Act was renewed annually. Then, with the 1918 Representation of the People Act, which further expanded the franchise in Great Britain, voting by ballot became the permanent norm for all kinds of elections, including parliamentary ones, even as open voting has remained standard practice among elected officials in assembly halls for reasons of public accountability.[108]

What's more, during these same years, the practice of mandating privatized and secretized suffrage by ballot in all official elections spread widely among other nations: New Zealand in 1870–71 (and thus in advance of Great Britain, though after Australia), Belgium in 1877, Italy in 1882, Norway in 1884, the Netherlands in 1887, all across Canada by the end of the 1880s and four-fifths of U.S. states by the century's close, then Japan in 1900, Demark in 1901, Austria in 1907, Argentina in 1912, and France, which, in 1913, finally added to the paper ballot an envelope and the *isoloir*, or curtained voting booth, with the promise that it would permit the elector his "freedom" (*liberté*) at the precise moment when he went to cast his vote.[109] Not surprisingly, the technology continued to change throughout these years, and a high degree of heterogeneity characterized its employment, from the source and design of ballots, to the steps involved in filling them out, to the nature of the ballot boxes and urns themselves.[110] But around much of the world, the formalization of secret voting in national elections added a critical new arena in the aftermath of 1870 for the activity of individual choice-making already familiar, in variant forms, from the world of consumer goods, ideas and beliefs, mates, and educations and careers.

The revolutions of the late eighteenth century revived the very old idea of popular sovereignty, rooting it in the collective virtue and wisdom of the indivisible people as an operative idea and then making it the key to political freedom. The late nineteenth century, in what our same Dublin correspondent observing the elections in Pontefract went so far as to call (unusually) another "revolution" at the end of another "old regime," grafted this eighteenth-century notion together with a new, less recognized one. Any guess what the newer one was? That ensuring this liberty required not only accepting conflict over choices among the varied and individual beings who made up "the people" but also allowing for their free expression on a person-by-person basis as a step in their ultimate rectification. By tallying all those individually generated choices, state agents did not necessarily help produce better

outcomes (despite what some democratic theorists today claim); this
was not an argument about any invisible hand, in the Adam Smithian
sense, necessarily shaping all those individual transactions into something beneficial to the community as a whole. But the new election system ensured, our Dublin correspondent continued, that state-organized
proceduralism—in the case of Pontefract, the establishment of "the
most unexciting and decorous of public proceedings"—would be fully
compatible with the experience of "freedom" that he claimed also to
have witnessed in that fateful Yorkshire by-election at the same time.[111]
Fair and free were twinned, with process as key.

    Just a few years later, in a famous lecture of 1881, the great Victorian
philosopher T. H. Green argued something similar: the seemingly para-
doxical position that growing government intervention (as in voting
reform and oversight) would ultimately enhance rather than compromise "true freedom." The reason was that government could work to
eliminate circumstances that would otherwise prohibit opportunities
for "the full exercise of the faculties with which man is endowed."[112]
For his contemporaries, that included the ability to choose in the
political arena without external constraint or fear of the consequences.
Never mind that both the choices themselves and the mechanism for
adjudicating between them would henceforth be laid out by national
political parties in conjunction with state officials, not generated by
those individual people themselves. (One of the only ways to object to
either the options or the process itself was to, in a sense, throw away
one's vote and refuse to choose at all, a choice with its own history.)[113]
Never mind that majority rule would mean that, compared to the world
of taste or beliefs or even emotions, the realization of one's choice
would always be limited and often thwarted by the choices of others.
With the secret ballot, choosing-as-freedom, a fantasy about individual
preference and agency being realizable without concern for the desires
or moral strictures of others, became a political ideal with the full backing of the state regulatory apparatus. Insofar as there was little resistance
and little even to witness (that is, beyond individual entrances and exits
at the polling place), it quickly became, and remains, an ordinary, unremarkable one at that.

Political Choice and Women

Then it was up to women to prove, against the odds, that the vote—and especially the private and personal preference-based vote—befit women as well. Indeed, it became necessary, in the age of rights, to establish that women, or some subset of women, were entitled to this particular form of choice-making as a basic right. It, too, was a matter of what advocates were to call "political freedom."[114]

Resistance, especially from men, was intense. For in certain ways, the spread of the secret ballot set back the cause of female suffrage. Sure, gaining the franchise for women had existed as a theoretical demand since the French Revolution—think of Olympe de Gouges's *Declaration of the Rights of Woman*, as well as the comments of a few English and Dutch radicals of the 1790s who, early on, turned their attention to the state rather than the family as a key source of women's oppression. Moreover, as we've seen, this particular demand had been at the center of a small number of organized, transatlantic political movements rooted primarily in women's collective agency since the Seneca Falls Women's Rights Convention and the short-lived revolutions that convulsed many European cities, both in 1848. Some women had even briefly garnered the vote in places as disparate as parts of New Jersey (1790–1807) and Sierra Leone (1792–1808, just prior to it becoming a British Crown colony). By the last decades of the nineteenth century, the argument that as long as women were among the governed, they had a right to choose their governors had, in fact, become *the* major issue of the burgeoning bourgeois women's rights movement in many parts of the world, reflecting the growing status of voting more generally (Wollstonecraft had other concerns a hundred years earlier). That said, garnering voting rights for women in national elections long remained a fringe cause—in Britain as elsewhere—in terms of political life as a whole. Despite Mill's proposal of an amendment to the 1867 Reform Bill enfranchising women who met the new, more generous criteria for male enfranchisement (by changing "man" to "person"), and despite other political leaders proposing almost annually through the 1870s women's suffrage bills geared toward national elections, nothing happened in Britain on the legislative front.

Instead, a long period of almost total parliamentary inaction was to follow, as it did in most places where the issue was raised early on. Mill can, in fact, be said to have been largely out of step in both his early public advocacy for women's suffrage *and* his late fear of secret balloting, even as he became the great nineteenth-century philosophical advocate for individual choice. The thrust of suffrage expansion and secret ballot bills across the first three quarters of the nineteenth century in Britain and its empire was precisely the opposite: to make the vote and independent manhood across class, if not race or age, coterminous, and to define the exclusions ever more sharply.[115] In the aftermath of the Ballot Act, the new association of the self-governing, autonomous individual with the adult male British person who did his civic duty by entering the voting booth to express his private, decontextualized, and independent views, or "conscience," surely further eroded support for the always-marginal notion of the adult female person exercising her political rights directly by becoming a "chooser" in this very public realm.

Postcards, which entered what is often called their golden age right around the turn of the century, make this gendered distinction particularly apparent insofar as intensifying international fights about the who and the how of suffrage played out on their front sides. In the French context, in a collectable 1913 series called "Le Nouveau Vote Secret," photographic depictions of the new *isoloir* only heightened the sense of voting as a new kind of formal choreography for men alone. In each of the images, a proper-looking, white, metropolitan gentleman or group thereof is featured performing a particular ritual that depends upon a distinctive epistemic capacity that is itself beyond the eye's power to see, but that is also clearly taking place apart from all external "influence," including that of the women in their lives and other dependents (fig. 4.7). By contrast, increasingly organized opponents of women's enfranchisement at the start of the twentieth century often used humorous and cartoonish postcard imagery—of a female brain filled to the brim with superficial distractions or of a mock female voter who is ostensibly exercising her right to vote without being able to provide any reason for her choices—to ridicule the idea of real female citizens trying to do just that (figs. 4.8 and 4.9).

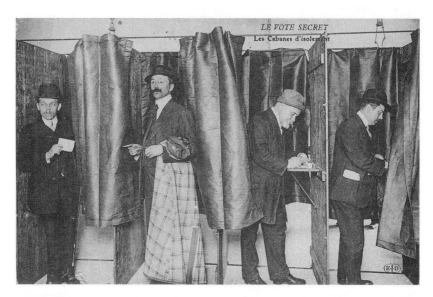

Fig. 4.7. "Le Vote Secret," one of many postcards from 1913 in which French men are shown engaging in orderly fashion in every stage of a new form of voting centered on what are here called *les cabanes d'isolement*, or isolation booths, an innovation of that year.

Figs. 4.8 and 4.9. "A Woman's Mind Magnified" (1906) and "Votes for Women" (1911), with the tagline "We don't know what we want but we'll 'ave it!!!," both British anti–women's suffrage postcards ridiculing women's thought processes.

Fig. 4.10. "When Women Vote—A Proposal" (1907), a British anti–women's suffrage postcard suggesting that women, by taking up voting, will succeed in reversing the natural order of choice.

Once again, to the task of choice, women brought all their old negative psychological traits rooted in their bodies: impulsiveness, superficiality, dependency, arbitrariness, distractedness, a basic inability to know their own minds, and a tendency to operate by sentiment or attention to appearances alone. (These were characteristics frequently attributed to colonial subjects as well.) Or conversely, women as choosers turned into quasi-men themselves—to the detriment of actual men, their families, and society as a whole. Witness yet another anti–women's suffrage postcard, this one playing on the common theme of role reversal: enfranchising women triggers the advent of an inverted society in which women are now doing *all* the choosing, including asking for (fully feminized and dependent) men's hands in marriage and thereby thwarting even "The Choice" (fig. 4.10). It was hard for pro–female suffrage forces to find ways to depict dignified, womanly women in parallel but not identical choice-making situations to their fathers, husbands, and sons, especially if those female voters were to be called upon to select, in public spaces, among various men bidding to be their chosen representatives in determining the nation's future course.

Yet there is a different way to look at this story. In another sense, the earlier reformulation of voting as an individualized and routinized process, albeit one with significant consequences for collective life, probably helped finally make possible the enfranchisement of women at the national level.[116] For with the establishment of the secret ballot as the new norm came the slow erosion of many of the major obstacles to women's full participation in election culture that had long stood in their way.

These were, in part, theoretical. As the idea of the vote as a public trust that one exercised on behalf of dependent others essentially became defunct, and as "independence" came to have more to do with intellectual capacity than status acquired through property, all the most obvious justifications for this specific sex-based form of disqualification started to evaporate. Gone was the old conceptual clarity about what distinguished those with the vote from those without. Women's suffrage advocates pounced. In particular, they exploited the possibilities inherent in the idea that if, as the Liberal party and suffrage activist Millicent Garrett Fawcett put it already in 1871, voting rights had become "nothing else than freedom to exercise the faculties,"[117] they might as readily be accorded to women as to men (despite anti–women's suffrage propaganda). The connection was made most bluntly at almost the same time and in the American context by the great Black abolitionist and women's rights advocate to whom we return: Frederick Douglass. In the same article in which he insisted "our natural powers are the foundation of our natural rights" and "the fact that woman has the power to say 'I choose *this* rather than *that*' is all-sufficient proof that there is no natural reason against the exercise of that power," he went on to conclude: "The power that makes her [woman] a moral and an accountable being gives her a natural right to choose the legislators who are to frame the laws under which she is to live, and the requirements of which she is bound to obey."[118]

Of course, as Douglass was acutely aware, this attention to mental capacity came everywhere rife with its own forms of exclusions. Those could be related to race, nationality, profession, virtue, economic status, marital status, and/or educational attainment, not to mention age. In the Americas, the cause of women's voting at times aided and at times thwarted that of Black people of both sexes aiming to do the same.[119] Ditto for other non-European colonial subjects in other places, including British India. But with this shift toward the epistemic in the criteria for enfranchisement, the right to vote for (some) women became generally easier to package and sell as a matter of interchangeability between the sexes and thus a matter of equal rights.

Furthermore, and maybe just as importantly, with the introduction of the ballot as a new norm, a pragmatic case could also be made that the *act* of voting in parliamentary elections had become as respectable and as devoid of rough-and-tumble antics as any number of other middle- and upper-class extramural, leisure-time pursuits. In other words, it had become fully suitable for women of every sort and no longer a prerogative of male courage. According to Fawcett's contemporary, suffragist Helen Blackburn, "The argument that [parliamentary] elections are too tumultuous has been nullified since the ballot has made it easier to vote at an election than to attend her Majesty's drawing-room."[120] Jacob Bright noted similarly that balloting as an organized form of choice had produced such "peace and order at the poll" that a woman could now vote "with far greater ease than she experiences in making her way out of a theatre or a concert room."[121] Some early advocates for female enfranchisement, like the Liberal party–affiliated Susan Gay, even made the argument that women would themselves be morally and intellectually elevated by the opportunity, that the exercising of "free choice" would collectively make them, like working-class men, into the fully morally and intellectually independent individuals they yearned to be.[122] In a way, this was an adaptation of Wollstonecraft's original argument. Voting, now reformed, was to be the path out of positions of unnatural dependency and a tool in the creation of a society of reasonable, informed choosers of both sexes.

Still, such abstract arguments can hardly have been sufficient even as a domestic ideology resting on notions of separate spheres for men and women declined more generally around the turn of the century. What we should not ignore (though it generally has been) is how women advocates for the vote eventually both punctured the association of preference-based choice with negative feminine traits that had always dogged it *and* drew strategically on those old associations to make the case for their enfranchisement. The key point is that they did not do so initially, *pace* Mill or his direct disciples like Susan Gay of the "free choice" comment above, by harnessing or instrumentalizing choice as a term or by linking it to any particular party or creed. They did so primarily as they had always done: as a form of enactment or bodily practice.

For an instructive example, let's pause for a moment on a minor episode in the history of the women's suffrage campaign, again in Britain, but one with echoes in many places where this cause was taken up in the years just before World War I. By the start of the twentieth century, as we've seen, the secret ballot was starting to become a settled matter, increasingly a requirement of democratic governance at the national level across much of the globe. So was something close to universal manhood suffrage with the end, in many places, of property requirements for the franchise. In contrast, that women were denied the vote was not—and would not be, from France to Japan, for almost half a century more—treated as a critical issue in need of remedy. Yet in practice and in many places, not least Britain, women had been chipping away at this exclusion for years, not to mention participating in both local and national politics in a variety of other ways, including on their own behalf as a specific constituency.[123]

Based on the idea that the specific "issues" at hand were natural extensions of women's particular concerns, single female ratepayers in Britain had won the vote in municipal elections in 1869. All female ratepayers, including married ones, were then empowered to participate in school board elections in 1870, in poor law board elections in 1875, in county council elections in 1888, and in parish and district council elections in 1894, some of which used forms of balloting not dissimilar to those used in parliamentary elections to determine the winners.[124] Something parallel can be said to have occurred—despite state-by-state variations and changing patterns of racial exclusion—in the United States, too, in the second half of the nineteenth century; hence the manufacture of separate "women's ballot boxes" for use in various districts

Fig. 4.11. A tin, mule-mounted women's ballot box of a type manufactured by George D. Barnard in St. Louis and used in the last three decades of the nineteenth century in places throughout the Midwest and West where women had partial (usually school board and occasionally municipal) voting rights only.

that drew a distinction between which kinds of votes were open to women as well and which were restricted solely to men (fig. 4.11).[125] By the turn of the century, New Zealand and much of Australia, again in the forefront just as with the secret ballot, had gone all the way. Both nations enfranchised women in national elections, though conspicuously not aboriginal ones in the case of Australia, and provided new examples for the rest of the world of both a mixed-sex and racialized franchise in practice.[126] So did certain western U.S. states. At the same time, white women and women of color around the world had been forming their own party-like organizations, with women playing all the roles, including hosting international congresses of the like-minded in cities from Berlin to Amsterdam to Buenos Aires.[127]

What was so clever about events like the Women's Exhibition held in London in 1909 was how it turned the act of middle-class white women making choices about matters of national import into a participatory political spectacle while also stressing its mundaneness. Founded by the Pankhurst family in Manchester, England, in 1903, the self-declared militant suffrage organization called the Women's Social and Political Union (WSPU) figured out, with this event among many others, how to make visible what would be otherwise be hard to see in the age of balloting. Through collective action, its members created something like a temple for the practice and worship of everyday, independent, and individualized female choice-making.

The setting was the Prince's Skating Rink in the fashionable London neighborhood of Knightsbridge. Alongside a stage for plays about women's suffrage, a jujitsu display in which a small woman threw a large policeman over her shoulder, and a full-sized facsimile of the notorious prison cell already being used for imprisoned suffragettes, the Pankhursts decked out the cavernous space as one giant shopping bazaar, complete with an "American" ice cream soda fountain. Every day over two weeks in May, women members of the WSPU and their patrons and supporters browsed, bought, and sold at stalls laden with consumer goods and foods from around the world, handcrafted and manufactured alike. In other words, they participated in a traditional feminine form of provisioning and choice-making that had already been repeatedly harnessed by women in the course of the nineteenth century to promote philanthropic causes. Visitors could even, in a throwback to eighteenth-century fashion, attend live auctions. In the end, WSPU reports demonstrate, these activities raised considerable funds for the cause.

It was, though, also impossible to miss the connection between all the shopping and the politics. Many of the goods "temptingly displayed," from tea sets to scarves to dolls and leather work, were branded with WSPU colors and symbols, a practice that would continue in official WSPU suffrage shops both in London and in smaller British cities, as well as in that temple of consumption, Selfridges, up to World War I.[128]

Fig. 4.12. "The Sweets Stall," one of a number of photographs of goods for sale at the 1909 Women's Exhibition taken by Christina Bloom and, in many cases, repurposed as souvenir postcards.

(Documentary postcards on sale at the exposition, many of them actually showing other goods for sale, are one major source for seeing now the commercial spectacle that was this enormous bazaar [fig. 4.12].)

More directly, in one of the corners of the Skating Rink, right across from the facsimile cell, stood a tribute to another, now analogic form of choice, in this case intellectual and political. That was a voting booth containing a ballot box, set up exactly as in parliamentary elections, into which all visitors, male *and* female, were every day urged to cast their completed ballots announcing their opinion or preference on a key issue of the moment. Totals were reported at the exposition on the following day and in the feminist press.[129]

The topics open to visitors' determinations at the Women's Exhibition of 1909 ranged from the serious to the silly, from explicitly feminist to general interest. One day the question was "should women serve on juries" (622 for, 62 against). Another was "should the state subsidize the opera" (223 yes, 130 no). Still another, described as "amusing," was "should women be policemen" (which produced only a 1-vote difference, 197 against, 196 for).[130] The point was obviously the spectacle itself, with its participatory and performative dimension, more than the quantifiable rendering of public opinion. That, and what the WSPU called "breaking down prejudice in many directions."[131] In the doing, women in favor of female suffrage displayed, to themselves and to onlookers alike, their own epistemic capacities, from framing the questions, to making up their minds, to actually marking and casting an Australian-style ballot, with the question in place of the candidate name, in exchange for a numbered check that turned the holder into an official elector. All of these were actions which, the organizers pointed out, were hardly a "high mystery" for British women (or the women of Tasmania or Wyoming) at the start of the twentieth century. As the organizers put it a bit facetiously to the readers of Votes for Women, "Having marked the ballot papers in the prescribed place, folded the paper in the prescribed way, and dropped it into the provided receptacle, you will then have achieved the adventure of casting a vote by ballot!"[132] The message was clear: in advocating for suffrage, they had already mastered its performance.

We remember the radical wing of the British women's suffrage movement just before World War I chiefly for its more dramatic actions and images. Militants like the women of the WSPU took literally their motto "Deeds, not Words," essentially an antirhetorical position. And many of their deeds were indeed both spectacular and effective. Between 1909 and 1914, "suffragettes," as they were dubbed in the press, famously put their own bodies on the line, courting arrests and going on hunger strikes that were often followed by painful (and equally visually arresting) force feedings on the part of the state. These same women also engaged in acts of strategic violence, from physically attacking politicians to smashing the windows of government offices and hundreds of fashionable West End shops and department stores. And they came up with nonviolent, ballot-related stunts with clever symbolic resonance too, like undermining the census by sending in dummy returns, stating "If I am intelligent enough to fill in this Census Form, I can surely make an X on a ballot paper" and disrupting real elections by pouring strange liquids into ballot boxes while they were otherwise in use.[133] Collectively, British suffragists demonstrated a marvelous sense of how to win attention, even negative attention, whether from political leaders or an all-too-willing press, and then benefit. Women, so obviously acting outside the boundaries of feminine behavioral norms to make their case, were bound to hold a certain lurid fascination.

Plus, reportage and related images, whether positive or not, helped highlight their capacity as historical agents. Consider, for example, an antisuffrage image of 1912 in which that eighteenth-century coinage "Going Shopping" becomes visually matched with a desexed older woman, hammer in hand, on her way to break shop windows rather than peer into them and make consumer choices (fig. 4.13). So much for women's presumed moral superiority (which had helped women win the vote in New Zealand and Australia) or sense of the boundaries of propriety when it came to action in the public sphere.

Nevertheless, even the most radical British suffragists recognized from the beginning that a second strategy was required in the larger battle over opinion. That was getting pro-suffrage women to simultaneously act in properly (and equally visibly) genteel and feminine ways that could also be linked directly in the collective public mind to the act of voting. The goal was to counter propaganda like "Going Shopping," no matter its truth or falsity, through an alternative set of images and deeds. The women of the WSPU chose also to engage in various forms of pageantry, like shopping and mock voting in the context of an exposition, that would make their ambitions, not to mention the people acting on them, seem reassuring, even prosaic. Writing just a few years after the 1909 bazaar, Sylvia Pankhurst, the daughter of WSPU founder Emmeline Pankhurst and eventually an anticolonial, socialist activist in her own right, was very clear on the purpose of this mixture. It was not to undermine the seriousness of the cause but rather to associate the act of women's suffrage—for all the moral arguments about freedom and slavery that informed its rhetoric—with traditional and pleasurable ("happy") feminine pursuits, including displaying, regarding, and acquiring inessential material goods.[134] Women, this exhibition suggested,

Fig. 4.13. A British anti–women's suffrage postcard and poster, designed by John Hassall and published by the National League Opposing Women's Suffrage in 1912, making novel use of the classic eighteenth-century neologism "going shopping."

could harness toward the good of the nation the very same, highly gendered choice-making abilities that "lighthearted" women routinely used in everyday life outside the workplace, including in various markets. Moreover, they could do so without the sky falling in and the loss of any of their traditional feminine qualities or inclinations. They were, in fact, already adept at doing so. That was because respectable femininity was perfectly compatible with all forms of deliberate, orderly, and informed selection.

Pro-suffrage women, in other words, were ultimately successful, despite the considerable obstacles in their way, in "winning" the right to political choice in part because they embraced what historian Joan Scott has influentially termed the essential "paradox" of all women's rights struggles: the need to stress difference and equality at the same time.[135] Suffragists regularly sought to demonstrate that, with the vote, women would bring their own special kind of feminine know-how and concerns to decision making—to the benefit of their compatriots as a whole. But simultaneously these same suffragists took pains to illustrate that little distinguished these same voters, except convention, from men. Which meant women were as deserving of freedom of choice as their male counterparts and would ultimately be voters in much the same sense. Female advocates of female suffrage also made this case in a context in which the nature of what counted as a manly choice—even in politics, that last domain of the idea of civic virtue—was shifting as well.

And in fact, when some newly enfranchised British women (those thirty and over) were finally able to vote in parliamentary elections in the aftermath of World War I, their actions caused little immediate stir. The press readily and repeatedly took up the old saw, even in the late 1920s as women's minimum voting age dropped to twenty-one, about the lack of excitement and the lack of any obvious effects of female suffrage at all, though considerable legislation benefiting women's welfare was actually to follow.[136] The same was the case when eligible (i.e., over twenty-one and generally white) women voted across the United States after the ratification of the Nineteenth Amendment to the Constitution in 1920. The vote itself resulted in little real change in either the dominant political ideology or the nature of partisan alignments of the day; conservative Republicans dominated the next decade.

Women were not suddenly rendered equal or emancipated by enfranchisement in any real sense either. Many newly eligible voters chose not to participate (as is still the case today). In the United States, most African American women, Native American women, and immigrant women of Asian descent were formally denied the opportunity for decades more (and frequently still are through voter suppression efforts), whether they hoped to vote or not. White women voters, including key suffrage leaders like Susan B. Anthony and Elizabeth Cady Stanton, were often complicit in upholding or even instrumentalizing white supremacy rather than seeking any cross-racial alliance of women or trying to broaden suffrage eligibility more generally, despite the origins of the women's movement in abolitionism. Some socialists and anarchists like Emma Goldman downplayed the value of suffrage ("our modern fetish") in any case, arguing that it would have little effect on freedom without a revolution to proceed it. As the editor of her journal and her sometime partner Alexander Berkman put it sarcastically regarding ballot options, "The sensation of being eaten by Mr. Lion or Mr. Tiger is essentially the same."[137] Maybe we make a mistake if we expect voting alone, or even the triumph of the suffrage cause, to have produced sudden, radical, and positive change for men or women, Black or white.[138] After all, even British militants' arguments were ultimately for inclusion in the world of individualized, then aggregated choice, not the overthrow of it; radical gestures on the part of suffrage activists were always deemed a means suited to an extralegal situation, or "just war," not an end unto themselves. As with the secret ballot, male support for (some) women's enfranchisement finally only increased when it seemed likely that the change in election law would have limited impact on policymaking or socioeconomic stratification afterward—that, ultimately, nothing would happen.

Instead, by the end of World War I, the cause of women as citizens selecting electoral representatives through the ballot had become, especially in the United Kingdom and the United States, part of the larger struggle for progress and "civilization" (an approach that often ended up further reinforcing existing racial and cultural hierarchies, including colonial ones). It also came to stand for democracy and liberty in marked contrast to both German and Bolshevik alternatives. Or at least that's how Christabel Pankhurst, Sylvia's less radical sister, packaged it in 1918, proclaiming in newfound support of the British state, "Let us remember that our Suffrage Victory will not be final until the war is won, because Germany, at once if completely victorious, and in the near future if successful in getting a compromise Peace, would sweep away for ever the votes of British women as well as of British men."[139] White Americans too similarly insisted in the shadow of World War I that women's suffrage—despite explicit exclusions that would require another fifty or so years of Black and white activism to rectify—marked nothing less than the triumph of Lady Liberty herself.[140] Look no further than Charles Dana Gibson's October 1920 cover illustration for *Life* magazine showing Columbia, the slightly oversized personification of liberty, handing a ballot to an elegant but real-looking, modern, white woman suffragist and offering "congratulations" (fig. 4.14).

This, too, was to prove an exportable analogy. It took decades more and, in many cases, another world war before women in most countries around the world were accorded the right to vote. Gradually other nations began to fall into line. By 1920, enfranchised women in thirty nations around the world were dropping ballots into boxes. Many more nations saw active pro–women's suffrage movements emerge soon thereafter, and victories came by the end of the first half of the century in nations ranging from Mongolia to Turkey to Brazil, as well as virtually all of Europe.[141]

The cause of women at the polls was generally not, at least initially, coterminous with any specific political or religious orientation, as had also been the case for the secret ballot. Socialist states, beginning with Russia in 1917, were actually in the forefront (with the exception of the former British colonies in the South Pacific). Definitions of eligible voters, as well as of the excluded, varied too, undermining the very idea of "women" as a single coherent category. And again, lest we romanticize even the promise of this development, we need keep in mind that the whole business of adding voters to the rolls was, everywhere, heavily

Fig. 4.14. Charles Dana Gibson, "Congratulations," designed as the cover of the American magazine *Life* (October 28, 1920).

dependent on an increase in rules and formal procedures controlling menus and behavior alike at the moment of decision making. Some commentators, like the political theorist Benjamin Barber, have gone so far as to equate the act of voting in the modern world to using a public toilet (a traditional point of comparison, along with huts, confessionals, and jail cells, for critics of secret voting): one enters the booth, closes the door, relieves oneself in solitude of one's burden, pulls the lever, and leaves.[142] The point for Barber was not just the loss of any aesthetic or festive dimension in what should be "an occasion for celebration as well as choice," as he put it. It was that the whole act of political choice-making, even when the product of mass suffrage, had ceased to link the voter or chooser to any larger community. That might be even more the case today, when online voting means the whole process can, in some places, be undertaken from the kitchen table.

Other critics go further and claim that in today's capitalist democracies, these sporadic and isolated enactments of political choice also have decreasingly little practical utility in terms of realizing citizens' collective desires and objectives; most policymaking now happens very far from the voting booth. What's more, political life for most of us has been reduced almost entirely, if one discounts social media postings, to this occasional act. The ballot, in other words, has been offered to more people, but self-rule in any tangible, sustained sense has itself increasingly been rendered moot.[143] The Russian joke about elections—that they feature "vybory bez vyborov," or choice without choice, playing on the identity of the Russian word for choice and elections—seems potentially apt for other places too. These are all reasonable critiques.

Still, voting—and especially voting by women—has not shed its status as an emblem of modern liberty, and it shouldn't. That is the case whether triggered initially by male franchise reforms, or new notions of female equity, or even interparty competition. And that's rooted as much as anything in the enduring symbolic value of the act itself, especially in its post-Pontefract form. Recall Walt Whitman's great poem "Election Day, November 1884," a stirring tribute to what he calls "America's choosing day" in which he insisted "The heart of it not in the chosen—the act itself the main, the quadrennial choosing."[144] Or look closely at Jacob Lawrence's depiction of the symbolic victory of 1920s northern Black voters, male and female, formally but freely lined up to cast their ballots despite the obvious presence of law enforcement, in one of the great images of his Migration series called *In the North they had the freedom to vote* (fig. 4.15). Choosing here is as much an end unto itself as a means to something else. With the expansion of voting—and specifically with

Fig. 4.15. Jacob Lawrence, *The Migration Series, panel no. 59: In the North they had the freedom to vote* (1940–41), tempera on hardboard, The Phillips Collection, Washington, D.C.

women's ultimately successful efforts to gain the franchise as it was re-made in the latter part of the nineteenth century—choosing by oneself was finally established not just as *the* way to realize one's ideas and aims but also what gives one standing as a full, autonomous, adult person in the first place. Bounded choice was, through this act, fully transformed into the dominant form of freedom in modern life.[145]

And in this vein, women's inclusion in the business of enacting political choice has, a hundred years later, become part of the gold standard for modernity and human rights, just like the secret ballot before it. Nations that long refused to enfranchise women, like Saudi Arabia, paid a price in terms of their international stature. Now even Saudi women can vote (in municipal elections)—as can, in principle, women everywhere in the world except the Vatican. The General Assembly of the United Nations adopted in 1979 an international *women's* bill of rights, the first of its kind, which spells out universal female political rights, starting with the right to participate in elections.[146] In the course of the twentieth century, voting—one of the last forms of choice-making made routinely available to women—turned into the basic form of choice on which all other choices must rest for every adult. The next frontier then became determining what all these modern forms of choosing actually meant, not least in the so-called land of Lady Liberty. That's also when the moral stakes started to creep back in.

CHAPTER 5

THE SCIENCES OF CHOICE

CAPITALISM. DEMOCRACY. By the start of the twentieth century, the making of small-bore choices was well on its way to being an ordinary feature of adult experience in North America, western and central Europe, and parts of Latin America, Africa, and Asia. In all of these places, a growing number of people regularly inserted themselves into certain kinds of markets as objects for selection, whether as job seekers, candidates for office, or potential spouses, lovers, or even friends. These same people also chose among existing possibilities, both live and inert, exclusive and not, including foods for dinner, entertainment options, people to contract with, and more. Some subset—an expanding realm of "choice architects"—helped make all this picking and choosing happen.

The significance accorded to these activities evolved in tandem. As the rules and procedures around the business of selection got more formal and standardized, the external moral strictures on the choices themselves started to fall away. They became more and more personal, driven by one's own predilections, or so at least it seemed. But simultaneously, this very particular kind of decision making, in its increasingly value-neutral and individualized but highly managed form, became an anchor concept within two ascendant and equally abstract systems for organizing human lives: market-based consumer culture and democratic governance. Arguably, in the mid-twentieth-century "free world," it became a focal point for their convergence, even or maybe especially as it remained largely absent from the workplace. As the French philosopher Simone Weil stated flatly in the 1940s, conveying the standard wisdom of her moment in places characterized by both, "Liberty, taking the word in its concrete sense, consists in the ability to choose."[1] That meant doubly what one wants to do and what one wants to be.

In practice, needless to say, both options and opportunities to make selections—even apart from those more obviously regimented and coercive hours spent in wage labor—were still wildly disproportionately distributed at the start of the twentieth century. They remain so today even as that Weil quote about freedom-as-choice maintains its transatlantic political currency.[2] Despite increases in voting access and the concurrent rise of public education and the welfare state in much of the world over the last hundred and fifty years, subordinated segments of the population have continued everywhere to be denied an equal share of either good alternatives to choose among or occasions for doing so. That includes women across the boundaries of race, class, age, religion, or ethnicity. Even in light of the advances of the nineteenth century in terms of new spaces for female choice-making in certain segments of the world, it would take decades more, everywhere, before even white, propertied women living in democracies secured anything like the full range of both possibilities and opportunities for choosing available formally to white men. For Black women and other racial and ethnic minorities of both sexes, it took—or more accurately, is taking—even longer, as the concept of separate gender spheres and racial discrimination have together shaped existence at every turn, especially in white-dominated places.

Moreover, money continues to hinder choice-making for the poor of all races—and maybe even more than in the past, as wealth becomes ever more the key modern facilitator of choice in multiple domains. (Democratic politics, where a formal equality of choice-making opportunities is still mandated at the level of the vote, is coming to seem increasingly anomalous.) Indeed, in practice, some people gaining in independent choices has as often worked to limit them for others as to expand them across the board, as in when, say, one person's decision to corner the market on a commodity like radio stations or to buy something dangerous like a gun ends up restricting the options available to others. Choice has rarely been a synonym for equality.

Nevertheless, what is worth noting is also that formal restrictions on participation in the full arena of regulated and structured choice, and especially suffrage, had, by the outbreak of World War I, become a specific and established political grievance in much of the world. Or, to put it another way, expanded choice-making opportunity was on its way to becoming a standard and collective aspiration—for men and women alike—in a variety of types of societies. It is in this context that a very old set of questions came back to the fore. These were, arguably, conundrums about human motivation, or what was now called psychology, that novelists had been probing since the eighteenth century, if not earlier: When do we—individually and collectively—choose to choose? And when we do, how and why does each of us decide to make the particular choices that we make, given the available options?

Even before the start of World War I and its profound challenge to older notions of human rationality, such mysteries began to garner new attention. Then, in the first decades of the 1900s, an auxiliary question became part of the broad intellectual landscape of the West, inspired in good measure by the Darwinian idea that human beings could be studied just like any other species: Can there be a "science" of the kind of reasoning and decision making known as choice?[3]

The search for an answer produced new kinds of experts: social scientists, inside and outside of academia, from psychologists to marketers to statisticians to economists, who took their job to be uncovering, explicating, and, in a good number of cases, redirecting the (already familiar) choice-making behavior of others. The particular methods these authorities used, however, just as much as the answers they came to, were to change widely held conceptions of the self, with the full participation of ordinary choosers, just in time for the emergence of what some now call the last form of utopianism.[4] That is the ideology of human rights, including feminism. Choice, remade as freedom from others' desires and demands, for women as well as men, ultimately became a key component of modern morality too. Indeed, the value of choice unto itself turned into a *doxic* notion for our times, seemingly without a backstory, even as feminism as a political movement has had its ups and downs. It is this late development, most fully realized in the United States but hardly confined to it, that this final chapter will recount.

Calling Freud

One of the most prominent—and striking—arguments at the turn of the century could perhaps be seen as a form of backlash. In Europe's major cities, there was no denying even in that moment that more and more people appeared to be availing themselves—crucially, primarily away from the workplace in terms of time or space—of the chance to participate in various kinds of individualized selection processes. It was also widely apparent that the possibility of doing so was, fitfully, expanding to new classes of people previously excluded from the realm of choice, though more often in metropoles than in hinterlands or colonies. Both developments were widely associated by then with a nascent political liberalism, combined with imperialism, that prized "free" expression, "free" trade, "free" association, and "free" elections, albeit governed by a wealth of formal and informal rules and prohibitions. But just as the new century was beginning, the Viennese doctor Sigmund Freud, eager to understand human motivations, came to a startling conclusion about all this urban choice-making activity. Based on his clinical work with patients suffering from nervous disorders, not to mention a considerable literary imagination of his own, he challenged the idea that modern people, male or female, were really in charge of their own destinies at all. That was despite what he called their "deeply rooted *belief* in psychic freedom and choice."[5]

For according to Freud's early works, when we humans think that we are acting of our own "free" will, especially in the making of affective and sexual choices, we are generally doing anything but. Our choices are not only largely irrational in the sense of uncorrelated with what seem to be our own, freely chosen preferences and desires; they are governed in good part by processes over which we have no control or, often, even knowledge. Worse, much of the time these processes actually inhibit our ability to achieve what we wish, making free choice an illusion that must, as Freud put it, "give ground before the claims of a determinism which governs even mental life."[6]

One of Freud's earliest and most enduring propositions, derived in good part from his work with female patients in the last decade and a half of the nineteenth century and already evident in his *Three Essays on the Theory of Sexuality* (1905), was that one's personality, including libido or sexual drive, was shaped very early on in childhood. According to the Viennese doctor, in each developmental stage, children focused their desires on a different sexual "object."[7] Initially, that object was a part of their own bodies, and children were quite flexible about what would do the trick. But as early as the toddler years, children were driven to pick another person as the dominant object of their desires. This process had everything to do with their unacknowledged feelings toward their own parents of the same and opposite sexes, even if it didn't subsequently seem that way. These early choices then set a pattern that would harden in puberty, as self-preservation typically (but certainly not always) directed them to attach themselves to someone else of the same sex as the desired parent. Indeed, these choices ultimately determined the very person one would become. And ironically, that meant that what Freud in his *Introductory Lectures on Psychoanalysis* (delivered in 1915–17 and published in 1916–17) was to call "object-choice"—the selection in childhood of a type of person toward whom libidinal energy would henceforth extended—was not really a choice at all.[8] It was not motivated or even conscious at the moment of its initial formation. Nor was it subject to deliberate manipulation later on.

On the contrary, all of this early history of object choice was naturally "repressed," in Freud's terms, or stored away in our "unconscious." There it remained, largely inarticulable and unavailable to our adult selves. Yet the unconscious continued to shape our lives as individuals, affecting our psychic health and often our behavior too. At best, sublimation of our unfulfilled desires allowed for the flourishing of elements of civilization, including the production of great works of art and other forms of human ingenuity, as Freud was later to propose in *Civilization and Its Discontents* (1930).[9] Mainly, as Freud explained in the wake of World War I, repression accounted for our misery—and not just for the seriously neurotic. At the extreme, people developed compulsions, which are situations in which one's thoughts and intentions end up making no difference in terms of what one actually does.[10] But even in less severe cases, individual freedom, on the one hand, and civilization, with all its implicit taboos, laws, and customs starting with its restricted menu of object choices, on the other, were permanently opposed, the one the direct antagonist of the other.

Karl Marx had already famously insisted in the mid-nineteenth century that "men make their own history, but they do not make it just as they please; they do not make it under circumstances chosen by themselves, but under circumstances directly encountered, given and transmitted from the past."[11] He meant mainly the external, material conditions of their lives. Freud added the extra weight of circumstances internal to the self that were often equally, if not more, opaque. Over more than three decades of theoretical texts, case studies, public appearances, training sessions, and other opportunities for proselytizing and debate, Freud leveled a profound attack on late nineteenth-century liberal verities about what made for an autonomous self.

Many other intellectuals influenced by and responsible for variants of Freud's ideas would continue to advance these arguments well into the middle of the twentieth century. We might even say that just as choice was taking off as an organizing principle for modern, Western existence, Freud and his acolytes detached it from conventional notions of autonomy and agency. Think of all of those twentieth-century novels—a good example is *Children's Bach* (1984) by the Australian novelist Helen Garner—that are full of characters who don't actually know why they have made the choices they have and find themselves suffering the consequences.

And yet, importantly, this isn't the full story. Psychoanalysis (as Freudians termed this way of seeing) was not exclusively a theory of human nature. It was also a method—and a potential escape hatch from this deterministic and potentially defeatist view of human mental and physical life. For according to Freud and subsequent psychoanalysts (as practitioners of Freud's method and variants became known), the individual, with the guidance of this kind of professional in the science of human choice, *could* arrive at greater knowledge of him- or herself. By way of techniques like "free" association, which meant saying whatever comes to mind without regard for any of the proprieties and within the self-contained space of the psychoanalyst's clinic, the patient could begin to access, via traces, the remote strata of the mind called the unconscious where that which is normally sublimated makes its home.[12] It was a matter of defeating the censors within as well as without. With greater understanding of one's own mind and, consequently, the sources of one's (bad) prior choices, one became capable of taking an important step toward genuine control over one's own future. Or, to put it slightly differently, one could use free will to recover free choice, which, for Freud, meant emancipation tout court. Freedom from inner bondage or repression required, for the patient, getting out of one's own way so as to be able to (a) make the choices one actually wanted (colloquially: "be oneself"), and (b) experience the moral agency of a full-fledged, self-sovereign adult rather than the dependency and impulsiveness associated more and more with children. This might not produce anything like happiness, in Freud's estimation. But it would help restore an individual's capacity to function as a truly autonomous being.

Furthermore, this path to liberation was not restricted to men. Yes, it's true: Freud clearly viewed women as having a less strong urge to choose; just one of the many feminine stereotypes he would employ in the pursuit of science was that women's inherent narcissism "affects women's choice of object, so that to be loved [i.e., chosen by another] is a stronger need for them than to love [i.e., choose an object for themselves]."[13] Yet women could still get in on the game. Women too could come to consciousness of themselves and the particular kind of modern freedom this entailed. What is more, they could, with the right training, serve as experts in choice and even agents of improved choice-making, aka psychoanalysts, themselves, much as Freud's daughter Anna was famously to do.[14] In the end, part of Freud's appeal—as his ideas spread rapidly from beyond central Europe and entered popular consciousness from London to Dakar to Mexico City[15]—was surely not just that he explained behavior that seemed otherwise inexplicable. It was also that he invented, just as the new century was beginning, a self-professed "science" focused on knowing the individual choosing subject, that emerging icon of the liberal, capitalist order, better than it might have otherwise seemed possible.[16]

We might conclude, then, that for all the talk of the death of man and for all the attention to determinist philosophies of human behavior with which he is often associated, Freud had a second legacy. It was the idea that we humans can develop rigorous, quasi-scientific methods not just to structure the making of choices but also to understand how and why, not to mention when and where, men or women, individually and collectively, choose as they do. Talk therapy in the clinic proved, ulti-mately, to be only one such tool for getting there. Multiple methods, from individualized questionnaires about motivations shaping future choices to the statistical study of choices already made, were employed in the course of the twentieth century for the study of choice behavior. In practice, such methods helped generate new conceptions of human nature. They also reinforced the idea that the human is, at his or (even-tually) her core, fundamentally capable of being a rational chooser de-spite the profound interior as well as exterior obstacles that had to be confronted along the way. Indeed, a variety of quasi-scientific studies of choice, corralling ordinary men and women into service as willing par-ticipants, helped make it seem as if this were, in fact, what nature in-tended of humans all along.

Marketers' Psychology, or the Measuring of Choice

Advertisers and marketers, especially those a world away from Vienna in the American Midwest, got there at almost the same moment. The growth of thinking in terms of markets, including metaphorical ones, was, in part, an effect of an era characterized in the United States by specific economic developments on the supply side, namely, new kinds of manufactured products, sold in new kinds of retail outlets, and pro-moted by new forms of advertising in novel spaces. Sewing machines, bicycles, and chewing gum; department stores, chain stores, and book-sized mail-order catalogs; electric signs, streetcar cards, and bill-boards: the end of the nineteenth century and the start of the twentieth was the dawn of the age of mass production *and* consumption. If the endless supermarket cereal aisle is today the visual emblem of the superfluity of choice, this is when it all began. Transportation and communications innovations helped. So did state encouragement of consumption, including infrastructure investment but also financial regulation and consumer protection and basic welfare provisions, all increasingly vital elements of modern liberalism.[17] But the size, makeup, and tastes of the pool of potential buyers changed in the United States at the same time. Consider that, by the 1920s, even parts of the working class began to have the capacity to buy branded products for personal use. And as the business and practice of selling grew in scale and competitiveness, and both goods and the advertising attached to them became increasingly national, so did the practical need to "understand" the customer-turned-consumer and his or her mentality.

Once again, that meant, largely, desires. However, the desires that preoccupied businesspeople in the age of mass consumption were chiefly commercial (and thus monetizable) rather than strictly sexual, though they were never really all that separate. What was needed were solid answers to such questions as: What motivates a wife, in need of clean clothes for her family, to choose one brand of soap over another? Why does her husband choose to purchase a car—or refrain from doing so entirely? How, in other words, can we explain various individuals' basic decisions in the realm of material consumption but also, more generally, about how to live in those limited free hours during which one hopes to govern oneself?

As myriad historians have demonstrated before me, psychology became entwined in the business of American advertising starting right after the turn of the new century in good part to answer these questions.[18] Of particular significance here was Walter Dill Scott, who billed himself initially as "Director of the Psychological Laboratory" of Northwestern University in Chicago, before adding in 1909 the very new-sounding title of "Professor of Advertising" at the Commerce School. In an earlier series of talks, articles in trade journals, and then books aimed at the growing ranks of ad men (still something of a new job description at the start of the last century), Scott repeatedly made the same case: that psychology, which he called "nothing but a stubborn and systematic attempt to understand and explain the workings of . . . [people's] minds," could be a "stable foundation for a theory of advertising."[19] That's because the laws of human choice-making, which had "always been assumed to be unknown, to be the one indeterminable factor in the universe," could now actually be ascertained. In fact, they could be used to stoke, even manufacture desire for one thing rather than another, the essential precursor to making a sale.[20] Because customers were open to suggestion, which is to say, manipulation, they could, in the famous words of the American journalist Samuel Strauss in the 1920s, be produced rather than found.[21]

Other early advertising gurus soon followed Scott's suit, insisting that generating effective advertising meant first becoming a student of human nature. With the right tricks—appealing to the senses, triggering feelings like sympathy or pride rather than sticking with logic—advertisers could, according to industry cheerleaders like Earnest Elmo Calkins and Ralph Holden, generate "certain effects on the minds of possible customers" and thus get them to "buy, believe and think the things that the advertiser wants them to buy, believe and think." For advertising itself, Calkins and Holden continued, was nothing but "that subtle, indefinable, but powerful force whereby the advertiser creates a demand for a given article in the minds of a great many people or arouses the demand that is already there in latent form."[22] The right advertisements, directed to the right people with the right techniques, could—as Josiah Wedgwood and many a shopkeeper already knew in the eighteenth century—shape "wills" so as to get people to think *and* behave differently, whether that meant deciding to purchase a novel gadget or to try different foods at breakfast time. The promise was nothing less than health, happiness, maybe even excitement, albeit with lighter pocketbooks afterward. Manufactured dissatisfactions, including discovering what one lacked, could—by a new category of skilled choice agents like Scott—be turned into manufactured satisfactions.

However, a counterargument also ran through early twentieth-century American advertising discourse: though the buying public could sometimes be persuaded to choose this over that, it was never *fully* controllable. The most sophisticated analysts, going back to Scott himself, emphasized that there were limits to public malleability. Potential consumers were, in fact, often in on the game, succumbing to the sales pressure—that is, to actually closing the deal—only intermittently and only when they actually chose to do so.

One fictious image (maybe more than any piece of fictious writing) makes this point clear already in 1885, just before modern advertising really took off. That year, Philadelphia painter John Peto, long obscure before his mid-twentieth-century rediscovery, produced a remarkable painting of a heap of very used books and other paper ephemera that appear to be spilling out of the picture plane, beyond the frame, into the viewer's space. The viewer feels him- or herself to be only inches away from a disorderly but intriguing country book sale. Indeed, some of Peto's other canvases of this moment are labeled "job-lot" or "store" to make their commercial nature clear. And in this case, going back to an old tradition in both advertising and political contest, the painter titled the work himself with an ironic command, "*Take Your Choice!*," in effect calling attention to the way the image implicated the viewer, pushing that person to resist reaching out his or her hand and grabbing the object that most appealed on a personal level (fig. 5.1).

In soliciting the viewer so directly, Peto wasn't alone. Over the next decade, other American painters working in a similar style and genre encouraged their audience to "Leave Your Order Here" on a realistically rendered but faux grocery blackboard, complete with a dangling piece of chalk for the viewer to write down his selection (fig. 5.2). Or they beckoned "Free Sample, Take One," with a simulation of a cupboard filled with peanuts behind broken glass, as in a famous painting by S. S. David of that same name. A few years earlier, Peto's own *Help Yourself* (1881) had similarly featured a bag of candy of many kinds spilling tantalizingly right toward the viewer, promising fulfillment if its boundaries were broached.

Yet of course, the possibility of picking out, mentally or physically, one of those peanuts or candies or one of the books in "*Take Your*

Fig. 5.1. John Peto, *Take Your Choice!* (1885), oil on canvas.

Choice!" was actually an impossibility, a product of the kind of illusion in which the trompe l'oeil painters popular in late nineteenth-century America specialized. The appeal for the audience (and we know that many of the purchasers of these paintings were merchants who hung them both at home and in commercial establishments, including the windows of Philadelphia's Wanamaker Department Store, though Peto himself never sold much) was the way such paintings simultaneously commanded and thwarted the familiar act of choosing as a step toward getting. That is, they created a game, knowing the viewer would ultimately see it as such. In seducing with objects ripe for plucking but calling attention to their artifice at the same time, *"Take Your Choice!"* and related works actually accorded considerable psychological agency to the chooser standing in front of the illusionistic canvas.[23]

And according to more sophisticated commentators on the business of advertising after the turn of the century, customers' ability to see beyond surfaces when they so desired was not all that made most advertising campaigns ineffective in determining customers' choices with anything like precision. For one, noted economist-turned-advertiser

Fig. 5.2. John Haberle, *The Slate* (c. 1895), oil on canvas, MFA Boston.

Joseph French Johnson in 1910 in the advertising industry's main journal, the *Printers' Ink*, "man is a bundle of potential wants, infinite in number," that change all the time. Just ask anyone in the fashion business, he noted. For another, when a customer satisfied one desire, it usually meant letting another go unrealized, thus potentially creating internal as well as external competition among the options: "If we buy an auto we will not be able to flash the gold, the silver, the silk and the fine linen which we might otherwise have flashed. In our sub-conscious way we put the things on the scales and we decide which we want most."[24]

Finally, in what sounds like a precursor of what was to come—here on the part of Harvard business professor Paul T. Cherington, who would subsequently leave academia to go to work in the J. Walter Thompson ad agency's fledgling research division—the purchaser, newly armed with disposable income in many cases, wants ultimately to feel he is making his own selections and thus defining himself by himself: "When the consumer buys, *he* does the *choosing*. He asserts his particular individuality. He expresses his likes or dislikes down to the most subtle differences. He weighs values between this and that brand of a similar product. He discriminates; he wants *what* he wants—and he gets it."[25]

The idea of using commodities to fabricate a distinctive identity rooted in one's personal style and tastes was, of course, partly the invention of advertisers in the first place, going back to the nineteenth century. Still, advertisers also saw it as a natural fact that the buyer desired to feel in control of his or her choices regardless of advertisers' ongoing efforts in manipulation. That experience soon became possible in new ways—and for women as well as men. By the end of the 1920s, an advertising-generated yearning for unmediated choice was enshrined in the first "self-serve" stores, namely, supermarkets. There the possibility of selecting goods entirely on one's own and without any external pressure (albeit once the options for sale had been carefully preselected by so-called experts) became a new selling point for customers of both sexes as well as retailers. So did the idea of satisfying personal tastes directly. No one emphasized that the purchaser would now be doing, unpaid and unaided, the work once done by others for a wage. Instead, promoters of the supermarket deemed it the ultimate space of autonomy and, consequently, pleasure and freedom. It was the place where, as an early ad for the memorably named American supermarket chain Piggly Wiggly put it, "You [the customer] take anything you please from the attractive open shelves, examine it leisurely, decide. There, the choice foods of the five continents have been assembled . . . for you to single out what you wish."[26] Consider, too, the contrast to the regimented world of work, where only the boss had much volition. All you needed for this new leisure-time experience was a rolling basket or cart—still the emblem of the independent shopper, even in the virtual marketplace of today—to gather all your personally made selections.

But what that meant in the first decade and a half of the twentieth century, and even more during World War I and the decade to follow, was that vague theories about the function of the human mind, or a universal consumer ethos, were not going to suffice. The actual consumer, in all of his or her particularity and growing autonomy, needed to become an object of study, singly and in the aggregate. For in order to know what to produce more of or anew, how to package it, where to place it in a shop, how much to sell it for, how to extend its appeal, and, ultimately, how to coax further (consumer) choices that translated into sales out of the future buyer, the manufacturer or distributor or storeowner or advertiser had to understand his or her specific target audience, as subject and object, in the here and now. And that required learning not just who lived where and how much money they had, all data available from various national censuses. It also meant uncovering what were soon called their "buying habits" or what they had previously purchased or planned to purchase when and where. What had to be discovered were the influences and motivations, conscious and not, behind all those acts of both routine and exceptional commercial choice-making. Advertisers, it turned out, needed to know how to mold preferences and also how to meet them, in a reciprocal dance with their customers.

Studying the customer necessitated first paying attention to differences in preference or taste or disposition—whether for goods, places to shop, or the kinds of advertising campaigns built around them—that were linked to race, ethnic identity, nationality of origin, place of residence, religion, age, occupation, class, and, especially, gender. The goal was to identify what were thought to be both sociologically and biologically determined patterns. Scott had already, in his early work, stressed the centrality of women as consumers. He had also called attention to the different psychology that women—or, as they were often referred to in the magazines and advertising literature of the era that invented them, "housewives"—brought to the act of consumption.[27] Female consumers, Scott noted, were more susceptible to suggestion, made more decisions about purchases that could be called spontaneous and emotional, and, in what might seem like a contradiction, showed greater interest in reading the fine print of advertisements closely.[28]

Subsequent advocates of the application of psychology to advertising, like University of Michigan psychology professor Henry Foster Adams, added other traits, many of them purportedly based on laboratory experiments, that he claimed were vital to take into account when considering the divergent consumption habits of the two sexes. Men are more likely to notice blue, for example, whereas red works better on women; men's attention is more likely to be fixed on pictures, though women remember them better; women prefer personal appeals, not to mention things labeled "bargain" and "cheap," while men are partial to "special sales"; women have more pride, whether for themselves or for the political and social groups of which they are a part, but when it comes to persuasion, men are more interested in the recommendations of persons of authority, appeals to their occupational group, or flattery of their intelligence; and, quoting one of his contemporaries in the field of applied psychology, "men agree more closely in their preferences and women are more alike in their dislikes."[29]

Again, much of the rhetoric about tailoring products to meet the specifications of men and women separately would have been commonsensical already to those who had developed products for the book or textile trade in London or Amsterdam going back to the early eighteenth century; market segmentation was not, in practice, new, whether the goods initially came from China, India, or Milwaukee.[30] But now, comprehension of what Adams called these "mental sex differences" born of both natural and vocational difference between men and women turned into a problem to be studied, a question of science.[31] That was especially the case as domestic markets, particularly in urban settings, grew more diverse according to various metrics. Generalizations about men and women now required correlation with other sorts of data, including both demographic and economic facts, on the one hand, and what often amounted to cultural stereotypes about immigrants or the poor or people of color, on the other (though close study of those deemed less likely to consume, including all of the above categories, was comparatively limited everywhere until at least the 1920s).[32] Class differences were long understood to be a significant variable in shaping buying preferences, starting with sources of persuasion. As Scott himself noted, attention to price point was not enough: "It is a well-observed fact that different classes of society think differently and that arguments which would appeal to one class would be worthless with another."[33] Others now stressed attention to racial, ethnic, and national roots too. For as a writer in *Printers' Ink* put it in 1915, "while human nature is the same under every sky, the overlying veneer differs widely, East and West and North and South. It is quite as important to study racial and national characteristics as it is to inform one's self about business laws and customs of foreign peoples."[34]

Thus was born consumer research. By the start of World War I, special departments devoted to the study of aspects of commercial markets, including purchasers themselves, had already been forged within some of the biggest advertising agencies in the nation, including Mahin Advertising in Chicago, N. W. Ayer & Son in Philadelphia, and J. Walter Thompson in New York. A number of newspaper and magazine publishers who depended on both subscriptions and advertising for revenue had done the same internally, hoping as a result of their work to sell both more space in their pages and their own services as business consultants. Independent research organizations such as the Business Bourse (1908), the Eastman Research Bureau (1916), and the Market Research Company (1918) followed suit, as did Harvard Business School with the establishment of its Bureau of Business Research (1911). What all of these enterprises offered up to those with a pecuniary interest in aligning supply and demand were expert middlemen, specialists in fostering the relationship between what we would now call the "choice set" being offered, on the one hand, and the tastes and habits of choosers in various segments of the population, on the other. Practitioners in the area of advertising concerned with marketing, as it was increasingly known in the first two decades of the twentieth century, would, for cash, help others cater to the customer and his or her discernment by exposing him or her to scrutiny in ways never experienced before.[35]

The *Chicago Tribune*, the paper of record on the home terrain of Scott and many other early leading figures of the new "scientific" advertising, promised even before World War I broke out that it could, for the right fee, reveal to business clients not just who and where their readership was, district by district across Chicago, but also what that readership desired and what that readership did when it entered the market. The question was how. Freudians got to know the minds of their subjects through sustained one-on-one conversation, albeit in the artificially controlled space of the therapy session and conducted by a professional on unequal terms with the patient. The new experts in consumer research, including those at the *Tribune*, largely took a different tack, one designed to learn about many people at once and in a way that could then become generalizable by type, though detailed in-person interviews were still widely used too. Borrowing once again from contemporary psychologists in terms of method, the *Tribune's* market researchers took up the practice of garnering what they claimed was reliable intelligence on customer choices through direct consumer surveys done in the field.[36]

Starting in 1913, the *Tribune's* Merchandising Service Department developed a questionnaire that could be used to learn its own readers' "buying and reading habits" as well as what shaped those habits, household by household, neighborhood by neighborhood. The information was so specific and factually exact, claimed its spokespeople, that "this Department can tell you, for example, whether Mrs. R. M. Lansing, 4722 Woodlawn Avenue, buys her merchandise at her neighborhood stores or in the loop [the main shopping area in downtown Chicago]; whether or not she prefers bulk to package goods and whether window displays, newspaper advertisements, street car cards or circulars make the greatest appeal to her." By then aggregating and anonymizing this data, they could reveal patterns by area, by ethnicity, or by class, though these were often the same, as researchers drew conclusions about Chicago consumers and their enclaves based on whether they were "American," German, Italian, "Negro," Lithuanian, Jewish, Polish, Bohemian, Irish, Scandinavian, or "mixed."[37]

Another *Tribune* experiment of just a bit later promised to reveal readers' responses to four more specific questions: "What are your favorite brands of food and why do you buy them? How was your attention first called to each? What has your experience been with each? and How much are you influenced by the labels and by the known purity of food products?" The answers were then tabulated and classified to show general trends in relation to yet more demographic facts.[38] Other businesses, including the Kellogg Company in Michigan, did the same with mail-in postcard questionnaires, in a sense updating the voluntary straw poll format that had been a feature of American newspapers since the 1820s. A century later, paid market panels and juries were employed to related ends. Historians have even found evidence that the credit departments of some American department stores did something similar starting in the 1920s, establishing retail data mining along lines of market segmentation as one more way to glean actionable intelligence about the buying habits of American consumers.[39]

Yet before we think of this as an entirely top-down or coercive enterprise, it is important to recognize that customers themselves, from subscribers to major national magazines to purchasers of all those Kellogg breakfast cereals, willingly participated in large numbers in these new endeavors, almost all of them without compensation. Whether at the door of their homes, on street corners, in stores, or via a stamp and a trip to the mailbox, they freely offered up personal information to strangers. What is more, the information they supplied went well beyond the demographic data traditionally given to census takers. With checked boxes, filled-out forms, and even copies of their household budgets, they shared what they aspired to own, what they believed, what they did.

Advertisers speculated that members of the public, across various social divides, agreed to do so in response to some combination of flattery, personal interest, and a desire to be useful. Incentives like a free cookbook occasionally helped. Yet what respondents' answers also suggest is a certain unspoken agreement between researcher and subject: that subjects were not looking to fight material temptations in the vein of Hercules at the crossroads but were instead defining themselves in good part by their desires and choices about which to realize. Moreover, they wanted to publicly "express" their "views" on these questions, in the words of mid-century marketing expert Mildred Parten, and to be noticed and heard for who they were.[40] Twentieth-century American consumers, in other words, also freely commodified themselves, further advancing the understanding that the world was made up of markets and they were the sum of their consumption choices within those markets. Or at least they collaborated in the making of this idea.[41] We do the same today every time we turn on a computer and browse the web, knowingly and usually willingly producing metadata about ourselves from which others will surely profit.

Not that it was always so easy to establish this working connection in the print era. Consumer research by paper survey was labor-intensive and expensive. By the time a *Tribune* survey taker talked to Mrs. Lansing at 4722 Woodlawn, this same interviewer had found the lady of the house out at two other addresses on the same street, another refusing to talk, and yet another unhelpful because "deaf as a door-nail." But Mrs. Lansing, whose husband was a vice president at the National City Bank and was herself a member of several clubs, was frank about her preferences. She liked to buy locally and in bulk when it was cheaper, but she was hostile to being labeled a "bargain hunter." She also preferred to shop for clothing downtown for the greater variety afforded. She characterized herself as a "believer" in advertising from way back who nevertheless did not see ads ever causing her to buy something she hadn't thought of before. It was window displays that impacted her choices most, she volunteered. By contrast, an Irish motorman named Peter Conway of 2637 Rice Street bought mainly in the neighborhood and at sales. He also trusted the recommendations of the dealer over advertisements. He thought most advertisements were best described as "fakes," though he admitted to using coupons taken from magazines to get some bookcases, and he claimed to read ads in the papers. Like Mrs. Lansing's, his answers (whether free form, selected from a list, or ranked) were not always consistent from question to question.[42]

Indeed, no sooner had such surveys been launched as a modern business practice than "marketing" turned into an academic discipline, a subfield of business education, in which methods of effective data collection and even question design and analysis were increasingly topics of scrutiny. Textbooks on the subject, which started to appear in the late

1910s and blossomed in the 1920s, remained steeped in the psychology of the consumer or "buying motives."[43] J. George Frederick, for example, originally an editor at *Judicious Advertising* in Chicago and then at *Printers' Ink* in New York, insisted in one of the first such guides to the nascent discipline that "field investigations" be accompanied by study of the consumer's "unconscious reaction," since "the conscious self is a censor," an idea he had clearly borrowed from an unnamed Freud.[44] The celebrity Viennese analyst made a tentative appearance in Columbia professor Albert Poffenberger's *Psychology in Advertising* (1925) as well, this time in relation to the consumer's "suppression" of unpleasant memories as a finding of "questionnaire studies," and eventually, in the 1940s, the Viennese Jewish émigré advertiser Ernest Dichter brought the conversation fully back to sex and hidden motivations from the perspective of Freudian psychoanalysis.[45] But American marketing gurus, whose graduate training more often stemmed in the first years from economics or psychology as developed at German and then American research universities, increasingly took their cues from an ascendant behavioralism.[46] That meant shifting the focus, as psychologist Henry Link was to put it in *The New Psychology of Selling and Advertising* (1932), from the "old psychology [which] was the study of *how* the mind *thinks*" to "the new psychology [which] is a study of how the mind *acts*"—or observable behavior in the marketplace. The way to accomplish the goal of accessing consumers' subjectivity was through the actual record of purchases—or concrete, enacted choices in real circumstances—made by what behavioral-psychologist-turned-advertising-executive John Broadus Watson called, in the preface to Link's key text, "Mr. and Mrs. Consumer."[47]

But that also meant even greater attention to market segmentation—and especially to the behavior of the female half of this couple, Mrs. Consumer, and her children. In 1919, Carson S. Duncan, professor of commerce and administration at the University of Chicago, a hotbed of the new approach, insisted on the need to focus, across regional, racial, and ethnic differences, on women as well as youths, who were now experiencing "greater freedom of choice" too.[48] So did a host of other commentators, including a corps of female copywriters and advertisers with specialties in women's buying habits, all of whom helped further skew the gender focus of market research—and often equated women with children even as they also celebrated women's mental independence and sovereignty within the home.[49] By 1930, another Columbia marketing professor, Paul Nystrom, could declare in a new edition of his innovative *The Economics of Retailing*, originally published in 1915, that the woman has to be recognized as the key figure in the "choice and purchase of consumer goods." For where both sexes once shopped, now "the woman is in a very real sense the purchasing agent for the American home"—and hence the very model of the modern consumer—no matter what the product, including radios, cars, and musical instruments.[50] That was her job and vocation. "At last," announced a 1928 ad for the Piggly Wiggly supermarket, the home of self-serve, "she is entirely free to choose for herself."[51] Moreover, Mrs. Consumer was generally imagined as a well-off, leisured white woman at that; a *Vogue* magazine reader "questionnaire," produced without commentary in a contemporaneous marketing text by the first president of the Market Research Council, starts by asking women how much autonomy in purchasing or planning they give to their hired help.[52]

Could there be a more clear-cut example of how preexisting class and gender norms entered twentieth-century social science?[53] Of course, the naturalization of woman's role as consumer was not new either; Mary Wollstonecraft had objected already to that facile assumption in the 1790s. So had scores of moral critics, male and female, as the nineteenth century drew to a close and the twentieth began, some blaming advertisers and marketers for what they saw as a drift into crassness and false values of all kinds, many of them coded female.[54] In 1912, the novelist Edith Wharton pilloried poor, vain Undine Spragg, the fictional midwestern social climber of *The Custom of the Country*, who treated her whole life as if it were taking place in a vast store, buying things she neither needed nor really wanted once she scored them and selling herself, like a shiny toy, through repeated marriages to the highest bidder.

Yet Wharton, for all her snobbery toward her own invention, can also be read to be suggesting that Undine (and legions of other young women like her) operated in this transactional, calculating way because that was actually the only option they had, whether in New York, in Paris, or back in the American Midwest.[55] Instead of the world turning in Wollstonecraft's preferred direction and giving women more opportunities to engage in pursuits long monopolized by men, the opposite had happened. The prosperous world had caught up with society women: *everyone* was now living in a world made up of autonomous consumers, segmented and classified by their buying power and store-bought possessions more than by any traditional status or character markers. The larger environment had, outside the confines of the workplace or its primary training ground, the schoolhouse, become one giant marketplace inhabited by clusters of independent choosing subjects. What's more, the fad of survey research—as exemplified by grand studies like *The New Housewives Market*, purportedly based on responses to "questionnaire cards" from more than 23,000 women magazine readers in 269 cities in 43 states—helped from the 1920s onward to make the model into a social reality (fig. 5.3).[56]

Multiple Choice

But what if the data were not reliable? Marketing experts in the late teens and 1920s also went back to the drawing board on the survey itself, including the design of the all-important questionnaire. To satisfy the demand for the new academic discipline to operate as a "social science," as well as industry needs regarding getting to the bottom of human behavior in the marketplace, the questions—it was proposed—had to be crafted differently than in the early days of the questionnaire. So did the answers. Walter Dill Scott had encouraged researchers to ask open-ended questions so as to make sure the responses they got did not conform to the investigators' own expectations and biases. Scientists of choice-making, like practitioners of other sciences, were expected from the start to operate with detached neutrality in the face of the observed. Increasingly, though, marketing teachers and organization leaders proposed presenting test subjects with a set of fixed alternatives to simple queries. By that they meant scripted choices about how to describe their previous thoughts and actions, including in the realm of choices. They

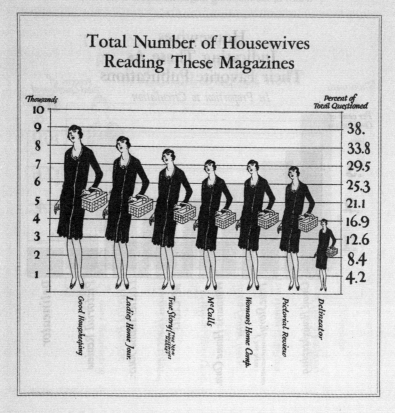

7. Combined Answers to Questions
Number 1 and Number 2:

Total Number of Housewives
Reading These Magazines

Magazine	Housewives	Per cent of Total Questioned
Good Housekeeping	9117	39.5
Ladies' Home Journal	8426	36.5
True Story (The New Housewives Market)	7808	33.8
Woman's Home Companion	7513	32.5
McCall's	7512	32.5
Pictorial Review	7078	30.6
Delineator	4225	18.3

Fig. 5.3. A page of *The New Housewives Market* (1927) showing the results of a survey of "housewives" on their reading choices where representations of them (as identical contemporary white women carrying shopping baskets) are deployed as the bars of the graph conveying this information to potential advertisers.

also urged that the options be presented in a popular ballot-like design—a "simple check list method" that "permits the reader to run along the possible answers and pick out the one he feels is right," as one influential text of the 1920s aimed at the "marketing investigator" put it[57]—or in what was coming to be known as a "multiple choice" format. After all, variants of this format had already entered popular culture. Consider "Australian" and "American" versions of "ballot postcards," a fad among both men and women in the early 1900s (and thus before women had access to real ballots in most places except sometimes in local elections) that required nothing more than putting Xs in the appropriate spots as a way to share generic news and sentiments with loved ones and friends (figs. 5.4 and 5.5). Such ephemera suggest that the paper menu of options format filtered both up and down in commercial culture in the early twentieth century in ways that made sense to researchers and test subjects alike.

One advantage of asking respondents to pick among preexisting answers, however arranged on the page, was that it would make the whole process of surveying quicker and easier for respondents and their proxies. Another was said to be improvement in the quality of the responses themselves. After all, no one liked to present or even think of him- or herself as vulnerable to sales pitches, and subjects could not really be trusted to explain or even to know their own motives in ways that weren't obfuscating unless given set options determined by experts. The goal (especially for those commentators still worried about the unconscious and sublimation) was to find ways to get closer to an honest declaration of the consumer's state of mind. What is more, the results would inevitably be more efficient for the researcher to tabulate and, ultimately, compare if there were a controlled number of established possibilities for the responses. Students of the history of social science research often point to "sampling," or ensuring a representative group of respondents so as to limit the size of the survey while increasing its reliability, as one major step toward the development of scientific survey techniques in this era. But equally important in the eyes of writers of interwar marketing texts was the advent of highly structured choice-making frameworks that could be used by professionals in the empirical study of test subjects' choice-making habits.[58]

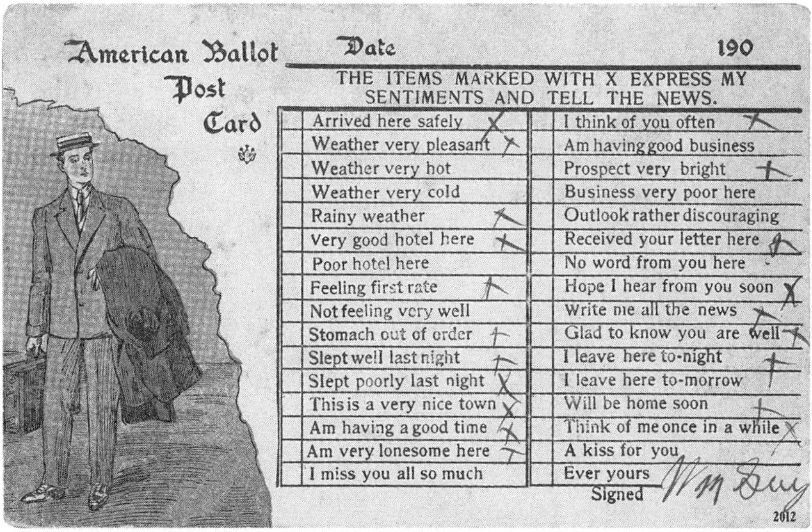

American Ballot Post Card — Date 190

THE ITEMS MARKED WITH X EXPRESS MY SENTIMENTS AND TELL THE NEWS.

Arrived here safely	I think of you often
Weather very pleasant	Am having good business
Weather very hot	Prospect very bright
Weather very cold	Business very poor here
Rainy weather	Outlook rather discouraging
Very good hotel here	Received your letter here
Poor hotel here	No word from you here
Feeling first rate	Hope I hear from you soon
Not feeling very well	Write me all the news
Stomach out of order	Glad to know you are well
Slept well last night	I leave here to-night
Slept poorly last night	I leave here to-morrow
This is a very nice town	Will be home soon
Am having a good time	Think of me once in a while
Am very lonesome here	A kiss for you
I miss you all so much	Ever yours

Signed

2012

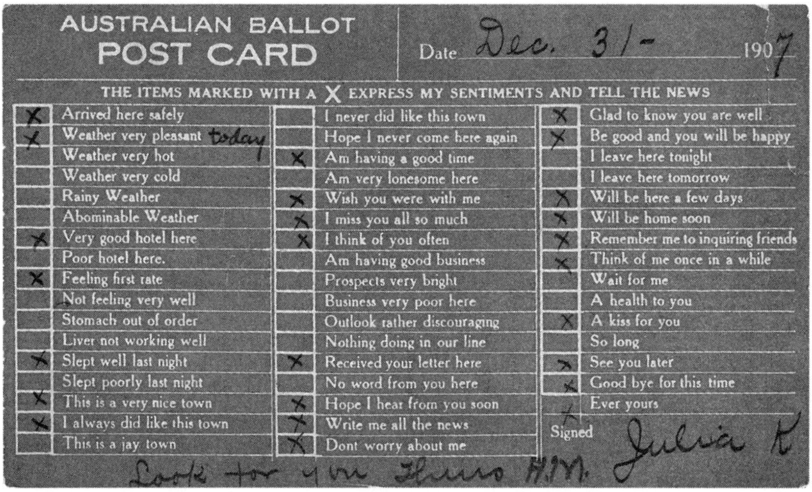

AUSTRALIAN BALLOT POST CARD — Date Dec. 31- 1907

THE ITEMS MARKED WITH A X EXPRESS MY SENTIMENTS AND TELL THE NEWS

Arrived here safely	I never did like this town	Glad to know you are well
Weather very pleasant today	Hope I never come here again	Be good and you will be happy
Weather very hot	Am having a good time	I leave here tonight
Weather very cold	Am very lonesome here	I leave here tomorrow
Rainy Weather	Wish you were with me	Will be here a few days
Abominable Weather	I miss you all so much	Will be home soon
Very good hotel here	I think of you often	Remember me to inquiring friends
Poor hotel here.	Am having good business	Think of me once in a while
Feeling first rate	Prospects very bright	Wait for me
Not feeling very well	Business very poor here	A health to you
Stomach out of order	Outlook rather discouraging	A kiss for you
Liver not working well	Nothing doing in our line	So long
Slept well last night	Received your letter here	See you later
Slept poorly last night	No word from you here	Good bye for this time
This is a very nice town	Hope I hear from you soon	Ever yours
I always did like this town	Write me all the news	Signed Julia K
This is a jay town	Dont worry about me	

Look for you Thurs A.M.

Figs. 5.4 and 5.5. Ballot postcards, used c. 1900–1910 by men and women alike in the United States, to convey news to family and friends at a distance.

For the rethinking of survey and questionnaire design, from type of question to sequence of options, coincided with another fundamental (and lasting) development in applied psychology and social science methodology in the 1910s and 1920s: the rise of the so-called multiple-choice format as a foundation for new kinds of mental testing. Here

Fig. 5.6. A battery-operated "multiple choice" apparatus designed in 1913 by Robert Yerkes to assess ideational behavior in animals and humans.

World War I really was transformative. Psychologist-turned-advertiser Walter Dill Scott, now at Carnegie Mellon Institute of Technology, was tapped to head the Army's Committee on the Classification of Personnel and devise an appropriate personality test for the purpose. Psychologist Robert Yerkes—Harvard professor, president of the American Psychological Association, and an expert in animal intelligence who had built a "multiple-choice" apparatus in 1913 to measure and compare under laboratory conditions the ideational behavior of humans and a variety of animals—took up a different and ultimately more influential charge as chairman of the Army's Committee on the Psychological Examination of Recruits. That was coming up with an exam that tested recruits' intelligence (fig. 5.6).

The initial plan, when the National Research Council subcommittee on the psychology of recruits first convened in 1917, was simply to screen for mental deficiency. But collaborating with Stanford's Lewis Terman and other prominent psychologists, Yerkes's group soon made two fateful decisions. One was to turn testing into a mass effort, screening every new recruit—ultimately more than 1.7 million men—so as to identify not only those at the bottom of the scale but also those superior men who would be suitable for officer training.[59] The other was to use a novel form of test in which there were several fixed options for every answer, and each subject had only to pick the one that he was most convinced was correct. The Alpha would be word-based and given to literate men. Beta, for illiterate ones, would depend on images. The conceit of Terman and others was that such tests could be crafted to be elemental both to administer and to score when given to an enormous number of people in a compressed period of time. Plus, when designed by a social science professional with expertise in devising menus, such tests could potentially eliminate bias and thus variability in the all-important results.[60]

For the other, perhaps dominant, impetus behind the turn to this new format was not Yerkes's lab-based, multiple-choice experiments with pigs, crows, and monkeys. Here we need also recall Frederick J. Kelly, a now largely forgotten midwestern school administrator and education professor. Kelly had, in the 1910s, developed a form of standardized achievement test that required selection of the one right answer among several predetermined ones as a way to measure the reading ability of schoolchildren in Kansas.[61] Now Terman, working with Yerkes but also building directly on work like Kelly's, offered up an innovation that, in addition to introducing new levels of efficiency and cost-effectiveness in terms of production and marking, promised to become an objective tool of measurement at the individual level. Technology, namely scoring by way of stencils and, eventually, machines, would replace a professional and his (or often her, when it came to schools and teachers) expert but still subjective judgment. Moreover, the standardized, multiple-choice exam looked like a way to garner a wealth of statistics for quantitative analysis afterward, whether that meant performance over time for a single student, or a snapshot of a cohort (say, voters, workers, students, or shoppers) at a particular moment, or comparisons across institutions, geography, or kinds of people.[62]

Multiple-choice testing was here to stay, though it must initially have seemed like yet another fad. Soon after the Great War ended, the multiple-choice format saw its fortunes rise well beyond army intelligence testing as it was appropriated as both a diagnostic and predictive tool in a wide variety of settings and for a wide variety of ages—and quite often with an explicitly eugenicist dimension. Standardized academic aptitude and achievement testing, based on determining the right answers among the typically four or five options offered and coloring in a circle corresponding to the chosen one with a pencil, all while a clock ticked along, came of age in the 1920s. So did academic, and frequently racialized, tracking. The College Entrance Examination Board (now College Board), which continues to produce the Scholastic Achievement Test (now Scholastic Aptitude Test or SAT) that is used by many U.S. colleges and universities to vet applicants to this day, was a prominent early adopter of this format.[63] But the multiple-choice technique also made its way into academic and corporate survey research to measure a wide variety of subjective responses too. In addition, after the war ended, it became a feature of various kinds of what was increasingly called polling, including on questions related to political as well as commercial preferences. Following the philosopher Michel Foucault, it is easy to see here the nexus of standardization, objectification, and new hierarchies of power that went hand in hand over the course of the modern era with new forms of ostensible individualization.[64]

But here, too, as Foucault fails to notice, women as well as men found themselves on both sides of the equation, albeit differentially. Starting in the nineteenth century, women played a greater role in social survey work than they did in many other professional capacities; they were frequently employed as interviewers and researchers, laying out the questions and the options and then recording and tabulating the answers.[65] (Just after World War II, marketing professor Mildred Parten was still urging those designing surveys in the United States to look for recruits at college women's clubs and among "wives of professors, who are frequently interested in survey work.")[66] Women also played significant roles in the expansion of multiple-choice testing, applying Yerkes's methods, for example, to new subjects, including young children.[67] But even more, women, including those elusive "housewives," continued to serve a key function as subjects of study. They were people who could be observed both in controlled experiments and in daily life trying to sort out all the options. And in all these roles, they actively helped draw lines between consumer and political culture that they were ultimately to exploit to their advantage as well as find themselves lastingly hindered by.

Consider the social survey designed in 1923 by two faculty members in the University of Chicago's Political Science Department to better understand nonvoters in that city's mayoral race earlier that same year. The project of Charles Edward Merriam and Harold Foote Gosnell might seem remote from the work of prior marketers. Not only were these academics invested in what was fundamentally a study of American political behavior, not consumption habits. The framing itself was also novel. Merriam and Gosnell's primary question was why did so many people—despite finding themselves all equally eligible and despite the best efforts of party workers using every device and appeal possible to get them to the polls—actually *refuse* this opportunity to make a choice? What these social scientists wanted to know in this first real study of this new question was about the "obstacles," understood as the antithesis of animating "drives," when it came to men's and women's decisions about participating in a municipal election.[68] Why, precisely, did almost 700,000 of 1.4 million eligible Chicago voters not bother to show up?

Yet putting those distinctions aside for the moment, the commonalities between this endeavor and early twentieth-century consumer research now seem striking. For one, the analogy between voting and buying, politics and consumption, was already well worn in American culture. A tradition of boycotts going back to the American Revolution had turned the decision not to engage in choice in the commercial sphere, or "nonconsumption" as it was then known, into a potential political act, much like nonvoting. Giving up tea in the 1760s or buying exclusively "free produce" in protest against slavery in the nineteenth century functioned in two distinct ways: as means to materially harm producers and sellers engaged in undesirable practices and as means to turn a decision about consumption into an expressive statement about ethical choice-making in the public sphere.[69] Women's suffrage activists on both sides of the Atlantic had done something similar. In a bid for respectability, they had long equated casting a ballot with shopping as similarly natural female pastimes, as we've seen in the British case. Furthermore, in an effort both to support and to spread the cause, they had filled their own markets with a variety of homely goods available for purchase, from greeting cards to dolls to buttons and badges and umbrellas, all marked with pro–women's suffrage messages.[70]

Companies took note early on, enlisting this equation to sell everything from cereal to soap. Just glance at a 1914 print advertisement, with the tagline "Votes for Women," in which a parade of little girls, arrayed as mock suffragists, carry boxes of Kellogg's Corn Flakes as pickets (fig. 5.7). One could read it either as a pro–women's suffrage statement or as a way of suggesting that women were already "voting" in a style that suited them, that is, over breakfast options in the grocery store. And once white women gained the franchise in the United States, popular culture routinely encouraged them to keep the analogy alive in order to elevate consumption as a patriotic act.[71] Even effectively disenfranchised Black people were wooed to shop in places like Birmingham, Alabama, by ads that treated buying as a form of election participation. In 1924, the city's leading Black newspaper ran an ad for Madam C. J. Walker's Toilet Preparations that entailed a contest in which the more one spent, the more "votes" one got for the "candidate" of one's choice among a list of pastors who were eligible to win a visit to the Holy Land at the company's expense. The mail-in coupons, maintaining the parallel, took the form of ballots.[72] If advertising copy is any indication, Cartwright's old slogan of radical suffrage politics—Take Your Choice!—was at the start of the twentieth century more likely to read as a consumer command than anything else (figs. 5.8 and 5.9).

Needless to say, there was little mention in mainstream political or commercial discourse of the structural inequalities on which this notion of choice was built. There was also little talk of the frustrations that mass consumption created or the ways consumerism and political goals could

Fig. 5.7. Kellogg's Toasted Corn Flakes advertisement linking voting and consumer purchasing with the tagline "Votes for Women" (1914).

Figs. 5.8 and 5.9. "Take Your Choice" was employed as an advertising tagline for products aimed at men (e.g., headlights, from *The Independent Magazine*, 1899) and equally at "housewives" (e.g., cleaning products, from *The Outlook*, 1913).

be at odds, for example, in failing to account for consumption's social costs.[73] These concerns stayed on the fringes even as certain ideas about the crassness of commerce and the dangers of a society built on such shoddy ideals continued to be heard. Democracy and consumer culture, according to boosters, both led to and were fueled by the same telos: the right to unfettered choice in marketplaces of varied kinds.

But it was also at the level of method that academic researchers and social scientists, in the wake of marketers and ad men, played their own role, along with their subjects, in reinforcing this association. Conceptually, Merriam and Gosnell's study of nonvoters, or those who stubbornly refused political choice, was very much in keeping with the kind of large-scale, collaborative, empirical, survey-based consumer choice research for which Chicago, the city, and Chicago, the university, had already become known.[74] In this case, political scientists simply substituted voters for customers.

The evidentiary centerpiece of the nonvoting project called for trained investigators—primarily political science graduate students of both sexes—to collect detailed information about a representative set or "sample" of adult Chicago residents who, in the last mayoral race, had either failed to register or registered but not shown up at the polls. Age, sex, race, country of birth, nationality, economic status, occupation, length of residence at current address and in state, prior voting experience: all were deemed important. These same researchers were then to read to all their test subjects, from a single and brief survey form, a list of 20 potential rationales, ranging from sickness to fear to disinterest, for their action or, in this case, inaction. Nonvoters had only to pick from this ostensibly comprehensive list (which is to say, have proxies put checkmarks with a pencil in small boxes, alone or in over 150 combinations) those that best represented their own situation. Additional space existed so that, if they so chose, those same nonvoters could expound on their choice(s)—in terms of both what they did and what box they picked—in their own words too. Then, finally, our experts were to take the results of all 6,000 interviews as registered on an equal number of cards, code them, and sort and tabulate them using an electronic machine that the authors identify as a Hollerith key-punch, a critical tool in the interwar information explosion (fig. 5.10).[75]

In the ensuing volume summarizing their findings, Merriam and Gosnell offered up a lot of statistical information—such as the fact that women, enfranchised locally since 1913, were still much more prevalent within the ranks of nonvoters than were men, in good part because of their own distaste for the business of electoral politics. But just as importantly, Merriam and Gosnell also gave their readers capsule vignettes about a wide variety of specific named and unnamed individuals from all walks of life who, it seemed, were willing to talk about their own mental processes in choosing whether or not to engage in this kind of choice-making—just as Mrs. Lansing had in her encounters with the *Tribune*'s marketing department a decade earlier. So we meet women like Mrs. Olson, a German-born Chicagoan from the northwestern part

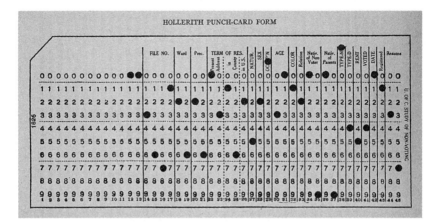

Fig. 5.10. A sample "Hollerith punch-card form" used to tabulate survey results, reproduced in Charles Edward Merriam and Harold Foote Gosnell, *Non-Voting: Causes and Methods of Control* (1924).

of the city, who refused to vote because her husband and son felt politics should not be women's concern. We meet specific Black voters of both sexes, most of them new to the city, whose memory of disenfranchisement in the South kept them wary of the polls or who saw no point in the whole enterprise, as in the case of a "junk man, born in Tennessee thirty-six years ago, a resident of Chicago for the last six" who said, "Day by day the world is getting worse and worse. Down South you can't vote and you haven't got anything; up here you can vote, but still haven't got anything. What's the use?"[76] We meet still others, including Russian Jews and young socialists, for whom nonvoting was itself a political act, a refusal to engage in a corrupt or rigged system in the hopes of undermining the system itself. And we encounter individuals like Mrs. Foucek, "a Bohemian woman who was naturalized through her husband's papers," and Mrs. Davis, "a young colored woman living in the congested negro district," who say they simply don't know enough to decide.[77]

The list goes on, rationale by rationale, from practical obstacles, to legal and administrative ones, to questions of personal belief. There is even an appearance by a Nazarene Apostolic preacher who not only resists the franchise himself but urges his congregants to do the same because it is God, not man, who is in charge of everything that happens.

Readers never learn the sentiments of those who refused to engage with Merriam and Gosnell's intrepid, anonymous researchers as well as refused to vote. However, taken together, these varied findings promised to be exploitable beyond the merely anecdotal or even the development of social theory.

For all these survey results, just like those of the *Tribune*, rooted as they were in the shared, voluntary recollections of thousands of Chicagoans of all backgrounds, were intended as fodder for others: in this case, future policymakers and party leaders. Moreover, those future policymakers and party leaders were assumed to have a vested interest in stimulating more individualized choice-making down the road, especially around election time. Running through this study and others that followed in the 1920s was the strong sense that the prevalence of nonvoters, like nonpurchasers, was a sign of a moral crisis—especially among establishment groups convinced (quite mistakenly) that abstainers were more common among the well-off classes than among the poor, radicals, or immigrants. If one group (nonpurchasers) threatened the health of the economy, the other (nonvoters) was, as the *Tribune* put it in 1924, "more dangerous than communists or kings. They are passive resistance to [democratic] government."[78] The point, touted by male and female academics and business consultants alike, was that with the employment of scientific methods of acquiring data about human motivations, it would be possible to discern how best to increase participation in rituals of choice-making, including voting as much as buying.[79]

Some of the same people actually promoted both. The major "Get Out the Vote" campaign of 1924, with its ostensibly neutral tagline "Vote as you please," was sponsored by the National Association of Manufacturers, the National Association of Credit Men, the American Bankers Association, and a variety of other business interests, along with such organizations as the League of Women Voters.[80] Among ideas discussed in this moment of consternation were easier registration processes, shorter ballots, voting by mail, publicity campaigns aimed at changing mindsets about the franchise, and even compulsory voting, a legal requirement that all citizens engage in political choice-making. The latter solution, which would have turned a right to choose into a duty to choose, never took off in the United States (as opposed to, say, Belgium, Brazil, or, again, Australia). That's probably because the association of choice with freedom, including the possibility of abstaining, was already too ingrained in the American context. The idea of pro-voting advocates was, though, not so much that *everyone* needed to be actively politically engaged. Rather, they insisted that the American political system as a whole only worked if all adult individuals, at least among the respectable classes, made the same decision to partake in the performance of political choice-making and do it well and without fear. Choice-making deserved to be a national cause as well as activity for both sexes.

The celebrated female anthropologist Margaret Mead made the case repeatedly, starting in the late 1920s, that choosing was, in fact, a distinctive and contemporary American preoccupation. But it needed more sustained attention. As she explained it first in her best-selling *Coming of Age in Samoa: A Psychological Study of Primitive Youth for Western Civilization* (1928) based on her year of living and observing local habits in the South Pacific, coming of age had become considerably more difficult in the United States than it was outside it. What's more, girls were the primary victims. That's because, at home, adolescents of both sexes, but especially teenage girls, were uniquely caught between a mythology that celebrated choice for everyone at every turn and a reality marked by economic, familial, and cultural pressures that mitigated free choice or made it severely limited in practice, unless one were to accept some rather severe social and emotional consequences. Thus a kind of battle ensued for which American adolescent girls were largely unprepared whether the issue was choice of future occupation, choice of religion or belief, or, with the rise of birth control, choice in the sexual domain.

According to Mead, though, the answer lay not in reducing access to all these possibilities or picking a single strand collectively. "Primitive" Samoa could not be a model for a pluralist United States. (This was, after all, the same moment as the birth of the children's restaurant menu, one of many early twentieth-century efforts to give even the young a circumscribed way to actualize their burgeoning consumer, if not political, preferences within a set of limited options designed specifically for them.)[81]

Instead, Americans needed to devise what Mead called an "education for choice," including teaching the young to recognize and embrace the multiplicity of options before them prior to making a selection. Such an education would make the whole business of "coming of age"—again, especially for girls—significantly less fraught, she believed, and also prepare them for real life in an advanced society.[82] For considered choice, rooted in the rational, autonomous individual, was *the* form of modern, Western freedom, a point that Mead—echoing John Dewey's emphasis on cultivating a democratic disposition in students—continued to make in increasingly political fashion through World War II.

Choice, of course, did come to education, as to most other sectors, in some of the ways Mead advocated: as options within one's studies and as part of curricula associated with progressive education. I am a product of the "open" elementary school movement that swept public education across the United States in the 1970s and which, in its emphasis on choice in reading matter, could be said to hark all the way back to Rousseau, Wollstonecraft, and Godwin.[83] Today's college students, every time they pick their courses from a large menu of options, are heirs of Harvard president Charles Eliot's late nineteenth-century advocacy of "electivism."[84] Some of them, as at Yale and Stanford, still describe this activity colloquially as "shopping." But just as importantly, as choice became a field of inquiry in its own right, something similar to Mead's vision was accomplished by other means. From being routinely queried about their choices and in a format that stressed this kind of mental work, Americans learned how to think in terms of choices. More and more, they also had reason to see themselves as naturally comfortable, even adept in this realm.

And all the while, the prevalence of such studies in American culture was also only growing. After the Depression, the federal government began to get in on the act, creating new bureaucracies for various kinds of statistics and data-collecting entities and expanding the web of subjects. So did more and more private businesses and universities, claiming public utility for survey and polling methods, whether in understanding the past or in prediction and planning, including the shaping of consumer and political behavior in the future.

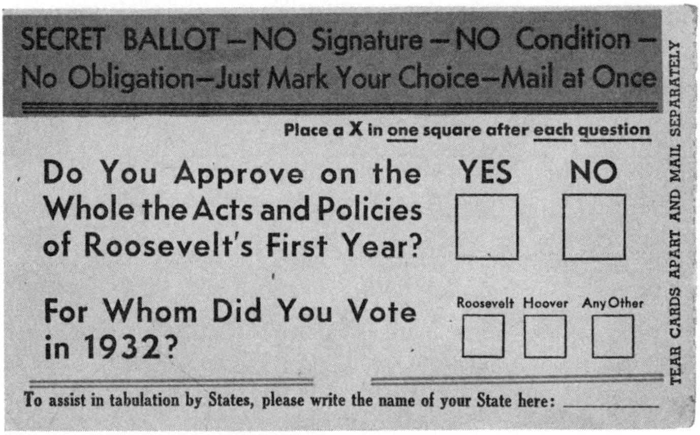

Fig. 5.11. A mail-in "secret ballot" produced in the wake of the 1932 U.S. presidential election by *Literary Digest*, which was famous for its straw polling methods in the era before modern polling began.

Indeed, one important shift happened in the mid-1930s, when market researchers George Gallup, Elmo Roper, and Archibald Crossley entered the political stage and turned their attention to electoral competition. First, they collectively rejected the mail-in ballot method of straw voting traditionally employed most successfully before presidential contests by the magazine *Literary Digest* (fig. 5.11). Then, in its place, they promoted surveying a small number of respondents selected according to the principles of scientific sampling and engaging them individually in interviews about political issues. Under the leadership of Gallup and his cohort, political polling caught up with consumer polling with lasting consequences for American public life.

Historian Sarah Igo claims that one of the reasons for the popularity of all kinds of polling in the mid-twentieth-century United States, whether conducted by survey researchers, political pollsters, or marketers, was that the "averaged American," living in what had become a heterogeneous commercial and democratic society, liked looking in the mirror and seeing the reflection back. Pollsters showed society, or "the public mind" (in Gallup's words), to itself, including what people in the aggregate bought, how they voted, whom they loved, and what they believed. In doing so, pollsters created both "a culture of surveying" and "a surveyed culture" in which, Igo says, public opinion had pride of place.[85]

But what she does not emphasize is that all this opinion research, through its very techniques, also had an effect on humans at the level of the self, making them more and more into the quasi-autonomous choosers, shaped by both subgroup identities and individual psychologies, that social scientists and pollsters saw them as being. In survey culture, women became acknowledged as choice-makers in politics, just as men increasingly became acknowledged as choice-makers in consumer affairs. (Back to the supermarket: perhaps it's not accidental that this story coincides with the expansion of this new kind of shopping environment, where men, going it alone and anonymously, felt newly welcome.) This kind of affirmation, in turn, helped shape self-understanding about what it is natural to perceive, think, feel. People, both as test subjects and the audience for polls, may have been encouraged to see difference and distinction, the varied tastes of different segments of the population. But they seem to have ended up also believing in an underlying and shared preference for choice itself as a defining feature of self and society alike.

The most famous of these studies—conducted by Paul Lazarsfeld, Bernard Berelson, and Hazel Gaudet of the Bureau of Applied Social Research at Columbia University and conducted on the citizens of Erie County, Ohio, in the lead-up to the 1940 contest for the U.S. presidency—was actually called *The People's Choice: How the Voter Makes Up His Mind in a Presidential Campaign* when the results were published just after World War II. This analysis of political choice-making in a precise geography drew, much like consumer research, on a combination of objective facts, organized in the form of statistics, and psychological data drawn from verbatim quotes collected through interviews with around 3,000 local residents, including four panels of 600 who were requestioned and observed more intensively over a six-month period. Still, the authors called it "the first study of the people's choosing," insisting it was unique in exploring how and why individual voters "decided to vote as they did" or the reasoning behind their specific political behavior in pulling the lever for one candidate over another (in this case, FDR v. Wendell Willkie).[86] What is more, women—despite the assumption of masculine normativity in the "his" in the title—were among the study's authors, made up the majority of interviewers, and constituted an almost equal number of subjects studied (since sampling required representativity), though women were still, the authors remark, unfortunately overrepresented among nonvoters.

What did it all add up to? The team of authors was mainly eager to demonstrate something counterintuitive: that though people of both sexes are open to persuasion and often want to vote for the person they think will ultimately win, party loyalty is much like brand loyalty, and advertising more often reinforces latent dispositions than actually changes minds. Mainly, however, it is the subtext of this study that makes it, in retrospect, so revealing. For both the framers and their respondents seem to have internalized the notion that in a liberal democracy, as Roger Smith puts it in his history of psychology, "each person has the right and duty to make choices, founded on individual differences in inward feeling and outward capacity, as the basis of social life."[87] This is how a free society works.

In international terms, by the 1940s, this had become a politics (despite the vaunted neutrality and objectivity of the empirical social scientist) in its own right, a specific kind of ideology. As Lazarsfeld and company point out about their wartime study and its popular appeal: "The wholesale suppression of civil rights in the totalitarian countries [i.e., Germany, the Soviet Union] highlighted the picture of a nation democratically choosing a leader amid free discussion."[88] Capitalism had long been said to do something similar, especially in contrast to the material deprivations of communism. And if freedom was, by definition, "the experience of choosing from among possible courses of action," as the author of one article in a popular 1940 anthology on the subject put together by the American philosopher Ruth Nanda Anshen noted, then the American way of life, precisely because of the premium placed on choice in economic, political, and cultural terms alike, became a beacon of freedom for the world.[89] It was an argument reinforced in Allied propaganda of various kinds, even advertisements for war bonds.[90] It was also an argument made by a host of intellectuals, including a number of women, during and just after wartime, even as some intellectuals in both the United States and Europe also worried about individual choice in the capitalist-democratic mode being compromised by pressure to keep up with the neighbors and conform (i.e., David Riesman), or becoming a mirage or even a form of oppression in light of rampant consumerism (i.e., Max Horkheimer and Theodor Adorno or Jeanne Hersch), or occurring without reference to some stable, general, and limited rules (i.e., Simone Weil).[91]

A favored metaphor was once again food. Mead insisted in the era of World War II that Americans, with their multiple cultures of origin, would never be satisfied by a single restaurant; they needed to have an array of choices set before them, cafeteria-style, so they could select the diet they wanted.[92] Riesman, in the best-selling postwar study *The Lonely Crowd*, conjured the world of cookbooks, arguing that in America instructions on how to make staples had given way to variety, allowing everyone to pick out the particular recipes that appealed to their tastes and thus to personalize the food they served.[93] The point? Active and unfettered choice-making—albeit from a set of options provided by others and within internalized and thus naturalized boundaries that Weil analogized to an ingrained habit of "not eating disgusting or dangerous things"[94]—was now not just an increasingly common leisure-time activity. It was the distinguishing feature of life in a certain kind of "open" society of which America was the chief example. The old republican or civic humanist idea of consumer culture drawing people away from the moral universe of citizenship rather than toward it was long in the rearview mirror.

What happened next is that choice-making, as an activity and especially as an area of quasi-scientific inquiry, became one of America's great postwar exports, a tool of market capitalism and democracy promotion alike. The process actually started in the interwar period, building on locally inflected but international phenomena like the growth in the 1920s and 1930s of the so-called modern girl from Beijing to Johannesburg. What distinguished her from her forebears (except maybe the original French *coquette*) is that she potentially had choice—or *erabu*, as popular Japanese women's magazines of the period termed it—when it came to lifestyles and advertised products alike.[95] But the scope of such ideals accelerated continuously and exponentially and reached a variety of new places after 1945 and through the 1950s and 1960s, where these ideals were variously met with enthusiasm and denounced. We might think of it as part of a larger postwar attempt, once the threat of fascism seemed to have subsided, to "seduce" (as journalist Pankaj Mishra puts it) postcolonial states in Asia, Africa, and Latin America, as well as Europe, away from engagement in communist revolution.[96] Freedom of choice, with its very particular commercial, religious, sexual, and political roots, became the key calling card of the capitalist, democratic alternative.

That also meant Western Europe, and then much of the world, was flooded in the postwar years with American consumer goods, American media and advertising, and American-style or "Australian-ballot" elections (fig. 5.12). Many places even got American *libre-service* food stores, promising, as the Roosevelt-sponsored Italian supermarket chain Esselunga did, that "the choice is the same for everyone" (albeit often designed to accommodate local tastes and habits and often meeting with fierce local resistance even as the myth of American bounty took root) (fig. 5.13).[97] There was no contradiction in the immediate postwar era between social democracy and state-sponsored freedom from want, on the one hand, and the expansion of choice, on the other; the 1950s to early 1970s was a period of unprecedented economic growth in global terms, even as social obligations were increasingly taken under consideration. But the ostensible appeal of this new kind of store and similar forms of marketing was no longer just convenience, abundance, and variety. It was also the promise of autonomy and fulfillment on equal terms for everybody, assuming they could each meet the price.

That wasn't all, either. Between the wars, *studies* of voters and consumers as choice-makers on the participatory American marketing and polling model became the foundation for an international export industry as well (and that was despite the fact that the social survey traced its real origins to nineteenth-century Britain and Germany). Gallup was no sooner established in 1935 as a leader in public opinion and election forecasting research in the United States than a British arm was set up in the form of the British Institute of Public Opinion in 1936 (an early

Fig. 5.12. Jan van Eyk, 1960 photograph of young woman choosing a record at a coin-operated vending machine called, in Dutch, a *Grammofoonplatenautomat*, an image that stands for the burgeoning American-style consumer culture of postwar Europe and its increased choices for young men and women.

question was "If you had to choose between Fascism and Communism, which would you choose?"), followed by a French one, L'Institut fran-çais de l'opinion publique, in 1938. In the postwar period, other versions were created around the world, including in Germany, Italy, and Japan. Their purpose was querying potential voters and consumers in sophis-ticated new ways but also promoting American-style democratic political culture.[98] (Until the 1950s, to "faire un Gallup" was the standard way in France to refer to opinion polling, even though results met with a fair amount of skepticism.)[99] And while consumer research on live subjects had already spread in interwar Europe, not least to Germany

Fig. 5.13. One of a series of posters from 1966 touting the new Italian supermarket chain Esselunga, each showing a hat belonging to a different social or professional group superimposed on a supermarket sales slip and the tagline "the choice is the same for all."

and Austria, the other global center for applied psychology,[100] those same nations had then promptly exported back alternate versions to the United States following the arrival, starting in the 1930s, of Jewish scholars seeking refuge from the Nazis. That émigré community soon included key figures like Lazarsfeld, a Viennese socialist with an expertise in mathematics and sociology who developed a specialty in opinion research once he couldn't return to his place of origin, and Dichter, who was forced to flee the University of Vienna's famed Psychoeconomic Institute and then set up shop in advertising stateside.

Finally, standardized, often multiple-choice testing, with its easy-to-grade, quantifiable results, became a regular feature of education in many nations in the latter half of the twentieth century, often with American impetus. Soon individuals around the world were participating not just for the sake of assessments of their own learning or capacity to do so but also as a data point in planning the reorganization of national education systems, another example of the malleability of the practice of choice across different domains.[101] Today the format of the multiple-choice test is recognizable globally, from driving to citizenship tests, as is our collective acquiescence to it.

In fact, seeing life as a series of multiple-choice exams is, by now, something of a cliché internationally, though maybe still especially so in the United States. Consider the 2014 novel *Facsímil*, translated as *Multiple Choice* for an Anglophone audience, by the Chilean author Alejandro Zambra and written entirely in a version of the format made famous by Yerkes, Terman, and others just about a hundred years earlier. Its very translatability suggests our familiarity, in the Americas and in much of the world, with choosing among limited sets of options labeled A, B, C, D, E, and maybe F as a way to navigate our own lives and construct stories about them. (Most of the world has evolved a long way from the freer choice paradigms of the open classrooms of the United States and United Kingdom in the 1970s.) Here, Zambra cleverly constructs a full portrait of himself and his travails, using only this extremely familiar technology—in this case derived specifically from the Chilean verbal aptitude test that the author took in 1993, just prior to going to university and just after the Pinochet era came to an end.[102]

But there is also a certain absurdity on deliberate display here in the global novel *Multiple Choice*. For the choices that Zambra presents are often not straightforward or even possible to choose among. How can we, his readers, know without context which is the best, often in the sense of the truest, of the options before his protagonist? Sometimes we confront these options without enough information. Some of them are choices no one would ever impose on oneself. Some confuse facts and opinions or find still other ways to frustrate rational choice-making. Ultimately, the novel not only reinforces common criticisms of such tests today (e.g., that they don't allow people to be creative or define themselves in their own terms, that they stress facts without context or the full complexity of real life, that all answers have to be solely right or solely wrong when nuance is called for, that they reinforce existing biases, and more). Zambra's novel also amounts to a critique of a whole way of seeing the world and both its practical and its moral dilemmas. What are we to do with the option "the correct choice is almost always D" when the question concerns what is the author trying to say about multiple-choice tests? Or "I hate you" when there is no question at all? In Zambra's hands, the multiple-choice format condenses language in such a way as to become a form of modern poetry—and precisely because of the ubiquity of the form. In the end *Multiple Choice* is as much a game as Peto's great painting *Take Your Choice!*: you, the consumer of this fiction, must pick one, as instructed in this familiar format, even though you can't. The writer/artist as choice architect is, once more, both manipulating the audience *and* displaying the mechanism of manipulation, including the built-in politics, for all who are willing to look.

The Ultimate Science of Choice

It wasn't artists, however, who ultimately sealed the deal on choice in the twentieth century. It was economists. What is important from our perspective is that they did so while largely giving up on psychology—or at least most of them did until behaviorism, albeit of a new kind, made a strong return in the 1980s. Well before that moment, mainstream economists helped cement the choice-as-freedom paradigm as critical to modern life, while largely rejecting engagement with or even thinking about specific humans and their particular values, desires, obligations, commitments, insecurities, or conflicts at all.

As we have seen, in the culture of the human or social sciences that developed in the first half of the last century, the self was sometimes imagined as chiefly a product of internal forces (for example, by psychologists) and sometimes chiefly of exterior ones (for example, by sociologists). Most often it was both at once, much as it was for novelists eager to work out their interplay. Autonomy, even what we moderns have since the 1920s called "individuality," emerged within these double parameters.

In the discipline of economics, though, something quite different happened over this same period: both psychological *and* sociological ways of understanding behavior largely disappeared, as did the study of what the Italian economist Vilfredo Pareto referred to dismissively just after the turn of the past century as "Mrs. So and So" and her buying habits.[103] In fact, Pareto argued, professional students of the economy had no reason to clamor to know why she, aka Mrs. So and So, purchased a particular good or didn't; the very question had become irrelevant. They also had no business worrying about whether what she bought was a good, in the sense of morally upstanding, or socially beneficial, or respectable, or even personally fulfilling, choice. Quite the contrary. All of this shunting aside, including of actual test subjects, was understood to be part of remaking the discipline of economics as, finally, a real science—and a mathematical one at that. It was hard numbers, not inscrutable people, that would be at its heart.

And yet, something very different happened. Science bled into real life again. Over the last hundred and twenty years or so, mainstream "neoclassical" economists both drew on existing practices and ended up reinforcing a conception of the human subject as essentially an individualized choice-maker even more than psychology-obsessed advertisers and marketing gurus like Lazarsfeld and Gaudet, with whom economists uneasily coexisted, ever did.[104] In economists' hands and those of their disciples in other fields, an investment in personally satisfying choice was reconceived as humans' *dominant* characteristic for the dual purpose of understanding the world as it is and of prophesizing what's next. Economics thus became the twentieth century's premier science of choice. Even reason was rethought and redefined. The result, long-term, should be seen as yet another example of what the philosopher of science Ian Hacking called a "looping effect" in which ordinary people, being naturally adaptive, increasingly both understand themselves and behave as the scientific experts expect they will, thereby requiring yet more study and classification.[105] By light of this theory, modeling humans as choosers and labeling them as such, in a context in which choosing from menus of options was already playing more and more of a role in mundane, reflexive experience, further helped remake the self-perception and, ultimately, actions of the core object of scrutiny: modern men and women. If all those yellow-pencil-wielding test takers and questionnaire respondents and fans of the psychoanalytic couch became choosers and choice agents themselves at one and the same time, economics finally gave them tools for imaginatively naturalizing the whole.

What is more, even before the so-called neoliberal turn of the 1970s and 1980s, practitioners of economics, more than other kinds of social scientists, turned choice-making, de facto, into an indisputable or commonsense positive value, just like markets. What's rarely recognized is that this shift would ultimately shape the way we have come to view human rights in general and women's rights more specifically. And this time, the story took place—albeit highly unevenly and episodically across multiple decades and with many different local variations—all over the wealthier parts of the globe, remaking the world as a whole in the process.

Homo Economicus: The Model Chooser

The idea of *homo economicus*—a model man or ideal type with which one can effectively theorize—arguably also goes back to John Stuart Mill, though he never used the term. Mill was not the first scholar of political economy, itself an invention of the eighteenth century, to imagine man in all times and places as naturally motivated to increase his wealth, whether in the form of money, goods, family size, leisure time, or all of the above. The English philosopher was, though, the first to try to reduce his model man, for the purposes of analysis, to this primary fact. As Mill explained circa 1830 in "On the Definition of Political Economy; and of the Method of Investigation Proper to It," political economy "does not treat of the whole of man's nature as modified by the social state, nor of the whole conduct of man in society. It is concerned with him solely as a being who desires to possess wealth, and who is capable of judging of the comparative efficacy of means for obtaining that end."[106]

Homo economicus started to change his stripes, however, even before the end of the nineteenth century. First, this hypothetical creature was reborn as a model consumer, or chooser of goods, rather than producer of them. Credit is usually given to a number of economists working in different professional spaces in the 1870s, including William Stanley Jevons in England, Carl Menger in Austria, and Léon Walras in French-speaking Switzerland. Key here was the shift to a focus on *utility*, understood as the value that a commodity holds for the individual purchaser as opposed to the labor value needed to produce it. The advantage was that the "marginal utility of the commodity," which meant the additional utility associated with an individual's consumption of an additional unit of the commodity in question, could be measured and thus used to explain not just pricing but also consumer behavior and the sphere of economic activity as a whole. For as Jevons put it in reference to *homo economicus* deciding what to use his limited resources to choose, for him "value depends entirely upon utility."[107]

But how was that utility to be understood in terms of the subject himself? Just some decades later, as *homo economicus* became ever more schematic and less recognizably a full-fledged human as opposed to analytic tool, he lost even the remaining traces of his psychology that had been related to the idea of utility. For Jevons, for example, it made sense to think of this model man as a seeker of "pleasure," a hedonist at heart; choosing what he wanted was his way to make himself happy. Economist Irving Fisher, writing several decades later, still took economic man's motivation for his selections to be loosely his "desires." But other turn-of-the-century economists, in an effort to clear economics of dependency on any kind of unscientific introspection, increasingly tried to sideline *all* discussion of interior sentiment as unobservable and thus unmeasurable. Utility, it was now argued, need not have any particular correlate in the individual's mind. Whatever the various and complex motivations or desires behind the purchases or acts of consumption of the chooser, they were outside the ambit of the economist's concern.[108] Psychological man thus became decidedly unpsychological man; choice, that old hinge between interior thought and exterior action, was all but drained of the former, along with many other of model man's traditional defining characteristics.

Finally, whatever *homo economicus* chose, there were to be no value judgments, no "oughts" in play. Even reason itself—once the foe of the irrational passions for many thinkers—would be recast in the early twentieth century as any decision that satisfies any preference, without concern for inner or outer conflicts, and just a few decades later, nothing more than consistency over time in picking. Whether one choice was better than another, and for whom and when and why, wasn't the business of the up-to-date economist. The economist was only to describe what is or was.[109] His model figure (unlike that of his predecessors going back to Adam Smith) lived increasingly in an ethics-free and historically and psychologically indeterminate world where choices had neither reasons nor consequences beyond themselves.

The Russian writer Fyodor Dostoevsky, very much a man of the nineteenth century, anticipated most famously in his experimental *Notes from Underground* (1864) what he referred to as the future reign of "statisticians," when "all human actions will then be calculated according to these laws, mathematically." The narrator, a self-described "educated and developed man of our times" tormented by these increasing pressures, famously rails against this unnatural state, asking "what sort of will of one's own can there be if it comes to tables and arithmetic" and acting out in the bluntest of terms the incompatibility of desire and reason and the many ways "one can want even against one's own profit."[110] The novella has been read ever since as a screed against hyper-rationalism and a revelation of the dark inner life that ultimately exerts its force on all of us. But at the turn of the new century, this was indeed the direction in which the social sciences concerned with "the economy,"[111] and choice within it, were going.

A key figure in this turn was, in fact, Pareto, a liberal industrialist and avid reader of Mill, who followed in Walras's footsteps by becoming, late in life, a professor of economics in Lausanne. There, in the last years of the 1890s, Pareto got to work creating a new image of the rational economic actor, admittedly as a new kind of fiction designed with mathematical modeling, not accuracy in terms of human experience, as the goal. Henceforth, Pareto proposed, *homo economicus* should have no psychology or personality, that is, no beliefs, values, emotions, or tastes. Similarly, he should display no adherence to any social norms, cultural codes, personal relationships, or obligations. That's because the economist does not actually need to know *why* this figure wants what he wants within any choice set. What defined this actor was solely that he was invested, within a context of finite resources, in utility maximalization, now called "ophelimity" to suggest that the consequences of his action(s) need not be directly beneficial to anyone, according to what were now called orderable "preferences" to distinguish them from desires or pleasures. Indeed, such a vision of choice-making, Pareto insisted, could apply equally to the behavior of any living being, whether "man, ass or ant."[112]

Pareto made this case in a famous argument with the historian and philosopher Benedetto Croce that ran in an Italian economics journal in 1900, just a few years before the appearance of Pareto's great treatise *Manuale di economica politica*, published in Italian in 1906 and in expanded French form in 1909. Croce's position in this debate was that of a skeptic in face of the modernizer. While similarly eager to make economics into a science independent of history and metaphysics, Croce revealed himself to be unsure if it were really possible to take psychology out of the study of economics or to ignore the conditions under which consumer choices are made. Surely, Croce reasons in this debate, they vary depending on the individual and the circumstances. As such, he rejects Pareto's earlier comments to the effect that "political economy only concerns itself with choices, which fall on things that are variable in quantity and capable of measurement," that is, choices which can be effectively expressed mathematically and "independently of the ideas of pleasure and pain." After all, states Croce, "to choose means to choose consciously," or to will something, and thus choice is "inseparable from the feeling of pleasure and displeasure" even if, conversely, pleasure can be separated from choice.[113]

But in response, the economist Pareto dug in his heels. He counters once again that the goal of those working in the field of economics must be to reduce its arena and to simplify even further if it is to become a pure science, which is to say, a study of "objective relations." The problem with pleasure, he notes, is that it cannot be measured. The solution is, however, clear to him: "In place of the hedonistic hypothesis I have substituted the material fact of choice," the only record that allows for correlations, meaning equations which express the interdependence of unrelated phenomena, and thus also predictions. In this view, there is actually no need to explore motives or reasons behind those choices, which he had previously called "only a matter of taste." There is also no need to consider whether they are logical or illogical; economics, unlike sociology, can simply assume rationality. And there is no need to consider choices from the point of view of ethics. What Pareto and Croce actually agree upon is that "the data of economics are the practical activities of men in so far as they are considered as such, independent of any moral or immoral determination." For Pareto, even standard terms like "value" and "utility" were too weighted down by their associations with complex human feelings and variable meanings, including ones with moral significance; hence his new vocabulary.[114] As he explains in his *Manuale di economica politica* in an effort to make the distinction clear, "Will Mrs. So and So buy a certain diamond today, or will she not? This may well be a psychological problem, but it is certainly not an economic one. How many diamonds are sold, on the average, in England, in a month or in a year? Here we have an economic problem."[115]

All of which leads us to ask (though it was hardly Pareto's question): Is this newfangled *homo economicus* distinctly a *man*? Or has he become so stripped down and schematic that he could really be either sex? The answer is surprisingly complex.

On the one hand, Pareto, despite his then-unusual public agreement with Mill on the value of women's suffrage,[116] was clearly hostile to the value of exploring women consumers per se, whether of jewels or anything else. His discussion of marriage markets in his debate with Croce suggests further his openness to thinking of women as objects for sale just as much as economic actors. While dismissing the related question "will So-and-So who lives in France marry a fair or a dark girl?" as merely of aesthetic interest and thus irrelevant, he offers by way of contrast "a country where polygamy is the rule and where rich men buy female slaves" and his comparative willingness in such circumstances to address "how many blonde slaves and how many brunette ones will be bought."[117] And in yet another place in the same debate, quoting the famed Italian Renaissance writer Boccaccio, Pareto makes it clear that he does not see women, with their many spiritual and household obligations, among his potential readers either.[118] All these references track with the development of a "scientific" field of academic inquiry—economics, in contrast to various forms of commercial and academic survey research—in which women were increasingly pushed to the margins in every way in the course of the first half of the twentieth century.[119]

On the other hand, there *is* another way to see the situation. The conception of the chooser had become so abstract as a result of the so-called marginal revolution in economics that the subject of scrutiny could now potentially also refer to anyone, anywhere, value free. The chooser was meant to be a universal type, with the same essential needs and capacities, as well as ways of thinking and acting, as any other human being. This was a possibility that opened up, at least in theory, the role of neutral chooser, apart from any institutions, values, conventions, or emotional commitments, to women as well as men, regardless of background. It could even be appropriated, as Mill had shown, to feminist ends precisely because—in contrast with a feminism rooted in essential femininity and thus difference—it so thoroughly lacked distinction.

But that's getting ahead of ourselves. The trend toward the reduction of *homo economicus* to essentially a shell of a human, potentially male *or* female, continued apace, if not directly, in the interwar period.

Historians of economics like Nicola Giocoli see but the further escape of economics from psychology in the Vienna Circle and the "pure logic of choice" that dominated the economic field in the 1930s.[120] Contemporaries clearly viewed it similarly. Economic historian Mary Morgan quotes John Maurice Clark, an American institutionalist economist of the 1930s, who quipped satirically, "Our old friend, the 'economic man,' is becoming very self-conscious and bafflingly non-committal . . . he says, 'I may behave one way and I may behave another, but what is that to you? You must take my choices as you find them: I choose as I choose and that is all you really need to know.' The poor thing has been told that his psychology is all wrong, and he is gamely trying to get on without any and still perform as many as possible of his accustomed tasks."[121] The trend was carried yet further in almost the same moment by the American economist Paul Samuelson with his concept of "revealed preferences"; economists could finally jettison the study of the economic actor altogether, he argued, in favor of the only observable and measurable indicator of preferences, concrete choices themselves.[122] There was nothing more one needed to know about human behavior. The laws of economics could best be understood as the effects, indeed the unintended consequences, of model man's choices to select one thing or action rather than another, in aggregate form, regardless of motives and desires before or afterward.

But if *homo economicus*, from Mill onward, had fewer and fewer discernable qualities, that did not make him totally false either. Maybe we can say he became more like an exaggeration of an increasingly recognizable type. As Lionel Robbins, the British author of the field-defining text *An Essay on the Nature and Significance of Economic Science*, was also already well aware in the early 1930s, he—or perhaps she—could never shed all presumed inner experience entirely, much as economists might try.[123] Arguably, that was true for *homo economicus*'s sociological bearings as well (the existence of free markets seems to have been the unacknowledged precondition for his flourishing as well as integral to his aspirations). We can thus still tease out the presuppositions that ran through mainstream economic thinking about our model chooser before World War II even as the scholarly focus turned, especially in advanced capitalist settings, to the enacted choices themselves.

First, it was still largely taken for granted by most mainstream economists that this figure, the chooser, has volition or free will. Choice is, for the chooser, real. Second, model economic man goes through life almost entirely as an individual, and an atomized one at that, meaning he or she thinks, decides, and acts entirely on his or her own and only worries about others if it affects his or her own welfare. Interdependency is not a factor in decision making or actions. Nor is the larger world. Egocentrism, along with self-reliance, is, however, assumed. As the feminist economist Julie Nelson puts it: "Homo economicus is the personification of individuality run wild . . . [he] is the central character in a romance of individuality."[124] Third, he or she has identifiable, even rankable, individual preferences and both knows those preferences before making a choice and can predict the outcome of that choice based upon them. No indecision, no impulsiveness, and no regrets ever enter the story.

Fourth, these preferences are, at once, exogenously given and resistant to change over time; *homo economicus* is consistent in taste and temperament even as he or she ages and gains life experience of all sorts. Fifth, this model human lives in a world in which he or she understands and is comfortable with markets of all kinds and experiences no barriers in entering or navigating them to get what is wanted; even information about options is easily and accurately processed. Sixth, he or she naturally sees all chosen goods as exchangeable, but fundamentally nonsharable with others. Interpersonal utility is not something much contemplated either. Seventh, this economic actor will behave in the same way in all times and places and regardless of his own social position or the larger socioeconomic context. He may live in society, but specific social and cultural obligations or expectations do not matter at all. Only resources do. Assuming markets are competitive and information is equally available to all (which is to say, a perfectly functioning capitalist order), the extent to which one chooses, as well as what one chooses, is variable only because we have different limits on what we can spend. He or she, as a human, is naturally something of a choice-making machine, experiencing little friction between inner life and outer action.

Now it is worth repeating that these assumptions are rarely spelled out in full even by those who work or worked in this domain. They are better described as hidden in plain sight. It is also worth repeating that *homo economicus* exists (and is best thought of) primarily as a tool; he is designed so as to make explanation and prediction possible in mathematical terms. But this stock figure must have appeared to have some basis in lived experience and real-life perceptions to be broadly recognizable. Otherwise, he would not have been plausible even as a scientific instrument. Most economists ultimately admitted as much. As Robbins noted in defense of the claim that individuals can arrange their preferences in order, this much is "obvious" based simply on "our everyday experience."[125] As a rule, according to the contemporary philosopher Philip Pettit, decision theory "explicates certain well-chosen platitudes of folk psychology, the alleged core of our commonsense theory of persons," though he doesn't say where or when or how this folk psychology emerged.[126] In the writings and lectures of modern economists, the way humans were increasingly likely to act in a liberal, capitalist environment—that is, participating in things structured like markets and engaging, ostensibly obstacle-free, in rituals of selection using small-scale technologies of choice within them—was used to redefine human nature in general. And that new definition then, conversely, helped solidify and indeed normalize both the structures and the practices within them in real life. We might call this a textbook tautology or self-fulfilling prophecy. The long, technical process of economists draining utility of all content and turning it into nothing more than preference satisfaction matters to our story because it set the stage for thinking about a host of preexisting choice-making activities, and the people who performed them, in novel ways.

For following Robbins, who hinted already in the 1930s that the principles and methods of economics starting with *homo economicus* were potentially applicable to any situation shaped by scarcity, this way of conceiving of self and world spread beyond the discipline of economics. It did so during World War II and considerably more in the immediate postwar context. The neoclassicists' market model, it turned out, could be effectively adapted to analyze and, consequently, to manipulate what were not strictly market settings in any conventional way. So could the model of the chooser and his or her behavior, whether the subject in question was a consumer, a citizen, or, for that matter, an elected official, a criminal, a diplomat, a student, a churchgoer, a business leader, a job seeker, a romantic partner, or a family member.[127] The consequence? The theory of choice came to seem a potential tool for changing the choice landscape itself, including efforts to increase what and when it is legal to choose, as well as the rules governing the competition—and, again, all well before the neoliberal turn of the mid-1970s and 1980s that is now so closely associated with the triumph of the idea of choice.[128]

The story has much in common with the parallel one, told earlier in this chapter, about the invention of marketing. Partly the growth of the human-as-chooser model depended on the emergence of new areas of academic social science research centered on choice or, more specifically, what came to be known, based on a revised understanding of reason, as "rational choice."[129] What defined these new endeavors was not just adopting the analytic methods of economics. It was also repurposing the figure of *homo economicus*, with his relentless orientation toward strategic choice-making, or the weighing of the costs and benefits of various courses of action, as foundational for other areas of investigation.

Those domains included social and political life, broadly construed. The influential American economist Kenneth Arrow, for example, inaugurated circa 1950 the study of what he called "social choice," arguing that "in a capitalist democracy there are essentially two methods by which social choices can be made: voting, typically used to make 'political' decisions, and the market mechanism, typically used to make 'economic' decisions." Because both involve individuals selecting among a "limited range of alternatives" and both take the collective choice to be "a composite of the desires of individuals," or sum of individual choices, they could be studied with the same techniques. Different voting methods could, for example, be analyzed as different forms of private preference aggregation. For by this logic, societies, political cultures, and markets were ultimately not that different from one another. Neither were the people operating within them, at least on a mathematical model. All of these settings were ultimately transactional realms governed by choices made by individuals in competition with each other.[130]

The growing fascination with analyzing the world in this fashion was helped along by continued formal work on various forms of interactive choice-making too. Just a half decade earlier, as World War II was finally drawing to a close, the émigré mathematicians John von Neumann and Oskar Morgenstern worked together in central New Jersey to lay out the foundations of game theory. This was a new area of study that extended the rational choice paradigm by focusing on optimal choice-making under conditions of uncertainty arising from the fact that in certain choice scenarios, as in many strategy games, one is dependent upon but cannot conclusively predict the choices of others. The implication of game theory, as expressed in von Neumann and Morgenstern's *Theory of Games and Economic Behavior* (1944), was that its theorems could be applied to "decision making" more broadly, leading to the establishment of rules for interactive choice similarly stripped of moral and political considerations as well as psychological ones. After the war, game theory seemed to open up new possibilities for collaboration across standard academic fields and national boundaries as well as new applications.[131]

For this is also a story about the growth of institutions, especially in the United States, eager to sponsor and support this particular kind of inquiry. Those institutions ranged from think tanks like RAND, to nonprofits like the Ford Foundation, to university-based research institutes, to, especially, the greatly expanded administrative machinery of the federal government, starting with the U.S. military. Sponsorship of this new work came in the form of dollars as well as prestige.[132] By the logic of rational choice itself, this combination of rewards (namely, money and power) had to have been a motivating factor for ambitious social scientists of all kinds. Indeed, with this backing, administrative elites had every incentive to recast themselves as "decision makers" as well as experts in decision making.[133] Some years before the war, the Austrian émigré economist Joseph Schumpeter had already argued that more mathematical rigor would make it possible for academic economists to have more sway with political leaders.[134] After the war, this began to happen, albeit in often odd ways. Drawing on their new methodological sophistication, economists and allies argued, the public could be steered not just to make choices but to choose more effectively, including in dangerous situations. Experts in decision theory became, in a sense, the latest incarnation of choice architects, often at the behest of the state. Today's libertarian paternalists, getting people to act "rationally" through "nudges" like putting apples rather than candy next to the cash register or making organ donation the default from which one must opt out rather than in, are in many ways the heirs.[135] The goal was similarly to use state power to shape human decision making in ways that were ultimately beneficial from the vantage point of the state and its planners.

For finally, the triumph of this social science paradigm became, symbiotically, also about meeting political needs in a moment of a "hot" followed by "cold" war.[136] What began in the first decades of the twentieth century as primarily an academic method of analysis and accompanying abstract philosophy, albeit always with an unstated liberal cast, turned into a form of political myth-making as well. Despite Pareto's, Robbins's, and others' warnings against mixing up positive description and prediction with "oughts" and urgings, and despite an ostensible scientific commitment to objectivity and professional detachment, quasi-economic social sciences in the immediate postwar period turned normative. What is more, they became boosters of a very particular form of democracy and capitalist consumer culture in which even equality could be recast as the equal opportunity to make choices and freedom as the possibility of doing so. At the center of both stood this new view of the rational self, continually pursuing his or her own version of happiness in accordance with varied, individual aims. Though economists were well aware that this isn't how the world really works, the expansion of this model and its application to so many fields effectively helped normalize and, in the end, valorize it.

The Critics

Criticism of this model started early, too. It hasn't let up, especially within academic circles. Dissenting scholars across numerous disciplines have decried both the empirical falseness and the political and ethical consequences built into elements of the autonomous economic man and his free-range free will that seem to have ruled the second half of the twentieth century and endured in the twenty-first.[137] Some of the critique has come from sociobiologists and those influenced by their findings, who have consistently downplayed the degree to which we ever control our choices, regardless of how we see them.[138] But challenges to *homo economicus* and the reign of free choice also run through the modern social and human sciences where the possibility of real agency on the part of humans has been taken more seriously. One key charge is that reliance on a crude and simplistic version of economic man has made theory too disconnected from real life: *homo economicus* doesn't really correspond to *homo sapiens* at all.[139] Another is that, regardless of realism, there are myriad negative consequences of thinking with this liberal model of consumption, where the focus is always individual choice under conditions of scarcity and different kinds of choice-making, with different moral weights, are treated as equivalent acts.

Such views, of course, build on a very old line of critique going back to Frankfurt School Marxism and before that, most religious traditions, including early modern Protestantism, which has also been identified as one point of origin for this view of humankind in the first place. But in the postwar era, it is behavioralists who have been among the most vocal critics of model economic man, as we saw in this book's introduction. Already in the 1950s, the Carnegie Mellon economist, psychologist, and computer science pioneer Herbert Simon made the case for seeing our rationality as limited—or what he called "bounded." Simon was convinced that understanding choice-making was the key to a unified science of human behavior, including efforts to perfect decision making through formal modeling. But he insisted that analysts needed as a starting point a less "God-like" and more "rat-like" chooser, that is, a less exalted view of human capacity.[140]

A now better-known critique got going in the early 1970s, as the Israeli army duo of psychologists Daniel Kahneman and Amos Tversky tried to test some of the precepts of rational choice theory in actual decision-making situations. What they learned is that, once one looks under the hood, the boundaries between the rational and the irrational are very hard to maintain. Or as the contemporary philosopher Elizabeth Anderson puts it, "we systematically violate just about every logical implication of decision theory."[141] With experiments rather than mathematical models, behavioralists have demonstrated that even when people have all the information they need to make "rational" decisions, they are generally inconsistent in their preferences. They make errors in framing. They don't think about risk or judge probabilities very well. They let their biases, impulses, and emotions rule their thinking. They open themselves up to manipulation by others. And they continually make choices that harm themselves rather than further their interests. That is, they (as marketers and Freudians already knew) often act against their better judgment. All of us humans—and not just children—are ultimately much less skilled at the optimization of choice than we might think.[142] That we don't generally recognize this lack in a way proves the point.

Once again, there is nothing here to surprise a novelist, even if novelists generally have less by way of scientific proof. A whole strain of contemporary fiction centers on characters who are depicted as such bad judges of situations that, over and over, they make poor choices, picking options that (readers quickly surmise) will lead to misery of various kinds despite their agency as actors. Swedish writer Lena Andersson's widely translated novels *Willful Disregard: A Novel about Love* (2013) and *Acts of Infidelity* (2014) are a case in point. Andersson's intelligent and professionally and financially independent heroines are led astray not by following their passions but rather by the way their passions cloud their rational, considered judgments, or what literary critic Sheila Heti calls "mistakes of deduction,"[143] in a world notably devoid of guardrails. The reader's pleasure, a combination of fascination mingled with horror, stems from watching such characters do so repeatedly—and reap the consequences. Humans are not really best understood as calculating machines, as Dostoevsky told us long ago. We are way too psychologically complicated.

But other critics have pointed to situations, rather than ingrained habits and behaviors, that effectively make "rational" choice irrelevant in any case. Those include moments where ostensibly rational agents are paralyzed and cannot bring themselves to make a choice because they have been presented with too many options. My sample size of one—myself—recognizes this scenario; like many people, I have a very hard time making up my mind when confronted with plentiful possibilities, something our own tech-driven world has exacerbated. That's in part because I can so easily come up with different rationales for different options or imagine better ones around the corner or anticipate regret down the line. Alternately, sometimes the value of one element of a menu over another is simply not apparent, as for the protagonist in novelist John Barth's *The End of the Road* (1958, revised 1967) who finds himself stuck indefinitely in the Baltimore train station, unable to come up with any reason to buy a thirty-dollar ticket for one destination versus another. That scenario also feels deeply familiar.

Let's remember, too, that there are situations in life where individuals are required to make choices that reasonable people might well refuse as unreasonable and a perversion of the very idea of choice, such as those confronting prisoners in the death camps of World War II; literary scholar Lawrence Langer calls them "choiceless choices."[144] Or where a prior choice (say, whom to marry or whether to leave one's homeland) impacts how one would make a subsequent one (say, what kind of job one seeks or even what to wear). Or where two different choices— picking a new bicycle as opposed to a new husband—are likely to be made on very different and maybe even conflicting grounds and with possibly conflicting aims.[145] Most of all, there are many very ordinary circumstances, even in capitalist economies, in which self-interest is simply not the chooser's highest priority when electing to do one thing or another.

That the motivation behind our choices is not always selfishness and that the record of our choices is not always an indicator of utility maximization has long seemed obvious to sociologists, anthropologists, historians, even institutional economists. This isn't only a matter of noting that different emotions—say, pride, self-loathing, altruism, curiosity, a sense of fairness, or even anger and vengeance—can come to the fore at different moments in life and effectively override self-interest or that some of our "choices" result from compulsions that in no way improve our lives. All choices, starting with preferences themselves, are, in the view of many social scientists outside mainstream economics, deeply conditioned and even to a considerable degree determined by the specific environment(s) in which they emerge and reverberate. This isn't just a matter of the realities of daily life either. They are shaped by the pressures of institutions, of political and legal regimes, and of residual social, cultural, and ethical customs, values, and expectations prescribed according to one's social position and status in all the communities and groups to which one belongs: familial, occupational, religious, ethnic and racial, neighborhood, and more. They are also shaped by existing prejudices. John Stuart Mill noted despondently (though this might well have seemed a plus to many others) that most people, even in conditions of political freedom, are inclined most of the time simply to follow others; when it comes to pleasure, he noted, "conformity is the first thing thought of . . . they exercise choice only among things commonly done," until they cease to have any real desires of their own.[146] Pareto himself wore a second hat as a social theorist when it was clear that his own model of *homo economicus*, rationally choosing among all the options before him, was insufficient for understanding the early twentieth-century world in all its dimensions.[147] Today Pareto is as well known in this second role as he is in his first as a pioneer in the discipline of economics.

Moreover, students of economic thought have largely overlooked the ways in which a small cohort of women, writing between the two world wars under the banner of the marginalized field of "home economics," also drew attention to the environmental pressures shaping twentieth-century decision-making behavior, especially when it came to consumption. Among the factors that scholars like Hazel Kyrk pointed to in limiting homemakers' ostensible "freedom of choice" were corporate culture and advertising.[148] This was also a theme for many mid-century critics of mass culture and "propaganda," who bemoaned its homogenizing social effects and the way it manipulated people into doing voluntarily precisely what extended family, churches, and neighbors had always demanded of them, namely, preserving the status quo.[149] To fail to see this was, for many postwar social critics, to exhibit a kind of bias of one's own. This was a bias that stemmed from living so thoroughly under the yoke of capitalism or inside Western consumer-derived norms that what was actually a symptom— a conviction about the social value of individual preference-based choice—came (erroneously) to seem like a root cause.

Furthermore, if we want to understand behavior in parts of the world or within subcultures with different value or economic systems than the dominant, modern Western capitalist-democratic one, late twentieth-century social scientists have said, we need to pay more attention to situations of intersubjectivity and even interdependence. Economist and philosopher Amartya Sen, for example, famously insisted in an influential article of the 1970s titled "Rational Fools" that economists needed to find a way to account for deliberate choices made as a result of social and moral "commitments," or other-regarding considerations, that were contrary or irrelevant to one's own, individual welfare.[150] Other scholars, following historian E. P. Thompson's lead at the same moment, urged more attention to the play of "moral economies," or concerns with fairness and communal welfare, even within market-places.[151] Subjects in many times and places, it turns out, cooperate or cooperated more than we might expect. What's more, these critics long insisted, rectifying such interpretive errors is not just a matter of reflecting reality more accurately or avoiding sins like anachronism and Euro-centrism. Ethically, we also need to move away from models in which a narrowly self-involved and free-floating *homo economicus* reigns no matter the topic. Otherwise, we will continue to naturalize, or at least justify, selfishness in political terms.[152] That is, we will fail to recognize the larger ramifications resulting from our many private choices, and we will continue to underproduce public goods and services.

Above all, though, various strains of self-conscious feminist thought have been a source of profound critiques of economic man and the models built from his example. The chief charge is that a modern, Western, capitalist bias has been accompanied by a masculinist one, not least when it comes to the assumptions baked into this prototype. For though the model is meant to be universal and untethered from sociological, ethical, and even psychological parameters, and though it is imagined to be primarily devoted to the original feminine act of choice—consumption of goods—*homo economicus* is male at its core. What's worse, modeling with this type ends up reaffirming masculine norms with real-world discriminatory effects.

How so? In always assuming voluntary decision making rooted in personal preferences, the *homo economicus* paradigm fails to account for the ways that women are always disproportionally constrained, practically but also imaginatively, when it comes to both when and what to pick. The weight of their history of disempowerment goes unacknowledged in most economic discourse. But at the same time and for the same reasons, this model also ignores, misinterprets, or treats as deviant women's sometimes deliberate but also nonutilitarian motivations for their choices when they do have more agency. That includes such relational values as love, social solidarity, and even obligation and dependency, as well as the related forgoing of income they often entail. As a result, many of women's most important roles in the world—for example, as (unpaid) laborers and caregivers within the home, not to mention producers of children—go unrecognized. These omissions then generate the further marginalization and undervaluing of women, as they fail to seem like true economic actors, which has become a way of saying autonomous beings.[153] Plus, by insisting upon *homo economicus*'s universality despite evidence to the contrary, this model's advocates also fail to address the ways it excludes many women *and* men around the world on the basis of class, race, age, religion, geography, custom, and especially income. Ultimately, *homo economicus* is best understood as a specific and parochial historical phenomenon.

Consider the story "Marcovaldo at the Supermarket." The great Italian writer Italo Calvino, as early as the 1960s, offered readers a harrowing if humorous picture of a poor family that infiltrates, at the end of a long workday, a new self-service market in an unnamed northern Italian industrial city. Aping the "busy maidservants" and "be-furred ladies," every member of the family individually fills a new-style wheeled basket with heaps of desirable goods selected from among the copious offerings, just as desirous of engaging in a ritual of feverish choice-making and thus preference fulfillment as everyone else. Each of them, young and old, male and female, has recently learned to imagine pleasure and, ultimately, freedom from their otherwise confined circumstances in this particular act. But they have no money to render their choice-making more than a fleeting performance. Thus when each of them finally gets to the check-out counter, they have to give it all up—and make their humiliating escape. "Marcovaldo at the Supermarket" is a story about the left-out or, really, the left-behind in the new frenzy of aspirational choice.[154]

Where We Are: The New Morality

We are, though, putting the cart before the horse with this discussion of nascent critiques here. The emergence after World War II of, first, a new notion of human rights, and second, a post-suffrage version of feminism occurred largely in alliance with the world-as-supermarket and individual-as-self-sufficient-choice-maker ethos, even as they moved well beyond questions of material consumption. This was not initially a matter of women making new inroads in economics depart-ments or revising existing models of *homo economicus*. Rather, what we are talking about is the development, first and foremost, of a new, largely secular moral project, rooted, paradoxically, in the rise of the practice and theory of value-neutral choice. Freedom may have once been identified with the making of certain (good or legally, socially, and reli-giously sanctioned) choices rather than other (bad or disfavored and outlawed) ones. But by the late 1940s, this was no longer the case: as we've just seen, it was widely postulated in the "free" world that libera-tion lay in the experience of choosing itself. A key progressive postwar goal became extending this idealized possibility to more kinds of people in more kinds of places as a value unto itself.

From this vantage point, two particularly influential texts of postwar history require a new look. One is the Universal Declaration of Human

Rights, an international endeavor led by Eleanor Roosevelt in the role of commission chair, that established the basic outline for human rights to this day. The other is Betty Friedan's *The Feminine Mystique*, which inaugurated so-called second-wave feminism in the United States. In very different forms and in very different registers, these two texts repurposed the practices *and* the sciences associated with an expanded menu of acceptable options and turned them into recipes for human flourishing in universal ethical terms. Both, in other words, can be read as manifestos in favor of the modern understanding of choice.

The Universal Declaration of Human Rights—which passed a United Nations vote unanimously in 1948, but ultimately without the support of the Soviet Union and its allies, or South Africa or Saudi Arabia—was not an immediate landmark success. The final version was a compromise, like most things ever written by a committee. It was also skeletal, lacking in examples, evidence, or even much by way of explanation. It was, furthermore, not much remarked upon in its moment. It has certainly never been very effective in practice; essentially a formal bill of rights, the text was constructed without the establishment of any enforcement mechanism or even suggestion of one in the future. Yet what has come to distinguish the Universal Declaration is not just its ostensible global scope compared to previous such exercises. Repeated hints of a highly historically particular moral program run through the whole.

First, the committee's focus, in the wake of World War II, was resolutely on individuals, abstracted from any context and untethered from collectivities of any kind, from family to nation to cultural group. The latter, though discussed by the committee, disappeared entirely from the final text. It is the dignity and liberty of the individual that, in principle, is being protected in the face of the threat of totalitarianism or other forms of authoritarianism.[155]

Second, the fundamental guarantee in its articles became not the fulfillment of basic needs, as some Communists on the committee had hoped, but rather the opportunity to pursue those needs, from housing to education to job to marriage partner, as one sees fit and in whatever version one chooses, given one's existing resources and situation. In fact, beyond the plentiful articles into which choice language carried the day—those about employment, education, and political representation, as mentioned in this book's introduction—we know that there were additional debates about the validity of even more categories of rights that might be framed in this particular, self-interested way. These categories extended from the right to "the free choice of residence within the borders of each state" (suggested initially by the Canadian lawyer John Humphrey) to, more broadly, the individual right to "free choice of work and . . . mode of life" (suggested by the Lebanese delegation), all rooted in the idea that every individual should be "free" to craft their own experience and trajectory in keeping with their personal values and tastes.[156]

Of course, there was a certain irony in the language of the marketplace as much as democracy shaping this text, which stayed away from any explicit discussion of consumer issues. There was a certain irony, too, in the fact that its framers' goal was ultimately to establish that it was prohibited, or beyond a matter of choice, for any state leader to deny anyone, anywhere, the right to choose the key elements of their individual lives. But we understand now that this was the decisive moment when human rights became framed primarily, if not exclusively, as an exercise in freedom from interference—or negative freedom rather than positive freedom, to use Isaiah Berlin's almost contemporaneous terms.[157] In the Universal Declaration of Human Rights of 1948, the moral doctrine of human rights became coterminous, in ways it never had been before, with unlimited and unimpeded freedom of choice.

Finally, in the finished text, the rights of man were now taken to pertain to women too, but mainly tacitly, which is to say, through the additive principle and in the name of universality. The Soviet delegation and the United Nation's own Commission on the Status of Women, created in 1946, had tried and failed to get attention specifically to women's rights into the document. The only exception was finally article 2, an antidiscrimination statement, which mentions sex in a long list of other distinctions, from race and color to religion to property to birth to political opinion, that are not to be countenanced in terms of the extension of rights and freedoms. But there was widespread agreement on the necessity of substituting gender-neutral language in place of traditional talk of "mankind" or the "rights of man," which Eleanor Roosevelt and others feared would be taken literally in many parts of the world. In the end, "all human beings" and then "everyone" took pride of place throughout the text (though there remained a few references in the text to "brotherhood" and "himself and his family," specifically in articles 23 and 25, which deal with wage labor and social welfare, respectively).[158] We are all, in this view, abstract, fungible subjects, versions of *homo economicus* in principle even if not in practice.

And while crafted by an international panel, these categories and terms were imposed on the world largely by representatives of capitalist, democratic, and historically Christian nations. All the key architects of the Declaration—Eleanor Roosevelt of the United States, Peng-Chun Chang of China, Charles Malik of Lebanon, René Cassin of France, and the key staff person, John Humphrey of Canada—had been educated at least in part in North America or Western Europe. Most were academics. Non-Western philosophical traditions were not much considered even as commentators from Chang onward tried to find parallels, including a similar emphasis on choice here and there, in traditions from Confucianism to Islam.[159] In fact, it is hard not to see in the Universal Declaration the triumph of a logic that remained alien in much of the world in the 1940s but that had already become *doxic* in powerful areas of it. That was partly through habit and partly through new conceptualizations of that habit under the rubric of the new sciences of choice.

The same went for terminology, just as it would for framers of abortion rights in the early 1970s. Eleanor Roosevelt said in 1947 about her own role in the process: "I may be able to help them [the rest of the international committee] put into words the high thoughts which they can gather from past history and from the actuality of the contemporary situation, so that the average human being can understand and strive for the objectives set forth."[160] Her "real value" on the drafting commission, as she saw it, was that she could translate from everyday experience to abstraction and back again, all in plain terms. For Roosevelt was also quite convinced that it was at the microcosmic level of the household and its practices that human rights would ultimately take root as a set of moral claims to live by: "Where, after all do human rights begin? In small places, close to home—so close and so small that they cannot be seen on any maps of the world. . . . Unless these rights have meaning there they have little meaning anywhere."[161]

In a very different way, translation from everyday lived experience to theory and back again was central to Betty Friedan's self-conscious, choice-based feminism a little more than a decade later too. But the starting point was quite specifically the front lines of mid-century suburban American life from which she reported on a looming crisis. As Friedan explained in her heated 1963 nonfiction bestseller, *The Feminine Mystique*, women (by which she meant postwar, middle-class, white, heterosexual, college-educated American women) had already won the basic comforts and legal rights they needed, including access to schools and colleges, workplaces, and government seats. Yet they had been collectively sold a kind of false consciousness, which she called the "feminine mystique," that made it seem as if they had very limited options or, actually, no real options at all for themselves beyond reveling in full-time domesticity.

Encouraged by battalions of Freudian psychologists and sexologists, market researchers, writers of advertising copy, and even educators like Margaret Mead, and reinforced from women's colleges to the pages of women's magazines, that titular ideal had overwhelmingly steered the well-educated women of mid-century America into default roles as housewives and mothers as their highest destiny. It had then pushed these same women to occupy themselves and find "true feminine fulfillment" solely in what Friedan took to be trivial forms of choice-making, like deciding which dishwasher to buy or what to make for dinner. That, and "wait[ing] to be chosen" themselves, or found sexually appealing by their partners. As a result, a disproportionate number were deeply unhappy, trapped in the "comfortable concentration camp" (to repeat her famously overwrought metaphor) of the modern suburban home, self-medicating with incessant pills and, yes, shopping. Thanks to what we might now call twentieth-century variants of choice agents combined with women's own docility, middle-class American women had, Friedan announced, become unwitting and unselfconscious participants in their own oppression.[162]

How did Friedan know any of this to be the case? Just as Margaret Mead had learned from her Samoan and then American informants, Friedan drew, she claimed, not only from her long experience as a mid-century suburban mother on the outskirts of New York City but also from substantial evidence collected from her own set of informants. That included responses to a detailed proto-feminist "questionnaire" about "life choices" that she had distributed in 1957 to her former Smith College classmates on the occasion of their fifteenth reunion and then subsequent in-depth "interviews" with dozens of female subjects of varied ages.[163] She also read deeply in contemporary social science and psychology.

It was there that Friedan also found a solution of sorts. The answer lay not in more varied or artisanal baking (Friedan was a lot less enthusiastic about cooking or dining as an emblem of freedom than many of her mid-century contemporaries). But neither did it lie in politics or the remaking of institutions, despite Friedan's earlier days as a labor journalist and activist.[164] Friedan also had little time in the pages of *The Feminine Mystique* for those structurally without much choice, like the "cleaning woman" that Friedan urged her readers to hire, or for any kind of collective action on the part of women writ large, though she praised her feminist forebears for their organizational skills. Instead, she urged individual women (again, meaning white, middle-class, well-educated, heterosexual women) to seize the initiative and to engage in self-realization—a form of "growing up"—that would amount to self-liberation. Echoing Mill as much as fashionable mid-century French existentialist philosophers including Simone de Beauvoir,[165] Friedan argued that what her female subjects as well as most commentators had failed to grasp was that a full existence requires conscious determinations about who to be—or a "life plan," as she put it in her final chapter. Otherwise, one was left a shell of a person.

For men, she noted, this much was already obvious, an established part of American mythology. From the "brilliant" psychoanalyst Erik

Erikson to the sociologist David Riesman to existentialist philosophers like Jean-Paul Sartre, big-name contemporary intellectuals had repeatedly insisted on the importance of each of their male counterparts courageously "choosing his identity" and becoming a full-fledged "individual." But in Friedan's hands, the message was not only redirected toward women (as de Beauvoir had already done a number of years earlier); it was also rendered concrete and mundane, rooted in postwar American sociological detail and the everyday language of the popular women's magazines that she also rejected.[166]

Perhaps in keeping with this end, Friedan, unlike de Beauvoir and more like Eleanor Roosevelt and contemporary economists, chose in *The Feminine Mystique* to adopt the linguistic and conceptual category of "choice" for all of this business of preference-realization, from the smallest decisions of the housewife to the largest of decisions about how to live and who to be. The last line of the book's preface reads: "in the end, a woman, as a man, has the power to choose, and to make her own heaven or hell." All Friedan really meant was that women should consider adding meaningful extramural work to their housewifely and childcare duties, that they should entertain more options for how to spend their days and be less judged for which they picked. But Friedan ultimately reinforced the message already latent in the Universal Declaration of Human Rights that we are all—women included—defined by how often and what we choose, whatever the situation. In fact, she opened a new horizon for women: "The problem for many [before now] was money, race, color, class, which barred them from choice—not what they would be if they were free to choose." This was a far cry from Wollstonecraft's vision of women's rights. For Friedan, it was also a different goal than that of her suffragist foremothers. The key now was less to attack the supermarket than to demand a larger set of offerings, that is, to see liberation in repeated acts of deliberate, self-conscious, and preference-based choice-making among a wider array of options when it came to *all* aspects of life.[167]

Women responded almost immediately. Though some saw only the threat of communism in Friedan's upsetting of gender norms (this was also a critical moment for the birth of the New Right), hundreds of

American women wrote to Friedan in the early 1960s extolling how her words had made them personally "feel" free.[168] It is easy to see the roots here of late 1960s and early 1970s feminist consciousness raising, which took revising personal narratives of one's own experience and trajectory in light of structural forms of sexism to be the essential first step toward new forms of collective self-determination for women.[169]

And what began as a cultural phenomenon ultimately became, with the founding in 1966 of the National Organization for Women (NOW) with Friedan at the helm, political too. The organization's original statement of purpose, written by Friedan, attaches the women's movement directly to the "world-wide revolution of human rights now taking place within and beyond our national borders." It also insists, using that same idiom, that "the time has come to confront, with concrete action, the conditions that now prevent women from enjoying the *equality of opportunity and freedom of choice which is their right*, as individual Americans, and as human beings."[170] The point is not just that human rights campaigns and the allied feminist political organizing of the late 1960s and early 1970s in the United States and Europe were both shaped by the rhetoric, ideals, practices, and, ultimately, sciences of their times. More significantly, in liberal second-wave feminism, choice was turned into a form of secular salvation. Feminism ultimately served, like human rights more generally, to help render choice the moral core of modern times, at least in the land of plenty.

Yet that mainstream take also helps explain why, today, resistance to feminism has become a stand-in for resistance to a whole worldview, in the United States and around the globe. In opponents' hands, choice as opportunity for inventiveness or self-fulfillment or even emancipation and transformation has turned into something else. It has become suggestive of an amoral, selfish universe, where the self and its profoundly individualistic desires is the whole horizon and material abundance is the expected norm even as many are left out. *Roe v. Wade*, the Supreme Court case that legalized abortion in the United States just ten years after the publication of *The Feminine Mystique* and did more than any other legal event domestically to propagate this moralized language about individualized choice, has often been described as a new beginning in feminist struggles for women's liberation, as it was then known. But it was really the culmination of this story. What's more, as the epilogue will show, "choice"—the era's great rhetorical prop—was already in the early 1970s pretty weak tea for securing an essential element of justice, equality, and, indeed, freedom for women. This book draws to a close with a reflection on this recent past as a gateway to reconsidering the ethics of choice going forward.

EPILOGUE

The Past and Future of a "Right to Choose"

The idea of liberty is one which each epoch reshapes to its own liking.

—MARC BLOCH

IN THE MID-1970S, just after the case of *Roe v. Wade* was heard and decided in the U.S. Supreme Court, several national organizations in favor of legalized abortion made a strategic decision. They threw their weight behind the idea that, when it came to the possibility of carrying through or terminating a pregnancy, women had a "right to choose."

This decision does not, of course, shock or even surprise us now. It didn't actually come as much of a bombshell then either. Quite the contrary: the choice to employ the language of choice and then attach it to a cause seen as particular to women and their reproductive lives was rooted in precedents, some quite old by the 1970s and some quite recent.

"Choice" was hardly a critical term for feminism or any rights-based political movement even well into the twentieth century. Yet, as we've seen, the story isn't linear. Choice-making (as opposed to production or invention) had long been women's special domain, especially when connected to consumption and idea of the frivolous and fickle *coquette*. Since well before the triumph of capitalism, that association had worked on two sides of the Atlantic both to link and to taint all three: women, consumer culture, and the very modern business of making individual, self-motivated choices. At the same time, though, opportunities to exercise a personal preference in the face of two or more options had also always been only partially open to women, whatever their class and background. And when it came to ideas and beliefs, even when choice *was* available to some (largely bourgeois or elite) women in practice, it was almost always coded male or, later, gender neutral, which often meant masculine by default. So as similar forms of choice-making grew in significance, practically as well as conceptually in arenas from religion to family and career to, finally, politics, they became a focus for the ambitions of a growing number of women by the start of the twentieth century. That was even with all the limitations, exclusions, and unacknowledged constraints that I've been describing as characteristic of modern or "bounded" choice. The goal of affording more women more alternatives from which they might select what they desired, whether in things or people or worldviews or "lifestyles," also accelerated and spread across a wide geography in the aftermath of first one, then a second world war, especially as the victors made a fetish of a new, geopolitical conception of freedom-as-choice and choice-as-freedom. Eventually, with many setbacks along the way, feminists extended this enduring ideal once again, this time to a very particular kind of gendered labor: birthing babies.

The concept of parenthood by choice ran, pre-*Roe v. Wade*, from the socialist birth control pioneer Margaret Sanger's 1919 argument that "No Woman can call herself free until she can choose consciously whether she will or will not be a mother" to the "Children by Choice" demonstrations held by a fledgling National Association for the Repeal of Abortion Laws (NARAL) in 1969. Both were themselves outgrowths, in new language, of the radical nineteenth-century idea of voluntary motherhood.[1] In addition, the nascent "women's liberation" movement of the 1960s—born at the same moment as the birth control pill introduced a novel kind of sexual freedom into daily life—was rife with stories of women who felt they had had no options except to get a back-room, illegal abortion, which they frequently described as no real choice at all.[2] Attaching choice to the campaign for the legalization of abortion in the context of second-wave feminism could thus already serve in the late 1960s as a kind of shorthand for an old idea: Women required not only more and better alternatives when it came to various aspects of their lives, including family planning. They also needed the basic autonomy to consider and pursue, unimpeded, their own preferred course of action, based on their own circumstances, desires, values, interests, and, it must be said, pocketbooks. It was an idea that fit well, potentially, within a politically democratic and economically capitalist world that had already made a habit, science, and, finally, virtue of self-interested choice.

Indeed, the victorious jurists of *Roe v. Wade* had already succeeded in channeling aspects of this basic idea to their advantage, along with a few other forms of justification, as the case was heard in 1971–73. Sarah Weddington, the young Texas lawyer for the plaintiff Roe, had argued before the Supreme Court that "a pregnancy to a woman is perhaps one of the most determinative aspects of her life. . . . And we feel that, because of the impact on the woman, this certainly—in as far as there are any rights which are fundamental—is a matter which is of such fundamental and basic concern to the woman involved that she should be allowed to make the choice as whether to continue or to terminate her pregnancy."[3] Justice Harry Blackmun, author of the majority opinion, had picked up on that argument, among others, which he translated into legal terms as a "right of privacy," or space beyond the reach of government, where individual women and (critically) their doctors could to a considerable degree make their own decisions—much as they already could, post-*Griswold v. Connecticut* (1965) and then *Eisenstadt v. Baird* (1972), when it came to birth control.[4]

In his concurrence, Justice Potter Stewart had also reinforced the centrality of the Fourteenth Amendment to this line of reasoning. Though he had conceded that "The [U.S.] Constitution nowhere mentions a specific right of personal choice in matters of marriage and family life," he had insisted that "the 'liberty' protected by the Due Process

Clause of the Fourteenth Amendment covers more than those freedoms explicitly named in the Bill of Rights." Furthermore, Stewart had
noted that several earlier decisions of the Court, including *Eisenstadt v.
Baird* in the previous term, had demonstrated that "freedom of personal
choice in matters of marriage and family life is one of the liberties protected by the Due Process Clause."[5] The right to abortion had, in other
words, already been construed by jurists in *Roe v. Wade* not as a right to
equal protection or really as a right *to* anything tangible, but rather as a
negative right, a right to noninterference. The law was to protect
the freedom, specifically of women, to make their own decisions about
the future of their pregnancies, at least in the first few months. The
passage of *Roe v. Wade* had put the power of the state behind this fundamentally liberal but also very late twentieth-century idea.[6]

It was, though, the intense backlash to *Roe v. Wade*, including the
mobilization of a growing political and religious right against the legalization of abortion on any grounds, that led defenders of abortion to
decide that the movement required a commitment to a single, consistent formulation or, really, value that would resonate widely both politically and culturally. In the aftermath, rather than at the heart of *Roe*, that
value became choice. We know from reading feminist meeting tran-
scripts of the era that the major swing toward choice rhetoric in the
mid-1970s was part of a deliberate deescalation strategy in what became,
ironically, an escalating and enduring culture war that would reshape
American politics for the long haul. In the wake of the growing negative
reaction to the Supreme Court's legalization of first- and second-term
abortion in early 1973, mainstream pro-abortion and women's rights
groups in the United States decided to consciously steer the conversation away from more controversial and previously implicated issues.
The list included state-based neonatalism, feminism and the Equal
Rights Amendment, sexual freedom, and even abortion itself, with its
potential associations with sacrilege (in religious terms) or communism
(in political ones).[7] The subsequent turn to talk of choice was intended
pragmatically to shift the debate to the considerably less fraught idea,
by the standards of the United States in the 1970s, of respect for women
as decision makers—or, ultimately, choosers.[8]

Precedent wasn't the only reason either. From a public relations or advocacy perspective, the story could now be spun as something like common sense. If women were already "free"—thanks to a combination of changing laws, mores, and social practices—to make their own choices among multiple alternatives when it came to consumer goods, ideas, entertainments, jobs, partners, candidates for office, and more, why not this choice as well? In fact, it could be argued that sexually active women needed to have this initial choice—about whether and when to bear children if they found themselves pregnant—in order to be free to make all the subsequent ones that would shape other facets of their lives. Opposition to legal abortion, by this logic, meant nothing less than opposition to freedom: freedom for women to make independent determinations about their own bodies and selves, just like men. Who could object?

Furthermore, talk of being "pro-choice" or, even more, having the "right to choose" had the perceived advantage by the middle years of the 1970s of being now rooted in a broadly consensual set of values that increasingly cut across the conservative/progressive divide. Such lingo was consonant with the human rights language of the postwar era, from the Universal Declaration of Human Rights (1948) to the Helsinki Accords (1975), and the subsequent expansion of constitutional democracy across the globe. It also accorded well in the United States with newer conceptions of small government, antipaternalism, and a kind of market-based individualism that insisted people generally know their own interests best. (Milton and Rose Friedman's *Free to Choose*, which aired on public television in 1980, summed up the growing conviction, rooted in three-quarters of a century of neoclassical economic thought, that "reliance on the freedom of people to control their own lives in accordance with their own values is the surest way to achieve the full potential of a great society," as well as the system that has prevailed for most of "our" history.)[9] It even seemed in harmony with the contemporaneous, more left-leaning liberal egalitarian political theory of John Rawls, which took the academic world by storm in the 1970s.[10] The slogan "my body, my choice," first coined around the time of *Roe v. Wade*, was not intended to mean absolute freedom to do whatever one wanted with one's physical self, no matter the consequences to others, any more than, say, the right to drive a car includes the right to drive in a state of inebriation; *Roe v. Wade* clearly laid down limits, including the number of weeks after which the choice of abortion was off the table. Nevertheless, the rise of the linkage between abortion and choice under the guise of women's empowerment happened in concert with and perhaps as the ultimate expression of what has come to be known as neoliberalism.[11] That is an approach to politics characterized by the gradual undoing of elements of the welfare state and its redistributive and regulatory policies that had previously been part and parcel of liberal governance—or the spillover of neoclassical economists' thinking into democracy itself.

It was largely a matter of affinity. In legal theorist Robin West's cynical telling, the logic of *Roe*, rooted in making a virtue of individual preferences and "free" markets for their realization, could potentially be extended just as well to "the sale and purchase of labor . . . subprime mortgages, high interest loans, prostitution services, surrogacy services, babies, gambling contracts, guns, or kidneys."[12] In one way, this might appear to be a world washed clean of moral concerns, replaced with nothing more than prices and cash. In another, though, it seems the site of an increasingly hegemonic vision of morality in which having a choice is itself a moral good, maybe even *the* moral good, because it is the source of our collective freedom to each live as we wish and, ultimately, to "be ourselves." In the absence of agreement on the good and the right, choice went from being a benefit of freedom to freedom's very essence.

The paper trail is deep for this turn in the United States toward the harnessing of choice to the purposes of women's rights in the realm of abortion. It has also been well reconstructed by a number of legal scholars in recent years, including Reva Siegel, Linda Greenhouse, and especially Mary Ziegler. The story picks up almost exactly where *Roe* leaves off. In December 1972, just before the final decision was handed down the following month, Jimmye Kimmey, executive director of the Association for the Study of Abortion (ASA), founded in 1965 and the leading pro-legalization association of the time, wrote a memo to her colleagues under the heading "education campaign re: abortion rights." Then she made a persuasive case for why "right to choose" was the best and most persuasive slogan available at that moment for advocating for abortion rights. As she saw it, it was a punchy counter to the "right to life" slogan already in use by opponents. Also, unlike talk of conscience, choice "has to do with action—and it is action we are concerned with." Finally, it moved the conversation away from moral judgments; for as she bluntly put it, "What we are concerned with is, to repeat, the woman's right to choose—not her right (or anyone else's right) to make a judgment about whether that choice is morally licit."[13]

But it was the next year, after the *Roe* decision had already changed the legal landscape, that mainstream abortion access advocacy groups like Planned Parenthood, the National Association for the Repeal of Abortion Laws (NARAL), and Friedan's NOW, not to mention liberal religious groups like Catholics for a Free Choice, saw their fortunes really rise. It was then, too, that their leaders came to rely on the loose connections among abortion rights, freedom, and choice in an attempt both to rally potential supporters and to gain political traction against the burgeoning opposition. In one sense, the whole subsequent story of choice could be seen to depend on the decisional autonomy argument of *Roe v. Wade*. Mainly, though, as Ziegler persuasively shows, the strategy and its chief talking points were developed in the ruling's aftermath—and largely outside of courtrooms. According to a confidential memorandum, in late 1973, in a strategy session in Denver, Planned Parenthood's leaders made the self-conscious decision to henceforth draw very little on *Roe* directly. Instead, it was similarly determined that the best approach would involve "the reaffirmation of commitment to freedom of choice in parenthood." For as conference organizer Robin Elliott proposed, "an important thematic idea to be stressed is that abortion in a pluralistic society is to be considered as a matter for determination according to personal choice." The idea stuck. By the late 1970s, under the directorship of the Black feminist healthcare advocate Faye Wattleton, this had become Planned Parenthood's main talking point nationally.[14]

As for NOW, which didn't touch the abortion question for some time after its founding in 1966: gradually arguments that associated abortion with women's freedom of choice ruled the day too. In 1974, NOW adopted a Bill of Women's Rights to Choose Abortion and dedicated a lobbying day to this idea.[15] Its formal debating handbook of that same year suggested that advocates draw connections between a woman's right to limit childbearing and First Amendment rights, including freedom of religion and of speech.[16] (It is worth noting that this was a strategy that was also adopted slightly earlier by the National Association of Laity, a progressive Catholic organization, which endorsed the old idea of "the free exercise of a conscience" and framed abortion as a "personal option.")[17] NOW supporters were urged *not* to argue "the moral rights or wrongs of abortion" but rather a foundational form of personal choice. Further, just like the architects of Planned Parenthood's strategy, NOW's leaders saw an advantage by the middle of the decade in placing the story of abortion rights within a larger historical narrative, starting with Margaret Sanger (despite her unmentioned eugenicist past). That way, an older, seemingly settled campaign for women's rights could be framed as just one node in an ongoing effort to win women, regardless of race and income, the legal right to be choosers in all aspects of their lives.[18]

NARAL, which Friedan also helped launch in 1969, finally did much the same. In its guide for speakers and debaters published almost a decade later in 1978, defenders of abortion rights were encouraged to stress that "the decision to have an abortion is and should be a private one, free from outside pressures or interferences. In a democratic, nonsectarian society, women should be free to make their own decisions regarding childbearing and contraceptive use."[19] It is hard not to hear this as a derivative mashup of debates about the advantages of the secret ballot with arguments for women's suffrage. Once again, the idea was to avoid taking up a moral defense of abortion itself, especially as the stigma around abortion grew, or mentioning abortion's positive social effects in an instrumental fashion. Rather, advocates were to draw on a kind of atomistic liberalism in which the individual (woman) had a natural right to form her own conceptions of the good apart from the state, the pressure of churches, or even relations with her intimates. For in the end, as a 1979 NARAL fund-raising campaign explained, the struggle over abortion is really best seen as "a test of whether our society will protect the rights of the individual to lead his or her life, free of the dictates and dogma of others."[20]

Enter a variety of catchy slogans, songs, and images intended to cement the relationship between reproductive freedom and choice. These were tools for fund-raising, lobbying, and public education, not to mention protesting, that harked back very directly to national women's suffrage campaigns in both the United States and Britain. Even before *Roe v. Wade*, women's groups had started to invent a vocabulary and imagery for the cause that made use of the concept of choice (figs. E.1 and E.2). After *Roe*, a mass movement dedicated to the defense of abortion access and rooted in choice-themed paraphernalia was launched as well. By the mid-1970s, "pro-choice kits" were made widely available to abortion rights spokespeople as part of NOW's extensive media campaign. So were choice-themed postcards, bumper stickers, and buttons to affix to one's clothing (like NARAL's "I'm pro-choice . . . and I vote," which, at a literal level, sounds redundant) for everyone else.[21]

The U.S. movement in defense of abortion rights also got an explicitly patriotic spin, thanks to new efforts to link choice with freedom both rhetorically and iconographically. In 1977, when President Jimmy Carter invited NARAL members to the National Women's Conference in Houston to discuss gender inequalities, they took up the chant "choice, choice, choice." Then, according to Friedan's recollections of that event, "when Right to Life men led a noisy demonstration in the galleries, carrying pictures of pickled fetuses, the National Abortion Rights Action League raised a single blue and white banner with the Statue of Liberty raising a torch over 'the right to choose.' . . . [Then] some women stood to sing 'God Bless America' with them."[22] And in a further turn toward the invocation of a national creed in defense of women's reproductive independence, state abortion rights organizations held rallies in the late 1970s with titles and accompanying banners reading "Freedom Is the Right to Choose" and "Freedom to Choose Is the American Way."[23]

Mainstream political parties took notice—and reinforced the fight along partisan lines. At the time of *Roe*, party alignment on abortion

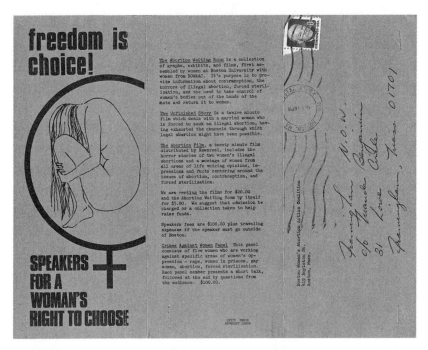

Fig. E.1. "Freedom Is Choice! Speakers for a Woman's Right to Choose" (1972), an early effort, designed by the Boston Women's Abortion Action Coalition, to link both freedom and choice to the question of abortion rights.

Fig. E.2. Photograph by Bettye Lane of an abortion rights demonstration held in May 1972 in Union Square, New York, in defense of that state's liberal abortion law before the *Roe v. Wade* verdict. Signs and banners included "The Right to Choose Abortion" (pictured) and "Mrs.—had no choice in 1968. Now she does" (not pictured).

wasn't clear in the United States. But by the late 1970s and, even more, 1980s, all of these choice-based catchphrases were becoming the distinctive property of the Democratic Party, as the two major American political parties began to divide along the lines of two distinct sets of talking points on the abortion question.[24] What's more, the feminist story about abortion began to take on a life of its own. As Ziegler and other historians point out, some efforts were made in the early years to try to combine discussion of abortion with the promotion of larger social goals, with talk of the "preconditions of free choice," like equal pay for women and an end to workplace discrimination; this was especially the case among feminist groups with large representations of people of color, as it was for most abortion-rights groups outside the United States.[25] However, that approach gained little mainstream domestic traction. Ultimately, abortion rights became something of a single-issue movement in the United States, like women's suffrage some sixty years earlier. And while many have detailed this struggle's outsized effects on American political culture, from national events like presidential campaigns to local efforts to organize the options through lobbying for hospitals and clinics, on the one hand, or pregnancy crisis centers and adoption agencies, on the other, it is important not to neglect its second impact. The fight over abortion and choice would ultimately reshape arguments about "women's liberation" as a whole, with lasting implications for how we understand women's relationship to the idea and practice of choice today.

The language of choice, meanwhile, was quickly internationalized and used—sometimes successfully and sometimes not—to rally a broad public in many parts of the world behind similar campaigns for the legalization of abortion in the early stages of pregnancy. That was certainly the case in Europe, even as the feminist revival from the 1960s onward became focused as much on political-economic constraints on women's lives as on personal emancipation. In 1971, for example, one of the most visible French women's rights organizations, for which Simone de Beauvoir served as the first president, took the name Association Choisir. Choisir (literally, to choose) was to play a central role in the legalization of abortion a few years later, thanks in good part to

Tunisian-born lawyer and founder Gisèle Halimi, whose defense of a teenage girl charged in 1972 in the working-class Parisian suburb Bobigny with an illegal abortion became a cause célèbre about the girl's lack of choice. (To capture the mood of cheerful celebration around free-spirited feminist choice in France that was soon to follow, see Agnès Varda's film *One Sings, the Other Doesn't*, memorably reviewed in the *New Yorker* by Pauline Kael in 1977 as "Scrambled Eggs.") Choisir's agenda, shaped by Halimi, also quickly became considerably more radical, especially about sexuality, than that of its American counterparts—an ironic development, perhaps, considering women did not garner the right to vote in France until after World War II.[26]

France was not an outlier either. Later in the same decade, doctors in Britain, where a medical approach to the subject was generally more common and abortion had already been legalized in the late 1960s, banded together behind the slogan "Doctors for a Woman's Choice on Abortion."[27] In Sweden, the feminist organization Group 8 adopted in the 1970s the theme of women's right to determine matters related to their own bodies, in marked contrast to older arguments in favor of the decriminalization of abortion.[28] So did Italian women, aligning themselves with new international norms under the banner "La Decisione Alla Donna" or "It's Women Who Decide."[29] By the start of the twenty-first century, the association of choice and self-determination with women's right to abortion, not to mention right to IVF, to assisted suicide, and to other newer issues connected to bodily autonomy, had gone global, from Argentina to Zambia to Pakistan, where the Urdu slogan "Mera Jism Meri Marzi"—literally, "my body, my choice"—ensures continual controversy. The phrase has also ceased to have a particularly American ring, though it has remained (often problematically from the perspective of various corners of the world) largely associated with the Global North and the West.[30]

Indeed, such slogans have also stuck around in the United States, now half a century later, despite the *actually* shocking reversal of *Roe v. Wade* in the subsequent Supreme Court case of *Dobbs v. Jackson Women's Health Organization* (2022). NARAL Pro-Choice America, as it called itself until very recently, still sends literature to my mailbox with messages about the importance of fighting for women's right to choose, along with the argument that *Roe* constituted "one of the great landmarks of freedom in the United States."[31] So does Planned Parenthood, where the phrase "pro-choice" has largely been jettisoned but the reign of choice endures in institutions like Houston's Planned Parenthood Center for Choice.[32] Meanwhile, the Democratic National Committee is busy raising money for senatorial campaigns in 2024 through a site called Defendchoice.org, and the organization Marie Stopes International dedicated to providing contraception and safe abortions around the globe changed its name just a few years ago to MSI Reproductive Choices. And if anyone wonders if this rhetoric has been picked up by ordinary people, male and female alike, I'd suggest they need look no farther than the handmade signs that I spotted at local protests in Philadelphia directed at the overturning of *Roe v. Wade* in the context of the *Dobbs* decision in summer 2022 and in newspaper photos of protests elsewhere: "Forced Birth Is Enslavement"; "Our Future, Our Choice, Our Fight"; "It's Pro-Choice or No Choice"; "Choice Is Patriotic"; "Don't Trust Me with a Choice but with a Child?"; "My Body, My Choice, My Freedom, My Voice"; and "By Choice (with downward arrow) Pregnant." Or, as the original Jane Roe (Norma McCorvey) put it more colloquially in 2020 in a striking deathbed confession about her shift from anonymous plaintiff to paid anti-abortion crusader: "If a young woman wants to have an abortion, fine. That's no skin off my ass. You know, that's why they call it 'choice.' It's your *choice*."[33] Fifty years after *Roe*, this is still the dominant way Americans think about freedom.

Right Critique—and Left

That said, we still have to conclude that the attachment of women's autonomy to a "right to choose" has, from another vantage point, been surprisingly unsuccessful both politically and as a framing device. Not only has this commitment failed to permanently secure American women legal access to abortion. It has also prompted withering (and at times surprisingly similar, considering the polarization around this issue) critiques on both the right and left of the U.S. political spectrum.

Fig. E.3. Barbara Kruger, *Untitled (Your body is a battleground)*, photographic silkscreen on vinyl, made initially in Kruger's signature graphic style for the 1989 Women's March on Washington and repeatedly deployed in defense of abortion rights since that moment.

And through it all, the concept of choice itself has been at the center of the attacks as much as the defense, with women bearing the brunt of the criticism (fig. E.3).

All over the world for the last fifty or sixty years, the most prevalent challenges to the legalization of abortion have been those of cultural and religious conservatives. So have the most potent in political terms. That has been especially true in the United States. For one of the unanticipated effects of the *Roe v. Wade* decision was to give new energy to a right-wing countermovement that put *Roe*'s feminist champions on the defensive almost from the start. The main strategy of the American anti-abortion movement, which first got going within the Catholic Church, also has roots in the 1960s. But it remained marginal to the debate leading up to *Roe*, and it, too, only really became linked to national politics after the Supreme Court's ruling in 1973. That's also when its social base started to expand to encompass evangelical Protestants and cultural conservatives as well.

The counterargument began from a simple but powerful idea: that some things are too valuable or, frankly, sacred to be subject to personal choice. Critical to this category is the idea of life itself. By this way of seeing things, the "right to life" (on the part of a potential or "unborn" child) necessarily trumps any "right to choose" (on the part of a potential mother). Individual choice—the core of a woman's independence—may matter a lot in some contexts, but it is not always the most important value at hand. That's especially the case when she has a potential other life, seen by many as an expression of God's will, within her.[34] For some, the correct analogy here is to chattel slavery. But rather than compare women's lack of choice with the situation of those enslaved—an old feminist strategy, as we've seen—the counterargument associates women seeking abortions with slave owners and compares the fight against abortion to abolitionism, or the fight against slavery, on moral grounds.

Now, I can imagine many readers jumping up to object right about now and declaring that this line of argument has always been disingenuous, that all of this right-to-life discourse is simply a way to disguise the policing of women's sexuality and to elevate the autonomy of others, from husbands to fetuses, over that of women themselves. This is potentially persuasive, as fear of women's growing sexual independence seems fundamental to antichoice arguments about abortion much as it once did to arguments about women, luxury, and shopping or reading. Women's choices have always been judged and found wanting, especially when it comes to anything connected to sex. So is the idea that this whole line of argument is only instrumental, a way for politicians, religious leaders, and allied interest groups to build and feed larger grievances and resentments and to win over adherents in a bid for political spoils.

However, intentions aside, it is important to recognize the significance of this conservative critique in reframing the larger question of choice in public life. What the turn to the phrase "right to life" did for many citizens was offer a way, rhetorically, to bracket off abortion, much like rape (for its harmful effect on another) or even suicide (for its harmful effect on oneself), as outside the boundaries of personal discretion on moral and religious grounds. Or maybe it is more accurate to say that this new formulation presented a chance to reimpose a version of Hercules's Choice—to take the right or the wrong path in a strict binary—around both the decision about whether or not to engage in nonprocreational sex *and* the decision about how to deal with the consequences. Here, for its proponents, was the opportunity to suggest, once again, that the law could be used to reinforce clear moral distinctions, and even more, that freedom could be reconfigured as the chance to do what one ought rather than simply what one desired.[35] That included preserving the integrity of the traditional heterosexual family, conceived of as undermined when too much choice is available to anyone but the paternal head. As such, the right-to-life position became the place of a concerted attack on the (still-gendered) modern choice paradigm, an attack that has had large repercussions for thinking about the meaning, extent, and validity of choice and its vaunted moral neutrality for adult women certainly, but ultimately for everyone.

For in order to bolster their message, a growing swath of anti-abortion activist groups like the National Right to Life Committee (founded in 1968) and Americans United for Life (founded in 1971) went all the way back to some foundational critiques of women as choosers. Take, for example, the insistence that pro-choice women sought "abortion on demand," heard even before *Roe*.[36] The implication, even if not usually spelled out, was that such women saw no difference between weighing reproductive options and consumer ones; everything was equally about selfish wants and their own convenience, which is to say, indistinguishable from shopping. Other critiques were more direct, as when right-wing critics characterized women themselves as dangerously prone to making bad choices about reproduction for lack of knowing their own minds in any steady way. The choice of abortion, it was also argued in the 1970s but drawing on a very old register, could potentially be the result of nothing more than the "whim or caprice of the putative mother," not to mention irresponsibility or manipulability.[37] Certainly, there were class and racial assumptions built into such claims too (though they have often been deliberately obfuscated by allusions to abolitionism as of late).[38] The lasting implication of much antichoice discourse is that, when it comes to women, and especially poor and ill-informed ones, long-standing moral categories like virtue, on the one hand, and individual choice, on the other, run in opposite directions. Consider the alternative bumper sticker (for these are the years of their triumph on America's highways and back roads): "It's not a choice; it's a life."

This is a message that has, over the past fifty or so years, been found in variations all over the world, frequently pitting religious groups and leaders, whether as outliers or aligned with ruling parties, against liberal reformers. The same logic has prevailed whether the topic is abortion, birth control, veiling and other female sartorial requirements, or really any domain in which restricting women's choices connected to sexuality could work to encourage a world less thoroughly permeated by pluralist democratic and capitalist norms and more invested in local "traditions." Stabilizing existing ways of doing things, even if not that long-standing, and rendering them impervious to too much choice has become ground zero in that effort. For those with authoritarian tendencies, like Russia's Vladimir Putin, promises of a return to a pre-feminist past, where families were sacrosanct, gender roles were clear and distinct, and women were not considered fully autonomous beings, have become a large part of the appeal.

Nevertheless, it's important to recognize a second strand in the anti-abortion rhetoric on the right that also has historical roots but which took off in the United States specifically in the 1980s. That was an effort to salvage individual choice and its modern association with human rights, but to turn this association against abortion and, more generally, against women's demands as a whole. As such, anti-abortion groups also made a point of posing tough questions about how conflicting personal choices might be reconciled when it came to unwanted pregnancy. What, they asked, about the preferences—and, indeed, "rights" in the newer sense of a guarantee of freedom of choice—of boyfriends and husbands? Of the parents of pregnant women and girls? Of "unborn" children? Why should a woman's preferences necessarily triumph over those of others invested in a specific birth and, indeed, the family as a whole?[39]

Some anti-abortion forces further insisted that other kinds of freedom of choice mattered, and mattered more, than those seized upon by feminist activists, including the same notion of religious choice that had sometimes been touted by religiously affiliated abortion-rights groups in the 1970s. Starting with the so-called Hyde Amendment of 1976, anti-abortion activists and political representatives turned the old liberal, Protestant idea of freedom of conscience, or religious choice, *against* choice in the reproductive realm in a battle of what would otherwise seem to be allied rights or freedoms.[40] The argument was again quite basic: Not only is Congress not obligated to provide abortions to those so desiring. Congress has no business forcing, via taxation, those who are opposed to abortion for reasons of "conscience" (i.e., religious Christians) to pay for others to choose abortion. The argument also worked all too well. Upon the Hyde Amendment passing, it was declared illegal in the United States for federal funding to be used *for* abortions—even though that decision, de facto, made abortion akin to a luxury good that was available as a real option only to those with the (often substantial) funds to pay for it themselves. Arguably, the Hyde Amendment even turned increased choice for some, as in those participating in a growing adoption marketplace, into coercion for others.[41]

Feminists in the late 1970s were apoplectic—and with good reason. But some of them also saw the writing on the wall. A few argued, presciently, that "choice" was ultimately the wrong term for the situation and that hitching the reproductive rights wagon to this concept was seriously misguided. For one, it could be used to devalue deformed fetuses or even ordinary female ones, making everything a (mere) choice. Eugenics, or the controlling and limiting of undesirables, whether by families or the state, has always haunted discussions of abortion and reproductive options just as racism has, often in combination.[42] Advances in genetic engineering will likely continue to open up new frontiers in this debate. But even more broadly, socialists, health-care advocates, and especially more radical feminists, many of them feminists of color, insisted as early as the mid-1970s that the modern concept of choice offered a constricted and overly legalistic notion of liberation.

Yes, women in organizations like the National Women's Health Network (founded 1975) emphasized: it is important, even essential, to stress *all* women's right to make their own decisions about their own bodies, including about whether to bear children. As Mary Treadwell Barry, executive director of Pride Inc., put it already in the early 1970s, "As a black woman, I support the abortion campaign for reasons inherent in being a member of the black minority in racist America.... Every woman should have the right to control her body and its usage, as she so chooses. Every woman should have the right to conceive, when she so chooses. Every woman should have the right to sexual fulfillment without fear of conception, if she so chooses. Women must secure these rights by liberating the minds of those legislators opposed to the personal freedoms of any of America's second-class citizens—women."[43] One can't help but be reminded here of claims about women's bodily autonomy going all the way back to abolitionist movements of the mid-nineteenth century and both Black and white women's suffrage movements after that.

However, Black feminists, in particular, sensed early on that talk of choice in this context was insufficient, a bare minimum only and a potentially pernicious one at that. The mainstream feminist position set the stage for thinking of abortion as solely a civil right, a right to fulfill individual desires without government interference, not a social or economic right framed in response to essential needs or a matter of social justice. Moreover, the mainstream position denied the way most women's lives were embedded in families and communities and existing systems of custom and belief that typically constrained their choices considerably further in practice. What that meant, more radical feminists and feminists of color pointed out, was that in its dominant packaging, the fight for access to abortion likely both appealed to and pertained disproportionately to those who already had a wide range of choices in other regards, namely, middle- and upper-class, educated white women. Thus, like their conservative opponents, some left-wing feminists chafed early on at the seemingly bourgeois, consumerist framing that was partly the legacy of *Roe* and the organizations fighting for it: abortion as something for sale exclusively to those who had the resources—financial, familial, *and* psychological—to select it in a reproductive marketplace. Or, as the writer and activist Rickie Solinger noted, a framing in which motherhood was less a right than "a consumer's privilege."[44]

By contrast, nonmainstream feminists argued from the 1970s onward, *real* choice would require access to decent wages, to childcare, to health care, to education, to environmental protections, to freedom from sexual and racial discrimination, harassment, or violence, and to freedom from pressure toward sterilization (a particular worry of women of color). It would, in other words, necessitate a slew of additional public policies that, first, diminished existing constraints on meaningful choice before any child was conceived and, then, expanded the possibilities for women, including poor ones, afterward once any child was born. As Dorothy Roberts memorably argued two decades later, invoking the history of the regulation of Black women's reproductive bodies going back to the slave auction: "Reproductive liberty . . . must acknowledge that we make reproductive decisions within a social context, including inequalities of wealth and power," and thus it must address them in concert.[45] Otherwise, the pro-choice movement was in danger of not just leaving some people out or keeping them from being able to exercise the options that they wanted through various forms of soft coercion. It was actually helping legitimate racial and economic inequality and injustice. By offering up the charade of "free" choice and then opening up poor women to blame and other backdoor moral judgments when they couldn't make good ones, whether that meant having too many abortions or too many offspring, the mainstream pro-choice movement was punishing those it claimed to be aiding. What's more, it was legitimating lack of public support for essential caregiving, throwing back into private life the kind of matters that should concern us all collectively.[46]

For the next generation on the left in the early twenty-first century, this has been reason enough to throw in the towel on the whole framing

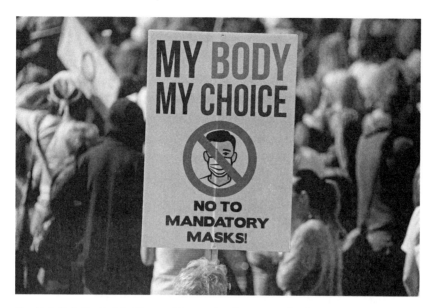

Fig. E.4. "My Body My Choice. No to Mandatory Masks!," a September 2020 photograph of a protestor in Trafalgar Square, London, holding up a made-to-go-viral sign, in a "Resist and Act for Freedom" protest against mandatory coronavirus vaccines, mask wearing, and a second lockdown at the time of the Covid-19 pandemic.

(despite all those mailers from NARAL Pro-Choice America and DefendChoice.org).[47] Some argue that choice, like personal freedom, is a "euphemism," and a dated one at that.[48] Others say that it is, for the disadvantaged, a "taunt" or even a "threat."[49] (One is reminded of the old political critique, forcefully made in the Harlem Renaissance socialist magazine *The Messenger* in the 1920s, that electoral choice is meaningless if you don't make the options and all the ones you are given are rotten.)[50] It is also easy to find evidence that both the word and the concept have been captured or co-opted or even weaponized, like much human rights talk today, including to right-wing effect. Who wasn't horrified to see antivaccine and antimasking protestors during the outbreak of Covid-19 rallying behind the phrase "My Body, My Choice"? Here was the now classic expression of modern, global feminism turned into the battle cry of extreme libertarianism in the face of public health directives to the contrary (fig. E.4).[51] But even in the before-times, the

sentiment behind phrases like "my body, my choice"—with its suggestion of radical bodily autonomy combined with antistatism—had
already spilled over into other domains, from work-life balance (Linda
Hirshman's example) to New Age wellness cures (my example).[52] As
such, the abortion rights movement's great slogan reinforced as much
as benefited from a climate in which the "right to choose" had long
ago, for those vested with the power to act on it, become the coin of
the realm.

And Now . . .

Are these naysayers right? Is choice now, a quarter of the way into the
twenty-first century, a useless or exhausted idiom, lacking all critical
edge? Today, that's almost another way of asking if we are done with
capitalism and democracy and their special offspring, human rights. But
this *is* the question increasingly being posed, for different reasons and
with different alternatives in mind, on the right and on the left in many
parts of the world. Responding to the globalization of the concept and
its extension now to artificial reproduction technologies as well, the
Indian women's health advocacy network Sama is not alone in insisting
that "an urgent need has been felt to demystify the concept of choice,"
starting with "distinguish[ing] between latent choice and social choice
shaped by family, market, and other agents."[53] What can the historian
add to this discussion, aside from telling us the story of how we got here
and, maybe, how difficult it remains to pull these strands apart? That is,
of course, a question with which this book began.

Some would reply that the proper response is "nothing," that the historian's job is, at this point, done. According to this view, the work of
the historian is primarily descriptive: telling us what happened and how.
Others, though, would likely insist there remains more to accomplish.
Conventionally, historians can, once all the "background" is out of the
way, take one of several possible routes in assessing the legacy of the past
from the vantage point of now. All involve tiptoeing toward the normative, or general lessons learned, that is the lifeblood of most other
disciplines.

A historian can, for example, decide to mount a high-minded defense of preserving the particular tradition of thought and behavior that has just been laid out for inspection. In this instance, that's not altogether unappealing as a prospect. Since liberal democracy seems to be under severe strain and governments are turning increasingly authoritarian in many parts of the world as I write, we may well wish to keep choice around, warts and all. Indeed, in light of attacks specifically on rights now associated with choice—from populist movements that place little stock in popular elections (the *ur*-choice mode of democratic politics) to new forms of antifeminist policies that deny choice in family planning—the appeal of this old idea and associated practices will likely grow again in opposition. Those who have been denied choice, whether because they live in repressive states or in the limbo of statelessness, frequently remind us that we should not, in any case, be too cavalier about abandoning it as either practice or goal. The Russian American critic Masha Gessen, for example, in defense of what they call "the choicefulness of life," points out in a 2018 personal essay aimed at those frustrated by Western fealty to the choice ideal that it is still hardly a universal prerogative. Whereas totalitarian governments explicitly eliminated it, autocratic ones, like that of contemporary Russia, now profit by conjuring an imaginary past in which choice was simply unnecessary; the new promise is "to relieve one of the need to choose" once again. As a result, engaging in individuated, preference-based choice-making, even among unacceptable options, should, according to Gessen, be considered a form of resistance.[54]

Moreover, for those truly without any freedom to decide much for themselves, choice remains aspirational like nothing else: it is *the* way to realize one's humanity. In German writer Jenny Erpenbeck's extraordinary novel translated as *Go, Went, Gone* (2015), a retired former East German professor, after living through both World War II and the end of communism, finds himself comfortable but "trapped in his cage of free agency, imprisoned by the luxury of free choice." That condition extends all the way to questions of reproduction. Even the old food metaphor for abundance and taste has gone sour, as "for him, refusing to eat would be just as capricious as gluttony." But the discovery of a group of African refugees living temporarily in Berlin shifts his perspective. It reveals to him a previously unseen world of people whose real pain comes not from lack of the necessities for survival but rather from being trapped in a bureaucratic system in which, practically and ultimately psychologically, as various refugees repeatedly tell him, "you don't have a choice anymore."[55] The novel is a powerful statement about the loss of personhood that accompanies the loss of the protections of human rights, understood as the right to make choices about one's own future, especially for the earth's least powerful people. Maybe there is a good reason why "freedom to make life choices" is one of six factors used today by the World Happiness Report to measure national well-being on a global scale.[56]

Another possibility for historians of this subject, though, is to join critics of so-called choice feminism in calling for a real break with the past. That means trying to persuade others that the particular tradition linking freedom to choice has run its course, practically and conceptually, and that it is time to move on to new goals, as some feminists, including explicitly anticapitalist and anti-imperialist ones, have proposed. Today, choice, despite its global proliferation, is—from this alternative perspective—usually an illusion and a dangerous one at that. Why? Either because there are, regardless of rhetoric to the contrary, no meaningful or even truly different options available to most people in the world, making this aspiration a farce *or* because the process is so ridden with unrecognized constraints, internal and external, formal and informal, on when and where and how that it no longer holds out the promise of resistance, much less liberation.[57] Think of the person, for example, who is told that the choice of abortion is possible, but there are no doctors or clinics available, no money or transportation to get to where such things do exist, no chance of a break from work or childcare for the purpose, and no support from others around them for their decision. Or think of the person who has access and funds but is ultimately thwarted by all the attendant rules and restrictions drawn up by choice architects imperceptibly shaping their actions and even their wishes. These are hardly meaningful examples of freedom.

We must acknowledge, too, that this situation is likely only to increase with the advancement of algorithmic choice, where menus of options are both ubiquitous and invisibly curated just for us. After all, "personalization" requires not just ceding power to others to establish the options and the rules of engagement; it demands ongoing surveillance and the building up of a record of previous choice-making (both our own and that of others deemed like ourselves) about which survey makers and marketers a hundred years ago could only have dreamed.[58] Mr. Cock, the choice agent responsible for those remarkable early eighteenth-century English auctions, is now a computer program watching your every keystroke and then rearranging the offerings to get you to do what it wants in response. In years to come, artificial intelligence will likely just up the ante.

Then there are the psychic and political burdens. The contemporary obligation of continuous personal choice-making in daily life—whether about sneakers or health care—has turned into a source of exhaustion, distress, even loneliness and alienation.[59] It has also, everywhere, become a wellspring for failed policies that bolster existing inequalities and fracture any cultural common ground.[60] And especially in the United States, where a peculiar blend of authoritarianism and libertarianism has come to characterize extreme right-wing positions on topics such as taxes, guns, and public health, choice is now a strategic asset. It has helped engender a distinctive kind of conservatism characterized by indifference toward our collective well-being and the many aspects of our lives that we share with others. Simone Weil famously warned in the middle of the last century, even as she celebrated the fact of having options, that "when the possibilities of choice are so wide as to injure the commonweal, men cease to enjoy liberty."[61] Arguably, that is where we have arrived today. The historian might well conclude that choice, after a long run, has now irremediably lost its way.

Or, one could split the difference, as a third potential strategy for the historian would involve recuperation. Might we be able to resuscitate elements of a path not taken or once taken but now obscured by time? In this instance, that would mean avoiding throwing the baby out with the bathwater. On the contrary, we might think about trying to restore to choice, right now, some of the possibility for critique and even disruption that previously inhered in both the idea and the practice, not least for women in the formative years of their struggle for emancipation.

Of course, the risk of choice being taken as a synonym for whim, or selfishness, or being unconcerned with any larger good was present, as we've seen, from the start. That was especially the case when it was associated with perceived female pursuits, from shopping to reading fiction to finding love. It was also always limited in its social reach, sometimes working to exacerbate class differences as much as erase them. But in its earliest forms, the demand for choice also stood for an opening up of possibilities beyond the status quo, including the possibility of self-governance and, later, self-definition for women as well as men of all races, creeds, and backgrounds, that ended up at the heart of liberal feminism along with abolitionism. It also stood for doing so potentially in concert with others—hence all the elaborate rules—and, if not with the moral absolutism of the Hercules metaphor, then with concern for the impact on others psychologically as well as materially. Think back on Henry James's Isabel Archer and her desire to know the options even if they were not all equally actionable from the perspective of an upper-class nineteenth-century lady worried about her reputation in the public realm. After all, it was only very late in the day—say, the last sixty years—that anyone came to imagine *fully* individualized, frictionless, and judgment-free choice, as introduced by voting by secret ballot or, later, neoclassical economic models, as the ultimate form of freedom and, indeed, what humans live to make and do. In Sylvia Plath's *The Bell Jar*, the heroine is only defeated once numerous "lifestyle" options seem to be staring her in the face without any hierarchy among them or anyone telling her which is best, a thoroughly modern predicament. Maybe—a historian could argue—the excitement and sense of forward-lookingness inherent in an earlier liberal conception of choice could, without either its Victorian cultural baggage or the late twentieth-century neoliberal assumption that more is always better, be revived and repurposed for today, even as circumstances have changed. Then it might be made meaningful once again for men and women alike.

But another, far less common game plan for historians would be to see the present as a moment begging for intellectual creativity in which, in effect, we select none of the above. The historian with the license to dream but without an obligation to paths already identifiable in the historical record might instead pose new questions for new times, using the past, in all its specificity, as simply a mental springboard. What would it look like to preserve existing choice practices, from shopping to supply our homes to voting for public officers, but to remake them in a more equitable form, so that choice was more real for more people than at any time before? What would it look like to allow more imaginative alternatives, including ones invented by oneself, rather than sticking with the idea that we must take the banquet of possibilities as it comes, whether crafted by the state, business interests, or other powerful choice agents? UBI, or universal basic income, for example, starts from the radical idea that people are "experts on their own lives," but also that having the agency to design the menu of options affects their well-being as a whole.[62] A new conception of autonomy might be the result.

This isn't just a question of the redistribution of money either. The arts, too, involve the potential for innovation beyond existing selections—think of Emily Dickinson's great nineteenth-century poem "I Dwell in Possibility." Or consider the twentieth-century American sociologist C. Wright Mills's argument that "Freedom is, first of all, the chance to formulate the available choices, to argue over them—and then, the opportunity to choose."[63] That's an argument about the organization of intellectual life that similarly calls for crafting the alternatives oneself quite apart from existing choice purveyors. But conversely, maybe we could also begin to think about certain kinds of group choice in ways that don't entail simple aggregation of individual selections until a winner can take all but instead require all those affected by certain decisions to manufacture solutions through compromise. That might go some way toward addressing climate change, immigration issues, and other large-scale problems for which the existing liberal order seems powerless and which are driving both intense polarization and the nihilistic political climate of today. What, finally, if indecision were more acknowledged as a strength, a liminal position that has the upside of requiring one to consult others, to ponder again, and to accept the difficulties of being human and acting in the world?

Then there is the whole question of our time on the job. As the now traditional bifurcation of work, on the one hand, and leisure, on the other, starts to evaporate under the technologically enhanced pressures of "remote" employment and a "gig" economy, might we start to think about both spheres and their relationship to choice differently? Perhaps the distinct kind of freedom and unfreedom associated with each of these kinds of time is the product of a distinct historical era—and one that is no longer entirely relevant to our postindustrial age, when the two sides of this coin have, for many people, colonized each other. Without its traditional foil, one might start to wonder if the supposed open-endedness of choice-making outside working hours will or indeed should remain so coveted as a goal. That might especially be a question for women, nowadays often balancing family and employment with diminishing guardrails or even coworkers with whom to conspire. Conversely, one might also wonder if the assumed redemptive power of work and the workplace, the distinctive activity and space in the modern world long governed by hierarchy and command rather than free-range choice, isn't due for an overhaul too. (The term "free labor," after all, always only referred to the moment when the contract got signed or broken, not what happened in between, as critics of "wage slavery" have long pointed out.) Could we imagine a more cooperative model that guarantees both more autonomy *and* more ways of protecting each other from the vicissitudes of life across the waning work/life divide?

These are philosophical rather than political questions, more utopian than anything else. But they are also moral ones—which is where choice becomes so complicated. In certain ways, we obviously require a way of existing ethically in the world in which choice is not always the highest goal and sometimes other values matter more, including our shared well-being and concern for others (which is precisely why "my body, my choice" is so misplaced as a mantra against masking during a pandemic). In other ways, though, choice itself needs, within the framework of pluralism, to be more explicitly linked to basic moral considerations rather than set in opposition to them or evoked as a means of evading them. To say abortion should be a choice is, in a sense, to kick the can down the road, not to make the question any easier. What feminists like Dorothy Roberts have made clear is that arguing for choice as such, whether we are talking about opportunities or options, is generally hollow. There will always be ethical stakes to our decisions even as their contours evolve over time. There will always be good outcomes and bad ones too. Choice, whether about babies or baubles or beliefs, *should* be a means, not an end unto itself.

History

Maybe this project starts with our descriptive modes. Historians are, after all, already in the choice analysis business. As the leading contemporary guide to historical practice puts it bluntly, "History Is the Study of People and the Choices They Make."[64] And these days we, meaning both amateurs and professionals, have a default position for doing so. Whether we are concentrating on medieval peasants, early modern mercenaries, nineteenth-century bourgeois housewives, or our own grandparents, we historians generally imagine those people as rational agents, engaged at every turn in making deliberate, instrumental, and largely comprehensible determinations, given the range of options available to them. That is, we turn the people we think and talk and write about, regardless of time and place and social particulars, into liberal subjects: aware of what they wanted and needed and acting of their own accord to effectively realize those preferences or ambitions through a process of what economists might call constrained optimization.[65]

Working backward from consequences to causes, historians of all kinds tend, therefore, to see their own job as finding pragmatic and consistent rationales for various kinds of documented choice-based behavior in the past. Even human sacrifice gets this treatment nowadays, as in Camilla Townsend's remarkable 2019 study, *Fifth Sun: A New History of the Aztecs*. We do so in a worthy effort to make sure no group of social actors is accorded a greater degree of rationality and thus dignity than any other, even or especially when it is clear those actor(s) were

operating in severely constrained circumstances or suffering from subjugation. There is, after all, good reason not to reduce anyone to their
condition alone (such as "slave" or "prisoner") or to deny anyone autonomy as a full-fledged choice-maker when we value this status so
much today in economic, political, and psychological terms.

This is not to say, though, that historians typically resort to as thin a
model of the human as that which we associate with *homo economicus*,
all personal volition and independence from others. On the contrary, like
most observers of social life, including anthropologists and sociologists,
historians largely see their task as discerning the circumstances—
structural, cultural, and contingent—that shape or shaped how much
choice any individual or group had, what those choices were, and why
a given option got picked. This is especially the case when we cannot
know motives firsthand. Listen to how some prominent contemporary
historians explain it. Arlette Farge proposes that the historical actor constructs her "own agency out of what history and society put at her disposal," thereby revealing how people can "belong to society but not be
subjugated by it."[66] Marcia Chatelain goes further: "History encourages
us to be more compassionate toward individuals navigating few choices,
and history cautions us to be far more critical of the institutions and
structures that have the power to take choices away."[67]

Still, it is the context within which choice-making happens that is
almost always considered the historical variable today. It is not the re-
course to or nature of the choice-making itself, nor the particular weight
attached to this activity, nor the picture of human nature underwriting
any of it. For all our investment in historicization, or treating the past as
distinct from the present, we rarely historicize, never mind psycholo-
gize, any of these latter developments—or their implicit ethics.

The consequences are considerable. By translating all people into
modern-style choosers, we fail to treat either the existence of or the
standing that is widely accorded today to what philosopher Elizabeth
Anderson calls "subjective utilities," or preferences that people hold
apart from any feeling of obligation to hold them, as products of a host
of contingent and temporally specific factors.[68] We also fail to illuminate
how people could have existed (and might still) quite apart from this

modern *doxa*. (Here is where we should not forget Burney's *Evelina*, struggling with how to perform even a basic choice, or Austen's Fanny Price, still a bit stunned to see herself as a "chuser" in any realm.) We miss, too, the irrational, the perverse, and the huge range of often clashing values and aims at play in our ordinary processes of selection, which behavioral economists have long made clear, but which take on different meanings and values in different circumstances as well.[69] And we frequently neglect to account for the consistent appeal of limited autonomy, or simply going with the flow, whether we are talking about early modern Aztecs or mid-twentieth-century Americans, men or women. Perhaps we should start thinking about renarrating some of our stories of the past with some of those elements back in place.

One last detour into the realm of fiction is suggestive. In a famous Japanese science fiction story of the 1960s called "Take Your Choice" written by the pseudonymous Sakyo Komatsu, a steady stream of people seek out what appears to be an underground shop in the hopes of choosing their own future for themselves. But when shown a glimpse of each of the options, they don't pick the most desirable; rather, they routinely pick the only one with a sure end, even though they know it will mean a catastrophic occurrence like a nuclear holocaust. They do so in an effort to avoid the greater agony of uncertainty. Ultimately those who wander into this unusual emporium want choice when it comes to their own destinies, but not for any reason having to do with freedom.[70] Yet looking back on life in a very different if almost contemporaneous setting—suburban Connecticut in the 1970s—all the ordinary choices made along life's way seem both to have mattered and not. Here is the American writer James Salter, in the novel *Light Years*, capturing the thinking of his bourgeois architect protagonist toward the end of his existence: "There is no complete life. There are only fragments. . . . For whatever we do, even whatever we do not do prevents us from doing the opposite. Acts demolish their alternatives, that is the paradox. So that life is a matter of choices, each one final and of little consequence, like dropping stones into the sea. We had children, he thought; we can never be childless. We were modest; we will never know what it is to spill out our lives."[71] Only in fantasy fiction and video games does the character (and, consequently, the reader/player) ever get to experience a do-over, the chance to choose again, with or without hindsight, in pursuit of a new and different outcome. It is not only a matter of external obstacles. Reality is messier in part because we humans are so complex.

Capital-H History now aims to show the particularity and contingency of choices people made in the past. Ideally, it can also demonstrate the particularity and contingency of our own fixation on independent choice-making, starting with both its gendered contours and its effects on real women as well as men. Encouraging that possibility has been one basic goal of this book. My hope is that taking a more historical view of choice in action—especially when it comes to the people long most thwarted and enabled and thwarted again by its possibilities—might help change the way we write causation and motivation into our stories of the past more broadly.

More significantly, though, history written with choice as itself a key construct, but a variably practiced and variably understood one, might open up a different possibility: that our attachment to choice in its current form is ripe for rethinking *outside* of historical precedent, setting the stage for new kinds of politics and subjectivities. That is something behavioral economists and libertarian paternalists, for all their concern with tweaking the choice architecture all around us to our individual and collective benefit, rarely contemplate. It is also my larger ambition. As a historian of the taken-for-granted, I remain convinced that exposing the constructed nature of that which seems most natural to us in the present is at least a first step in the battle against complacency or the failure to even ask.

I thus leave you, as a reader, with no survey, no standardized quiz, no kind of menu at all, only the invitation to make choice a problem to be wrestled with before it is a default solution. Rather than continually asking how we might choose more or better, let's start wondering, without prejudgment, if choice as we know it is really what freedom should be all about.

ILLUSTRATION CREDITS

COLOR PLATE CREDITS

Plate 1. © Ashmolean Museum, University of Oxford.

Plate 2. Gift of the Print and Drawing Club, Art Institute of Chicago.

Plate 3. Gift of Mrs. Horace Havemeyer in memory of her mother-in-law, Louisine W. Havemeyer, National Gallery of Art, Washington, D.C.

Plate 4. *The Humours of an Election II: Canvassing for Votes* © Sir John Soane's Museum, London.

Plate 5. The Phillips Collection, Washington, D.C. © 2024 The Jacob and Gwendolyn Knight Lawrence Foundation, Seattle/Artists Rights Society (ARS), New York.

Plate 6. John Wilmerding Collection, Courtesy National Gallery of Art, Washington, D.C.

Plate 7. Nationaal Archief/Collectie Spaarnestad/Jan van Eyk.

Plate 8. The Broad Art Foundation/Sprüth Magers.

ACKNOWLEDGMENTS

I have an abundance of friends, colleagues, and institutions to thank.

Sponsorship or support for parts of this project came from three universities—the University of Virginia, Yale University, and the University of Pennsylvania—as well as the Institute for Advanced Study in Princeton, the American Philosophical Society in Philadelphia, the Center for Ballet and the Arts at New York University, the Kluge Center at the Library of Congress, and the John Simon Guggenheim Memorial Foundation. Thank you to all.

Many superb graduate students helped over the years in ways big and small, and I am especially grateful to Arielle Alterwaite, Javier Ardilla, Paige Pendarvis, Francis Russo, and Sasha Zborovsky.

I am very much indebted to the Wolf Humanities Center at Penn for providing me with the opportunity to devote a year's worth of discussion and programming to the theme of choice; sustained conversations, even mid-Covid-19, with Karen Redrobe, Nancy Hirschmann, Shira Brisman, and Lisa Mitchell, among many others, were invaluable. In my own department and across Penn, I am also grateful to Ben Nathans, Sigal Ben-Porath, Michael Hanchard, Zita Nunes, Melissa Teixeira, Fred Dickinson, Eric Orts, John Pollack, Allison Hoffman, Andrea Goulet, and Peter Agree for vital tips, as well as, in many cases, their encouragement and friendship as they pursued related projects.

Elsewhere I have benefited enormously from fruitful exchanges (probably many of them no longer recalled except by me) with François Furstenberg, Peter Mandler, Rita Felski, Karl Ameriks, Benjamin Friedman, Henry Cowles, Neeti Nair, Naomi Lamoreaux, Deborah Coen,

Ajay Skaria, Daniel Mandell, Cori Field, Maylis Avaro, Chad Wellmon, Daniel Heller-Roazen, Lynn Hunt, Deborah Dinner, Gideon Rosen, Barry Schwartz, Joan Scott, Natalie Caron, Gabriel Abend, Michael Meranze, Duncan Kelly, Michael Kwass, Danielle Allen, Jonathan Sheehan, and Michael Walzer. The same goes for organizers and audience members at talks and seminars that I've given on aspects of the project at, in no particular order, the University of Warwick, the University of Sydney, Northwestern University, Oxford University, Johns Hopkins University, the Center for Ballet and the Arts at NYU, the Catholic University of Australia, the Intellectual History Seminar at the Research Triangle in North Carolina, the Institute for Historical Studies at the University of Texas-Austin, the Institute for Historical Research in London, the Amsterdam Global Intellectual History Seminar, Concordia University-Montreal, CRASSH at Cambridge University, the Columbia/ NYU Consortium on Intellectual History, the Heyman Center at Columbia, Swarthmore College, the New York Area Seminar on Cultural and Intellectual History at the CUNY Grad Center, the University of Michigan Law School, the Center for the Study of Representative Institutions at Yale University, the Eighteenth Century Seminar at Princeton University, the National History Center in Washington, the School of Social Science at the Institute for Advanced Study, and an America2026 meeting at the Tocqueville Château, in addition to plenary sessions at the annual meetings of the Society for French Historical Studies and the Nineteenth-Century French Studies Association, the Faber Lecture in the Program in European Cultural Studies at Princeton University, and the Stourzh Lecture on the History of Human Rights and Democracy at the University of Vienna.

Furthermore, I am extremely lucky to have a number of friends and colleagues who are marvelous critical readers as well as terrific writers themselves. My biggest thanks go without a doubt to Darrin McMahon, Carolyn Dean, David Bell, Francesca Trivellato, Natalie Dohrmann, and Don Herzog for their generosity in reading and commenting on the entire manuscript. Equally, I am grateful to have had the steadfast support in writing this book of Rob Tempio at Princeton University Press as well as the highly able assistance of Chloe Coy and the rest of the

Princeton team. Winky Lewis added her wonderful photographs to the mix, including one with a fortune reading "Vote," at just the right minute. The cherished "Book Club" in Philadelphia will see its impact here too.

Then there is family. Lucinda Rosenfeld, Jerry Seigel, and especially Zoë Affron and Isaiah Affron get my heartfelt thanks in this category for reasons I hope they each know. There is every reason that this book, like the others before it, is dedicated to Matthew Affron.

NOTES

Introduction

1. Susan Sontag, "Fascinating Fascism" [1975], *Under the Sign of Saturn* (Picador, 2002), 104–5, notes that in an "affluent society" there is a "tendency to turn every part of people's lives into a taste, a choice; to invite them to regard their very lives as a (life) style." Similarly, Anthony Giddens, *Modernity and Self-Identity: Self and Society in the Late Modern Age* (Stanford University Press, 1991), 81, proposes that today "we have no choice but to choose" what he, too, calls a "lifestyle," meaning "an integrated set of practices which an individual [deliberately] embraces . . . because they give material form to a particular narrative of self-identity."

2. The key distinction between freedom as an "opportunity concept" involving having choices and freedom as an "exercise concept" involving getting to make choices is well explained in Ian Carter, "Choice, Freedom, and Freedom of Choice," *Social Choice and Welfare* 22, no. 1 (2004): 61–81.

3. Pierre Bourdieu, *Distinction: A Social Critique of the Judgment of Taste* (Routledge, 1984), 471. A *doxa* is variously categorized as a form of common sense, a normative idea, or a metaconcept; typically, it only becomes subject to scrutiny when a larger crisis undermines its self-evidence.

4. See Sophia Rosenfeld, "Human Rights and the Idea of Choice," 2018 Stourzh Lecture, http://culturahistorica.org/wp-content/uploads/2020/05/rosenfeld_human_rights.pdf. The text of the UDHR is available at http://www.un.org/en/universal-declaration-human-rights/.

5. See Paul Taylor, "Religion and Freedom of Choice," in *Religion and Human Rights: An Introduction*, ed. John Witte Jr. and M. Christian Green (Oxford University Press, 2012), 170–87, on the evolving language related to religious choice from article 18 of the UDHR (1948), which implies but does not use the term "choice," to article 18 of the International Covenant on Civil and Political Rights (1966), which does, to the Declaration on the Elimination of All Forms of Intolerance and of Discrimination Based on Religion or Belief (1981), where the new wording is "religion or whatever belief of his choice," implying the right to choose atheism or the practice of no religion as well. See chapter 2 of this book on this formulation's debt to a Protestant model according to which religion is a set of propositions or beliefs to which one gives assent.

6. See article 16, 1b and 1g, of the Convention on the Elimination of All Forms of Discrimination against Women (1979), which revises the language of article 16 of the UDHR: http://www.un.org/womenwatch/daw/cedaw/text/econvention.htm#.

7. The text of various constitutions can be found at https://www.constituteproject.org/. Almost all contemporary constitutions lay out a mixture of rights related to the freedom to choose alongside rights related to the provision of necessities.

8. Michael Ignatieff, *Human Rights as Politics and Idolatry* (Princeton University Press, 2001), 57.

9. Gerald Dworkin, "Is More Choice Better than Less?" in *Midwest Studies in Philosophy VII: Social and Political Philosophy*, ed. Peter A. French, Theodore E. Uehling Jr., and Howard K. Wettstein (University of Minnesota Press, 1982), 47–61, see 60. On how choice and autonomy reinforce one another, see Meir Dan-Cohen, "Conceptions of Choice and Conceptions of Autonomy," *Ethics* 102, no. 2 (January 1992): 221–43.

10. On democracy and procedural freedom, see John Rawls, *A Theory of Justice* (Oxford University Press, 1971).

11. On the concept of market freedom, see Eric MacGilvray, *The Invention of Market Freedom* (Cambridge University Press, 2011).

12. See Kent Greenfield, *The Myth of Choice: Personal Responsibility in a World of Limits* (Yale University Press, 2011) and Yascha Mounk, *The Age of Responsibility: Luck, Choice and the Welfare State* (Harvard University Press, 2017). The columnist Bret Stephens, for example, argues in "The Conversation [with Gail Collins]," *New York Times*, March 20, 2023: "If the government is expected to backstop everybody's bad or dumb decisions, the country would bankrupt itself in a week. Part of living in a free society is being responsible for your choices, including your mistakes."

13. Jonathan Safran Foer and Nathan Englander, eds., *New American Haggadah* (Little, Brown, 2014): "We are chosen, the Haggadah tells us. . . . As modern people, we are used to choosing; being chosen is much more difficult, at least for many of us. Some of us do not accept it at all." For the background here, see David Novak, "Mordecai Kaplan's Rejection of Election," *Modern Judaism* 15, no. 1 (1995): 1–19.

14. Henry James, *The Portrait of a Lady*, first serialized in *Atlantic Monthly* in 1880. In the scene in question, Isabel's aunt promises to tell her "whenever I see you taking what seems to me too much liberty." Isabel replies, "Pray do . . . I always want to know the things one shouldn't do." The crucial exchange then reads as follows: "'So as to do them?' asked her aunt. 'So as to choose,' said Isabel."

15. For more on these abortion debates of the 1970s, see the epilogue to this book.

16. For the range of contemporary opinion on what free will is and whether it exists, see Robert Kane, ed., *The Oxford Handbook of Free Will* (Oxford University Press, 2002) for a start.

17. See, for example, John Tooby and Leda Cosmides, "The Psychological Foundation of Culture," in *The Adapted Mind: Evolutionary Psychology and the Generation of Culture*, ed. L. Barkow, J. Tooby, and L. Cosmides (Oxford University Press, 1992), 19–136, but also the critique of such approaches in Richard Harper, Dave Randall, and Wes Sharrock, *Choice: The Sciences of Reason in the 21st Century: A Critical Appraisal* (Polity, 2016), chap. 5 ("Evolutionary Choice").

18. For different perspectives on female choice from an evolutionary perspective, see Randy Thornhill and Steven W. Gangestad, *The Evolutionary Biology of Human Female Sexuality* (Oxford University Press, 2008); Evelleen Richards, *Darwin and the Making of Sexual Selection* (University of Chicago Press, 2017); and Richard Prum, *The Evolution of Beauty: How Darwin's Forgotten Theory of Mate Choice Shapes the Animal World—and Us* (Doubleday, 2017), who argues controversially for the significance of subjective desires in evolution and that "freedom of choice matters to animals" too (13).

19. See chapter 4 for more on Cartwright.

20. For the argument that an earlier conception of freedom depended less on the idea of opportunities for choice, or noninterference, than it did on the idea of independence, or lack of dependence on anyone else as a representative of a preferred status category, see notably Quentin Skinner, *Liberty before Liberalism* (Cambridge University Press, 1998) and "Freedom as the Absence of Arbitrary Power," in *Republicanism and Political Theory*, ed. C. Laborde and

J. Manor (Oxford University Press, 2008); and Philip Pettit, *Republicanism: A Theory of Freedom and Government* (Oxford University Press, 1997), "Agency-Freedom and Option-Freedom," *Journal of Theoretical Politics* 15 (2003): 387–403, and "Free Persons and Free Choices," *History of Political Thought* 28, no. 4 (2007): 709–18. Skinner uses the term "neo-Roman" and Pettit the term "republican" to distinguish this kind of freedom from later, more liberal conceptions. Arguably, however, the distinction between these two different conceptions of freedom was not always so neat in theory or, especially, in practice, and elements of the nondomination model endure in a variety of civil rights struggles.

21. For an overview of the value system of the traditional European nobility, see Jonathan Dewald, *The European Nobility, 1400–1800* (Cambridge University Press, 1996). But on the particular "liberties" afforded to gentlemen as a consequence of their status, see Constance Griffejoen-Cavatorta, *Noblesse et franchise: La valeur de liberté dans les écrits des aristocrates au Grand Siècle* (Classiques Garnier, 2017).

22. A key example is Joseph Addison, "The Choice of Hercules," *The Tatler*, no. 97 (November 22, 1709), but also see chapter 1 of this book.

23. See Elaine Pagels, *Adam, Eve, and the Serpent: Sex and Politics in Early Christianity* (Random House, 1988), as well as Stephen Greenblatt, *The Rise and Fall of Adam and Eve* (Norton, 2017), on understandings of Eve's (free) choice and its consequences. There is also an alternative tradition, stemming from Augustine, of viewing free will as always an illusion; for more on this, see chapter 2 of this book.

24. See Robert H. Taylor, ed., *The Idea of Freedom in Asia and Africa* (2002) and William C. Kirby, ed., *Realms of Freedom in Modern China* (2003), both in Stanford University Press's The Making of Modern Freedom series, as well as David Kelly and Anthony Reid, eds., *Asian Freedoms: The Idea of Freedom in East and South East Asia* (Cambridge University Press, 2009) and Ajay Skaria, "Revisiting Non-Willing Freedom: How Gandhi Matters Today" (2022), https://manifold.umn.edu/read/cc-frame-002-revisiting-non-willing-freedom-how-gandhi-matters-today/section/1b88aa78-2ced-47f6-8725-797b1012c218. Conversely, on the nonuniversality of the aspiration toward choice from the perspective of cultural psychology, see Sheena S. Iyengar and Sanford E. DeVoe, "Rethinking the Value of Choice: Considering the Cultural Mediators of Intrinsic Motivation," in *Cross-Cultural Differences in Perspectives on the Self* (University of Nebraska Press, 2003), 129–74; and Hazel Rose Markus and Barry Schwartz, "Does Choice Mean Freedom and Well-Being?" *Journal of Consumer Research* 37, no. 2 (2010): 344–55.

25. On thinking about European modernity without resorting to Eurocentrism, see Carol Gluck, "The End of Elsewhere: Writing Modernity Now," *American Historical Review* 116, no. 3 (June 2011): 676–87.

26. See, for example, David Harvey, *A Brief History of Neoliberalism* (Oxford University Press, 2005).

27. See, for example, Timothy Breen, *The Marketplace of Revolution: How Consumer Politics Shaped American Independence* (Oxford University Press, 2004) or Colin Jones, "The Great Chain of Buying: Medical Advertisement, the Bourgeois Public Sphere and the Origins of the French Revolution," *American Historical Review* 101 (1996): 13–40. For a critique, see Sophia Rosenfeld, "Of Revolutions and the Problem of Choice," in *Rethinking the Age of Revolutions: France and the Birth of the Modern World*, ed. David Bell and Yair Mintzker (Oxford University Press, 2018), 236–72.

28. On synchronicity as a historical development, see Helge Jordheim and Einar Wigen, "Conceptual Synchronisation: From Progress to Crisis," *Millennium* 46, no. 3 (June 2018): 421–39.

29. Leisure time was increasingly envisioned, starting in the 19th century, as a distinct set of hours, apart from those taken up by work or school or the required tasks of daily life, during

which one was "free" to make one's own choices about what to do and where and with whom; see Alain Corbin, *L'Avènement des loisirs, 1850–1960* (Aubier, 1998). By contrast, the capitalist workplace itself and the activities that go on within it during working hours have not generally been understood to have much to do with choice; see E. P. Thompson, "Time, Work-Discipline, and Industrial Capitalism," *Past & Present*, no. 38 (December 1967): 56–97, on the growing distinction.

30. For some of these micro-technologies, instructions on their use are a key part. Many are also preprinted but meant to be modified with a pen in hand (checking a box, crossing out what's rejected, writing in a name, for example) to be become functional. On paper as an "everyday technology" whose uses grew as its cost dropped in the 19th century, see Carla Bittel, Elaine Leong, and Christine von Oertzen, eds., *Working with Paper: Gendered Practices in the History of Knowledge* (University of Pittsburgh Press, 2019), though choice technology is not specifically mentioned.

31. See Reinhart Koselleck, "Structures of Repetition in Language and History," in *Sediments of Time: On Possible Histories*, ed. Sean Franzel and Stefan-Ludwig Hoffmann (Stanford University Press, 2018), esp. 167, on the historical significance of repetition.

32. On taking seriously Hannah Arendt's attention to the history of habits of mind in shaping political life (though Arendt does not specifically take up choice-making except in passing), see Sophia Rosenfeld, "On Lying: Writing Philosophical History after the Enlightenment and after Arendt," in *The Worlds of American Intellectual History*, ed. Joel Isaac, James Kloppenberg, Michael O'Brien, and Jennifer Ratner-Rosengarten (Oxford University Press, 2018).

33. Pierre Bourdieu, *Outline of a Theory of Practice*, trans. Richard Nice (Cambridge University Press, 1977 [1972]), 93–94.

34. On the physical orchestration or "choreography" of social practices and how it helps foster both social organization and abstract thinking, see Andrew Hewitt, *Social Choreography: Ideology as Performance in Dance and Everyday Movement* (Duke University Press, 2005).

35. I introduce the term "bounded choice" as an extension of behavioral economists' terms like "bounded self-interest" and "bounded rationality." It is intended as a way to recognize that even situations promising "free" choice inevitably come with boundaries not of one's own making.

36. This argument accords with Lawrence M. Friedman, *The Republic of Choice: Law, Authority and Culture* (Harvard University Press, 1990). But see, too, Lorraine Daston, *Rules: A Short History of What We Live By* (Princeton University Press, 2022), on the variety of kinds and their various functions across time.

37. See Isaiah Berlin, *Two Concepts of Liberty* (Oxford University Press, 1958). Useful critiques of this distinction include the classic essay by Charles Taylor, "What's Wrong with Negative Liberty?" in *The Idea of Freedom: Essays in Honour of Isaiah Berlin*, ed. Alan Ryan (Oxford University Press, 1979) and Tim Gray, *Freedom* (Palgrave Macmillan, 1990), esp. chap. 1.

38. See Cass Sunstein, *Choosing Not to Choose: Understanding the Value of Choice* (Oxford University Press, 2015), 5, on the concepts of "choice architecture," defined as the social context that enables and constrains choice in different circumstances, and "choice architects" (also "choice agents" in others' hands), defined as those people who get to determine or shape the social context in which choices are made, not to mention the choices themselves. I borrow from the language of contemporary choice theory intermittently in this book even as I also seek to historicize the concepts behind this language.

39. This book makes the case in practice that feminism needs to be seen as part and parcel of larger ideological and political struggles, not as a distinct strain of thought and activism best studied in isolation, as it often is. But I also follow Geneviève Fraisse (e.g., *Féminisme et philosophie* [Gallimard, 2020]) in taking the position that exploring together historical techniques of

women's domination and historical strategies of women's liberation reveals otherwise hidden aspects of larger political and social visions.

40. On freedom's meaning in relationship to slavery, see Edmund Morgan, "Slavery and Freedom: The American Paradox," *Journal of American History* 59, no. 1 (1972): 5–29; Orlando Patterson, *Freedom*, vol. 1: *Freedom in the Making of Western Culture* (Basic Books, rev. ed., 1992); Eric Foner, *The Story of American Freedom* (Norton, 1999); and Tyler Stovall, *White Freedom: The Racial History of an Idea* (Princeton University Press, 2021). But also see François Furstenberg, "Beyond Freedom and Slavery: Autonomy, Virtue, and Resistance in Early American Political Discourse," *Journal of American History* 89, no. 4 (March 2003): 1295–1330, who shows how slavery and freedom were not always pitted against each other.

41. Accessible accounts of the psychological factors that shape choice-making behavior include Amos Tversky and Daniel Kahneman, "The Framing of Decisions and the Psychology of Choice," *Science* 211 (January 20, 1981): 453–58; Daniel Kahneman, *Thinking, Fast and Slow* (Farrar, Straus and Giroux, 2011); Daniel Ariely, *Predictably Irrational: The Hidden Forces That Shape Our Decisions* (Harper, 2009); and Sheena Iyengar, *The Art of Choosing* (Twelve, 2010).

42. On the problem of too much choice in wealthy parts of the world, key books include Barry Schwartz, *The Paradox of Choice: Why More Is Less* (Harper Perennial, 2005); Edward Rosenthal, *The Era of Choice: The Ability to Choose and Its Transformation of Contemporary Life* (MIT Press, 2006); and Iyengar, *The Art of Choosing*. There are also versions that concentrate on choice in a specific domain, such as Amalia McGibbon et al., *The Choice Effect: Love and Commitment in an Age of Too Many Options* (Seal Press, 2010). For an overview, see Sophia Rosenfeld, "Free to Choose?" *The Nation*, June 3, 2014.

43. Professions associated today with helping people choose range from personal shoppers to financial planners to matchmakers. Some help you define your own tastes; some help you fit in better with those like you; and some help you make the optimal choice in terms of a larger goal like wealth accumulation or enhanced experience. The proliferation of "experts" in choice deserves its own literature.

44. Immanuel Kant, *Conjectures on the Beginning of Human History* [1786], in *Kant: Political Writings*, ed. Hans Reiss and trans. H. B. Nisbet, 2nd ed. (Cambridge University Press, 1991), 224.

45. [Sylvia Plath], *The Bell Jar* (Heinemann, 1963), 73. But see, too, Søren Kierkegaard, *The Sickness unto Death*, trans. Walter Lowrie (Princeton University Press, 1954 [1849]), 169, on how, when everything appears possible, "the soul goes astray in possibility." This may be particularly true when cultures cease to provide much guidance in the form of traditions, customs, or religious strictures about what constitutes a *good* option in the variety of circumstances requiring choice that one is likely to confront.

46. The claim here is not that all choices we make are experienced as freedom *or* that all forms of freedom that matter to us involve choice; it is simply that this is the dominant understanding of our times and rarely challenged as such.

47. The work of psychologists in these domains has prompted a raft of self-help books designed to help readers either choose better (e.g., Chip Heath and Dan Heath, *Decisive: How to Make Better Choices in Life and Work* [Crown, 2013]) or choose less for the value of self-control (e.g., Joanne Heim, *Living Simply: Choosing Less in a World of More* [Multnomah, 2006]). It has also prompted a literature designed to encourage public policies that will, through the redesign of "choice architecture," help choosers make better choices for themselves or "nudge" them toward certain options over others; see especially Richard Thaler and Cass Sunstein, *Nudge: Improving Decisions about Health, Wealth, and Happiness* (Yale University Press, 2008) and Sunstein, *Choosing Not to Choose*, as well as the commentary on this approach in Sigal Ben-Porath, *Tough Choices: Structured Paternalism and the Landscape of Choice* (Princeton University

Press, 2010) and Samuel Moyn, "The Nudgeocrat: Navigating Freedom with Cass Sunstein," *The Nation*, June 3, 2019.

48. Vivek Shanbhag, *Ghachar Ghochar*, trans. Srinath Perur (Penguin, 2017 [2013 in Kannada]).

49. On the negative effects, especially on politics, of an overemphasis on personal choice, see—in addition to the works of Pettit cited above—such varied liberal and left critiques as Dworkin, "Is More Choice Better than Less?"; Andrew Bard Schmookler, *The Illusion of Choice: How the Market Economy Shapes Our Destiny* (State University of New York Press, 1993); and Renata Salecl, *The Tyranny of Choice* (Profile Books, 2011), as well as the critiques of earlier Marxists like Herbert Marcuse, who labels choice one of the "deceptive liberties" of capitalism (*One Dimensional Man* [Beacon, 1964], 7). But there are also conservatives, like Alasdair MacIntyre, and communitarians, like Michael Sandel and Charles Taylor, who insist a culture that prioritizes individual choice over tradition or community will be a culture without purpose or direction.

50. See Giddens, *Modernity and Self-Identity*, 5–6, on how having choices makes class mobility possible, but also on how differential access to different kinds of choice-making has itself become an element of class distinction in the contemporary world.

51. Greenfield, *The Myth of Choice*, 24.

52. Margaret Wilkerson Sexton, *A Kind of Freedom: A Novel* (Counterpoint Press, 2017).

53. See Brian Daugherity, *Keep on Keeping On: The NAACP and the Implementation of Brown v. Board of Education in Virginia* (University of Virginia Press, 2016), chap. 6; and Martha Minow, "Confronting the Seduction of Choice: Law, Education, and American Pluralism," *Yale Law Journal* 120, no. 4 (January 2011): 814–48, on the long, checkered history of school choice plans. Today these laws, and economist Milton Friedman's past support for them under the banner "freedom of choice," are often cited to make a case for the racial roots of neoliberalism in the United States; see Diane Ravitch, "The Dark Side of School Choice," *New York Review of Books*, January 14, 2021.

54. See Elaine R. Thomas, *Immigration, Islam, and the Politics of Belonging in France: A Comparative Framework* (University of Pennsylvania Press, 2011), chap. 5. The expression in French is "une manifestation de volonté."

55. Allison Hoffman, "The ACA's Choice Problem," *Journal of Health Politics, Policy and Law* 45, no. 4 (2020): 501–15.

56. Linda R. Hirshman, *Get to Work: A Manifesto for Women of the World* (Viking, 2006), referring to the writing of Gloria Steinem, among others. The term was coined by her initially in "Homeward Bound," *American Prospect*, November 21, 2005.

57. Additional critiques of "choice feminism" include Michaele Ferguson, "Choice Feminism and the Fear of Politics," *Perspectives on Politics* 8, no. 1 (March 2010): 247–53; Miranda Kiraly and Meagan Tyler, *Freedom Fallacy: The Limits of Liberal Feminism* (Conor Court, 2015); Jennifer M. Denbow, *Governed through Choice: Autonomy, Technology, and the Politics of Reproduction* (New York University Press, 2015); and, more broadly, Nancy Fraser, *Fortunes of Feminism: From State-Managed Capitalism to Neoliberal Crisis* (Verso, 2013).

58. Clare Chambers, *Sex, Culture and Justice: The Limits of Choice* (Penn State University Press, 2008), argues against the idea of choice as a catchall justification, especially when it comes to forms of body modification from genital mutilation to breast implants.

59. Dorothy Roberts, *Killing the Black Body: Race, Reproduction, and the Meaning of Liberty* (Pantheon, 1997), 294. This more expansive view of what feminism demands is also characteristic of the work of Nancy Hirschmann, who proposes in *The Subject of Liberty: Toward a Feminist Theory of Freedom* (Princeton University Press, 2003) that women's freedom requires changing power structures, not just adding more choices, because both women's self-conceptions and desires and the options available to them are already shaped by patriarchy, capitalist forms of

inequality, racism, and other types of oppression. However, see, too, Saba Mahmood, *Politics of Piety: The Islamic Revival and the Feminist Subject* (Princeton University Press, 2005), who argues that seeing adherence to traditional values and practices as necessarily evidence of patriarchal constraints on women's choices leads to misunderstanding the lives of women operating outside white, Western norms and animates mainstream Western feminist support for imperialism.

60. Meghan Murphy, "Choice Feminism," *Herizons* (summer 2012), https://herizons.ca/archives/cover/choice-feminism.

61. The model here is more the work of historically minded political theorists, from Hannah Arendt to Pierre Rosanvallon and Axel Honneth, than it is the work of historians of political thought.

62. Dror Wahrman, *The Making of the Modern Self* (Yale University Press, 2004), argues that, at least in the British context, certain kinds of identity (racial, gendered, national) hardened from the last quarter of the 18th century onward, coming to seem more immutable and thus less subject to choice than previously. One implication is clearly that this turn away from identitarian choice helped fuel subsequent forms of exclusion and inequality that now need undoing. However, claims about naturally occurring forms of difference have also worked in recent years to bolster claims for equal treatment; see, for example, Joanna Wuest, "From Pathology to 'Born Perfect': Science, Law, and Citizenship in American LGBTQ+ Advocacy," *Perspectives on Politics* 19, no. 3 (September 2021): 838–53, on the effects of the shift from the language of "sexual preference," with its suggestion of willed choice, to "sexual orientation."

63. Rogers Brubaker, in *Trans: Gender and Race in an Age of Unsettled Identities* (Princeton University Press, 2016), compares contemporary thinking about gender and racial identity and tries to explain why, at present, essentialist and voluntarist understandings play out differently in these two domains.

64. See especially Nancy Armstrong, *How Novels Think: The Limits of British Individualism from 1719–1900* (Columbia University Press, 2005), 4.

Chapter 1

1. The *Oxford English Dictionary* gives 1757 as the date of the first appearance of this term in print. However, Samuel Johnson included the verb "to shop" in the 1756 edition of his dictionary and defined it as "to frequent shops: as, they are shopping"; quoted in Nancy Cox and Karin Dannehl, *Perceptions of Retailing in Early Modern England* (Ashgate, 2007), 145. Online databases suggest a surge in the employment of both "to go a shopping" and "shopping" in the 1780s and 1790s. The English term "shopping" can be found in French texts as well, starting in the mid-19th century, though older terms for visiting stores—"courir de boutique en boutique," for example—continued to be used in French as well; see Joan DeJean, *How Paris Became Paris: The Invention of the Modern City* (Bloomsbury, 2014), 144–69. German writers, too, used the English term in the 19th century when they wanted to emphasize the novelty of the activity and distinguish it from simply buying; in 1829, for example, a German prince explained in an otherwise German-language text for German readers that "to go *shopping*" is a modern thing to do in Paris (quoted in Jan Hein Furnée and Clé Lesger, eds., *The Landscape of Consumption: Shopping Streets and Cultures in Western Europe, 1600–1900* [Palgrave Macmillan, 2014], 13). The Dutch only started using the term *winkelen* as a substitute at the end of the 19th century.

2. On British American slave auctions or "vendues" from New York to the Caribbean, see Gregory O'Malley, *Final Passages: The Intercolonial Slave Trade of British America, 1619–1807* (University of North Carolina Press, 2014). On North American auctions more generally, see Ellen Hartigan-O'Connor, "Public Sales and Public Values in Eighteenth-Century North America," *Early American Studies* 13, no. 4 (fall 2015): 749–73. In the 18th century, the French and Dutch employed auctions for sales of the enslaved in the New World as well.

3. The limited literature on 18th-century English auctions includes Robin Myers, "Sale by Auction: The Rise of Auctioneering Exemplified in the Firm of Christopher Cock, the Langfords, and Henry, John and George Robins (c. 1720–1847)," in *Sale and Distribution of Books from 1700*, ed. Robin Myers and Michael Harris (Oxford Polytechnic Press, 1982), 126–63; Brian Learmount, *A History of the Auction* (Barnard and Learmount, 1985), 23–28; Iain Pears, *The Discovery of Painting: The Growth of Interest in the Arts in England, 1680–1768* (Yale University Press, 1988), 57–67; Cynthia Wall, *The Prose of Things: Transformations of Description in the Eighteenth Century* (University of Chicago Press, 2006), chap. 6; and Jeremy Warren and Adriana Turpin, eds., *Auctions, Agents and Dealers: The Mechanisms of the Art Market, 1660–1830* (Wallace Collection, 2008).

4. On the importance of the secondhand trade to early modern commerce, see Laurence Fontaine, ed., *Alternative Exchanges: Second-Hand Circulations from the Sixteenth Century to the Present* (Berghahn Books, 2004); Jon Stobart and Ilja Van Damme, eds., *Modernity and the Second-Hand Trade: European Consumption Cultures and Practices, 1700–1900* (Palgrave Macmillan, 2010); and Daniel Roche, *The Culture of Clothing: Dress and Fashion in the Ancien Regime*, trans. Jean Birrell (Cambridge University Press, 1997), 344–63.

5. [Christopher Cock], *The Last Sale for this Season: Being the Most Valuable Part of the Collection of Elihu Yale, Esq.; (late governor of Fort St. George) deceas'd* (London, 1722).

6. [Christopher Cock], *Catalogue of Several Curious Figures of Human Anatomy in Wax, taken from the life ... will be sold by auction* (London, 1736).

7. [James Ralph], *The Touch-Stone: or, Historical, Critical, Political, Moral, Philosophical, and Theological Essays on the reigning Diversions of the Town* (London, 1728), 231–32.

8. See both [Henry Fielding], *The Historical Register, for the Year 1736* (London, 1737), act 2, where Cock is represented by the character Mr. Hen, and William Hogarth's engraving reproduced here. Earlier works in which Hogarth portrayed his neighbor and sometimes salesman for his canvases include *A Scene from The Beggar's Opera* (1728–29, National Gallery of Art, Washington, DC) and *Conversation Piece (Portrait of Sir Andrew Fountaine with Other Men and Women)* (c. 1730–35, Philadelphia Museum of Art).

9. On the history of book sales catalogs, see Annie Charon and Élisabeth Parinet, eds., *Les Ventes de livres et leurs catalogues, XVIIe–XXe siècle* (Ecole des Chartes, 2000).

10. See Wall, *The Prose of Things*, on the format of novels and auction brochures compared.

11. [Christopher Cock], *A Catalogue of the Rich Furniture of the Right Honourable the Earl of Cadogan, Deceas'd* (London, 1727), no. 4.11; lot 16; and lot 83. Her name is properly spelled Sofonisba Anguissola.

12. See, for example, the following catalogs associated with London sales held by Mr. Cock: *A Catalogue of the Entire Goods of Gilbert Clarke Esq; (deceased) [...] As likewise a choice Parcel of Books* (1726); *A Catalogue of an exceedingly fine library of books in several arts and sciences [...] the Beauties of the Copies, the Choiceness and Scarceness of the Editions, and all other Excellancies will easily be discover'd and approv'd by the Curious* (1730?); *A Catalogue of the Entire Library of Mrs. Katherine Bridgeman: (of Cavendish Square) deceas'd: consisting of a choice collection of books* (1743); and *A Catalogue of the Entire and Choice Library of Thomas Pelham junior, Esq.: (late Member of Parliament for Lewes in Sussex, and one of the commissioners of trade and plantations) deceas'd, consisting of Variety of Curious and Uncommon Books in most branches of Polite Literature, and in several Languages* (1744).

13. See, too, the following Cock catalogs: *A Catalogue of the Valuable and Exceeding Fine Collection of Mr. Geminiani's Choice Pictures* (London, 1725); *A Catalogue of the Valuable Picture of the Right Honourable Archibald, late Earl of Roseberry [...] As Likewise, very Choice and Curious parcel of old Japan and other China* (London, 1725); *A Catalogue of the Rich Furniture of the Right Honourable the Earl of Cadogan, (deceas'd) [...] together with Sundry choice, and valuable Jewels* (London, 1727); *Rich Household Furniture: Fine Side-Boards of Plate and Other Choice Effects*

(London, 1733); *A Catalogue of Signor Sterbini's Curious Collection Lately brought from Rome, Consisting of the greatest variety of choice and noble Pieces of Antiquities* (London, c. 1733); and *A Catalogue of Mons. Beauvais's Collection ... [including] a choice collection of medals in gold and silver [...] and other curious effects* (London, 1739).

14. Fielding, *The Historical Register, for the year 1736*, 13. On the idea, from the late 17th century onward, of the *cabinet choisi*, a book collection that included titles valuable not just for their intellectual or moral contents but also for their worth as material objects, see Jean Viardot, "Naissance de la bibliophilie: Les cabinets de livres rares," in *Histoires des bibliothèques françaises*, ed. Claude Joly, vol. 2: *Les bibliothèques sous l'Ancien Régime, 1530–1789* (Éditions du Cercle de la Librairie, 1988), 269–89.

15. For "choice cargo," see *Charleston, April 27, 1769. To Be Sold, On Wednesday, the Tenth Day of May next, A Choice Cargo of Two Hundred and Fifty Negroes: Arrived in the Ship Countess of Sussex ... directly from Gambia, by John Chapman and Co*, reproduced here. This broadside also refers to this "cargo" as a "parcel," as does this advertisement: "To Be sold on Monday next, the 15th ... at public Vendue, under the New Market House, a parcel of choice house and plantation slaves," *South Carolina Gazette*, January 13, 1733. Compare *Charleston, February 3rd, 1768. The Sale of Negroes belonging to Mr. John Miles ... by publick Outcry at Mr. Nightingall's on Charlestown-Neck, and are in Number upward of Seventy Negroes. All seasoned, young and healthy, most of them born in this Country, among whom are Coopers, Sawyers, Housewenches, handy Boys and Girls, and all the others very good Field Slaves*. In market terms, these "negroes" are here both thoroughly commodified in the sense of stripped of all particularities and relations to others for the purposes of sale *and* differentiated (by age, gender, capabilities and experience, place of origin, and often physical appearance) as products among which buyers (i.e., enslavers) can choose.

16. *A Catalogue of Part of the Valuable Spanish Silks and Other Effects of the St. Joachim Prize, taken by His Majesty's Ship the Monmouth, Capt. Charles Wyndham ... which will be sold by Auction, by Mr. Cock* (London, 1744), 1, 3.

17. [Christopher Cock], *A Catalogue of the particulars of the dwelling house, coach-house, and stables ... of Sir Joesph Eyles, Deceas'd. Likewise, all the household and other furniture; consisting of ... great Choice of the old fine Japan China ...* (London, 1740) and *A Catalogue of the Collection of Italian, Flemish and French Books of Prints of the Rt. Hon. Edward Earl of Oxford and Mortimer, Deceas'd ... with great Choice of the finest Editions of the C[las]sicks* (London, 1746). See, too, the ad run by Cock in the *London Evening Post*, March 8–10, 1739, for the sale of the stock of a bankrupt "laceman," including "great Choice of Embroider'd and Brocaded Waistcoats, and Short Aprons" (Learmount, *A History of the Auction*, 22–23).

18. For French examples, see *Catalogue d'une collection d'estampes de choix des plus célèbres graveurs* (March 13, 1770), but also *Vente d'un choix de ... tableaux et dessins* (Paris, December 29, 1777), *Notice d'estampes d'un beau choix, toutes sous verres* (September 20, 1779), and *Notice d'un choix de livres* (November 12, 1784). See, too, *The Cream of All Sorts of the Best Winter Goods, just imported in the last ship from London by Albert Dennie ... He imports the choice of goods, and has fresh supplies in every ship ... His warehouse is upon Dyer's Wharf ...* (Boston, c. 1745); the advertisement for Forster's Linen Warehouse, promising "a great Choice of ready-made Shirts of all Prices," in *The Public Advertiser*, February 14, 1764, cited in Beverly Lemire, *Fashion's Favorite: The Cotton Trade and the Consumer in Britain, 1660–1800* (Oxford University Press, 1991), 192; and the advertisement for Thomas Bromilow, Linen-Draper and China-Man, saying "that he is just come down from London, and has brought the greatest choice of under-mentioned articles," in *Gote's Liverpool Advertiser*, April 5, 1770, cited in Jon Stobart and Bruno Blondé, eds., *Selling Textiles in the Long Eighteenth Century: Comparative Perspectives from Western Europe* (Palgrave Macmillan, 2014), 166.

19. On the history of cotton in a global framework but with an emphasis on local differences, see Giorgio Riello and Prasannan Parthasarathi, eds., *The Spinning World: A Global History of*

Cotton Textiles, 1200–1850 (Oxford University Press, 2009) and "From India to the World: Cotton and Fashionability," in *The Oxford Handbook of the History of Consumption*, ed. Frank Trentmann (Oxford University Press, 2012), 145–72. See, too, Sven Beckert, *Empire of Cotton: A Global History* (Knopf, 2014) and, for a specialized study of the growth of demand outside Europe starting in the 18th century, Kazuo Kobayashi, *Indian Cotton Textiles in West Africa: African Agency, Consumer Demand and the Making of the Global Economy* (Palgrave Macmillan, 2019).

20. Pears, *The Discovery of Painting*, 52–60.

21. On the politics of cotton regulation in 18th-century Europe, see Natalie Rothstein, "The Calico Campaign of 1719–1721," *East London Papers* 7 (1964): 3–21; Felicia Gottmann, "Textile Furies: The French State and the Retail and Consumption of Asian Cottons, 1686–1759," in *Goods from the East, 1600–1800: Trading Eurasia*, ed. Maxine Berg et al. (Palgrave Macmillan, 2015), 244–58; and the works of Beverly Lemire: *Fashion's Favourite*; "Fashioning Cottons: Asian Trade, Domestic Industry and Consumer Demand, 1660–1780," in *The Cambridge History of Western Textiles*, vol. 1 (Cambridge University Press, 2003), 493–512; and ed., *The British Cotton Trade*, vols. 1–4 (Pickering and Chatto, 2009). As an example of a locally made substitution that itself became available for export, see the discussion of Mexican printed cottons called *indianillas* in Amelia Peck, ed., *Interwoven Globe: The Worldwide Textile Trade, 1500–1800* (Metropolitan Museum, 2013), 41.

22. On this point, see John Styles, *The Dress of the People: Everyday Fashion in Eighteenth-Century England* (Yale University Press, 2007).

23. On the "democratization" of luxury goods, see Maxine Berg and Helen Clifford, eds., *Consumers and Luxury: Consumer Culture in Europe, 1650–1850* (Manchester University Press, 1999); Berg, *Luxury and Pleasure in Eighteenth-Century Britain* (Oxford University Press, 2005); Berg, *Goods from the East*; and Frank Trentmann, *Empire of Things: How We Became a World of Consumers, from the Fifteenth Century to the Twenty-First* (Harper, 2016). On the rise of "populuxe" goods, see Cissie Fairchilds, "The Production and Marketing of Populuxe Goods in Eighteenth-Century Paris," in *Consumption and the World of Goods: Consumption and Society in the Seventeenth and Eighteenth Centuries*, ed. John Brewer and Roy Porter (Routledge, 1993), 228–49.

24. Michael Kwass, *Contraband: Louis Mandrin and the Making of a Global Underground* (Harvard University Press, 2014), 2.

25. See Roche, *The Culture of Clothing*, 108–11, on how the value of working-class French women's wardrobes increased in the 18th century both in absolute terms and as a percentage of total assets.

26. On the idea of a consumer revolution, see most famously Neil McKendrick, John Brewer, and J. H. Plumb, *The Birth of a Consumer Society: The Commercialization of Eighteenth-Century England* (Europa Publications/Indiana, 1982), but also Lorna Weatherill, *Consumer Behavior and Material Culture in Britain, 1660–1760* (Routledge, 1988); Brewer and Porter, *Consumption and the World of Goods*; and Daniel Roche's pioneering *The Culture of Clothing* and *A History of Everyday Things: The Birth of Consumption in France, 1600–1800*, trans. Brian Pearce (Cambridge University Press, 2000 [1997]). On the dating and extent of this revolution, see Peter N. Stearns, "Stages of Consumerism: Recent Work on the Issues of Periodization," *Journal of Modern History* 69 (March 1997): 102–17; François Crouzet, "Some Remarks on the *métiers d'art*," in *Luxury Trades and Consumerism in Ancien Régime Paris: Studies in the History of the Skilled Work Force*, ed. Robert Fox and Anthony John Turner (Ashgate, 1998), 263–86; and the more recent challenge to this narrative by one of its founders, John Brewer, "The Error of Our Ways: Historians and the Birth of Consumer Society" (Cultures of Consumption Working Paper no. 12, June 2004). Michael Kwass summarizes this literature in *The Consumer Revolution, 1650–1800* (Cambridge University Press, 2022).

27. On luxury debates in the 18th century, see Christopher Berry, *The Idea of Luxury: A Conceptual and Historical Investigation* (Cambridge University Press, 1994); Maxine Berg and Elizabeth Eger, eds., *Luxury in the Eighteenth Century: Debates, Desires and Delectable Goods* (Routledge, 2003); and John Shovlin, *The Political Economy of Virtue: Luxury, Patriotism, and the Origins of the French Revolution* (Cornell University Press, 2006).

28. See Nicholas Alexander and Gary Akehurst, eds., *The Emergence of Modern Retailing, 1750–1950* (Routledge, 1998); Nancy Cox, *The Complete Tradesman: A Study of Retailing, 1550–1820* (Ashgate, 2000); John Benson and Laura Ugolini, eds., *A Nation of Shopkeepers: Five Centuries of British Retailing* (I. B. Tauris, 2002); Andrew Hann and Jon Stobart, "Sites of Consumption: The Display of Goods in Provincial Shops in Eighteenth-Century England," *Cultural and Social History* 2 (2005): 165–88; Jon Stobart, Andrew Hann, and Victoria Morgan, *Spaces of Consumption: Leisure and Shopping in the English Town, c. 1680–1830* (Routledge, 2007); and Ian Mitchell, *Tradition and Innovation in English Retailing, 1700 to 1850: Narratives of Consumption* (Ashgate, 2014).

29. See Carolyn Sargentson, *Merchants and Luxury Markets: The Marchands Merciers of Eighteenth-Century Paris* (Victoria and Albert Museum, 1996); Robert Fox and Anthony John Turner, eds., *Luxury Trades and Consumerism in Ancien Régime Paris: Studies in the History of the Skilled Workforce* (Ashgate, 1998); Jennifer Jones, *Sexing "La Mode": Gender, Fashion and Commercial Culture in Old Regime France* (Berg, 2004); and especially Natacha Coquery, ed., *La Boutique et la ville: Commerces, commerçants, espaces et clientèles, XVIe–XXe siècle* (Tours, Centre d'histoire de la ville moderne et contemporaine, 2000) and Coquery, *Tenir boutique à Paris au XVIIIe siècle: Luxe et demi-luxe* (Editions du Comité des travaux historiques et scientifiques, 2011).

30. See Danielle van den Heuvel and Sheilagh Ogilvie, "Retail Development in the Consumer Revolution: The Netherlands, c. 1670–c. 1815," *Explorations in Economic History* 50, no. 1 (2013): 69–87; van den Heuvel, "New Products, New Sellers? Changes in the Dutch Textile Trades, c. 1650–1750," in *Selling Textiles in the Long Eighteenth Century*, ed. Stobart and Blondé, 118–37; and Clé Lesger, "Urban Planning, Urban Improvement and the Retail Landscape in Amsterdam, 1600–1850," in *The Landscape of Consumption*, ed. Furnée and Lesger, 104–24.

31. On Europe as a whole, including smaller towns, see the volumes edited by Bruno Blondé with an international team of scholars, including *Retailers and Consumer Changes in Early Modern Europe: England, France, Italy and the Low Countries* (PUFR, 2005); *Buyers and Sellers: Retail Circuits and Practices in Medieval and Early Modern Europe* (Brepols, 2006); and *Fashioning Old and New: Changing Consumer Patterns in Western Europe, 1650–1900* (Brepols, 2009).

32. Hoh-Cheung Mui and Lorna Mui, *Shops and Shopkeeping in Eighteenth-Century England* (Routledge, 1989), 29, cite Gregory King's claim there were 50,000 shopkeepers in England and Wales in 1688, and by the 1750s, 142,000, including over 21,000 in London alone. They also (see 38–40) use the excise records for 1759 to suggest a ratio of shops to population for England and Wales of 1 shop for every 43.3 people and, for southern England, of 1 shop for every 34.

33. On drapers' shops as precursors to department stores in this regard, see Claire Walsh, "Shop Design and the Display of Goods in Eighteenth-Century London," *Journal of Design History* 8, no. 3 (1995): 157–76; and "The Newness of the Department Store: A View from the Eighteenth Century," in *Cathedrals of Consumption: The European Department Store, 1850–1939*, ed. Geoffrey Crossick and Serge Jaumain (Ashgate, 1999), 46–71.

34. Hentie Louw, "Window-Glass Making in Britain c. 1660–c. 1860 and Its Architectural Impact," *Construction History* 7 (1991): 47–68.

35. Daniel Defoe, *The Complete English Tradesman, in Familiar Letters; Directing him in all the several Parts and Progressions of Trade* (London, 1726), 312–13. Even earlier, the importance of display in shops was emphasized by Jacques Savary in *Le Parfait négociant ou instruction générale pour ce qui regarde le commerce des marchandises de France et des pays étrangers* (Paris, 1675); see

Clare Haru Crowston, *Credit, Fashion, Sex: Economies of Regard in Old Regime France* (Duke University Press, 2013), 187–88.

36. See, for example, Uwe Spiekermann, "Display Windows and Window Displays in German Cities of the Nineteenth Century: Towards the History of a Commercial Breakthrough," in *Advertising and the European City: Historical Perspectives*, ed. C. Wischermann and E. Shore (Ashgate, 2000), 139–71.

37. Olivier Dautresme, "Une Boutique de luxe dans un centre commercial à la mode: L'exemple du 'magasin d'effets précieux à prix fixe' au Palais-Royal à la fin du XVIIIe siècle," in *La Boutique et la ville*, ed. Coquery, 239–47, esp. 240. Clearly indicated price differences became one major way of structuring consumer choice henceforth.

38. Styles, *The Dress of the People*, 169–71. In this regard, one can certainly compare the shop with other 18th-century spaces, such as urban boulevards, that historians take to have opened up, de facto, horizontal social relations within vertically arranged cultures (see William Sewell, *Capitalism and the Emergence of Civic Equality in Eighteenth-Century France* [University of Chicago Press, 2021]). However, as I hope to make clear in this chapter and the next, I take the experience of individuated choice and the new kinds of hierarchies it engendered to be just as important in terms of reshaping conceptualizations of social relations in this period; I consider the growth of capitalism alone to be insufficient to explain an investment in either civic equality or individuation (see chapter 2 on religious culture for the other side of this story); and mainly, I see gender as complicating all of these generalizations.

39. Kathryn Morrison, *English Shops and Shopping: An Architectural History* (Yale University Press, 2004), 37.

40. See Brewer and Porter, *Consumption and the World of Goods*, on the difference between the more expansive idea of consumption, on the one hand, and consumerism, which has as its focus only the moment of purchase, not what happens before or after, on the other.

41. *Verslag over den toestand* (1852), 64, cited in Jan Hein Furnée, "'Our Living Museum of Nouveatés': Visual Social Pleasures in The Hague's Shopping Streets, 1650–1900," in *The Landscape of Consumption*, ed. Furnée and Lesger, 208–31, see 218.

42. See the travel diary of Sarah Kemble Knight (1704), cited in Ann Smart Martin, *Buying into the World of Goods: Early Consumers in Backcountry Virginia* (Johns Hopkins University Press, 2008), 156.

43. T. H. Breen points out in *The Marketplace of Revolution*, 62–63, that finished cloth made up half of all goods transported to North America in the 18th century, and colonists increasingly consumed cloth that was imported rather than homemade.

44. On the growth of shops, shopping, and consumerism in North America, see Carole Shammas, *The Pre-Industrial Consumer in England and America* (Oxford University Press, 2000); Richard Bushman, "Shopping and Advertising in Colonial America," in *Of Consuming Interests: The Style of Life in the Eighteenth Century*, ed. Cary Carson, Ronald Hoffman, and Peter J. Albert (University of Virginia Press, 1994), 233–51; Ann Smart Martin, "Frontier Boys and Country Cousins: The Context for Choice in Eighteenth-Century Consumerism," in *Historical Archeology and the Study of American Culture*, ed. LuAnn DeCunzo and Bernard Herman (Winterthur, 1996), 71–102; and Christina J. Hodge, *Consumerism and the Emergence of the Middle Class in Colonial America* (Cambridge University Press, 2014). There is also a well-developed literature on shopkeepers, including Thomas Doerflinger, *A Vigorous Spirit of Enterprise: Merchants and Economic Development in Revolutionary Philadelphia* (University of North Carolina Press, 1986).

45. See Richard Bushman, *The Refinement of America: Persons, Houses, Cities* (Knopf, 1992), 359.

46. On sample books, see Mary Elizabeth Burbidge, "The Bower Textile Sample Book," *Textile History* 14, no. 2 (1983): 213–21; and Natalie Rothstein, ed., *A Lady of Fashion: Barbara Johnson's Album of Styles and Fabrics* (Norton, 1987). See also Sargentson, *Merchants and Luxury*

Markets, 105–7, on bans so as to avoid knock-offs. *The Spinning World*, ed. Riello and Parthasarathi, reproduces a page from a European textile sample book that was one of many imported (especially by the Dutch) to Japan between 1799 and 1859.

47. The best source on the early history of the restaurant, including the advent of the menu, is Rebecca Spang, *The Invention of the Restaurant: Paris and Modern Gastronomic Culture* (Harvard University Press, 2000). See Francis Blagdon, *Paris as it was and as it is: A Sketch of the French Capital, illustrative of the Effects of the Revolution . . . in a series of letters, written by an English traveler, during the years 1801–2, to a friend in London* (London, 1803), 1:438–60, specifically on the experience of a meal at Beauvilliers's fashionable restaurant in the Palais Egalité (!). Blagdon reproduces the full menu, with "prix des mets pour une personne" (444–52) and describes it as "a printed sheet of double *folio*, of the size of an English newspaper. It will require half an hour at least to con over [consult] this important catalogue" (442–43).

48. See, for example, Thavolia Glymph, "The Irretrievable Past?" *Perspectives* 62, no. 1 (January 2024): 5–6, for a meditation on mail-order catalogs, as opposed to brick-and-mortar stores, as refuges for Black people in the 20th-century United States.

49. Berg, *Luxury and Pleasure*, 274.

50. On trade cards and newspaper advertising, primarily in England, see Maxine Berg and Helen Clifford, "Selling Consumption in the Eighteenth Century: Advertising and the Trade Card in Britain and France," *Cultural and Social History* 4 (2007): 145–70; Jon Stobart, "Selling (through) Politeness: Advertising Provincial Shops in Eighteenth-Century England," *Cultural and Social History* 5 (2008): 309–28; Chloe Wigston Smith, "Clothes without Bodies: Objects, Humans and the Marketplace in Eighteenth-Century It-Narratives and Trade Cards," *Eighteenth-Century Fiction* 23, no. 2 (2010–11): 347–80; and, for examples, Theodore Crom, *Trade Catalogues, 1542–1842* (T. R. Crom, 1976); Ambrose Heal, *London Tradesmen's Cards of the XVIII Century: An Account of Their Origin and Use* (Dover, 1968); and Anne Lambert, *A Nation of Shopkeepers: Trade Ephemera from 1654 to the 1860s in the John Johnson Collection* (Classic Clenery Press, 2001).

51. On the emergence of the idea of fashion, see Gilles Lipovetsky, *The Empire of Fashion: Dressing Modern Democracy*, trans. Catherine Porter (Princeton University Press, 2002); Beverly Lemire, ed., *The Force of Fashion in Politics and Society: Global Perspectives from Early Modern to Contemporary Times* (Ashgate, 2009); Michael Kwass, "Big Hair: A Wig History of Consumption in Eighteenth-Century France," *American Historical Review* 111, no. 3 (June 2006): 631–59; and Sewell, *Capitalism and the Emergence of Civic Equality*.

52. Bushman, "Shopping and Advertising in Colonial America," 245. That customers absorbed too this view of shopping is evident in the comments of one Mrs. Reed, who wrote from the English provincial city of Chester in 1775 to say "there is no occasion to be in a violent hurry, for there is always great variety of choice in the shops and full as cheap as what people bring to the fair" (Berg, *Luxury and Pleasure*, 260).

53. Defoe, *The Complete English Tradesman*, 60.

54. See Iyengar, *The Art of Choosing*, chap. 6.

55. Cox, *The Complete Tradesman*, 200. "The Bower Textile Sample Book," compiled in Manchester in the 1770s, includes 121 sorts of cottons and cotton-linens and linen checks, 78 sorts of Holland stripes, and 192 kinds of fustian, to give one example.

56. Blagdon, *Paris as it was and as it is*, 453.

57. Thomas Sheraton, *Cabinet Dictionary* (1805), quoted in Amanda Vickery, "Neat and Not Too Showy: Words and Wallpaper in Regency England," in *Gender, Taste and Material Culture in Britain and North America, 1700–1830*, ed. John Styles and A. Vickery (Yale Center for British Art, 2006), 216; this advice is imagined specifically in the case of a gentleman who is so vain as to order furniture that is not suitable to his rank and fortune.

58. Louis-Sébastien Mercier, *Le Tableau de Paris* (Amsterdam, 1783), chapter DLV: "Le Petit-Dunkerque," 82–83.

59. See the introduction to this book on the use of this vocabulary.

60. Anon., *The Tea Purchaser's Guide; or, The Lady and Gentleman's Tea Table and Useful Companion, in the Knowledge and Choice of Teas* (London, 1785).

61. Albert Bendix, *Guide dans la choix des étrennes: Almanach du Palais-Royal pour 1824* (Paris, 1824), 13, which functioned mainly as a shopper's guide to types of businesses, from *armuriers* to *restaurateurs*.

62. See note 27 on the history of the critique of luxury.

63. On the connections between polite behavior and notions of gentility or refinement in 18th-century England, see Paul Langford, *A Polite and Commercial People: England, 1727–1783* (Oxford University Press, 1992); and Soile Ylivuori, *Women and Politeness in 18th-Century England: Bodies, Identities and Power* (Routledge, 2019). For their translation to American soil, see Bushman, *The Refinement of America*; and Daniel Walker Howe, *Making the American Self: Jonathan Edwards to Abraham Lincoln* (Oxford University Press, 2004).

64. Cited in Pears, *The Discovery of Painting*, 41.

65. On taste, see especially Robert W. Jones, *Gender and the Formation of Taste in Eighteenth-Century Britain: The Analysis of Beauty* (Cambridge University Press, 1998); and Jennifer Tsien, *The Bad Taste of Others: Judging Literary Value in Eighteenth-Century France* (University of Pennsylvania Press, 2012). This is the same moment, of course, as the birth of the science of aesthetics.

66. This point is also consonant with arguments made in the first chapters of Jonathan Sheehan and Dror Wahrman, *The Invisible Hands: Self-Organization and the Eighteenth Century* (University of Chicago Press, 2015), about the social conditions that occasioned reflection on self-organizing systems in the 18th century.

67. See Amanda Vickery, *Behind Closed Doors: At Home in Georgian England* (Yale University Press, 2010), chap. 4; similar patterns can be found in some shopkeepers' accounts too, but note that married women's choices were concealed in many such accounts, as well as manufacturers' ledgers, because married women's debts were harder to recover in common law (5). On gendered patterns of consumption in 18th-century England, see, too, G. J. Barker-Benfield, *The Culture of Sensibility: Sex and Society in Eighteenth-Century Britain* (University of Chicago Press, 1992), 152–214; and Margot Finn, "Men's Things: Masculine Possession in the Consumer Revolution," *Social History* 25 (2000): 133–55.

68. See, for example, the comments of traveler Johanna Schopenhauer, just after 1800, to the effect that, in the Danzig of her youth, "no [respectable] lady went to the shops to make her purchases" alone (i.e., without a manservant), in marked contrast to London; cited in Helen Berry, "Polite Consumption: Shopping in Eighteenth-Century England," *Transactions of the Royal Historical Society*, 6th ser., 12 (2002): 375–94, see 380.

69. Lesger, "Urban Planning," 130–31, points out that, in The Hague in the 18th century, women actually made up the majority of shop owners as well as purchasers, especially in less capital-intensive trades like cotton selling.

70. On shopping and gender, see especially Jennifer Jones, "Coquettes and Grisettes: Women Buying and Selling in Ancien Régime Paris," in *The Sex of Things: Gender and Consumption in Historical Perspective*, ed. Victoria de Grazia and Ellen Furlough (University of California Press, 1996), 25–53; Amanda Vickery, *The Gentleman's Daughter: Women's Lives in Georgian England* (Yale University Press, 1998); and Claire Walsh, "Shops, Shopping and the Art of Decision Making in Eighteenth-Century England," in *Gender, Taste, and Material Culture*, ed. Styles and Vickery, 151–77. On free Blacks and enslaved people in stores in backcountry Virginia, see Martin, *Buying into the World of Goods*, chap. 6.

71. By the last decades of the 18th century, the production of cotton cloth in Europe was directly linked to slavery in the New World insofar as the raw cotton was picked by enslaved

laborers in the French and British Caribbean and, increasingly, South Carolina and Georgia; it was worn in finished forms, as a result of exportation in two directions, by many of those same enslaved peoples; and it was traded for new chattel slaves—people refashioned as consumer objects for purchase by enslavers—on the West African coast; see Beckert, *Empire of Cotton*.

72. See Jan de Vries, *The Industrious Revolution: Consumer Behavior and the Household Economy, 1650 to the Present* (Cambridge University Press, 2008). This argument, while influential, is not without detractors; Frank Trentmann in *The Empire of Things* points out, for example, that rising food prices, not materialism, could also explain the new household work ethic that de Vries identifies.

73. On the history of sumptuary laws, see Giorgio Riello and Ulinka Rublack, eds., *The Right to Dress: Sumptuary Laws in Global Perspective, c. 1200–1800* (Cambridge University Press, 2019) and Daston, *Rules*, 155–68, where it is noted that dress regulations have been defended variously as (a) stabilizing the social order through the symbolic display of difference and hierarchy, (b) saving families and individuals from impoverishment, (c) helping one avoid God's wrath, (d) upholding general standards of modesty, (e) checking luxury, and (f) a necessary form of economic protectionism. On negro cloth, including its relationship to the dehumanization of the auction block, see Tiya Miles, *All That She Carried: The Journey of Ashley's Sack, A Black Family Keepsake* (Random House, 2021), 133, 179. The last such laws in Europe were passed in Poland in 1776 and Bavaria in 1818, according to *The Right to Dress*, 32. In their place, dress increasingly became regulated by schools, clubs, companies, and other institutions, all with their own distinctive internal rules, as well as by affordability and social norms.

74. On the importance of administrative states in creating commercial society, see Trentmann, *The Empire of Things*; Furnée and Lesger, *The Landscape of Consumption*; David Ormrod, *The Rise of Commercial Empires: England and the Netherlands in the Age of Mercantilism, 1650–1770* (Cambridge University Press, 2003); and Christiane Eisenberg, *The Rise of Market Society in England, 1066–1800* (Berghahn, 2013).

75. See Joanna Innes and Nicholas Rogers, "Politics and Government, 1700–1840," in *The Cambridge Urban History of Britain*, vol. 2: *1540–1840*, ed. Peter Clark (Cambridge University Press, 2000), on various urban "improvement schemes," though some British initiatives were, unusually, privately funded.

76. On the case of street lighting, which spread from Paris, where it was established in the late 17th century, to the French provinces; then from London to many of Britain's good-sized towns; and finally, via the Amsterdam model, which was originally the best in Europe, to cities like Berlin, Leipzig, and Cologne, see Darrin McMahon, "Illuminating the Enlightenment: Public Lighting Practices in the *Siècle des Lumières*," *Past and Present* 240, no. 1 (August 2018): 119–59. On the underside of similar developments, in this case in North America, see Jeremy Zallen, *American Lucifers: The Dark History of Artificial Light, 1750–1865* (University of North Carolina Press, 2010).

77. William Alexander, M.D., *The History of Women, from the earliest antiquity, to the present time* (Philadelphia, 1796 [Dublin, 1779]), 1:108.

78. [Robert Southey], *Letters from England by Don Manuel Alvarez Espriella* (London, 1808), 1:39, 58.

79. Clare Williams, ed., *Sophie in London, 1786, being the Diary of Sophie v. la Roche* (Jonathan Cape, 1933 [1788]), 87. Sophie van La Roche also published in the 1780s, as commercial ventures, accounts of her travels with various companions through the Netherlands, Switzerland, and France, as well as edited the periodical *Pomona: Für Teutschlands Töchter*, another source of travel writing for women. See especially Alison E. Martin, *Moving Scenes: The Aesthetics of German Travel Writing on England, 1783–1830* (Modern Humanities Research Association and Maney Publishing, 2008), chap. 2.

80. On this connection, see Pamela Cheek, *Heroines and Local Girls: The Transnational Emergence of Women's Writing in the Long Eighteenth Century* (University of Pennsylvania Press, 2019), esp. 1–2, 9.

81. Mary Ann Hanway, *Ellinor; or, The World As It Is: A Novel* (London, 1798), 162.

82. ECCO is the key source here for this corpus. Authors' given names here range from "a young lady" to "Mrs. Gomersall of Leeds."

83. An American Lady, *The Hapless Orphan; or, Innocent Victim of Revenge: A Novel* ([Boston], 1793), 93.

84. See, for example, Albinia Gwynn, *The Rencontre; or, Transition of a Moment: A Novel* (Dublin, 1785), 2:223, on the practice of shopping by proxy, depending on those "better versed in those matters" to go "chuse them [the articles] for me." Amanda Vickery makes the case, in *Women, Privilege and Power: British Politics, 1750 to the Present* (Stanford University Press, 2002), 22, for English women gaining a kind of de facto independence through their role as consumers as early as the 1720s.

85. Among works on consumption and the British novel, most of which also concentrate on the gendered dimension of the experience but not specifically choice, see Elizabeth Kowaleski-Wallace, *Consuming Subjects: Women, Shopping and Business in the Eighteenth Century* (Columbia University Press, 1997); Deidre Shauna Lynch, *The Economy of Character: Novels, Market Culture and the Business of Inner Meaning* (University of Chicago Press, 1998) and "Counter Publics: Shopping and Women's Sociability," in *Romantic Sociability: Social Networks and Literary Culture in Britain, 1770–1840*, ed. G. Russell and C. Tuite (Cambridge University Press, 2002), 211–36; and E. J. Clery, *The Feminization Debate in Eighteenth-Century England: Literature, Commerce and Luxury* (Palgrave Macmillan, 2004). More generally on the novel and the development of the modern individual, understood as female, see Nancy Armstrong, *How Novels Think* and *Desire and Domestic Fiction: A Political History of the Novel* (Oxford University Press, 1987).

86. See, for example, the work of the historians Daniel Roche and Timothy Breen. Roche insisted in the late 1980s that consumption in 18th-century France had led not to alienation, as Marxist critics had long argued, but to liberation, that is, "a new state of mind, more individualistic, more hedonistic, in any case more egalitarian and more free," as well as a trend toward self-expression ("Apparences révolutionnaires ou révolution des apparences," in *Modes et révolutions, 1780–1804* [Editions Paris-Musées, 1989], 111). Breen, in *The Marketplace of Revolution*, 151, similarly imagined American political independence in the 18th century as springing from the independence of the consumer: "the act of choosing could be liberating, even empowering, for it allowed them [ordinary men and especially ordinary women] to determine for themselves what the process of self-fashioning was all about." On the contemporary politics fueling such claims, see, too, François Furstenberg, "Atlantic History in the Neoliberal Age" (unpublished talk, 2015) and David Steigerwald, "All Hail the Republic of Choice: Consumer History as Contemporary Thought," *Journal of American History* 93, no. 2 (September 2006): 385–403.

87. Mrs. Gomersall, *The Citizen, A Novel* (London, 1790), 2:111–12.

88. Southey, *Letters from England*, 1:59.

89. Theresa Braunschneider, *Our Coquettes: Capacious Desire in the Eighteenth Century* (University of Virginia Press, 2009), 11.

90. As this anxiety applied especially to calico, see Chloe Wigston Smith, "'Callico Madams': Servants, Consumption and the Calico Crisis," *Eighteenth-Century Life* 31, no. 2 (2007): 29–53.

91. Sieur Louis Liger, *Le Voyageur fidèle, ou le guide des étrangers dans la ville de Paris* (Paris, 1715), 364. Similarly, Sophie von La Roche marvels, in a positive sense, that at a lamp seller's shop in London, "The highest lord and humble labourer may purchase here lamps of immense beauty and price or at a very reasonable figure, and both receive equally rapid and courteous attention" (*Sophie in London*, 142).

92. McKendrick, Brewer, and Plumb, *The Birth of a Consumer Society*, 53.

93. Here I follow William Sewell, in *Capitalism and the Emergence of Civic Equality*, to the extent that I imagine the advent of fashion did produce some new sense of social leveling and threats to privilege in the 18th-century public sphere; but it is worth noting that traditional status markers, like accent and manners, remained in play throughout this period and also that new status indicators came to the fore even if fabric was relatively democratized—to the advantage of yet more competitive consumption rooted in social differentiation.

94. Jones, "Coquettes and Grisettes," 36–38.

95. John Trusler, *The Way to Be Rich and Respectable: Addressed to Men of Small Fortune*, 4th ed. (London, 1776), 11.

96. On novelists' investment in highlighting *akrasia* at a moment when it was not central to philosophy, see Thomas Salem Manganaro, *Against Better Judgment: Irrational Action and Literary Invention in the Long Eighteenth Century* (University of Virginia Press, 2022).

97. Robert Campbell, *The London Tradesman* (1747), 115, cited in Lemire, *Fashion's Favorite*, 84. On the modification of products to suit taste, including whim, see, too, John Styles, "Product Innovation in Early Modern London," *Past and Present* 168, no. 1 (August 2000): 124–69.

98. Bernard Mandeville, *The Fable of the Bees: Part II* (London, 1729), 286, and *The Fable of the Bees; or, Private Vices, Public Benefits: [Part I]*, 3rd ed. (London, 1724), 406.

99. [Mrs. Margaret Holford], *Fanny, a novel, in a series of letters: Written by a lady* (London, 1785), 1:254–55.

100. [Frances Burney], *Camilla; or, A Picture of Youth* (London, 1796), book 6, chap. 2.

101. On the idea of addiction as a "willed compulsion," see Carl Erik Fisher, *The Urge: Our History of Addiction* (Penguin, 2022), though shopping addiction is not his focus. Another variant, described at the time, is the compulsive stealing of consumer goods, especially by well-heeled women unmotivated by need.

102. Helen Maria Williams, *Julia: A Novel* (Dublin, 1790), 1:33.

103. [Jane Austen], *Sense and Sensibility: A Novel. By a Lady* (London, 1811), chap. 26.

104. Mandeville, *The Fable of the Bees . . . [Part I]*, 405.

105. Kant, *Conjectures on the Beginning of Human History*, esp. 224.

106. von La Roche, *Sophie in London*, 87.

107. [Frances Burney], *Cecilia; or, Memoirs of an Heiress* (London, 1782), vol. 1, book 1, chap. 5.

108. [Frances Burney], *Evelina; or, The History of a Young Lady's Entrance into the World*, new ed. (London, 1784 [orig. 1778]), 1:21 (letter X).

109. Ibid., 1:235, 236 (letter XLV).

110. See *A Lady Travels: Journeys in England and Scotland from the Diaries of Johanna Schopenhauer*, ed. Ruth Michaelis-Jena and Willy Merson (Routledge, 1988), 138–39.

111. Jones, *Sexing "La Mode,"* 145.

112. David Owen, "What Happens to All the Stuff We Return?" *New Yorker*, August 14, 2023.

113. Alexander, *The History of Women*, 1:108.

114. *The Spectator*, August 11, 1712, no. 454, cited in Berry, "Polite Consumption," 387. See also "Lady Praise-All," in *The Female Tatler*, no. 67 (December 7–9, 1709), for whom "everything [in an India House] was displaced to oblige her ladyship's curiosity" but who "protested she shouldn't grudge to spend an estate on such things so prodigiously fine, drank a gallon of tea, and marched off without laying out Six-Pence" (*The Commerce of Everyday Life: Selections from The Tatler and The Spectator*, ed. Erin Mackie [Bedford/St. Martin's, 1998], 294). Defoe, too, complained in *The Complete English Tradesman*, 61, of ladies who go from one mercer's shop to another "to look upon their fine silks, to rattle and banter the shopkeepers, having not so much the least occasion, much less the intention, to buy anything."

115. Schopenhauer, *A Lady Travels*, 151.

116. Louis-Sébastien Mercier, *Parallèle de Paris et de Londres: Un inédit*, ed. Claude Bruneteau and Bernard Cottret (Didier Érudition, 1982), cited in Jones, *Sexing "La Mode,"* 167.

117. Burney, *Camilla*, book 7, chap. 1.

118. Mrs. [Jane] West, *A Tale of the Times* (London, 1799), 2:114–15.

119. [Frances Burney], *The Wanderer; or, Female Difficulties* (London, 1814), vol. 3, book 5, chap. 45. The description continues: "though they [ladies who frequented the shop] tried on hats and caps, till they put them out of shape; examined and tossed about the choicest goods, till they were so injured that they could only be sold at half price; ordered sundry articles, which, when finished, they returned, because they had changed their minds; or discovered they did not want them; still their consciences were at ease . . . if after two or three hours of lounging, rummaging, fault finding and chaffering, they purchased a yard or two of ribbon, or a few skanes of netting silk."

120. See Martín Monsalve Zanatti, "The History of Retailing in Latin America," in *Routledge Companion to the History of Retailing*, ed. Jon Stobart and Vicki Howard (Routledge, 2018), esp. 434; Benjamin Orlove, ed., *The Allure of the Foreign: Imported Goods in Postcolonial Latin America* (University of Michigan Press, 1997); and Jürgen Osterhammel, *The Transformation of the World: A Global History of the Nineteenth Century*, trans. Patrick Camiller (Princeton University Press, 2015), 234–36.

121. See Steven Bunker, *Creating Mexican Consumer Culture in the Age of Porfirio Díaz* (University of New Mexico Press, 2012) and María Isabel Baldasarre, "Fantasías parisienses y sastrerías londinenses: Moda, comercio y publicidad en Buenos Aires a fines del siglo XIX," *d'Obras* 14, no. 29 (2020): 270–93.

122. The original allegory, by the 5th-century BC Sophist Prodicus of Ceos, was known from Xenophon's *Memorabilia* and often evoked throughout the early modern era, especially once it was taken up by Renaissance Humanists. Important 18th-century versions include J. S. Bach, *Hercules at the Crossroads/Hercules auf dem Scheidewege* (secular cantata, 1733); Georg Friederich Handel, *The Choice of Hercules* (opera, 1750); Paolo de Matteis, *The Choice of Hercules* (painting after the Third Earl of Shaftesbury's instructions, intended as an illustration of his *A Notion of the Historical Draught or Tablature of the Judgment of Hercules according to Prodicus* published in French in 1712 and English in 1713); Joseph Addison, "The Choice of Hercules" (essay, 1709); William Shenstone, "The Judgement of Hercules" (poem, 1740?); Robert Lowth, "The Judgment of Hercules" (poem, 1743); Benjamin West, *The Choice of Hercules between Virtue and Pleasure* (painting, 1764); and even garden designs after this motif, as in the gardens of Stowe in Buckinghamshire. See Erwin Panofsky, *Hercules am Scheidewege und andere antike Bildstoffe in der neueren Kunst* (Teubner, 1930); Maren-Sofie Rostvig, "*Tom Jones* and the Choice of Hercules," in *Fair Forms: Essays in English Literature from Spenser to Jane Austen*, ed. Rostvig (D. S. Brewer, 1975), 147–77; and Peter N. Miller, "Hercules at the Crossroads in the Seventeenth and Eighteenth Centuries: Neo-Stoicism between Aristocratic and Commercial Society," in *République des Lettres, République des Arts: Mélanges offerts à Marc Fumaroli de l'Académie française*, ed. Christian Mouchel and Colette Nativel (Droz, 2008), 168–92.

123. [Rev. Joseph Spence], "The Choice of Hercules: A Lesson of Socrates; recorded by Xenophon," in *Moralities: or Essays, Letters, Fables; and Translations* (London, 1753), 141.

124. Joseph Spence, *Polymetis; or, An Enquiry Concerning the Agreement between the Works of the Roman Poets and the Remains of the Antient [sic] Artists* (London, 1747), 140.

125. See the most important abolitionist pamphlet of the century, [William Fox], *An Address to the People of Great Britain, on the Consumption of West-India Produce* (London, c. 1791), 3. Fox goes on to say: "The case now fully lies before us; and we have to make our choice, either to join ourselves with these manufacturers of human woe, or to renounce the horrid association" (11). Breen, in *The Marketplace of Revolution*, 190, takes boycotts in prerevolutionary North America as evidence that "the concept of freedom of choice was elevated into a right" prior to 1776; however, though boycotts can only be effective in a world in which consumer choice is

established practice, Breen does not make the necessary distinction between notions of private, personalized choice undergirding modern human rights principles and an older model of moral choice closer to the Hercules paradigm. Most later boycotts, including those associated with civil rights and nonconsumption models, follow on the old paradigm, remoralizing certain market choices over others, even as engagement is open to a wider public than some other forms of political protest.

126. Jonathan Sheehan and Dror Wahrman do not mention Hercules in *Invisible Hands*; but they do point out that "Judeo-Christian free will had always meant the freedom to choose between good and evil, right and wrong: that is to say, the freedom to make moral choices between weighted options that a prior determination had already placed in strict hierarchy to each other" (79), a way of seeing morality that was entirely consonant with the Hercules myth of the 18th century. Moreover, later retellings of the myth often incorporated reference to Matthew 7:13–14 on the choice between two gates and two roads. But see, too, the more secular distinction drawn between a republican, civic humanist or neo-Roman conception of freedom, on the one hand, and a market view focused on the exercise of "discretionary choice," on the other, as laid out in MacGilvray, *The Invention of Market Freedom*, 134.

127. See Tristram Hunt, *The Radical Potter: The Life and Times of Josiah Wedgwood* (Metropolitan Books, 2021). Among the many medallions that Wedgwood's company offered were ones depicting both abolitionist themes and the Choice of Hercules.

128. Sheldon Garon and Patricia Maclachlan, eds., *The Ambivalent Consumer: Questioning Consumption in East Asia and the West* (Cornell University Press, 2006), 88. See, too, Yamazaki Masakazu, "Signs of a New Individualism," *Japan Echo* 11, no. 1 (spring 1984), reproduced in *Years of Trial: Japan in the 1990s*, ed. Masuzoe Yoichi (Japan Echo, 2001), 297–314; and *Individualism and the Japanese: An Alternative Approach to Cultural Comparison*, trans. Barbara Sugihara (Japan Echo, 1994) on indigenous strains of individuality in different cultures. The focus here is on the 1970s, but many of the sales techniques associated with this consumer outlook—including an emphasis on display and female sales help—date from the advent, in the early 1900s, of the major Japanese department stores, which themselves drew on both Western models and retail traditions associated with 17th-century Japanese drapery stores; see esp. Brian Moeran, "The Birth of the Japanese Department Store," in *Asian Department Stores*, ed. Kerrie MacPherson (University of Hawaii Press, 1998), 141–76.

129. Trentmann, *Empire of Things*, 488. For a negative account of the ever-increasing commodification of childhood, see Juliet Schor, *Born to Buy: The Commercialized Child and the New Consumer Culture* (Scribner, 2004).

130. Commodity fetishism is described in the first chapter of Marx's *Capital: A Critique of Political Economy*, first published in 1867.

131. See Paul Lerner, *The Consuming Temple: Jews, Department Stores, and the Consumer Revolution in Germany, 1880–1940* (Cornell University Press, 2015), on how the ultimate modern choice purveyors—the Jewish owners of the great department stores of the Belle Époque—stood accused by critics of commercial culture of foisting a seductive and dangerous secular religion on vulnerable women.

132. There is a large literature on the history of critiques of consumer culture from Albert Hirschman, *Rival Views of Market Society and Other Recent Essays* (Viking, 1986) to Daniel Horowitz, *The Morality of Spending: Attitudes toward the Consumer Society in America, 1875–1940* (Ivan R. Dee, 1992).

133. Iris Murdoch, *The Sovereignty of Good* (Routledge, 2001 [1970]), 8.

134. Ibid., 34, 8.

135. On the distinctive forms of consumerism in the USSR, see, for example, Sheila Fitzpatrick, *Everyday Stalinism: Ordinary Life in Extraordinary Times, Soviet Russia in the 1930s* (Oxford

University Press, 1999), esp. 54–62; Amy Randall, *The Soviet Dream World of Retail Trade and Consumption in the 1930s* (Basingstoke, 2008); and Timo Vihavainen and Elena Bogdanova, eds., *Communism and Consumerism: The Soviet Alternative to the Affluent Society* (Brill, 2015).

136. Kunitz's comments in the 1962 Pop Art Symposium—cited in *Pop to Popism*, ed. Wayne Tunnicliffe and Anneke Jaspers (Prestel, 2015), 61—come just two years before the seminal *American Supermarket* exhibition at the Bianchini Gallery in New York, including works by six of the leading Pop artists (Warhol, Oldenberg, etc.), turned shopping into an art form; see Christoph Grunenberg, "The American Supermarket," in *Shopping: A Century of Art and Consumer Culture*, ed. Grunenberg and Max Hollein (Tate Liverpool, 2002), 171–78. It is worth noting that female Pop artists more often tackled the subject of woman herself, and especially her body, as a consumer item; see Angela Stief, *Power Up: Female Pop Art* (DuMont, 2011).

137. Michel Sanouillet and Elmer Peterson, eds., *The Essential Writings of Marcel Duchamp* (Thames and Hudson, 1975), 74.

138. Herbert Molderings, *Duchamp and the Aesthetics of Chance: Art as Experiment*, trans. John Brogden (Columbia University Press, 2010). On the subsequent history of chance as an artistic practice opposed to conscious choice, see, too, Margaret Iversen, *Chance* (MIT Press, 2010).

139. Louise Norton, "The Richard Mutt Case," *The Blind Man*, no. 2 (May 1917): 5.

140. Duchamp noted that "the choice [*le choix*] of these 'readymades' was never dictated by an aesthetic delectation. This choice was based on a reaction of visual indifference with at the same time a total absence of good or bad taste . . . in fact a complete anesthesia"; see *The Art of Assemblage*, ed. William C. Seitz (Museum of Modern Art, 1961). On the same question, see also Octavio Paz, "The Ready-Made," in Joseph Masheck, *Marcel Duchamp in Perspective* (Prentice Hall, 1975), 88.

141. See Helen Molesworth, "Rrose Sélavy Goes Shopping," in *The Dada Seminars*, ed. Leah Dickerman (National Gallery of Art, 2005), 173–89.

142. Claude-Rigobert Lefebvre de Beauvray, *Singularités diverses, en prose et en vers* ([Cosmopolis], 1753), 44.

Chapter 2

1. What Jefferson called "The Life and Morals of Jesus of Nazareth," completed primarily in 1819–20, is reproduced in facsimile as *The Jefferson Bible* (Smithsonian Books, 2011). The text is composed of cuttings related to moral teachings and history from printed New Testaments in four languages (English, French, Greek, and Latin), which Jefferson pasted in four columns onto blank pages and subsequently had bound as a book—an early example of what, since the 1970s, is sometimes called Cafeteria Christianity to emphasize that all the elements, whether precepts or practices, have been treated as "à la carte."

2. The (Protestant-derived) idea that religion is equivalent to a set of beliefs or propositions to which one gives assent as an individual and which one freely chooses in a kind of religious marketplace, unfettered by authority or social pressures, is fundamental to global norms concerning religious freedom today. But this conception of religion has been widely criticized as of late for the way in which it has, via European colonialism, missionary efforts, and then human rights initiatives, been imposed on the non-Protestant world, including parts of it in which religion is understood, attained, and experienced quite differently. See Talal Asad, "Thinking about Religion, Belief and Politics," in *The Cambridge Companion to Religious Studies*, ed. Robert Orsi (Cambridge University Press, 2012), 36–57; and Elizabeth Shakman Hurd, *Beyond Religious Freedom: The New Global Politics of Religion* (Princeton University Press, 2015).

3. The idea of freedom of expression is similarly subject to new scrutiny at the moment for its potential Western bias; for its falsity given the extent of speech regulations necessary for a

functioning democracy; and for the way it could be said to protect lying, the interests of the monied, and various forms of hate speech directed against minorities, all in the context of shifts in global technology that challenge its original justifications; see, for example, Brian Leiter, "The Case against Free Speech," *Sydney Law Review* 38 (2016): 407–39.

4. On the extent of human freedom in early Protestant teachings, see Martin Luther, "On Christian Freedom" (1520) and John Calvin, "Christian Freedom" (*The Institutes of Christian Religion*, chap. 19, book 3, 1536), as well as Hilary Gatti, *Ideas of Liberty in Early Modern Europe: From Machiavelli to Milton* (Princeton University Press, 2015), esp. chap. 2. On the significance of *adiaphora*, or things indifferent, see Ethan H. Shagan, *The Rule of Moderation: Violence, Religion and the Politics of Restraint in Early Modern England* (Cambridge University Press, 2011), 76; and Roland Bainton, *Erasmus of Christendom* (Scribner's, 1969), 184–85.

5. See Willem J. van Asselt et al., eds., *Reformed Thought on Freedom: The Concept of Free Choice in Early Modern Reformed Theology* (Baker Academic, 2010).

6. On the history of baptism from the Reformation onward, see Bryan D. Spinks, *Reformation and Modern Rituals and Theologies of Baptism: From Luther to Contemporary Practices* (Routledge, 2006). On the debate among 17th-century dissenters in British North America, see Holly Brewer, *By Birth or Consent: Children, Law, and the Anglo-American Revolution in Authority* (University of North Carolina Press, 2005), chap. 2.

7. For a clear explanation of this doctrine, see Andrew R. Murphy, *Conscience and Community: Revisiting Toleration and Religious Dissent in Early Modern England and America* (Penn State University Press, 2001).

8. John Locke, *A Letter Concerning Toleration* [written in Latin in Holland in 1685, published in Latin and English in 1689], ed. Ian Shapiro (Yale University Press, 2003), 219 for both. On this text, see, too, Mark Goldie, introduction to *A Letter Concerning Toleration and Other Writings* (Liberty Fund, 2010); John Dunn, "The Claim to Freedom of Conscience: Freedom of Speech, Freedom of Thought, Freedom of Worship?" in *From Persecution to Toleration: The Glorious Revolution and Religion in England*, ed. Ole Peter Grell, Jonathan Israel, and Nicholas Tyacke (Clarendon Press, 1991), 171–94; and John Marshall, *John Locke, Toleration, and Early Enlightenment Culture* (Cambridge University Press, 2006). For a contrary view, see Don Herzog, *Happy Slaves: A Critique of Consent Theory* (University of Chicago Press, 1989).

9. [Jonathan Clapham], *A Guide to The True Religion; or, A Discourse Directing to make a wise Choice of that Religion Men venture their Salvation upon* (London, 1668), 8.

10. There is an enormous literature on the history of toleration; see Ole Peter Grell and Robert W. Schribner, eds., *Tolerance and Intolerance in the European Reformation* (Cambridge University Press, 1996); Ole Peter Grell and Roy Porter, eds., *Toleration in Enlightenment Europe* (Cambridge University Press, 2006); Alexandra Walsham, *Charitable Hatred: Tolerance and Intolerance in England, 1500–1700* (Manchester University Press, 2006); and Hans Erich Bödeker, Clorinda Donato, and Peter Hans Reill, eds., *Discourses of Tolerance and Intolerance in the European Enlightenment* (University of California Press, 2009).

11. Pierre Bayle, *A Philosophical Commentary on These Words of the Gospel, Luke 14:23, "Compel Them to Come In, That My House May Be Full"* (Liberty Fund, 2005 [1686]), 209. According to David Wootton (see *John Locke: Political Writings* [Liberty Fund, 1993], introduction and 188), Locke also thought in market terms insofar as he argued in his earlier *An Essay Concerning Toleration* (1667) that if God cannot "compel me to buy a house," God cannot "force me his way to venture the purchase of heaven"; but the commercial analogy is less drawn out in this context.

12. William Temple, *Observations upon the United Provinces of the Netherlands* (London, 1673), 207, cited in Brad Gregory, *The Unintended Reformation: How a Religious Revolution Secularized Society* (Harvard University Press, 2012), 164, who does not discuss the rise of the marketplace metaphor, though he does note the novelty of treating religion as a matter of individual preference.

13. See Judith Pollmann, *Religious Choice in the Dutch Republic: The Reformation of Arnoldus Buchelius, 1565–1641* (St. Martin's Press, 1999) on the origins of this distinctiveness, but see also Ronnie Po-Chia Hsia and Henk Van Nierop, eds., *Calvinism and Religious Toleration in the Dutch Golden Age* (Cambridge University Press, 2009) on the limits.

14. Johan Meerman, *De Burgerlyke Vryheid* (Leiden, 1793), 16, cited in Wyger R. E. Velema, *Republicans: Essays on Eighteenth-Century Dutch Political Thought* (Brill, 2007), 165–66.

15. On the "free Choice" of "rational and free Agents," see Charles Chauncy, A.M., *The only Compulsion proper to be made Use of in the Affairs of Conscience and Religion: A Sermon Preach'd at the Old Brick Meeting-House in Boston, September 2d 1739* (Boston, 1739), 11. On "The special Endowment of his [man's] Nature, which constitutes him such, is the Power of Self-Determination, or Freedom of Choice; his being possessed of which is as self-evident, as the Explanation of the Manner of its operating, is difficult," see Ebenezer Gay, *Natural Religion as Distinguished from Reveal'd: A Sermon Preach'd … at Harvard-College in Cambridge, May 9. 1759* (Boston, 1759), 12, cited in John Corrigan, *The Hidden Balance: Religion and the Social Theories of Charles Chauncy and Jonathan Mayhew* (Cambridge University Press, 1987), 36.

16. Gilbert Tennent, *The Blessedness of Peace-Makers represented; and the Danger of Persecution considered; In Two Sermons, on Mat. V.9 preach'd at Philadelphia … in May 1759* (Philadelphia, 1765), 21–22, cited in J. William Frost, *A Perfect Freedom: Religious Liberty in Pennsylvania* (Cambridge University Press, 1990), 53.

17. On this argument in Leveller women's petitions, see Jacqueline Broad and Karen Green, *A History of Women's Political Thought in Europe, 1400–1700* (Cambridge University Press, 2009), chap. 10. It is important to note that this was not an argument for greater rights for women per se but rather a birthright claim for all humans.

18. In addition to Sir Kenelm Digby, *A Conference with a Lady about Choice of Religion* (Paris, 1638) and Edward Weston, *The Englishman Directed in the Choice of His Religion* (London, 1740), see Robert Manning, *England's Conversion … The Young Gentleman Directed in the Choice of His Religion* (Antwerp, 1725); George White, *The Englishman's Rational Proceedings in the Choice of Religion* (London, 1742); and [Daniel Turner], *Common Sense, or the Plain Man's Answer to the Question, whether Christianity be a Religion Worthy of our Choice in this Age of Reason* (London, n.d. [18th century]).

19. John Gother (a convert to Catholicism) suggests in *The Sincere Christian's Guide, in the Choice of Religion* (London, 1734) a parallel between shopping and picking a religion, while also insisting that there is a right course of action in all areas of choice-making that depends on ascertaining the right information; the passage quoted in the text continues: "For this we examine and look over Markets and Shops; for this we compare Houses, Situation and Air; for this we take all the best Information we can, and spare no Pains in asking Advice, that so we may not be deceiv'd in taking the worst, when better may be had" (5–6). On attitudes toward conscience in Catholicism in this period, see Nicole Reinhardt, "How Individual Was Conscience in the Early Modern Period? Observations on the Development of Catholic Moral Theology," *Religion* 45, no. 3 (2015): 409–28.

20. Barry Alan Shain, *The Myth of Individualism: The Protestant Origins of American Political Thought* (Princeton University Press, 1994), rightly stresses how differently liberty was understood in 18th-century North America, when it was still closely tied to Protestant thinking, than it is today—though this argument can be overdrawn too.

21. James McLachlan, "The Choice of Hercules: American Student Societies in the Early Nineteenth Century," in *The University in Society*, vol. 2: *Europe, Scotland and the United States from the 16th to the 20th Century*, ed. Lawrence Stone (Princeton University Press, 1974), 489.

22. Karl Marx, "On the Jewish Question" [1844], in *Marx on Religion*, ed. John Raines (Temple University Press, 2002), 58.

23. See Charles Taylor, *Sources of the Self: The Making of Modern Identity* (Harvard University Press, 1992), esp. part 2; and Jerrold Seigel, *The Idea of the Self: Thought and Experience in Western Europe since the Seventeenth Century* (Cambridge University Press, 2005), esp. chap. 6, for different takes on the development of this conception of self.

24. Ethan Shagan, *The Birth of Modern Belief: Faith and Judgment from the Middle Ages to the Enlightenment* (Princeton University Press, 2018), argues that, after the Reformation, belief went from being a "privileged condition" to a "private judgment, a space of autonomy in which one is ultimately answerable to no one but oneself." He labels the latter "modern belief" (4–6).

25. On the pragmatic reasons for the growth of religious pluralism in Europe starting in the 16th century, see Benjamin J. Kaplan, *Divided by Faith: Religious Conflict and the Practice of Toleration in Early Modern Europe* (Harvard University Press, 2007).

26. Voltaire, "The Ecclesiastical Ministry," in *The Philosophical Dictionary* (1764), in *The Works of Voltaire* (DuMont, 1901), 7:114–17.

27. See Immanuel Kant's famous essay "What Is Enlightenment?" (Berlin, 1784), but also Carl Friedrich Bahrdt, *On Freedom of the Press and Its Limits: For Consideration by Rulers, Censors, and Writers* (Vienna, 1787), in which "freedom to think" is linked to "freedom to share one's insights and judgments verbally or in writing" as "a sacred and inviolable human *right* that, as a *universal* human right, is above all the right of princes" (reproduced in full in *Early French and German Defenses of Freedom of the Press*, ed. John Christian Laursen and Johan van der Zander [Brill, 2003], see 127).

28. In the encyclical "Mirari Vos: On Liberalism and Religious Indifferentism" (1832), Pope Gregory XVI condemned, in order, indifferentism (the idea that salvation is possible by professing any religion as long as morality is maintained), liberty of conscience ("a pestilence"), freedom to publish and disseminate, and, finally, separation of church and state: https://www.papalencyclicals.net/greg16/g16mirar.htm. Compare with the rhetoric of Nicolas-Sylvestre Bergier (cited in Thomas Kselman, *Conscience and Conversion: Religious Liberty in Post-Revolutionary France* [Yale University Press, 2018], 25), who was still railing well into the 19th century against "the absurdity that every individual ought to decide for himself whether or not to have one [religion]."

29. Constitution of Year III (France), art. 354, reads: "Nul ne peut être empêché d'exercer, en se conformant aux lois, le culte qu'il a choisi."

30. John Brewer, *The Pleasures of the Imagination: English Culture in the Eighteenth Century* (Farrar, Straus and Giroux, 1997), 169.

31. On Protestant imperialism and early propaganda designed to attract new colonists from both Great Britain and continental Europe to different parts of the globe, see Owen Stanwood, *The Global Refuge: Huguenots in an Age of Empire* (Oxford University Press, 2020), 54–57; and, more specifically, Bertrand Van Ruymbeke, *From New Babylon to Eden: The Huguenots and Their Migration to Colonial South Carolina* (University of South Carolina Press, 2006), 25–60.

32. See Peter Berger, *The Heretical Imperative: Contemporary Possibilities of Religious Affirmation* (Anchor Press, 1979), 30–31, for a variant of this argument.

33. James Lackington, *Memoirs of the Forty-Five First Years of the Life of James Lackington*, 7th ed. (London, 1794), 251.

34. William Penn, *The Great Case of Liberty of Conscience* [London and Dublin, 1670], in *The Political Writings of William Penn*, ed. Andrew Murphy (Liberty Fund, 2002), 94, 233.

35. William Penn, *The Frame of Government of the Province of Pennsylvania in America* (London, 1682). See, too, his slightly earlier *England's Great Interest in the Choice of This New Parliament, Dedicated to all Her Freeholders and Electors* ([London], 1679), 4, in which he claimed "blind obedience" in religious matters was parallel to "blind obedience" in government and condemned both.

36. On the formation of Penn's colony, see Mary Maples Dunn, *William Penn: Politics and Conscience* (Princeton University Press, 1967) and Andrew Murphy, *Liberty, Conscience and Toleration: The Political Thought of William Penn* (Oxford University Press, 2016). On Pennsylvania's religious foundations, see, too, Sally Schwartz, *"A Mixed Multitude": The Struggle for Toleration in Colonial Pennsylvania* (New York University Press, 1987); Frost, *A Perfect Freedom*; and Murphy, *Conscience and Community*, chap. 5.

37. For the argument for the existence of market-based choice in multiple domains of early American life, including religion, see T. H. Breen and Timothy Hall, "Structuring Provincial Imagination: The Rhetoric and Experience of Social Change in Eighteenth-Century New England," *American Historical Review* 103, no. 5 (December 1998): 1411–39; and R. Laurence Moore, *Selling God: American Religion in the Marketplace of Culture* (Oxford University Press, 1994), chap. 1. For critiques, see Steve Bruce, *Choice and Religion: A Critique of Rational Choice Theory* (Oxford University Press, 1999) and especially Chris Beneke, "The Free Market and the Founders' Approach to Church-State Relations," *Journal of Church and State* 52, no. 2 (2010): 323–52. On the commodification of religion today, see James B. Twitchell, *Shopping for God: How Christianity Went from In Your Heart to In Your Face* (Simon & Schuster, 2007).

38. Beneke, "The Free Market," 335.

39. Jane Calvert, *Quaker Constitutionalism and the Political Thought of John Dickinson* (Cambridge University Press, 2009), 140.

40. Schwartz, *A Mixed Multitude*, 1.

41. See Theodore Thayer, "Town into City, 1746–1765," in *Philadelphia: A 300-Year History* (Norton, 1982), 101, though Thayer stresses that this was a small number in relation to the population as a whole.

42. Schwartz, *A Mixed Multitude*, 154.

43. On patterns of women's religious behavior in Anglophone North America, see Harry S. Stout and Catherine A. Brekus, "Declension, Gender, and the 'New Religious History,'" in *Belief and Behavior: Essays in the New Religious History*, ed. Robert P. Swierenga and Philip R. Vander-Meer (Rutgers University Press, 1991), 15–37; Catherine A. Brekus, *Strangers and Pilgrims: Female Preaching in America, 1740–1845* (University of North Carolina Press, 1998); and Chris Beneke, *Beyond Toleration: The Religious Origins of American Pluralism* (Oxford University Press, 2006), 13–14.

44. Richard Pointer, *Protestant Pluralism and the New York Experience: A Study of 18th-Century Religious Diversity* (Indiana University Press, 1988), 11 (Rev. Michael Christian Knoll in *Protocol of the Lutheran Church in New York City, 1702–1750* [United Lutheran Synod of New York and New England, 1958]) and 38 (Field Horne, ed., *The Diary of Mary Cooper: Life on a Long Island Farm, 1768–1773* [Oyster Bay Historical Society, 1981]).

45. Calvert, *Quaker Constitutionalism*, 145. The journal is printed as "The Journal of William Black," *Pennsylvania Magazine of History and Biography* 1, no. 3 (1877): 233–49.

46. See Frank Lambert, *"Pedlar in Divinity": George Whitefield and the Transatlantic Revivals, 1737–1770* (Princeton University Press, 2002), 47, 93, 179, on these negative terms. But Lambert also details how much Whitefield himself, who claimed to be on a mission to bring to the colonies a "choice cargo of heavenly wares" (47), made use of mercantile language and techniques in his revivals.

47. For various views on the First Great Awakening in North America, see Jon Butler, *Awash in a Sea of Faith: Christianizing the American People* (Harvard University Press, 1990); Timothy D. Hall, *Contested Boundaries: Itinerancy and the Reshaping of the Colonial American Religious World* (Duke University Press, 1994); Frank Lambert, *Inventing the "Great Awakening"* (Princeton University Press, 1999); and Douglas Winiarski, *Darkness Falls on the Land of Light: Experiencing Religious Awakenings in Eighteenth-Century New England* (University of North Carolina Press, 2017).

48. On women and evangelical religion in the 18th century and into the 19th, see Susan Juster, *Disorderly Women: Sexual Politics and Evangelicalism in Revolutionary New England* (Cornell University Press, 1994); Marilyn Westerkamp, *Women and Religion in Early America, 1600–1859: The Puritan and Evangelical Traditions* (Routledge, 1998); Catherine Brekus, "The Revolution in the Churches: Women's Religious Activism in the Early American Republic," in *Religion and the New Republic: Faith in the Founding of America*, ed. James H. Hutson (Rowman and Littlefield, 2000), 115–36; and, more generally, Nicole Eustache and Ann M. Little, "'Ineradicably Untidy': Women and Religion in the Age of Atlantic Empires," *Early American Studies* 17, no. 4 (fall 2019): 397–413.

49. Beneke, *Beyond Toleration*, 75.

50. Samuel Davies to John Brunskill, January 4, 1750, cited in Hall, *Contested Boundaries*, 120.

51. Beneke, "The Free Market," 336.

52. Tennent, *The Blessedness of Peace-Makers represented; and the Danger of Persecution considered*, 21.

53. See Juster, *Disorderly Women*, 199–200. That this pattern had deep roots is made evident in Sherrin Marshall Wyntjes, "Women and Religious Choices in the Sixteenth-Century Netherlands," *Archiv für Reformationsgeschichte* 75, no. 1 (1984): 276–89, which documents that some prominent women made religious choices on their own considerably earlier, albeit as often for political, social, and economic reasons as for spiritual ones. On the continuation of this pattern into the 19th century, when women across classes continued to attend multiple meetings of different sects and to choose, independently in some cases of their husbands or family tradition, the one that responded most to their needs, see Rachel Cope, "'Our Piety Began to Be a Little Different than the Old Way': How Three Nineteenth-Century Women Made Personal Religious Choices," *New York History* 92, no. 4 (fall 2011): 247–67; John H. Wigger, *Taking Heaven by Storm: Methodism and the Rise of Popular Christianity in America* (Oxford University Press, 1998); and Lincoln Mullen, *The Chance of Salvation: A History of Conversion in America* (Harvard University Press, 2017).

54. David D. Hall, ed., *Lived Religion in America: Toward a History of Practice* (Princeton University Press, 1997).

55. Corrigan, *The Hidden Balance*, 38, 42–43.

56. Beneke, "The Free Market," 336–37.

57. See Brewer, *By Birth or Consent* and Courtney Weikle-Mills, *Imaginary Citizens: Child Readers and the Limits of American Independence, 1640–1868* (Johns Hopkins University Press, 2013).

58. Isaac Stiles, *A Looking-glass for Changlings* (New London, 1743), 15, cited in Hall, *Contested Boundaries*, 67, 115.

59. See *Equiano's Travels* (originally *The Interesting Narrative of the Life of Olaudah Equiano*), ed. P. Edwards (Heinneman, 1996 [1789]): "On a signal given, (as the beat of a drum) the buyers rush at once into the yard where the slaves are confined, and make choice of that parcel they like best. . . . In this manner, without scruple, are relations and friends separated, most of them never to see each other again" (28).

60. On the growing religious pluralism of early America, see Pointer, *Protestant Pluralism*; Beneke, *Beyond Toleration*; and William Hutchinson, *Religious Pluralism in America: The Contentious History of a Founding Ideal* (Yale University Press, 2003). Kevin Butterfield, in *The Making of Tocqueville's America: Law and Association in the Early United States* (University of Chicago Press, 2015), states that the proportion of Americans belonging to churches roughly doubled between 1776 and 1850 (21–22) and cites Jon Butler's claim that 10,000 new churches were built between 1780 and 1820, then another 40,000 in the next forty years (33).

61. Nathan Hatch, *The Democratization of American Christianity* (Yale University Press, 1989), 25, notes that the number of newspapers in the United States similarly went from 90 to 370 between the years 1790 and 1810 alone.

62. On printing and bookselling in early Philadelphia, see Rosalind Remer, *Printers and Men of Capital: Philadelphia Book Publishers in the New Republic* (University of Pennsylvania Press, 1996).

63. On lending libraries (commercial and social) and women patrons in 18th-century North America, see Hugh Amory and David D. Hall, eds., *A History of the Book in America*, vol. 1: *The Colonial Book in the Atlantic World* (University of North Carolina Press, 2007), 402–3. In the 19th century, the distinction between commercial and social or membership libraries started to decline. For Britain, see Giles Mandelbrote and K. A. Manley, eds., *The Cambridge History of Libraries in Britain and Ireland*, vol. 2: *1640–1850* (Cambridge University Press, 2006) on various types and their different patrons and lending practices.

64. For these quotes, see James Raven, "Social Libraries and Library Societies in Eighteenth-Century North America," in *Institutions of Reading: The Social Life of Libraries in the United States*, ed. Thomas Augst and Kenneth Carpenter (University of Massachusetts Press, 2007), 51, 44, respectively.

65. On modernity meaning "the choice of what *sort* of Jew to be within an increasingly wide and varied range of religious, cultural, and social possibilities" (italics mine), see Tony Michels and Mitchell Hart, eds., *The Cambridge History of Judaism*, vol. 8: *The Modern World, 1815–2000* (Cambridge University Press, 2017), introduction, 3–4.

66. On the combination of evangelical religion, with its emphasis on taking moral responsibility for one's own salvation, and moral reform efforts, especially among women, see Teresa Anne Murphy, *Ten Hours' Labor: Religion, Reform and Gender in Early New England* (Cornell University Press, 1992) and Christine Stansell, *City of Women: Sex and Class in New York, 1789–1860* (University of Illinois Press, 1987).

67. Howe, *Making the American Self*, 116.

68. See Bryan Garsten, "Constant on the Religious Spirit of Liberalism," in *The Cambridge Companion to Constant*, ed. Helena Rosenblatt (Cambridge University Press, 2009), 286–312.

69. Emma Griffin, *Liberty's Dawn: A People's History of the Industrial Revolution* (Yale University Press, 2013), 200–201, documents that in England too, evangelical Christianity or nonconformity brought to the working class, starting in 1790s, more options in churches (meaning both multiple denominations and different chapels of any given faith), more opportunities for the sampling of different preachers on different occasions, and more effort on the part of ministers to court those who showed up. In the United States, the Second Great Awakening differed from the first in terms of its scale, its increasing relationship to markets and print, and its greater institutionalization; see Robert Abzug, *American Reform and the Religious Imagination* (Oxford University Press, 1994).

70. For the text of the popular early 19th-century American hymn "Freedom of the Human Will" ("Know then that every soul is free / To choose his life and what he'll be / For this eternal truth has giv'n / That God will force no man to heav'n"), see Hatch, *The Democratization of American Christianity*, 231. On Charles Finney, see James E. Block, *A Nation of Agents: The American Path to a Modern Self and Society* (Harvard University Press, 2002), 394–96, who quotes Finney's "Sinners, Bound to Change Their Own Hearts" from *Sermons on Important Subjects* (1836) to the effect that "he [every human] has the understanding to perceive and weigh; he has conscience to decide upon the nature of moral opposites; he has the power and liberty of choice." On Finney's conception of conversion as "voting" for the Lord and against the Devil, see Michael Kazin, *The Populist Persuasion: An American History*, 2nd ed. (Cornell University Press, 2017), 11. According to Gregory Wills, *Democratic Religion: Freedom, Authority and Church Discipline in the Baptist South, 1785–1900* (Oxford University Press, 2003), 51, in the antebellum period, Baptist churches even granted voting privileges to female members, and often to enslaved people of both sexes, with the idea that ecclesiastical power resided in every member equally.

71. Specifically on women's involvement, see Rodney Hessinger, *Smitten: Sex, Gender and the Contest for Souls in the Second Great Awakening* (Cornell University Press, 2022).

72. Mullen, *The Chance of Salvation*, 4–5. On the broader theme of the growth in the 19th-century United States of the idea of the autonomous self controlling his (or, less often, her) own destiny through choices made, see Robert Wiebe, *The Opening of American Society: From the Adoption of the Constitution to the Eve of Disunion* (Vintage, 1984), esp. chap. 8 ("Revolution in Choices"); Howe, *Making the American Self*; and Block, *A Nation of Agents*.

73. Though religious tests for federal officeholding are banned in the Constitution, it was not until *Torcaso v. Watkins* in 1961 that the U.S. Supreme Court held that religious tests for state officeholding violate the First Amendment.

74. Robert Baird, *Religion in America* (New York, 1856 [1844]), 79, cited in Block, *A Nation of Agents*, 378.

75. On attachment to community and social institutions rooted in rules and regulations and its consistency with strains of individualism in the early republic, see Butterfield, *The Making of Tocqueville's America*. This is in contrast to critiques of communitarians like Charles Taylor (see *The Ethics of Authenticity* [Harvard University Press, 1992] and *A Secular Age* [Harvard University Press, 2007]), who insist that if all choices are equally valid and none are more worthy or significant than others since the only framework for assessment is the self, fulfillment in community attachment becomes impossible, and we are reduced to what he calls "atomism."

76. On the history of commonplacing in early modern Europe, see Ann Moss, *Printed Commonplace-Books and the Structuring of Renaissance Thought* (Clarendon Press, 1996); Kevin Berland, Jan Kirsten Gilliam, and Kenneth A. Lockridge, eds., *The Commonplace Book of William Byrd of Westover* (University of North Carolina Press, 2001), introduction; and Adam Smyth, "Commonplace Book Culture: A List of Sixteen Traits," in *Women and Writing, c. 1340–c. 1650: The Domestication of Print Culture*, ed. Anne Lawrence-Mathers and Phillipa Hardman (University of York Press, 2010).

77. The Bodleian Library lists among John Locke's papers, for example, the following manuscripts: Locke c. 42A: medical and scientific commonplace book, 1676–94; Locke c. 42B: non-scientific commonplace book, 1679–92; Locke d. 1: commonplace book primarily on ethical issues, 1679–92; and Locke e. 17: commonplace book including material from student years.

78. Rick Kennedy, "Historians as Flower-Pickers and Honey Bees: Cotton Mather and the Commonplace-Book Tradition of History," in *Cotton Mather and Biblia Americana: America's First Bible Commentary: Essays in Reappraisal*, ed. Reiner Smolinksi and Jan Stievermann (Baker Academic, 2011), 261–76, esp. 263.

79. See *Jefferson's Legal Commonplace Book*, ed. David Konig and Michael Zuckert (Princeton University Press, 2019 [orig. 1762–67]) and *Jefferson's Literary Commonplace Book*, ed. David Wilson (Princeton University Press, 1989 [orig. 1758–72]).

80. John Locke, *A New Method of Making Common-Place-Books* (London, posthum., 1706). The original French version was published in Amsterdam in 1686 in the second volume of Jean Le Clerc's *Bibliothèque universelle*. See Richard Yeo, "John Locke's 'New Method' of Commonplacing: Managing Memory and Information," *Eighteenth-Century Thought* 2 (2004): 1–38; Michael Stolbert, "John Locke's 'New Method of Making Common-Place Books': Tradition, Innovation and Epistemic Effects," *Early Science and Medicine* 19, no. 5 (special issue: A Natural History of Early Modern Writing Technologies) (2014): 448–70; and Ellen B. Brewster, "Locke, Stock and Booksellers: Commonplace Book Fashions in the Long Eighteenth Century," *Oxford Research in English* 6 (spring 2018): 11–37.

81. At least ten different ones were published on the two sides of the Atlantic between 1770 and 1820; see Earle Havens, *Commonplace Books: A History of Manuscripts and Printed Books from Antiquity to the Twentieth Century* (Yale University Library, 2001), 58.

82. See Adam Smyth, *"Profit and Delight": Printed Miscellanies in England, 1640–1682* (Wayne State University Press, 2004) and Leah Price, *The Anthology and the Rise of the Novel from Richardson to George Eliot* (Cambridge University Press, 2000).

83. [Vicesimus Knox, ed.], *Elegant Extracts; or, Useful and Entertaining Pieces of Poetry, Selected for the Improvement of Youth, in Speaking, Reading, Thinking, and Composing; and in the Conduct of Life* (London, 1789 and many other editions), iii. Not surprisingly for an 18th-century English compendium, Robert Lowth's "The Choice of Hercules" is included among the offerings.

84. See "Monsieur Le Clerc's Character of Mr. Lock's [*sic*] Method, with his Advice about the Use of Common-Places," in Locke, *A New Method of Making Common-Place-Books*, ii.

85. Jonathan Swift, *A Complete Collection of Genteel and Ingenious Conversation, according to the Most Polite Mode and Method, Now Used at Court, and in the Best Companies of England* (1738), cited in the introduction to *The Commonplace Book of William Byrd*, 32.

86. Michel de Montaigne, "Of Books" [1578–80], in *The Complete Essays of Montaigne*, ed. and trans. Donald Frame (Stanford University Press, 1958), book 2, chap. 10, 296.

87. Ann Blair, *Too Much to Know: Managing Scholarly Information before the Modern Age* (Yale University Press, 2010), notes that cutting from the printed or manuscript page and pasting excerpts into new books was already a reading practice in the early modern era and had some parallels in manuscript culture; the 16th-century humanist scholar Conrad Gesner, for example, cut up his letters to distribute them among his papers by subject (217). But cutting and pasting as an intellectual practice clearly grew in frequency as print became more abundant and also cheaper over time.

88. See Locke, *An Essay Concerning Human Understanding* (Oxford University Press, 1975 [1694]), 238, 328–48, in which he explains (a) that consciousness is inseparable from thinking or mental activity and it is "this that makes every one to be, what he calls *self*; and thereby distinguishes himself from all other thinking things, in this alone consists *personal identity*" (chap. 27, 335), but also (b) that "Liberty" is "having the Power of doing, or forebearing to do, according as the Mind shall chuse or direct" (chap. 21, 238) and lack of liberty is having that mental power checked.

89. On newer uses and forms of commonplacing, including in the production of a self, see Kenneth Lockridge, *The Commonplace Books of William Byrd and Thomas Jefferson and the Gendering of Power in the Eighteenth Century* (New York University Press, 1992); Havens, *Commonplace Books*; Lucia Dacome, "Noting the Mind: Commonplace Books and the Pursuit of Self in Eighteenth-Century Britain," *Journal of the History of Ideas* 65 (2004): 603–25; and David Allan, *Commonplace Books and Reading in Georgian England* (Cambridge University Press, 2010).

90. See Stephen Simpson, "MS being a choice Farrago of new poems" (July 16, 1773), Beinecke Library (Yale University), Osborn Collection, MS c 563.

91. Michael Merill and Sean Wilentz, eds., *The Key of Liberty: The Life and Democratic Writings of William Manning, A Laborer, 1747–1814* (Harvard University Press, 1983). See, too, Martyn Lyons, "New Readers in the Nineteenth Century: Women, Children, Workers," in *A History of Reading in the West*, ed. Guglielmo Cavallo and Roger Chartier (University of Massachusetts Press, 1990), 313–44.

92. According to Heidi Brayman Hackel and Catherine Kelly, eds., *Reading Women: Literacy, Authorship, and Culture in the Atlantic World, 1500–1800* (University of Pennsylvania Press, 2008), 2, by 1800 nearly half of English and Anglo-American women had alphabetic literacy, and by the mid-19th century, U.S. census data indicates that 90 percent of white women and men were literate. The latter statistic just about matches the German Reich, where literacy reached about 88 percent by 1871. Moreover, by the end of the 19th century, the gap between male and female literacy rates had all but disappeared across most of the West, though rural rates were much lower than urban ones everywhere (Lyons, "New Readers," 313, 315).

93. Price, *The Anthology*, 38. See, too, Tom Keymer, *Richardson's Clarissa and the Eighteenth-Century Reader* (Cambridge University Press, 1992), 76.

94. Price, *The Anthology*, 13–14.

95. According to the *History of the Book in America*, 1:397, in England by the first third of the 18th century, and in the North American colonies after about 1750, both writers and booksellers began specifically to court women readers. They did so in booksellers' catalogs and newspaper ads, as well as in the title pages and introductions of collections of poetry, sermons, essays on moral conduct, and works of fiction.

96. See Anon., *A New Commonplace Book; being an improvement on that recommended by Mr. Locke ... Equally adapted to the Man of Letters and the Man of Observation, the Traveller and the Student, and forming an useful and agreeable Companion, on the Road; and in the Closet*, 2nd ed. (London, 1799).

97. Rebecca Bushnell, "Harvesting Books," in *A Culture of Teaching: Early Modern Humanism in Theory and Practice* (Cornell University Press, 1996), 117–43. See, too, Kennedy, "Historians as Flower Pickers and Honey Bees"; pickers has, of course, a double meaning, one related to conscious selection among alternatives and one not.

98. On Englesing's claims about a "reading revolution" directed toward extensive reading of a wide variety of published work rather than intensive reading of a small corpus of great books, as well as the ensuing debate among historians, see Robert Darnton, "First Steps Towards a History of Reading," in *The Kiss of Lamourette: Reflections in Cultural History* (Norton, 1990), 165–66.

99. See *A Common-Place Book of John Milton*, ed. John Horwood (Camden Society, 1876). Dissenters figure heavily among Anglophone commonplacers in both the 17th and 18th centuries.

100. John Milton, *Paradise Lost* (London, 1667), book 3, lines 122–23.

101. See *Areopagitica; a speech of Mr. John Milton for the liberty of unlicenc'd printing, to the Parlament of England* [London, 1644], ed. John Hales (Clarendon Press, 1889), 25. On this idea of the reader as chooser, see Stephen Dobranski, *Readers and Authorship in Early Modern England* (Cambridge University Press, 2005), 208; and Thomas Fulton, *Historical Milton: Manuscript, Print and Political Culture in Revolutionary England* (University of Massachusetts Press, 2010), esp. 98–107.

102. On the Swedish law (which critically did not extend to religion) and on the Danish one (which was rescinded shortly thereafter), see Ulla Carlsson and David Goldberg, eds., *The Legacy of Peter Forsskal: 250 Years of Freedom of Expression* (Nordicom, 2017), esp. 39–70; and Ulrick Langen and Frederik Stjernfelt, *The World's First Full Press Freedom: The Radical Experiment of Denmark-Norway, 1770–1773* (De Gruyter Oldenbourg, 2022). The idea of listeners' or readers' rights runs through many 18th-century discussions of freedom of expression; see, for example, Elie Luzac, *An Essay on Freedom of Expression* (Leiden, 1749), reproduced in *Early French and German Defenses of Freedom of the Press*, in which the Huguenot author states that everyone has a right and obligation to seek the truth, "but since this search cannot be made without knowing ideas opposed to our own, it is abundantly clear that men must not be deprived of the means to know the ideas of others" (46).

103. Milton, *Areopagitica*, 19, 17–18.

104. Stephen Colclough, "Recovering the Reader: Commonplace Books and Diaries as Sources of Reading Experience," *Publishing History* 44 (January 1998): 5–37, suggests something similar but is more focused on the specific act of reading.

105. The first manuscript is labeled "Memorable Facts, Events, Opinions, Thots [*sic*], Etc., Recorded by Benjamin Rush in the Years 1789–1791" and the second is labeled "Benjamin Rush Commonplace Book, 1792–1813." They can be found in the American Philosophical Society, Philadelphia as, respectively, Mss.B.R89me and Mss.B.R89c. They are also reproduced as *The*

Autobiography of Benjamin Rush: His "Travels through Life" Together with His Commonplace Book for 1789–1813, ed. George W. Corner (Greenwood Press, 1948); for quotations and encounters, see 302, 303, 242, 239, and 244.

106. Ibid., 164–65.

107. See "Of the Mode of Education Proper in a Republic" (1798), in *Selected Writings of Benjamin Rush*, ed. Dagobert D. Runes (Philosophical Library, 1947), 89.

108. See "On the Different Species of Mania" (1786), in *Selected Writings of Benjamin Rush*, 211–20. Rush's "Commonplace Book" also incorporated some of his own lectures, including "On the Medical Jurisprudence of the Mind" (1810), which further detailed the doctor's thoughts on the sources and social effects of faulty reasoning.

109. Rush's *An Enquiry into the Effects of Spirituous Liquors upon the Human Body, and their Influence upon the Happiness of Society* was first published in Philadelphia in 1784 and came out in many subsequent editions. On the distinctiveness of Rush's take on alcohol addiction as a problem not of habit but of loss of free agency, including control over one's choices, and thus a disease of the will, see Fisher, *The Urge*, esp. 49.

110. Deborah Norris Logan diaries, Philadelphia, 1815–1839, Historical Society of Pennsylvania, Logan Family Papers, coll. 0379, vols. 28–44. See here vol. 28 (January 1, 1815–January 17, 1816). The best text on this subject is Susan M. Stabile, "Female Curiosities: The Transatlantic Female Commonplace Book," in *Reading Women*, ed. Hackel and Kelly. Deborah Norris Logan married the grandson of the well-known book collector (and first secretary of the colony under William Penn) James Logan, whose family published, following the gift of his books to the Philadelphia public, an inventory titled *Catalogus Bibliothecae Loganianae* in 1760.

111. Stabile, "Female Curiosities," 221–23.

112. Elizabeth Phillips Payson notebook/commonplace book, Charlestown, Massachusetts, 1806–1825, Schlesinger Library, Radcliffe Institute, Harvard University, A/P347; on this example, see Hackel and Kelly, *Reading Women*, 58.

113. Amy (Hornor) Coates commonplace book, Philadelphia, 1790–1810, Historical Society of Pennsylvania, Coates and Reynell Family Papers, box 57, vol. 106, folder 3.

114. Elizabeth Galloway commonplace book, Philadelphia, 1819–26, Historical Society of Pennsylvania, Ms. Am. 06866.

115. See, for example, Anna Lowell commonplace book, Massachusetts, 1839, and Charlotte Haven Brooks commonplace book, no location, 1826–32, both in Harvard Libraries, Ms. Am 1206 and Ms. Am 889.20, respectively.

116. See Anna Jane Mitchell McAllister commonplace book, Philadelphia, 1832–36, Penn Libraries, Ms. Coll. 947. French literary journals figure similarly in the reading diary and commonplace book kept by an anonymous French woman in Versailles; see her reading diary and commonplace book of 1819–22 in Penn Libraries, Ms. Coll. 865. It is not uncommon to find excerpts in different languages in the same books.

117. For examples of women's incorporation of images of their own making, see Ann Perrin commonplace book, New Jersey or New York, 1824–66, Penn Libraries, Ms. Coll. 369 (which includes a drawing of her own notebook, labeled "Album"), and Anon., commonplace book, Scotland, 1823–26, Penn Libraries, Ms Coll. 1129. For an example of extensive incorporation of satirical engravings alongside newspaper clippings, see Lady Harriet Plunkett's commonplace book, possibly Ireland, c. 1815–20, Yale Libraries, Osborn fd5, which also includes her own decorations.

118. See Logan's first commonplace book (1808), described in Stabile, "Female Curiosities," 221.

119. Logan diaries, vol. 33 (January 1, 1823–May 31, 1824).

120. Ibid., vol. 28 and vol. 35 (March 19, 1825–October 29, 1825), respectively.

121. Ibid., vol. 28.

122. Ibid., vol. 44 (December 11, 1838–January 17, 1839), which is the final volume. Her late life complaints include such exclamations as "I have not even the pleasures of a pen and ink worth a button." Writing is for her a very material practice.

123. See Antonia Forster, "Book Reviewing," in *The Cambridge History of the Book in Britain*, vol. 5: *1695–1830*, ed. Michael Suarez and Michael Turner (Cambridge University Press, 2009), 631–48, which focuses on the founding of the *Monthly Review* in 1749. On antecedents, see Patricia Gael, "The Origins of the Book Review in England, 1663–1749," *The Library* 13, no. 1 (March 2012): 63–89. Subsequent British journals included the *Critical Review* (f. 1756), the *Edinburgh Review* (f. 1802), and the *Quarterly Review* (f. 1809), all containing an early form of product reviews.

124. For the former, see Thaddeus Mason Harris, *A Selected Catalogue of Some of the Most Esteemed Publications in the English Language Proper to Form a Social Library; with an Introduction upon the Choice of Books* (Boston, 1793), iv, which promised to follow the dictates of the late 18th-century Anglican essayist Vicesimus Knox to "attempt to suggest some general habits, which may tend to facilitate selection" for those at a distance from the city or for those who "find it extremely difficult to separate the most valuable compositions from the many worthless works among which they are crouded [sic] in shops." For the latter, see Charles Joseph Gloriot and Claude-Marie Paul Tharin, *Bibliothèque d'un littérateur et d'un philosophe chrétien; ou, Recueil propre à diriger dans le choix des lectures* (Besançon, 1820), who developed a scale by which to measure a specific book's qualities (piq = piquant, orig = original, vér = true, etc.) and promised to distinguish what choices were most suitable for young people, women, Christians, and even well-informed people who were wracked with doubt. Similar titles include [probably John Whiston], *Directions for a Proper Choice of Authors to Form a Library, which may both improve and entertain the mind, and be of real use in the conduct of Life* (London, 1766) and Thomas Frognall Dibdin, *The Library Companion; or, The young man's guide, and the old man's comfort, in the choice of a library* (London, 1824), as well as a host of etiquette books for both sexes. Catalogs of distinguished older private collections were also frequently used as models for building one's own library; see Alicia Montoya, "Building the *Bibliothèque choisie*, from Jean Le Clerc to Samuel Formey: Library Manuals, Review Journals, and Auction Catalogues in the Long Eighteenth Century," in *Book Trade Catalogues in Early Modern Europe*, ed. Arthur Der Weduwen, Andrew Pettegree, and Graeme Kemp (Brill, 2021), 426–62.

125. *Critical Review*, cited in Brewer, *The Pleasures of the Imagination*, 193.

126. On the various dangers associated with women's reading, see Jacqueline Pearson, *Women's Reading in Britain, 1750–1835: A Dangerous Recreation* (Cambridge University Press, 1999); Suellen Diaconoff, *Through the Reading Glass: Women, Books and Sex in the French Enlightenment* (State University of New York Press, 2005); and Patricia Howell Michaelson, *Speaking Volumes: Women, Reading and Speech in the Age of Austen* (Stanford University Press, 2002), esp. 152–53.

127. The caption to this image reads, in a parody of female choice-making logic, as follows: "'Pray, my dear Mr. Page,' cried a pretty lisper, looking over a Catalogue, 'will you let me have that dear *Man of Feeling*, I have so long waited for: Well, this will do for one. No. 1889, *Cruel Disappointment*, for another. *Reuben, or Suicide*, high ho! No. 1746, I suppose he killed himself for love. *Seduction*, yes, I want that more than any thing. *Unguarded Moments*, ah we all have our unguarded moments. *True Delicacy*, No. 2 that must be a silly thing by the title. *School of Virtue*, heaven knows mamma gives me enough of that. *Test of Filial Duty*, at any rate she puts me to that test pretty often. *Mental Pleasures*, worse and worse! I'll look no longer. Oh! stay a moment—*Mutual Attachment, Assignation, Frederick or the Libertine*, just add these Mr. Page, and I shall not have to come again until the day after to-morrow.'"

128. Weikle-Mills, *Imaginary Citizens*, 115.

129. Mary Wollstonecraft, *A Vindication of the Rights of Woman*, ed. D. L. Macdonald and Kathleen Sherf (Broadview, 1997 [London, 1792]), 332, 195.

406   NOTES TO CHAPTER 2

130. Jean-Jacques Rousseau, *Emile, or Education*, trans. Barbara Foxley (Dent, 1911 [1762]), book 4.

131. William Godwin, "Of Choice in Reading," in *The Enquirer, Reflections on Education, Manners and Literature, in a series of essays* (London, 1797), 129–46.

132. Wollstonecraft, *A Vindication*, 333, 195, 105. Resistance to fashion bound together many religious and political radicals of the 1790s.

133. Mrs. [Anna] Jameson, *A Commonplace Book of Thoughts, Memories, and Fancies, Original and Selected*, 2nd ed. (London, 1855), preface.

134. Virginia Woolf, *A Room of One's Own* (London, 1929).

135. Jane Austen, *Mansfield Park* (London, 1814), chap. 40.

136. Ellen Gruber Garvey, *Writing with Scissors: American Scrapbooks from the Civil War to the Harlem Renaissance* (Oxford University Press, 2013), chap. 5.

137. Sue Davis, *The Political Thought of Elizabeth Cady Stanton* (New York University Press, 2008), 185–95, see 189 for this citation from Stanton, *The Woman's Bible* (Northeastern University Press, 1993 [orig. 1895–98]), part 2, 8.

138. John Stuart Mill, *The Subjection of Women* [1869], reproduced in *The Basic Writings of John Stuart Mill*, introduction by J. B. Schneewind (Random House, 2002), 140, 210.

139. Harriet Taylor, "The Enfranchisement of Women" (review essay on *New York Tribune for Europe*, issue of October 29, 1850), originally published in *Westminster and Foreign Quarterly Review* 55, no. 109 (July 1851): 149–61, reproduced in *Women, the Family, and Freedom: The Debate in Documents*, vol. 1: *1750–1880*, ed. Susan Groag Bell and Karen M. Offen (Stanford University Press, 1983), see 292 for quotation.

140. Compare resolution seven of the Second Wooster Convention (in Elizabeth Cady Stanton, Susan B. Anthony, and Matilda Joslyn Gage, eds., *History of Woman Suffrage* [New York, 1881], 1:826): "That we deny the right of any portion of the species to decide for another portion, or of any individual to decide for another individual what is and what is not their 'proper sphere'; that the proper sphere for all human beings is the largest and highest to which they are able to attain; what this is, can not [*sic*] be ascertained without complete liberty of choice; woman, therefore, ought to choose for herself what sphere she will fill." The theme of no distinct woman's sphere was already central to the American women's rights movement, especially as defined by Stanton, but it had not been previously linked so explicitly to choice. Wendell Phillips, speaking at the opening of the Second Wooster Convention, noted "in drawing up some of these resolutions, I have used very freely the language of a thoughtful and profound article in the *Westminster Review* . . . [which] states with singular clearness and force the leading arguments for our reform, and grounds of our claim in behalf of woman" (ibid., 1:227). Taylor's essay also entered French discourse after being published by Jeanne Deroin in *L'Almanach des Femmes* in 1852.

141. Mill, *The Subjection of Women*, 176.

142. Ibid., 142.

143. Ibid., 141.

144. On these non-English editions, see Eileen Hunt Botting and Sean Kronewitter, "Westernization and Women's Rights: Non-Western European Responses to Mill's *Subjection of Women*, 1869–1908," *Political Theory* 40, no. 3 (August 2012): 466–96, see 469. For a more focused study of international impact, see Douglas Howland, *Personal Liberty and Public Good: The Introduction of John Stuart Mill to Japan and China* (University of Toronto Press, 2005), esp. chaps. 3 and 4.

145. On socialist women's rights arguments in the 19th century, see Barbara Taylor, *Eve and the New Jerusalem: Socialism and Feminism in the Nineteenth Century* (Pantheon, 1983); and for the later period, Charles Sowerwine, *Sisters or Citizens? Women and Socialism in France since 1876*

(Cambridge University Press, 1982) and Anne Lopes and Gary Roth, *Men's Feminism: August Bebel and the German Socialist Movement* (Humanity Books, 2000). Socialist and liberal women's rights arguments in this era should be thought of less as antithetical than as related forms of critique and aspiration; the former stretched the case of the latter to include more criticism of institutions themselves, starting with marriage, and more emphasis on the provision of social rights, as will become clear in the next chapter.

146. Frederick Douglass, "Woman Suffrage Movement," *New National Era* (October 20, 1870), in *Frederick Douglass on Women's Rights*, ed. Philip S. Foner (Greenwood Press, 1976), 94.

147. Maria Deraismes, *Eve dans l'humanité*, ed. Laurence Klejman (Côté Femmes, 1990 [1891]), 41.

148. On the history of the term "feminism," see Karen Offen, "Sur l'origine des mots 'féminisme' et 'féministe,'" *Revue de l'histoire moderne et contemporaine* 34, no. 3 (1987): 492–96. For a counterhistory that does not root feminism entirely in Western trends or terms, see Lucy Delap, *Feminisms: A Global History* (University of Chicago Press, 2020).

149. See *The Autobiography of John Stuart Mill*, ed. Charles W. Eliot (P. F. Collier and Son, 1909), 161, in which the philosopher claimed that *On Liberty* was fully "our joint production," written together by Taylor (who died the year before publication) and himself. Scholars have been debating the extent of Taylor's contribution ever since.

150. On John Stuart Mill's distinctive conception of liberty (and its differences from that of Kant), see Gerald Dworkin, ed., *Mill on Liberty: Critical Essays* (Rowman and Littlefield, 1997) and Nancy Hirschmann, *Gender, Class and Freedom in Modern Political Theory* (Princeton University Press, 2008), chap. 5.

151. Mill, *On Liberty* [1859], in *The Basic Writings of John Stuart Mill*, 60.

152. *Autobiography of John Stuart Mill*, 34. According to one of his more recent biographers, Mill was an exceptionally "autobiographical thinker: for him the political and the personal were inseparable"; see Richard Reeves, *John Stuart Mill: Victorian Firebrand* (Atlantic, 2007), 8.

153. F. A. Hayek, ed., *John Stuart Mill and Harriet Taylor: Their Correspondence and Subsequent Marriage* (Routledge and Kegan Paul, 1951), 168.

154. Charles Darwin, *On the Origin of the Species by Means of Natural Selection* (London, 1859), 61. On this choice of metaphor, see Robert M. Young, "Darwin's Metaphor: Does Nature Select?" *The Monist* 55, no. 3 (July 1971): 442–503. Darwin is referring in this passage primarily to the selection process used by humans in domestic breeding and in the cultivation of plants, but his own choice of term is clearly an effort to explain a complex and invisible process by means of an analogy that builds on something familiar and bodily. To that end, Darwin repeatedly gives intentions and goals to something he calls "Nature," while also anthropomorphizing it as "she."

155. On this connection, see especially Alan Ryan, *The Making of Modern Liberalism* (Princeton University Press, 2012), part 3.

156. Charles Dupont-White, *Essai sur les relations du travail* (Paris, 1846), 346, quoted in Helena Rosenblatt, *The Lost History of Liberalism: From Ancient Rome to the Twenty-First Century* (Princeton University Press, 2018), 148.

Chapter 3

1. There is not much serious literature on dance cards, but see *Collection de 124 carnets de bal du XVIIIe siècle formée par M. Bernard Franck* (Gerschel, 1902); Fritz Bernhard and Elke Dröscher, *Ballspenden* (Harenberg, 1979); Brigitte Holl, ed., *Ballspenden: Kostbarkeiten aus galanter Zeit: Katalog* (Heeresgeschichliches Museum [Vienna], 1990); Uwe Schlottermüller, "Zwischen unentbehrlich und unbekannt: Die TanzKarte," *Tanzen* 11, no. 3 (1993): 16–19; and

especially Monika Fink, *Der Ball: Eine Kulturgeschichte des Gesellschaftstanzes im 18. und 19. Jahrhundert* (Studien Verlag, 1996), 52–59; and Henri Joannis-Deberne, *Carnets de bal: Mémoire de l'ephémère* (Musée de Carouge, 2004). They shared formal properties in the 19th century with restaurant menus, which sometimes took the form of a printed piece of paper and other times appeared as a leather-bound book with a silk cord attached to the spine.

2. See Émile Zola, "The Ball-Program," in *Stories for Ninon*, trans. Edward Vizetelly (Heinemann, 1895 [orig. *Contes à Ninon*, Paris, 1864]), 16–27.

3. See Christopher Bayly, *The Birth of the Modern World, 1780–1914* (Wiley Blackwell, 2003), on the global factors that increased knowledge of elite habits among the wider population during the 19th century.

4. On the development of *contracts*, or mutual transfers of rights, as the basic tool and standard of market exchange, rooted in *consent*, or the meeting of individual minds or wills when it came to such agreements, the standard work is Patrick Atiyah, *The Rise and Fall of Freedom of Contract* (Oxford University Press, 1979), but see, too, Herzog, *Happy Slaves* and Amy Dru Stanley, *From Bondage to Contract: Wage Labor, Marriage and the Market in the Age of Slave Emancipation* (Cambridge University Press, 1998).

5. Marx's own critique focused in part on the limits of rights as a language for creating conditions of true equality. For an example of how this line of argumentation developed into a discussion of the deceptiveness of free choice in the context of social and economic inequality, see Marcuse, *One Dimensional Man*, esp. 7.

6. The term "Hobson's Choice," which dates from the 17th century, refers possibly to Thomas Hobson, a late 16th-/early 17th-century stable owner in Cambridge, England, who reputedly always offered his customers the choice of the horse closest to the door or no horse at all. Hobson's Choice came to mean a particular kind of false choice structured in this way, a scenario that Mill decried on more than one occasion.

7. On the idea that the self-determining individual was a role only open to men in the emerging liberal order and, further, that the new social contract was built on the subordination of women, see Carole Pateman, *The Sexual Contract* (Stanford University Press, 1988); Christine Fauré, *Democracy without Women: Feminism and the Rise of Liberal Individualism in France*, trans. Claudia Gorbman and John Berks (Indiana University Press, 1991 [1985]); Geneviève Fraisse, *Muse de la raison: La démocratie exclusive et la différence des sexes* (Alinéa, 1989); and Isabel V. Hull, *Sexuality, State, and Civil Society in Germany, 1700–1815* (Cornell University Press, 1996). For the extension of this argument to race too, see Carole Pateman and Charles W. Mills, *Contract and Domination* (Polity, 2007).

8. Jane Austen, *Northanger Abbey* (London, 1817), chap. 10. This is the fourth of five ball scenes that structure this novel, moving the key protagonists, with advances and setbacks, inexorably toward sorting out who should marry whom. For two different takes on the larger theme of choice in Austen's work, see Richard Handler and Daniel Segal, *Jane Austen and the Fiction of Culture* (University of Arizona Press, 1990), chap. 4; and Michael Suk-Young Chwe, *Jane Austen, Game Theorist* (Princeton University Press, 2013).

9. Mary Astell, *Some Reflections upon Marriage* (London, 1700), 22.

10. "Consent" is sometimes used synonymously with "choice"; but generally, consent is a much more limited ideal—it means agreeing to someone else's terms—and does not suggest either the range of defined options or the autonomy associated with active choice-making. On the limits of consent, a key word in today's sexual ethics, see Geneviève Fraisse, *Du Consentement: Essai* (Seuil, 2017).

11. See Braunschneider, *Our Coquettes*, 97–98, on the meaning of the term "The Choice." See, too, plays like Paul Hiffernan's *The Lady's Choice* (originally performed in 1756 as *The Maiden Whim* in London) and novels like *The Precipitate Choice; or, The history of Lord Ossory and Miss*

Rivers... by a lady (London, 1772, but also Boston and Dublin editions), in which "choice" in the title necessarily links the text to the classic marriage plot.

12. John Witte, *From Sacrament to Contract in Marriage, Religion and Law in the Western Tradition*, 2nd ed. (Westminster John Knox Press, 2012), insists on continuity up until the middle of the 20th century.

13. John Winthrop, Speech to the Massachusetts General Court (July 3, 1645), cited in Nancy Cott, *Public Vows: A History of Marriage and the Nation* (Harvard University Press, 2000), 13. See, though, Don Herzog, *Household Politics: Conflict in Early Modern England* (Yale University Press, 2013), for the importance of thinking about the gap between theory and lived experience regarding such norms.

14. On the rise of the idea of companionate marriage in England, see esp. John R. Gillis, *For Better, For Worse: British Marriages, 1600 to the Present* (Oxford University Press, 1985). On the history of this idea more generally, see Anthony Giddens, *The Transformation of Intimacy: Sexuality, Love and Eroticism in Modern Societies* (Stanford University Press, 1992); Stephanie Coontz, *Marriage, a History: How Love Conquered Marriage* (Penguin, 2006); and Sabine Melchior-Bonnet and Catherine Salles et al., eds., *Histoire du mariage* (R. Lafont, 2009). A summary of the historiographical debate can be found in Jeffrey Watt, *The Making of Modern Marriage: Matrimonial Control and the Rise of Sentiment in Neuchâtel, 1550–1800* (Cornell University Press, 1992), 1–23.

15. On marital choice as revealed by correspondences, see Dena Goodman, "Marital Choice and Marital Success: Reasoning about Marriage, Love, and Happiness," in *Family, Gender, and Law in Early Modern France*, ed. Suzanne Desan and Jeffrey Merrick (Penn State University Press, 2009), 26–61; and, for a slightly later moment, Denise Z. Davidson, "'Happy' Marriages in Early Nineteenth-Century France," *Journal of Family History* 37, no. 1 (2012): 23–35, though it is important to keep in mind that sentimental norms could have invaded the language of courtship and marriage but not necessarily extended to social practices.

16. Michaelson, *Speaking Volumes*, 160, points out that the question in Richardson's *Clarissa* is "Do women have the right to refuse the partner chosen by their parents?" and the question in Jane Austen's novels is more often "Can a woman find a marriage partner of whom her parents will approve?"

17. On the history of the idea of companionate marriage specifically in France, see James Traer, *Marriage and Family in Eighteenth-Century France* (Cornell University Press, 1980); David Denby, *Sentimental Narrative and the Social Order in France, 1760–1820* (Cambridge University Press, 1994); and Maurice Daumas, *Le Mariage amoureux: Histoire du lien conjugal sous l'Ancien Régime* (Armand Colin, 2004).

18. See Denis Diderot, *Supplément au voyage de Bougainville, ou dialogue entre A et B sur l'inconvénient d'attacher des idées morales à certaines actions physiques qui n'en comportent pas* (written in 1772, published posthum. in 1796). Compare Morelly's *Code de la Nature, ou le véritable esprit des lois* (1755) and also Voltaire's articles "Divorce," in his *Dictionnaire philosophique* (1764) and "Adultère," in *Questions sur l'Encyclopèdie* (1770).

19. On libertine thinking in 18th-century France, see Peter Cryle and Lisa O'Connell, eds., *Libertine Enlightenment: Sex, Liberty, and License in the Eighteenth Century* (Palgrave Macmillan, 2004). The expression "plaisirs de choix" figures in the Marquis de Sade's *La Nouvelle Justine, ou les malheurs de la vertu, suivie de l'histoire de Juliette, sa soeur* (Paris, 1797), 6:221. One question is how much libertinism should be seen as a philosophical position versus a form of justification for practices that already existed among aristocratic men in the late Old Regime.

20. For overviews of feminist thought in 18th-century France, especially around the terms of marriage, see Karen Offen, *European Feminisms, 1700–1950: A Political History* (Stanford University Press, 2000), esp. 35–37; and Karen Green, *A History of Women's Political Thought in Europe, 1700–1800* (Cambridge University Press, 2014).

21. On the Revolution's effects on family law and ideals alike, see Traer, *Marriage and the Family in Eighteenth-Century France*; Irène Théry and Christian Biet, eds., *La Famille, la loi, l'état: De la Révolution au Code Civil* (Imprimerie nationale, 1989); Lynn Hunt, *The Family Romance of the French Revolution* (University of California Press, 1992); and esp. Suzanne Desan, *The Family on Trial in Revolutionary France* (University of California Press, 2004).

22. On early debates around divorce, as well as its gradual institutionalization, see Roderick Phillips, *Putting Asunder: A History of Divorce in Western Society* (Cambridge University Press, 1988) and, for comparison, Lawrence Stone, *The Road to Divorce: England, 1530–1987* (Oxford University Press, 1995) and Norma Basch, *Framing American Divorce: From the Revolutionary Generation to the Victorians* (University of California Press, 1999). For the quotation, see *Loi qui détermine les causes, le mode et les effets du Divorce* (Paris, September 20, 1792).

23. Charles-Louis Rousseau, *Essai sur l'éducation et l'existence civile et politique des femmes, dans la constitution françoise* (Paris, 1790), 31.

24. Desan, *The Family on Trial*, 16.

25. Madeleine de Scudéry, *Clélie, histoire romaine* (Paris, 1660), book 2, cited in Karen Offen, *The Woman Question in France, 1400–1870* (Cambridge University Press, 2017), xv.

26. On the relationship of feminism to abolitionism in both French and Anglo-American contexts, see Stanley, *From Bondage to Contract*; Karen Sánchez-Eppler, *Touching Liberty: Abolition, Feminism and the Politics of the Body* (University of California Press, 1993); Karen Offen, "How (and Why) the Analogy of Marriage with Slavery Provided the Springboard for Women's Rights Demands in France, 1640–1848," in *Women's Rights and Transatlantic Antislavery in the Era of Emancipation*, ed. Kathryn Kish Sklar and James Brewer Stewart (Yale University Press, 2007), 57–81; Claire Midgely, *Women against Slavery: The British Campaigns, 1780–1870* (Routledge, 1992); and Kathleen Brown, *Undoing Slavery: Bodies, Race, and Rights in the Age of Abolition* (University of Pennsylvania Press, 2023). It is important to note that claims of "slavery" remained potent even after the era of abolitionism as a way to challenge all forms of servility, a rhetorical conflation that is sometimes criticized now as having worked to minimize the unique horrors of chattel slavery in practice.

27. Harriet Jacobs, *Incidents in the Life of a Slave Girl, Written by Herself* (Boston, 1861), cited in Amy Dru Stanley, "Slave Breeding and Free Love: An Antebellum Argument over Slavery, Capitalism and Personhood," in *Capitalism Takes Command: The Social Transformation of Nineteenth-Century America*, ed. Michael Zakim and Gary J. Kornblith (University of Chicago Press, 2012), 119–44, see 142.

28. On Garrison's arguments, see Henry Mayer, *All on Fire: William Lloyd Garrison and the Abolition of Slavery* (St. Martin's, 1998). See, too, Robert Finley's lecture of 1839, "True and False Religion," in which he claimed that the essence of slavery is "being obligated to choose against our feelings and inclinations," cited in Stanley, "Slave Breeding," 143.

29. Claire Démar, *Appel d'une femme au peuple sur l'affranchissement de la femme* (Paris, 1833), in *Textes sur l'affranchissement des femmes (1832–33)*, ed. Valentin Pelosse (Payot, 1976), esp. 21.

30. Hollis Clayson, *Painted Love: Prostitution in the Art of the Impressionist Era* (Yale University Press, 1991), discusses how the illusion of independent choice on the part of both parties was central to the whole conceit, giving way to moral condemnations of women who participated in prostitution but also, variously, exposés of their exploitation and celebrations of their modernity.

31. See Anon., *Lettre à Madame *** sur le divorce* (n.p., 1790), cited in Desan, *The Family on Trial*, 36, translation lightly modified based on the original.

32. Recent accounts of the ideals and practices upholding marriage in 19th-century France include Patricia Mainardi, *Husbands, Wives and Lovers: Marriage and Its Discontents in Nineteenth-Century France* (Yale University Press, 2003); Agnès Walch, *Histoire du couple en France de la*

Renaissance à nos jours (Ouest-France, 2003); Michelle Perrot, *La Vie de famille au XIXe siècle* (Points, 2015); and Jean-Claude Bologne, *Histoire du couple* (Perrin, 2016).

33. In the United States, too, the Revolution was a turning point in the forging of new—and lasting—notions of self-fulfillment and voluntary contractualism; see Jay Fliegelman, *Prodigals and Pilgrims: The American Revolution against Patriarchal Authority, 1750–1800* (Cambridge University Press, 1982), esp. chap. 5; Ellen K. Rothman, *Hands and Hearts: A History of Courtship in America* (Basic Books, 1984); Karen Lystra, *Searching the Heart: Women, Men, and Romantic Love in Nineteenth-Century America* (Oxford University Press, 1989); and Hendrik Hartog, *Man and Wife in America: A History* (Harvard University Press, 2002).

34. Guillaume Le Roberger, *Bureau de confiance pour les mariages, ses bases et son organisation,* also called *Établissement national pour faciliter les mariages* ([Paris, March 1790]), 12. On the history of such agencies, see also Jean-Claude Bologne, *Histoire du célibat et des célibataires* (Fayard, 2007), 217–18.

35. On this journal, see Jennifer Jones, "Personals and Politics: Courting *la citoyenne* in *Le courrier de l'hymen,*" *Yale French Studies,* no. 101 (2001): 171–81.

36. See Jean-Claude Bologne, *Histoire de la conquête amoureuse: De l'antiquité à nos jours* (Seuil, 2007), 240, on the rise of "want-ads" related to marriage.

37. Hansun Hsiung and Elena Serrano, in "Introduction: Epistemologies of the Match," *Isis* 12, no. 4 (December 2001): 760–65, attempt to historicize algorithmically driven dating platforms as products of a long search for a technical solution to a particular knowledge problem: identifying and securing amorous partners.

38. On "foires aux amoureux" in various towns in Belgium and on the "marché aux filles" in Artois in France, see the brief discussion in Melchior-Bonnet and Salles et al., *Histoire du mariage,* 793. See, too, E. P. Thompson, "The Selling of Wives," in *Customs in Common: Studies in Traditional Popular Culture* (New Press, 1991), 404–66.

39. On social dancing in the 19th century, and especially the significance of the ball (public or private) as a social site, see François Gasnault, *Guinguettes et lorettes: Bals publics à Paris au XIX siècle* (Aubier, 1986); Fink, *Der Ball*; [Claire Rousier], *Histoires de bal: Vivre, représenter, recréer le bal* (Cité de la musique, 1998); and Henri Joannis-Deberne, *Danser en société: Bals et danses d'hier et d'aujourd'hui* (Bonneton, 1999). There is not much scholarship specifically on dancing masters, but they were often treated both as authorities in the ways of elites *and* as untrustworthy on account of their aping of social prestige that they did not have and their excessive, bordering on effeminate attention to manners.

40. The literature on social dance in the 19th-century novel, much of which focuses on the novels of Jane Austen, includes Timothy Dow Adams, "To Know the Dancer from the Dance: Dance as Metaphor of Marriage in Four Novels of Jane Austen," *Studies in the Novel* 14, no. 1 (spring 1982): 55–65; Handler and Segal, *Jane Austen and the Fiction of Culture*; Cheryl Wilson, *Literature and Dance in Nineteenth-Century Britain: Jane Austen to the New Woman* (Cambridge University Press, 2009); Sarah Davies Cordova, *Paris Dances: Textual Choreographies in the Nineteenth-Century French Novel* (International Scholars Publishers, 1999); and Sylvie Jacq-Mioche, "Le bal dans la littérature romanesque française," in *Histoires du bal,* ed. Rousier, 141–52. See, too, the excerpts in Allison Thompson, *Dancing through Time: Western Social Dance in Literature, 1400–1918, Selections* (McFarland, 1998).

41. On the quadrille and especially its late years and decline, see Jean-Michel Guilcher, *La Contredanse: Un tournant dans l'histoire française de la danse* (Editions Complexe et Centre national de la danse, 2003 [1969]), 177–92.

42. F[élicien] de Ménil, *Histoire de la danse à travers les âges* (A. Picard & Kaan, 1905), 189.

43. Elizabeth Aldrich, "Social Dancing in Schubert's World," and Enno Kraehe, "The Congress of Vienna," both in *Schubert's Vienna,* ed. Raymond Erickson (Yale University Press, 1997),

119–40 and 55–76, respectively. Aldrich points out how highly regulated all aspects of dancing, from hours to masks, were in early 19th-century Vienna.

44. Sections of the narrative of Robert Schumann's *Carnaval*, Op. 9 (1834–35), include "Valse noble," "Valse allemande," and "Coquette." Dance manuals make clear that popular waltzes called "Coquette" were in circulation in the same era as well (see de Ménil, *Histoire de la danse*, 192).

45. On the waltz, see Eduard Reeser, *The History of the Waltz*, trans. W.A.G. Doyle-Davidson (Continental Book Co., 1949); P.J.S. Richardson, *The Social Dances of the Nineteenth Century in England* (Herbert Jenkins, 1960); Ruth Katz, "The Egalitarian Waltz," in *What Is Dance? Readings in Theory and Criticism*, ed. Roger Copeland and Marshall Cohen (Oxford University Press, 1983), 521–32; and esp. Rémi Hess, *La Valse: Révolution du couple en Europe* (A. M. Métailié, 1989) and "Waltz," in *The International Encyclopedia of Dance*, ed. Selma Jeanne Cohen (Oxford University Press, 1996), 6:359–62.

46. For example, Domingo Ibarra, in *Colección de bailes de sala, y método para aprenderlos sin Ausilio de Maestro*, 2nd ed. (Mexico, 1862), 12–14, discusses the waltz in a special section dedicated to "dances performed by two people forming a single couple."

47. [Henri] Cellarius, *La Danse des salons* (Paris, 1847), 14, 8. Translations immediately spread the work widely. One English version, called *Fashionable Dancing*, was published in 1847 by David Bogue in London, and another was published, also in 1847, as *The Drawing Room Dances* by E. Churton in London and again, by Dinsmore and Co., in New York in 1858. A Swedish edition, titled *Etthundra moderna Parisiska Cotillon-turer*, was published in 1847 in Stockholm, and a German edition called *Hundert neueste Pariser Cotillon-Touren* was published in 1847, and again in 1855, in Leipzig, followed by an Erfurt edition circa 1860. Others, in multiple languages, copied Cellarius's dance descriptions without credit.

48. See, on Germany but applicable to France too, David Sabean, "Aesthetics of Marriage Alliance: Class Codes and Endogamous Marriage in the 19th-Century Propertied Classes," in *Family History Revisited: Comparative Perspectives*, ed. Richard Wall et al. (University of Delaware Press, 2001), 122–32. Guilcher, in *La Contredanse*, esp. 144–45, discusses dancing as a particularly socially beneficial skill for early 19th-century parvenus because it could be learned.

49. Cordova, *Paris Dances*, 225.

50. On fears of the effects of social dancing and, especially, the waltz, see Hess, *La Valse*; Elizabeth Aldrich, *From the Ballroom to Hell: Grace and Folly in Nineteenth-Century Dance* (Northwestern University Press, 1991); Mark Knowles, *The Wicked Waltz and Other Scandalous Dances: Outrage at Couple Dancing in the 19th and Early 20th Centuries* (McFarland, 2009); and more generally, Ann Wagner, *Adversaries of Dance: From the Puritans to the Present* (University of Illinois Press, 1997).

51. On waltzing leading to vertigo and spasms, see, for example, Donald Walker, *Exercises for Ladies* (London, 1836), 149, cited in Aldrich, *From the Ballroom to Hell*, 19–20.

52. De Maistre, cited in Joannis-Deborne, *Danser en société*, 14; and Charles Fourier, *Théorie des quatre mouvements et des destinées générales* [originally 1808 but especially influential in the 1830s and 1840s], in his *Oeuvres complètes* (1966–68), 1:130. Utopian socialists were often eager to eliminate competition from marriage markets as well as from markets for workers.

53. See, for example, the Saint-Simonian tract *Paris dansant, ou les filles d'Hérodiade, folles danseuses des bals publics* (Paris, 1845).

54. Similar expressions exist in other languages; for example, women stuck on the margins of a ball in French are said to "faire tapisserie" and in German they are similarly "Mauerblümchen."

55. Anon., *A Guide to the Ball Room: Being a Complete Compendium of the Etiquette of Dancing . . . by a Man of Fashion* (London, [184-]), xii–xiii.

56. Honoré de Balzac, "The Sceaux Ball," in *The Works of Honoré de Balzac*, ed. George Saintsbury (Jefferson Press, 1901), 5:18, 21. The novella was originally published as "Le Bal de Sceaux ou le Pair de France" in *Scènes de la vie privé* in 1830.

57. Ibid., 41–42.

58. See the critical apparatus to Gustave Flaubert, *Madame Bovary*, trans. Eleanor Marx Aveling, ed. Margaret Cohen, 2nd ed. (Norton, 2004 [1857]), as well as Dominick LaCapra, *Madame Bovary on Trial* (Cornell University Press, 1982) and Christine Haynes, "The Politics of Publishing during the Second Empire: The Trial of 'Madame Bovary' Revisited," *French Politics, Culture and Society* 23, no. 2 (summer 2005): 1–27, see 4. It is worth noting that ball scenes figured in Flaubert's work from its earliest days, much as they did for Balzac; see Eric Gans, *The Discovery of Illusion: Flaubert's Early Works, 1835–1837* (University of California Press, 1971) and Juliette Azoulai, "Flaubert dansomane: Scènes de bal des années 1840," in *Flaubert, histoire et étude de moeurs*, ed. Azoulai and Gisèle Séginger (Presses universitaires de Strasbourg, 2019), 125–38.

59. Flaubert, *Madame Bovary*. This passage was read in full by the prosecutor, Ernest Pinard, who claimed this as one of the "lascivious paintings" that characterize this novel and make it a celebration of adultery (see 318, 320–21).

60. By contrast to the prosecutor, who condemned Flaubert for not condemning his heroine, the defense lawyer argued that it is the waltz itself, not Mme. Bovary's response, which is lascivious, and that Flaubert was actually a strict moralist—which was probably not true either (see ibid., 356).

61. Gasnault, *Guinguettes et lorettes*.

62. See the trial record, in Flaubert, *Madame Bovary*, 635.

63. Cellarius, *The Drawing Room Dances*, 6.

64. See J. H. Gourdoux-Daux, maître de danse, *De l'Art de la Danse, considéré dans ses vrais rapports avec l'éducation de la jeunesse*, 3rd ed. (Paris, 1823 [orig. 1804 and 1811]). The English translation comes from *Elements and principles of the art of dancing, as used in the polite and fashionable circles, also rules of deportment and descriptions of manners of civility, appertaining to that art: from the French of J. H. G., by V. G.* (Philadelphia, 1817), 89.

65. See Eugène Giraudet, *La Danse, la tenue, le maintien, l'hygiène et l'éducation* (Paris, 1882), 23–29, on the bodily decorum associated with invitations, and 32–33, on verbal formulas for invitations depending on the type of ball, and the age and status of the lady being invited, and whether one wants to ask for the next dance or, via dance card, one later in the evening. See similarly Anon., *True Politeness: A Handbook of Etiquette for Gentlemen* (Philadelphia, 1849), on rules for what to talk about and with whom in varied scenarios.

66. Anon., *The Ballroom Preceptor and Polka Guide; comprising the most esteemed quadrilles, galopades, mazourkas and the other fashionable dances of the season*, 6th ed. (London, 1846), 16–17.

67. Mrs. H. O. Ward, *Sensible Etiquette of the Best Society, Customs, Manners, Morals, and Home Culture* (Philadelphia, 1878), cited in Aldrich, *From the Ballroom to Hell*, 114.

68. Zola, "The Ball-Program," 21.

69. *The Ball-Room Guide, A Handy Manual for All Classes of Society* (New York and London, 186-), 30, cited in Aldrich, *From the Ballroom to Hell*, 113.

70. Zola, "The Ball-Program," 19, 20.

71. Eugène Giraudet, *Traité de la danse, vol. 2: Grammaire de la danse et du bon ton à travers le monde et les siècles depuis le singe jusqu'à nos jours* (Paris, 1900).

72. For descriptions of the purpose and function of cotillons, the best sources are dance manuals, some of which, starting in the 1850s (post-Cellarius), specialize; see, for France: Laborde, *Le Cotillon* (Paris, 1853); Gustave Desrat, *Le Cotillon* (Paris, 1855) and *Le Cotillon:*

Vade-mecum du conducteur de cotillon (Paris, 1881); Philippe Gawlikowski, *Guide complet de la danse, contenant . . . toutes les figures du cotillon . . .* (Paris, 1858); Charles Périn fils, *Le Cotillon: Soixante figures choisies* (Paris, [1876]) and *Le Cotillon: Théorie et musique* (Paris, [1881]); and Henri de Soria, *Le Cotillon: Théorie complète* (Paris, [1899]). Similar guides were published in the second half of the 19th century in London, New York, Philadelphia, Florence, Vienna, and Madrid, among other cities. The phenomenon took off in the 1820s (it was admitted at court in 1827), and the first guide to their form and music seems to be the now rare *Le Cotillon: Danse nouvelle avec douze figures variées, et choréographie* (Paris, c. 1825), in Harvard's Houghton Library, which already includes figures like "La Trompeuse" and "Le Prisonnier." See, too, the American guide *The German: How to Give It. How to Lead It. How to Dance It* (Chicago, 1879).

73. Cellarius, *Drawing Room Dances*, 96 (#23).

74. Ibid., 88–89 (#7).

75. Laborde, *Le Cotillon*, 2.

76. Cellarius, *Drawing Room Dances*, 109 (#47).

77. Desrat, *Le Cotillon: Vade-mecum du conducteur de cotillon*, 15. This dance is also described in other terms in Desrat's *Méthode de la Danse de Salon* (Paris, [c. 1861]) and *Le Cotillon* (1855), 16.

78. These dances can all be found in Girardet's or Desrat's collections. English equivalents come largely from William B. de Garmo, *The Prompter: Containing full descriptions of all the quadrilles, figures of the German cotillon, etc.*, 4th ed. (New York, 1868). Edward Ferrero, in a popular American guide called *The Art of Dancing* (New York, 1859), 165, refers to still more figures that end with "a gentleman victim."

79. See *Coulon's Hand-Book containing all the last new and fashionable dances* (London, c. 1873) by the ex–dancing master of the royal family of Holland, Eugène Coulon; in "The Coquette," 13–14, if the woman declines the gentleman in question, he has to stand behind her chair with the other "rejected partners."

80. See, for example, Emile DeWalden, *Dewalden's Ball-Room Companion* (New York, c. 1870).

81. De Menil, *Histoire de la danse*, 193. For example, despite their thoroughly European origins and associations, the theme of one of the cotillon figures proposed by Alfredo Franco Zubicueta in his *Tratado de Baile*, 7th ed. (Santiago de Chile, 1908) is the nationalist one "Viva Chile."

82. *Cotillon*, an old French term for petticoat, seems also to have been revived as a literary synecdoche for women just as the new meaning of it as a dance game was coming into favor; see, for example, *Culotte et cotillon*, a vaudeville by Jeanne Hauteville (Paris, [1847]), with a strong feminist undercurrent, or *Les Mystères de l'Amour et de la galanterie, ou le règne du cotillon: Anecdotes scandaleuses et divertissantes de la cour de France . . .* (Paris, also 1847), in which the author speaks of the new "reign of the *cotillon*" beginning with the Restoration in 1815.

83. Lily Grove, *Dancing* (London, 1901 [orig. 1895]), 427–28. See, too, Wilson, *Literature and Dance*, on this question of gender and the cotillon.

84. Alphonse Karr, *Encore les femmes*, 2nd ed. (Paris, 1858), 89–90.

85. Périn fils, *Le Cotillon*, introduction.

86. *Aux Tuileries. Guide du Cotillon. Fabrication spéciale des accessoires* (Paris, 1885), but see, too, the following guides also published by manufacturers: *Catalogue des figures nouvelles et des accessoires pour la danse du cotillon*, 3rd ed. (Paris, 1870); *Nouveau guide de la danse du cotillon: Catalogue et explication des principales figures et de leurs accessoires* (Bordeaux, 1874); *Nouveau Manuel du Cotillon: Explication de diverses figures avec accessoires* (Bordeaux, 1877); and *Le Cotillon: Accessoires et figures* (Paris, 1886). One by "Cellarius, neveu," who went into the family business, was called *Guide du Cotillon* and published in Paris by the Magasin des Enfants in 1874. Eugène Clément's *Manuel du cotillon* (Paris, 1892) has on every page an advertisement for Au

Paradis des Enfants, a shop that specialized in party accessories, including tambourines for the leader, ball cards, hair ornaments, decorations, roulette wheels, and paper lanterns; see, too, *Aux Paradis des Enfants. Manuel du Cotillon. Vente et location des accessoires* (Paris, 1885). Similar examples can be found for London, e.g., Ardern Holt, *The Cotillon: Details of all the newest figures with and without accessories* (London, [1894]). Other authors also complain that gewgaws have become the centerpiece of the dance, whereas once one used what was at hand (cushions, mirrors, handkerchiefs, chairs).

87. See Gary Becker, *A Treatise on the Family* (Harvard University Press, 1981).

88. Charlotte Perkins Gilman, *Women and Economics: A Study of the Economic Relation between Men and Women as a Factor in Social Evolution* (University of California Press, 1998 [1898]), 71.

89. Caroline Dall's 1856 speech was later published as part of her book *The College, the Market, and the Court; or, Woman's Relation to Education, Labor, and Law* (Boston, 1867).

90. In *The Subjection of Women*, Mill argued for letting women into a competitive economy and letting them decide themselves how much and where they want to compete, based on the idea that economic independence was key to other forms of independence. But he also assumed few women would want more than home and children; women would not pick careers if they were interested in child-rearing; and only exceptional ones would ever really choose to defy the norm (see the previous chapter).

91. On the rise of new forms of choice regulation in labor contracting (and the coercion usually involved at every stage), see Sigrid Wadaver et al., eds., *The History of Labor Intermediation: Institutions and Finding Employment in the Nineteenth and Early Twentieth Centuries* (Berghahn Books, 2015), on Europe; and Walter Licht, *Getting Work: Philadelphia, 1840–1950* (University of Pennsylvania Press, 2000) and Brian P. Luskey, "Special Marts: Intelligence Offices, Labor Commodification, and Emancipation in Nineteenth-Century America," *Journal of the Civil War Era* 3, no. 3 (September 2013): 360–91, on the United States.

92. On both socialist and liberal women's arguments for protective labor regulation as vital to emancipation in the 19th century, see, for example, Sonya Rose, "Protective Labor Legislation in 19th-Century Britain: Gender, Class, and the Liberal State," in *Gender and Class in Modern Europe*, ed. Laura Frader and Sonya Rose (Cornell University Press, 1996), 193–210; and Alice Kessler Harris, *Out to Work: A History of Wage Earning Women in the United States*, 20th anniversary ed. (Oxford University Press, 2003), 180–214.

93. See Linda Gordon, *The Moral Property of Women: A History of Birth Control Politics in America*, 3rd ed. (University of Illinois Press, 2007), chap. 4.

94. Madeleine Pelletier, *L'Emancipation sexuelle de la femme* (Paris, 1912), cited in Offen, *European Feminisms*, 245.

95. On the history of birth control methods since the 19th century, see Donna J. Drucker, *Contraception: A Concise History* (MIT Press, 2020). But also see Sanjam Ahluwalia, *Reproductive Restraints: Birth Control in India, 1877–1947* (University of Illinois Press, 2008), who warns against treating women's choices, rather than national well-being and other topics, as necessarily the central issue in debates around birth control in this period.

96. See *Goodridge v. Department of Public Health* (2003), https://casetext.com/case/goodridge-v-dept-of-public-health. The majority opinion drew on *Loving v. Virginia* (1967), in which the U.S. Supreme Court had struck down barriers to interracial marriage using an argument about choice as well. However, in *Loving* the kind of choice in question was the choice to marry at all, not the choice to marry someone of the same sex. On the evolution in thinking about gay marriage, as well as the backlash engendered by each of the key cases, see Michael Klarman, *From the Closet to the Altar: Courts, Backlash, and the Struggle for Same-Sex Marriage* (Oxford University Press, 2013) and William Eskridge Jr. and Christopher Riano, *Marriage Equality: From Outlaws to In-Laws* (Yale University Press, 2020).

97. Anti–gay marriage spokespeople also often engage with the idea of choice, albeit in contrary ways, arguing that (a) acting on homosexual desire is, in fact, a personal choice, and a perverse or sinful one at that, which should not be underwritten by the institution of marriage; and/or (b) approving gay marriage opens the door to the legalization of any sexual choice, including, for example, plural marriage or underage marriage, as long as it is based on personal desires.

Chapter 4

1. *Bristol Mercury*, August 17, 1872.
2. *Daily News* (London), August 16, 1872.
3. *The Times* (London), August 16, 1872.
4. *The Times*, August 15, 1872; *Leeds Mercury*, August 16, 1872.
5. *Freeman's Journal and Daily Commercial Advertiser* (Dublin), August 16, 1872.
6. The Borough of Pontefract included the towns of Knottingley and Ferry Bridge as well as Pontefract. Of the five required polling stations, four were schoolrooms and one was the town hall of Knottingley. See the *Daily News*, August 15, 1872.
7. *Freeman's Journal*, August 16, 1872.
8. "Pontefract, There and Thereabout," *Freeman's Journal*, August 15, 1872.
9. *The Times*, August 19, 1872.
10. *Freeman's Journal*, August, 16, 1872.
11. *Leeds Mercury*, August 19, 1872.
12. *Pall-Mall Gazette* (London), August 28, 1872, also in *The Times*, August 28, 1872.
13. *Lloyd's Weekly Newspaper* (London), September 22, 1872.
14. According to the London-based *Times*, August 19, 1872, the few ballots deemed "spoiled" were the result of an elector voting for more than one candidate, making uncertain markings on the paper, identifying himself in writing, or leaving the whole thing blank. However, the *Times*' correspondent also noted that it was impossible to know how many ballots, though seemingly correctly completed, did not, as a result of elector incompetence, actually correspond to voters' choices.
15. *The Examiner* (London), August 17, 1872.
16. *The Times*, August 19, 1872.
17. Anthony Trollope, *The Way We Live Now* (Panther Books, 1967 [1875]), 527, 526. Trollope himself had lost badly in a parliamentary election in Beverly in 1868, just a few years before the publication of this novel.
18. *Leeds Mercury*, August 16, 1872.
19. For the text of the Universal Declaration of Human Rights (1948), article 21 (3), which states: "The will of the people shall be the basis of the authority of government; this will shall be expressed in periodic and genuine elections which shall be by universal and equal suffrage and *shall be held by secret vote or by equivalent free voting procedures*" (italics mine), see the link in the introduction, n4.
20. On the meanings attached to the secret ballot, see Romain Bertrand, Jean-Louis Briquet, and Peter Pels, eds., *Cultures of Voting: The Hidden History of the Secret Ballot* (Indiana University Press, 2006), introduction; and Alain Garrigou, "Le Secret de l'isoloir," *Actes de la recherche en sciences sociales*, nos. 71–72 (1988): 22–45. But see, too, Louis Massicotte, André Blais, and Antoine Yoshinaka, *Establishing the Rules of the Game: Election Laws in Democracies* (University of Toronto Press, 2004), chap. 5, on variation in procedure at the national level today, and Sarah Birch, *Full Participation: A Comparative Study of Compulsory Voting* (University of Manchester Press, 2009), on the particular question of where and why citizens are compelled to choose today in about a quarter of the world's democracies but not others.

21. With this claim, I am arguing neither for the celebration of 1872 as a victory in the steady advance of English democracy nor for this example as evidence of Victorian social control or a ruse designed to curtail popular participation in English political life in the supposed era of mass politics. Following Pierre Rosanvallon and Richard Dunn, among others, I consider democracy to be a set of related beliefs, claims, practices, laws, and institutions that have evolved over space and time rather than as an ideal from which a polity is always moving closer or further; see Rosenfeld, "Of Revolutions and the Problem of Choice."

22. James Harrington, *The Commonwealth of Oceana*, ed. J.G.A. Pocock (Cambridge University Press, 1992 [London, 1656]), 33–34. Further explanation and an engraving of the process were printed as the broadside *The Use and Manner of the Ballot* (London, 1658) and included in subsequent editions of *Oceana*.

23. *The Times*, August 15, 1872.

24. On the varied voting methods in use in France and the United States into the 19th century, see Malcolm Crook and Tom Crook, "The Advent of the Secret Ballot in Britain and France, 1789–1914: From Public Assembly to Private Compartment," *History* 92 (2007): 449–71, and "Reforming Voting Practices in a Global Age: The Making and the Remaking of the Modern Secret Ballot in Britain, France and the US, c. 1600–c. 1950," *Past and Present* 212, no. 1 (2011): 199–237. On the United States, see, too, Robert Dinkin, *Voting in Provincial America: A Study of Elections in the Thirteen Colonies, 1689–1776* (Praeger, 1977) and *Voting in Revolutionary America: A Study of Elections* (Praeger, 1982); Richard Bensel, *The American Ballot Box in the Mid-Nineteenth Century* (Cambridge University Press, 2004); and Alec C. Ewald, *The Way We Vote: The Local Dimension of American Suffrage in the Original Thirteen States, 1776–1789* (Vanderbilt University Press, 2009). On France, see Alain Garrigou, *Histoire sociale du suffrage universel en France (1848– 2000)* (Seuil, 2002); Philippe Tanchoux, *Les Procédures électorales en France de la fin de l'Ancien Régime à la Première Guerre Mondiale* (CTHS Editions, 2004); Yves Déloye and Olivier Ihl, *L'Acte de vote* (Presses de Sciences Po, 2008); Olivier Christin, *Vox Populi: Une histoire du vote avant le suffrage universel* (Seuil, 2014); "Special Issue: Voting and Electoral Culture," ed. Malcolm Crook, *French History* 29, no. 3 (2015); and the unpublished papers for the colloquium "Scrutin secret et vote public, huis clos et débat ouvert," organized by Jon Elster, Collège de France, Paris, June 3–4, 2010.

25. Thomas Jefferson to Thomas Lee Shippen (Paris, March 1789) in https://founders .archives.gov/documents/Jefferson/01-14-02-0389.

26. Pamphlets like *Qui faut-il élire? Ou conseils au peuple sur le choix de ses députés aux Etats-Généraux* (March 1789), calling political choice a sacred duty and explaining how to do it well, started to appear even before the meetings of the Estates-General in spring 1789. That same how-to literature (often framed as *Avis aux citoyens sur le choix . . .*) continued into the Revolution with a focus on principles for choosing judges and municipal officers as well as national representatives. At almost the same moment in the United States, the federal Constitution was being framed as the people's "choice," and Alexander Hamilton was insisting in the third sentence of *Federalist, no. 1* (1787) that Americans, "by their conduct and example," will be able to decide the important question "whether societies of men are really capable or not of establishing good government from reflection and choice" or whether they are destined to depend on "accident and force." But the *practice* of voting is not discussed in any of these texts or in most constitutions of the era.

27. See Jean Bart et al., eds., *La Constitution de l'an III, ou l'ordre républicain* (Presses universitaires de Dijon, 1998) on the exceptional terms of this constitution. Specifically on the secret ballot provision in it, see Sophia Rosenfeld, "The Social Life of the Senses: A New Approach to 18th-century Politics and Public Life," in *A Cultural History of the Senses in the Age of Enlightenment, 1650–1800*, ed. Anne C. Vila (Bloomsbury, 2014), 21–39. For the text of article 31, which

reads simply "all elections will be conducted by *scrutin secret*," see Serge Aberdam et al., eds., *Voter, élire pendant la Révolution française, 1789–1799: Guide pour la recherche* (CTHS Editions, 1999).

28. *Archives parlementaires* XV, 704, cited in Malcolm Crook, "Le Candidat imaginaire, ou l'offre et le choix dans les élections de la Révolution française," *Annales historiques de la révolution française*, no. 321 (2000): 91–110. Apart from a brief experiment in 1797, declared candidates were only formally required in French elections starting in 1889. On the significance of this policy, see Patrice Gueniffey, *Le Nombre et la raison: La Révolution française et les élections* (Editions de l'EHESS, 1993) and Christophe Voilliot, *La Candidature officielle: Une pratique d'Etat de la Restauration à la Troisième République* (Presses universitaires de Rennes, 2005).

29. Gary Nash, *The Urban Crucible: Social Change, Political Consciousness and the Origins of the American Revolution* (Harvard University Press, 1979), 367, provides a brief overview of the conflict. See, too, the following sample broadsides making the case for the ballot as a means to enhance voters' liberty by preventing extensive external pressure from the "rich and powerful" on their choices: *To the Freeholders and Freedmen of the City and Province of New York. Gentlemen, the method of taking the suffrages of the people, for places of trust, by ballot, is so manifestly conducive to the preservation of liberty* [1769]; *To the Freeholders, and Freemen of the City and Country of New-York; Gentlemen, Every good citizen must necessarily desire to preserve the peace of the city, and the freedom of elections* [1769]; and *New-York, January 8, 1770: All the real friends of liberty, and our happy Constitution, having with the greatest regret, beheld at several of our late elections, the most infamous bribery and corruption with the most brutal debauchery and riot* [1770].

30. For example, as early as 1763, members of a prominent colonial settler family in the mission town of Stockbridge, Massachusetts, tried to assert political control by replacing viva voce voting with balloting precisely so as to sideline Native peoples who had previously voted orally in their native language as well as English; see Daniel Mandell, "Behind the Frontier: Indian Communities in Eighteenth-Century Massachusetts" (PhD diss., University of Virginia, 1992), 234–37. For the later history of this tradition in the United States, where Black people were the main targets, see Alexander Keyssar, *The Right to Vote: The Contested History of Democracy in the United States*, rev. ed. (Basic Books, 2009).

31. Gordon Wood, *The Creation of the American Republic, 1776–1787*, new ed. (University of North Carolina Press, 1998), 170, points out that the New York constitution of 1777 calls for an "experiment" with the ballot because voting in this fashion, as opposed to viva voce, "would tend more to preserve the liberty and equal freedom of the people" (New York Constitution, 1777, VI). Similar measures were adopted in North Carolina, Georgia, Virginia, Pennsylvania, and some New Jersey counties. But Kentucky, to take an opposite example, voted viva voce until 1891. Such variance was made possible by the federal Constitution, which left the "conduct of elections" to the states and gave Congress only the power of oversight.

32. Eric J. Evans, *Parliamentary Reform in Britain, c. 1770–1918* (Routledge, 2000), 8, notes that though twenty-nine general elections took place between 1701 and 1831, some small boroughs held no electoral contests during that whole period.

33. This kind of thinking still governed the creation of the categories of active and passive citizen in France in 1789. Active citizens were individual agents seen as capable of making moral choices; passive citizens, excluded from this role by either a natural distinction (age, gender) or an artificial one (wealth), were to have their interests protected by active citizens voting in the interest of all. See William Sewell Jr., "Le Citoyen/La Citoyenne: Activity, Passivity, and the French Revolutionary Concept of Citizenship," in *The French Revolution and the Creation of Modern Political Culture*, vol. 2, ed. Colin Lucas (Oxford University Press, 1989), 105–23.

34. See Derek Hirst, "A Culture of Voting in Seventeenth-Century England," in *Cultures of Voting in Pre-Modern Europe*, ed. Serena Ferente, Lovro Kunčević, and Miles Pattenden (Routledge, 2018), 129–40. Christin, in *Vox Populi*, notes that in early modern French elections,

whether held by communes, guilds, charities, religious confraternities, universities, academies, or Church bodies, voting was similarly primarily a social ritual designed to achieve consensus, not a way to measure the relative strength of different opinions.

35. Mark Kishlansky, *Parliamentary Selection: Social and Political Choice in Early Modern England* (Cambridge University Press, 1986), 10–11.

36. Frank O'Gorman, "Campaign Rituals and Ceremonies: The Social Meaning of Elections in England, 1780–1860," *Past and Present*, no. 135 (1992): 79–115, see 80. On the tradition of open voting in parliamentary elections and its meaning from the 18th century onward, see, too, O'Gorman, *Voters, Patrons and Parties: The Unreformed Electoral System of Hanoverian England, 1734–1832* (Oxford University Press, 1989); John A. Phillips, *Electoral Behavior in Unreformed England: Plumpers, Splitters, and Straights* (Princeton University Press, 1982); Jeremy Mitchell, *The Organization of Opinion: Open Voting in England, 1832–68* (Palgrave Macmillan, 2008); Jon Lawrence, *Electing Our Masters: The Hustings in British Politics from Hogarth to Blair* (Oxford University Press, 2009), introduction and chap. 1; and specifically on Yorkshire, John Markham, *Nineteenth-Century Parliamentary Elections in East Yorkshire* (East Yorkshire Local History Society, 1982).

37. "English Affairs," *New York Times*, August 29, 1872, 4.

38. O'Gorman, "Campaign Rituals," 89.

39. James Vernon, *Politics and the People: A Study in English Political Culture, c. 1815–1867* (Cambridge University Press, 1993), 92.

40. See, for some famous examples, Charles Dickens's *Pickwick Papers* (1836); George Eliot's *Felix Holt: The Radical* (1866) and *Middlemarch* (1871–72, but set forty years earlier); and many of Trollope's political novels of the 1870s. See, too, Herbert George Nicholas, *To the Hustings: Election Scenes from English Fiction* (Cassell, 1956) and J. R. Dinwiddy, "Elections in Victorian Fiction," *Victorian Newsletter* 45 (1974).

41. Hunt, *The Radical Potter*, especially 211–15.

42. [John Cartwright], *Take Your Choice! Representation and Respect: Imposition and Contempt. Annual Parliaments and Liberty: Long Parliaments and Slavery* (London, 1776), 1. On Cartwright's politics, see, too, Frances Dorothy Cartwright, ed., *The Life and Correspondence of Major Cartwright* (London, 1826); John Cannon, *Parliamentary Reform, 1640–1832* (Cambridge University Press, 1973); and Ray Hemmings, *Liberty or Death: The Story of Thomas Hardy, Shoemaker, and John Cartwright, Early Landowner, in the Early Struggles for Parliamentary Democracy* (Lawrence and Wishart, 2000).

43. [John Cartwright], *American Independence: The Interest and Glory of Great Britain; or, Arguments to prove, that not only in Taxation, but in Trade, Manufactures, and Government, the Colonies are entitled to an entire Independency on the British Legislature* (London, 1774).

44. In this sense, Cartwright could be said to blur the distinction between freedom as nondomination, or not being subject to the will of another, and freedom as noninterference, or the capacity to make choices, as laid out by Quentin Skinner and Philip Pettit; see the introduction to this book.

45. David Bindman, David Ekserdjian, and Will Palin, eds., *Hogarth's Election Entertainment: Artists at the Hustings. Sir John Soane's Museum* (Apollo Magazine, 2001) demonstrates how Hogarth's election images both build on and advance an English tradition of satirical election paintings and prints, partisan and not, that use the Hercules theme. In James Gillray's slightly later caricature also drawing on Hercules imagery, *John Bull in a Quandary* (1788), the elector (i.e., John Bull) confronts a different problem than the elector in *Canvassing for Votes*: an inability to make up his mind when presented with the options of Tory or Whig (the subtitle for the print, from John Gay's *The Beggar's Opera*, is "which way shall I turn me, how shall I decide?").

46. Major John Cartwright, *The People's Barrier against Undue Influence and Corruption: Or the Commons' House of Parliament according to the Constitution* (London, 1780), 10.

47. Cartwright, *Take Your Choice!*, 22.

48. Ibid., 21.

49. Ibid., 70.

50. Tennessee Acts of 1796, title VI, chapter 2, article VII: Proceedings of the Polls, sect. 847, in *A Compilation of the Statute Laws of the State of Tennessee*, ed. Seymour D. Thompson and Thomas M. Steger (St. Louis, MO, 1871), 1:542.

51. Major [John] Cartwright, *A Bill of Rights and Liberties; or, An Act for a Constitutional Reform of Parliament* (London, 1817), 15. John W. Osborne, *John Cartwright* (Cambridge University Press, 2008), 119–20, notes that Cartwright had a model built for his home.

52. On George Grote's dispatching of models of this machine around the country and its display in the House of Commons, see Crook and Crook, "Reforming," 215, though the role of his wife, Harriet, in this process is not sufficiently developed in this account.

53. See Matthew McCormack, *The Independent Man: Citizenship and Gender Politics in Georgian England* (University of Manchester Press, 2005), esp. 13–19, 48–50, on the traditional, class-based linkage between independence and manliness as manifested in voting. On the later rise of the idea of the "independent" workingman as also dependent on a gender distinction, see Patrick Joyce, *Democratic Subjects: The Self and the Social in Nineteenth-Century England* (Cambridge University Press, 1994) and Keith McClelland, "Rational and Respectable Men: Gender, the Working Class, and Citizenship in Britain, 1850–1867," in *Gender and Class in Modern Europe*, ed. Laura Frader and Sonya Rose (Cornell University Press, 1996).

54. *The Spectator* (London), February 25, 1837, 184, which includes pictures of the Grotes' prototype for a new kind of voting machine too.

55. Geoffrey Brennan and Philip Pettit, "Unveiling the Vote," *British Journal of Political Science* 20, no. 3 (July 1990): 311–33, see 313.

56. Melissa Schwartzberg, in "Shouts, Murmurs and Votes: Acclamation and Aggregation in Ancient Greece," *Journal of Political Philosophy* 18, no. 4 (2010): 448–68, makes the point that any voting system based on counting votes person by person presupposes not only that individual judgments are distinctive and of value but also that honoring them confers "epistemic dignity" on individual voters. This dual motive seems to be at the base of Cartwright's demands too.

57. See John A. Phillips, *The Great Reform Bill in the Boroughs: English Electoral Behaviour, 1818–1841* (Oxford University Press, 1992), on these techniques.

58. McCormack, *The Independent Man*, 47.

59. *Narrative of the Proceedings at the Stamford Election, February, 1809*, appendix 11.

60. O'Gorman, *Voters, Patrons*, 277.

61. Ibid., 259–85. This rhetoric, like Cartwright's, remained largely unchanged from its 18th-century foundations; see the brief remarks of an "Independent burgess" in *To the Worthy Electors of Colchester* ([Colchester], 1781) to the effect that if "free choice" is ever extinguished, "your liberty is gone forever."

62. See, for example, the highly polemical broadside *To the Electors of Pennsylvania: Take your choice!* (1799), which gives a decidedly biased list of differences between two candidates, before then urging readers-turned-voters to "Take Advice! Look well at your tickets! Look well at your Boxes! Look well at your Tallies! Look well at your Returns!" as they make their choices. In England, too—witness John Bowdler, *Reform or Ruin: Take Your Choice!* (London, 1798)—voters were presented with highly partisan arguments about hot-button issues while also being urged to "judge for themselves." Persuasion, no matter how forceful, was considered distinct from coercion and arguably still is.

63. Key texts making the case for the secret ballot in this tradition include Jeremy Bentham, *Plan of Parliamentary Reform* (1817) and the co-authored broadside *The Ballot: Cure for the*

Ballotophobia (1830?); James Mill, *History of British India*, vol. 3 (1817); George Grote, *Statement on the Question of Parliamentary Reform* (1821); and finally, *The People's Charter* (1838), all published in London.

64. James Mill, "The Ballot," *Westminster Review* 13, no. 25 (July 1830): 1–37, reproduced in *James Mill: Political Writings*, ed. Terence Ball (Cambridge University Press, 1992), 11. This text is also known as "Thoughts on Modern Reform in the House of Commons."

65. On the introduction of the secret ballot in the states of Tasmania, Victoria, New South Wales, Queensland, and South Australia between 1856 and 1859, see Mark McKenna, "Building 'a Closet of Prayer' in the New World: The Story of the Australian Ballot," in *Elections, Full, Free and Fair*, ed. Marian Sawer (Federation Press, 2001), 45–62; and Judith Brett, *From Secret Ballot to Democracy Sausage: How Australia Got Compulsory Voting* (Text Publishing Co., 2019), which explains the multiple ways in which Australia led the world in electoral reform between the 1850s and the 1920s.

66. Hugh Childers, *The Ballot in Australia: A Speech Delivered in the House of Commons on the 9th of Feb, 1860* (London, 1860), 8. On Childers's efforts to draw attention to the Australian example, see Crook and Crook, "Reforming," 222–23, but they do not remark on the connection to Pontefract.

67. On the early legislative history of the ballot in England, see Joseph H. Park, "England's Controversy over the Secret Ballot," *Political Science Quarterly* 46, no. 1 (1931): 51–86; Bruce Kinzer, *The Ballot Question in Nineteenth-Century English Politics* (Garland, 1982); Christophe Jaffrelot, "L'Invention du vote secret en Angleterre," *Politix* 6, no. 22 (1993): 43–68; and Frank O'Gorman, "The Secret Ballot in Nineteenth-Century Britain," in *Cultures of Voting*, 16–41. See, too, the interesting discussion of the subject in Elaine Hadley, *Living Liberalism: Practical Citizenship in Mid-Victorian Britain* (University of Chicago Press, 2010), chap. 4.

68. John A. Phillips, "England's 'Other' Ballot Question: The Unnoticed Political Revolution of 1835," *Parliamentary History* 24, Supplement S1 (December 2005): 139–63, as well as Bryan Keith-Lucas, *The English Local Government Franchise: A Short History* (Blackwell, 1952).

69. See Vernon, *Politics and the People*, on the role of paper in the privatization of politics in the 19th century more generally.

70. On the rise of political parties, see Frank O'Gorman, *The Emergence of the British Two-Party System, 1760–1832* (Edward Arnold, 1982) and Philip Salmon, *Electoral Reform at Work: Local Politics and National Parties, 1832–1841* (Royal Historical Society, 2002). On their growing importance in political life from the 1860s, see John Belchem, *Class, Party and the Political System in Britain, 1867–1914* (Blackwell, 1990) and Angus Hawkins, *British Party Politics, 1852–1886* (Palgrave Macmillan, 1998). But Jon Lawrence, *Speaking for the People: Party, Language and Popular Politics in England, 1867–1914* (Cambridge University Press, 1998), also cautions against attributing too much power to political parties before World War I. For different national examples, see Daniele Caramani, *The Nationalization of Politics: The Formation of National Electorates and Party Systems in Western Europe* (Cambridge University Press, 2014) and Daniel Peart and Adam I. P. Smith, eds., *Practicing Democracy: Popular Politics in the United States from the Constitution to the Civil War* (University of Virginia Press, 2015), which focuses on parties too.

71. Salmon, *Electoral Reform at Work*, 224–32. On the discussion and institution of electoral reform in 19th-century England, there is an important older literature, including Cornelius O'Leary, *The Elimination of Corrupt Practices in British Elections, 1868–1911* (Oxford University Press, 1962); Harold Hanham, *The Reformed Electoral System in Great Britain, 1832–1914* (Historical Association, 1968); and T. J. Nossiter, *Influence, Opinion and Political Idioms in Reformed England: Case Studies from the North East, 1832–1874* (Harvester Press, 1975), as well as a revisionist literature including Phillips, *The Great Reform Bill*; Salmon, *Electoral Reform at Work*; and Lawrence, *Electing Our Masters*, chap. 2.

72. Evans, *Parliamentary Reform in Britain*, 32–33.

73. See, for example, such prescriptive works as James Cappock, *Electors' Manual; or, Plain Directions by which every person may know his own rights, and preserve them* (London, 1835) and Thomas Paynter, *The Practice at Elections, being plain instructions for the guidance of . . . all persons concerned in the election of members of the House of Commons for Counties and Places in England and Wales* (London, 1837).

74. Mill, *On Liberty*, 60.

75. John Stuart Mill, *Considerations on Representative Government*, ed. Geraint Williams (Everyman, 1993 [1861]), chap. 9, 318–19. Mill's discussion of voting in this text builds directly on his *Thoughts on Parliamentary Reform* (London, 1859). Specifically on the ballot question in Mill's thought, the subject of chap. 10, see Nadia Urbinati, *Mill on Democracy: From the Athenian Polis to Representative Government* (University of Chicago Press, 2002), 104–22. On the very different arguments made against the secret ballot in late 19th-century France, including the claim that it was too physically taxing for workingmen, see Garrigou, "Le Secret de l'isoloir."

76. A recurrent theme in the 19th-century discussion of the secret ballot was that the so-called power of choice should remain primarily with "men of property and intelligence," as Lord John Russell bluntly put it (see Cannon, *Parliamentary Reform*, 208)—and the poor would benefit from the guidance of their social and financial superiors or from not voting at all. Mill, too, insisted that the poor would be better off having an "indirect influence" on politics than a direct one (*Considerations*, 330). Even the *Report from the Select Committee on Parliamentary and Municipal Elections* (March 15, 1870) that was ultimately to encourage adoption of the secret ballot as national policy clarified that "undue influence" was different from "legitimate influence" in that the former was an influence "exceeding in a greater or less degree the legitimate influence which a popular and respected landlord must always exercise in his neighborhood." See *British Parliamentary Papers. Government. Elections* (Irish University Press, 1970), 4:752–53.

77. Mill, *Considerations*, 325.

78. Ibid., 327, 328, 332.

79. See Anthony Trollope, *An Autobiography*, 2nd ed. (Oxford, 2014 [1883]), 187, in which he calls the secret ballot both "unworthy of a great people" and "unmanly."

80. *The Times*, March 8, 1850.

81. *The Times*, December 10, 1856.

82. See, for example, Isabela Mares, *From Open Secrets to Secret Voting: Democratic Electoral Reforms and Voter Autonomy* (Cambridge University Press, 2015), 133, which notes that opponents of the secret ballot in Germany—where it was established for national (but not all) elections in a preliminary way, along with universal manhood suffrage, in 1871—also described it as incompatible with the "manly honor of the German *Volk*." See, too, M. L. Anderson, *Practicing Democracy: Elections and Political Culture in Imperial Germany* (Princeton University Press, 2000) and Hubertus Buchstein, *Öffentliche und geheime Stimmabgabe: Eine wahlrechtshistorische und ideengeschichtliche Studie* (Nomos, 2000), 347–96.

83. By the 1870s, just under 60 percent of adult males in boroughs could vote in parliamentary elections; see J. Davis and D. Tanner, "The Borough Franchise after 1867," *Historical Research* 69 (1996): 306–27. Full adult male suffrage, along with the enfranchisement of women over age thirty, was not instituted in the case of parliamentary elections until 1918, full adult female suffrage until 1928. The appendix, 129–35, in Evans, *Parliamentary Reform in Britain*, lists the terms of every major Act related to elections.

84. On these debates in the context of the 1867 Reform Act, see Catherine Hall, Keith McClelland, and Jane Rendall, *Defining the Victorian Nation: Class, Race, Gender and the British Reform Act of 1867* (Cambridge University Press, 2000).

85. James Thompson, *British Political Culture and the Idea of "Public Opinion," 1867–1914* (Cambridge University Press, 2013), 59.

NOTES TO CHAPTER 4   423

86. See Jennifer Pitts, *A Turn to Empire: The Rise of Imperial Liberalism in Britain and France* (Princeton University Press, 2005), esp. 249–54, on how the expansion of the franchise at home was linked in liberal thought to distinguishing British voters from colonial subjects in terms of political worthiness. British suffrage policy in India, in which the very few enfranchised colonial subjects were understood to be representatives of specific communities rather than individual decision makers, reinforced this distinction; see David Gilmartin and Robert Moog, "Introduction to 'Election Law in India,'" *Election Law Journal* 11, no. 2 (June 2012): 136–48.

87. Gladstone's comments can be found in *Hansard's Parliamentary Debates*, 3rd ser., 194 (March 1869): 648–63.

88. William Dougal Christie, *The Ballot and Corruption and Expenditure at Elections: A collection of essays and addresses of different dates* (London, 1872), 6–7, 23.

89. "The Ballot, a speech of E. A. Leatham in the House of Commons," March 16, 1869, in *Hansard's Parliamentary Debates*, 3rd ser., 194 (1489–90); quoted too in Hadley, *Living Liberalism*, 212.

90. Hadley, *Living Liberalism*, 208–9.

91. This phrase comes from the comments of Sir Henry James in the *Times*, June 27, 1871, quoted in Ben Griffin, *The Politics of Gender in Victorian Britain: Masculinity, Political Culture and the Struggle for Women's Rights* (Cambridge University Press, 2012), 247. What's important here is not only the effort to protect the voter from the influence of the boss, when not on the job, or the priest or minister, when not in church, but also the idea of each of these being a separate and distinct sphere.

92. See *Hansard's Parliamentary Debates*, 3rd ser., 118 (July 8, 1851), 357.

93. George Jacob Holyoake, *A New Defence of the Ballot, In Consequence of Mr. Mill's Objections to It* (London, 1868), 3, 5, 8, 4, 7.

94. There is a certain irony in the fact that reform efforts aimed at taking money out of elections by curtailing corruption and bribery ultimately made it easier to imagine voter behavior as analogous to consumer behavior, that is, driven by personal preferences that need not be justified as in the interests of the whole community. See chapter 5 on the importance of this analogy in 20th-century political science.

95. There are scholars who contest voter rationality, for example, Bryan Caplan, *The Myth of the Rational Voter: Why Democracies Choose Bad Policies* (Princeton University Press, 2008). There also exists a school of so-called epistemic democrats who posit that, collectively, citizens are not just able to choose in their own interests but effectively come to better conclusions; see, for example, Hélène Landemore, *Democratic Reason: Politics, Collective Intelligence, and the Rule of the Many* (Princeton University Press, 2013). But neither kind of normative claim has had much impact on historians' approaches to the analysis of elections.

96. In addition to the texts cited already by Christie, Leatham, and Holyoake, see especially Henry Romilly, *Public Responsibility and Vote by Ballot* (1865); William Hepworth Dixon, *Free Voting: An address delivered at the Public Hall, Guildford* (1868); A Member of the Council, *The Ballot: Its Uses and Effects* (1868); A Westminster Elector, *Mr. John Stuart Mill and the Ballot: A Criticism of his Opinions* (1869); and John Thomas Ball, *Ballot Considered in Connexion with Extension of the Franchise* (1872), all published in London.

97. *Report from the Select Committee on Parliamentary and Municipal Elections*, March 15, 1870, in *British Parliamentary Papers. Government. Elections* 4 (1970): 751.

98. Ibid., 298 ("convictions"); 69 ("dictates of their conscience"); 226 ("just"); 144 ("a man's whole life").

99. With the earliest Australian ballots, the voter crossed off the names of the candidates that he rejected. In later models, following the practice started in Western Australia, the voter typically colored in a circle or put an X next to the option(s) he chose. But the key feature is that the selections had not yet been made for the voter, unlike with a prepared party ticket.

100. The *Report from the Select Committee* had included detailed reporting on the Australian example, emphasizing its differences from the French and Italian cases in which there was considerably less attention either to ballot design or to secrecy. On the specific features of the Australian ballot, see Peter Brent, "The Australian Ballot: Not the Secret Ballot," *Australian Journal of Political Science* 41, no. 1 (March 2006): 39–50. On the unusualness of Australian examples being used in British parliamentary debates at this time, see Jeremy Finn, "'Should we not profit from such experiments when we could?' Australasian Legislative Precedents in British Parliamentary Debates, 1858–1940," *Journal of Legal History* 28, no. 1 (April 2007): 31–56, esp. 33–35.

101. Examples of guides issued in the immediate aftermath include William Cunningham Glen, *The Ballot Act, 1872, with Copious Notes and Index* (London, 1872), in which it is noted on the back page, "Poll books to be used in 'counting the votes,' as well as ballot boxes, stamping instruments, and all necessary books and forms may be obtained from the publishers of this work"; Richard Aubrey Essery, *Parliamentary and Municipal Elections by Ballot* (London, 1873); and Gerald A. R. Fitzgerald, *The Ballot Act, 1872, with an Introduction. Forming a Guide to the procedure at Parliamentary and Municipal Elections*, 2nd ed. (London, 1876).

102. *The Times*, September 3, 1872.

103. *The Times*, August 15 and 17, 1872.

104. See the *Report from the Select Committee on Parliamentary and Municipal Elections; together with the Proceedings of the Committee, Minutes of Evidence, and Appendix* (April 7, 1876), in *British Parliamentary Papers. Government. Elections* 5 (1971). Richard Ellis, the returning officer in the Borough of Hackney, claimed the ballot did away with "noise" (336). The town clerk of Manchester, Sir Joseph Heron, similarly reported on "the quietness and orderly manner in which elections are now carried on . . . the interest, I think, is shown by the number of votes which is recorded . . . [not] popular excitement outside" (292, 293). From Leeds, Liverpool, Kent, Sheffield, and elsewhere, the committee heard similar reports in similar language. There is work to be done on the different sound registers associated with different forms of modern politics.

105. Lawrence, *Electing Our Masters*, 65. See, too, Graeme Orr, "Suppressing Vote-Buying: The 'War' on Electoral Bribery from 1868," *Journal of Legal History* 27, no. 3 (2006): 289–314, who notes how not only practical concerns, like the rising cost of elections, but also changing conceptions of fairness in competition and of voter independence helped shift the ground on corruption.

106. Crook and Crook, "Reforming," 209–10.

107. [Major John Cartwright], *The Commonwealth in Danger* (London, 1795), 91.

108. On the early significance of "the people" surveilling their representatives' choices rather than the inverse, see Katlyn Carter, *Democracy in Darkness: Secrecy and Transparency in the Age of Revolutions* (Yale University Press, 2023).

109. Garrigou, "Le Secret de l'isoloir."

110. On further changes in mandated electoral technology from the 1870s on to reduce the visibility of the vote in Germany, Belgium, Norway, Italy, and Spain, as well as France, see Mares, *From Open Secrets to Secret Voting*, esp. 15, 133–35. On the constant remaking of the *urnes* themselves, see Olivier Ihl, "L'Urne électorale: Formes et usages d'une technique de vote," *Revue française de science politique* 43, no. 1 (1993): 30–60, who notes both their changing materiality and the way they got personalized with names, coats of arms, and logos in various locations in France.

111. *Freeman's Journal*, August 16, 1872.

112. Thomas Hill Green, *Works* (London, 1885–88), 3:371, inaccurately quoted in James Thompson, "Modern Liberty Redefined," in *The Cambridge History of Nineteenth-Century Thought*, ed. Gareth Stedman Jones and Gregory Claeys (Cambridge University Press, 2011), 720–24, see 721. It is worth considering the similarities between Green's position and Pettit's

present-day republicanism since Pettit too proposes that the state can use laws both to limit the choices available and to make some choices more costly than others but still enhance freedom overall (see Pettit, *Republicanism*, 93).

113. On the doctoring of ballots, including "knifing," "bolting," and using "pasters" to circumvent party choices in the United States, see Bensel, *The American Ballot Box in the Mid-Nineteenth Century*, as well as Jill Lepore, *The Story of America: Essays on Origins* (Princeton University Press, 2012), chap. 5. Today, some states allow what New Jersey calls "Personal Choice," or the opportunity to write in the name of a person not on the ballot, and one state (Nevada, like India, Spain, and a number of other nations) allows the voter to pick "none of the above." On the history of resistance through *le vote blanc* and spoiled votes in France, see Yves Déloye and Olivier Ihl, "Des voix pas comme les autres: Votes blancs et votes nuls aux élections législatives de 1881," *Revue française de science politique* 41 (1991): 141–70; and Crook and Crook, "The Secret Ballot," 468. On ways of registering an objection to the choices with which one has been presented in a context in which voting is compulsory, as in 20th-century Australia, see Graeme Orr, "The Choice Not to Choose: Commonwealth Electoral Law and the Withholding of Preferences," *Monash University Law Review* 23, no. 2 (September 1997): 285–311.

114. Constitution of the WSPU, reprinted in the *Women's Exhibition: Programme* (London: Women's Press, 1909); see the Sylvia Pankhurst Papers, International Institute for Social History (Amsterdam), https://access.iisg.amsterdam/universalviewer/#?manifest=https://hdl.handle.net/10622/ARCH01029.199?locatt=view:manifest.

115. The Great Reform Act of 1832 created the middle-class franchise but specified for the first time that voters were to be male. The Fourteenth Amendment to the U.S. Constitution did the same. As previously noted, Mill and a small number of radical liberals argued against such restrictions in the middle of the century; see Jane Rendall, "John Stuart Mill, Liberal Politics, and the Movement for Women's Suffrage, 1865–1873," in *Women, Privilege and Power: British Politics, 1750 to the Present*, ed. Amanda Vickery (Stanford University Press, 2001), 168–200.

116. Campaigns for the secret ballot and for women's suffrage are rarely linked in scholarly discussions, but two exceptions are: Hadley, *Living Liberalism*, chap. 4; and Griffin, *The Politics of Gender*, chap. 8.

117. Millicent Garrett Fawcett, "Electoral Disabilities of Women," lecture in New Hall, Tavistock, March 11, 1871, reproduced in *Before the Vote Was Won: Arguments for and against Women's Suffrage*, ed. Jane Lewis (Routledge, 2010 [1987]), 108.

118. "Woman Suffrage Movement," *New National Era* (Washington, 1870), in *Frederick Douglass on Women's Rights*, 94.

119. For a cogent argument about how, in the American case, women's exclusion from the franchise was never a separate question from that of the exclusion of free Blacks, including men, see Jan Lewis, "'Of Every Age Sex and Condition': The Representation of Women in the Constitution," in *Family, Slavery, and Love in the Early American Republic: The Essays of Jan Ellen Lewis*, ed. Barry Bienstock et al. (University of North Carolina Press, 2021), 185–211. On the difficulties of maintaining the link between gender equality and racial equality in practice, see Hélène Quanquin, "Women's Rights," in *Frederick Douglass in Context*, ed. Michael Roy (Cambridge University Press, 2021), 172–81.

120. Helen Blackburn, "Some of the Facts of the Women's Suffrage Question" (1878), in *Before the Vote Was Won*, 326. By contrast, the sense that open elections were inappropriate settings for respectable women was reinforced by comments like those of Mr. Henry Davies, a bookstore owner in Cheltenham, who told the Select Committee in 1869 that though local women could now vote in some local elections, "ladies voting in either of these wards is a very difficult thing to do. There are a very great number of women who vote in those wards; but I should hardly call them ladies" (*Report from the Select Committee*, in *Parliamentary Papers. Government. Elections*, vol. 4).

121. Cited in Griffin, *The Politics of Gender*, 239. Bright was the rare figure who explicitly linked, at the parliamentary level, enthusiasm for the ballot with advocacy for expanding the franchise to include women.

122. See Susan Elizabeth Gay (on behalf of the Women's Liberal Federation, a party off-shoot), *A Reply to Mr. Gladstone's Letter on Woman Suffrage* (London, 1892), reproduced in *Women, the Family, and Freedom: The Debate in Documents*, vol. 2: *1880–1950*, ed. Susan Groag and Karen Offen (Stanford University Press, 1983), 227.

123. On women's involvement in electoral politics without the vote, see, for example, Matthew Cragoe, "'Jenny Rules the Roost': Women and Electoral Politics, 1832–68," in *Women in British Politics, 1760–1860: The Power of the Petticoat*, ed. Kathryn Gleadle and Sarah Richardson (Basingstoke, 2009). Vickery, in *Women, Privilege and Power*, stresses attention to women's political engagements beyond electoral politics as well.

124. On women voting in local elections before getting the vote at the parliamentary level, see the detailed study by Patricia Hollis, *Ladies Elect: Women in English Local Government, 1865–1914* (Oxford, 1987). In Sweden, women were given the right to vote in municipal elections in 1862—earlier than in Britain—but it took sixty more years before they were also able to vote in national elections in Sweden.

125. Kenneth Florey, *Women's Suffrage Memorabilia: An Illustrated Historical Study* (McFarland, 2013), 17.

126. New Zealand granted all women who were British subjects, twenty-one and over, including Maori women, the right to vote in parliamentary elections in 1893, though Chinese women were excluded. South Australian women won the vote in 1894 and Western Australian women in 1899, and then the Australian Parliament passed the Commonwealth Franchise Act in 1902, which similarly enabled Australian women to vote in federal elections and also to stand for Parliament but excluded "aboriginal natives" from the same protections. See Patricia Grimshaw, "Settler Anxieties, Indigenous Peoples, and Women's Suffrage in the Colonies of Australia, New Zealand, and Hawai'i, 1888–1902," *Pacific Historical Review* 69, no. 4 (2000): 553–72. See, too, Neill Atkinson, *Adventures in Democracy: A History of the Vote in New Zealand* (University of Otago Press, 2003), on the evolution of Maori voting laws, and especially Patricia Grimshaw, *Women's Suffrage in New Zealand* (Aukland University Press/Oxford, 1987).

127. Leila J. Rupp, "Constructing Internationalism: The Case of Transnational Women's Organizations, 1888–1945," *American Historical Review* 99, no. 5 (1994): 1571–1600. The first Women's Pavilion at an international exposition was at the Centennial Exposition held in Philadelphia in 1876. The first international congress on women's rights was held in Paris in 1878, one of a series that would be held from the 1880s on in a variety of other cities on both sides of the Atlantic. Of course, despite the focus on internationalism, participation and attendance were limited by religion, class, language, race, and nationality as well as cost.

128. See "The Women's Exhibition," *Women's Franchise* 2, no. 47 (May 1909): 3. On the radical suffrage movement and consumerism, including the development of themed merchandise and specialized shops known for their window displays, see John Mercer, "Shopping for Suffrage: The Campaign Shops of the Women's Social and Political Union," *Women's History Review* 18, no. 2 (April 2009): 293–309. See, too, Erica Rappaport, *Shopping for Pleasure: Women in the Making of London's West End* (Princeton University Press, 2001), epilogue ("The Politics of Plate Glass") on how suffragists sought, through the smashing of store windows, to use their position as shoppers to force shopkeepers to support their cause, but also how many stores, including the major London department stores like Selfridges and fashionable West End shops, similarly exploited their connection to women's suffrage, whether through advertising in *Votes for Women* and other movement publications or through selling branded merchandise, such as tricolor underwear, in the hopes of courting suffragist business.

129. On this exposition, see E. Sylvia Pankhurst, *The Suffragette: The History of the Women's Militant Suffrage Movement, 1905–1910* (London, 1911), 373–76, as well as *The Women's Exhibition Programme, Women's Franchise,* and esp. the WSPU journal, *Votes for Women.* See, too, Diane Atkinson, *Suffragettes in Pictures* (Sutton, 1996), for photos of WSPU shop-window displays.

130. Topics are detailed in "Close of the Women's Exhibition," *Votes for Women* 2, no. 64 (May 1909): 8–9; and "The Women's Exhibition," *Votes for Women* 2, no. 65 (June 1909): 8. Other topics included "should the income of wives and husbands be reckoned separately for Income Tax purpose" (643 against, 61 for), "should our colonies be represented in the Imperial Parliament (for Empire Day)" (432 yes, 80 no), and "should married women be excluded from teaching in the nation's schools" (by teacher request) (149 yes, 631 no). Still others focused on the creation of a tunnel under the Channel, censorship of plays, and validity of daylight savings, all deliberately issues unattached to any specific party platform.

131. "Close of the Women's Exhibition."

132. "Where Women Will Vote," *Votes for Women* 2, no. 59 (April 23, 1909): 21.

133. On the census tactic, see *Votes for Women* (March 31, 1911), cited in Martin Pugh, *The March of the Women: A Revisionist Analysis of the Campaign for Women's Suffrage, 1866–1914* (Oxford University Press, 2000), 197–98. On ballot-box spoiling (which French suffragists engaged in too), see Alison Neilans, *The Ballot Box Protest: Defence at Old Bailey* (London, 1910). On the range of spectacular tactics used in Britain by radical suffrage groups including the WSPU in the era before World War I (though the Women's Exposition largely goes unnoted), see, too, Lisa Tickner, *The Spectacle of Women: Imagery of the Suffrage Campaign, 1907–14* (University of Chicago Press, 1988); Sophia A. van Wingerden, *The Women's Suffrage Movement in Britain, 1866–1928* (St. Martin's, 1999), chap. 4; Laura E. Nym Mayhall, *The Militant Suffrage Movement: Citizenship and Resistance in Britain, 1860–1930* (Oxford University Press, 2003); and Andrew Rosen, *Rise Up, Women! The Militant Campaign of the Women's Social and Political Union, 1903–1914* (Taylor and Francis, 2012).

134. Pankhurst, *The Suffragette,* 376. The Pankhurst family also had its own past in retail; see Rachel Holmes, *Sylvia Pankhurst: Natural Born Rebel* (Bloomsbury, 2020), who argues that Emmeline had a strong sense of the role of shopping in women's psyches and how it could be exploited, positively and negatively, for publicity purposes.

135. See Joan Wallach Scott, *Only Paradoxes to Offer: French Feminists and the Rights of Man* (Harvard University Press, 1996).

136. Pat Thane, "What Difference Did the Vote Make?" in *Women, Privilege and Power,* ed. Vickery, 259–62. Thane cites too, on page 262, an article from the *Times* (London) of May 31, 1929, to the effect that, when the polls closed following the final extension of the vote to women twenty-one and older (by law in 1928, in practice in 1929), "There was every sign in many constituencies that [the female voter] has risen admirably to the occasion. Though stories were told of her nervous uncertainty about polling procedures, general observation suggested that she had no need to ask her way, but displayed the coolness attributed to the modern generation."

137. On Goldman's famous essay "Woman Suffrage" (1910), in which she dismissed suffrage in these terms, see Angela Shpolberg, "On the Vote: Emma Goldman and Women's Suffrage," *Los Angeles Review of Books,* October 24, 2020. See, too, Alexander Berkman, *Mother Earth* (November 1906): 5, who went on to write, "It is true that it does not matter whether you vote or not, since the result will be precisely alike. . . . Ho, freeman! come cast your votes! Oh, holy and precious privilege! Oh, marvel of the ages! the flock may choose by whom it shall be devoured!"

138. See Keyssar, *The Right to Vote,* 175–77.

139. *The Britannia* (February 8, 1918), quoted in Van Wingerden, *The Women's Suffrage Movement in Britain,* 170. During the war, Sylvia turned pacifist as did many other socialist feminists;

but the majority of British suffragettes, including Emmeline and Christabel, found themselves allied with their prior opponents, including Liberal feminists like Millicent Garrett Fawcett, as patriotic supporters of the war effort.

140. See Martha S. Jones, *Vanguard: How Black Women Broke Barriers, Won the Vote, and Insisted on Equality for All* (Basic Books, 2020) on how both ideas of white supremacy and the exclusion of Black men and women from the mainstream struggle for female suffrage fostered a separate fight, lasting from the 19th century through most of the 20th, for Black women's enfranchisement (among other racial justice issues) in the United States. Its roots lay primarily in antislavery conventions, Black Methodist conferences, and the colored convention movement; see, too, Manisha Sinha, *The Slave's Cause: A History of Abolition* (Yale University Press, 2017) on those links.

141. On women and suffrage in global or comparative terms, see Jad Adams, *Women and the Vote: A World History* (Oxford University Press, 2014) and Dawn Langan Teele, *Forging the Franchise: The Political Origins of the Women's Vote* (Princeton University Press, 2018), which concentrates on the United States, Britain, and France. David Stasavage, *The Decline and Rise of Democracy: A Global History from Antiquity to Today* (Princeton University Press, 2020), esp. 271–74, points out that from none to almost all of Europe's nations adopted universal female suffrage in the first half of the 20th century, an effect that he attributes to the transformations of two world wars but also to the growing realization that women's suffrage would not result in the redistribution of property away from elites, social unrest, or the imposition of new values.

142. Benjamin Barber, in *Strong Democracy: Participatory Politics for a New Age* (University of California Press, 1984), 187–88. There are also commentators who seek either a return to some form of open voting or the introduction of lotteries in place of elections as more just and more efficient ways to determine political representation; see, for example, Brennan and Pettit, "Unveiling the Vote" and Bart Engelen and Thomas R. V. Nys, "Against the Secret Ballot: Toward a New Proposal for Open Voting," *Acta Politica* 48 (2013): 490–507. However, this remains a highly theoretical and minority viewpoint with little to no support in the public sector despite heated debates about voting methods in the 2020s.

143. See the conclusion to Aziz Rana, *The Two Faces of American Freedom* (Harvard University Press, 2010).

144. Walt Whitman, "Election Day, November 1884," https://poets.org/poem/election-day -november-1884.

145. The philosopher Thomas Scanlon, in "Responsibility and the Value of Choice" (*Think* 12, no. 33 [March 2013]: 9–16), initially lays out the different grounds on which appeals to choice can be made. Here, using his terms, we might say that women's suffrage is initially less significant on instrumental grounds (i.e., if I vote, I will be happier with the results or the results will be better) than on symbolic ones (i.e., if I vote, I will be representing myself, and I will have the status of a competent, full person in both the world's eyes and my own).

146. The Convention on the Elimination of All Forms of Discrimination against Women (CEDAW) was adopted by the UN General Assembly in 1979, the culmination of more than thirty years of work begun by the UN Commission on the Status of Women in 1946. Article 7 states that "Parties shall take all appropriate measures to eliminate discrimination against women in the political and public life of the country and, in particular, shall ensure to women, on equal terms with men, the right: (a) To vote in all elections and public referenda and to be eligible for election to all publicly elected bodies." For the link, see the introduction to this book, n6.

Chapter 5

1. Simone Weil, *The Need for Roots* (first part, "The Needs of the Soul," written in 1942–43, published in 1949 in French and 1952 in English), in *Simone Weil: An Anthology*, ed. Siân Miles (Grove Press, 1986), 95.

2. I last heard this quotation read on Bastille Day 2022, at the French Embassy residence in Washington, D.C., by Deputy Secretary of State of the United States Wendy Sherman, as an emblem of what connects the two nations.

3. Harper, Randall, and Sharrock, *Choice: The Sciences of Reason in the 21st Century*.

4. Samuel Moyn, *The Last Utopia: Human Rights in History* (Harvard University Press, 2010).

5. Sigmund Freud, *Introductory Lectures on Psycho-Analysis*, trans. Joan Riviere (George Allen & Unwin, 1949 [1916–17]), 87–88 (italics mine).

6. Ibid.

7. See Sigmund Freud, *Three Essays on the Theory of Sexuality*, trans. James Strachey (Basic Books, 1962). Allan Compton, "The Development of the Drive Object Concept in Freud's Work: 1905–1915," *American Psychoanalysis Association* 33, no. 1 (1985): 93–115, is also helpful.

8. In his *Introductory Lectures on Psycho-Analysis*, Freud laid out for doctors and for "laymen of both sexes" the different stages of object-choice and also the various types. See, too, "A Special Type of Choice of Object Made by Men (Contributions to the Psychology of Love I)" (1910), in the *Penguin Freud Library*, vol. 7: *On Sexuality* (Penguin, 1977), in which Freud noted that "up till now we have left it to the creative writer to depict for us the 'necessary conditions for loving' which govern people's choice of an object and the way in which they bring the demands of their imagination into harmony with reality" but that it is now time for "science" to "concern herself with the same materials whose treatment by artists has given enjoyment to mankind for thousands of years, though her touch must be clumsier and the yield of pleasure less" (230). In this text, the focus is on men who routinely "choose" for an object either an unavailable woman or a woman of bad reputation, whom Freud described as a "cocotte," ostensibly because she chooses too often.

9. See Sigmund Freud, *Civilization and Its Discontents*, trans. and ed. James Strachey (Norton, 2010 [1930]).

10. Sebastian Gardner, *Irrationality and the Philosophy of Psychoanalysis* (Cambridge University Press, 1993), 164.

11. Karl Marx, *The Eighteenth Brumaire of Louis Bonaparte* (International Publishers, 1963 [1852]), 15.

12. On the invention and development of psychoanalysis up to World War II, see George Makari, *Revolution in Mind: The Creation of Psychoanalysis* (Harper Collins, 2008).

13. Sigmund Freud, *New Introductory Lectures on Psychoanalysis*, trans. James Strachey (Norton, 1964 [1932]), 132.

14. On the heated topic of Freud's sympathy to women, including his daughter, as practitioners of psychoanalysis, but also the tensions between psychoanalysis and feminism, see Elisabeth Young-Bruehl, *Anna Freud: A Biography*, 2nd ed. (Yale University Press, 2008), 52, 429–30.

15. Joy Damousi and Mariano Ben Plotkin, eds., *The Transnational Unconscious: Essays in the History of Psychoanalysis and Transnationalism* (Palgrave Macmillan, 2009).

16. On Freud's ultimate embrace of free will in light of his deterministic philosophy, see Ilham Dilman, *Free Will: An Historical and Philosophical Introduction* (Routledge, 1999), 179–82; and Alfred Tauber, *Freud: The Reluctant Philosopher* (Princeton University Press, 2010).

17. Trentmann, *Empire of Things*, esp. 285–88.

18. On the advertising business in the early 20th-century United States, see Susan Strasser, *Satisfaction Guaranteed: The Making of the American Mass Market* (Pantheon Books, 1989); James D. Norris, *Advertising and the Transformation of American Society, 1865–1920* (Greenwood Press, 1990); Richard Tedlow, *New and Improved: The Story of Mass Marketing in America* (Basic Books, 1990); and Jackson Lears, *Fables of Abundance: A Cultural History of Advertising in America* (Basic Books, 1994). The backstory can be found in Stephen R. Fox, *The Mirror Makers: A History of American Advertising and Its Creators* (William Morrow, 1984), chap. 1.

19. Walter Dill Scott, *The Theory of Advertising: A Simple Exposition of the Principles of Psychology in Their Relation to Successful Advertising* (Small, Maynard, 1903), 3, 2, which was drawn heavily from Scott's earlier talks at the Agate Club and articles for *Mahin's Magazine.*

20. See the expanded version published by Scott as *The Psychology of Advertising* with the same subheading (Small, Maynard, 1908), 116.

21. Samuel Strauss, "Things Are in the Saddle," *Atlantic Monthly* (November 1924): 579.

22. Earnest Elmo Calkins and Ralph Holden, *Modern Advertising* (New York: D. Appleton, 1907), 280 (citing Scott), 8, 4.

23. On Peto and his contemporaries, see John Wilmerding, *Important Information Inside: The Art of John F. Peto and the Idea of Still-Life Painting in Nineteenth-Century America* (National Gallery of Art, 1986) and esp. Michael Leja, *Looking Askance: Skepticism and American Art from Eakins to Duchamp* (University of California Press, 2004), chap. 4 (see 147 re: Wanamaker).

24. Joseph French Johnson, "The New Economics and the Marginal Consumer," *Printers' Ink* 73 (December 15, 1910): 42–43.

25. Paul T. Cherington, *Advertising as a Business Force: A Compilation of Experience Records* (Doubleday, 1913), 89, quoting an "unsigned article in *Printers' Ink.*" Merle Curti, in "The Changing Concept of 'Human Nature' in the Literature of American Advertising," *Business History Review* 41, no. 4 (winter 1967): 335–57, sees a shift around this moment from the predominant image of a rational consumer who wants to make his/her own decisions to one that stresses the irrationality of the consumer and his/her susceptibility to emotional appeals of all kinds. But it is also possible to see elements of both discourses overlapping and often within the same texts.

26. See Charles McGovern, *Sold American: Consumption and Citizenship, 1890–1945* (University of North Carolina Press, 2006), 47. See, too, Tedlow, *New and Improved*, 230, on other early slogans associated with supermarkets, such as "Pick Out the Merchandise You Like Best." On the history of supermarkets beyond the United States, see Kim Humphrey, *Shelf Life: Supermarkets and the Changing Cultures of Consumption* (Cambridge University Press, 1998) and Paul du Gay, "Self-Service: Retail, Shopping, and Personhood," *Consumption Markets and Culture* 7, no. 2 (2004): 149–63.

27. Trentmann, *Empire of Things*, esp. 254–56, points out how the idea of the housewife, which was adopted in many parts of the world in the first half of the 20th century, linked women more directly than ever with consumption, including of new technologies like washing machines and refrigerators that promised ultimately to provide them with more leisure time for other forms of consumption.

28. Scott, *The Psychology of Advertising*, 87, 111, 138.

29. Henry Foster Adams, *Advertising and Its Mental Laws* (Macmillan, 1916), 317–19.

30. On early forms of market segmentation, see Ronald Fullerton, *The Foundations of Marketing Practice: A History of Book Marketing in Germany* (Routledge, 2016).

31. Adams, *Advertising and Its Mental Laws*, 317.

32. Douglas Ward, "Capitalism, Early Market Research, and the Creation of the American Consumer," *Journal of Historical Research in Marketing* 1, no. 2 (July 2009): 200–223, see 214, in which he quotes a 1914 Curtis primer on using census statistics to gauge the consumer market to the effect: "As a whole the colored peoples have fewer wants, lower standards of living, little material prosperity and are not generally responsive to the same influences as the whites." Ditto for the foreign-born, who are also described as having "lower standards of living and lesser wants," making consumer research on them less essential.

33. Scott, *The Theory of Advertising*, 204.

34. Thaddeus S. Dayton, "Foreign Opportunity and Difficulties in the Way," *Printers' Ink* 90 (January 7, 1915): 80–81, cited in Curti, "The Changing Concept of 'Human Nature,'" 352, with small modifications.

35. See Lawrence C. Lockley, "Notes on the History of Marketing Research," *Journal of Marketing* 14, no. 5 (April 1950): 733–36; McGovern, *Sold American*, 25–26; and Peggy Kreshel, "Advertising Research in the Pre-Depression Years: A Cultural History," *Journal of Current Issues and Research in Advertising* 15, no. 1 (spring 1993): 59–65.

36. On the turn within American psychology in the early 20th century toward understanding the psychological characteristics of the collective, or large populations, rather than individual subjects, and the accompanying shift from laboratory experiments administered to individuals to quantitative social science methods associated with the questionnaire, the social survey, and the rise of statistics, see Kurt Danziger, *Constructing the Subject: Historical Origins of Psychological Research* (Cambridge University Press, 1990). On the growth of survey research more generally, see Jean M. Converse, *Survey Research in the United States: Roots and Emergences, 1890–1960* (University of California Press, 1987) and Martin Bulmer, Kevin Bales, and Kathryn Kish Sklar, eds., *The Social Survey in Historical Perspective, 1880–1940* (Cambridge University Press, 2001).

37. The *Tribune's* own Merchandising Service Department published a promotional text revealing some of its data ("advertising intelligence") to the public in an anonymous pamphlet titled *Winning a Great Market on Facts* in 1916; see 8, 26. For subsequent surveys of readers and their buying preferences, see also the *Tribune's* annual publication, starting in 1919, of the *Book of Facts: Data on Markets—Merchandising—Advertising, with Special Reference to the Chicago Territory and Chicago Newspaper Advertising.*

38. Adams, *Advertising and Its Mental Laws*, 7–8, describes this *Tribune* experiment based on an article in *Judicious Advertising* (December 1913): 63. Other texts comment on the *Tribune's* efforts positively as well.

39. See Josh Lauer, "Making the Ledgers Talk: Customer Control and the Origins of Retail Data Mining, 1920–1940," in *The Rise of Marketing and Market Research*, ed. Hartmut Berghoff, Philip Scranton, and Uwe Spiekermann (Palgrave Macmillan, 2012), on how this information allowed one to track a single customer over time rather than a snapshot approach.

40. Mildred Parten, *Surveys, Polls, and Samples: Practical Procedures* (Harper Brothers, 1950), 2: "More than a million people are interviewed annually by pollers. The public has given freely of its time and has even seemed to enjoy expressing its views."

41. Miguel De Beistegui, *The Government of Desire: A Genealogy of the Liberal Subject* (University of Chicago Press, 2018), suggests that, in the modern world, desires have been created, organized, and distributed by markets, changing subjectivities in the process. Jackson Lears, "The Ad Man and the Grand Inquisitor: Intimacy, Publicity and the Managed Self in America, 1880–1940," in *Constructions of the Self*, ed. George Levine (Rutgers University Press, 1992), 107–41, similarly links advertising, in particular, to an array of "sorting and categorizing institutions" that have reshaped human subjectivity and produced the "managed subject" (109–10). But such Foucauldian accounts, as important as they are, rarely have much interest in subjects' own reasons for participation in this process and thus deny them much conscious agency.

42. Sample "Newspaper Directory Blanks," filled in for Lansing (February 1913) and Conway (February 1914), are reproduced in *Winning a Great Market on Facts*, 14, 16.

43. See the chapter titled "Consumers' Buying Motives" in Melvin T. Copeland, *Principles of Merchandising* (A. Shaw Company, 1924), which focuses on both rational and emotional motivations among buyers, in contrast to sellers' more obvious financial motivations.

44. J. George Frederick, *Business Research and Statistics* (D. Appleton, 1920), 178–79.

45. Alfred T. Poffenberger, *Psychology in Advertising* (A. Shaw Company, 1925), 354–55. On Dichter's significance as the founder of what would become motivational research in the 1950s, see Stefan Schwarzkopf and Rainer Gries, eds., *Ernest Dichter and Motivation Research: New Perspectives on the Making of Post-War Consumer Culture* (Palgrave Macmillan, 2010).

46. See D.G.B. Jones and D. D. Monieson, "Early Development of the Philosophy of Marketing Thought," *Journal of Marketing* 54 (1990): 102–13.

47. Henry C. Link, *The New Psychology of Selling and Advertising* (Macmillan, 1932), 79, and the foreword by John Broadus Watson, vii.

48. C. S. Duncan, *Commercial Research: An Outline of Working Principles* (Macmillan, 1919), 152.

49. See McGovern, *Sold American*, 36–48, on women's roles within advertising, including in the famed "women's department" of J. Walter Thompson, as well as advertisers' conception of women as, alternately, naturally skilled as consumers and childlike. As the marketing consultant and Scott disciple Christine Frederick put it in 1929, "Mrs. Average Consumer does not know more, intellectually, than the present 14-year-old adolescent, if as much" (39).

50. Paul Nystrom, *The Economics of Retailing* (Ronald Press Company, 1915), described the whole field as consumed with two questions: Who are the consumers? What do they want? (42). By the third edition in 1930, the answer was focused on women (see 1:26–27).

51. See McGovern, *Sold American*, 45.

52. Percival White, *Market Analysis: Its Principles and Methods* (McGraw-Hill, 1921), 29. The question posed, among others on hired help, is "Do you give your servants discretion in purchasing?"

53. Helene Silverberg, ed., *Gender and American Social Science: The Formative Years* (Princeton University Press, 1998), does not dwell on marketing but aims to show how gender became encoded within the analytic tools, investigative practices, and conceptual categories of social science in general.

54. See especially Daniel Horowitz, *The Morality of Spending* and, for its continuing validity after World War II, *The Anxieties of Affluence: Critiques of American Consumer Culture, 1939–1979* (University of Massachusetts Press, 2004).

55. Edith Wharton, *The Custom of the Country* (Charles Scribner's Sons, 1913). This was, of course, a long-standing critique of marriage itself, going back to the 17th and 18th centuries and further developed by socialists of many varieties in the 19th; see chapter 3.

56. *The New Housewives Market* (New York, 1927), itself a luxury volume, insisted that (a) the masses, meaning not just white-collar families, now have the power to buy in "automobile salesrooms, radio shops, home furnishing departments, clothing establishments, grocery and drug stores"; and (b) "the American worker's selection" was no longer a function of price alone but also depended upon beauty, quality, and how much it will enhance the purchaser's life.

57. William Reilly, *Marketing Investigations* (Ronald Press Company, 1929), 130. See, too, on questionnaire design, Percival White, *Market Analysis: Its Principles and Methods* (McGraw-Hill, 1925) and *Marketing Research Technique* (Harper and Brothers, 1931), as well as Parten, *Surveys, Polls, and Samples*, who announced she had been collecting material for this volume since the 1930s and walked her readers through the pros and cons of "check-list" questions (such as "which brand of cigarette do you like best? Brand A, Brand B, Brand C, Brand D, Other, No Preference"), "ranking or order of method" questions, and finally "multiple-choice questions," also known as "cafeteria questions." This is the same moment as the rise of a larger category of books on social science methods, including Carol Aronovici, *The Social Survey* (Harper Press, 1916), Dorothy Swain Thomas and Associates, *Some New Techniques for Studying Social Behavior* (Teachers College, 1929), and many more in the 1930s, and a good number by women. On social science methods more generally in this period, see Jennifer Platt, *A History of Sociological Research Methods in America, 1920–1960* (Cambridge University Press, 1996).

58. On the historical evolution of marketing thought, including in textbooks, see Robert Bartels, *The Development of Marketing Thought* (R. D. Irwin, 1962); Jonathan Augustus Silva, "The Development of American Marketing Thought and Practice, 1902–1940" (PhD diss., Ohio State University, 1998); Coleman Harwell Wells, "Remapping America: Market Research and American Society, 1900–1940" (PhD diss., University of Virginia, 1999); and Douglas B. Ward, *A New Brand of Business: Charles Coolidge Parlin, Curtis Publishing Company, and the Origins of Market Research* (Temple University Press, 2010).

59. Clarence S. Yoakum and Robert M. Yerkes, *Army Mental Tests* (Henry Holt, 1920), 12. See, too, Henry Minton, *Lewis M. Terman: Pioneer in Psychological Testing* (New York University Press, 1988) and Leila Zenderland, *Measuring Minds: Henry Herbert Goddard and the Origins of American Intelligence Testing* (Cambridge University Press, 1998), 282–88.

60. On the link between Yerkes's earlier work with animals and his engagement in mental testing, see James Reed, "Robert M. Yerkes and the Mental Testing Movement," in *Psychological Testing and American Society, 1890–1930*, ed. Michael Sokol (Rutgers University Press, 1990), 75–94; and Alfred H. Fuchs and Shae A. Trewin, "History of Psychology: Robert Yerkes' Multiple-Choice Apparatus, 1913–1939," *American Journal of Psychology* 120, no. 4 (winter 2007): 645–60. Yerkes's "multiple-choice apparatus" became commercially available in the 1920s for use in other labs once it was manufactured by CH Stoelting Co.

61. Frederick J. Kelly, *The Kansas Silent Reading Test* (Kansas State Printing Plant, 1915).

62. On the relationship of mental testing to subsequent educational experiments with multiple-choice testing, see Franz Samelson, "Was Early Mental Testing: a) Racist Inspired, b) Objective Science, c) A Technology for Democracy, d) The Origin of Multiple-Choice Exams, e) None of the Above? (Mark the RIGHT Answer)," in *Psychological Testing and American Society*, ed. Sokol, 113–27. See, too, John Carson, *The Measure of Merit: Talents, Intelligence, and Inequality in the French and American Republics, 1750–1940* (Princeton University Press, 2007), chap. 6; and Paul Davis Chapman, *Schools as Sorters: Lewis M. Terman, Applied Psychology, and the Intelligence Testing Movement, 1890–1930* (New York University Press, 1988).

63. Carl Brigham, who had previously worked with Yerkes as an army tester, devised the SAT in 1926; see Nicholas Lemann, *The Big Test: The Secret History of the American Meritocracy* (Farrar, Straus and Giroux, 1999), which also underlines the link to eugenics. See, too, Mark Garrison, *A Measure of Failure: The Political Origins of Standardized Testing* (State University of New York Press, 2009), who sees such tests as an "ideological tool for justifying social inequality (fair competition)" and "a political tool for securing state power and affirming the power of public office and the professions (accountability)" (2), at the expense of democracy.

64. Michel Foucault, *Discipline and Punish: The Birth of the Prison*, trans. Alan Sheridan (Knopf, 1989).

65. Christine von Oertzen, "Machineries of Data Power: Manual v. Mechanical Census Compilation in Nineteenth-Century Europe," *Osiris* 32 (2017): 129–50, points out that as early as the 1870s, Prussian women, engaged in home-based labor, were central to the filling out and sorting of the mass-produced, card-sized questionnaires used for the Prussian census. Later women played an important role as expert users of the first punch-card systems in the United States and Europe.

66. Parten, *Surveys, Polls, and Samples*, 135–36.

67. See, for example, Eleanor Rowland Wembridge and Priscilla Gabel, "Multiple Choice Experiment Applied to School Children," *Psychological Review* 26, no. 4 (1919): 294–99; and Warner Brown and Florence Whittell, "Yerkes' Multiple Choice Method with Human Adults," *Comparative Psychology* 3, no. 4 (1923): 305–18.

68. See Charles Edward Merriam and Harold Foote Gosnell, *Non-Voting: Causes and Methods of Control* (University of Chicago Press, 1924). In an era of anxiety about nonvoters, it was

followed by Ben Arneson, "Non-Voting in a Typical Ohio Community," *American Political Science Review* (November 1925), and Arthur M. Schlesinger and Erik M. Eriksson, "The Vanishing Voter," *New Republic* 40 (October 1924), plus much discussion in the popular press.

69. See Lawrence B. Glickman, *Buying Power: A History of Consumer Activism in America* (University of Chicago Press, 2009).

70. See Margaret Finnegan, *Selling Suffrage: Consumer Culture and Votes for Women* (Columbia University Press, 1999), for the U.S. context. Note, too, that both British and American suffragists published cookbooks in the same era including recipes for delicacies like "Election Cake."

71. See, for example, Christine Frederick (a female advertising consultant and home economics specialist), *Selling Mrs. Consumer* (Business Bourse, 1929), 322–23, cited in McGovern, *Sold American*, 68, who claimed that women consumers "vote in broad democratic fashion at great popular elections, the polls being open every day at a million or more retail stores."

72. Liette Gidlow, *The Big Vote: Gender, Consumer Culture and the Politics of Exclusion, 1890s–1920s* (Johns Hopkins University Press, 2007), 125.

73. For an argument about the underrecognized costs of consumption, see Juliet Schor, *Do Americans Shop Too Much?* (Beacon Press, 2000).

74. See Martin Bulmer, *The Chicago School of Sociology: Institutionalization, Diversity and the Rise of Sociological Research* (University of Chicago Press, 1986), on the innovations in sociological methods developed at the University of Chicago between 1915 and 1935.

75. Merriam and Gosnell, *Non-Voting: Causes and Methods of Control*, 11. See, too, Lars Heide, *Punched Card Systems and the Early Information Explosion, 1880–1945* (Johns Hopkins University Press, 2009), esp. chap. 1. By the 1960s, such punch cards were being used to tabulate voting.

76. Merriam and Gosnell, *Non-Voting: Causes and Methods of Control*, 133.

77. Ibid., 188.

78. See Michael McGerr, *The Decline of Popular Politics: The American North, 1865–1928* (Oxford University Press, 1986), 191. However, other political scientists have also embraced low voter turnout at other moments, worrying about the effects of mass participation.

79. Gosnell himself soon turned to this task; see his own *Getting Out the Vote: An Experiment in the Stimulation of Voting* (University of Chicago Press, 1928).

80. McGerr, *The Decline*, 195–96.

81. On the rise of children's menus since the 1920s, see "Children's Menus" on the blog "Restauranting through history": https://restaurant-ingthroughhistory.com/2018/04/22/childrens-menus/, including examples of menus with taglines such as "And now . . . for boys and girls a treat . . . just pick from these good things to eat" (ellipses in 1947 original). This is one element of what might be called "choice training" for middle-class American children, along with allowances and opportunities to "pick" their favorite treats, outfits (sometimes), entertainments, activities, and friends, though children are currently prohibited from a range of other standard choice-making activities, including voting in elections, marrying or having sexual relations with adult people, changing genders (in some places), buying certain products, choosing to perform certain jobs, and spending their days doing something other than attending school.

82. Margaret Mead, "Education for Choice," in *Coming of Age in Samoa: A Psychological Study of Primitive Youth for Western Civilization* (William Morrow, 1928). On this argument, see, too, Peter Mandler, *Return from the Natives: How Margaret Mead Won the Second World War and Lost the Cold War* (Yale University Press, 2013), esp. 12, 27. Mead further developed these points in a 1931 talk to the American Association of University Women, Philadelphia Chapter, and in "An Anthropologist Looks at America," given at the Progressive Education Association in Philadelphia in 1941.

83. On the principles behind this movement, which began in the UK, see Charles Silberman, *The Open Classroom Reader* (Vintage, 1973), who emphasizes that "a child's enjoyment of school

is related to his having significant choice in determining the act in which he will be engaged" (174), as well as the specific materials he will work with.

84. The idea of choice in curriculum offerings or "electives" is associated first with a group of U.S. university presidents of the latter half of the 19th century. Brown University's Francis Wayland explained that "the various courses should be so arranged that, in so far as it is practicable, every student might study what he chose, all that he chose, and nothing but what he chose"; see his *Report to the Corporation of Brown University on Changes in the System of Collegiate Education* (Providence, 1850), 52. Harvard's Charles Eliot linked his own advocacy of "electivism"—or the student being empowered to "elect" or "select for himself" his courses of study according to his own "preferences" and "peculiar taste"—to both Protestantism and democracy ("political liberty"); see his essays "A Turning Point in Education" of 1869 and "The Elective System" of 1885.

85. Sarah E. Igo, *The Averaged American: Surveys, Citizens and the Making of a Mass Public* (Harvard University Press, 2007), 118, 4; see, too, Lears, *Fables of Abundance*, 244–45, on the rise of opinion polling out of market research and how it has been used to manage public debate.

86. Paul F. Lazarsfeld, Bernard Berelson, and Hazel Gaudet, *The People's Choice: How the Voter Makes Up His Mind in a Presidential Campaign* (Columbia University Press, 2021 [reprint of 1948 ed.]); quotes from preface to 3rd ed. (1967), v, and introduction, 1.

87. Roger Smith, *Between Mind and Nature: A History of Psychology* (Reaktion Books, 2013), 105.

88. Lazarsfeld, Berelson, and Gaudet, *The People's Choice*, 14.

89. Just as World War II was beginning, Ruth Nanda Anshen devoted the first of her many anthologies on pertinent philosophical topics to freedom and compiled the responses of thinkers including Albert Einstein, Benedetto Croce, Henri Bergson, Alfred North Whitehead, Paul Tillich, Bertrand Russell, Thomas Mann, Louis Brandeis, John Dewey, and Franz Boas (and no women); see *Freedom, Its Meaning* (Harcourt Brace, 1940), 487.

90. For example, a General Electric advertisement for war bonds called "Freedom of Choice" that ran in the *Saturday Evening Post* in March 1944 reads: "In large measure, freedom of choice is what this war is about. Freedom of choice means such ordinary things as trying soy beans in the south field next year, if *you* think it's the thing to do. It means buying the kind of flour *you* think gives you the best biscuits. It means *you and your boy* doing the deciding whether he'll go to college, or learn to be a tool-maker. . . . This freedom of choice—and its counterpart, a sense of responsibility for the decisions made—has done much to develop the character that is going to win this war—on the battle fronts, on the farm, in industry. And when the victory is won, the kind of America we have fought and worked to preserve must be a country in which every man and woman, and every boy and girl, will have freedom of choice in even greater measure." The text is topped by a drawing of a young white boy on a bicycle, all alone, contemplating two different paths across the horizon.

91. See David Riesman, with Nathan Glazer and Reuel Denney, *The Lonely Crowd: A Study of the Changing American Character* (Yale University Press, 2020 [1950, rev. ed. 1961]); Max Horkheimer and Theodor Adorno, "The Culture Industry: Enlightenment as Mass Deception," in *Dialectic of Enlightenment*, trans. Edmund Jephcott (Stanford University Press, 2002 [1947]), as well as the related comments of Jeanne Hersch, *The Old and the New World: Their Cultural and Moral Relations* (Unesco, 1956), esp. 198; and Weil, *The Need for Roots*, in *Simone Weil: An Anthology*.

92. On this wartime claim and its context, see Fred Turner, *The Democratic Surround: Multimedia and American Liberalism from WWII to the Psychedelic Sixties* (University of Chicago Press, 2013), 74–75.

93. Riesman, *The Lonely Crowd*, 125.

94. *Simone Weil: An Anthology*, 95.

95. Alys Eve Weinbaum et al., eds., *The Modern Girl around the World: Consumption, Modernity, and Globalization* (Duke University Press, 2008), esp. 282.

96. Pankaj Mishra, *Age of Anger: A History of the Present* (Farrar, Straus and Giroux, 2017), 42.

97. Emanuela Scarpellini, *Material Nation: A Consumer's History of Modern Italy*, trans. Daphne Hughes and Andrew Newton (Oxford University Press, 2011), 213, and in greater detail, *La spesa è uguale per tutti: L'avventura dei supermercati in Italia* (Marsilio, 2007). On commercial Americanization more generally, see Richard Kuisel, *Seducing the French: The Dilemma of Americanization* (University of California Press, 1993) and Victoria De Grazia, *Irresistible Empire: America's Advance through Twentieth-Century Europe* (Harvard University Press, 2005); but see also "Americanization?" (348–54) in Trentmann, *Empire of Things*.

98. On opinion polling beyond the United States, see Robert M. Worcester, ed., *Political Opinion Polling: An International Review* (St. Martin's, 1983), esp. 61 for the 1937 question cited; Nick Moon, *Opinion Polls: History, Theory, Practice* (University of Manchester Press, 1999); and John G. Geer, ed., *Public Opinion and Polling around the World: A Historical Encyclopedia* (ABC-CLIO, 2004). For specific national contexts, see Sandro Rinauro, *Storia del sondaggio d'opinione in Italia, 1936–1994: Dal lungo rifiuto alla repubblica dei sondaggi* (Instituto Veneto di Scienze, Lettere ed Arti, 2002); Löic Blondiaux, *La fabrique de l'opinion: Une histoire sociale des sondages* (Seuil, 1998); and Hartmut Berghoff, "Von der 'Reklame' zur Verbrauchslenkung: Werbung im nationalsozialistischen Deutschland," in *Konsumpolitik: Die Regulierung des privaten Verbrauchs im 20. Jahrhundert*, ed. Berghoff (Vendenhoeck & Ruprecht, 1999), 77–112. Polling was slower to take off in Latin America; see Daniel Robinson, *The Measure of Democracy: Polling, Market Research, and Public Life, 1930–1945* (University of Toronto Press, 1999).

99. Blondiaux, *La fabrique de l'opinion*, 321.

100. On marketing in the German-speaking world, see Ronald A. Fullerton, "When the Owl of Minerva Flew at Dusk: Marketing in Greater Germany, 1918–1939," *European Business Review* 21, no. 1 (2009): 92–104. More generally, see de Grazia, *Irresistible Empire*, chap. 4.

101. See Martin Lawn, ed., *An Atlantic Crossing? The Work of the International Examination Inquiry* (Symposium Books, 2008) and Lawn, "Voyages of Measurement in Education in the 20th Century: Experts, Tools, Centres," *European Educational Research Journal* 12, no. 1 (2013). The United States has been unusual in outsourcing this task to independent entities, including for-profit ones; in most nations, testing is a government project.

102. Alejandro Zambra, *Multiple Choice*, trans. Megan McDowell (Penguin, 2016 [2014]). On the history of standardized testing in Chile, including the Prueba de Aptitud Académica (PAA), see María Teresa Flórez PetoNur, "High-Stakes Assessment Systems as a Historical Barrier in the Struggle for Change in Education: The Case of Chile," in *Assessment Cultures: Historical Perspectives*, ed. Cristina Alarcón and Martin Lawn (Peter Lang, 2018).

103. Vilfredo Pareto, *Manual of Political Economy, A Critical and Variorum Edition*, ed. Aldo Montesano et al. (Oxford University Press, 2014 [1906]), 73.

104. On those commonalities, see Paul Lazarsfeld, "The Empirical Analysis of Action," in *The Language of Social Research: A Reader in the Methodology of the Social Sciences*, ed. Lazarsfeld and Morris Rosenberg (Free Press, 1955), who stresses that though many kinds of social scientists resist any association with consumer research, people in his line of work know that all social scientists now have "one central topic in common: What are the factors which account for the choices which people make among a specified number of alternatives?" (387)

105. On Ian Hacking's looping effect, see the excellent description in Henry Cowles, *The Scientific Method: The Evolution of Thinking from Darwin to Dewey* (Harvard University Press, 2020), as well as Hacking, "The Looping Effects of Human Kinds," in *Causal Cognition: A Multidisciplinary Debate*, ed. Dan Sperber et al. (Oxford University Press, 1995), 351–83, and *The Social Construction of What?* (Harvard University Press, 1999), esp. 105–8.

106. John Stuart Mill, "On the Definition of Political Economy; and of the Method of Investigation Proper to It" [1829 or 1830], in *Essays on Some Unsettled Questions of Political Economy* (London, 1844). On the idea of *homo economicus* from Mill onward, see Harold K. Schneider, *Economic Man: The Anthropology of Economics* (Free Press, 1974); Joseph Persky, "The Ethology of *Homo Economicus,*" *Journal of Economic Perspectives* 9, no. 2 (spring 1995): 221–31; Mary S. Morgan, "Economic Man as Model Man: Ideal Types, Idealization and Caricatures," *Journal of the History of Economic Thought* 28, no. 1 (March 2006): 1–27; Irene C. L. Ng and Lu-Ming Tseng, "Learning to Be Sociable: The Evolution of *Homo Economicus,*" *American Journal of Economics and Sociology* 67, no. 2 (2008): 265–86; and Dante A. Urbina and Alberto Ruiz-Villaverde, "A Critical Review of *Homo Economicus* from Five Approaches," *American Journal of Economics and Sociology* 78, no. 1 (2019): 63–93.

107. William Stanley Jevons, *The Theory of Political Economy* (London, 1871), 1.

108. As the British economist Lionel Robbins colorfully explained in a masterful summation of the new economic theory, "With one slash of Occam's razor, it [the ordinal revolution] extrudes for ever [*sic*] from economic analysis the last vestiges of psychological hedonism" (*An Essay on the Nature and Significance of Economic Science*, 2nd ed. [London, 1952; 1st ed., 1932; 2nd ed., 1935], 56n2). On neoclassical economic theory and the rethinking of utility more generally, see especially Nicola Giocoli, *Modeling Rational Agents: From Interwar Economics to Early Modern Game Theory* (Edward Elgar, 2003) and Ivan Moscati, *Measuring Utility: From the Marginal Revolution to Behavioral Economics* (Oxford University Press, 2019). However, D. Wade Hands, "Economics, Psychology, and the History of Consumer Choice Theory," *Cambridge Journal of Economics* 34 (2010): 633–48, challenges Giocoli's story.

109. This position, too, is well summarized by Robbins, in *An Essay on the Nature and Significance of Economic Science*, who insists the new science of economics is "entirely neutral between ends" (24), keeping its focus on "ascertainable facts," not "valuations and obligations" that belong to the world of ethics (148) or "propositions involving 'ought'" (142).

110. Fyodor Dostoevsky, *Notes from Underground*, trans. Richard Pevear and Larissa Volokhonsky (Vintage Books, 1994 [orig. 1864 in two parts in *Epoch* magazine]), 21, 24, 108, 31, 25.

111. On the late (1930s–1950s) emergence of the idea of "the economy" as a self-contained structure or totality of relations of production, distribution, and consumption of goods and services within a geographical space, see Timothy Mitchell, "Origins and Limits of the Modern Idea of the Economy" (1995), https://blogs.cuit.columbia.edu/tm2421/files/2018/01/Mitchell-1995.pdf.

112. Letter from Vilfredo Pareto to Maffeo Pantaleoni, 1899, quoted by Giocoli, *Modeling Rational Agents*, 73. On Pareto's life and ideas, see Fiorenzo Mornati, *Vilfredo Pareto: An Intellectual Biography*, trans. Paul Wilson, 3 vols. (Palgrave Macmillan, 2018). Specifically on his thinking about choice, see Martin Gross and Vincent Tarascio, "Pareto's Theory of Choice," *History of Political Economy* 30, no. 2 (1998): 170–87; Luigino Bruni and Francesco Guala, "Vilfredo Pareto and the Epistemological Foundations of Choice Theory," *History of Political Economy* 33, no. 1 (2001): 21–49; and Ernesto Screpanti and Stefano Zamagni, *An Outline of the History of Economic Thought*, 2nd ed. (Oxford University Press, 2005), 223–27.

113. Pareto's full debate with Croce is reproduced in John Cunningham Wood and Michael McLure, eds., *Vilfredo Pareto: Critical Assessments of Leading Economists* (Routledge, 1999), 237–44, 245–61 (quotations, 240–41). The debate was originally published as "Sul principio economico" and "Sul fenomeno economico" in the *Giornale degli Economisti* in 1900.

114. Wood and McLure, *Vilfredo Pareto*, 253, 248, 244.

115. Pareto, *Manual of Political Economy*, 73.

116. Mornati, *Vilfredo Pareto*, 1:136.

117. Wood and McLure, *Vilfredo Pareto*, 254.

118. Ibid., 245, quoting Boccaccio to the effect "Let any woman who has prayers to say, or cooking to do for her beloved, leave them alone. These stories are not going to run after anybody begging to be read."

119. On the declining number of women employed in the United States after 1920 as professional economists (apart from home economics and social work programs), see Evelyn L. Forget, "American Women and the Economics Profession in the Twentieth Century," *OEconomia* 1, no. 1 (2011): 19–30. On the attitudes of early male economists regarding women, see Michèle Pujol, *Feminism and Anti-Feminism in Early Economic Thought* (Edward Elgar, 1992). Pareto was also convinced that feminism could only work in wealthy societies.

120. Giocoli, *Modeling Rational Agents*, 62, 79.

121. John Maurice Clark, *A Preface to Social Economics* (1936), 9, cited in Morgan, "Economic Man as Model Man," 20.

122. See Paul Samuelson, *Foundations of Economic Analysis* (Harvard University Press, 1947) and "Consumption Theory in Terms of Revealed Preferences," *Economica* (1948): 243–53.

123. Robbins, *An Essay on the Nature and Significance of Economic Science*, 87–88.

124. Julie Nelson, *Feminism, Objectivity, and Economics* (Routledge, 1996), 30–31.

125. Robbins, *An Essay on the Nature and Significance of Economic Science*, 78–79.

126. For the argument that rational choice theory is a formal-mathematical version of the "folk psychology" of individual behavior, see Philip Pettit, "Decision Theory and Folk Psychology," in *Foundations of Decision Theory: Issues and Advances*, ed. Michael Bacharach and Susan Hurley (Blackwell, 1991), 147–75, see 145.

127. On the expansion of economic thinking, including rational choice theory and game theory, into other domains, see Marion Fourcade, *Economists and Societies: Discipline and Profession in the United States, Britain, and France, 1890s to 1990s* (Princeton University Press, 2009) and Robert Backhouse, "Economics," in *The History of the Social Sciences since 1945*, ed. Backhouse and Philippe Fontaine (Cambridge University Press, 2010), 56–66.

128. On choice as a key cultural value in the late 20th century, see the wonderful overview in Daniel Rodgers, *Age of Fracture* (Princeton University Press, 2011); but see, too, specialized studies such as Alex Davies, James Freeman, and Hugh Pemberton, "'Everyman a Capitalist' or 'Free to Choose'? Exploring the Tensions within Thatcherite Individualism," *Historical Journal* 61, no. 2 (2018): 477–501, which examines the ideal of "maximizing individual freedom of choice within a competitive yet tightly regulated market environment"; and Eli Cook, "Rearing Children of the Market in the 'You' Decade: Choose Your Own Adventure Books and the Ascent of Free Choice in 1980s America," *Journal of American Studies* 55, no. 2 (2021): 418–45.

129. On the distinguishing features of rational choice theory, starting with the association of self-interest with rationality, see Jon Elster, ed., *Rational Choice* (New York University Press, 1986) and Shaun Hargreaves Heap et al., *The Theory of Choice: A Critical Guide* (Blackwell, 1992).

130. Kenneth J. Arrow, *Social Choice and Individual Values* (Wiley, 1951), 1, 6, 23.

131. On game theory, see Giocoli, *Modeling Rational Agents*, chaps. 4–6; E. Roy Weintraub, *Toward a History of Game Theory* (Duke University Press, 1992); and Paul Erickson, *The World the Game Theorists Made* (University of Chicago Press, 2015). See, too, Theodore M. Porter and Dorothy Ross, eds., *The Modern Social Sciences* (vol 7. of *The Cambridge History of Science*) (Cambridge University Press, 2008) on the internationalization of methods for the social sciences in the 20th century.

132. See, for example, Alex Abella, *Soldiers of Reason: The Rand Corporation and the Rise of the American Empire* (Houghton Mifflin, 2008).

133. Hunter Heyck, *Age of System: Understanding the Development of Modern Social Science* (Johns Hopkins University Press, 2015), chap. 4.

134. Schumpeter, first issue of the journal *Econometrica* (1933), cited in Timothy Mitchell, "Economics: Economists and the Economy in the Twentieth Century," in *The Politics of Method*

in the Human Sciences: Positivism and Its Epistemological Others, ed. George Steinmetz and Julia Adams (Duke University Press, 2005), 126–41, see 131.

135. See the discussion of Cass Sunstein and "nudges" in the introduction to this book.

136. The large literature on the interplay between Cold War politics and the social sciences concerned with rational choice includes: S. M. Amadae, *Rationalizing Capitalist Democracy: The Cold War Origins of Rational Choice Liberalism* (University of Chicago Press, 2003); Mark Solovey and Hamilton Cravens, eds., *Cold War Social Science: Knowledge Production, Liberal Democracy and Human Nature* (Palgrave, 2011), esp. Hunter Heyck, "Producing Reason," 99–116; Paul Erickson et al., *How Reason Almost Lost Its Mind: The Strange Career of Cold War Rationality* (University of Chicago Press, 2013); and Paul Erickson, "Mathematical Models, Rational Choice, and the Search for Cold War Culture," *Isis* 101 (2020): 386–92.

137. On the problems with economic man, see Urbina and Ruiz-Villaverde, "A Critical Review of *Homo Economicus* from Five Approaches"; Elizabeth Anderson, "Beyond *Homo Economicus*: New Developments in Theories of Social Norms," *Philosophy and Public Affairs* 29, no. 2 (2000): 170–200; and Justyna Brzezicka and Radosław Wiśniewski, "*Homo Oeconomicus* and Behavioral Economics," *Contemporary Economics* 8, no. 4 (2014): 353–64.

138. See the introduction to this book.

139. R. H. Thaler, "From *Homo economicus* to *homo sapiens*," *Journal of Economic Perspectives* 14, no. 1 (2000): 133–41. For critiques of rational choice models more generally, see the following: Donald Green and Ian Shapiro, *Pathologies of Rational Choice Theory: A Critique of Applications in Political Science* (Yale University Press, 1994); Jeffrey Friedman, ed., *The Rational Choice Controversy: Economic Models of Politics Reconsidered* (Yale University Press, 1996); Emily Hauptmann, *Putting Choice before Democracy: A Critique of Rational Choice Theory* (State University of New York Press, 1996); and G. M. Hodgson, *How Economics Forgot History: The Problem of Historical Specificity in Social Science* (Routledge, 2001). As Talal Asad summarizes, rational choice theory is "a very impoverished language for understanding life as it is actually lived" (*Secular Translations: Nation-State, Modern Self, and Calculative Reason* [Columbia University Press, 2018], 153).

140. On bounded rationality, see Herbert A. Simon, *Models of Man, Social and Rational: Mathematical Essays on Rational Human Behavior in a Social Setting* (Wiley, 1957). See, too, Hunter Crowther-Heyck, *Herbert A. Simon: The Bounds of Reason in Modern America* (Johns Hopkins University Press, 2005), where the key to Simon's work is found in the following quote: "if one could discover how and why the human social atom chose to do one thing rather than another—how the forces of heredity and personality and education and environment conspired to lead an individual to 'take the road to the right or to the left'—if one could understand the choices that individuals made, then perhaps one could assemble a true science of human behavior" (5). The quote about a "rat-like chooser" dates from 1954 and is cited by Crowther-Heyck in ibid., 6.

141. Anderson, "Beyond *Homo Economicus*," 173.

142. See, for example, Daniel Kahneman and Amos Tversky, "On the Psychology of Prediction," *Psychological Review* 80 (1973): 237–51; Tversky and Kahneman, "Judgment under Uncertainty: Heuristics and Biases," *Science* 185 (1974): 1124–31; Tversky and Kahneman, "The Framing of Decisions and the Psychology of Choice"; and Kahneman and Tversky, "Choices, Values, and Frames," *American Psychologist* 39, no. 4 (1984): 341–50. But already in the 1960s, consumer economists like Elizabeth Hoyt were calling for closer links between the study of "the field of choice" (economics) and the study of "the act of choice" (psychology); see "Choice as an Interdisciplinary Area," *Quarterly Journal of Economics* 79, no. 1 (February 1965): 106–12.

143. Sheila Heti, "Trouble in Paradise," *New York Review of Books*, March 24, 2022, reviewing Lena Andersson, *Willful Disregard: A Novel about Love*, trans. Sarah Death (Other Press, 2016) and *Acts of Infidelity*, trans. Saskia Vogel (Other Press, 2019).

144. Lawrence Langer, "The Dilemma of Choice in the Deathcamps," *Centerpoint: A Journal of Interdisciplinary Studies* 4, no. 1 (fall 1980): 53–58, who suggests that choices made in the absence of freedom or the ability to consider moral questions, and thus just for the sake of survival, challenge the meaning of the term.

145. There is also a literature showing how we battle ourselves when it comes to choices to be made, but also how little we are able to think of our choices as in any way comprehensively linked. See, for example, Albert Hirschman, "Against Parsimony: Three Easy Ways of Complicating Some Categories of Economic Discourse" (1982), in *The Essential Hirschman*, ed. Jeremy Adelman (Princeton University Press, 2013), in which Hirschman argues that our preferences are also subject to metapreferences, which can cause profound arguments within the self that lead to changes in our choices over time—something which mainstream economists also rarely recognize.

146. Mill, *On Liberty*, 63, who sounds very close to Tocqueville here. Marx saw ideology playing a similar role.

147. See especially Pareto, *Trattato di sociologia generale*, known in English as *The Mind and Society*, published originally in Florence in 1916.

148. See Hazel Kyrk, *A Theory of Consumption* (Houghton Mifflin, 1923), which is focused on "freedom of choice," as well as Agnès Le Tollec, "Finding a New Home (Economics): Towards a Science of the Rational Family, 1924–1981" (PhD diss., Université Paris-Saclay, 2020).

149. See, for example, Seymour Martin Lipset, "Forcing a Free Choice," *New York Times Book Review*, March 6, 1966, 47, on Jacques Ellul and the forces of conformity.

150. Amartya Sen, "Rational Fools: A Critique of the Behavioral Foundations of Economic Theory," *Philosophy and Public Affairs* 6, no. 4 (summer 1977): 317–44. This work builds on the earlier *Collective Choice and Social Welfare* (Harvard University Press, 1970).

151. Tim Rogan, *The Moral Economists: R. H. Tawney, Karl Polanyi, E. P. Thompson, and the Critique of Capitalism* (Princeton University Press, 2017); Thompson coined the phrase in 1971.

152. See esp. Elizabeth Anderson, *Value in Ethics and Economics* (Harvard University Press, 1995); Debra Satz, *Why Some Things Should Not Be for Sale: The Moral Limits of Markets* (Oxford University Press, 2010); and Michael Sandel, *What Money Can't Buy: The Moral Limits of Markets* (Farrar, Straus and Giroux, 2012), on the hazards of both libertarian and utilitarian "market thinking" in terms of crowding out nonmarket values.

153. Some key texts in this tradition include Paula England and Barbara Stanek Kilbourne, "Feminist Critiques of the Separative Model of Self: Implications for Rational Choice Theory," *Rationality and Society* 2, no. 2 (April 1990): 156–71; Marianne A. Ferber and Julie A. Nelson, *Beyond Economic Man: Feminist Theory and Economics* (University of Chicago Press, 1993); Gillian J. Hewitson, *Feminist Economics: Interrogating the Masculinity of Rational Economic Man* (Edward Elgar, 1999); and especially Ferber and Nelson, *Feminist Economics Today: Beyond Economic Man* (University of Chicago Press, 2003). More broadly on the rational choice tradition, see both Elizabeth Anderson, "Should Feminists Reject Rational Choice Theory?" and Ann E. Cudd, "Rational Choice Theory and the Lessons of Feminism," in *A Mind of One's Own: Feminist Essays on Reason and Objectivity*, ed. Louise M. Antony and Charlotte E. Witt (Westview, 1993), 369–417.

154. Italo Calvino, "Marcovaldo at the Supermarket," in *Marcovaldo; or, The Seasons in the City*, trans. William Weaver (Houghton Mifflin Harcourt, 1983 [1963]).

155. On what these individualist principles also elided in practice, see the important revisionist article of Mark Mazower, "The Strange Triumph of Human Rights: 1933–1950," *Historical Journal* 47, no. 2 (2004): 379–98.

156. Johannes Morsink, *The Universal Declaration of Human Rights: Origins, Drafting, and Intent* (University of Pennsylvania Press, 2000), 73–74, 160. It is worth noting that whereas Marxists on the committee generally saw economic well-being as a prerequisite to enjoying

political and civil rights, liberals tended to see political and civil rights, with a focus on choice, as the priority out of which a state dedicated to social rights could emerge. The major statement on this question was article 25.

157. See the introduction to this book on Berlin's distinction, which was elaborated just a few years after the passing of the UDHR. On the limited but not entirely absent role of social and economic rights in the UDHR, see Jessica Whyte, *The Morals of the Market: Human Rights and the Rise of Neoliberalism* (Verso, 2019).

158. See Morsink, *The Universal Declaration of Human Rights*, 128–29, on these debates. See, too, "Eleanor Roosevelt Speeches, on Gender Neutral Language in the UDHR, date unknown," *Eleanor Roosevelt Papers* (2019), https://www2.gwu.edu/~erpapers/speech/doc.cfm?_p =record&_f=sp_unknowndate_genderneutral-udhr. For a different read, stressing the endurance of the male breadwinner family model and a very gendered social vision underpinning the whole text, as revealed by these exceptions, see Whyte, *The Morals of the Market*, 93–95. Only in 1993 did the United Nations World Conference on Human Rights, held in Vienna, confirm that women's rights were human rights.

159. See Hans Ingvar Roth, *P. C. Chang and the Universal Declaration of Human Rights* (University of Pennsylvania Press, 2018), 210, in which Chang is described as invested in bringing together the Confucian idea "Never impose on others what you would not choose for yourself" with Jesus's formulation of the Golden Rule: "Do unto others what you want them to do to you." Nevertheless, the critique of the UDHR as dependent on racist, colonial, and Eurocentric logic began almost immediately after its adoption, building on the nascent work of postcolonial critics.

160. M. Glen Johnson and Janusz Symonides, *The Universal Declaration of Human Rights: A History of Its Creation and Implementation, 1948–1998* (Unesco Publishing, 1998), 21n2.

161. Ibid., 71.

162. Betty Friedan, *The Feminine Mystique* (Norton, 2013 [1963]), 5, 77, 337.

163. See Judith Hennessee, *Betty Friedan: Her Life* (Random House, 1990), 70–71, but also the preface to *The Feminine Mystique*, xxi, on Friedan's sources, starting with this questionnaire. There is a long prior history of alumnae questionnaires; one was, for example, distributed in 1928 in honor of Radcliffe's looming semicentennial, and over two thousand women, with graduation dates from the 1880s to the 1920s, responded. See Barbara Miller Solomon, *In the Company of Educated Women: A History of Women and Higher Education in America* (Yale University Press, 1985), 182–85.

164. See Daniel Horowitz, *Betty Friedan and the Making of the Feminine Mystique: The American Left, the Cold War, and Modern Feminism* (University of Massachusetts Press, 1998), for this context.

165. On the fashionableness of existentialism in the United States in the mid-century as a philosophy of authenticity that encouraged individuals to create their own identities and take responsibility for their lives through conscious, enacted choices in a world without fixed moral foundations, see Casey Nelson Blake, Daniel Borus, and Howard Brick, *At the Center: American Thought and Culture in the Mid-Twentieth Century* (Rowman and Littlefield, 2019), esp. 69 and 117–18; and Louis Menand, *The Free World: Art and Thought in the Cold War* (Farrar, Straus and Giroux, 2021), 63–91. On Friedan's borrowing specifically from Simone de Beauvoir's *The Second Sex*, trans. H. M. Parshley (Knopf, 1952 [1949]), which urged women to seek "self-fulfillment in transcendence" (51) or full subjecthood, see Sandra Dijkstra, "Simone de Beauvoir and Betty Friedan: The Politics of Omission," *Feminist Studies* 6, no. 2 (summer 1980): 290–303.

166. Friedan, *The Feminine Mystique*, 416, 78, 373.

167. Ibid., xxv, 79.

168. See, for example, letter to Friedan from a reader in Sioux City, Iowa (March 12, 1964): "Thanks to this fascinating and delightful book I am fully confident of myself and my desire to launch the career I've always wanted for so long. The last of the cobwebs of guilt have been swept

away and what a marvelous free feeling!"; and letter to Friedan, n.p. (March 23, 1964): "After re-reading your book, the *Feminine Mystique*, I simply have to respond to you in order to congratu-late you and thank you for setting me free! Really free!" Both are reproduced in *The Feminine Mystique: The Norton Critical Edition*, ed. Kirsten Fermaglich and Lisa M. Fine (Norton, 2013), 380, from the Betty Friedan Papers, Schlesinger Library, Harvard University. On contemporary responses, see, too, Stephanie Coontz, *A Strange Stirring: The Feminine Mystique and American Women at the Dawn of the 1960s* (Basic Books, 2011).

169. See Lisa Maria Hogeland, *Feminism and Its Fictions: The Consciousness-Raising Novel and the Women's Liberation Movement* (University of Pennsylvania Press, 1998).

170. NOW's 1966 Statement of Purpose, https://now.org/about/history/statement-of -purpose/ (italics mine).

Epilogue

1. Margaret Sanger, "A Parents' Problem or Woman's?" *Birth Control Review* (March 1919), 6–7, available at https://www.m-sanger.org/items/show/1434. The expression "children by choice—not chance" was already associated at mid-century with Planned Parenthood, the organization that Sanger founded as the American Birth Control League in 1921 and which was renamed in 1942; see Isabel Heinemann, "From 'Children by Choice' to 'Families by Choice'? 20th-Century Reproductive Decision-Making between Social Change and Normative Transi-tions," in *Children by Choice? Changing Values, Reproduction, and Family Planning in the 20th Century*, ed. Ann-Katrin Gembries (De Gruyter, 2018). On NARAL's "Children by Choice" demonstrations, held with press conferences in eleven cities on Mother's Day 1969, see Suzanne Staggenborg, *The Pro-Choice Movement: Organization and Activism in the Abortion Conflict* (Ox-ford University Press, 1991), 51. Note that Stella Browne was using similar language in England, circa 1915, arguing that women needed "absolute freedom of choice" in deciding both on a partner and on whether or not to have children; see Barbara Brookes, *Abortion in England, 1900–1967* (Routledge, 1988), 81–82.

2. On the pill as producing new forms of choice in practice, see Elizabeth Siegel Watkins, *On the Pill: A Social History of Oral Contraceptives, 1950–1970* (Johns Hopkins University Press, 1998) and Elaine Tyler May, *America and the Pill: A History of Promise, Peril and Liberation* (Basic Books, 2010). On 1960s feminists' arguments about lack of acceptable choice under conditions of pregnancy, see Celeste Michelle Condit, *Decoding Abortion Rhetoric: Communicating Social Change* (University of Illinois Press, 1990), 68.

3. Condit, *Decoding Abortion Rhetoric*, 99–100. Sarah Weddington called her own book, in which she also described her own abortion, obtained in Mexico in 1967, *A Question of Choice* (Putnam's, 1992).

4. See the transcript of *Roe v. Wade*, 410 US 113, available at https://supreme.justia.com/cases /federal/us/410/113/. Blackmun defines the "right of privacy" as one that "is broad enough to encompass a woman's decision whether or not to terminate her pregnancy. The detriment that the State would impose upon the pregnant woman by denying this choice altogether is apparent."

5. Ibid.

6. On the arguments made in *Roe v. Wade*, see David J. Garrow, *Liberty and Sexuality: The Right to Privacy and the Making of Roe v. Wade* (University of California Press, 1998); N.E.H. Hull, *Roe v. Wade: The Abortion Rights Controversy in American History* (University Press of Kansas, 2001); and N.E.H. Hull, Williamjames Hoffer, and Peter Charles Hoffer, eds., *The Abortion Rights Con-troversy in America: A Legal Reader* (University of North Carolina Press, 2004). Mae Kuykendall, in "Liberty in a Divided and Experimental Culture: Respecting Choice and Enforcing Connection in the American Family," *UCLA Journal of Gender and Law* 12, no. 2 (2003), argues more generally that "a record of our cultural and historical attachment to choice is found in the efforts throughout

the history of the justices of the Supreme Court, even those regarded as both jurisprudentially and culturally conservative, to fashion nuanced and even poetic statements about the extent to which we equate choice in constructing our families with our traditions of liberty" (268).

7. Abortion was legalized earlier in Russia, Eastern Europe, and China, but under the banner of collective needs, including the well-being of the nation, not individual choice. On the changing justifications for legal reform, see Nick Hopwood, Rebecca Flemming, and Lauren Kassell, eds., *Reproduction: Antiquity to the Present Day* (Cambridge University Press, 2018), esp. 231–32; and Matthew Connelly, *Fatal Misconception: The Struggle to Control World Population* (Harvard University Press, 2008).

8. Linda Greenhouse and Reva Siegel, eds., *Before Roe v. Wade: Voices That Shaped the Abortion Debate before the Supreme Court's Ruling* (Kaplan, 2010), xii–xiii. There are interesting parallels here with contemporaneous movements against rape and coercive sex, which is to say, for the importance of women's consent as well.

9. Milton and Rose Friedman, *Free to Choose: A Personal Statement* (Harcourt Brace Jovanovich, 1980), 309–10. The book and TV show were popular reprisals of their more scholarly argument for economic liberalism, *Capitalism and Freedom*, of 1962.

10. On Rawls and choice, see the introduction to this book.

11. Fraser, in *Fortunes of Feminism*, only mentions abortion in passing but argues that second-wave feminism has lost, since the 1980s, its more emancipatory, utopian qualities as it has become not just allied with but a form of legitimation for the extreme individualism associated with neoliberalism.

12. Robin West, "From Choice to Reproductive Justice: De-Constitutionalizing Abortion Rights," *Yale Law Journal* 118 (2009): 1394–1430, see 1424.

13. Jimmye Kimmey, "Right to Choose Memorandum," reproduced in Greenhouse and Siegel, *Before Roe v. Wade*, 33–34.

14. See Mary Ziegler, "The Framing of a Right to Choose: Roe v. Wade and the Changing Debate on Abortion Law," *Law and History Review* 27, no. 2 (summer 2009): 281–330, esp. 308–9 for the citations of the Denver Conference Memorandum (November 2, 1972) in the Schlesinger Library, Harvard University; and Ziegler, *After Roe: The Lost History of the Abortion Debate* (Harvard University Press, 2015), 122–23 and chap. 4 ("The Rise of Choice: Single-Issue Politics and Privacy Arguments").

15. Right to Choose Timeline, 1974, in Records of the National Organization for Women, MC 496, Schlesinger Library, Harvard University.

16. Debating the Opposition, NOW Right to Choose Lobbying Kit, 1974, in Records of the National Organization for Women, MC 496, M-152, 29.6, Schlesinger Library, Harvard University.

17. Statement of the National Association of Laity, January 1974, Records of the National Organization for Women, MC 496, Schlesinger Library, Harvard University.

18. Ziegler, "The Framing of a Right to Choose," 321–22.

19. NARAL, *Legal Abortion: A Speaker's and Debater's Notebook* (1978); also cited in Ziegler, "The Framing of a Right to Choose," 317.

20. Ziegler, *After Roe*, 139.

21. Staggenborg, *The Pro-Choice Movement*, 202.

22. Betty Friedan, "Houston: How the Women's Movement Survived," Betty Friedan Papers, Schlesinger Library, Harvard University; also cited in Ziegler, "The Framing of a Right to Choose," 316.

23. Mary Ziegler, *Roe: The History of a National Obsession* (Yale University Press, 2023), 19.

24. On the relationship of the abortion issue specifically to party alignment, see Matthew Levendusky, *The Partisan Sort: How Liberals Became Democrats and Conservatives Became Republicans* (University of Chicago Press, 2009), 13–14, 64–69; and Andrew Lewis, *The Rights Turn*

in Conservative Christian Politics: How Abortion Transformed the Culture Wars (Cambridge University Press, 2017).

25. Ziegler, *After Roe*, 141–48.

26. On this organization, see Gisèle Halimi, *La Cause des femmes* (B. Grasset, 1973), translated as *The Right to Choose* (University of Queensland, 1977). Halimi's defense relied upon the claim, "When I speak of freedom I mean being in possession of the power to practice that freedom; and the great lack in our system of society is that we do not grant women the power to make a choice in the matter of parenthood." By the 1970s, Simone de Beauvoir, too, had started to talk about "the right to choose" motherhood and the need for collective action on the part of women to secure such rights, though this had not been her preferred idiom before; see Alice Schwarzer, *After the Second Sex: Conversations with Simone de Beauvoir*, trans. Marianne Howarth (Pantheon, 1984). In France, abortion up to the tenth week of pregnancy was legalized in 1975 under the Loi Veil or "loi sur l'interruption volontaire de grossesse." Choisir was tagged as "reformist," but as Halimi argued, its strategy was always revolutionary—to work for radical changes in *mentalité*—and its agenda expanded considerably after 1974 to include educational, political, economic, and social rights for women too.

27. On Britain, see Fran Amery, *Beyond Pro-Life and Pro-Choice: The Changing Politics of Abortion in Britain* (Bristol University Press, 2020). There, abortion up to the twenty-eighth week, with doctors' permission, was legalized in 1967.

28. See Lena Lennerhed, "Sherri Finkbine's Choice: Abortion, Sex-Liberalism, and Feminism in Sweden in the 1960s and 1970s," *Women's History Magazine* 73 (2013): 13–18. In 1975, Swedish women won the right to an abortion on demand until the twelfth week, and after evaluation by a counselor, the eighteenth; but Swedish women had already had limited access to abortion for medical purposes since 1938.

29. Louise Vandelac, *L'Italie au féminisme* (Editions Tierce, 1978), 51, but see, too, the contemporary challenges to the idea of "autodeterminazione" under capitalism and patriarchy as meaningless (52–54). Abortion in the first ninety days of pregnancy became legal in Italy in 1978, though the law also allowed medical personnel to opt out of performing abortions for reasons of "conscience," as did French law.

30. On abortion rights movements internationally, see Colin Francome, *Abortion Freedom: A Worldwide Movement* (Allen and Unwin, 1984); Andrzej Kulczycki, *The Abortion Debate in the World Arena* (Routledge, 1999); and Penny A. Weiss, ed., *Feminist Manifestos: A Global Documentary Reader* (New York University Press, 2018). Between 1967 and 1978, forty-two countries made it easier to terminate pregnancies (Connelly, *Fatal Misconception*, 244), and many others have passed legislation to this effect subsequently. Some countries—Poland, the United States—have moved the opposite direction in recent years. Protesters against restrictions on access and defenders of abortion rights, according to AP photos, also continue to trot out the English-language saying "My Body, My Choice" from Krakow to Athens to Jakarta in an effort to generate international media coverage.

31. As I was finishing this book in the fall of 2023, NARAL changed its name to Reproductive Freedom for All, a change described as a "rebranding" to suit the post-*Roe* climate: https://apnews.com/article/abortion-advocates-rebrand-naral-reproductive-freedom-ccd0d424a5578aad9d7ce0dc9151afc9.

32. On this center, see https://www.plannedparenthood.org/planned-parenthood-center-for-choice/who-we-are.

33. Adrian Horton, "AKA Jane Roe: Behind the Headline-Making Abortion Documentary," *The Guardian*, May 22, 2020.

34. See, for example, Ramesh Ponnuru, *The Party of Death: The Democrats, the Media, the Courts, and the Disregard for Human Life* (Regnery, 2006). For left-leaning accounts of conservative opposition in the late 20th-century United States, see William Saletan, *Bearing Right: How*

Conservatives Won the Abortion War (University of California Press, 2003); Condit, *Decoding Abortion Rhetoric*; and Keith Cassidy, "The Right to Life Movement: Sources, Development, Strategies," *Journal of Policy History* 7, no. 1 (1995): 128–59. Evangelicals were initially more concerned about lax morality in contemporary culture than the inalienable rights of the fetus, but the latter quickly became a central theme of the movement as a whole; see Sara Dubow, *Ourselves Unborn: A History of the Fetus in Modern America* (Oxford University Press, 2010).

35. For the latter argument, see, for example, John C. Garvey, *What Are Freedoms For?* (Harvard University Press, 1996).

36. Daniel K. Williams, *Defenders of the Unborn: The Pro-Life Movement before Roe v. Wade* (Oxford University Press, 2016), chap. 5.

37. Condit, *Decoding Abortion Rhetoric*, 106. There are, of course, some structural similarities between this kind of argument and the arguments of feminists who critique, from a different political vantage point, women's decisions to, say, engage in plastic surgery to enhance their sex appeal as frivolous or even socially harmful forms of consumer choice.

38. See, for example, Elizabeth Dias, "Inside the Extreme Effort to Punish Women for Abortion," *New York Times*, July 1, 2022, who cites Jeff Durbin, an Arizona pastor and advocate of "abortion abolition," to the effect: "There were people arguing against the abolitionists at the time. They were saying 'well, sure, it's wrong. But if you don't want a slave, don't get one.' You know, so everything was sort of 'That's their plantation, their choice.'"

39. On the compatibility of neoliberal, free market framings not only with a kind of moral libertarianism but also with socially conservative, patriarchal family values positions and disinterest in equality, see Wendy Brown, *In the Ruins of Neoliberalism: The Rise of Antidemocratic Politics in the West* (Columbia University Press, 2019); Whyte, *The Morals of the Market*; and Melinda Cooper, *Family Values: Between Neoliberalism and the New Social Conservatism* (Zone, 2017), who alone discusses abortion in this context.

40. See Lewis, *The Rights Turn in Conservative Christian Politics*, esp. 93–96; and Condit, *Decoding Abortion Rhetoric*, 113–15. Very similar claims about threats to "religious liberty" figured prominently in the winning case against the birth control mandate in Obamacare (*Burwell v. Hobby Lobby Stores, Inc.* (2014)) and the losing side on same-sex marriage (*Obergefell v. Hodges* (2015)). On the compatibility and historical entanglement of conservative strands of Christianity with human rights claims more generally, see Sam Moyn, *Christian Human Rights* (University of Pennsylvania Press, 2015).

41. The marketplace model, in which abortion became available at a price, became even more clear after the Hyde Amendment was upheld in the U.S. Supreme Court (in *Harris v. McRae* [1980]) with Justice Stewart's argument that "although government may not place obstacles in the path of a woman's exercise of her freedom of choice, it need not remove those not of its own creation: Indigency falls in the latter category"; see Rickie Solinger, *Pregnancy and Power: A Short History of Reproductive Politics in America* (New York University Press, 2005), 201.

42. The *Oxford Handbook of the History of Eugenics*, ed. Allison Bashford and Philippa Levine (Oxford University Press, 2010), illustrates the frequently close historical alliance between progressive birth control and/or abortion policies, on the one hand, and eugenics, on the other. In Sweden, for example, laws as early as the 1930s permitting women to obtain abortions in certain circumstances were accompanied by mandatory sterilization policies for those "incapable of rational decisions" (Connelly, *Fatal Misconception*, 104), and different rules around reproductive health were routinely established in colonial settings than in metropoles (Johanna Schoen, *Choice and Coercion: Birth Control, Sterilization, and Abortion in Public Health and Welfare* [University of North Carolina Press, 2005]). But see, too, Jonathan Anomaly, "Defending Eugenics: From Cryptic Choice to Conscious Selection," *Monash Bioethics Review*, no. 35 (2018): 24–35, for a controversial contemporary defense of "liberal eugenics," prioritizing individual rather than state-based choice for prospective parents.

43. Statement of Mary Treadwell Barry, Executive Director of Pride, Inc., Women's National Abortion Action Coalition, January 17, 1974, in Records of the National Association for Women, MC 496, Schlesinger Library, Harvard University.

44. Rickie Solinger, *Beggars and Choosers: How the Politics of Choice Shapes Adoption, Abortion, and Welfare in the United States* (Farrar, Straus and Giroux, 2001). On more radical feminist groups' engagement in the abortion question, see Jennifer Nelson, *Women of Color and the Reproductive Rights Movement* (New York University Press, 2003); Zakiya Luna, "From Right to Justice: Women of Color Changing the Face of US Reproductive Rights Organizing," *Societies without Borders* 4, no. 3 (2009): 343–65; Kimala Price, "What Is Reproductive Justice: How Women of Color Are Redefining the Pro-Choice Paradigm," *Meridians* 10 (2010): 42–65; and Jael Silliman, Marlene Gerber Fried, Loretta Ross, and Elena Gutiérrez, *Undivided Rights: Women of Color Organize for Reproductive Justice*, 2nd ed. (Haymarket Books, 2016). DeGrazia, in *Irresistible Empire*, stresses that there were strains of the women's movement in both the United States and Europe that were also anticonsumerist in the 1970s.

45. Dorothy Roberts, *Killing the Black Body: Race, Reproduction, and the Meaning of Liberty*, 2nd ed. (Penguin, 2017), 6, as well as "Reproductive Justice, Not Just Rights," *Dissent* (fall 2015), a term coined by Black feminists in 1994, and "Reproductive Freedom" (interview) in *Penn Today* (July 26, 2022), in which she calls for a shift away from a framework that centers choice "to one of justice that recognizes the human right not to have a child as well as the right to have children and to raise them in a safe and supportive community, and also calls for the social economic, and political conditions that are needed to lead free reproductive lives."

46. See here especially West, "From Choice to Reproductive Justice," 1412, 1416.

47. See, for example, Jackie Calmes, "Advocates Shun 'Pro-Choice' to Expand Message," *New York Times*, July 28, 2014. On more philosophical grounds, see Denbow, *Governed through Choice*, and from a British perspective, Marie Fox, "A Woman's Right to Choose? A Feminist Critique," in *The Future of Human Reproduction: Ethics, Choice, and Regulation*, ed. John Harris and Søren Holm (Clarendon Press, 1998), 77–100. Silliman et al., in *Undivided Rights*, ix–xi, notes that the turn to "reproductive justice" as an alternative to "choice" gained momentum in the United States in the context of the SisterSong conference in 2003 and was reinforced by the renaming of the annual March for Freedom of Choice as the March for Women's Lives in 2004.

48. Marlene Gerber Fried, "Abortion in the United States: Legal but Inaccessible," in *Abortion Wars: A Half Century of Struggle, 1950–2000*, ed. Rickie Solinger (University of California Press, 1998), 219, for choice as "euphemistic" language in the context of abortion debates. Charles Taylor makes a similar argument in *A Secular Age*, 479, calling choice an "empty term" and "argument-stopping universal" that generally "occludes everything important," including "the real moral weight of the [given] situation"; but he does not mention abortion directly.

49. Solinger, *Beggars and Choosers*, 223.

50. A. Philip Randolph and Chandler Owen, "The New Negro—What Is He?" *The Messenger* 2 (August 1920): 73–74, reproduced in *The Harlem Renaissance: A Brief History with Documents*, ed. Jeffrey B. Ferguson (Bedford/St. Martin's, 2008), 39–41.

51. Rachel Bluth, "My Body, My Choice: How Vaccine Foes Coopted the Abortion Rallying Cry," *Shots: Health News from NPR*, July 4, 2022. The appropriation of this well-known phrase in this context can be seen as a strategic move to make antimasking and antivaccination positions consonant with larger fights for bodily autonomy in the face of government oppression. However, it can also be seen as part of an effort to undermine the effectiveness of this well-known rhetoric for its original purpose and/or to troll its liberal supporters.

52. Hirshman, *Get to Work*.

53. Sama-Resource Group for Women and Health, *ARTs and Women: Assistance in Reproduction or Subjugation* (New Delhi, 2006), 101, cited in Margaret McLaren, *Women's Activism,*

Feminism, and Social Justice (Oxford University Press, 2019), 74. Sama, founded in 1999, means equality in Sanskrit.

54. Masha Gessen, "To Be, or Not to Be," *New York Review of Books*, February 8, 2018.

55. Jenny Erpenbeck, *Go, Went, Gone*, trans. Susan Bernofsky (New Directions, 2017 [2015]), 63, 67, 80.

56. See John F. Helliwell et al., *World Happiness Report* (2023), but published annually since 2012 as a result of a partnership among Gallup, Inc., the Oxford Wellbeing Research Centre, the UN Sustainable Development Solutions Network, and the World Happiness Report's Editorial Board.

57. This is a theme that recurs in editorial cartoons, where choice scenarios are often presented as fake despite the billing, because (a) all the options are terrible; (b) all the options are identical; (c) only one of the options is decent, so that in practice there are no real options; (d) what looks like choice is actually predetermined as a result of corruption or scheming; or (e) what looks like choice is actually random and a matter of chance, whether for everyone or for some subset of people ostensibly being given an opportunity to make a free choice.

58. See Jonathan Cohn, *The Burden of Choice: Recommendations, Subversion, and Algorithmic Culture* (Rutgers University Press, 2019) and Ed Finn, *What Algorithms Want: Imagination in an Age of Computing* (MIT Press, 2017), including on the creation and making of "user data" and "consumer history."

59. On this point, see especially Salecl, *The Tyranny of Choice*, who stresses that today "we are on our own" (146) when it comes to both figuring out the goals behind all our fragmented choices (a task for which we are psychologically ill-prepared) and coping with the consequences.

60. Critics of the current celebration of choice often point to how it opens up new differentials within and between societies, groups, and individuals; see, for example, Friederike Fleischer, "'To Choose a House Means to Choose a Lifestyle': The Consumption of Housing and Class Structuration in Urban China," *City and Society* 19, no. 2 (December 2007): 287–311.

61. Weil, *The Need for Roots*, 96.

62. David Zeitlin, "Fighting Poverty with Cash" (on Amy Castro Baker's UBI experiments), *Pennsylvania Gazette*, April 20, 2021, https://thepenngazette.com/fighting-poverty-with-cash/.

63. C. Wright Mills, *The Sociological Imagination* (Oxford University Press, 1959), 174.

64. Zachary M. Schrag, *The Princeton Guide to Historical Research* (Princeton University Press, 2021), 10–14.

65. Walter Johnson, "On Agency," *Journal of Social History* 37, no. 1 (fall 2003): 113–24, makes a similar point about the desire of those writing the "new social history" to imagine even enslaved people as endowed with considerable autonomous decision-making power.

66. Arlette Farge, *The Allure of the Archives* (Yale University Press, 2013), 93, 94.

67. Marcia Chatelain, quoted in Schrag, *The Princeton Guide*, 13.

68. Anderson, "Beyond *Homo Economicus*," 189–90.

69. In ways that are potentially helpful to historians, behavioral economists undermine the idea of a consistent rational actor across all circumstances and draw attention to external as well as internal factors that affect decision-making capacity; see, for example, Avner Offer, *The Challenge of Affluence: Self-Control and Well-Being in the United States and Britain since 1950* (Oxford University Press, 2006), a rare example of a study that draws on behavioral economic ideas to interpret the past. So do, in very different ways, political theorists like Arendt, who insist that our psychologies and mental "faculties," and not just our beliefs, adapt themselves to different technologies, political situations, mores, and more—and vice versa.

70. Sakyo Komatsu is a pseudonym of the writer Minoru Komatsu, whose story "Take Your Choice," trans. Shiro Tamura and Grania Davis, is reprinted in *Best Japanese Science Fiction Stories*, ed. John L. Apostolou and Martin H. Greenberg (Dembner Books, 1989), 85–103.

71. James Salter, *Light Years* (Random House, 1975), 35–36.

INDEX

abolitionism, 13, 75, 108, 111, 138–39, 160, 244; and abortion, 349, 351; and women's movement, 244, 254, 349, 353, 360, 410n26

abortion, 5, 22, 194, 329, 347–48, 354; and advocacy groups, 340–43, 346–47, 353–54; as a civil right, 353; in Britain, 346; and eugenics, 352; in France, 345–46; and freedom, 338–39, 341–44; and Hyde Amendment, 352; in Italy, 346; and legalization of, 333, 335, 337–38, 348; and linkage with choice, 21, 339–44, 347, 350, 356, 358, 363; and Margaret Sanger, 342; and Mary Treadwell Berry, 353; and opposition to, 338–39, 348–52; and party alignment, 343, 345; and "pro-choice kits," 343; and slavery, 349; and socialist women, 193; in Sweden, 346; and women's liberation, 345. *See also* anti-abortion movement; National Association for the Repeal of Abortion Laws (NARAL); Planned Parenthood; "right to choose"; *Roe v. Wade*

academic aptitude and achievement testing, 287, 288

Adams, Henry Foster, 275

Adams, John, 95

addiction, 15, 125, 132, 391n101

Adorno, Theodor, 301

advertising, 2, 10, 163, 188, 268–82, 270; agencies, 276; and art, 81, 270; and cloth, 48, 64; and customers, 274, 277–78; and dance manuals, 176; and elections/voting, 237, 290–92, 300, 302; and feminism, 20, 330; gurus, 269–71, 305; and invention of shopping, 27, 42, 44, 48, 73; and Joseph

French Johnson, 271–72; and manipulation, 273; and marketing, 267, 276, 280; and mass consumption, 80; and *Printers' Ink*, 272, 276; and psychology, 268–69, 275, 280, 286, 305, 307; as "scientific," 276–80; and slave auctions, 33; and supermarkets, 273; for war bonds, 300; and women, 80, 274–75, 280–81, 283, 290, 292, 301, 323. *See also* Scott, Walter Dill

affective choice, 21, 149, 153, 164, 179, 187–88, 190, 263. *See also* interdependent choice

age of revolutions, 8–9, 98, 133, 136, 149, 162, 195, 207, 210; and affective choice, 153; and consumer choice, 72; and women, 195. *See also* American Revolution; French Revolution

akrasia, 64

Alexander, William, 56

algorithms, 13, 16, 131, 156, 163, 359

American Psychological Association, 286. *See also* psychology

American Revolution, 95, 103, 106, 109–10, 208, 226, 289, 411n33

Americans United for Life, 350

Amish, 91, 103

Anabaptists, 90–91

Anderson, Elizabeth, 321, 364

Andersson, Lena, 321

Anglicans, 101, 103–4

Anshen, Ruth Nanda, 300, 435n89

Anthony, Susan B., 254

anti-abortion movement, 338–39, 347–52; and freedom, 342

anticapitalist critiques, 79–80, 140, 358

arcades, 40, 50, 76